BEST PLACES®

SAN FRANCISCO

★

BEST PLACES®
SAN FRANCISCO

★

Edited by
REBECCA POOLE FORÉE
MATTHEW RICHARD POOLE

EDITION **1**

SASQUATCH BOOKS
SEATTLE

Printed in the United States of America
Distributed in Canada by Raincoast Books Ltd.

First edition.
02 01 00 99   5 4 3 2 1

ISSN: 1526-9663
ISBN: 1-57061-186-6

Series editor: Kate Rogers
Cover and interior design: Nancy Gellos
Cover photograph: Harald Sund/The Image Bank
Fold-out and interior maps: GreenEye Design

SPECIAL SALES

BEST PLACES' guidebooks are available at special discounts on bulk purchases
for corporate, club, or organization sales promotions, premiums, and gifts.
Special editions, including personalized covers, excerpts of existing guides,
and corporate imprints, can be created in large quantities for specific needs.
For more information, contact your local bookseller or Special Sales,
BEST PLACES' Guidebooks, 615 Second Avenue, Suite 260, Seattle, Washington
98104, 800/775-0817.

SASQUATCH BOOKS
615 Second Avenue
Seattle, WA 98104
206/467-4300
books@SasquatchBooks.com
www.SasquatchBooks.com

CONTENTS

Contributors   viii
About Best Places® Guidebooks   ix
How to Use This Book   x
  Best Places® Star Ratings   xi

PLANNING A TRIP   1
How to Get Here   2
When to Visit   8
General Costs   10
Tips for Special Travelers   11
Calendar of Events   14
  The Golden Gate Bridge   3
  San Francisco's Literary Legends   6

LAY OF THE CITY   19
Orientation   20
Visitor Information   24
Getting Around   24
Essentials   28
Local Resources   33
Important Telephone Numbers   37
  Low-Priced Parking   21
  San Francisco's Ferry Fleet   29

TOP 200 RESTAURANTS   39
Restaurants by Star Rating   40
Restaurants by Neighborhood   41
Restaurants by Food and Other Features   43
Restaurant Reviews   48
  Amazing Grazing   51
  San Francisco on Celluloid   63

LODGINGS   139
Union Square   140
Financial District   149
SoMa (South of Market Street)   151
Nob Hill   152
North Beach   155
Fisherman's Wharf   156
Civic Center and Japantown   157

Pacific Heights   160
Haight-Ashbury   163
The Castro   164
Airport Area   165
   San Francisco Reservation Services   141
   The Chain Gang   147

EXPLORING   167
Top 25 Attractions   168
Neighborhood Districts   194
Museums   233
Parks and Beaches   238
Organized Tours   239
   Top 25 Attractions   169
   Family Attractions   203

SHOPPING   241
Shops from A to Z   248
   San Francisco's Street Fairs   244
   Golden Gate Bridge by the Numbers   259

PERFORMING ARTS   297
Theater   298
Classical Music and Opera   304
Dance   309
Film   312
Literature   315
   Coffeehouse Culture   301
   Fun for Free   308

NIGHTLIFE   317
Nightlife by Feature   318
Nightlife by Neighborhood   319
Music and Clubs   321
Bars, Pubs, and Taverns   332
Coffee, Tea, and Dessert   343
   The Barbary Coast   325
   Swanky Hotel Bars   337
   Where Do You Want to Go Tonight?   341

ITINERARIES 347
Days One Through Seven   348
The 49-Mile Scenic Drive   349
San Francisco Day by Day   351

DAY TRIPS 355
Berkeley   356
Wine Country   362
Marin County   375
Palo Alto   378
Half Moon Bay   380
Santa Cruz   382
Marin Coast   385
Point Reyes National Seashore   390
Angel Island State Park   391
Napa Valley Wineries   364
Sonoma Valley Wineries   372
See Life at the Farallon Islands   388

RECREATION 393
Outdoor Activities   397
Spectator Sports   410
The Two-Wheel Route: Bicycling in Marin   396
The Best Views of San Francisco and the Bay   401

CONFERENCES, MEETINGS, AND RECEPTIONS 413

Index   421
Money-back Guarantee   435
Best Places® Report Form   436

Contributors

REBECCA POOLE FORÉE and **MATTHEW RICHARD POOLE**, a sister-and-brother writing team, have together written and edited more than 50 travel books on California and many of the world's great cities. More than half a million of their travel tomes are currently available in major bookstores around the world. Forée and Poole also share their travel news and reviews online and on various radio and television shows throughout California.

KRISTINE M. CARBER is a magazine editor and guidebook writer who spends her free time exploring San Francisco's colorful neighborhoods and streets—at last sighting, she was sipping espresso while people-watching at one of the hot new cafes.

Freelance writer **FELICIA CLARK**, a long-time resident of the city, has been exploring the streets of San Francisco for more than a decade.

DARA COLWELL is an investigative reporter who enjoys trekking through San Francisco's varied landscapes. You'll most likely find her in the Mission District, attempting to speak Spanish with the locals.

A writer and editor for a San Francisco magazine, **ROB FARMER** has managed to transform his life-long love affair with the city into a full-time job.

TANYA HENRY is senior food editor at Cooking.com and a trained chef who has lived and eaten in the city for more than 15 years.

DAVID HILL is a writer and novelist who has been residing in San Francisco for more than 20 years; he can be reached at uphill186@aol.com.

DIANNE JACOB is a foodie who first dined in San Francisco as a child at Chinatown restaurants, where her aunts and uncles passed liquor under the tables in brown paper bags.

PERSIS NAKONECHNY lives and plays in San Francisco, where she is always in pursuit of excellent food, choice drinks, and good times.

CYNTHIA RUBIN, a freelance editor and writer, has been dining, shopping, and checking out the views in San Francisco for the past 17 years.

About Best Places® Guidebooks

People trust us. BEST PLACES® guidebooks, which have been published continuously since 1975, represent one of the most respected regional travel series in the country. Each guide is written completely independently: no advertisers, no sponsors, no favors. Our reviewers know their territory, work incognito, and seek out the very best a city or region has to offer. Because we accept no free meals, accommodations, or other complimentary services, we are able to provide tough, candid reports about places that have rested too long on their laurels, and to delight in new places that deserve recognition. We describe the true strengths, foibles, and unique characteristics of each establishment listed.

San Francisco Best Places is written by and for locals, and is therefore coveted by travelers. It's written for people who live here and who enjoy exploring the city's bounty and its out-of-the-way places of high character and individualism. These are the very characteristics that make *San Francisco Best Places* ideal for tourists, too. The best places in and around the city are the ones that denizens favor: independently owned establishments of good value, touched with local history, run by lively individuals, and graced with natural beauty. With this premier edition of *San Francisco Best Places*, travelers will find the information they need: where to go and when, what to order, which rooms to request (and which to avoid), where the best music, art, nightlife, shopping, and other attractions are, and how to find the city's hidden secrets.

We're so sure you'll be satisfied with our guide, we guarantee it.

NOTE: *The reviews in this edition are based on information available at press time and are subject to change. Readers are advised that places listed may have closed or changed management, and, thus, may no longer be recommended by this series. The editors welcome information conveyed by users of this book. A report form is provided at the end of the book, and feedback is also welcome via email: books@SasquatchBooks.com.*

How to Use This Book

This book is divided into twelve chapters covering a wide range of establishments, destinations, and activities in and around San Francisco. All evaluations are based on numerous reports from local and traveling inspectors. BEST PLACES° reporters do not identify themselves when they review an establishment, and they accept no free meals, accommodations, or any other services. Final judgments are made by the editors. Every place featured in this book is recommended.

STAR RATINGS *(for Top 200 Restaurants and Lodgings only)* Restaurants and lodgings are rated on a scale of one to four stars (with half stars in between), based on uniqueness, loyalty of local clientele, performance measured against the establishment's goals, excellence of cooking, cleanliness, value, and professionalism of service. Reviews are listed alphabetically, and every place is recommended.

★★★★ The very best in the city

★★★ Distinguished; many outstanding features

★★ Excellent; some wonderful qualities

★ A good place

(For more on how we rate places, see the BEST PLACES° Star Ratings box.)

PRICE RANGE *(for Top 200 Restaurants and Lodgings only)* Prices for lodgings are based on peak season rates for one night's lodging for two people (i.e., double occupancy). Off-season rates vary but can sometimes be significantly less. Prices for restaurants are based primarily on dinner for two, including dessert, tax, and tip. When prices range between two categories (for example, moderate to expensive), the lower one is given. Call ahead to verify, as all prices are subject to change.

$$$ Expensive (more than $100 for dinner for two; more than $150 for one night's lodgings for two)

$$ Moderate (between expensive and inexpensive)

$ Inexpensive (less than $35 for dinner for two; $80 or less for one night's lodgings for two)

ADDRESSES AND PHONE NUMBERS Every attempt has been made to provide accurate information on an establishment's location and phone number. But it's always a good idea to call ahead and confirm. For establishments with two or more locations, we try to provide information on the original or most recommended branches.

CHECKS AND CREDIT CARDS Most establishments that accept checks also require a major credit card for identification. Note that some places accept only local checks. Credit cards are abbreviated in this book as follows: American Express (AE); Carte Blanche (CB); Diners Club (DC); Discover (DIS); Japanese credit card (JCB); MasterCard (MC); Visa (V).

EMAIL AND WEB SITE ADDRESSES With the understanding that more people are using email and the Internet to access information and to

BEST PLACES® STAR RATINGS

Any travel guide that rates establishments is inherently subjective—and BEST PLACES® is no exception. We rely on our professional experience, yes, but also on a gut feeling. And, occasionally, we even give in to a soft spot for a favorite neighborhood hangout. Our star-rating system is not simply a AAA-checklist; it's judgmental, critical, sometimes fickle, and highly personal. And unlike most other travel guides, we pay our own way and accept no freebies: no free meals or accommodations, no advertisers, no sponsors, no favors.

For each new edition, we send local food and travel experts out to review restaurants and lodgings anonymously, and then to rate them on a scale of one to four, based on uniqueness, loyalty of local clientele, performance measured against the establishment's goals, excellence of cooking, cleanliness, value, and professionalism of service. That doesn't mean a one-star establishment isn't worth dining or sleeping at—far from it. When we say that *all* the places listed in our books are recommended, we mean it. That one-star pizza joint may be just the ticket for the end of a whirlwind day of shopping with the kids. But if you're planning something more special, the star ratings can help you choose an eatery or hotel that will wow your new clients or be a stunning, romantic place to celebrate an anniversary or impress a first date.

We award four-star ratings sparingly, reserving them for what we consider truly the best. And once an establishment has earned our highest rating, everyone's expectations seem to rise. Readers often write us letters specifically to point out the faults in four-star establishments. With changes in chefs, management, styles, and trends, it's always easier to get knocked off the pedestal than to ascend it. Three-star establishments, on the other hand, seem to generate healthy praise. They exhibit outstanding qualities, and we get lots of love letters about them. The difference between two and three stars can sometimes be a very fine line. Two-star establishments are doing a good, solid job and gaining attention, while one-star places are often dependable spots that have been around forever.

The restaurants and lodgings described in *San Francisco Best Places* have earned their stars from hard work and good service (and good food). They're proud to be included in this book—look for our BEST PLACES® sticker in their windows. And we're proud to honor them in this, the first edition of *San Francisco Best Places*.

plan trips, BEST PLACES has included email and Web site addresses for establishments, where available. Please note that the World Wide Web is a fluid and evolving medium, and that Web pages are often "under construction" or, as with all time-sensitive information, may no longer be valid.

MAP INDICATORS The letter-and-number codes appearing at the end of most listings refer to coordinates on the fold-out map included in the front of the book. Single letters (for example, F7) refer to the downtown San Francisco map; double letters (FF7) refer to the Greater San Francisco map on the flip side. If an establishment does not have a map code listed, its location falls beyond the boundaries of these maps.

HELPFUL ICONS Watch for these quick-reference symbols throughout the book:

FAMILY FUN Family-oriented places that are great for kids—fun, easy, not too expensive, and accustomed to dealing with young ones.

GOOD VALUE While not necessarily cheap, these places offer you the best value for your dollars—a good deal within the context of the city.

ROMANTIC These spots offer candlelight, atmosphere, intimacy, or other romantic qualities—kisses and proposals are encouraged!

UNIQUELY SAN FRANCISCO These are places that are unique and special to the city, such as a restaurant owned by a beloved local chef or a tourist attraction recognized around the globe. (Hint: If you want to hit several of these special spots at once, turn to the Top 25 Attractions in the Exploring chapter. They're all uniquely San Francisco!)

  Appears after listings for establishments that have wheelchair-accessible facilities.

INDEXES In addition to a general index at the back of the book, there are five specialized indexes: restaurants are indexed by star-rating, features, and location at the beginning of the Restaurants chapter, and nightspots are indexed by features and location at the beginning of the Nightlife chapter.

READER REPORTS At the end of the book is a report form. We receive hundreds of reports from readers suggesting new places or agreeing or disagreeing with our assessments. They greatly help in our evaluations, and we encourage you to respond.

MONEY-BACK GUARANTEE See "We Stand by Our Reviews" at the end of this book.

PLANNING A TRIP

PLANNING A TRIP

How to Get Here

BY PLANE

Two major airports serve the Bay Area: San Francisco International (SFO) and Oakland International (OAK) Airports.

SAN FRANCISCO INTERNATIONAL AIRPORT

SFO (650/876-2377; map:KK5-LL5) lies 14 miles south of San Francisco directly off the Bayshore Freeway (Hwy 101). The fifth-busiest airport in the United States and the seventh busiest in the world, SFO is the stopping-off point for more than 1,000 flights a day. And with the new international terminal in the works, the airport will soon be bigger and far more user-friendly. All major domestic airlines and many international ones fly into SFO, and each of the three main terminals is linked by adjoining walkways. Most gates are no more than a 10-minute walk from the check-in counters.

For travel information once you've hit the ground, go to the **INFORMATION DESK** on the terminal's lower level near baggage claim. You can also call the toll-free hot line (800/736-2008) from 7am to 5pm weekdays for information on how to find your way into the city.

SFO's **PARKING COMPLEX**, which currently holds 7,000 cars, is undergoing a massive expansion and the construction has further complicated what was already barely controlled chaos. Scarce space and high prices can make parking a chore, and passengers are advised to call ahead (650/877-0227) for availability. There is also a **CONSTRUCTION HOT LINE** (650/635-4000) for information on which parking lots have been temporarily closed (this can change at short notice). Short-term parking costs $1 for 20 minutes, with a maximum of $22 for the first 24 hours. Long-term parking, limited to 30 days, costs $12 per day for the first week and $15 per day thereafter. Valet parking is also available for $32 per day with a minimum of one day's stay. MasterCard, Visa, American Express, and Discover cards are accepted. For those who have a disability, parking is offered on the first four levels of the short-term parking area at a reduced rate of $12 per day. Passengers with a disability are required to show their special ID card, placard, and dashboard driver's license when they exit.

If the airport parking lots are full, a number of more affordable nearby **COMMERCIAL LOTS** offer free shuttle service to the airport (a 5- to 7-minute drive). **SKY PARK** (650/875-6655), **PARK & FLY** (650/877-0304), **PARKING COMPANY OF AMERICA** (650/877-0250), and **PARKS SHUTTLE & FLY** (650/871-7275) are open 24 hours a day and do not require reservations, though at peak travel times it's wise to call ahead about availability. Rates range from $9 to $16 per day.

THE GOLDEN GATE BRIDGE

San Francisco's most famous landmark took 13 years to plan and build and is a masterpiece of engineering and design. More than a mile long, the bridge was conceived by engineer Joseph Strauss to withstand winds of more than 100 miles an hour and is supported by cables that measure more than 3 feet in diameter. Standing 220 feet above the channel, the bridge has endured the wind, fog, more than 1,000 suicides, and the misconception that it was ever truly golden. It's painted with 5,000 gallons of International Orange each year, a weather-resistant paint chosen by consulting architect Irving F. Morrow because he thought it would accentuate the area's natural beauty (that, and it's visible through fog). In contrast to the gray hue of most bridges, orange is a great change of pace, and it glows like gold in the setting sun.

You can get one of the best views of the bridge by walking across it, where you can admire the metal gussets that allow it to sway more than 27 feet at its center. The bridge's engineering was put to a test in 1987 when, during the structure's 50th birthday, nearly one-third of San Francisco's population showed up to celebrate by strolling across. The mass of people literally flattened the span, making bridge officials noticeably nervous. Fortunately, Big Red held firm.

Airport Transportation

While public transportation via **BAY AREA RAPID TRANSIT (BART)** will not extend to the airport until 2002, there are several ways to get to and from SFO without driving, the cheapest being the bus. **SAMTRANS** (800/660-4BUS) buses 7F and 7B run every half hour from the airport's upper departure level to the Transbay Terminal at Mission and First Streets. 7F costs $3 and takes 30 minutes; passengers are restricted to one carry-on bag. 7B costs $1.10 and takes 55 minutes, with no luggage restrictions. Another cheap (but more complicated) bus route: Take either the 3X to Colma BART station or the 3B to Daly City BART station (for $1), then catch BART (510/464-6000) into San Francisco. The ride takes roughly 40 minutes and costs only $2.25 to downtown, but it might be a strain on travelers with heavy luggage.

The SFO **AIRPORTER BUSES** (415/495-8404) serve the downtown area and run every 15 to 30 minutes, stopping in the Union Square area and the Financial District. The service operates from 5am to 11pm and costs $10 one-way. No reservations are required.

And of course, there's **GREYHOUND/TRAILWAYS** (800/231-2222), which can get you to San Francisco from just about anywhere. Round-trip fares vary; all buses go to the Transbay Terminal in San Francisco (425 Mission St; map:N2).

An equally inexpensive option is to take the free **CALTRAIN** (800/660-4287) shuttle from the airport's North and South Terminals to Millbrae Station. The trains run frequently during the day, and from there it's only a 25-minute ride ($2) to the CalTrain Depot on Fourth and Townsend Streets in San Francisco (map:O4). This is not recommended at night; although the neighborhood is rapidly improving, it's pretty isolated after dark.

AIRPORT SHUTTLES are the most convenient door-to-door transit service and the Bay Area's favorite way to travel. Of the variety of reasonably priced shuttle companies, most charge around $10 to $16 (one-way) and will take you anywhere in the city. Reduced rates apply for pickups of two or more people, and rides are shared with other passengers, so expect multiple stops en route. Shuttles leave every 10 to 15 minutes from the upper level of each airport terminal; look for the red signs posted on the curb.

SUPERSHUTTLE (415/558-8500), whose ubiquitous blue-and-yellow vans can be found at all major California airports, serves SFO from San Francisco and the Peninsula and charges $10 per person to a hotel, $12 to a residence, and $8 for each extra person in your party.

Equally reliable services (often with shorter waiting lines) are the **BAYPORTER EXPRESS** (415/467-1800), which runs to the East and South Bay from SFO for $16 per person; **LORRIES AIRPORT SERVICE** (415/334-9000), a 20-year-old business that whisks travelers into the city for $11 per person; and **QUAKE CITY SHUTTLE** (415/255-4899), which runs from 5am to 11pm (reservations are required only for the SFO-bound). No reservations are needed for shuttle rides from SFO, but you should definitely make them traveling to the airport from your hotel or home; you can call anytime, day or night. For service from the airport, most passengers just get in line after they've landed and hop on the next available shuttle; the wait is usually no longer than half an hour. While most shuttles operate until midnight, they're few and far between in the wee hours; service picks up again around 5am.

TAXIS are a reliable but expensive option, costing approximately $35 to $40 plus tip. You'll find them outside the lower level of the terminal.

OAKLAND INTERNATIONAL AIRPORT

Another often overlooked way to fly into San Francisco is through Oakland International Airport (1 Airport Dr, off Heggenberger Rd; 510/577-4000; map:JJ2-KK2), or **OAK** for short, located off Interstate 880 in the East Bay. The midsize airport serves 9.1 million passengers a year, and a $600 million expansion project should enable it to handle another 5 million, anticipated as a result of greater air traffic and overcrowding at SFO.

OAK, far less hectic than SFO, has only a fraction of the maddening delays that SFO incurs daily. Its two terminals serve 10 domestic airlines (including **UNITED** and **ALASKA AIRLINES**) along with international flights to Europe and the Pacific. **SOUTHWEST AIRLINES** (800/435-9792) offers more than 80 flights in and out of Oakland each day, much of it commuter service to Los Angeles. Terminal 1 houses most of the kiosks and restaurants. A walk to Terminal 2 from the check-in counters takes no longer than 10 minutes.

For ground information, visitors to OAK can call the **VISITOR SERVICES VOLUNTEERS** (510/577-4015 from 8am to 8pm, or 510/577-4000 after hours). Transportation into San Francisco and the surrounding Bay Area is straightforward. Hotel shuttles, taxis, rental cars, and shuttles into Oakland are all available outside the baggage claim area; signs are clearly marked. The **AIR-BART SHUTTLE** (510/577-4294) runs every 15 minutes until midnight between the airport and the Coliseum BART station in Oakland. Tickets cost $2 and must be bought inside the airport from machines marked Air-BART. Once you arrive at the BART station, you then need to buy a ticket to your next destination. Private shuttle services will take passengers into San Francisco for about $20; the journey takes half an hour to 45 minutes, depending on traffic. Late-night shuttles are scarce, so grab the first one you can find. A taxi to or from downtown San Francisco costs around $45, so unless money's not a concern, it's advisable to take a shuttle instead.

SHORT-TERM PARKING (510/633-2571) costs $1 every 20 minutes or $20 per day; **LONG-TERM PARKING** costs $5 an hour or $10 per day; **ECONOMY PARKING** (located across from Terminal 1) costs $4 an hour or $8 per day—a big savings compared to the lots at SFO. That makes the Oakland Airport quite popular with those who fly down to LA for a few days. All lots are directly across from the airport, and shuttle service is provided. Parking lots fill up quickly, so you may want to get there early to make sure you secure a spot.

BY TRAIN

Two train services go to and from San Francisco. **CALTRAIN** (800/660-4BUS) offers regular service from the city along the Peninsula down to San Jose and stops at major cities, including Palo Alto (Stanford University) and Mountain View. The trip to San Jose costs $4.50 one-way and takes an hour and a half. Other slower trains make several stops and take longer. Bikes are allowed on all trains.

AMTRAK (800/USA-RAIL) trains from major cities, including Chicago, San Diego, Seattle, and Sacramento, stop at four East Bay stations: Richmond (16th St and MacDonald Ave), Berkeley (3rd St and University Ave), Oakland (245 2nd St at Jack London Square), and Emeryville (5885 Landregan St). A free connecting Amtrak shuttle bus from the Emeryville station drops passengers off at the San Francisco Ferry Building, at the intersection of Market Street and the Embarcadero. The shuttle also makes stops at Pier 39, the Union Square area, and SFO.

SAN FRANCISCO'S LITERARY LEGENDS

Like any artistic enclave, San Francisco has drawn its share of literary talent. Great authors such as Mark Twain, Dashiell Hammett, Robert Louis Stevenson, Oakland-born Jack London, Jack Kerouac, and Allen Ginsberg have all written about the city, lending their genius to the backdrop of its rolling hills. San Franciscans in general are well read, which explains the hundreds of bookstores here: the city has more than 200—new and used, intimate and colossal, nonprofit and corporate—for every political bent, sexual leaning, and cultural interest. Many well-known authors live and work in the area, including Amy Tan (*The Joy Luck Club*), Isabel Allende (*The House of the Spirits*), Dorothy Allison (*Bastard Out of Carolina*), and Armistead Maupin (famous for his *Tales of the City* series). New writers are always making their presence known, including cyber-authors Po Bronson and Martha Baer.

Here's a short list of works that will enliven your understanding of the area.

Nonfiction

California: An Interpretive History by Walton Bean (McGraw Hill, 1993) is an account of California's (sometimes shady) past.

California Coastal Access Guide by the University of California (Seven Hills, 1997) provides, true to its title, a guide to the coastal regions.

Literary San Francisco by Lawrence Ferlinghetti and Nancy Peters (Harper & Row, 1980) is also out of print but available through amazon.com; it's an account of the writerly circles that have helped shape the city's history.

The Mayor of Castro Street by Randy Shilts (St. Martin's Press, 1988). A landmark work on the political career of Harvey Milk and the development of gay politics.

San Francisco Confidential by Ray Mungo (Birch Lane Press, 1995). A look at what goes on behind the city's closed doors.

San Francisco Stories: Great Writers on the City by John Miller (Chronicle Books, 1990) includes contributions by locals Herb Caen, Anne Lamott, Amy Tan, and many others.

San Francisco: The Ultimate Guide by Randolph Delehanty (Chronicle Books, 1995) is a meticulously researched compendium of 13 walking tours through the city. Unfortunately, it's out of print, but copies can be ordered through amazon.com.

16th Street: Faces in the Mission by Bert Katz (Gulliver Books, 1997) is a photo collection of Mission residents. Local coffee shops on 16th and Valencia Streets tend to have a copy lying around.

Fiction

As Francesca by Martha Baer (Bantam Doubleday Dell, 1998). An exploration of the allure of cybersex.

Beyond Definition: New Writing from Gay and Lesbian San Francisco by Marci Blackman and Trebor Healey, editors (Manic D Press, 1994). Poetry and fiction from a cross-section of queer San Francisco.

The First $20 Million Is Always the Hardest by Po Bronson (Avon, 1998). A high-tech novel from the Silicon Valley chronicler and writer for *Wired* magazine.

The Grapes of Wrath by John Steinbeck (Turtleback, 1976). The classic epic of California during the Depression, by one of America's best observers.

The Joy Luck Club by Amy Tan (Ivy Books, 1994). The lives of several generations of Chinese and Chinese-American women are explored in this sensitive novel.

The Maltese Falcon by Dashiell Hammett (Vintage Crime/Black Lizard, 1992). A great detective novel set in a dark and dangerous San Francisco.

On the Road by Jack Kerouac (Penguin, 1991). Sex, drugs, and rock 'n' roll in San Francisco and across the world, from the notorious Beat.

Tales of the City (6 volumes) by Armistead Maupin (Harperperennial Library, 1994). A soap opera following the lives and loves of a group of friends in the sexually liberated 1970s right on into the post-AIDS '80s.

Fares vary accordingly. The average one-way train ticket from Los Angeles to the Bay Area (a 12-hour trip) costs $70.

BY BUS

GREYHOUND (800/231-2222) operates out of the Transbay Terminal in San Francisco (415/495-1569) at First and Mission Streets (map:N2), traveling to cities around the Bay Area and throughout the United States. For popular destinations such as Lake Tahoe, it's an efficient way to travel, but local out-of-town destinations are better served by SamTrans buses (San Mateo County Transit District; 800/660-4287). You'll find Greyhound on the third floor of the Transbay Terminal—but since this isn't the best part of town, you should plan your trip so you get there during the day.

BY CAR

San Francisco can be accessed by several major highways. US Interstate 80 is the major artery from the east and the turnoff for those heading south via **INTERSTATE 5**. Expect major traffic and a $2 toll as you approach the Bay Bridge from the eastern side. More scenic yet often equally congested is **US HIGHWAY 101**, which snakes north-south from Marin County across the Golden Gate Bridge (a $3 toll), through San Francisco, and on down to San Jose. Known as the Pacific Coast Highway, **HIGHWAY 1** is a narrow, winding coastal road that passes along the majestic Pacific both north and south of the city, merging with 101 on the Golden Gate Bridge and, up north, eventually heading back toward the coast at the Stinson Beach exit in Marin County. Yes, it's a gorgeous drive, but it's recommended only for those who have plenty of time and don't get carsick.

Driving up from Los Angeles, there are two main routes. The longer coastal route along Highway 101 (437 miles and an 11-hour drive) is a beautiful scenic ride until you reach San Jose, at which point traffic, even under good conditions, slows things down to a crawl. From there it will take an hour and a half to reach the city. The inland route, Interstate 5 (389 miles and 8 hours), is a long, flat, boring stretch, but it will get you there in good time. From Sacramento it's 88 miles to San Francisco (1½–2 hours); from Yosemite it's 210 miles (4–5 hours).

San Francisco Parking Tips

Driving around San Francisco presents a formidable challenge. The combination of hills, traffic, aggressive drivers, and a notable lack of parking will tax your driving skills and patience. To avoid runaway cars on steep hills, curb your wheels! Turn the tires *away* from the curb and toward the street when facing uphill, and *toward* the curb when facing downhill—otherwise your car may find itself on a surprise journey or, at best, slapped with a parking ticket. Also, towaway zones and time limits proliferate, and parking regulations are strictly enforced. The best way to chalk up tickets is to either ignore parking signs or assume any degree of flexibility. Ultimately, the best way to see the city is on your feet or using public transportation. Taxis are few and far between, so much so that locals joke that there are only four or five cabs in the whole town—which doesn't seem so far-fetched when you try to find one. Instead, buy a bus map and a day pass and take Muni, our unreliable but essential public transport system of buses, streetcars, and cable cars. For information about the Muni system, including rates and routes, call 415/673-6864.

When to Visit

WEATHER

If you've decided to come to San Francisco in the summer because you expect it to be warm and sunny, think again. Epitomized in Mark Twain's infamous (mis)quote, "The coldest winter of my life was the summer I spent in San Francisco," the city's weather should be factored into the timing of your visit—although you never really know what to expect. In recent years, flash flooding and El Niño's storms ravaged the area during the winter, followed by an unusually (for San Francisco) hot summer. But the city normally enjoys mild weather year-round, with temperatures seldom rising above 70°F (21°C) or falling below 40°F (5°C). Be forewarned, however, about the morning and evening fog, which makes the temperature dip precipitously when it rolls in. Locals tend to dress in layers of clothing, and lightweight clothes often aren't enough, especially during the foggy summer months.

Typically, San Francisco enjoys its best weather in September and October. January is when the rain hits hardest, although it rains often throughout the winter, and it's windy year-round. The Bay Area is home to several "microclimates," which means that while one part of the city may be hot (typically the Mission District), another part (the Sunset District) will be blanketed in icy fog. The National Weather Service Forecast (650/364-7974), therefore, may not suffice; bring an extra sweater instead.

Average temperature and precipitation by month

Month	Daily Maximum Temp. degrees F	Daily Minimum Temp. degrees F	Monthly Precipitation in inches
JANUARY	56.1	46.2	4.48
FEBRUARY	59.4	48.4	2.83
MARCH	60.0	48.6	2.58
APRIL	61.1	49.2	1.48
MAY	62.5	50.7	0.35
JUNE	64.3	52.5	0.15
JULY	64.0	53.1	0.04
AUGUST	65.0	54.2	0.08
SEPTEMBER	68.9	55.8	0.24
OCTOBER	68.3	54.8	1.09
NOVEMBER	62.9	51.5	2.49
DECEMBER	56.9	47.2	3.52
ANNUAL AVERAGE	62.5	51.0	19.33

Source: San Francisco Convention and Visitors Bureau

TIME

San Francisco is on Pacific Standard Time (PST), which is three hours behind New York, two hours behind Chicago, one hour behind Denver, and two hours ahead of Honolulu.

WHAT TO BRING

Be ready for anything by wearing layers, layers, layers. In the winter, dress for rain and carry an umbrella, but in Indian-summer autumn you may want to have a T-shirt on hand. In the summer months, wear shorts only if you're brave or visiting the Mission District. Always bring a lightweight jacket or sweater with you just in case. If you're sitting on crowded public transportation, you can take it off; if you're walking along the windy streets to do a bit of shopping, you can put it back on.

As for clothing style, in San Francisco anything goes. This being home to Levi Strauss and Esprit, the fashion is casual, clean chic. Suits and ties are worn solely in the Financial District; most people—even those working for billion-dollar Internet companies—dress as if they've just dashed out of the house for a cup of coffee. This is not to say San Franciscans dress down:

in a town where Banana Republic rules, expensive T-shirts and khakis are considered good taste. Areas like Haight-Ashbury ("the Haight") still attract leather-clad punks and tie-dyed hippies, while secondhand clothing stores are popular everywhere, and '50s retro fashion still makes a splash.

General Costs

California's economy has been booming, thanks mostly to the continued success of the computer industry in Silicon Valley, the proliferation of aspiring Internet start-ups, and flourishing national companies such as the Gap, which originated and have their headquarters here. In short, San Francisco draws an incredible amount of money—and people—to this small, windswept peninsula.

The high-tech industry is big business in San Francisco. Hewlett-Packard, Intel, Sun Microsystems, Apple Computer, and Adobe Systems all reside in Silicon Valley. There are 1,931 computer companies in the area, and new software, multimedia, communications, and networking companies launch literally every day. Then, of course, there's the big banking industry: Wells Fargo and Charles Schwab & Co., for example, are all longtime city residents.

The high cost of living (San Francisco's is one of the highest in the country) coupled with the housing crunch stands as a glaring contradiction to the city's 14,000 homeless people. Nonetheless, San Francisco has always drawn—and continues to draw—a diverse, well-educated, and creative workforce. Thousands move to the city every month to start a business or a lucrative Internet-oriented career. Many are lured by the city's history of open-minded thinking and an entrepreneurial spirit that has prevailed here since the Gold Rush.

It is worth mentioning that the record-low 1 percent tenant vacancy rate and the climbing (indeed, astronomical) rent in nearly all neighborhoods has changed the housing market in recent years. Those who opt to stay are compromising their budgets to live here, while old-timers who bought their homes decades ago for $40,000 are guaranteed a comfortable retirement. The introduction of live/work spaces to former industrial neighborhoods is also changing the housing game. In short, affordable housing has all but disappeared as the economy keeps steamrolling right along.

Average costs for lodging and food

Double room:	
CHEAP	$99
MODERATE	$120–$150
EXPENSIVE	$220

Lunch for one:	
CHEAP	**$5–$8**
MODERATE	**$10–$15**
EXPENSIVE	**$15–$25**

Beverage in a restaurant:	
GLASS OF WINE	**$3.50–$7**
PINT OF BEER	**$3.50–$5**
COKE	**$1.50**
DOUBLE LATTE	**$2.75**

Other common items:	
MOVIE TICKET	**$8.75**
ROLL OF FILM	**$6**
TAXI PER MILE	**$1.80** in town, **$2.30** out of town
SOUVENIR T-SHIRT	**$10**

Tips for Special Travelers

FAMILIES WITH CHILDREN

In an emergency call 911, 24 hours a day. For questions about your child's health call Lucile Packard Children's Health Services at UCSF (415/476-3921, or 415/476-1037 for emergency service). You will have to pay for any emergency service, so you may want to contact your medical insurance carrier before seeking treatment. Emergency rooms are at San Francisco General Hospital (415/206-8111), UCSF Medical Center (415/476-1037), Davies Medical Center (415/565-6060), and California Pacific Medical Center (415/600-0600). In addition, downtown Medical/ Travel Medicine (415/362-7177) offers immediate, same-day appointments for travel-related medical conditions and is open from 8am to 6pm.

Watch for this icon throughout the book; it indicates places and activities that are great for families.

SENIORS

Seniors are well looked after in the city and receive discounts at museums and tourist attractions and on public transportation. The Senior Citizen Information line (415/626-1033) offers info on city services, and the Friendship Line for the Elderly (415/752-3778) is a support service that also offers crisis intervention.

PEOPLE WITH DISABILITIES

California is one of the leading states when it comes to providing social services for people with disabilities. Transportation organizations have created an ID card that gives people with disabilities discounts on travel throughout the Bay Area. For information, contact San Francisco Muni's Elderly and Handicapped Discount ID Office (415/923-6070).

11

For information on disability-related needs and referrals to state and national resources, call Direct Link for the Disabled (800/221-6827, ext. 7130). A crisis line for the disabled offers advice on everything from public transportation to stress and operates 24 hours a day (800/426-4263). Locally, the American Foundation for the Blind (415/392-4845) offers catalogs to help people access resources. Lighthouse for the Blind and Visually Disabled (415/431-1481) has devices such as walking canes to help people get around the city.

Most of San Francisco's major tourist attractions are wheelchair accessible, and many hotels offer services for visitors with wheelchairs or other special needs. The San Francisco Visitor Information Center (900 Market St, lower level Hallidie Plaza; 415/391-2000; map:N3) has the most up-to-date information.

WOMEN

San Francisco is a safe place for female travelers, but as in any major city, it's advisable to take more precautions at night. Many women's services are tied to lesbian resources, and the most comprehensive center for both is at the Women's Building (3543 18th St; 415/431-1180; map:L6). The building houses nine women's organizations and offers everything from classes in yoga and aerobics to social services. Another important health resource is Planned Parenthood (815 Eddy St between Van Ness and Franklin Sts; 415/441-5454; map:L3), which offers contraception and the morning-after pill at sliding rates. The Bay Area Women's and Children's Center (318 Leavenworth St; 415/474-2400; map:M4) also offers specialized services to women. The Rape Crisis Hotline (415/647-7273) is open 24 hours a day.

PET OWNERS

San Franciscans love their dogs, some to the point of militancy. Organized groups like to express their views to the city council, and the focus tends to be on one thing: letting canines roam freely through city parks. The Recreation & Park off-leash task force even maintains a Web site and a lively email network where like-minded owners can come together and wag their tongues.

San Francisco's off-leash areas are well delineated in *The Bay Area Dog Lover's Companion* (Foghorn Press), available at most local bookstores. Dogsbythebay.com is another good resource, providing info on hotels and restaurants that will welcome your pooch. Off-leash areas within San Francisco include:

FORT FUNSTON, along Skyline Bouelvard next to Lake Merced.
CRISSY FIELD, on the north edge of the Presidio, at Marina Boulevard.
MISSION DOLORES PARK, on Dolores Street between 18th and 20th.
ALTA PLAZA PARK, at Steiner and Clay Streets.
BUENA VISTA PARK, on Haight Street between Baker and Central.

GAYS AND LESBIANS

San Francisco is renowned as a mecca for gay and lesbian travelers. Its large gay community is centered in the Castro neighborhood (at Castro and 18th Sts), where festive rainbow flags fly and the streets are lined with upscale shops and well-dressed men. The neighborhood is extremely close-knit and supportive, and its vitality owes much to its denizens' long struggle for equality and civil rights. The city's lesbian population tends to concentrate around 16th and Valencia Streets in the Mission District. You can find clubs and bars catering to the gay community in all parts of San Francisco, however—this is a tolerant, gay-friendly city, and proud of it.

There are literally too many resources for gays and lesbians to list here. Several local publications and online resources cover news, culture, and events, including **DAMRON LESBIAN AND GAY TRAVEL GUIDES**, which provide information for lesbian and gay people looking for travel and accommodations; **GAY-MART** (www.gaymart.com), a gay and lesbian travel and resource guide that lists accommodations, bars and clubs, tea rooms, and cafes; **GAYCITY SAN FRANCISCO** (www.citycentral.net/ gaycity), with links to nightlife coverage, community news, live chat, classifieds, and discussion boards; **QSF GUIDE** (www.qsanfrancisco.com); and **SANFRANCISCO-LEATHER.COM**. *The Bay Area Reporter*, the community paper, can be found stacked in bars, bookshops, and various stores around town.

For those eager to chat it up in person, Cafe Flore (2298 Market St; 415/621-8579; map:K6) is a great spot. The restaurant, a favorite gathering place, has a good coffee selection, and you're bound to bump into a local enjoying their latte who can shoot the breeze or offer good advice. For guidebooks and other publications, check out the community bookstore A Different Light (489 Castro St; 415/431-0891; map:K6), which has a wide array of gay-oriented literature and a helpful staff.

For information on AIDS, contact the SF AIDS Foundation (415/864-2273) or the AIDS Nightline (415/434-AIDS).

FOREIGN VISITORS

The city has a number of services for travelers from abroad, including money exchange and translation services. Thomas Cook Currency Services (75 Geary St; 415/362-3452; map:N3) offers currency exchange, wire transfers, and sale and cashing of traveler's checks. Worldwide Foreign Exchange (150 Cyril Magnin St at 5th and Market Sts; 415/392-7283; map:M3) will exchange foreign currency and traveler's checks for U.S. dollars and vice versa.

Translation Express (51 Federal St, Suite 305; 415/284-9945; map:O3) can translate any document from any language overnight. International Effectiveness Center (690 Market St, Suite 700; 415/788-4149; map:N3), one of San Francisco's oldest translation services, provides simultaneous interpretation and guided tours with interpreters.

For a complete list of consulates, consult the yellow pages.

AUSTRALIA	I Bush St	415/362-6160
AUSTRIA	41 Sutter St	415/951-8911
CANADA	50 Fremont St	415/543-2550
FRANCE	88 Kearny St	415/781-0986
GERMANY	1960 Jackson St	415/775-1061
GREAT BRITAIN	I Sansome St	415/981-3030
IRELAND	44 Montgomery St	415/392-4214
ITALY	2590 Webster St	415/931-4924
MEXICO	870 Market St	415/392-5554
NETHERLANDS	901 Mariners Island Blvd, San Mateo	650/349-8848
NEW ZEALAND	I Maritime Plaza	415/399-1255
NORWAY	20 California St	415/986-0766
RUSSIA	2790 Green St	415/202-9800
SPAIN	1405 Sutter St	415/922-2995
SWEDEN	120 Montgomery St	415/788-2631
VENEZUELA	455 Market St	415/512-8340

WEB INFORMATION

For the savvy and not-so-savvy Web surfer, just about any info involving San Francisco is easily accessible online—from local news to traffic reports to hotel reservations. The following Web pages are a good place to start when planning your visit:

WWW.SFBAY.YAHOO.COM for general information

WWW.SFGATE.COM for coverage by the *Chronicle* and *Examiner* newspapers

WWW.SFVISITOR.ORG for the SF Convention and News Bureau

WWW.HOTELDISCOUNT.COM for a complete list of hotels and rates

WWW.BERKELEY.EDU for the University of California at Berkeley

Calendar of Events

JANUARY

SAN FRANCISCO SPORTS AND BOAT SHOW / Cow Palace; 415/469-6065 Over a nine-day period in mid-January, the show draws thousands of boating enthusiasts wanting to test the waters.

FEBRUARY

CHINESE NEW YEAR / Chinatown; 415/982-3000 (call for exact date) A huge procession through Chinatown marked by an endless array of marching bands, beautifully decorated floats, an immense writhing dragon nearly a block long, and earsplitting fireworks, the Chinese New Year parade rings in the day, but the festivities go on for a week. A must-see.

MARCH

ST. PATRICK'S DAY PARADE / Along Market St; 510/644-1164 Thousands of Irish in San Francisco—the city seems to be their home away from home—gather the Sunday before March 17 in good drinking spirit, and anyone who's willing to party is recruited on the spot. The parade starts at 12:45pm at Market and Second Streets and moves on to City Hall, but the fun doesn't stop there. While the post-party takes place at the nearby Civic Center, the pub crawl winds its way toward the Embarcadero and continues long after sunset.

APRIL

 CHERRY BLOSSOM FESTIVAL / Japantown; 415/563-2313 Held for over two weeks in mid- to late April, this celebration of Japanese arts—including traditional drumming, flower arranging, and origami—celebrates the cherry blossom so prized in Japanese culture.

SAN FRANCISCO INTERNATIONAL FILM FESTIVAL / AMC Kabuki 8 Cinemas, Fillmore and Post Sts, and other venues; 415/931-FILM America's oldest film festival, held mid-April to early May, screens enough movies to reflect an eclectic world experience. This event is extremely popular with locals, who often book far in advance. Don't worry if you just landed in town—there are more than 200 films to choose from, and tickets are relatively inexpensive. Whatever you end up seeing will give you a feel for the richness of cinema.

MAY

CINCO DE MAYO CELEBRATION / Mission District; 415/826-1401 The Sunday before May 5. Join the mariachi bands, parades, and dancers as the Latino community celebrates General Ignacio Zaragoza's defeat over the French at Puebla, Mexico, in 1862. The parade starts at 10am at 24th and Bryant Streets and winds its way to the Civic Center.

BAY TO BREAKERS FOOT RACE / Golden Gate Park; 415/777-7770 Traditionally sponsored by the *San Francisco Examiner*, the run from downtown to Ocean Beach attracts more than 100,000 athletes, joggers, (in)appropriately attired nudists, and leftover Halloween trick-or-treaters, all with one goal in mind—reaching the end. For many, it's not when you get there but how much fun/booze/comments on your costume/media coverage you had along the way. Held the third Sunday of May, it's a true San Francisco occasion.

CARNAVAL PARADE AND FESTIVAL / Mission between 14th and 24th Sts and Harrison St between 16th and 21st Sts; 415/826-1401 The South American festival is one of San Francisco's greatest events, with more than half a million spectators eagerly lining the route to watch the parade and join in the dancing. Steel drums, samba, and sangría transform the Mission into Río de Janeiro every Memorial Day weekend, and even the tightest shirts loosen up.

JUNE

UNION STREET ART FESTIVAL / Along Union St; 415/441-7055 A theme-filled celebration, full of music, arts and crafts, and gourmet food, held the first weekend of June.

NORTH BEACH FESTIVAL / Grant Ave; 415/989-2220 The North Beach Festival wines, dines, and serenades close to 100,000 visitors who can browse the arts and crafts booths, listen to poetry, or sit down and relentlessly people-watch.

 SAN FRANCISCO LESBIAN, GAY, BISEXUAL, TRANSGENDER PRIDE PARADE AND CELEBRATION / Market St; 415/864-3733 Usually the third or last weekend of June, this is an outlandish ode to gay pride. The parade sports drag queens, transvestites, gay marching bands, habit-wearing nuns, and a profusion of exposed skin and studded leather. While the parade is flamboyant fun and a photographer's dream, the popular occasion reflects a serious commitment to assert a queer-positive identity.

STERN GROVE MIDSUMMER MUSIC FESTIVAL / Sloat Blvd at 19th Ave; 415/252-6252 If you want to enjoy a day filled with free classical, jazz, and ethnic music and dance, show up with a blanket and a picnic in tow. Get here early and dress warmly: the Sunset District does not earn its name till September. Held mid-June through August.

JULY

FOURTH OF JULY CELEBRATION AND FIREWORKS / Along the northern waterfront; 415/777-7120 (call for exact location) On Independence Day, come join the patriotic celebration with hot dogs and baked beans. More often than not, the evening fog obscures some of the million-dollar fireworks display, and while locals swear they won't trek down to see another one, they always do.

JAZZ AND ALL THAT ART ON FILLMORE / Fillmore St; 415/346-4446 Fillmore Street closes itself off to traffic in early July and pays tribute to its jazz history with several blocks of arts and crafts booths, gourmet food, and, of course, jazz. The music is live and so is the vibe.

SAN FRANCISCO MARATHON / 800/698-8699 Usually held the second weekend in July, this is one of the largest marathons in the world. Call for entry and course information.

CABLE CAR BELL-RINGING COMPETITION / Union Square; 415/923-6217 Muni cable car operators compete for top bell-ringer in this annual competition.

AUGUST

RENAISSANCE PLEASURE FAIRE / North of San Francisco; 800/52-FAIRE (call for location) Fling yourself back to the Middle Ages with games, plays, food booths fit for a king, and elaborate arts and crafts. Actors with English accents and cutting wit entertain the thousands that flock here. Runs on Labor Day and six to eight weekends after.

ABSOLUT A LA CARTE, A LA PARK / Golden Gate Park; 415/458-1988 (call for exact location) This huge outdoor food fair, held Labor Day weekend, features over 40 of the city's favorite restaurants offering an impressive array of edibles in this eater's city. The wine flows equally, too, with 20 wineries and another 20 microbreweries offering their own liquid fare. Bring Alka-Seltzer and $9 for admission.

SEPTEMBER

OPERA IN THE PARK / Golden Gate Park; 415/861-4008 A free concert to launch the opera season. Call for location and to confirm the date.

SAN FRANCISCO SHAKESPEARE FESTIVAL / Golden Gate Park; 415/422-2221 Weekends in September, the festival offers free performances on outdoor stages featuring the musings of the Bard.

SAN FRANCISCO BLUES FESTIVAL / Fort Mason Center; 415/826-6837 During the third or fourth weekend in September, this weekend-long concert takes place. The largest outdoor blues festival on the West Coast, the festival features a dizzying array of local and national talent. You can charge tickets by phone through BASS Ticketmaster (510/762-2277).

FOLSOM STREET FAIR / Folsom and Harrison Sts; 415/861-3247 For the leather-clad aficionado, this can be an R-rated affair that makes other gay parades look like a Disney show. A San Francisco tradition for the Castro crowd and the curious, it happens the last Sunday in September.

OCTOBER

REGGAE IN THE PARK / Golden Gate Park; 415/458-1988 The first weekend in October, big-name artists thump bass grooves to large crowds, making this festival hard to miss. One of the city's best-attended festivals (no doubt due to good Indian-summer weather), the event costs $15 in advance and $17.50 on site. Two-day passes are available at a discounted rate, and it's free for children under 12.

FLEET WEEK / The Embarcadero; 415/395-3928 On Columbus Day weekend the U.S. Navy's Blue Angels tear up the skies over the Marina district and Fisherman's Wharf in a display of daring and speed. You'll find pedestrians glued to the spot looking up, trying to catch a glimpse as the planes disappear between buildings.

HALLOWEEN / A San Francisco favorite. It starts October 30, when the Exotic Erotic Halloween Ball attracts thousands of scantily clad partiers.

17

On Halloween proper, the spooks come out all over the place, especially in the Castro. While parties around the Civic Center can get disrupted by violence and theft, uptown the streets are clogged with amazing costumes, and Elvis lives on. Check the local papers to see what's happening when.

NOVEMBER

SAN FRANCISCO BAY AREA BOOK FESTIVAL / Concourse Exhibition Center, 8th and Brannan Sts; 415/487-4550 It's only $2 for adults, and kids under 17 get in free to the biggest book fair of the year, usually held over a weekend in October.

SAN FRANCISCO JAZZ FESTIVAL / 415/398-5655 This city loves its jazz, and the nearly two-week event in early November meanders through its best jazz venues. Past events have featured artists such as Herbie Hancock, Wayne Shorter, and Dave Brubeck.

DECEMBER

THE NUTCRACKER / War Memorial Opera House; 415/703-9400 Performed annually by the San Francisco Ballet, this classic holiday production is a perennial favorite. Tickets should be bought in advance.

LAY OF THE CITY

LAY OF THE CITY

Orientation

You need only open your eyes to discover why San Francisco is one of North America's top tourist destinations—and to understand why so many people, once they've seen it, want to stay in this beautiful city by the bay. Like the consummate hostess, San Francisco is possessed of charm, grace, natural good looks, and a captivating wit. And she is welcoming to all guests, eager to provide amenities for a visit you'll not soon forget. Situated at the tip of a peninsula, the city has huge expanses of water on three sides—most notably the Pacific Ocean to the west. The northern border, home to the stunningly beautiful Golden Gate, is adorned with two of the world's most impressive bridges, the **GOLDEN GATE BRIDGE** and the **SAN FRANCISCO–OAKLAND BAY BRIDGE**. On the east, the San Francisco Bay entrance is dotted by the natural wonders of **ALCATRAZ ISLAND, ANGEL ISLAND,** and **YERBA BUENA ISLAND** as well as the human-made **TREASURE ISLAND**. The city itself packs a bounty of beauty into its compact 47 square miles. From rolling hills and eucalyptus groves to towering skyscrapers and a colorful urban fabric, it's a harmonious balance between natural and human-made attractions.

Incorporated in 1850, San Francisco was a Gold Rush town, built on the wishes and whims of citizens who came here from around the world seeking their share of the new wealth. Much of that pioneering freewheeling spirit still thrives in the many diverse neighborhoods, each with a flavor and texture uniquely its own. The grid of the city's streets originated at Chinatown's Portsmouth Square and emanated from there; **MARKET STREET** diagonally intersects the grid from the waterfront to Twin Peaks and beyond. **SOUTH OF MARKET**, or **SOMA**, as it's known today, has long cultivated a sort of "other city" identity. Flatter than much of this notoriously hilly city, and with wider streets, SoMa now is home to large, low-slung warehouses, industrial and high-tech businesses, artists' lofts, funky and hip restaurants, lively nightspots (many along 11th and Folsom Sts), and the new **PACBELL BALLPARK** (2nd and Townsend Sts; map:O4). Still being developed in leaps and bounds, SoMa has also become a high-culture focal point with the building of the new **SAN FRANCISCO MUSEUM OF MODERN ART** and **YERBA BUENA CENTER FOR THE ARTS** (3rd and Mission Sts; map:N3), where a verdant park provides a tranquil spot to study the city's fascinating skyline.

Just north of Market Street are two areas that form the city's commercial core. The **FINANCIAL DISTRICT** (Kearny St to the Embarcadero) is marked by such mercantile monuments as the **TRANSAMERICA PYRAMID** (Montgomery and Washington Sts; map:N2), the **BANK OF**

LOW-PRICED PARKING

It borders on the absurd what some garages charge for parking in the city. In the Financial District, for example, rates go as high as $5 per 20 minutes, and a day's parking at the Pier 39 Garage will set you back a whopping $30. Heck, that's a decent lunch for two.

That's why you'll want to keep this page earmarked if you're touring the city by car, because the best parking deals are the city-owned garages, which charge a fraction of what the private parking sharks demand for a tiny patch of oily cement. We've put together the following list of city-owned garages to save you both time and lunch money.

Note: After you park, take your ticket with you, because you'll have to present it and pay up before you return to your car (and be sure to remember where you parked it, because some of the garages are huge). The parking rates below may have increased since this book went to press, but they're still the cheapest in the city.

Chinatown Area

Portsmouth Square Garage: Entrance is on Kearny Street between Washington and Clay Streets. $1 per hour for the first 4 hours. 504 spaces.

Golden Gateway Garage: Entrances are on Washington and Clay Streets, between Battery and Davis Streets. $3 per hour for the first 4 hours. 1,000 spaces.

Nob Hill/Union Square Area

St. Mary's Square Garage: Entrances are on Pine, Kearny, and California Streets, bordered by Grant Avenue. $1 per hour for the first 4 hours on weekends, $4 per hour for the first 4 hours on weekdays. 828 spaces.

Sutter-Stockton Garage: Entrances are on Stockton and Bush Streets, bordered by Grant Avenue and Sutter Street. $1 per hour for the first 4 hours. 1,865 spaces.

Union Square Garage: Entrance is on Geary Street, bordered by Powell, Post, and Stockton Streets. $1 per hour for the first 4 hours. 1,100 spaces.

Ellis-O'Farrell Garage: Entrances are on O'Farrell and Ellis Streets, bordered by Powell and Stockton Streets. $1 per hour for the first 4 hours. 1,263 spaces.

South of Market (SoMa) Area

Fifth & Mission Garage: Entrances are on Mission and Minna Streets, bordering Fourth and Fifth Streets. $1 per hour for the first 4 hours. 2,622 spaces.

Moscone Center Garage: Entrance is on Third Street, between Howard and Folsom Streets. $1 per hour for the first 4 hours. 732 spaces.

Civic Center and Hayes Valley Area

Civic Center Garage: Entrance is on McAllister Street between Polk and Larkin Streets. $1 per hour for the first 4 hours. 840 spaces.

Performing Arts Garage: Entrance is on Grove Street between Gough and Franklin Streets. $1 per hour for the first 4 hours. 612 spaces.

AMERICA building (Kearny and California Sts; map:N2), and the four shopping and high-rise office complexes of **EMBARCADERO CENTER** (bounded by Battery St and the Embarcadero and Sacramento and Clay Sts; map:N2). To the west are the department stores and luxury hotels of **UNION SQUARE** (an area bounded by O'Farrell and Sutter Sts and Powell St and Grant Ave; map:N3). The square itself is a terraced green expanse surrounding the granite Dewey Monument, which commemorates Admiral Dewey's 1898 victory over the Spanish navy at Manila Bay in the Spanish-American War.

Northeast of Union Square are the endlessly fascinating alleys and streets of **CHINATOWN**. Enter through the arching, dragon-adorned Chinatown Gate (Bush St at Grant Ave; map:N3) to explore this city-within-a-city, where the herb shops, Taoist temples, and strains of numerous Chinese dialects combine for an intoxicating effect. Along Stockton Street, this exotic enclave flows seamlessly into the Italian neighborhood of **NORTH BEACH**, where excellent restaurants and espresso cafes vie for your attention on Columbus Avenue. North Beach is also home to the remnants of the Beat generation, best exemplified at City Lights Bookstore (Columbus Ave and Broadway; map:N2), where poet-proprietor Lawrence Ferlinghetti still keeps shop.

Head farther north to the waterfront and you come to San Francisco's most popular tourist attraction, **FISHERMAN'S WHARF** (Jefferson St between Mason and Hyde Sts; map:M1). Once the true domain of fishermen and their nets, the neighborhood is now a collection of knick-knack shops, restaurants, souvenir stands, and walk-away crab cocktail vendors. Rising above it all is affluent, mostly residential Russian Hill, named for the immigrant Russian population that settled here a century ago, now boasting a fine array of restaurants, coffee shops, bars, and book and antique stores along Polk Street. To the south is posh **NOB HILL**, whose pinnacle atop California Street is home to the city's grande dame hotels—the Fairmont, the Mark Hopkins, the Huntington, and the Stanford Court—and the soaring, neo-Gothic Grace Cathedral, modeled after Notre Dame in Paris.

To the west, the city's residential areas have plenty to offer the eager sightseer. **PACIFIC HEIGHTS** (anchored by Fillmore St between Jackson and Post Sts) is a tony enclave replete with chic shopping boutiques, small but popular restaurants, and a mix of beautiful old Victorians and sleek modern homes. Visit Alta Plaza Park (Jackson and Steiner Sts; map:K2) for breathtaking views in every direction. Stroll down the hill along **FILLMORE STREET** and you'll go through the youngish, postcollegiate neighborhood of **COW HOLLOW**, so named because dairy farms once flourished here. The main drag is **UNION STREET**, turf of savvy boutique shoppers by day, single bar-hoppers by night. Farther down Fillmore is the **MARINA DISTRICT**, as famous for its great views and warm micro-climate as for its instability in earthquakes (it's built almost entirely on landfill and sustained major damage in the Loma Prieta quake of 1989). The Marina nowadays is generally a calm, sun-washed sea of Mediterranean-style homes along small, meandering streets. On weekends, though, the main artery of **CHESTNUT STREET** is a riot of folks in college alma-mater sweatshirts jockeying for a healthy breakfast in one of the many trendy juice joints and cafes. The Marina is also home to the Palace of Fine Arts, the Exploratorium, and the Golden Gate Promenade.

On the south side of town, the outlying neighborhoods have an entirely different feel. The **HAIGHT-ASHBURY** district (Divisadero St to Stanyan St and Oak St to Frederick St) hasn't lost touch with its '60s flower-power roots; in today's undeniably seedy yet gentrified Haight, an eclectic mix of shops, restaurants, and vintage clothing stores attracts an equally eclectic mix of locals and tourists. South of here is the famous **CASTRO** district, nerve center of the city's large, politically active gay and lesbian population. You can experience a good cross section of this interesting, vibrant neighborhood on Castro Street between Market and 17th Streets, anchored by the fabulous Castro Theatre, one of San Francisco's best repertory film houses.

Westward still, **GOLDEN GATE PARK** stretches from the Haight-Ashbury area at Stanyan Street to the Great Highway and the Pacific Ocean. This immense swath of green (between Fulton St on the north and Lincoln Ave on the south) is home to the M. H. de Young Memorial Museum, the Asian Art Museum, the California Academy of Sciences, and a slew of other botanical and cultural sights. South of the park, the **SUNSET DISTRICT**, a quiet residential bastion of postwar middle-class homes, is currently in the throes of becoming trendy. North of the park, the **RICHMOND DISTRICT**, another up-and-coming working-class neighborhood, boasts a mind-boggling assortment of ethnic restaurants, from Russian to Thai to kosher delis; just travel down Clement Street or Geary Boulevard and take your pick. The Richmond, also known informally as Chinatown West, has an Asian population bigger than Chinatown's. Its northern neighbor is the **PRESIDIO**, a former military base converted a few years ago into a national park, with walking and biking trails and historic sites galore. At the Presidio's northernmost tip is Fort Point, a Civil War fortress that still houses the San Martín Cannon, cast in Peru in 1684. And directly above the fort looms the city's biggest crown jewel of all: the **GOLDEN GATE BRIDGE**.

Visitor Information

Visitors to San Francisco have never been ashamed of acting like visitors. Which only makes sense: after all, on any given day, about half the people they see on the sidewalk are just like them—from out of town. With tourism the city's number-one source of revenue, it's not unusual to see people trying to get their bearings on street corners as they battle with huge maps flailing about in the wind. Locals are known for their willingness to help—and there are ample resources to turn to. Ground zero is the **SAN FRANCISCO VISITOR INFORMATION CENTER** (900 Market St at Powell St; 415/391-2000; map:N3), in the lower level of Hallidie Plaza, next to the cable car turnaround near Union Square. Open Monday through Friday 9am to 5pm, weekends 9am to 3pm, and closed major holidays, the center is a cornucopia of helpful expertise, from city maps and tour books to hotel and restaurant advice. There's also a hot line with schedules for citywide entertainment and events—in five languages, no less. For non-English events information, call 415/391-2003 (French); 415/391-2122 (Spanish); 415/391-2101 (Japanese); or 415/391-2004 (German). The center is operated by the **SAN FRANCISCO CONVENTION AND VISITORS BUREAU** (201 3rd St, Suite 900; 415/391-2000; map:N3), another valuable tourist resource; an easy way to access its font of information is on the Internet at www.sfvisitor.org. Other visitor information kiosks are sprinkled throughout town, including one near the front entrance to the San Francisco Shopping Centre (5th and Market Sts; map:N3) and at the San Francisco International Airport (800/736-2008; map:KK5-LL5).

Getting Around

BY BUS

With the possible exception of New York, no other U.S. city has more locals who pride themselves on living a sans-auto lifestyle. By foot, bike, or bus, it is relatively easy to get around in San Francisco without a car—especially if you're willing (and able) to hike up the many hills. In fact, given the scarcity of parking spots, walking is often preferred. The **MUNICIPAL RAILWAY SYSTEM** (415/673-6864 or 415/923-6336), or **MUNI** as it is known around here, is San Francisco's public transportation network. Efforts always seem to be under way to improve the system's punctuality, but if you need to be somewhere at a specific time, play it safe and hail a taxi (see the By Taxi section, below). Muni operates an extensive system of diesel- and electric-powered buses, as well as a handsome line of historic streetcars that amble up and down Market Street from First

Street to the Castro district. The streetcars, collected from cities around the world and restored to their original beauty, include a wood-sided car from 1920s Italy and a convertible car that locals call "the Boat."

The Muni system also operates light-rail trains as well as the famous cable cars, the nation's only moving national landmarks. Cable car fares are $2 one-way. Bus and streetcar fares are $1 for adults (ages 18–64); 65 cents for seniors (age 65 and up), youth (ages 5–17), and disabled persons; and free for children under 5. Exact change is required, except on cable cars, where conductors can make change for $20. Adults can save on fares by buying Muni tokens at 80 cents each in rolls of 10, 20, and 40. (Cable car conductors accept a token plus $1.)

An even better deal for frequent riders is the Muni Passport. Available for one day ($6), three consecutive days ($10), or seven consecutive days ($15), Passports allow you to ride buses, streetcars, and cable cars as many times a day as you wish. (A 30-day Fastpass, good for unlimited rides excluding cable cars, costs about $35 to $40.) Passports will also get you a reduced transit fare to ballgames at 3Com Park or the new PacBell Ballpark and other special events; the 3- and 7-day passes are good for discounts at various local attractions including the San Francisco Zoo, museums in Golden Gate Park, and some sights near Fisherman's Wharf. You can buy 1-day Muni Passports from conductors on cable cars; in addition, Passports and cable car tickets are sold at several locations throughout town, including the information booths in the baggage claim areas at San Francisco International Airport; the downtown Visitor Information Center; the cable car ticket booth at the turnaround at Powell and Market Streets; and TIX Bay Area (251 Stockton St on Union Square; 415/433-7827; map:N3). For a complete list of locations, call 415/923-6050 or 415/923-6051, or visit the Muni Revenue Department (949 Presidio Ave at Geary Blvd; 415/923-6336; map:J3).

BY BART

Bay Area Rapid Transit (insider tip: don't call it "the" BART, it's just BART) is an excellent way to travel longer distances. The clean, safe underground rail network links San Francisco to East Bay destinations including Berkeley, Oakland, Fremont, and Pleasanton, as well as cities as far south as Daly City and Colma. BART fares range from about $1.10 to $5, depending how far you're going. Call 650/992-2278 for schedules and more information.

BY TAXI

It's an ongoing debate: city officials say there aren't enough taxis in San Francisco, while cabbies say there are too many. Caught in the middle are everyday San Franciscans, standing on street corners with outstretched arms trying to flag down a cab. While you can usually hail a taxi from a downtown sidewalk without too much trouble, it can be a terribly frustrating endeavor during rush hour and on weekend evenings. Your best bet during these times is to call ahead from your hotel room, restaurant, or wherever you happen to be. Rates for most taxi companies are about $2.50 upon entering the cab, then either 30 cents for each sixth of a mile or 40 cents for each minute. Trips to and from the airport usually cost between $30 and $40; some drivers will offer a flat rate before the trip starts. A few of the bigger companies, all radio dispatched, are DESOTO CAB (415/970-1300), YELLOW CAB (415/626-2345), and CITY WIDE (415/920-0700).

BY CAR

About five years ago city officials estimated there were 450 registered automobiles in San Francisco for every mile of paved roadway. It doesn't take a civil engineer to figure out that that's too many cars. In spite of the city's reputation for good public transportation, cars still abound. The by-product, of course, is traffic—tons of it. And parking? Fuhgeddaboudit. Everyone here makes jokes about being tempted to stop and park if they see a good spot, even when they don't need one. Still, driving in San Francisco can be a convenient—if sometimes adventurous—way to get around. And a car definitely comes in handy for trips outside of town. The San Francisco International Airport has outlets for most RENTAL CAR COMPANIES; most have downtown and other San Francisco locations as well, including Avis (800/331-1212), Budget (800/527-0700), and Hertz (800/654-3131). The California State Automobile Association (CSAA), a division of AAA (800/272-2155), has a traveler's service providing information on rental cars, trips, and road and weather conditions, as well as tour books and maps. For CSAA emergency roadside assistance, call 800/222-4357.

Your best bet for PARKING downtown is in one of the many centrally located lots. Metered parking is available but hard to come by, and once you find a spot, you can't stay long; most downtown meters allow 30 to 60 minutes of parking or are located in loading or rush-hour tow-away zones. The garages on average charge $1.50 per hour, $7 for four hours, or about $15 to $25 for the day. There are a few relatively LOW-PRICED GARAGES in the Union Square area; see the "Low-Priced Parking" sidebar in this chapter for details. In outlying neighborhoods, street parking is usually easier to find. Most areas have 2-hour metered parking along the commercial strips at 25 cents (quarters only) for each half- or quarter-hour; noncommercial streets typically have 2-hour parking limits enforced by ever-vigilant patrolling officers of the Department of Parking and Traffic (415/554-7275), who time your visit by marking your tires with chalk. Parking tickets range from $25 or $30 for a minor violation to $250 and more for parking illegally in a space reserved for the disabled. If your car is towed, call the AUTO IMPOUND (415/553-1235) and expect to pay at least $100 to retrieve it. If you think your car may have been stolen, call the California Highway Patrol (415/557-1094), but always check first to see whether it has been towed.

BY BICYCLE

One look at the steep hills that rise and fall all over San Francisco, and you might think only an Olympic athlete or a fool would use a bicycle to get around. But bikes are actually one of the best ways to see the city. And there are plenty of places to ride that don't overtax your legs or lungs. Great **BIKE TRAILS** trace the Embarcadero along the waterfront, from the northern piers around to the Ferry Building and toward the South Beach Marina; the more rustic Golden Gate Promenade, along the northern edge of the city, takes you by the foot of the Golden Gate Bridge. Both offer flat terrain and spectacular views of the city and the bay. Bicycling is also an excellent way to see the Presidio. While this military-base-turned-national-park has its inclines, the Presidio trails—some of which are unpaved—offer a wooded, tranquil respite from the urban hubbub just a stone's throw away. Golden Gate Park is another great choice for leisurely biking, with a web of trails meandering throughout its length, many leading all the way out to the ocean. On Sunday the park is closed to auto traffic, so all you have to look out for are daredevil inline skaters (and other bikes). Riding the hilly streets in the heart of the city is more of a pastime for bike messengers than for pleasure bikers, but bikes are hugely popular just beyond the city limits.

MOUNTAIN BIKING was invented in Marin County, and that is where you'll find an army of enthusiasts keeping the tradition alive on any given day. You can ride across the Golden Gate Bridge to access the myriad trails in the Marin Headlands and Tennessee Valley, which begin just north of the bridge. Call the Golden Gate National Recreation Area (415/556-0560) for details and map information.

Another outstanding choice for trail riding is Angel Island State Park (415/435-1915), an oasis of tranquility in the center of the bay. Ferries will take you and your bike to and from the island (see the By Ferry section, below). Several places in San Francisco have good-quality **BIKES FOR RENT** at reasonable day and weekend rates. On Stanyan Street near the eastern entrance to Golden Gate Park, several bike shops coexist in neighborly harmony as a sort of "bicycle row"; among these, Start to Finish Bike Rentals (672 Stanyan St; 415/750-4760) offers one of the city's largest selections. Other good bets near the wharf and North Beach area are Adventure Bike Rentals (968 Columbus Ave; 415/771-8735) and Blazing Saddles Bike Rentals (Pier 41, at Fisherman's Wharf, and 1095 Columbus Ave; 415/202-8888).

BY FERRY

As you might imagine in a city bounded by water, passenger ferries populate the bay. In fact, before the bridges were built, ferries were the only way to reach the city from the east and the north without an overland detour of several hours. Now less widely used, they're still a scenic and fun way to get across the water. Commuters, tourists, and weekend bike warriors share the decks (alas, no automobiles are permitted). Ferries go to the Marin County towns of Sausalito, Larkspur, and Tiburon as well as to Alcatraz and Angel Island; East Bay destinations include Alameda, Oakland, Berkeley, and Vallejo farther to the north (you can even get as far as Davis and Sacramento via connecting buses). Boats for the various **FERRY SERVICES** depart from the Ferry Building at the foot of Market Street and from Piers 39, 41, and 43½. Services include Blue & Gold Fleet (415/705-5555), Red & White Fleet (877/855-5506), Golden Gate Ferries (415/923-2000), the Angel Island–Tiburon Ferry (415/435-2131), the Harbor Bay Ferry (510/769-5500), the Oakland/Alameda Ferry (510/522-3300), and Baylink Ferries (877/643-3779). Call ahead for fare, bicycle, and schedule information.

Essentials

PUBLIC REST ROOMS

The City of San Francisco spent a lot of money a few years back, and not without controversy, to put a handful of high-tech, self-cleaning public rest rooms in such well-trod spots as Market and First Streets, Fisherman's Wharf, and the cable car turnaround at Market and Powell Streets. Look for the olive-green boothlike kiosks. It costs 25 cents to enter, with no time limit. Many parks and public buildings also have rest rooms, including the San Francisco Public Library (100 Larkin St at Grove St; map:M4), the San Francisco Shopping Centre (5th and Market Sts; map:M4), most museums, and major department stores.

MAJOR BANKS

The easterly hub of San Francisco's downtown area is called the Financial District, and it's easy to find a banking institution here to meet your needs. All major banks can exchange currency. The self-proclaimed bank of the West is **WELLS FARGO**, founded right here in the city by the bay in the mid-1800s to handle the "new" money that folks were pulling down from the hills in the form of gold nuggets. Wells Fargo has many branches throughout the Bay Area along with several in downtown San Francisco, including its beautiful banking hall at the corner of Market and Montgomery Streets (415/477-1000). At 420 Montgomery Street you'll find an interesting History Museum in the Wells Fargo lobby

SAN FRANCISCO'S FERRY FLEET

One of the most fun and interesting ways to explore the Bay Area is by ferry. In addition to the popular ride over to Alcatraz, there are a number of options for cruising the bay. The **Blue & Gold Fleet** (415/705-5555) offers ferry service to Alcatraz, Angel Island, Sausalito, and Tiburon, as well as bay cruises throughout the week. All tours depart from Pier 39 or Pier 41 at Fisherman's Wharf; call for the latest schedules and rates. Also located on Fisherman's Wharf is the **Red & White Fleet** (415/447-0597). It offers a one-hour Golden Gate Bridge Cruise that takes in all the city's waterfront sites and also cruises under the Golden Gate Bridge, along the Marin Headlands, and past Sausalito, Angel Island State Park, and Alcatraz Island. Also offered is a 45-minute "Round the Rock" cruise that circles Alcatraz. It's based at Pier 43 on Fisherman's Wharf; contact them for schedules and rates.

(415/781-2235), with photographs and artifacts from the Gold Rush era and a genuine stagecoach. Until not very long ago, the world headquarters for Bank of America was in San Francisco, in the massive granite-clad skyscraper that still bears the bank's name (Pine and Montgomery Sts; map:N2). While the actual headquarters have moved east, the "BofA" building and the bank itself still exert a strong presence in San Francisco. Downtown you'll find branches of the bank at the corner of Market and New Montgomery Streets, in the One Market Plaza building (1 Market St; map:O2), and near Union Square (420 Powell Street). Call the 24-hour customer service number (800/227-5458) for a complete list of local branches and other recorded information.

POLICE AND SAFETY

In cases of emergency, dial 911 from any phone. In nonemergency situations, call the San Francisco Police Department (415/553-0123). San Francisco has a relatively good reputation for safety, though just as you would in any major urban area, keep your wits about you: pickpockets have been known to strike on busy sidewalks and buses, and deserted streets and unattended bags can attract more aggressive thieves. Fortunately, the police department maintains a high-profile presence, and most officers are friendly and approachable.

HOSPITALS AND MEDICAL/DENTAL SERVICES

San Francisco, one of the nation's leading health-care and research centers, is home to myriad top-quality hospitals and medical centers. The California Pacific Medical Center (2333 Buchanan St; 415/563-4321; map:K3) is based in the Pacific Heights area and offers a physician referral service (800/225-5637). The University of California at San Francisco (UCSF) (505 Parnassus Ave; 415/476-1000; map:I6), one of the nation's leading cancer research facilities, has a medical center on its campus. And the San Francisco City Health Center (800/533-7344) is a network of community health facilities offering the complete range of medical services. Call to locate a participating branch near you.

The Dental Referral Service (800/422-8338) can put you in touch with a dentist who accepts your insurance or can treat you in an emergency. The San Francisco Dental Society Referral Service (415/421-1435) also offers information on low-cost clinics and emergency care.

POST OFFICES

Call the 24-hour postal hot line (800/275-8777) for information on post office locations and hours, postal rates, sending valuables, and other mail-related questions. The main post office downtown is the Rincon Finance Station (180 Steuart St at Howard St; map:O2), open Monday through Friday 7am to 6pm, Saturday 9am to 2pm. The Chinatown Station (867 Stockton St at Clay St; map:N2) is open Monday through Friday, 9am to 5:30pm, and Saturday 9am to 4:30pm. Macy's at Union Square (180 O'Farrell St at Stockton St; map:N3) has a full-service post office in the store's lower level. It's the only post office in the city open on Sunday (11am to 5pm); Monday through Saturday hours are 10am to 5:30pm.

GROCERY STORES

If you can't find what you're looking for at one of the farmers markets held during the week in the city, several good grocery stores dot the downtown periphery. Whole Foods Market (1765 California St; 415/674-0500; map:L3) has a cultish following among locals, who flock to the bright, warehouselike store for its gourmet products, health-conscious inventory, and fresh-prepared foods to go. In Pacific Heights, Mollie Stone's Market and Deli (2435 California St; 415/567-4902; map:K3) is also popular for its fresh-made foods and its outstanding fish and meat department. Open daily till 10pm, this is a great place to stop for a huge deli sandwich and a good bottle of wine for a picnic in Golden Gate Park. The Safeway chain has several locations in San Francisco, including one in the Northpoint Centre (350 Bay St; 415/781-4374; map:M1), open daily until midnight, and a 24-hour store in the Marina district (15 Marina Blvd; 415/586-2421; map:J1).

PHARMACIES

Walgreens drugstores are in abundance in San Francisco, and in addition to a full-service pharmacy, you'll find a large assortment of sundries. Some stores are open 24 hours and have 24-hour prescription services. There are several locations downtown, including 825 Market Street at 4th Street (415/543-9534) and 141 Kearny Street (415/834-0231). For a complete list of store locations, call 800/925-4733. Other good locally owned full-service pharmacies include the One Market Plaza Pharmacy (1 Market St Plaza; 415/777-0404; map:N2), downtown in the Financial District; the Four-Fifty Sutter Pharmacy (450 Sutter St, 4th floor; 415/392-4137; map:N3), which will deliver your prescription anywhere in the city; and the Fairmont Hotel Pharmacy (801 Powell St; 415/362-3000; map:N3), in the lobby of the landmark Union Square hotel.

DRY CLEANERS AND LAUNDROMATS

Most hotels offer dry cleaning and laundry service for their guests. In addition, a good service in the Financial District is Embarcadero Cleaners (2 Embarcadero Center; 415/986-7627; map:N2), a full-service operation with express cleaning available. Ray's French Cleaners (1205 Union St at Hyde St; 415/885-4171; map:M2), on Russian Hill, offers same-day service for shirts as well as complete laundry service; it's open every day except Sunday.

You can find full-service and self-service laundries in almost every neighborhood in town, but you can clean your clothes *and* enjoy a social night out at Brain Wash (1122 Folsom St at Langton St, between 7th and 8th Sts; 415/861-3663; map:M4), a laundromat and cafe in the hip South of Market area. In addition to several self-serve laundry machines, the place has a full-fledged singles scene, complete with live music. Pinball and video games dot the flanks. The cafe menu offers burgers, salads, pastas, and a great beer selection; food is served until 10pm on weekends, 9pm weeknights. The laundromat is open until midnight on weekends and 11pm on weeknights.

LEGAL SERVICES

The Lawyer Referral Service (a branch of the Bar Association of San Francisco) offers attorney referrals (415/989-1616). The San Francisco Trial Lawyers Association provides free legal advice and referrals (415/956-6401). The AIDS Legal Referral Panel (582 Market St, Suite 910; 415/291-5454; map:N3), composed of volunteer attorneys, helps individuals with AIDS/HIV handle everything from wills to power of attorney to discrimination. Fees are based on a sliding scale; Spanish- and Farsi-speaking attorneys are available. Centro Legal de la Raza (474 Valencia St, Suite 295; 415/575-3500; map:L5) gives legal services to Spanish-speaking people and has 12 attorneys and dozens of volunteers on staff.

BUSINESS AND COPY SERVICES

HQ Global Work Places (44 Montgomery St; 415/781-5000; and 2 Embarcadero Center; 415/835-1300; map:N3, N2) has everything the traveling business executive could possibly need, from part- or full-time corporate office suites and videoconferencing facilities to secretarial, computer, and graphic services and high-speed Internet access. Vantas

Officing Solutions Worldwide (1 Sansome St; 415/951-4600 or 800/416-4600; map:N2) offers full office and secretarial services in suites with commanding bay views, along with word processing and desktop-publishing services and high-speed Internet connections. They even have a law library. For copy needs, Ascribe Business Services (234 Front St; 415/398-0330; map:O2) is a respected Financial District outfit specializing in legal documents, oversize printing, presentation blowups and mounting, and digital color printouts. They can also make booklets for you. Copy Central is a popular service center, with four locations downtown (Market and 3rd Sts; 415/882-7377; 603 Battery St at Jackson St; 415/433-5792; 110 Sutter St at Montgomery St; 415/392-6470; and 4 Embarcadero Center, lobby level, Drumm and Clay Sts; 415/576-0430; map:N3-O2). Copy Central can handle high-volume jobs, including oversize documents, and also has a self-service station. The city is rife with Kinko's outlets as well, all open 24 hours a day, including locations downtown (201 Sacramento St; 415/834-0240; map:N2), in Pacific Heights (3225 Fillmore St; 415/441-2995; map:K1), and in the Upper Market area (1967 Market St; 415/252-0864; map:L5).

MESSENGER SERVICES

More than just a delivery method, messengering in San Francisco is almost cultlike. The bicycle couriers that zip in and out of traffic, slipping at full speed through the tiniest openings between cars and trucks, have reached near-legendary status. One of the most reliable, quick, radio-dispatched services is Aero Special Delivery Service (415/621-7433 or 800/303-2376).

PHOTOGRAPHY EQUIPMENT AND SERVICES

Shutterbugs love the atmosphere at Discount Camera (33 Kearny St; 415/392-1100; map:N3), a large downtown store that offers everything from same-day camera repair to advice on proper f-stop settings. It also has a full line of cameras, video cameras, binoculars, and more. Metro Camera Service SF (953 Mission St; 415/356-0480; map:N3) will put a rush on the repair of any kind of camera—even a video camera—and have it back to you the same day, or the same afternoon in some cases. For film developing within an hour, some locals prefer Wolf Camera, with nine locations in the Financial District, including 229 Kearny Street, 415/421-0301; 650 Market Street, 415/788-5950; and 455 Powell Street, 415/421-8033; map:N3-M3.

COMPUTER REPAIRS AND RENTALS

The people at PC Repair Center (415/452-0955) will pick up your ailing laptop and give you a loaner while they fix it. They promise a 4-hour response time, with no charge for traveling to your location. For exclusive, factory-authorized Macintosh service, a good choice is ComputerWare

(Sansome and Pine Sts; 800/434-9622; map:N3), where the friendly, knowledgeable staff can often fix your problem while you wait. Rent-A-Computer (660 Davis St; 415/398-7800; map:N2), downtown, offers reasonable rental rates on a full line of products by Apple, Compaq, IBM, and Sun Microsystems.

PETS AND STRAY ANIMALS

If you see a stray or any animal in need of help, or if you've lost your furry or feathered travel companion, call San Francisco Animal Care and Control (1200 15th St; 415/554-6364; map:M5), which also has a lost pet service (415/LOST-PET). If the little critter gets sick or injured, Pets Unlimited (2343 Fillmore St; 415/563-6700; map:K3) is one of the top animal health-care facilities in the city, offering everything from 24-hour emergency service to grooming to flea control.

SPAS AND SALONS

Nearly every spa and salon service you could imagine—and some you probably can't—is available in San Francisco, much of it at the finer hotels. Spa Nordstrom (San Francisco Centre, 865 Market St; 415/977-5102; map:M4) and 77 Maiden Lane Salon & Spa (77 Maiden Ln; 415/391-7777; map:N3) are luxe establishments where you can get everything from a bikini wax to a Swedish massage (for more details on these spas, see Body Care in the Shopping chapter). At Zendo Urban Retreat (256 Sutter St; 415/788-3404; map:N2), a popular choice for personal relaxation and revitalization, services include hair and makeup styling, massage, and other body treatments. At the less-expensive Kabuki Springs and Spa (1750 Geary Blvd; 415/922-6000; map:K3), you can sink into a traditional Japanese group-style bath, have an exclusive hour-long private massage, or treat yourself to a facial, seaweed wrap, or salt scrub. The Kabuki's communal facilities are reserved for women only on Wednesday, Friday, and Sunday, and for men only on Monday, Thursday, and Saturday; on Tuesday it's co-ed.

Local Resources

NEWSPAPERS

As of this writing, San Francisco is one of the few American cities that can still call itself a two-paper town—but maybe not for long. For years the SAN FRANCISCO CHRONICLE (901 Mission St; 415/777-7000; www.sfgate.com; map:N3) has been the daily morning paper, providing local coverage as well as the usual national syndicated news. The SAN FRANCISCO EXAMINER (110 5th St; 415/777-2424; www.examiner.com; map:N3), the first paper in the empire founded by famed media magnate William Randolph Hearst, has been the afternoon daily, a bit more sensationalist but with a solid mix of national coverage and local flavor. A joint operating agreement crafted years ago has allowed the papers to share plant facilities and combine forces to publish a single Sunday paper. In late 1999, however, the Hearst Corporation bought the *Chronicle*, raising concerns that it might be just a matter of time before one paper (most likely the *Examiner*) goes the way of the teletype machine. The city also supports two weeklies. The muckraking **SAN FRANCISCO BAY GUARDIAN** (520 Hampshire St; 415/255-3100; www.sfbay.com; map:M6) has been a free source of lively political viewpoints and excellent nightlife and events coverage for decades; it's one of the largest and most respected alternative weeklies in the nation. **SF WEEKLY** (510/834-7717; www.sfweekly.com), although now owned by out-of-staters, still offers interesting features on controversial topics and an extensive entertainment and events section. The gay community is served by the magazine **Q SAN FRANCISCO** (415/764-0324; www.qsanfrancisco.com), a glossy monthly with well-written articles on all aspects of gay and gay-related life, and the **BAY AREA REPORTER** (395 9th St; 415/861-5019; www.ebar.com; map:M4), a good paper featuring editorials, columnists, local news and arts coverage, and events listings. For in-depth business news and investigation, the weekly **SAN FRANCISCO BUSINESS TIMES** (275 Battery St; 415/989-2522; map:N2) is a trusted and widely read source.

PUBLIC LIBRARIES

After more than a little controversy and extensive public debate, the new **SAN FRANCISCO PUBLIC LIBRARY** (100 Larkin St; 415/557-4400; www.sfpl.lib.ca.us; map:M4), or the New Main, as it has come to be known, opened in April 1996, just across the street from the Old Main. Love it or hate it, it's a sight to behold, a modernist temple of knowledge, with all the accoutrements in place for the ride into the 21st century. You enter the library through a breathtaking five-story spiraling atrium. The sleek hallways and various rooms are drenched in natural light, beckoning you to stay and feel at home. There's a 247-seat auditorium, a gallery, a cafe, and outdoor terraces. The book stacks contain special collections on subjects ranging from government and gay and lesbian history to music and environmentalism. There are sections on Chinese and African-American cultures and an area devoted entirely to San Francisco history. The New Main is as tech-savvy as any public library has ever been, with some 400 computer terminals, most offering **FREE INTERNET ACCESS**. And in a move lamented by a vocal group of traditionalists, much of the card catalog has been electronically converted, to be made available online at the library's Web site. Other sections worth noting are the Children's Center, which includes a computer education room; the Center for the Deaf and Hearing Impaired; the Library for the Blind and Print Handicapped; and the International Center, which contains materials for foreign-language-speaking patrons. The New Main is open Monday 10am to 6pm, Tuesday through Thursday 9am to 8pm, Friday 11am to 5pm, Saturday 9am to 5pm, and Sunday noon to 5pm. Call 415/557-4400 to locate one of the 26 neighborhood library branches throughout the city.

MAJOR DOWNTOWN BOOKSTORES

Borders Books & Music (400 Post St; 415/399-1633; map:N3) is an enormous store near Union Square with four floors of books and music CDs—more than 200,000 titles plus 2,000 CD-ROMs. There's also a great collection of periodicals from the United States and abroad, plus a cozy on-site cafe where you can sit and read them all. Perhaps the most celebrated bookstore in San Francisco is City Lights Bookstore (261 Columbus Ave; 415/362-8193; map:N2), founded by Beat generation icon Lawrence Ferlinghetti, who still reigns over the shop. The inventory is vast and varied, with an eclectic assortment of literary works by local and national authors, a comprehensive collection of political books, and of course everything ever written by Ginsberg, Kerouac, et al. The San Francisco outlet of Barnes & Noble (2550 Taylor St; 415/292-6762; map:M1) has two floors of stacks featuring books in every imaginable category—125,000 titles in all. As with all Barnes & Noble stores, the staff encourages browsing, with numerous work tables and comfy chairs set out for your convenience.

RADIO AND TV

The radio dial is jam-packed in the Bay Area, with stations of every stripe squeezed in shoulder to shoulder. If the pop hit of the moment is what you seek, you can find it on no fewer than three major stations. The area is also home to one of the nation's first classic rock stations, KFOG, which continues to be a trendsetter in that genre. One of the first urban contemporary stations in the country, Berkeley's KBLX, has spawned many an imitator from coast to coast. But for true diversity and a taste of local eccentricity, the lower end of the dial is the place to be. National Public Radio can be heard on two stations here (KQED and KALW), each emanating its own temperament in between national feeds. KPOO is one of the most truly eclectic stations in the region, airing everything from gospel to Latin jazz as well as good locally produced shows on community and political affairs. The arbiter of independent programming has long been Berkeley's KPFA, which as we write is battling very publicly with corporate powers-that-be for its independent soul. Here's a quick guide to the radio dial.

Radio stations

TALK / NEWS / SPORTS
KPIX–FM / 95.7
KSFO–AM / 560
KNBR–AM / 680
KCBS–AM / 740
KGO–AM / 810
KFBK–AM / 1530
KPIX–AM / 1550
KLIV–AM / 1590

PUBLIC / COLLEGE STATIONS
KQED–FM / 88.5
KPOO–FM / 89.5
KZSU–FM / 90.1
KUSF–FM / 90.3
KALX–FM / 90.7
KALW–FM / 91.7
KPFA–FM / 94.1

URBAN / SOUL / HIP-HOP
KBLX–FM / 102.9
KMEL–FM / 106.1
KDIA–FM / 1310

JAZZ / URBAN CONTEMPORARY
KSJS–FM / 90.7
KCSM–FM / 91.1
KJAZ–FM / 92.7
KKSF–FM / 103.7

ADULT CONTEMPORARY
KLLC–FM / 97.3
KIOI–FM / 101.3

KKIQ–FM / 101.7
KEZR–FM / 106.5

ROCK / CLASSIC ROCK / ALTERNATIVE
KSJO–FM / 92.3
KLCQ–FM / 92.9
KUFX–FM / 94.5
KFOG–FM / 104.5
KITS–FM / 105.3

OLDIES
KBGG–FM / 98.1
KFRC–AM / 610

COUNTRY
KYCY–FM / 93.3
KSAN–FM / 94.9
KRTY–FM / 95.3

CLASSICAL
KKHI–FM / 100.9
KDFC–FM / 102.1
KDFC–AM / 1220

SOFT HITS
KOIT–FM / 96.5
KBAY–FM / 100.3

SPANISH
KZWC–FM / 92.1
KSOL–FM / 98.9
KBRG–FM / 104.9
KOFY–AM / 1050

TV stations

FOX KTVU / 2
NBC KRON / 4
CBS KPIX / 5
ABC KGO / 7
PBS KQED / 9
WB KBWB / 20
UPN—INDEPENDENT KICU / 36

UNIVERSITIES

The University of San Francisco (USF) has a beautiful campus in the central part of the city and offers a full range of under- and postgraduate studies (2130 Fulton St; 415/422-5555; map:I3-J3). The University of

California at San Francisco (UCSF), with campuses and hospital facilities throughout the town, is part of the state's university program (415/476-9000). It's the only UC campus dedicated solely to graduate and professional study in the health sciences, and the school is world renowned for its scientific discoveries, research, and patient care. San Francisco State University (SFSU) is part of California's state college system, with a strong reputation for its psychology and business departments (1600 Holloway Ave; 415/338-1111). The City College of San Francisco (main campus: 50 Phelan Ave; 415/239-3000) has eight neighborhood campuses and offers a full range of courses leading to Associate of Arts and Science degrees, most of which meet the requirements of four-year colleges and universities. Free noncredit courses, such as English as a Second Language and Citizenship, are available as well. Golden Gate University (536 Mission St; 800/448-4968; map:N3) has campuses throughout the city offering courses in law, business, and public affairs, among other fields.

Important Telephone Numbers

EMERGENCIES	911
AAA CALIFORNIA (CSAA), MAPS AND ROAD INFO	415/565-2012
AAA EMERGENCY ROAD SERVICE (24 hours)	800/222-4357
AIDS HOTLINE	800/367-2437
AMBULANCE	911
AMERICAN RED CROSS (Bay Area chapter)	415/427-8000
AMTRAK	800/872-7245
ANIMAL CONTROL	415/554-6364
AUTO IMPOUND	415/553-1235
BETTER BUSINESS BUREAU	415/243-9999
BIRTH RECORDS	415/554-2700
BLOOD BANK	415/567-6400
CALIFORNIA HIGHWAY PATROL	415/557-1094
CHAMBER OF COMMERCE	415/392-4520
CHILD PROTECTIVE SERVICES	800/856-5553
CITY BOX OFFICE	415/392-4400
CITY OF SAN FRANCISCO INFORMATION	415/554-4000
COAST GUARD	800/438-8724
CUSTOMS (U.S.)	415/782-9210
DIRECTORY INFORMATION	411
DOMESTIC VIOLENCE HOTLINE	415/864-4722
EMERGENCIES	911
FBI	415/553-7400
FIRE	911
GREYHOUND BUS	800/231-2222

IMMIGRATION AND NATURALIZATION	800/375-5283
LOST PETS	415/567-8738
MARRIAGE LICENSES	415/554-4176
MISSING PERSONS	415/558-5500
MUNI BUS/RAILWAY INFORMATION	415/673-6864
PASSPORTS	415/538-2700
PLANNED PARENTHOOD	415/441-5454
POISON CONTROL	800/523-2222
POST OFFICE INFORMATION	800/275-8777
RAPE COUNSELING	415/821-3222
ROAD CONDITIONS	800/427-7623
SAN FRANCISCO CONVENTION AND VISITORS BUREAU	415/391-2000
SAN FRANCISCO DEPARTMENT OF PUBLIC HEALTH	415/292-1500
SAN FRANCISCO DEPARTMENT OF SOCIAL SERVICES	415/557-5000
SENIOR INFORMATION CENTER	415/626-1033
SUICIDE PREVENTION	415/781-0500
TICKETS (BASS)	510/762-2277
TIME	415/767-2676
TIX BAY AREA (discount tickets)	415/433-7827
WEATHER	510/562-8573
ZIP CODE INFORMATION	800/275-8777; www.usps.com

TOP 200 RESTAURANTS

Restaurants by Star Rating

★★★★
Fleur de Lys
La Folie
Masa's

★★★⯪
Boulevard
Fifth Floor
Fringale
Hawthorne Lane
Jardinière

★★★
Acquerello
Antica Trattoria
Aqua
Azie
Bizou
Cafe Kati
Campton Place
Charles Nob Hill
The Dining Room at the
    Ritz-Carlton
Eliza's
Eos Restaurant &
    Wine Bar
Farallon
Flying Saucer
42 Degrees
Gary Danko
Infusion Bar & Restaurant
Kokkari Estiatorio
Kyo-ya
MC²
The Meetinghouse
Oritalia
Pacific
Pane e Vino
PlumpJack Cafe
Postrio
Rose Pistola
Rubicon
The Slanted Door
Thep Phanom
Tommy Toy's
Universal Cafe
Woodward's Garden
Yank Sing
Zarzuela
Zinzino
Zuni Cafe

★★⯪
Aperto
Baker Street Bistro
Bix
Black Cat Cafe
Cafe Jacqueline
Cafe Marimba
Carnelian Room
Carta
Casa Aguila
Cha Cha Cha
Delfina
Doidge's
Ebisu
Ella's
Firefly
Gordon's House of
    Fine Eats
Grand Café
Hayes Street Grill
Kabuto Sushi
Khan Toke Thai House
Le Colonial
L'Osteria del Forno
LuLu
Manora's Thai Cuisine
Mecca
PJ's Oysterbed
Ristorante Ecco
Rumpus
Slow Club
South Park Cafe
Ti Couz
Timo's
2223 Restaurant and Bar
The Waterfront
    Restaurant & Cafe
Zax

★★
A. Sabella's
Absinthe Brasserie
    and Bar
Ace Wasabi's
Avenue 9
Bacco Ristorante
Betelnut
Bistro Aix
Blowfish Sushi to Die For
Brandy Ho's Hunan Food
Brasserie Savoy
Cafe Bastille

Cafe Majestic
Caffe Macaroni
Cypress Club
The Elite Cafe
Enrico's
Foreign Cinema
The Garden Court
Garibaldi's
Globe
Great Eastern
Greens
Harbor Village Restaurant
Harris's
Helmand
Hong Kong Flower
    Lounge
House of Nanking
Hyde Street Bistro
Il Fornaio
Jack's
Kan Zaman
Kuleto's
La Taqueria
Le Charm
Liberty Cafe
Mario's Bohemian
    Cigar Store
Millennium
Mom Is Cooking
Momo's
Moose's
North Beach Restaurant
One Market
Park Chow
Pastis
Pauline's Pizza
Plouf
Scala's Bistro
Shanghai 1930
Stars
Straits Cafe
Suppenkuche
Tadich Grill
Tavolino
Terra Brazilis
Thirsty Bear Brewing
    Company
Tokyo Go Go
Ton Kiang
Zazie

★★

Angkor Borei
Balboa Cafe
Cafe Pescatore
Caffe Sport
Dottie's True Blue Café
Eric's
Fog City Diner
Gordon Biersch Brewery
    Restaurant
Hamburger Mary's
Marcello's Pizza
Mel's Diner
Miss Millie's
Sears Fine Food
Swan Oyster Depot
Tu Lan

★

Alice's Restaurant
Barcelona
Brisas de Acapulco

Brother's Korean
    Restaurant
Cafe Claude
Cafe Niebaum-Coppola
Caffe Freddy's
Charanga
Chow
Citizen Cake
Crescent City Cafe
Dol Ho
Firewood Cafe
Florio's
Franciscan
Hard Rock Cafe
The House
Indian Oven
Indigo
Jackson Fillmore
Kate's Kitchen
La Villa Poppi
Laghi
Lhasa Moon
Maya San Francisco

Mifune
Moki Sushi and
    Pacific Grill
Montage
North Star
Pintxos
Potrero Brewing Co.
R&G Lounge
Red Herring
Rotunda
Sam's Grill & Seafood
    Restaurant
Sapporo-ya
Shalimar
Stinking Rose
Sushi Groove
Taqueria Cancun
Thai House
Tommaso Ristorante
    Italiano
XYZ
Zodiac Club

Restaurants by Neighborhood

BERNAL HEIGHTS
Liberty Cafe
Moki Sushi and
    Pacific Grill

CASTRO
Chow
Firewood Cafe
Marcello's Pizza
Mecca
2223 Restaurant and Bar
Zodiac Club

CHINATOWN
Dol Ho
Great Eastern
House of Nanking
R&G Lounge

CIVIC CENTER
Eliza's
Jardinière
Millennium
Stars

COLE VALLEY
Eos Restaurant &
    Wine Bar
Zazie

EXCELSIOR DISTRICT
Mom Is Cooking

FINANCIAL DISTRICT
Aqua
Barcelona
Bix
Boulevard
Cafe Bastille
Cafe Claude
Carnelian Room
Fog City Diner
The Garden Court
Globe
Gordon Biersch Brewery
    Restaurant
Harbor Village Restaurant
Il Fornaio
Jack's
Kokkari Estiatorio
Kyo-ya
One Market
Oritalia
Pastis
Plouf
Red Herring
Rubicon
Sam's Grill & Seafood
    Restaurant
Shanghai 1930

Tadich Grill
Tommy Toy's
The Waterfront
    Restaurant & Cafe
Yank Sing

FISHERMAN'S WHARF
A. Sabella's
Cafe Pescatore
Franciscan

HAIGHT-ASHBURY
Cha Cha Cha
Crescent City Cafe
Indian Oven
Kan Zaman
Kate's Kitchen
Thep Phanom

HAYES VALLEY
Absinthe Brasserie
    and Bar
Carta
Hayes Street Grill
Indigo
Suppenkuche
Terra Brazilis
Zuni Cafe

MARINA/ COW HOLLOW

Ace Wasabi's
Baker Street Bistro
Balboa Cafe
Betelnut
Bistro Aix
Cafe Marimba
Doidge's
Greens
Lhasa Moon
Mel's Diner
Pane e Vino
PlumpJack Cafe
Zinzino

MISSION DISTRICT

Angkor Borei
Brisas de Acapulco
Charanga
Citizen Cake
Delfina
Flying Saucer
Foreign Cinema
La Taqueria
La Villa Poppi
Pauline's Pizza
Pintxos
The Slanted Door
Taqueria Cancun
Ti Couz
Timo's
Tokyo Go Go
Universal Cafe
Woodward's Garden

NOB HILL

Charles Nob Hill
The Dining Room at the
    Ritz-Carlton
Fleur de Lys
Masa's

NOE VALLEY

Alice's Restaurant
Bacco Ristorante
Eric's
Firefly
Miss Millie's
Thai House

NORTH BEACH

Black Cat Cafe
Brandy Ho's Hunan Food
Cafe Jacqueline
Cafe Niebaum-Coppola
Caffe Freddy's
Caffe Macaroni

Caffe Sport
Cypress Club
Enrico's
Gary Danko
Helmand
The House
L'Osteria del Forno
Mario's Bohemian
    Cigar Store
MC²
Moose's
North Beach Restaurant
Rose Pistola
Stinking Rose
Tavolino
Tommaso Ristorante
    Italiano
Zax

PACIFIC HEIGHTS/ PRESIDIO HEIGHTS/ FILLMORE/ JAPANTOWN

Cafe Kati
Cafe Majestic
The Elite Cafe
Ella's
Florio's
Garibaldi's
Hard Rock Cafe
Jackson Fillmore
Laghi
The Meetinghouse
Mifune
Sapporo-ya

POLK GULCH

Swan Oyster Depot

POTRERO HILL

Aperto
Eliza's
42 Degrees
Gordon's House of
    Fine Eats
North Star
Potrero Brewing Co.
Slow Club

RICHMOND DISTRICT

Brother's Korean
    Restaurant
Hong Kong Flower Lounge
Kabuto Sushi
Khan Toke Thai House
Mel's Diner
Straits Cafe
Ton Kiang

RUSSIAN HILL

Acquerello
Antica Trattoria
Harris's
Hyde Street Bistro
La Folie
Mario's Bohemian
    Cigar Store
Sushi Groove
Zarzuela

SOUTH OF MARKET (SOMA)

Azie
Bizou
Blowfish Sushi to Die For
Fringale
Hamburger Mary's
Hawthorne Lane
Infusion Bar & Restaurant
Le Charm
LuLu
Manora's Thai Cuisine
Maya San Francisco
Momo's
Montage
Ristorante Ecco
South Park Cafe
Thirsty Bear Brewing
    Company
Tu Lan
XYZ

SUNSET DISTRICT

Avenue 9
Casa Aguila
Ebisu
Park Chow
PJ's Oysterbed

TENDERLOIN

Brasserie Savoy
Dottie's True Blue Café
Shalimar

UNION SQUARE

Campton Place
Farallon
Fifth Floor
Grand Café
Kuleto's
Le Colonial
Pacific
Postrio
Rotunda
Rumpus
Scala's Bistro
Sears Fine Food

Restaurants by Food and Other Features

AFGHAN
Helmand

ALL-NIGHT
Marcello's Pizza
Mel's Diner

AMERICAN
Bix
Cypress Club
Dottie's True Blue Café
Firewood Cafe
Fog City Diner
Globe
Gordon Biersch Brewery
    Restaurant
Gordon's House of
    Fine Eats
Hamburger Mary's
Hard Rock Cafe
Hawthorne Lane
Indigo
Jack's
Liberty Cafe
LuLu
Mel's Diner
The Meetinghouse
Miss Millie's
Momo's
Montage
Moose's
North Star
One Market
PlumpJack Cafe
Potrero Brewing Co.
Rubicon
Sears Fine Food
Universal Cafe
The Waterfront
    Restaurant & Cafe
Woodward's Garden

BAKERY
Citizen Cake
Dottie's True Blue Café
Ella's
Greens
Il Fornaio
Liberty Cafe

BARBECUE
Brother's Korean
    Restaurant

BREAKFAST
Absinthe Brasserie
    and Bar
Baker Street Bistro
Brasserie Savoy
Cafe Majestic
Cafe Niebaum-Coppola
Cafe Pescatore
Campton Place
Citizen Cake
Crescent City Cafe
Doidge's
Dottie's True Blue Café
Ella's
The Garden Court
Grand Café
Hamburger Mary's
Il Fornaio
Kate's Kitchen
Kuleto's
Mel's Diner
Mom Is Cooking
Pacific
Postrio
Scala's Bistro
Sears Fine Food
South Park Cafe
Taqueria Cancun
Universal Cafe
XYZ
Zazie

BREAKFAST ALL DAY
Doidge's
Dottie's True Blue Café
Hamburger Mary's
Mel's Diner
Sears Fine Food

BRUNCH
Absinthe Brasserie
    and Bar
Aperto
Baker Street Bistro
Carnelian Room
Carta
Crescent City Cafe
The Elite Cafe
Ella's
Florio's
The Garden Court
Greens
Kate's Kitchen

Liberty Cafe
The Meetinghouse
Miss Millie's
Moose's
Park Chow
PJ's Oysterbed
Postrio
Rotunda
Slow Club
Suppenkuche
2223 Restaurant and Bar
Yank Sing
Zazie

BURGERS
Balboa Cafe
Chow
Ella's
Fog City Diner
Hamburger Mary's
Hard Rock Cafe
Mel's Diner
Moose's
Park Chow
Slow Club
Zuni Cafe

CAJUN/CREOLE
Crescent City Cafe
The Elite Cafe
PJ's Oysterbed

CALIFORNIAN
Alice's Restaurant
Aperto
Aqua
Avenue 9
Black Cat Cafe
Cafe Kati
Cafe Majestic
Charles Nob Hill
Fog City Diner
The Garden Court
Garibaldi's
Gary Danko
Globe
Greens
Hayes Street Grill
Jardinière
Masa's
MC^2
Montage
Postrio

Ristorante Ecco
Rumpus
Slow Club
Stars
Zax
Zodiac Club

CAMBODIAN
Angkor Borei

CHINESE
Alice's Restaurant
Brandy Ho's Hunan Food
Dol Ho
Eliza's
Eric's
Great Eastern
Harbor Village Restaurant
Hong Kong Flower
    Lounge
House of Nanking
R&G Lounge
Shanghai 1930
Tommy Toy's
Ton Kiang
Yank Sing

COFFEE SHOP
Doidge's
Dottie's True Blue Café
Kate's Kitchen
Mel's Diner
Sears Fine Food

CONTINENTAL
Absinthe Brasserie
    and Bar
Baker Street Bistro
Bistro Aix
Bizou
Boulevard
Brasserie Savoy
Cafe Bastille
Cafe Jacqueline
Campton Place
Fifth Floor
Fleur de Lys
Foreign Cinema
42 Degrees
Fringale
Grand Café
Hyde Street Bistro
La Folie
Le Charm
Pastis
Plouf
South Park Cafe

Ti Couz
Zazie

**DESSERTS
(EXCEPTIONAL)**
Absinthe Brasserie
    and Bar
Acquerello
Aqua
Bistro Aix
Boulevard
Cafe Jacqueline
Campton Place
Citizen Cake
Cypress Club
Delfina
Eos Restaurant & Wine
    Bar
Farallon
Firefly
Flying Saucer
42 Degrees
Globe
Gordon's House of Fine
    Eats
Hawthorne Lane
Il Fornaio
Jardinière
Le Charm
Liberty Cafe
Masa's
The Meetinghouse
Momo's
Montage
North Star
One Market
Pane e Vino
Postrio
Scala's Bistro
Tavolino
Ti Couz

DIM SUM
Dol Ho
Harbor Village Restaurant
Shanghai 1930
Ton Kiang
Yank Sing

DINER
Dottie's True Blue Café
Fog City Diner
Hamburger Mary's
Hard Rock Cafe
Mel's Diner
Miss Millie's
North Star

Sears Fine Food

ECLECTIC
Carta
Firefly
Flying Saucer
Mecca
2223 Restaurant and Bar
XYZ
Zodiac Club

FAMILY
Eric's
Fog City Diner
Franciscan
Hard Rock Cafe
La Taqueria
Mel's Diner
Mifune
Mom Is Cooking
Montage
North Beach Restaurant
R&G Lounge
Sapporo-Ya
Sears Fine Food
Tommaso Ristorante
    Italiano

FIREPLACE
A. Sabella's
Kokkari Estiatorio
Park Chow

FRENCH
Absinthe Brasserie
    and Bar
Baker Street Bistro
Bistro Aix
Bizou
Boulevard
Brasserie Savoy
Cafe Bastille
Cafe Claude
Cafe Jacqueline
Campton Place
The Dining Room at the
    Ritz-Carlton
Fifth Floor
Fleur de Lys
Foreign Cinema
42 Degrees
Fringale
Grand Café
Hyde Street Bistro
La Folie
Le Charm
Pastis

Plouf
South Park Cafe
Ti Couz
Zazie

GERMAN
Suppenkuche

GOURMET TAKE-OUT
Greens
Yank Sing

GREEK
Kokkari Estiatorio

GRILL
Brother's Korean
    Restaurant
Hayes Street Grill
Jack's
Moki Sushi and
    Pacific Grill
Momo's
Sam's Grill & Seafood
    Restaurant
Tadich Grill

HEALTH-CONSCIOUS
Ace Wasabi's
Angkor Borei
Aqua
Blowfish Sushi to Die For
Chow
Ebisu
Gordon's House of
    Fine Eats
Greens
Kabuto Sushi
Kyo-ya
Millennium
Miss Millie's
North India Restaurant
Park Chow
Sapporo-Ya
Sushi Groove
Terra Brazilis
Tokyo Go Go
Zax

INDIAN
Indian Oven
Shalimar

**INVENTIVE ETHNIC
(FUSION)**
Azie
Betelnut
Eos Restaurant &
    Wine Bar

The House
Infusion Bar & Restaurant
Oritalia
Pacific
Tommy Toy's
XYZ

ITALIAN
A. Sabella's
Acquerello
Antica Trattoria
Aperto
Bacco Ristorante
Cafe Niebaum-Coppola
Cafe Pescatore
Caffe Freddy's
Caffe Macaroni
Caffe Sport
Delfina
Enrico's
Florio's
Franciscan
Il Fornaio
Jackson Fillmore
Kuleto's
La Villa Poppi
Laghi
L'Osteria del Forno
Marcello's Pizza
Mario's Bohemian
    Cigar Store
North Beach Restaurant
Pane e Vino
Ristorante Ecco
Rose Pistola
Scala's Bistro
Stinking Rose
Tavolino
Tommaso Ristorante
    Italiano
Zinzino

JAPANESE
Ace Wasabi's
Blowfish Sushi to Die For
Ebisu
Kabuto Sushi
Kyo-ya
Mifune
Sapporo-Ya
Sushi Groove
Tokyo Go Go

KITSCHY
Flying Saucer
Mel's Diner
Miss Millie's

Sears Fine Food
Straits Cafe

KOREAN
Brother's Korean
    Restaurant

LATE-NIGHT
Black Cat Cafe
Enrico's
Globe
Greens
Hamburger Mary's
Jardinière
Kan Zaman
Marcello's Pizza
Mecca
Mel's Diner
Rose Pistola
Zodiac Club
Zuni Cafe

LATIN
Cha Cha Cha
Charanga
Terra Brazilis

MEDITERRANEAN
Bizou
Florio's
42 Degrees
Garibaldi's
Kokkari Estiatorio
Zuni Cafe

MEXICAN
Brisas de Acapulco
Cafe Marimba
Casa Aguila
La Taqueria
Maya San Francisco
Mom Is Cooking
Taqueria Cancun

MICROBREWERY
Gordon Biersch Brewery
    Restaurant
Potrero Brewing Co.
Thirsty Bear Brewing
    Company

OUTDOOR DINING
Baker Street Bistro
Betelnut
Bistro Aix
Cafe Bastille
Cafe Claude
Cafe Niebaum-Coppola
Cafe Pescatore

Enrico's
Foreign Cinema
42 Degrees
Il Fornaio
Khan Toke Thai House
Le Charm
Mario's Bohemian
    Cigar Store
Momo's
Park Chow
Plouf
Potrero Brewing Co.
Rose Pistola
The Waterfront
    Restaurant & Cafe
Zazie
Zinzino

OYSTER BAR
Brasserie Savoy
The Elite Cafe
Farallon
Hayes Street Grill
LuLu
PJ's Oysterbed
Red Herring
Swan Oyster Depot

PAN-ASIAN
Betelnut
The House
Moki Sushi and
    Pacific Grill
Pacific
Shanghai 1930
Straits Cafe

PERSIAN
Kan Zaman

PIZZA
Cafe Niebaum-Coppola
Cafe Pescatore
Caffe Freddy's
Chow
Citizen Cake
Enrico's
Firewood Cafe
Il Fornaio
L'Osteria del Forno
LuLu
Marcello's Pizza
Momo's
Park Chow
Pauline's Pizza
Ristorante Ecco
Rose Pistola

Scala's Bistro
Tommaso Ristorante
    Italiano
2223 Restaurant and Bar
Universal Cafe

PRIVATE ROOMS
Azie
Boulevard
Carta
Ebisu
Tadich Grill
Zarzuela

ROMANTIC
Absinthe Brasserie
    and Bar
Cafe Bastille
Cafe Jacqueline
Cafe Majestic
Carnelian Room
Charles Nob Hill
The Dining Room at the
    Ritz-Carlton
Farallon
Fifth Floor
Fleur de Lys
The Garden Court
Jardinière
Khan Toke Thai House
La Folie
Masa's
The Meetinghouse
The Waterfront
    Restaurant & Cafe
Zarzuela

SEAFOOD
A. Sabella's
Absinthe Brasserie
    and Bar
Ace Wasabi's
Aqua
Black Cat Cafe
Blowfish Sushi to Die For
Brasserie Savoy
Brisas de Acapulco
Cafe Pescatore
Ebisu
The Elite Cafe
Farallon
Franciscan
Great Eastern
Harbor Village Restaurant
Hayes Street Grill
Hong Kong Flower
    Lounge

Kabuto Sushi
Kyo-ya
Manora's Thai Cuisine
Moki Sushi and
    Pacific Grill
PJ's Oysterbed
Plouf
R&G Lounge
Red Herring
Rose Pistola
Sam's Grill & Seafood
    Restaurant
Sushi Groove
Swan Oyster Depot
Tadich Grill
Tokyo Go Go

**SOUP/SALAD/
SANDWICH**
Caffe Freddy's
Chow
Citizen Cake
Dottie's True Blue Café
Ella's
Fog City Diner
Hamburger Mary's
Hard Rock Cafe
Mel's Diner
Montage
Park Chow
Rotunda
Sears Fine Food
Universal Cafe
Zazie

SOUTHERN
Crescent City Cafe
The Elite Cafe
PJ's Oysterbed

SPANISH
Barcelona
Pinxtos
Timo's
Zarzuela

STEAK
Carnelian Room
Harris's
Jack's
Sam's Grill & Seafood
    Restaurant

SUSHI
Ace Wasabi's
Blowfish Sushi to Die For
Ebisu

Kabuto Sushi
Kyo-ya
Mifune
Moki Sushi and
    Pacific Grill
Sushi Groove
Tokyo Go Go

TAPAS
Barcelona
Cha Cha Cha
Charanga
Enrico's
Fog City Diner
Pinxtos
Slow Club
Tavolino
Thirsty Bear Brewing
    Company
Timo's
Zarzuela

THAI
Khan Toke Thai House
Manora's Thai Cuisine
Thai House
Thep Phanom

TIBETAN
Lhasa Moon

**UNIQUELY SAN
FRANCISCO**
A. Sabella's
Bix
Cafe Majestic
Caffe Macaroni
Cha Cha Cha
Enrico's
Florio's
Franciscan

Greens
Jack's
Kuleto's
Lhasa Moon
Mario's Bohemian
    Cigar Store
Momo's
North Beach Restaurant
North Star
Potrero Brewing Co.
Rotunda
Sam's Grill & Seafood
    Restaurant
Sears Fine Food
Suppenkuche
Sushi Groove
Swan Oyster Depot
Tadich Grill
Tommaso Ristorante
    Italiano

VALUE, GOOD
Bistro Aix
Brother's Korean
    Restaurant
Cafe Pescatore
Caffe Freddy's
Chow
Dol Ho
Eliza's
Hamburger Mary's
House of Nanking
Hyde Street Bistro
Jackson Fillmore
Kan Zaman
Kate's Kitchen
La Taqueria
La Villa Poppi
Le Charm
Lhasa Moon

L'Osteria del Forno
Marcello's Pizza
Mifune
Mom Is Cooking
Park Chow
R&G Lounge
Sapporo-Ya
Shalimar
Tu Lan
Zarzuela

VEGETARIAN
Chow
Eric's
Greens
Lhasa Moon
Millennium
Miss Millie's
Park Chow

VIETNAMESE
Le Colonial
The Slanted Door
Tu Lan

VIEW
Boulevard
Carnelian Room
Franciscan
Greens
Red Herring
The Waterfront
    Restaurant & Cafe

WINE BAR
Eos Restaurant &
    Wine Bar
Liberty Cafe
Zinzino

RESTAURANTS

A. Sabella's / ★★

2766 TAYLOR ST; 415/771-6775

One of the long-established Fisherman's Wharf restaurants, A. Sabella's has that old-time San Francisco feeling that attracts tourists and locals alike. The Sabella family has owned this restaurant for four generations, ever since it was a fish market in 1887. The large dining room has floor-to-ceiling windows overlooking the wharf, and there's a massive fireplace in the lounge. With a remodel a few years ago, the restaurant traded in its 1960s decor for a sleeker, softer, less cavernous look, with slipcovered chairs and modern light fixtures. A tank harbors live Dungeness crab, abalone, and Maine lobster, used in traditional dishes such as cioppino, abalone dore, and bouillabaisse. Fortunately, the seafood has been updated along with the decor: the cioppino is fragrant, the clam chowder fresh and light, and the petrale sole is enhanced with toasted capers and a nutty brown butter sauce. For dessert, try the Sabella specialty: New York–style cheesecake with a walnut–graham-cracker crust. *$$$; AE, DC, DIS, JCB, MC, V; no checks; lunch, dinner every day; full bar; reservations recommended; map:M1* &

Absinthe Brasserie and Bar / ★★

398 HAYES ST; 415/551-1590

Stylish Absinthe, named for the green herbal liqueur so potent it was banned in turn-of-the-century France, re-creates the romance and mystery of the bygone Belle Epoque. The sumptuous decor begins at the entry with French rattan cafe chairs, copper-topped tables, and a mosaic checkerboard floor. Chef Ross Browne (who relocated here along with the owner and general manager from the now-shuttered Rosmarino) prepares a brasserie-style French and Italian menu with such starters as veal sweetbreads sautéed in a sweet marsala sauce, a delicious version of the classic pissaladière, and fluffy ricotta dumplings. A generous seafood platter loaded with Dungeness crab, shrimp, and mussels is a highlight. Entrees change daily and vary in consistency (much like, alas, the service). You'll find everything from roasted veal chops and seasonal risottos to inventive vegetarian creations. Desserts are more dependable: a Scharffen Berger chocolate pot de crème is sublime, as is the lavender crème brûlée. And while you won't find actual absinthe on the menu, professional bartenders mix a range of amusingly named cocktails, including one named after Hemingway's *Death in the Afternoon*—an unusual combination of Pernod and champagne. *$$; AE, DC, DIS, MC, V; no checks; breakfast Tues–Fri, lunch Tues–Fri, dinner Tues–Sun, brunch Sat–Sun; full bar; reservations recommended; map:L4* &

Ace Wasabi's / ★★

3339 STEINER ST; 415/567-4903

This sushi hot spot is a haven for the postcollege trust-fund society that has transformed the Marina into one of the most loved and loathed districts in the city. Owner Ken Lowe is savvy enough to know that in San Francisco, the food must come first, which is why he purchases only grade-A ingredients for his innovative Japanese dishes—and it shows. Saddle up to the bar for some sake bombers while a table frees up, then chow down on the wondrously tender calamari appetizer, the popular buckwheat-noodle/julienned-vegetable salad, the colorful Three Amigos roll (tuna, eel, and avocado), and the tasty Rock and Roll (unagi, avocado, and cucumber). The only drawbacks are the slow service and LOUD atmosphere on busy nights, but if you're into that kind of scene and sushi, you'll love Ace Wasabi's. *$$; AE, MC, V; no checks; dinner every day; full bar; reservations not accepted; map:K1* &

Acquerello / ★★★

1722 SACRAMENTO ST; 415/567-5432

Acquerello, which means "watercolor" in Italian, offers contemporary regional Italian cooking in a tranquil, refined setting. Co-owners Suzette Gresham and Giancarlo Paterlini worked together at Donatello during that restaurant's heyday, and they make a great team: Gresham in the kitchen turning out exceptionally flavorful and well-constructed *nuova cucina*; Paterlini in the 60-seat dining room pampering customers and offering expert advice on wines. The small, innovative menu changes often, but expect elegant dishes such as beef carpaccio with hearts of palm and black truffles to start, and pasta selections like triangular ravioli filled with swordfish in a light tomato-caper sauce. Entrees are beautifully presented and include such dishes as grilled quail with fresh oranges and sage or fillet of beef topped with Gorgonzola and walnuts. Gresham composes delicate dishes and light sauces, so you might have room for such knockout desserts as the chocolate "cloud cake" with pralines or the warm zabaglione scented with orange muscat. A converted chapel provides a serene setting for this stellar cuisine, with dramatic pointed archways, flower-filled planters, and a permanent collection of—what else?—watercolors. Jackets are suggested for gentlemen. *$$–$$$; AE, DC, DIS, MC, V; checks OK; dinner Tues–Sat; beer and wine; reservations recommended; gcp19@aol.com; www.acquerello.com; map:L3*

Alice's Restaurant / ★

1591 SANCHEZ ST; 415/282-8999

Mention Alice's Restaurant to locals and you're likely to get a nice warm reminiscent smile and hear a tale of the great time they had at the place down the Peninsula. *That* Alice's, a ramshackle biker hangout in Woodside, has been a Bay Area staple since the 1920s. *This* Alice's, in the heart of Noe Valley, while younger, is recalled nearly as fondly by some who have eaten here. The understated, cheery corner restaurant serves fabulous and affordable Hunan and Mandarin specialties. The dishes are prepared artistically, with a California-cuisine flair. There are many house specialties: among the best are Alice's spicy eggplant with chicken, shrimp, and chili peppers; the seafood delight, with prawns, scallops, fish, and fresh vegetables; and the Hunan smoked pork, with leeks, cabbage, and red and green chili peppers. The sweet-and-sour dishes and sizzling rice soups are also excellent. The best part is, nothing on the menu is over $10. No wonder people like it so much. *$; MC, V; no checks; lunch, dinner Tues–Sat; beer and wine; reservations not accepted; map:K8*

Angkor Borei / ★★☆

3471 MISSION ST; 415/550-8417
Situated in an Outer Mission District storefront, next to an Indian restaurant that also delivers pizza (really!), Angkor Borei is one of those small Asian restaurants with a loyal following. In a dining room with pink walls, red carpet, and intricate carvings, this family restaurant serves exquisitely spiced Cambodian fare (which is similar to Thai food but less spicy) with surprising refinement and finesse. For an appetizer, try the crispy spring rolls stuffed with a variety of vegetables or the huge lacy crepes folded omelet-style over a juicy vegetable-nut filling. Cold main dishes might include a medley of bean sprouts, chilies, basil, carrot, and julienned cucumbers, assembled over cold noodles and accompanied with a fragrant coconut-milk dipping sauce. For something hot and steamy, dip into the aromatic coconut-milk–laced curry with green Thai basil, lemongrass, Japanese eggplant, and straw mushrooms. A milder yet complex red curry enhances a plate of sautéed shrimp nestled on a bed of spinach. Beautifully charred chicken, beef, or pork, highly spiced by long marinating, is served with fresh sliced vegetables and sweet dipping sauces to cool the palate. Many vegetarian dishes are available, too. *$; AE, DC, MC, V; no checks; lunch Mon–Sat, dinner every day; beer and wine; reservations recommended for 5 or more; map:L8* &

Antica Trattoria / ★★★

2400 POLK ST; 415/928-5797
Soon after Antica Trattoria opened its doors in 1996, the surrounding Russian Hill neighborhood was abuzz with talk of chef Ruggero Gadaldi's incredible Italian fare (he previously wore the toque at the now-closed Etrusca). Occupying a moderately busy corner on Polk and Union Streets, this simply decorated restaurant with dark wood floors and cream-colored walls has developed a deserved reputation as one of the city's best Italian trattorias. Appetizers might include a purée of potato and vegetable soup seasoned with bacon, or delicate (and divine) slices of beef carpaccio enhanced with capers, arugula, mustard, and Parmesan shav-

AMAZING GRAZING

Even if you don't have a place to store a lot of farm-fresh fruits and veggies, it's still well worth your time to stroll through San Francisco's fantastic **Ferry Plaza Farmers Market** and sample some of Northern California's finest bounty. From award-winning homemade salami and Berkeley's famous Acme bread to organically grown produce, handcrafted sheep's-milk cheese, and locally made olive oils and vinegars, you'll find the makings for a great meal. In fact, most of San Francisco's top chefs do their shopping here. There's free live entertainment, too. The market is open year-round (rain or shine) every Saturday from 8am to 1:30pm and every Tuesday from 10:30am to 2:30pm in front of the Ferry Building on the Embarcadero; on Tuesday there's a second location at Justin Herman Plaza. Call 510/528-6987 for more information.

ings. A recent rendition of the creamy risotto was prepared with pears and Taleggio cheese, while a memorable chestnut-flavored fedelini (angel hair pasta) was dressed with leeks and a smoked-chicken cream sauce. Main dishes might include a savory monkfish wrapped in pancetta, potatoes, and wild mushrooms, or a perfectly grilled pork tenderloin with Gorgonzola, crispy pancetta, and polenta. It's not the most surprising Italian fare in the city, but it's some of the best prepared and reasonably priced. Top it off with the terrific tiramisu. *$$; AE, DC, MC, V; no checks; dinner Tues–Sun; beer and wine; reservations recommended; map:L2* &

Aperto / ★★☆
1434 18TH ST (AT CONNECTICUT ST); 415/252-1625
One of the Potrero Hill neighborhood's best restaurants, Aperto is a homey, friendly place popular with locals. In a small dining room adorned with paintings by a local artist, patrons enjoy unpretentious service and generous portions of California-Italian cuisine. The changing menu emphasizes simple, honest peasant cuisine with innovative touches and might include a superior roast chicken with preserved lemon, fish and meat specials, and more than a half-dozen daily pasta dishes, such as penne with cumin-roasted eggplant, tomato, and goat cheese, or the popular spinach-ricotta tortellini with pistachio, pancetta, and sun-dried tomatoes in a cream sauce. The crab-cake salad garnished with a cucumber-and-chickpea purée is another good choice. For dessert, the warm chocolate soufflé is worth every calorie. Aperto doesn't take reservations, so you may have to stand in line for a table on weekend nights; once you settle in with a basket of house-made focaccia and a good glass of red wine, however, the wait will soon be forgotten. *$$; DC, MC, V; local checks only; lunch Mon–Fri, dinner every day, brunch Sat–Sun; beer and wine; reservations not accepted; map:N6* &

Aqua / ★★★

252 CALIFORNIA ST; 415/956-9662
When it opened in September 1991, Aqua was the first restaurant in the city to elevate the humble seafood house to a temple of haute cuisine. Huge flower arrangements punctuate its attractive, sleek-as-a-shark dining room, where slipcovers on the chairs change with the seasons and the large mirrors and dramatic lighting reflect a well-heeled Financial District crowd. They're usually oohing and aahing over chef Michael Mina's creations, which are marked by a refreshingly light touch with herbs and sauces. Begin with a savory mussel soufflé or roasted spot prawns stuffed with spicy crabmeat—or, if you're really feeling flush, you could shell out 60 to 80 bucks for a parfait of Russian caviar. Segue into Hawaiian swordfish au poivre with pancetta-wrapped shrimp dumplings, grilled tuna draped with a layer of foie gras, or cabbage-wrapped king salmon. The dessert list is sure to include such delights as blackberry coffee cake, pumpkin cheesecake, and soufflés. A few non-seafood entrees are always available, and Mina demonstrates his tolerance for culinary landlubbers by offering a five-course vegetarian tasting menu alongside the regular six-course sampler. *$$$; AE, DC, DIS, MC, V; no checks; lunch Mon–Fri, dinner Mon–Sat; full bar; reservations recommended; map:N2* &

Avenue 9 / ★★

1243 9TH AVE; 415/664-6999
Duck into this bustling, cheery bistro any night of the week and you'll find the place packed with Sunset District locals. Avenue 9 exudes energy, and a friendly, efficient wait staff serves a hefty offering of well-prepared Cal-Med fare at neighborhood prices. Tables line the right-hand wall of the restaurant, with a long banquette for seating; an exposed kitchen fills the rest of the room. A 10-seat bar allows patrons to view Jeff Rosen, the owner and head chef, busily working behind the stoves. Orange- and yellow-toned walls with just a bit of stainless steel and exposed pipe take the decor beyond the cafe look without getting mired in industrial chic. The menu is decidedly eclectic, with a strong California sensibility that's partial to local products. Petaluma duck breast is served with a mound of black mission figs and grilled piadini; a flatbread appetizer comes with house-cured salmon and Sonoma farmer's cheese. A lusty Tuscan salad of heirloom tomatoes, kalamata olives, and anchovies hits the mark, as does a caramelized onion and roasted-garlic pizzetta. For dessert try the gingerbread cake studded with caramelized walnuts—you won't be disappointed. A reasonably priced wine list offers mostly California selections and Rhône varietals, with more than 10 options by the glass. *$$$; AE, MC, V; no checks; lunch, dinner every day; beer and wine; reservations recommended; map:H5* &

Azie / ★★★

826 FOLSOM ST; 415/538-0918

Chef-restauranteur Jody Denton wants to corner the culinary market on the up-and-coming scene on Folsom Street. By the looks of the brand-new Azie, wedged in next door to his wildly popular LuLu, he's well on his way. This stylish restaurant bears its South of Market surroundings in mind, with 22-foot ceilings vaulted by four huge columns. The dining room is split-level; in the booths on the main level, you can draw a set of curtains for a truly exclusive feel. The main level is also home to the exhibition kitchen, where chef Donnie Masterton prepares Asian-inspired French cuisine. One recent menu included such dishes as roulade of monkfish, grilled veal medallions with sea urchin–wasabi butter, and aromatic oxtail bundles. Adventurous, to be sure; if you have trouble making a decision, opt for the nightly tasting menu. Dining is also available at the bar, where a DJ plays music nightly. While it was open at first for dinner only, there are plans to offer lunch soon. *$$; AE, DC, MC, V; no checks; dinner every day; full bar; reservations recommended; map:N4*

Bacco Ristorante / ★★

737 DIAMOND ST; 415/282-4969

The enticing atmosphere of this modern Northern Italian–style trattoria, with its cheerful persimmon-colored dining rooms and small linen- and butcher-paper-covered tables, beckons to Noe Valley passersby on the lookout for a casual meal. Locals know it's the kind of neighborhood place where they can hang out with a plate of well-made pasta, authentic antipasti, and a decent Italian wine. Tables are perpetually full, service is smooth and efficient, and the food is fresh and tasty. Start with a terrine of eggplant, peppers, and goat cheese served with a green salad, or the excellent steamed clams and mussels seasoned with tomato and garlic. When it comes to pasta, the kitchen excels. Giant, thin ravioli are stuffed with chard and ricotta, drizzled with brown butter, and topped with crisp fried sage leaves. The classic bowl of orrechiette and slightly bitter broccoli rabe gets its zing from the anchovies, garlic, and red chili flakes. A couple of other good dishes are the grilled Italian sausages and polenta, served with a tomato and olive purée, and the tender broiled lamb chops dressed with garlic and rosemary. For dessert, dive into the opulent chocolate terrine with hazelnut custard sauce garnished with strawberries, or the espresso-infused tiramisu. *$$; MC, V; no checks; dinner every day; beer and wine; reservations recommended; map:K7* &

Baker Street Bistro / ★★½

2953 BAKER ST; 415/931-1475

This small, quiet Union Street storefront bistro is the quintessential neighborhood cafe. In good weather, grab a seat outdoors and pretend you're in a Parisian *arrondissement*. Jacques Manuera opened Baker Street Bistro in 1991 after working as a chef in France and Washington, D.C. His excellent fare is—you guessed it—classically inspired French bistro. Expect such entrees as rabbit in mustard sauce, snails on a bed of angel hair pasta with mushroom sauce, osso buco, and New York steak with lemon butter and potatoes. This bistro is also the perfect place for a leisurely brunch of eggs Benedict, mimosas, and strong coffee. *$$; AE, MC, V; no checks; breakfast, dinner Tues–Sun, brunch Sat–Sun; beer and wine; reservations recommended; map:J2* &

Balboa Cafe / ★☆

3199 FILLMORE ST; 415/921-3944

The Balboa has had a long history as one of the main "meet-markets" in San Francisco, and the song remains the same. Co-owners Billy Getty (of *the* Getty clan) and San Francisco Supervisor Gavin Newsom run this joint as well as the PlumpJack Cafe up the street, which explains all the self-impressed politicos, gold diggers, DINKs (Dual Income No Kids), suits, and post-fraternity/sorority types hobnobbing around the handsome polished-wood-and-brass bar. Oh, and there's food served here as well. The menu offers a few upscale dishes such as cabernet-braised short ribs with mashed potatoes and roasted root vegetables, but they're all done better at PlumpJack (see review) for about the same price. Instead, save a few dollars and order the kick-butt Niman Ranch Balboa Burger or a Caesar salad, both of which are among the best in town. *$$; AE, DC, MC, V; no checks; lunch, dinner every day; full bar; reservations recommended; map:K1* &

Barcelona / ★

7 SPRING ST (BETWEEN CALIFORNIA, SACRAMENTO, MONTGOMERY, AND KEARNY STS); 415/989-1976

Get to know "the margarita king" and you'll have a night to remember. That's the self-applied title of owner Giovanni, whose restaurant serves some of the best tapas downtown. And Giovanni is the consummate host, seemingly always there, and always with a welcoming smile. After 5pm the restaurant, decorated in lively, rich colors and dark wood accents, fills up with happy-hour revelers spilling out of the surrounding office towers. They clamor toward the bar for Giovanni's margaritas and the generous spread of complimentary appetizers. The regular menu is chock-full of Spanish and Catalan treats, many based on centuries-old recipes. Don't miss the *pimientos de piquillo* (beef-stuffed peppers with goat cheese) or the *gambas al ajillo* (shrimp with garlic and olive oil) appetizers. The paella is a specialty and is made with a wide selection of seafood and specialty meats. On Friday and Saturday nights, live flamenco shows provide a boisterous party atmosphere. *$; AE, DC, MC, V; no checks; lunch Mon–Fri, dinner every day; full bar; reservations recommended; map:N2* &

Betelnut / ★★

2030 UNION ST; 415/929-8855

A member of the Real Restaurants company (which includes such successes as Tra Vigne and Bix), this sumptuously decorated Asian "beerhouse" has the ever-so-slightly-tarty feel of an exotic 1930s Shanghai brothel. Named after a popular seed that is chewed throughout Asia for its intoxicating side effects, Betelnut became a huge success in a short time, and it's still on everyone's list of places to try (though, alas, the namesake nut is not offered here). Tall glass doors facing Union Street are opened on warm evenings to provide alfresco dining, and mechanized bamboo fans sway languorously above the busy bar. The mixed menu is pan-Asian, with an array of authentic dishes from Vietnam, Singapore, China, Thailand, Indonesia, and Japan. While the unusual concept entices diners, the reality is not always up to par. With more than a dozen cooks in the kitchen on busy nights, results can vary. Some dishes consistently get raves, including the spicy coconut chicken with eggplant, lemongrass, and basil; the crunchy tea-smoked duck; the succulent short ribs; and the sun-dried anchovies with peanuts, chilies, and garlic. But the green papaya salad gets mixed reviews, and Betelnut's dumplings can be downright disappointing. *$$; DC, DIS, MC, V; no checks; lunch, dinner every day; full bar; reservations recommended; www.citysearch7. com; map:K2* &

Bistro Aix / ★★

3340 STEINER ST; 415/202-0100

French-trained chef and owner Jonathan Beard runs this trendy Marina district bistro frequented by stylish Gen-Xers and baby boomers. With its creamy lime-green walls decorated with black-and-white photos of Italy and France, Aix is a charming, casual restaurant that attracts patrons from all corners of the city. Part of the bistro's draw is the inexpensive early-bird fixed-price dinners served Sunday through Thursday from 6–8pm. Diners choose from three entrees, such as grilled top sirloin with roasted garlic, linguine with clams and tomatoes, or a juicy roasted chicken with a crusty golden skin. The main menu features cracker-crust pizzas with various toppings, such as goat cheese and grilled eggplant or wild mushrooms and truffle oil; sirloin burgers; grilled fish, like ahi tuna with black-trumpet mushrooms; and pastas such as an excellent orrechiette with spinach, pancetta, and a peppery tomato sauce. The wine list is reasonably priced and primarily Californian, peppered with European varietals. Desserts can be staggeringly rich, including the warm macadamia-chocolate torte with espresso ice cream and caramel bananas. The dining room is small and sometimes cramped and noisy, so head for the heated back garden patio; it's romantically lit at night. *$$; AE, MC, V; no checks; dinner every day; beer and wine; reservations recommended; map:K1* &

Bix / ★★☆

56 GOLD ST; 415/433-6300

Somehow the martini never seems to go out of fashion, and neither does Bix, one of the sexiest and most sophisticated supper clubs in the city. It's modeled after a 1920s "New American" supper club, complete with massive silver columns, art-deco–style lighting, and oodles of hand-carved Honduran mahogany (it's truly a beautiful room). The restaurant's raison d'être, however, is the top-notch martinis that really sneak up on you. If you manage to make it to a dinner table (the ones on the intimate mezzanine are the best), it's de rigueur to order the crispy chicken hash, a Bix best-seller for more than a decade. Other popular choices include the grilled filet mignon with sautéed spinach and stuffed potato chips, day-boat scallops with black Perigord truffles pomme purée, and Beluga caviar on toast for a mere $118 a pop (c'mon, live a little). Finish the feast in high fashion with another Bix specialty, the bananas Foster. *$$–$$$; AE, CB, DC, DIS, MC, V; no checks; lunch Mon–Fri, dinner every day; full bar; reservations recommended; map:N2* &

Bizou / ★★★

598 4TH ST; 415/543-2222

Bizou means "a little kiss" in French, but San Francisco foodies seem to have planted a big fat wet one on this lively bistro with the rustic Mediterranean menu. Since April 1993, chef-owner Loretta Keller (formerly of Stars) has seduced even normally conservative diners into eating such exotica as beef cheeks, parsnip chips, cod ravioli, and house-cured anchovies (with the heads on, no less), winning them over with her deceptively simple, flavorful preparations. There are plenty of less adventurous items, to be sure, including a wonderful salad of pear, Gorgonzola, radicchio, frisée, and toasted walnuts; day-boat scallops with wild mushrooms, endive, and balsamic vinegar; stuffed young chicken with celeriac, grilled apples, and goat cheese; and desserts like French cream with persimmon and fig sauces and a Seville orange and Meyer lemon curd cake. Housed in a 1906 building, the corner storefront restaurant has an updated bistro feel, with window boxes, vintage light fixtures, weathered mustard-colored walls, large windows, and an oak bar. A few caveats, though: the tables are packed tightly together, the place can get very noisy, and the service can range from boffo to beastly. *$$; AE, MC, V; no checks; lunch Mon–Fri, dinner Mon–Sat; full bar; reservations recommended; map:N4* &

Black Cat Cafe / ★★☆

501 BROADWAY; 415/981-2233

Black Cat is restaurateur Reed Hearon's (LuLu, Rose Pistola) latest venture, which plays on San Francisco's ethnic diversity by serving dishes from around the city: Chinese spareribs, North Beach pasta, Fisherman's Wharf seafood, and so on. Unfortunately such a mixed bag of menu items is getting mixed reviews, so you'll probably want to go with something that's hard to screw up, such as their big ol' T-bone steak for four or the great selection of fresh seafood and shellfish—lobster, crab, shrimp, mussels—served by the pound and prepared in five different ways (we prefer it grilled with garlic and hot pepper). Or hedge your bets and order an array of smaller dishes and dine family style, washing it all down with a few Black Cat sake-spiked martinis. As for the decor, subtle it ain't: blazing red booths, checkered tablecloths, bright lighting, high ceilings, and more mirrors than Liberace's dressing room create an atmosphere of high-energy Parisian brasserie laced with classic San Francisco scenes. It's all still very popular with the local celebrities and CEOs, who always situate themselves in the dig-me booths so everyone can see how much fun it is to be wealthy. After dinner, take a gander at the soigné scene down in the Blue Bar jazz club below. Note: Black Cat is one of the few high-quality restaurants in the city that serves food until 2am. *$$–$$$; AE, DC, MC, V; no checks; lunch, dinner every day; full bar; reservations recommended; map:N2* &

Blowfish Sushi to Die For / ★★

2170 BRYANT ST; 415/285-3848

Japanese animation films play on two suspended television sets for the young and the hip who pack this place, lounging against a backdrop of velvet walls, techno dance music, and acid jazz. Clearly, Blowfish caters to a crowd that wants more than just good sushi. Located in the industrial northeast Mission District, the restaurant offers a combination of traditional and more adventurous sushi by chef Ritsuo Tsuchida. If you're intent on trying blowfish, the Japanese delicacy otherwise known as puffer fish, expect to fork over about $30 if it's in season, and be prepared for a letdown: it's fairly bland. Move on to the mavericks: Maui Maki (tuna, mango, and macadamia nuts); double crab salad with soft-shell crab; tempura-battered asparagus maki wrapped in rice; and the restaurant's namesake, Blowfish Maki (a roll of yellowtail, scallions, and tobiko, draped with salmon—but, ironically, no blowfish). Non-fish-eaters also have choices: filet mignon with rosemary garlic butter, chicken pot stickers, or asparagus spring rolls with duck. Chef Tsuchida likes to tempt his regular customers with some of his more unusual creations: seared ostrich on portobello-mushroom tempura, anyone? Service is friendly and efficient. *$$–$$$; AE, DC, DIS, MC, V; no checks; lunch Mon–Fri, dinner every day; full bar; reservations recommended; map:M6* &

Boulevard / ★★★☆

1 MISSION ST; 415/543-6084

Nancy Oakes, a self-taught chef whose cooking career began in 1977 at a scruffy San Francisco saloon, teamed up with nationally renowned restaurant designer Pat Kuleto in 1993 and created this glittering jewel that sits squarely in the center of the city's culinary crown. Hailed as one of the nation's 10 best chefs by *Food & Wine* magazine, Oakes has come a long way from her days of dishing out saloon-style grub to an audience of longshoremen. These days her patrons tend to be well-heeled gastronomes who have been fans ever since she opened her first restaurant, L'Avenue, in 1988. At big, bustling Boulevard, she now serves hearty American-style cuisine with French and Italian influences. Before you indulge in her fabulous fare, feast your eyes on Kuleto's fantastic Parisian-inspired interior design, which he has dubbed "industrial art nouveau." After a spin through the revolving entrance door, you'll find yourself standing under an impressive domed brick ceiling offset by a dizzying array of details including pressed-tin wainscoting, thousands of brightly colored mosaic tiles, and a sea of decorative ironwork that blends elegantly with the dark wood walls and chairs. This visual extravaganza is capped with a sweeping view of the Embarcadero and the Bay Bridge. On the seasonal menu you'll find a well-chosen mix of dishes. Oysters, giant beluga caviar, and fresh sautéed Sonoma foie gras served on an apple and fig strudel top the extensive appetizer list. Main courses might include a boneless rabbit stuffed with fresh chicken-and-sun-dried-tomato sausages, roasted to perfection in the wood-fired oven; asparagus risotto accompanied by roasted prawns and shiitake mushrooms filled with herbed goat cheese; and oven-roasted northern halibut resting on a large bed of wilted baby spinach sprinkled with chanterelle mushrooms and a side of buttery potato-chive fritters. For dessert, the ganache-mousse tart with fresh raspberries or pecan pie topped with vanilla ice cream and chocolate sauce push the sated diner over a blissful edge. *$$$; AE, DC, DIS, MC, V; no checks; lunch Mon–Fri, dinner every day; full bar; reservations recommended; blvd@sirius.com; www.kuleto.com/ boulevard; map:O3* &

Brandy Ho's Hunan Food / ★★

217 COLUMBUS AVE; 415/788-7527

If you've never experienced good, hot Hunan cuisine, you're due for a visit to Brandy Ho's. It's located on the busy intersection of Broadway and Columbus and, ergo, does a lot of tourist business, but that hasn't diminished the quality of its signature dishes: fried dumplings in sweet-and-sour sauce, cold chicken salad, fish-ball soup, and for your main course, Three Delicacies: a marvelous mix of scallops, shrimp, chicken, onion, bell peppers, and bamboo shoots, all seasoned with ginger, garlic, and wine and served with black-bean sauce. Unless you specify otherwise, most dishes come hot-hot-hot and require copious amounts of Chinese beer. The fancy black-and-white granite tabletops and large, open kitchen are a cut above the usual Chinese restaurant decor, but there's certainly no need to change out of your Levi's. It's not our favorite Chinese restaurant (Ton Kiang and

Eliza's get our vote), but it's the best in the North Beach neighborhood. *AE, DC, DIS, MC, V; no checks; lunch, dinner every day; beer and wine; reservations recommended; map:N2* &

Brasserie Savoy / ★★

580 GEARY ST; 415/441-2700
Brasserie Savoy has long been a favorite pre- and après-theater dinner and cocktail scene, partly because the food is always consistently good and reasonably priced, and partly because it's just so Euro-cool. The atmosphere is pure French bistro, right down to the black-and-white marble floors and tables with matching woven chairs. The menu follows suit, serving such Franco classics as halibut steak rôti with preserved lemon, olives, basil, and tomato; a hearty bouillabaisse made with local seafood; and grilled rib-eye with pommes frites and bordelaise sauce. A popular option is to sit at one of the banquettes or at the bar, order a glass of Alsace Riesling, and nosh on seafood appetizers—mussels marinière, oysters in champagne sauce, fish soup—or a frisée salad. Darn good crème brûlée as well. *$$; AE, CB, DC, DIS, MC, V; no checks; breakfast, dinner every day; full bar; reservations recommended; map:M3* &

Brisas de Acapulco / ★

3137 MISSION ST; 415/826-1496
Among the mishmash of Mexican restaurants in the Mission District, this one stands out by offering dishes with a Salvadoran influence. Its friendly, no-frills, family-style approach is evident from the minute you walk in. And although the staff speaks little English, they are quick to point to their menu favorites. Specialties are seafood (in particular, the excellent shrimp dishes) and *sopa de pollo*, a hearty chicken soup that shouldn't be missed. If you are really hungry, order the *Combinacion Brisas de Acapulco*, which comes with snapper fillets, squid, shrimp, and clams. The *bistec salvadoreo*, a grilled steak in an onion-tomato sauce, is another highlight. Most dishes are under $10. *$; cash only; lunch, dinner every day; full bar; reservations not accepted; map:L7*

Brother's Korean Restaurant / ★

4128 GEARY BLVD; 415/387-7991
It's not much to look at—just a wood-paneled room with overhead ceiling fans and bright lights—but the folks who line up for dinner here aren't too concerned about aesthetics. They've come for a taste of home, and the many Korean expatriates who dine here are like a living testament to the great food. You can grill your own food at your table or, if you're not feeling so ambitious, have the kitchen do it for you. Either way, the marinated beef and pork are succulent and delicious, best when rolled into a lettuce leaf and consumed by hand. The kitchen also offers a range of authentic Korean fare, from beef soups to pan-fried fish to

tempura. Entrees are served with side dishes including seaweed, kimchee, peanut sauce, and of course rice. Warning: Many of the dishes are so incredibly spicy that you might think the barbecue smoke in the air is coming from your mouth. *$; MC, V; no checks; lunch, dinner every day; beer and wine; reservations not accepted; map:H4*

Cafe Bastille / ★★

22 BELDEN PL; 415/986-5673

The narrow downtown alley known as Belden Place couldn't be a better spot for this ever-bustling Parisian-style cafe. Expats, Financial District workers, and in-the-know business folks seek out this cosmopolitan hangout for more than just the delicious crepes. Gregarious waiters, outdoor tables, and plenty of charm make Cafe Bastille a favorite lunchtime destination. During the day, sit outside and choose from sweet and savory crepes (the specialty here). Salads, croque monsieur sandwiches, and a variety of mussel dishes are also available. In the evening, listen to live jazz and enjoy the heartier dinner menu: roast chicken, *boudin noir* (black sausage) with sautéed apples, steak frites, or ratatouille. This inviting cafe's interior exudes a funky charm with its warm lighting, brightly tiled floor, and walls adorned with '50s French posters. Ask a friendly waiter for a recommendation from the moderately priced list of French and California wines and take in the always-interesting scene. *$$; AE, MC, V; no checks; lunch, dinner Mon–Sat; full bar; reservations not accepted; map:N3*

Cafe Claude / ★

7 CLAUDE LN; 415/392-3515

Take a turn down tiny Claude Lane and it's as if you've accidentally encountered a little Parisian street. The lane is anchored by Cafe Claude, where tables are set out with umbrellas, servers are rude and abrupt, and everyone loves it as they sit and sip espresso and listen to the man playing the accordion in the corner. Actually, the service is never all that rude, but it definitely can be, shall we say, "Parisian." And that fits right in with the authentic cafe fare. The salads (including a great niçoise) and baguette sandwiches are popular choices at lunch. We recommend the daily pizza, which comes with any number of surprising toppings, from eggplant to artichoke hearts. At dinner on Thursday through Saturday, a hip crowd files in to hear live jazz by local trios and enjoy such plates as beef braised in red wine with mushrooms; steamed mussels with garlic, tomatoes, and white wine; and the soup du jour. *$; MC, V; no checks; lunch, dinner Mon–Sat; beer and wine; reservations recommended; map:N3*

Cafe Jacqueline / ★★☆

1454 GRANT AVE; 415/981-5565

Tucked along a narrow North Beach street filled with boutiques and Italian shops, Cafe Jacqueline is a small, romantic restaurant that serves one amazing dish: the soufflé. Inside the lace-draped storefront windows, a softly lit room holds about a dozen linen-covered tables topped with long-stemmed roses in vases, where you'll often see starry-eyed diners holding hands. This is also where you'll eat soufflé for dinner and soufflé for dessert. That's all there is, except for salad and soup appetizers. You won't care, however, because the soufflés are impeccably made by French-born Jacqueline Margulis. She says creating the soufflés is like painting—she never tires of creating them because each is one of a kind. Pick your own combinations: in a recent visit, the white corn, ginger, and garlic concoction balanced crisp, sweet corn against a creamy-rich base. The leek and chanterelle creation was technically perfect, but had no detectable mushrooms. The crab and the truffle soufflés are house specialties. For the grand finale, the sweet soufflés arrive with a fresh-fruit topping or a dusting of powdered sugar. A smooth white-chocolate version might contain pudding and cakelike bits. Many people come to Cafe Jacqueline solely for dessert, so if you're on a budget (the soufflés aren't cheap), go after dinner and add a glass of champagne or an espresso for a memorable evening out. *$$$; AE, DC, DIS, MC, V; no checks; dinner Wed–Sun; beer and wine; reservations recommended on weekends; map:N2* &

Cafe Kati / ★★★

1963 SUTTER ST; 415/775-7313

Cafe Kati may not have the elbow room of some of San Francisco's other top restaurants, but there are few chefs on the West Coast who can match Kirk Webber—a California Culinary Academy graduate—when it comes to culinary artistry. Obscurely located on a residential block off Fillmore Street, this tiny, modest, 60-seat cafe has garnered a monsoon of kudos for Webber's weird and wonderful arrangements of numerous cuisines. Even something as mundane as a Caesar salad is transformed into a towering monument of lovely romaine arranged upright on the plate and held in place by a ribbon of thinly sliced cucumber. Fortunately, it tastes as good as it looks. Though the menu changes monthly, it always spans the globe: miso-marinated Chilean sea bass topped with tempura kabocha squash; pancetta-wrapped pork tenderloin bathed in a ragout of baby artichokes and chanterelle mushrooms; walnut-crusted chicken with Gorgonzola; crispy duck confit with sweet potato polenta and wild mushrooms. Complete the gustatory experience with the to-die-for butterscotch pudding. When making a reservation, request a table in the front room—and don't make any plans after dinner because the kitchen takes its sweet time preparing your objet d'art. *$$; MC, V; no checks; dinner Tues–Sun; beer and wine; reservations recommended; katikwok@ aol.com; www.cafekati.com; map:K3*

Cafe Majestic / ★★

1500 SUTTER ST; 415/441-1100

Well off the beaten path and tucked away within one of San Francisco's best historic hotels, Cafe Majestic is one of the city's most romantic restaurants. This intimate hideaway, with beautiful fixtures and white linens, combines turn-of-the-century elegance with chef Frank Palmer's excellent California cuisine. Palmer plays it fairly straight, letting the flavors speak for themselves. When he does get a bit inventive, it is to introduce a few Asian accents, such as with the pan-roasted Alaskan halibut, prepared with ginger consommé and served with cucumber noodles. The lime-crusted ahi tuna with tempura prawns is delightful, as is the crispy whole Thai snapper with sweet-and-sour sauce. The tomato consommé is an outstanding starter. Sit at the beautiful mahogany bar for one of the city's most perfect martinis (there you can also examine one of the world's rarest butterfly collections). A pianist performs nightly on the grand piano in the bar. This is a bit of old-world San Francisco, but with all the modern touches. *$$$; AE, DC, JCB, MC, V; no checks; breakfast, dinner every day; full bar; reservations recommended; map:L3* &

Cafe Marimba / ★★☆

2317 CHESTNUT ST (AT SCOTT ST); 415/776-1506

This exuberant little restaurant sandwiched between shops in the Marina district is easy to miss, despite its vibrant sunset-purple facade and the seemingly endless stream of people who squeeze through its lime-green doors every evening. Step inside and you'll be bowled over by a profusion of more screaming colors—pink, turquoise, green, orange—not to mention a fiery-red, 10-foot-tall papier-mâché *diablo* towering above the room. The secret to eating at Marimba, which packs more people into a small space than a yuppie-express Muni bus, is to make a reservation early in the evening so you won't have to wait long for a table. San Francisco chef Reed Hearon, famous for his Black Cat and Rose Pistola restaurants, pioneered this festive place, and although he has since moved on to other projects, Marimba still thrives under owners Louise Clement and Bill Susky's inspired creations. The quite reasonably priced fare here is real Mexican—not an overpriced upscale version of Taco Bell. Once you're seated, immediately order the wonderful guacamole and chips. The restaurant has a changing repertoire of more than 50 salsas; the nightly selections might include roasted corn, avocado-tomatillo, or tomato with smoked chilies. Have a margarita to douse the flames, or sip a delicious fresh-fruit juice. Then move on to the sublime shrimp *mojo de ajo*, drenched in garlic, chilies, and lime; spicy snapper tacos with pineapple salsa; or grilled chicken spiced with mild, smoky achiote seed. Even the more common fare has a twist: the seafood comes with a choice of five sauces, including garlic, caramelized onions, and fresh jalapeño sauces, or a combination of capers, olives, tomatoes, and jalapeños. Top it all off with the fantastic flan. *$$; AE, MC, V; no checks; lunch Tues–Sun, dinner every day; full bar; reservations recommended; map:J1* &

SAN FRANCISCO ON CELLULOID

As most film fans know, San Francisco's cinematic contributions are extensive. Time and time again, hotshot Hollywood producers and their entourages trek north to capture this seductive city on film. Here is a sampling of some of the more memorable movies made in the city by the bay—just in case you didn't recognize her in her many glamorous poses.

A View to a Kill	Foul Play	Nine to Five
American Graffiti	George of the Jungle	Pacific Heights
Another 48 Hours	The Graduate	The Parent Trap
The Bachelor	Guinevere	Patch Adams
Basic Instinct	Harold and Maude	Patty Hearst Story
Birdman of Alcatraz	High Anxiety	Phenomenon
The Birds	Interview with the Vampire	Play It Again, Sam
Black Stallion II	Invasion of the Body	Quicksilver
Bullitt	Snatchers	The Right Stuff
Butterflies Are Free	Jagged Edge	RoboCop II
The Candidate	James and the Giant Peach	The Rock
Chan Is Missing	The Jazz Singer	Shoot the Moon
City of Angels	The Joy Luck Club	Sister Act
Class Action	The Killing Fields	Sister Act II
The Conversation	Leonard VI	Sneakers
Copycat	Love Story	Star Trek IV
Crackers	Magnum Force	Sudden Impact
Cujo	The Maltese Falcon	They Call Me Mr. Tibbs
Dirty Harry	Mrs. Doubtfire	Tucker
Dying Young	Murder in the First	Vertigo
EDtv	The Net	What Dreams May Come
Escape from Alcatraz	The Night Before Christmas	When a Man Loves a
Flubber	Nine Months	Woman
48 Hours	1982	Woman in Red

Cafe Niebaum-Coppola / ★

916 KEARNY ST; 415/291-1700

Film director Francis Ford Coppola brought all the amenities of his hugely popular Napa Valley winery to the city and nestled them stylishly at the foot of the landmark Sentinel Building in North Beach. It may sound at first like a bit of a marketing ploy (and, in fact, it is), but once you sit down to eat you'll be convinced your stop was worthwhile. Coppola is known in these parts for his gourmet savvy, and it is reflected in the casual country Italian dishes served here—many are reportedly made from the director's favorite recipes. The pastas, pizzas, and panini are excellent, great for a light lunch or dinner. A large selection of Italian pastries is available early in the day, and the entire menu can be served outside. As you might expect, there are some 100 wines on the list, 24 of them available by the glass; many can be sampled at the wine-tasting bar. And who knows, after a couple of tastings, you may just talk yourself into buying a T-shirt. *$; AE, DC, MC, V; checks OK; breakfast, lunch, dinner every day; full bar; reservations recommended; map:N2* &

Cafe Pescatore / ★★☆

2455 MASON ST; 415/561-1111

It's hard to get a good meal at a fair price in the Fisherman's Wharf vicinity, which is why we're so fond of Cafe Pescatore. Okay, so it's not Rose Pistola (see review), but it's not trying to be. Rather, it's a modest yet attractively decorated trattoria-style restaurant that will leave you both stuffed and satisfied. The trick is to know what to order, which is basically anything cooked in the open kitchen's wood-fired oven. Our perennial favorites are the polenta al forno (oak-roasted cheese polenta topped with marinara sauce and fresh pesto), the puffy calzone primavera stuffed with spinach, goat cheese, sweet peppers and artichokes, any of the thin-crust pizzas, and for the big eater in your group, a sizzling slab of oven-roasted chicken. When the weather's warm the floor-to-ceiling windows are retracted, allowing for some very pleasant alfresco dining. *$$; AE, DC, DIS, MC, V; no checks; breakfast, lunch, dinner every day; full bar; reservations recommended; map:M1* &

Caffe Freddy's / ★

901 COLUMBUS AVE; 415/922-0151

Caffe Freddy's consistently reaffirms our belief that good Italian food shouldn't cost a fortune. So if you're wandering along Columbus Avenue and you're looking for some good, cheap but quality eats, pass through the painted palms that frame the doorway, situate yourself at a booth in the back, and ponder the extensive menu. Pastas, pizzas, sandwiches, salads, soups, and a large assortment of appetizers are available, as well as a few chalkboard surprises such as a thick cut of Atlantic salmon with all the trimmings for under $14. Start with the fresh warm cabbage salad with goat cheese, currants, walnuts, rosemary, and spinach, or the antipasto plate of bruschetta, fresh melon, ham, sun-dried tomatoes, and pesto. Then sample the seafood dishes, such as the fresh fish soup, a steaming bowl of fat mussels, or fresh Idaho trout. The open-faced sandwiches topped with melted mozzarella are excellent as well. On a typically cold and blustery day, the house-made stew and a real cup of Italian coffee are just the ticket to warm your budget-minded bones. *$; AE, MC, V; no checks; lunch Wed–Sun, dinner Tues–Sun; beer and wine; reservations recommended; map:N2* &

Caffe Macaroni / ★★

59 COLUMBUS AVE; 415/956-9737
Don't let the funky little facade or silly name fool you—Caffe Macaroni is one of the best southern Italian restaurants in the city. It's so bloody small you can't help but feel special, as if you've been invited to dine in some stranger's kitchen in Roma. (And if you think the main dining room is tiny, check out the one upstairs—bonk!) For such a diminutive kitchen, it churns out a surprising amount and variety of antipasti and pastas. The menu changes daily; we recently had an outstanding spinach-and-cheese ravioli dish served in a wild-mushroom sauce. Gnocchi fans will find happiness here as well. The soft polenta makes a good starter, and there's a wide selection of reasonably priced Italian wines. You'll adore the jovial and vivacious Italian waiters too—it's all part of the unique Macaroni experience. *$–$$; cash only; dinner Mon–Sat; beer and wine; reservations recommended; map:N2*

Caffe Sport / ★★

574 GREEN ST; 415/981-1251
Since 1969 owner-chef Antonio La Tona has been serving heaping plates of pasta and steaming hot bowls of cioppino to tourists and locals alike. Considered an institution by many, this North Beach restaurant serves lusty Sicilian dishes with more than a hint of the stinking rose on every plate. There's also often a heaping helping of attitude: the place is famous for obnoxious service bordering on rude. Even so, reservations are a good idea. The best way to experience this unique slice of North Beach is to go with a group. Order large family-style portions of any of the pasta dishes; the pesto and the seafood combo are consistently rich and tasty. The copious amounts of garlic, unusual Sicilian paintings, hanging hams, and brusque waiters might all add up to sensory overload, but it's definitely an experience you won't soon forget. *$$$; cash only; lunch, dinner Tues–Sat; beer and wine; reservations recommended; map:M1* &

Campton Place / ★★★

340 STOCKTON ST; 415/955-5555

Just off the lobby of a small, European-style luxury hotel, Campton Place pairs an ambience steeped in serene, old-money traditionalism with a kitchen that delights in inventive, newfangled ideas. Since its unveiling in 1983, the pricey restaurant has been the proving ground for such noteworthy chefs as Bradley Ogden (who went on to Lark Creek Inn fame), Jan Birnbaum (now the proud owner of Catahoula in Calistoga), and, most recently, Todd Humphries (now at Greystone). Humphries's replacement, Frenchman Laurent Manrique, is now at the chef's helm, and has been wowing hard-to-please San Franciscans with his simple yet sophisticated Gascony cooking. Recommended dishes include his tomato and ham tartare crouton appetizer, the foie gras ravioli in a clear duck-Parmesan bouillon, the roasted monkfish Basquaise, and one of his signature dishes, poached chicken Aurelie. Desserts are as decadent as one would expect from this lush brand of cuisine. The service is quietly attentive, and the decor is a study in understated elegance. Campton Place also serves a superb breakfast and a reasonably priced three-course prix-fixe dinner offered nightly until 7:30 and all night long on Wednesdays. *$$$; AE, DC, DIS, MC, V; no checks; breakfast, lunch, dinner every day; full bar; reservations recommended; reservations@campton.com; www. citysearch7.com; map:M3* &

Carnelian Room / ★★★

555 CALIFORNIA ST; 415/433-7500

When it's time to treat yourself to the finer things in life, tell your diet and budget to bugger off and reserve a table at the Carnelian Room. One of our favorite high-rise restaurants, it's perched on the top floor of the Bank of America building—a giddy 52 floors above the streets of San Francisco. The combination of dark oak paneling, brass chandeliers, and enormous windows with captivating city views makes for a very romantic setting (particularly if you can score a windowside table). By day the Carnelian Room is the exclusive Banker's Club, accessible only to members or by invitation, but at night we little people can max out our Visas on Grand Cru Burgundies, smoked sturgeon with caviar-whipped potatoes, and thick cuts of prime rib so tender you can cut them with a fork. (It's also a great place to have a drink and watch the sunset.) Okay, so it's an old-school dinosaur in a city brimming with stylish restaurants, but red meat is back in style and few restaurants can make a thick-cut New York steak taste as sinfully pleasurable as this one. Our all-time favorite dish is the rack of lamb with port wine and rosemary sauce, best accompanied by a glass of Silver Oak cabernet sauvignon. Since the wine cellar houses some 36,000 bottles, it's a good idea to let the sommelier help find the right match for your meal. Of course there are several fish, fowl, and pasta dishes as well, but none compare to the kitchen's deft handling of premium-quality beef and lamb. The Sunday brunch is quite popular as well. *$$$; AE, CB, DC, DIS, MC, V; no checks; dinner every day, brunch Sun; full bar; reservations recommended; map:N2* &

Carta / ★★☆

1772 MARKET ST; 415/863-3516

In a city teeming with restaurants offering every imaginable type of cuisine, this eclectic restaurant could be easily overlooked. Carta's ambitious concept showcases the dishes of a different country or region every other month, and surprisingly, it works quite well. From Morocco to Russia to the American Deep South, chef Rob Zaborny steps up to the challenge of creating remarkably good regional dishes. When Tuscany was the culinary destination not long ago, a sampling of small plates turned up deliciously prepared country-style rabbit stew infused with lovely hints of clove and red wine. A tart lemon vinaigrette perfectly complemented a salad of sweet figs, arugula, and shaved fennel. An eggy baked artichoke tart was disappointing, but a large plate of trout flamed with fresh herbs was cooked to perfection. Zaborny has converted a storefront on a nondescript block of Market Street to carry out his innovative vision. Wrought-iron light fixtures and brilliantly colored art hang from the sun-splashed yellow walls. A recently added private dining area with a long banquette and a warm color scheme give the room a distinctly Mediterranean feel. And live piano music played Thursday through Saturday adds a soothing touch. There's a large and changing selection of varietals from around the world, with offerings by both the glass and the bottle. Curious diners can go online for a sneak preview of the cuisine to come. *$$$; AE, DC, MC, V; no checks; lunch Mon–Fri, dinner every day, brunch Sun; full bar; reservations recommended; www.creative.net/~carta; map:L5* &

Casa Aguila / ★★☆

1240 NORIEGA ST; 415/661-5593

Laura Esquivel's sensual novel *Like Water for Chocolate* comes alive in Casa Aguila. The minute a mountainous plate of wildly imaginative Mexican food arrives at your table, it's evident chef Luis Angeles Hoffman cooks anything but ordinary fare. Beautiful, robust dishes you would expect to find only in inland Mexico bring diners from all over the city to this small Outer Sunset District gem. Don't expect anything to happen quickly here. Once you sit down (which itself can be preceded by a long wait if you don't have a reservation), nibble on complimentary tamales and warm chips and salsa. If you're really hungry, try the zesty lime-marinated ceviche appetizer. But keep in mind that portions are enormous, so you may want to just pick one of the more than 20 enticing entrees. The *pollo ranchera* is a dizzying, aromatic mound of sweet potatoes, apples, and prunes topped with sweet marinated chicken breasts and wonderfully spiced whole sticks of cinnamon. For pork lovers, whole orange slices top a chop dish teeming with apples, jicama, potatoes, and whole garlic cloves. If you have room for dessert, silky caramel-flavored flan is the perfect finish. At the end of the meal, you'll pay more than at your average taqueria, but everything here, including the tasty sangría, rates far above average. *$$; AE, MC, V; no checks; lunch, dinner every day; beer and wine; reservations recommended; map:G6* &

Cha Cha Cha / ★★☆

1801 HAIGHT ST; 415/386-5758
2327 MISSION ST; 415/648-0504
When we're asked which San Francisco restaurants are our favorites (and we're asked all the time), one of the first we mention is Cha Cha Cha. It's fun, it's festive, the Caribbean food is very good, the prices are totally reasonable, the sangría is addictive, and every meal ends with a free Tootsie Roll. What's not to like? The cafe is wildly decorated with Santeria altars and such, which blend in perfectly with the varied mix of pumped-up patrons quaffing pitchers of sangría while waiting for a table (which often takes up to an hour on weekends, but nobody seems to mind). The tapas-style dishes we always start with: sautéed mushrooms, fried calamari, fried new potatoes (dig the spicy sauce), Cajun shrimp, mussels in saffron (order more bread for the sauce), and plantains with black-bean sauce. Check the specials board for outstanding seafood dishes as well, but skip the so-so steak. A second branch, recently opened in the Mission, serves exactly the same food in a much larger space; not only is the wait shorter (if any), but there's also a full bar. Still, the original is our favorite simply for the only-in-SF Cha Cha Cha experience. *$; MC, V; no checks; lunch, dinner every day; beer and wine; reservations not accepted; map:I5* &

Charanga / ★

2351 MISSION ST; 415/282-1813
Chef Gabriela Salas left her post at the popular Cha Cha Cha restaurant (see review) after nine years to open her own place, named after a style of Latin music. And many people eagerly followed her to this new outpost tucked behind an unassuming facade on Mission Street. She has provided San Franciscans with one of the few—and one of the best—restaurants in town serving cuisine from Costa Rica and the Caribbean. Ultimately, it's a tapas experience—which isn't to say the cuisine is the slightest bit like what you'll find anywhere else. Salas's spicy vegetable *empanaditas* are out of this world, served with a yogurt-pineapple-mint salsa that quickly cools the palate. The ceviche is another good selection, as are the mussels and the sautéed mushrooms. Charanga is relatively

nondescript, but bring a large group, order a few pitchers of sangría, and you'll soon be creating your own atmosphere. *$; DC, DIS, MC, V; no checks; dinner Tues–Sat; full bar; reservations recommended; map:L6*

Charles Nob Hill / ★★★

1250 JONES ST; 415/771-5400
First things first: you'll never find parking here, so leave the car behind. OK, now we can tell you that this tucked-away little gem atop Nob Hill has for the past few years been turning itself into one of the elite dining spots in the city. And that has everything to do with chef Ron Siegel, whose uncommon skill earned him global recognition when he won Japan's prestigious Iron Chef competition in 1998. All that did was make tables harder to get at his elegant, refined restaurant. Siegel is a master of flavor combinations and presentation. On a recent visit, the lamb noisette with lentil ragout, caramelized salsify, and braised escarole was heavenly. Siegel's Hudson Valley foie gras is arguably the best foie gras in town. The menu varies with the season, planned around the best available local ingredients. A good way to dine here is with the Chef's Tasting Menu, a six-course journey in which you can leave yourself in Siegel's capable hands. The wine list contains many older vintages, great for a celebration. But perhaps the best thing about Charles Nob Hill is that you get all the trappings of fine dining without any of the stuffiness. It's all very civilized. *$$$; AE, DC, MC, V; no checks; dinner Tues–Sun; full bar; reservations required; map:M2* &

Chow / ★

215 CHURCH ST; 415/552-2469
Chow, the first of Tony Gulisano's no-frills cafes serving bargain-priced food, regularly has Castro dwellers lining up. The warm, 80-seat dining room, with a long mahogany bar stretching the length of it, offers a casual and relaxed atmosphere—a good match for the inexpensive food. This no-reservations restaurant is known for its robust wood-fired pizzas with such toppings as fennel sausage and red onions or a roast-chicken pie with pancetta. Vegetarians can easily find their way around the menu, with offerings like pasta with peppers and eggplant, grilled portobello mushrooms and polenta, or noodles with tofu and pesto. The desserts tend toward such classics as strawberry shortcake and a pie of the day. An impressive beer list includes several Belgian options and six microbrews on tap. A small list of wines by the glass is also available. A sister restaurant, Park Chow (see review), is located near Golden Gate Park. *$; MC, V; no checks; lunch, dinner every day; beer and wine; reservations not accepted; map:K5* &

Citizen Cake / ★

399 GROVE ST; 415/861-2228

When you're looking to impress your pals with a grand dessert, this chic little bakery is the place to get your cake. Locals love Citizen Cake, as much for its hip, modern feel as for its magnificent baked goods. Prices can be a bit steep, but they stop short of exorbitant. At lunch, folks who work in the area line up for the wood-fired pizzas and excellent sandwiches (but be sure to treat yourself to a fresh-made cookie—or a piece of cake—for an after-lunch snack). *$; MC, V; local checks only; breakfast, lunch Tues–Sun; no alcohol; reservations not accepted; map:L4*

Crescent City Cafe / ★

1418 HAIGHT ST; 415/863-1374

Step past the blue-tiled facade in the midst of the hippie-holdout Haight-Ashbury district, and it's as if you've stepped into the heart of New Orleans. This postage-stamp-size place—just four tables and about a dozen stools around an L-shaped bar—is like a little slice of Creole comfort, complete with jazz filling the air at all times. When you want spicy, come here and order the gumbo or the jambalaya, each rich, hearty, and fiery hot. The Southern fried chicken with mashed potatoes and corn bread is rib-sticking good, and there are some mighty fine blackened fish dishes. On weekends, neighborhood folks line up for the huge buckwheat pancakes, Southern-style biscuits and gravy, and Creole omelets with grits. Service is good and prompt, if just a bit frazzled. But it's worth getting shuffled out the door to save yourself the airfare to the Big Easy. *$; MC, V; no checks; breakfast, lunch Mon–Fri, dinner every day, brunch Sat–Sun; beer and wine; reservations not accepted; map:J5*

Cypress Club / ★★

500 JACKSON ST; 415/296-8555

Reviews of the Cypress Club invariably begin with descriptions of its dining room, and for good reason: everything in this sumptuous restaurant is over the top. Bulging archways are lined in hammered copper; glass light fixtures look like huge sundaes or a woman's breasts (you choose); low, serpentine partitions snake through the room; plump burgundy velvet covers booths and chairs; and columns resemble giant urns. It's almost as if a particularly impish animator, instead of an interior decorator, had gotten the design commission and decided to fashion a luxury restaurant that would be right at home in Toontown. All this visual drama could easily overshadow the food, and in some cases it does, depending on who's the chef that month. Unfortunately, the Cypress Club suffers from a revolving-door turnover of chefs and other personnel, leaving it difficult for diners to know exactly what to expect. Entrees range from monkfish baked with heirloom pear tomatoes in a saffron lobster broth to herb-kissed loin of lamb with roasted baby beets and potato purée to a whole oven-roasted trout stuffed with lemon, sage, and foie gras. Dinner comes to a reliably rousing finale with temptations like warm lemon cake with white chocolate–poppy seed ice cream, dark chocolate and hazelnut timbale with Tahitian vanilla cream and chocolate sauce, and almond crème brûlée topped with honey-whipped cream. Be sure to scan the room as you dine, because you'll likely find yourself with some interesting dinner companions—everyone from TV talk-show host Conan O'Brien to actor Don Johnson has graced the Cypress Club's velvet-cushioned chairs. *$$–$$$; AE, DC, MC, V; no checks; lunch Mon–Fri (in Dec only), dinner every day; full bar; reservations recommended; www.citysearch7.com; map:N2* ౹

Delfina / ★★☆

3621 18TH ST; 415/552-4055

Opening to rave reviews in 1998, this tiny Mission District restaurant with a clean, modern design and pea-green walls has been packed ever since. Partners Anne Spencer and Craig Stoll have extensive pedigrees at other Bay Area restaurants, and chef Stoll's daily-changing creations showcase his skills for cooking Italian regional cuisine. Top-notch starters have included nettles-and-ricotta ravioli; a salad studded with fresh cracked crab, fennel, and grapefruit segments; and the far-from-ordinary Ribollita da Delfina minestrone. Entrees are hearty and include rich, braised meat dishes, excellent pastas, and fish. Pancetta-wrapped rabbit loin bursts with flavor, as do the buttermilk-battered fried onions and polenta served on the side. A textbook spaghetti with tomatoes, garlic, olive oil, and chili flakes has a little heat to warm the throat. Swordfish rests on a bed of soft leeks; salmon may be served with fresh vegetables and a tangy citrus dressing. Desserts are simply delicious: profiteroles stuffed with coffee ice cream, creamy buttermilk panna cotta (baked custard), and Gorgonzola with chestnut honey. Delfina's wine list is a well-edited one, with many moderately priced bottles among the offerings. *$$; MC, V; no checks; dinner every day; beer and wine; reservations recommended; map:K6* ౹

The Dining Room at the Ritz-Carlton / ★★★

600 STOCKTON ST; 415/773-6198

For those special occasions (or when the other person is buying), few restaurants go the extra distance to spoil you rotten like the Dining Room at the Ritz-Carlton hotel. No less than five tuxedoed wait staff are at your beck and call, surreptitiously attending to your needs as you bask in your evening of opulence. The setting is, as one would expect, sumptuous and regal. The room was redecorated in the fall of '97: cushy high-backed chairs, rich brocade, crystal chandeliers, elegant table settings, and live harp music provide a definite air of formality (though the servers will lighten up if you prod them with humor). Celebrity chef Gary Danko left the Ritz in the summer of 1996 to open his own restaurant (see Gary Danko review); his replacement, chef Sylvain Portay (a Frenchman from the famed Le Cirque restaurant in New York), continues the Ritz-Carlton tradition of using only the finest, freshest ingredients from around the world, though he brings a more modern style of French cooking to the table. The seasonal menu is strictly prix fixe, offering a choice of three-, four-, or five-course dinners; the latter includes wine pairings per course by master sommelier Emmanuel Kemiji (one of only 31 master sommeliers in the United States) for a hefty additional fee. Notable dishes have included the frothy crayfish bisque, risotto with butternut squash and roasted squab, sweetbreads with scallions and bok choy, a juicy roasted rack of Colorado lamb, and grilled John Dory (a New Zealand fish) spiked with basil and olives. For the finale, indulge in the ultimate French dessert: dark chocolate soufflé with bitter almond ice cream. The Dining Room also features a unique rolling cheese cart, laden with at least two dozen individually ripened cheeses. $$$; AE, DC, DIS, MC, V; no checks; dinner Mon–Sat; full bar; reservations required; www.ritzcarlton.com; map:M3 &

Doidge's / ★★★

2217 UNION ST; 415/921-2149

If you thought it was hard to get a table at French Laundry in Wine Country, try Doidge's on a sunny Sunday morning—by the time you're seated it's well past lunchtime. Which explains why people sometimes make reservations weeks in advance for an opportunity to savor one of the best breakfasts both east and west of the Mississippi. Yes, it's that good. The decor is pure country cozy with cute little tables, bentwood furnishings, and flowers all around. Hot chocolate, for example, comes in such adorable little pots that most patrons can't resist a cup. Everything on the menu is good, but standout dishes have always been the eggs Benedict, breakfast casseroles, eggs Florentine, gourmet omelets, corned beef hash, and the thick stack of French toast, washed down with a refreshing mimosa. The portions are hefty and so is the price, but it's worth the splurge (though the slow service can be annoying). Lunch is served as well, but most come for the classic American breakfast. $$; MC, V; no checks; breakfast, lunch every day; beer and wine; reservations recommended; map:K2 &

Dol Ho / ★

808 PACIFIC AVE; 415/392-2828

Some contend the mark of authenticity and quality at an ethnic restaurant is when people of that ethnicity are filling the place. Given that benchmark, Dol Ho must be one of the best places in town for dim sum. And it is. Despite not having the polish and, well, cleanliness of the city's more popular dim sum parlors, this place serves up dim sum that's quite fresh and delicious. What's more, it's considerably cheaper than you'll find almost anywhere else. The trays of shrimp and pork dumplings, fried eggplant, custard tarts, and other delights roll out from the kitchen every few minutes; as at all dim sum restaurants, just point at what you want when it passes. *$; cash only; dim sum every day 7am–5pm; beer and wine; reservations not accepted; map:N2*

Dottie's True Blue Café / ★★☆

522 JONES ST; 415/885-2767
Don't let the dicey neighborhood deter you from venturing to one of the best breakfast cafes in the city, sequestered within the Pacific Bay Inn downtown. Though Dottie's serves lunch, it's the all-day, all-American morning fare everyone lines up for, such as hefty portions of French toast, cornmeal pancakes, bacon and eggs, and omelets that look especially appealing against the blue-and-white checkerboard tablecloths. Because it's all made from scratch they don't mind taking special orders, and they do wonders with bean cakes that double as meatless sausage patties. The clincher, though, is the fantastic fresh-baked breads, muffins, or scones that accompany your order. It's a great place to start your day, and the kind of diner you wish was just around the corner from home. *$; DIS, MC, V; no checks; breakfast, lunch Wed–Mon; beer and wine; reservations not accepted; map:M3* &

Ebisu / ★★★

1283 9TH AVE; 415/566-1770
It's a good bet that Ebisu would top anyone's short list of favorite sushi spots. Known for its consistently fresh ingredients, this compact restaurant has been pleasing sushi-lovers with its exquisite creations for more than 17 years. The best seat in the house at most sushi bars is the bar; that's true at Ebisu too, though you can opt for table seating or the tatami-covered private room as well. All will typically require a wait, so how hungry you are will usually determine where you decide to sit. If you're an adventurous eater, let the chef's recommendations be your guide. The tuna in every shape and form is always delicious: the buttery *toro* (or fatty tuna) is incredible, as are any of the nigiri-like maguro and hamachi. A number of whimsically named rolls are available; try the Tootsie Roll, made of tempura-fried salmon rolled in rice, or the Two Balls No Strikes—spicy tuna wrapped in thin avocado slices. Other Ebisu specialties include deliciously prepared chicken teriyaki and a unique and sumptuous seafood salad. *$$; AE, DC, MC, V; no checks; lunch, dinner every day; beer and wine; reservations not accepted; map:H5* &

The Elite Cafe / ★★

2049 FILLMORE ST; 415/346-8668

In a city where new restaurant openings are outnumbered only by Internet start-ups, the popular Elite Cafe (known as the E-light by many locals) has held its ground since 1981. A mostly local crowd comes to this bustling Fillmore institution for its fiery Cajun and Creole cuisine and fresh offerings from the oyster bar (be prepared to wait awhile for a table since reservations are not accepted). Handsome dark wood wainscoting and light-colored walls provide a comfortable, upscale setting for the gutsy Southern cuisine. Bountiful portions of thick and tasty gumbo, spicy baby-back ribs, and a signature blackened redfish will fill you to the gills. The à la carte seafood items, from oysters on the half shell and fried calamari to the divine creamy seafood chowder, consistently arrive fresh and generously portioned. For some of the best bread pudding in the city, try the Elite's version swathed in a rich bourbon sauce—it'll have you whistling Dixie. *$$$; AE, DC, DIS, MC, V; checks OK; dinner every day, brunch Sun; full bar; reservations recommended for 6 or more; map:K3* &

Eliza's / ★★★

2877 CALIFORNIA ST; 415/621-4819
1457 18TH ST; 415/648-9999

Eliza's is not only one of our favorite Chinese restaurants in San Francisco, it's one of our favorite San Francisco restaurants period. Where else can you get such fresh, high-quality cuisine in an artistic setting for under $7 a dish? You'll love the decor—oodles of gorgeous handblown glassware, orchids, and tasteful neon lighting create a soothing, sophisticated ambience despite the crowded dining room. The menu offers a large array of classic Hunan and Mandarin dishes, all served on beautiful Italian plates. Start with the assorted appetizer dish, which is practically a meal in itself. Two other recommended dishes are the kung pao chicken—a marvelous mixture of tender chicken, peanuts, chili peppers, hot sauce, and fresh vegetables—and the vegetable moo-shu (with sweet plum sauce). Regardless of what you order you're likely to be impressed, and the $5 lunch specials are a steal. The only drawback is the line out the door that often forms around 7pm, and they don't take reservations. *$; MC, V; no checks; lunch, dinner every day; beer and wine; reservations not accepted; map:J3, N6* &

Ella's / ★★½

500 PRESIDIO AVE; 415/441-5669

If carbo-loading is your idea of a good time, Ella's—a sunny, charming corner cafe in Laurel Heights—won't disappoint. An in-house master baker whips up fabulous goodies, especially for breakfast and lunch: moist banana-nut–cinnamon coffee cake, sticky buns thick with pecans and orange zest, buttery sweet potato–raisin muffins, and even the poached eggs come on thick slices of yeasty house-made white toast. The buttermilk, pumpkin and pecan, or lemon and ginger oatmeal pancakes are airy and flavorful, the orange juice is fresh, and the omelets are bursting with sausages, roasted peppers, and provolone. Even the lunch menu is enlivened by hamburgers served on house-made buns and flaky potpies, along with salads, sandwiches, grilled fish, and specials such as pot roast with gravy. Dinner dishes are more substantial: beef stew, sautéed pork medallions, and lots of salads, vegetables, and homey American heartland–type entrees. Expect a madhouse at the weekend brunch, with lines of hungry folks wrapping around the corner starting at 8:30am. Service is courteous and efficient, despite all the hustle and bustle. Try to sit at the counter if a table isn't available—and on your way out, be sure to buy a loaf of bread to go. *$$; AE, MC, V; no checks; breakfast Mon–Fri, lunch, dinner Mon–Fri, brunch Sat–Sun; beer and wine; reservations not accepted; map:J3* &

Enrico's / ★★

504 BROADWAY; 415/982-6223

Like a phoenix rising from the ashes, Enrico's is back on bawdy Broadway and better than ever. This restaurant/bar/coffeehouse/jazz club is named after Enrico Banducci, who owned the famous hungry i night-club during San Francisco's beatnik era and opened this eponymous place as well. (It was later closed in the '80s as the Broadway area went through a depression of sorts.) You can't help but love Enrico's, particularly when you're seated at the heated outdoor patio, sipping a cocktail, noshing on an array of delicious tapas, and listening to the cool jazz beat while a cross section of the world's cultures walks by. The menu items change monthly, but you're bound to find something that appeals: brick-oven pizzas, Tuscan soups, fresh pastas, fresh seafood, and thick-cut steaks. When in doubt, opt for the juicy Niman Ranch hamburger served on focaccia with house-made condiments, which is served until midnight on weekends. Enrico's is also the place to go for the best mint juleps anywhere (if you've never tried one, try this one). A live jazz band plays nightly with no cover charge, and valet parking is both available and necessary. *$$; AE, DC, DIS, MC, V; no checks; lunch, dinner every day; full bar; reservations recommended; map:N2* &

Eos Restaurant & Wine Bar / ★★★

901 COLE ST; 415/566-3063

One of the most talked-about restaurants in the city, Eos has everyone asking, "Where is Cole Valley?" It's not so much the menu—the Euro-Asian fusion theme is hardly original—as it is the portions (generous) and presentations (brilliant) that have brought throngs of visitors and residents to this once-little-known San Francisco neighborhood nestled near the southeast corner of Golden Gate Park. Owner-chef Arnold Wong, a California Culinary Academy graduate and a former architecture student, has taken the art of arrangement to a whole new level: every dish is masterfully crafted to take full advantage of the shape, color, and texture of each ingredient. And—egad!—it's a desecration simply to dig in to such culinary artwork, though one's guilt is soon assuaged after the assault begins, particularly when it's upon the tender breast of Peking duck, smoked in ginger-peach tea leaves and served with a plum-kumquat chutney. Other notable dishes are the almond-encrusted soft-shell crab appetizer dipped in spicy plum ponzu sauce, shiitake mushroom dumplings, blackened Asian catfish atop a bed of lemongrass risotto, five-pepper calamari, and the red curry–marinated rack of lamb. Desserts are as fetching as the entrees, particularly the Bananamisu (akin to tiramisu) with caramelized bananas and the warm bittersweet chocolate soufflé cake. Unfortunately, a quiet, romantic dinner is out of the question here, since the stark deco-industrial decor merely amplifies the nightly cacophony. After dinner, adjourn to the restaurant's popular wine bar around the corner, which stocks more than 400 bottles—many at reasonable prices—from around the globe. Nearly 50 red and white wines are available by the glass, too. *$$–$$$; AE, MC, V; no checks; dinner every day; beer and wine; reservations recommended; map:I5* &

Eric's / ★★☆
1500 CHURCH ST; 415/282-0919

The efficient service at this quaint, small corner restaurant in Noe Valley is mind-boggling. And while no one seems really hurried, the orchestration is actually essential to help expedite the feeding of Eric's Hunan specialties to the crowds lined up out the door. The mango beef and chicken are very good and come in sizable portions. Other good bets are Eric's soups, tiger prawns, and the five-taste chicken, battered and fried and served in a sweet-and-sour sauce. There are also some great vegetarian selections, including asparagus with black-bean sauce. And Eric's prices are incredibly reasonable—part of the reason this small spot packs 'em in. *$; MC, V; no checks; lunch, dinner every day; beer and wine; reservations not accepted; map:L8*

Farallon / ★★★
450 POST ST; 415/956-6969

Diving into the undersea world of chef Mark Franz (of Stars restaurant fame) and designer Pat Kuleto can leave one breathless. In the fall of 1997, the two co-owners opened a dazzling $4 million, 160-seat restaurant offering seafood dishes that are as innovative as Kuleto's elegant aquatic-themed decor. Giant handblown jellyfish chandeliers with glowing tentacles seemingly float beneath a sea-blue ceiling in the Jelly Bar cocktail lounge, where sculpted strands of kelp climb up illuminated pillars.

Upstairs, the marine motif continues with huge sea-urchin chandeliers dangling from the arched, painted mosaic ceiling—all a dramatic but enchanting stage for Franz's excellent coastal cuisine. For starters, consider delectable asparagus bisque with cardamom cream; truffled mashed potatoes with crab and salmon caviar artfully stuffed into a real sea-urchin shell; Maine lobster and wild-mushroom gnocchi with a leek, tarragon, and champagne lobster sauce; or giant tiger prawns—the best thing on the menu. Entrees change daily and might include ginger-steamed salmon and sea-scallop pillows with a prawn mousse or sautéed gulf prawns with potato risotto, English peas, pearl onions, and truffle portobello coulis. While Franz's forte is fish, he also has a flair for meat dishes such as a juicy grilled filet of beef served with a portobello mushroom and potato galette, haricots verts, and black truffle aioli. The 300-item wine list fits in swimmingly with the menu (though prices are high), and about two dozen wines are available by the glass. The attentive staff helps make Farallon a deep-sea affair to remember. *$$$; AE, DC, DIS, MC, V; no checks; lunch Mon-Sat, dinner every day; full bar; reservations recommended; map:M3* &

Fifth Floor / ★★★☆

12 4TH ST; 415/348-1555

Chef George Morrone was much beloved in San Francisco when he presided over the stoves at Aqua. When he departed for New York to run Robert DeNiro's famed River Cafe, local foodies wept in unison. So it was with great anticipation that the city greeted the news he would return to open Fifth Floor, the chic restaurant atop the stylish new Palomar Hotel near Union Square. The zebra-print carpet and ebony wood paneling on the walls perfectly complement the combination of playfulness and sophistication on Morrone's modern French menu. Start with the trio of tuna tartare (ahi, hamachi, and big-eye) or the decadent lobster consommé with lemongrass flan. Even the "simple salad" is prepared with 1970 Solera reserve sherry. The main course choices are anchored by Morrone's signature tuna foie gras, a delicate, indulgent affair. Or if you're really feeling celebratory, order the whole Saint Pierre, poached in olive oil and carved and served tableside. The wine list is excellent, and the bar area is an elegant, hip alcove. *$$$; AE, MC, V; no checks; dinner Mon–Sat; full bar; reservations recommended; map:M3* &

Firefly / ★★☆

4288 24TH ST; 415/821-7652

Hidden in a cluster of homes on the west end of 24th Street is Noe Valley's best restaurant—just look for a giant metal sculpture of its namesake nocturnal insect perched above a lime green and sizzling yellow door. Inside, an eclectic array of modern art surrounds small tables laden with an equally eclectic display of food, which might include steaming bowls of bouillabaisse de Marseilles bubbling over with monkfish, prawns, scallops, and bass; shrimp-and-scallop pot stickers accompanied by a spicy sesame-soy dipping sauce (Firefly's signature appetizer); and a portobello mushroom Wellington served with linguine that's swirled with fresh vegetables. Chef–co-owner Brad Levy and co-owner Veva Edelson, both formerly of Embarko, dub it "home cooking with few ethnic boundaries." They also proudly announce on every menu that their meat comes from the well-known Niman Ranch, home of "happy, drug-free animals with an ocean view," which leaves politically correct Noe Valley carnivores smiling as they savor the spicy pork stew. The changing roster of desserts is as good as it looks, especially the not-too-sweet strawberry shortcake and the banana bread pudding with caramel anglaise. *$$–$$$; AE, MC, V; checks OK; dinner every day; beer and wine; reservations recommended; map:J7* &

Firewood Cafe / ★

4248 18TH ST; 415/252-0999

Who says you can't get top-notch cuisine on a budget? Those who do have yet to visit Firewood, where you can satisfy your yen for such fresh fare as calamari with lemon-garlic aioli without breaking the bank. Just because the proprietors here are willing to save you money doesn't mean they don't bother to decorate: it's a handsome, comfortable dining room with enormous streetside picture windows. So what's the catch? No table service. Order at the counter and then retire to your seat. You'll quickly forget about the self-service once you sink your teeth into the succulent roast chicken and roasted new potatoes. Or try one of Firewood's gourmet pizzas. Salads here are large, fresh, and worthy of full-scale restaurants. The wine list is well edited and priced. By meal's end, if you haven't already gotten over the fact that there's no wait staff, you surely will when you walk out with your tip money in your pocket. *$; MC, V; checks OK; lunch, dinner every day; beer and wine; reservations not accepted; map:J6*

Fleur de Lys / ★★★★

777 SUTTER ST; 415/673-7779

Fleur de Lys is definitely a Grand Occasion restaurant, with fantastic food, formal service, breathtaking decor, and a superb wine list. Trained by such French superstars as Paul Bocuse and Roger Vergé, wunderkind chef and co-owner Hubert Keller displays a formidable technique—beautifully prepared ingredients accompanied by surprising garnishes and subtle sauces—and many of his contemporary French dishes are near-miracles. Recent standouts include the terrine of Hudson Valley foie gras in a fresh herb and black pepper gelée with brioche, fresh Atlantic salmon baked in a tender corn pancake topped with imperial caviar and a watercress sauce, marinated loin of venison with a mustard seed sabayon, and his five-course vegetarian feast, which prompted a flurry of favorable press when it debuted several years ago. Critics sometimes sniff that particular dishes are too complex, portions seem small, and prices loom large, but these are small dents in Fleur de Lys's mighty armor. The restaurant's decor matches the splendor of its food step for step: the romantic dining area is draped in a luxurious tentlike fashion with 700 yards of rich, red-and-gold hand-painted floral fabrics, and in the center of the room sits a spectacular crown of fresh flowers on a pedestal. Mirrored walls double this visual spectacle while simultaneously allowing you to admire yourself and your glitteringly attired companion. Fleur de Lys isn't always crowded, but reservations are required; this is the sort of establishment that doesn't want to guess who's coming to dinner. *$$$; AE, DC, MC, V; no checks; dinner Mon–Sat; full bar; reservations required; map:M3* &

Florio's / ★

1915 FILLMORE ST; 415/775-4300

When Oritalia left its longtime Fillmore Street location for a larger space in more populated territory near Union Square, Pacific Heights denizens mourned. Then Florio's moved into the space, and area foodies were happy once again. This friendly, stylish, unassuming spot wasted little time becoming a neighborhood anchor, with several regulars among the clientele. With just 47 seats, the brasserie-style place always seems crowded. Many head for the bar area to have a glass from the excellent wine list. There are ownership ties here to the downtown supper club Bix (see review), and the service is on a par with that impeccable restaurant. The Italian-Mediterranean dishes are even keeled—some very good, some less so. Try the lobster bisque or the steamed mussels for a taste of the chef's skill. Other dishes, such as classic steak frites or the roast chicken, are decent, but not so different from what you'd find at other San Francisco restaurants. Still, a unique experience is not what to look for when you visit Florio's—a comfortable "insider" feeling is the ticket here. Just don't drive: parking in these parts is notoriously tight. *$; AE, MC, V; no checks; dinner every day, brunch Sat–Sun; full bar; reservations recommended; map:K3*

Flying Saucer / ★★★

1000 GUERRERO ST; 415/641-9955

A few weeks after landing in the outer Mission District, Flying Saucer owner-chef Albert Tordjman tossed a well-known restaurant critic out onto the sidewalk. Why? Because Tordjman hates critics. The reviewer wrote a rave anyway, and the legend of Flying Saucer was launched. This hip bistro, dominated by a giant *Phantom of the Opera*–esque mask and a wacky spaceship-shaped bumper car hanging over the door, specializes in attitude as well as excellent food. And the credentials Tordjman brings to his enterprise are top-flight: an apprenticeship in his native Lyon, followed by jobs at such high-profile restaurants as London's Dorchester, New Orleans's Commander's Palace, and Napa Valley's Auberge du Soleil. Tordjman's menu can be quite eccentric and changes often, but most of it works rambunctiously well. The entrees are complicated, intense in flavor, and baroque in presentation: duck confit with black chanterelles on coconut-curry lentils, Creole mustard-crusted lamb chops with a chestnut-yam mash cake and Rainwater Madeira demiglace, and crisp-skin salmon topped with a tangerine-basil sauce. Desserts are out of this world, too, so don't leave Tordjman's planet without one. Unfortunately, the Saucer's bad attitude sometimes extends to the service, which can be maddeningly rude. But that doesn't seem to keep earthlings from eating here—at least once. *$$–$$$; MC, V; no checks; dinner Tues–Sat; beer and wine; reservations required; map:L7* &

Fog City Diner / ★☆

1300 BATTERY ST; 415/982-2000
Fog City is a fun place to meet with friends over a cheeseburger and a milk shake. The glimmering chrome, glass, polished woods, and neon decor à la restaurant designer Pat Kuleto is sleek and sophisticated, but it does a poor job of absorbing the decibels. Besides the usual diner fare (gourmet chili dogs, sandwiches, salads, and damn good onion rings), the kitchen offers a medley of savory "small plates" such as crab cakes, Asian-style prawns, and quesadillas with chili peppers and almonds. Full entrees are available as well, such as fresh fish, thick steaks, cioppino, and pot roast, but the best bet is to nosh on the small plates tapas-style. If you're feeling gluttonous, feast on Fog City's fat banana split, which can easily feed a threesome. *$–$$; CB, DC, DIS, MC, V; no checks; lunch, dinner every day; full bar; reservations recommended; map:N1* &

Foreign Cinema / ★★

2534 MISSION ST; 415/648-7600
Like a Steven Spielberg movie, the opening of this Mission District restaurant was anticipated at least a year in advance. The hype reached such a fevered pitch, locals were half expecting to see a line of product tie-ins in local stores. When the place finally opened, in the summer of 1999, it was quickly apparent the throngs hadn't waited in vain. The concept behind this contemporary French restaurant is to combine dinner and a movie in a single location. Accessed through an unassuming door along Mission Street, the restaurant has an industrial-chic appearance, with deliberately unfinished walls, exposed mechanics in the ceiling, and hard surfaces throughout. On one wall in a center courtyard, classic foreign films are projected in all their grainy black-and-white glory (early features included Fellini's *La Dolce Vita* and Bergman's *Seventh Seal*). Drive-in-movie–type speaker boxes are placed at each table so you can

listen along as you dine. But mostly the films are just an imaginative distraction from the main attraction: the food. The lobster and monkfish bouillabaisse is rich and decadent; the roasted Sonoma duck breast is tender and bursting with flavor; the rosemary-marinated lamb melts in your mouth. It's quite a production. As of this writing, a lunch menu is in development. *$$; MC, V; no checks; dinner every day; full bar; reservations recommended; map:L6* &

42 Degrees / ★★★

235 16TH ST; 415/777-5559

Like Caffe Esprit, the former occupant of this bayside site, 42 Degrees is popular with a relentlessly hip crowd of young professionals and boasts a spare, high-tech warehouse look, with a soaring ceiling and lots of concrete, metal, and glass. As night falls, however, candlelight, table linens, and strains of live jazz soften the effect, transforming the stark 100-seat space into an appealing supper club. The name refers to the latitude of Provence and the Mediterranean Sea, and chef-owner James Moffat's ever-changing menu reflects this sun-splashed influence with starters like watercress salad with duck confit, walnuts, and pomegranates; Medjool dates with Parmesan and celery; and grilled artichokes with Meyer lemons. Entrees might include risotto with shaved truffles and mushrooms, pan-roasted chicken with lemon and black olive sauce, or grilled pancetta-wrapped salmon. Lighter eaters can look to the chalkboard for small plates such as pizzettas, Iberian blood sausage, and herb-roasted potatoes with aioli. Desserts include a sublime chocolate pot de crème, milk chocolate crème brûlée, and a warm apple Napoleon with vanilla ice cream and huckleberry sauce. The service is courteous and professional, the mezzanine-level windows afford a view of the bay, and there's a large, pleasant courtyard patio for dining alfresco on warm days. *$$–$$$; MC, V; no checks; lunch Mon–Fri, dinner Wed–Sat; full bar; reservations recommended; map:O5* &

Franciscan / ★

PIER 43, FISHERMAN'S WHARF; 415/362-7733

This is one of the best restaurants on Fisherman's Wharf, with many pleasant surprises on its fresh seafood menu. The huge establishment has commanding views of the bay from most seats. Situated on three tiers, the tables in the recently remodeled dining room are mostly angled to face the massive floor-to-ceiling windows. The seafood is the best bet here, although the pasta dishes we've tried (such as the angel hair with rock shrimp) aren't bad. The roast Pacific snapper is tender and flaky, and the Maine lobster is super-rich. Portions are huge, served without a lot of fancy-shmancy flair. Kids will find much to like, too. Despite the throngs of tourists dining here, it's a pleasant respite from the madding crowd coursing through the wharf area outside. *$$; AE, DC, MC, V; no checks; lunch, dinner every day; full bar; reservations recommended; map:K1* &

Fringale / ★★★⯪

570 4TH ST; 415/543-0573

Chef–co-owner Gerald Hirigoyen, named one of the 10 best chefs in the nation by *Food & Wine* magazine, draws crowds to his tiny, boisterous 50-seat French restaurant tucked away in a charmless section of the city. Behind this restaurant's cheery yellow facade, however, there's plenty of charm emanating from the casual, blond-wood-trimmed interior, petite curved bar, and friendly, largely French wait staff. Hirigoyen was born and raised in the Basque country of southwest France, and his origins serve as the abiding inspiration for his gutsy, flavor-packed—and extremely reasonably priced—fare. Outstanding dishes include the frisée salad topped with a poached egg and warm bacon dressing, steamed mussels sprinkled with garlic and parsley, wild mushroom ravioli, rack of lamb, and his signature (and meltingly tender) pork tenderloin confit with onion and apple marmalade. Hirigoyen was originally a pastry chef, and he flaunts his talents with his incredible crème brûlée and rich chocolate Basque cake topped with chocolate mousse. Fringale (French for "a sudden pang of hunger") is perpetually packed with famished folks at dinnertime, so expect a noisy crowd and a wait for a table, even if you've made a reservation. *$$; AE, MC, V; no checks; lunch Mon–Fri, dinner Mon–Sat; full bar; reservations recommended; map:O4* &

The Garden Court / ★★

2 NEW MONTGOMERY ST (PALACE HOTEL); 415/546-5010 OR 415/512-1111

Dining at the Garden Court, showpiece of the grand 1875 Palace Hotel, is like entering a Victorian romance novel. One can almost picture scads of beauteous heroines perching straight-backed on the plush settees here, blushing as they avert their eyes from the steady gaze of roguish but tender-hearted young blades jostling each other near the potted palms. Ah, we digress—but you see what magic this incredibly romantic, old-fashioned room can work on you. Blame it on the soaring marble and gilt columns, the opulent furnishings, the mirrored doorways, or the rows of crystal chandeliers descending from the high, intricately patterned, domed ceiling of amber-stained glass. The food hasn't always lived up to the regal surroundings, but recently management has made it a priority, and executive chef Peter DeMarais presents an interesting California menu with European flourishes. Starters might include a French butter pear salad with Stilton cheese and a cracked-pepper vinaigrette or a velvety crab bisque; entrees range from grilled rack of lamb with sweet onions and basil mashed potatoes to freshwater prawns and rock shrimp served on a pumpkin risotto to grilled swordfish with Japanese sweet potato purée and ginger-butter sauce. In addition to lunch and dinner, the Garden Court serves an elegant afternoon tea to the strains of live harp and a lavish (and costly) Sunday brunch. *$$$; AE, DC, DIS, MC, V; no checks; breakfast, lunch every day, tea Wed–Sat, dinner Tues–Sat, brunch Sun and holidays; full bar; reservations recommended; map:N3* &

Garibaldi's / ★★

347 PRESIDIO AVE; 415/563-8841

Evocative of the great neighborhood-type restaurants in New York's Greenwich Village and SoHo, Garibaldi's seems like a place where everyone walked over from his or her house around the corner. The restaurant is small and the tables are jammed so close together that at times you feel like reaching over and trying something from your neighbor's plate. So it's a good thing the atmosphere is friendly and lively, if at times decidedly loud. The staff, polished yet down-to-earth, makes everyone feel like a regular. In fact, many people *become* regulars because the Italian-Mediterranean food is so good. The dishes are sophisticated without being highfalutin. The risottos (there are usually two on the menu, and sometimes one nightly special) are quite good. If you are looking to eat light, but don't want to forsake robust flavor, try one of the entree salads, such as the grilled prawns marinated in charmoula. Among the entree highlights are a Mediterranean lamb dish and a generous cut of tender filet mignon. And don't miss the rich desserts: the signature sweet is a white-chocolate cheesecake with a crunchy cookie crust. Sunday brunches are very popular here, too. *$$; AE, MC, V; local checks only; lunch Mon–Fri, dinner every day, brunch Sun; full bar; reservations recommended; map:J3* &

Gary Danko / ★★★

800 NORTH POINT; 415/749-2060

Call them the dynamic duo if you will. The culinary team of award-winning chef Gary Danko (of San Francisco's Ritz-Carlton fame) and well-connected maître d' Nick Peyton created quite a stir in San Francisco when they opened this highly anticipated restaurant. The concept sounds simple, but is surprisingly difficult to achieve: fine cuisine combined with impeccable service. At Gary Danko, it seems to be working like a well-oiled machine. The namesake chef fashioned a seasonally changing menu that is rooted in the classical school. His signature dishes include glazed oysters; seared foie gras with peaches, caramelized onions, and *verjus* sauce; roast lobster with chanterelle mushrooms; and an amazing herb-crusted lamb loin. Dinners are served in three tasting-menu formats: you choose either the three-, four-, or five-course meal. Sommelier Renee-Nicole Kubin shows a deft touch with her recommended pairings. Everything seems well thought out, including the understated elegance of the 75-seat room and the art collection curated by a local gallery owner. Dinner here can be a truly memorable experience. *$$$; AE, DC, MC, V; no checks; dinner every day; full bar; reservations recommended; map:L1*

Globe / ★★

290 PACIFIC AVE; 415/391-4132

With just 44 seats, this downtown restaurant sometimes seems to have at least twice that many people waiting for tables. Popular would be an understated way to describe it: there may not be another restaurant in town, pound for pound, that has created as much buzz. The chic little spot, near the city's advertising and media offices, is the ultimate power-lunch spot, where deals are made and black is worn. The hipness of it all does not overshadow the food, though, which is probably the real reason Globe is beating them away at the door. The menu changes weekly but usually includes variations on American and California classics: wood-fired roast lamb, pork chops with green-olive tapenade, pizzas, and the like. The wines, mostly from the Napa and Sonoma Valleys, are well chosen and priced. Desserts are to die for: the cheesecake will satisfy even the most stubborn purists. One more plus: Globe serves dinner later than a lot of spots in town. *$$; AE, MC; local checks only; lunch Mon–Fri, dinner every day; full bar; reservations recommended; map:N1*

Gordon Biersch Brewery Restaurant / ★☆

2 HARRISON ST (AT THE EMBARCADERO); 415/243-8246

This modern, two-level brewery located at the foot of the Bay Bridge is one of the most popular après-work watering holes in the city. It's mostly a well-dressed 20-to-late-30s crowd who come to catch a buzz, smoke on the front steps, and flirt (though you have to almost shout to be heard over the din). The lower level houses the shiny brewery equipment and horseshoe-shaped beer bar offering a variety of fresh lagers and ales. Upstairs is a full restaurant serving reasonably good bistro dishes such as lemon roasted half chicken with garlic mashed potatoes and baby-back ribs with garlic fries (our two favorites). Of course, each entree is paired with the proper brewski to wash it all down. If you're not up for a full meal, there's a wide array of smaller plates (try the crunchy calamari fritti appetizer) and salads. Unfortunately, the noise from below makes a quiet dinner for two out of the question. But if you like good beer, hearty food, and a high-energy environment, you'll like Gordon Biersch. *$$; AE, DC, DIS, MC, V; no checks; lunch, dinner every day; full bar; reservations recommended; map:O3* ᕦ

Gordon's House of Fine Eats / ★★☆

500 FLORIDA ST; 415/861-8900

Longtime Real Restaurants chef Gordon Drysdale (Bix, Caffe Museo) has brought his many passions together under one big industrial-size roof with exhilarating results. This 110-seat restaurant sizzles with energy, and a genuine conviviality prevails. The converted 1930s bilevel warehouse space boasts plenty of exposed piping, concrete floors, and high-tech halogen lighting, but warm mahogany tables and colorful original artwork keep the industrial-chic elements in check. The downstairs bustles with activity around an open kitchen and a long concrete-faced bar; upstairs is slightly more quiet and relaxed. The menu, or more accurately menus, are wholly original and aim to please everyone. You can choose both appetizers and entrees from five categories: healthful, comfort, local favorites, luxury, and international. A healthful selection of smoky vegan pea soup is simply exquisite. The cornflake-fried chicken, a popular comfort selection, already has a following, though the more inventive pork osso buco with spaetzle and the ham steak with grilled pineapple and sweet-potato pie are better flavor-packed choices. Desserts, equally imaginative, include Gordon's doughnut plate, a playful combo of fritters, fried custard, and doughnuts, as well as frozen grasshopper pie that oozes with mint and chocolate—both are utterly unforgettable. And as if all that weren't enough, there's live music five nights a week, and a lunch menu was recently added to the repertoire. This is clearly Gordon's very full house of fine eats. *$$$; DC, DIS, MC, V; no checks; lunch Mon–Fri, dinner every day; full bar; reservations recommended; map:M6* &

Grand Café / ★★☆

501 GEARY ST; 415/292-0101

The Grand Café is one of the most beautiful restaurants in the city, a magnificent mix of art deco, art nouveau, and Beaux Arts. The Kimpton Hotel & Restaurant Group has done a brilliant job refurbishing this turn-of-the-century grand ballroom into an objet d'art highlighted with Parisian-style chandeliers, intricate murals, and amusing bunny-esque sculptures. It's a pleasure just *being* here, though you're bound to enjoy chef Denis Soriano's classic French cooking as well. Be sure to start your experience with the rich, savory polenta soufflé and the baby-spinach salad with sliced pears, feta, walnuts, and fresh raspberry vinaigrette. Entrees we heartily recommend include the ultra-tender pan-seared duck leg confit with cabbage-walnut dressing, the grilled filet mignon in a mushroom-shallot sauce, and the roasted duck breast with mission figs and huckleberry sauce. You'll enjoy the friendly, professional service as well. Note: The equally impressive bar and lounge has its own exhibition kitchen and menu, offering similar dishes for about half the price. The grilled marinated skirt steak with whipped potatoes and red-wine sauce is fantastic, as are the pizzas from the wood-burning oven. *$$$; AE, CB, DC, DIS, MC, V; no checks; breakfast, lunch, dinner every day; full bar; reservations recommended; map:M3* &

Great Eastern / ★★

649 JACKSON ST; 415/986-2500

If you love seafood and Chinese food and have an adventurous palate, have we got a restaurant for you. The venerable Great Eastern restaurant in Chinatown is renowned for its hard-to-find seafood, yanked fresh from the myriad huge fish tanks that line the back wall. If it swims, hops, slithers, or crawls, it's probably on the menu. Frogs, sea bass, soft-shell turtles, abalone, sea conch, steelhead, and Lord only knows what else are served sizzling on large, round, family-style tables. Check the neon board in back to peruse the day's catch, which is sold by the pound. Our advice: Unless you're savvy at translating an authentic Hong Kong menu, order one of the set dinners (the crab version is fantastic) or point to another table and say, "I want that." (Don't expect much help from the harried servers.) The crystal chandeliers and glimmering emerald-and-black furnishings make an attempt at elegance, but it's the gaudy fish tanks filled with edible creatures that capture everyone's eye. *$$; AE, MC, V; no checks; lunch, dinner every day; beer and wine; reservations recommended; map:N2* &

Greens / ★★

FORT MASON CENTER, BLDG A (OFF MARINA BLVD AT BUCHANAN ST); 415/771-6222

As Le Tour d'Argent in Paris is to the dedicated duck fancier and the Savoy Grill in London is to the roast beef connoisseur, so is Greens at Fort Mason to the vegetarian aesthete. Not only is the food politically correct here, it's often so good that even carnivores find it irresistible. Part of the Greens treat is visual: located in a converted barracks in the historic Fort Mason Center, the enormous, airy dining room is surrounded by huge windows with a spectacular view of the bay and the Golden Gate Bridge, and a gigantic sculpted redwood burl is a Buddhist-inspired centerpiece in the waiting area. Yes, Greens is owned and operated by the Zen Center—but this is a restaurant, not a monastery. The menu changes daily: expect to see such dishes as mesquite-grilled polenta; filo turnovers filled with mushrooms, spinach, and Parmesan; pizza sprinkled with onion confit, goat cheese, and basil; and fettuccine with mushrooms, peas, goat cheese, and crème fraîche. Greens to Go, a takeout counter inside the restaurant, also sells baked goods, savory soups, sandwiches, and black-bean chili. An à la carte dinner menu is offered Monday through Friday; guests may order from the prix-fixe five-course dinner menu only on Saturday. The restaurant is also open for late-night desserts, coffee, and wine from Monday through Saturday, 9:30–11pm. *$$–$$$; DIS, MC, V; local checks only; lunch Tues–Sat, dinner Mon–Sat, brunch Sun; beer and wine; reservations recommended; map:K1* &

Hamburger Mary's / ★★

1582 FOLSOM ST; 415/626-1985

If you want to take a safe peek at San Francisco fringe society (bull dykes, heroin addicts, bike messengers, transvestites, tattoo artists, and such), head to Hamburger Mary's at Folsom and 12th Streets. For years this SoMa greasy spoon has been a popular meeting spot for those with alternative outlooks, but even normal, boring types like us drop in to have a fat, juicy burger (served on great whole wheat bread with a side of spicy home fries) and admire the wild decor, which looks like a flea market that imploded. Sandwiches, salads, and vegetarian dishes are available as well, all at low prices. Mary's also serves breakfast, and it's always interesting to see what stumbles in from an all-nighter. *$; DC, DIS, MC, V; no checks; lunch, dinner Tues–Sun; full bar; reservations accepted; map:M5* &

Harbor Village Restaurant / ★★

4 EMBARCADERO CENTER; 415/781-8833

A favorite of prosperous Pacific Rim businesspeople, middle- and upper-class Chinese-American families, and downtown office workers out for a lunchtime treat, this giant Hong Kong–style seafood and dim sum restaurant has great food, but it misses top honors because of minor inconsistencies in cooking and major flaws in service. Lunch is a state-of-the-art dim sum extravaganza, with master chefs from Hong Kong turning out plate after plate of sublime morsels in vast, interesting variety. At dinner, you can choose from an enormous Cantonese menu that includes dishes rarely found on this edge of the Rim, among them prized varieties of shellfish, kept alive in tanks until the moment they're ordered and served with exquisite simplicity (albeit at an exorbitant cost). Many of the more affordable seafood dishes are just as marvelous, though some of the standard Chinese dishes suffer from perfunctory preparation, and all too often entire orders are piled simultaneously on the undersize tables by the standoffish staff. Still, the food and upscale decor (this is one of San Francisco's prettiest Chinese restaurants) might make you forgive these lapses. So be adventurous: go with a gang and get a large table, order only a few dishes at a time, and then order more when the food is nearly gone. And in keeping with Chinese tradition, save the steamed whole fish for last—it's a Cantonese symbol of good luck. *$$$; AE, DC, DIS, MC, V; no checks; lunch, dinner every day; full bar; reservations recommended; map:N2* &

Hard Rock Cafe / ★

1699 VAN NESS AVE; 415/885-1699

 This San Francisco link in the Hard Rock chain is exactly what you would expect it to be: a loud, cavernous room filled with rock 'n' roll memorabilia, tourists, and a line for T-shirts. You'll have to speak up to be heard over the blaring rock music, but that's just part of the Hard Rock experience. Despite the often annoying ambience, the food is actually pretty good (not healthy, exactly, but good). The highlight of the menu is the Rock's juicy chicken sandwich, best accompanied with a side of addictive onion rings. Other diner-style menu items include fajitas, baby-back ribs, grilled fish, salads, sandwiches, and (of course) the all-American burger. Perhaps Hard Rock's strongest point, however, is that it's one of the few restaurants in the city that caters to teens and children. Otherwise, in a city with so many incredible restaurants, it's hard to justify a meal at the Hard Rock—particularly if you already have the shirt. *$–$$; AE, DC, DIS, MC, V; no checks; lunch, dinner every day; full bar; reservations recommended; map:L2* &

Harris's / ★★

2100 VAN NESS AVE; 415/673-1888

Not just another steak house, Harris's is a living monument to the not-quite-bygone joys of guiltless beef-eating. You can even get a sneak preview of your meal by peering at the deep-pink slabs in the showcase window facing the street. The hushed, formal club setting boasts dark wood paneling, plush carpets, large brown tufted booths, well-spaced white-draped tables, and chairs roomy enough to accommodate the most bullish build. Jackets are appreciated (though no longer required). Harris's choice midwestern beef, impeccably dry-aged for three weeks on the premises, bears the same relation to supermarket beef as foie gras bears to chicken liver; the tender steaks, grilled to order, can even be chosen by cut and by size. The larger bone-in cuts (such as the Harris Steak and the T-bone) have the finest flavor, but the pepper steak and the rare prime rib are great, too. Those who prefer calf brains to these sanguine beauties will find a flawless version here. You might want to skip the usual steak-house appetizers in favor of Harris's excellent Caesar salad. For true-blue traditionalists, the exemplary martini—served in a carafe placed in a bucket of shaved ice—makes an excellent starter course. *$$$; AE, DC, DIS, MC, V; no checks; dinner every day; full bar; reservations recommended; www.citysearch7.com; map:L2* &

Hawthorne Lane / ★★★☆

22 HAWTHORNE ST; 415/777-9779

When Hillary Rodham Clinton was in town to promote her book *It Takes a Village*, she ate a late dinner at Hawthorne Lane. Probably learned about it from hubby Bill, who supped here the year before and might have raved about the miso-glazed black cod with sesame spinach rolls, the special lobster tempura, the roasted Sonoma lamb with butternut squash and Parmesan risotto, or the house-made fettuccine with chanterelle mushrooms. Ever since it opened in June 1995, Hawthorne Lane has been one of the city's hottest restaurants, its popularity fueled by its lovely design, its proximity to the happening SoMa scene, and the pedigree of owner-chefs David and Anne Gingrass (formerly of Spago and Postrio fame). The dining room is a refined, beguiling space, with wrought-iron cherry blossoms, a massive skylight, giant urns with dazzling fresh floral displays, and light-colored woods creating an air of perennial spring. Hawthorne also wins raves for its varied selection of wonderful breads and desserts, both the work of pastry chef Nicole Plue, who worked at the Sheraton Palace and One Market before landing here. If you can't get a reservation, snag one of the seats at the long, oval bar, where you can order from the dining room menu, or sign up for one of the many tables set aside for walk-ins. *$$$; DC, DIS, MC, V; checks OK; lunch Mon–Fri, dinner every day; full bar; reservations recommended; dcg@hawthorne lane.com; www.hawthornelane.com; map:O3* &

Hayes Street Grill / ★★⯪

320 HAYES ST; 415/863-5545

San Francisco Examiner restaurant reviewer Patricia Unterman, one of the nation's best food critics, is part owner and chef of this spartan yet venerable and reliable fish house that specializes in simple yet perfectly prepared seafood. In a city where dining trends change monthly (and restaurants close weekly), the Grill is a citadel of consistency, offering impeccably fresh fish and straightforward preparations that highlight the quality of the ingredients. Whatever's the most fresh on the market is what's on the menu that day—Hawaiian swordfish, Alaskan king salmon, California red snapper—which is then prepared to your liking (mesquite grilled, lightly sautéed, braised), topped with a range of sauces (shallot butter, Sichuan peanut, tomatillo salsa), and served with a side of signature French fries cooked in peanut oil. Other seafood dishes are also available, such as savory fish soup, raw oysters on the half shell, and paella. And don't miss the wicked crème brûlée for dessert. We highly recommend this Civic Center institution for a pre-opera/symphony/ballet meal, or anytime you crave fresh fish done well. *$$; AE, DC, DIS, MC, V; no checks; lunch Mon–Fri, dinner every day; full bar; reservations recommended; map:L4* &

Helmand / ★★

430 BROADWAY; 415/362-0641

An oasis of good taste on Broadway's less-than-tasteful topless strip, Helmand serves delicious renditions of Afghan cuisine in a pretty room lit by brass chandeliers and small table lanterns. The restaurant's light and variously spiced house-made yogurts (a staple of Afghani cooking) dress several favorite appetizers, including *mantwo* (a house-made dumpling filled with sautéed onions and beef, topped with a carrot, yellow split pea, and beef sauce, and served on yogurt) and *kaddo borawni* (sweet baby pumpkin that's pan-fried, then baked, and tempered by a piquant yogurt-garlic sauce). For a main course, try the *chowpan*—a tender, juicy half rack of lamb marinated like a fine Armenian shish kebab, then grilled and served with sautéed eggplant and rice pallow. Other fine choices include *sabzi challow* (a wonderfully seasoned mixture of spinach with lamb), *mourgh challow* (chicken sautéed with split peas and curry), and *koufta challow* (light, moderately spicy meatballs with sun-dried tomatoes, peppers, and peas), each served with a ramekin of flavorful fresh cilantro sauce and aromatic white or brown rice. Servers are personable (if sometimes slightly scattered), and the wine list is well chosen and well priced. Parking is scarce in this neighborhood, so take advantage of the validated parking (time is limited) at the lot down the block. *$$; AE, MC, V; no checks; dinner every day; full bar; reservations recommended; map:N2* &

Hong Kong Flower Lounge / ★★

5322 GEARY BLVD; 415/668-8998

Hong Kong, probably the world's most competitive culinary arena, has hundreds of excellent restaurants vying to produce the freshest, subtlest, and most exciting flavors. In 1987 Alice Wong, whose family owns four Flower Lounges in and around that city, expanded the empire to California with several Bay Area restaurants, including this grand restaurant on lower Geary. Though the Flower Lounge has been around for years, it's still one of the better Chinese restaurants in San Francisco (and that's saying a lot), thanks largely to the Hong Kong chefs who continue to produce cuisine according to the stringent standards of their home city. The red, gold, and jade decor is pure Kowloon glitz (although the patrons are comfortably informal), and the service is fast and efficient. Among the best dishes on the vast menu are the exquisite minced squab in lettuce cups, the delicate crystal scallops in shrimp sauce, the fried prawns with walnuts, and any fish fresh from the live tank. An excellent Peking duck is served at a moderate price. *$$; AE, DC, DIS, MC, V; no checks; lunch, dinner every day; full bar; reservations recommended; map:G4* &

The House / ★

1230 GRANT AVE; 415/986-8612
1269 9TH AVE; 415/682-3898

Much is made of fusion cuisine in San Francisco, and it seems each month someone opens a new place to give it a whirl. But Larry Tse, chef-owner of the House in North Beach, has been quietly doing as well if not better than anyone else at creating fusion fare for years. Happily holding its own in a sea of Italian eateries, this little Asian-inspired restaurant is a wildly popular alternative. The dishes are fairly simple, given their East-meets-West concept. The Chinese chicken salad is one of the best-sellers, as is the Caesar, served with wok-seared scallops or spring rolls. The entree menu changes frequently; the daily specials are the safest bets. A ginger soy sauce–topped Chilean sea bass was a memorable recent selection. The wine list is interesting and well priced, though you might opt for a flavorful Chinese tea infusion to go with your fusion. The House has proved so popular that Tse and his wife opened another one on Ninth Avenue in the Inner Sunset. That is where he spends most of his time these days, leaving his brother-in-law at the helm on Grant Avenue. Be prepared for a noise level that can sometimes reach ear-splitting. *$; AE, MC, V; no checks; lunch Mon–Fri, dinner Mon–Sat (Grant Ave); lunch Tues–Fri, dinner Tues–Sun (9th Ave); full bar; reservations recommended; map:N2, H5*

House of Nanking / ★★

919 KEARNY ST; 415/421-1429
The dinnertime waiting line outside this tiny, greasy, wildly popular hole-in-the-wall starts at 5:30pm; by 6pm, you may face a 90-minute wait for a cramped, crowded, itsy-bitsy table with a plastic menu that lists only half of the best dishes served here. Lunchtime crowds make midday eating just as problematic. Here's a solution: arrive for a late lunch or a very early dinner (between 2:30–5pm) and walk right in. When owner-chef-head-waiter Peter Fang can give you his full attention, he'll be glad to apprise you of the day's unlisted specials: perhaps succulent chicken or duck dumplings, an exotic shrimp-and-green-onion pancake with peanut sauce, or tempura-like sesame-battered Nanking scallops in a spicy garlic sauce. Or just take a look at what the diners sandwiched around you are eating and point to what looks good (it's hard to go wrong in this place). Nanking, Fang's hometown, is at the inland end of the Shanghai Railroad, making it an exchange point for foods from Sichuan, Peking, Guangdong, and the local coast; Fang is famous for concocting wily revisions of many traditional dishes. While the food is usually very good and the prices are some of the most reasonable in the city, the service is downright terrible (you may not get your beer until 10 minutes after you've started eating), and it's the main reason this restaurant doesn't earn three stars. *$; cash only; lunch Mon–Sat, dinner every day; beer and wine; reservations not accepted; map:N2* &

Hyde Street Bistro / ★★

1521 HYDE ST (BETWEEN JACKSON AND PACIFIC STS); 415/292-4415
This little French bistro on Russian Hill sits right next to a cable car line, and you'll hear the famous bells clanging right outside the door. Owned by chef Fabrice Marcon, Hyde Street Bistro is definitely a neighborhood haunt. You'll see chef Marcon charging in and out of the kitchen all night, talking with patrons, his baseball-capped head enthusiastically bobbing up and down. The best deal (available weekdays only) may be the well-priced Neighbor's Dinner, which includes an entree du jour served with a wine of Marcon's choice. His standard menu is small and reflects both regional French cuisine and Americanized versions. Sample dishes include

a Lyonnaise salad with smoked bacon and an optional poached egg; tender hanger steak drenched in a green peppercorn sauce; perfectly roasted honey-lavender–glazed duck confit (Marcon's specialty); and seared tuna au poivre. The eclectic wine list is heavy with French varietals but reasonably priced. Save room for the tarte Tatin floating on caramel sauce, or the warm and dense chocolate cake. *$$; AE, MC, V; checks OK; dinner Tues–Sun; beer and wine; reservations recommended; map:L2* &

Il Fornaio / ★★

1265 BATTERY ST; 415/986-0100

Il Fornaio began as a baker's school in Milan, a project started by the Veggetti family to collect regional recipes and save the disappearing art of Italian baking. In the late 1980s the Veggettis expanded their operation to include several retail bakeries, wholesale bakeries, and restaurants in California and other western states. The San Francisco and Palo Alto restaurants were the first to make it to these shores, and although the staffs occasionally suffer from a too-sexy-for-my-hat attitude, there's no denying that Il Fornaio serves fantastic baked goods and good Northern Italian food in an airy, stylish setting. Breads and bread sticks, served with pungent, extra-virgin olive oil, provide simple and unpretentious proof that bread is an art form. The antipasti are generally very good (give the grilled eggplant with goat cheese, sun-dried tomatoes, sweet onions, and capers a whirl), and the pizzas and calzones are universally delightful, crisp and smoke-flavored from the wood-burning oven. Interesting pasta choices include ravioli di verdura (pasta stuffed with spinach, Swiss chard, pine nuts, and basil in a rich baby artichoke and tomato sauce). The rotisserie meats are consistently well prepared. Dessert tortes, cakes, and cookies offer further proof of the skills of Il Fornaio's bakers. Many of the Il Fornaio restaurants in the Bay Area have pretty patios, and the San Francisco branch offers one of the most pleasant outdoor dining areas in the city. *$$; AE, DC, MC, V; no checks; breakfast, lunch, dinner every day; full bar; reservations recommended; www.ilfornaio.com; map:N1* &

Indian Oven / ★

233 FILLMORE ST; 415/626-1628

In the culturally diverse Lower Haight, it isn't surprising to find the gamut of ethnic restaurants. What is surprising is to find one so very good and so very authentic. Indian Oven, a good-looking and affordably priced corner restaurant, is by many expert accounts the best Northern Indian restaurant in town. Roll up your sleeves and order the appetizer sampler plate: samosas (vegetable puffs stuffed with peas and potatoes), pakoras (deep-fried fritters filled with your choice of meat or vegetables), and pappadum crackers. The entrees are mostly outstanding, including a delicious *jheenga masala*—prawns sauteed in a spicy tomato sauce. The tandoori chicken and the chicken and lamb skewers are also good. When you've got to have your curry fix, there are few better places. *$; AE, DC, DIS, MC, V; no checks; dinner every day; beer and wine; reservations recommended; map:K4*

Indigo / ★

687 MCALLISTER ST AT GOUGH ST; 415/673-9353
Surprisingly, in a town so keen on the symphony, opera, and ballet, there is a startling dearth of quality places near the Performing Arts Center for pre-performance dining. So when Indigo opened a while ago, there was a citywide standing ovation. All it had to do was perform. As the name might indicate, this restaurant is very blue, with elegant velvet booths and a gorgeous plaster sculpture running the length of one wall—very dramatic indeed. And the food follows suit, with dishes prepared from fresh local ingredients. The daily ravioli is usually quite good, but for something a bit heartier, the grilled pork chop with herb bread pudding is your best choice. The wait staff will even hasten your order if you're rushing to make a theater engagement. So far, the show here has been worthy of its favorable reviews. *$; AE, MC, V; no checks; dinner Tues–Sun; full bar; reservations recommended; map:L4*

Infusion Bar & Restaurant / ★★★

555 2ND ST; 415/543-2282
Trendy, noisy, alcohol-oriented—these rather damning adjectives apply to Infusion, a relatively new SoMa bar and restaurant that nevertheless manages to establish itself as a place that's serious about good food. It was named after the house specialty, vodka-based infusions flavored with assorted fruits and vegetables, everything from jalapeño to pineapple, watermelon to cucumber (they have more than 50 flavors in stock). You can admire eight of them in their decanters behind the handcrafted Honduran mahogany bar that stretches along one side of the long, narrow room—or up close in an ice-cold martini glass, of course. The spare, modern furnishings stand in dramatic contrast to the intense, spicy complexity of the food. European, Asian, Mexican, and Caribbean influences add interesting grace notes to self-taught chef David Fickes's New American fare, with starters that range from guava empanadas with Brie to a ginger-cured tuna accented with wasabi-infused oil and tangerine essence. There are always a few imaginative pasta dishes, such as fusilli with chicken and chipotle chili sauce (Fickes has a fondness for chilies); entrees include a crisp walnut-crusted salmon with chardonnay-pear sauce and peppered filet mignon flamed with Wild Turkey. Fickes sometimes misses his mark with his innovative recipes, but when he hits it, he's incredible. Top off the fine feast with white-chocolate–bourbon mousse with pistachio shortbread or chocolate pecan pie. At 9:30pm Thursday

through Saturday a live band performs on the loft stage. *$$; AE, DC, MC, V; no checks; lunch Mon–Fri, dinner every day; full bar; reservations recommended; infusn@aol.com; www.citysearch.com/sfo/infusion; map:O3* &

Jack's / ★★

615 SACRAMENTO ST; 415/421-7355

Ernest Hemingway ate here. So did Alfred Hitchcock, Mark Twain, and Ronald Reagan. Opened in 1864, this venerable San Francisco institution is the city's oldest same-location restaurant. In late 1998 it reopened after an extensive refurbishing. The new owner took painstaking care to return the restaurant to its original splendor, with alabaster walls, gold-leaf reliefs, and a wrought-iron staircase. The top-floor dining room is capped by a magnificent Parisian-style skylight. To accommodate its landmark status, the menu relies heavily on American classic dishes, but the French influence is also apparent in such memorable selections as steak au poivre, duck confit, and the escargot appetizer. The menu is extensive, so be careful where you tread. If you stay within familiar territory—pork chop with spiced apples, Jack's New York steak—you can't go wrong. *$$$; AE, DC, DIS, MC, V; no checks; lunch Mon–Fri, dinner Mon–Sat; full bar; reservations recommended; map:N2* &

Jackson Fillmore / ★

2506 FILLMORE ST; 415/346-5288

If you like to make an entrance, go to Jackson Fillmore, the minuscule trattoria on Fillmore that's so small, everyone in the dining room can't help but stop eating and turn their heads to the door when somebody walks in. And then be prepared to wait. But that's part of the fun at this bright neighborhood restaurant, where chef-owner Jack Kreitzman is usually the one to greet you, with a smile and a suggestion for a great glass of wine. Once seated, you are quickly served a helping of the fresh-made bruschetta with a mouthwatering aroma of garlic. From ricotta ravioli to roast chicken with garlic (highly recommended) to portobello mushrooms, the recipes here are fairly straightforward and skillfully executed. This is a great place for a couple to dine, but larger groups can also be accommodated. As of this writing, there are plans to expand the restaurant into the space next door. We only hope the growth doesn't kill the boisterous charm we've come to love. *$; AE, MC, V; no checks; dinner every day; full bar; reservations accepted for parties of 3 or more; map:K2* &

Jardinière / ★★★½

300 GROVE ST; 415/861-5555

A native Californian, chef Traci Des Jardins worked in many notable restaurants in France, New York, and Los Angeles before co-opening Rubicon restaurant in San Francisco, which launched her culinary reputation nationwide. She won the prestigious James Beard Rising Star Chef of the Year award in 1995 and was named one of *Food & Wine*'s Best New Chefs in America. With those kudos, it's no wonder that her own restaurant, Jardinière (pronounced zhar-dee-NAIR), was a smashing success as soon as the highly stylized glass doors swung open in September 1997. With award-winning designer-restaurateur Pat Kuleto as her business partner, Des Jardins was assured of an impressive setting for her French-California cuisine. Formerly home to a jazz club, the two-story interior is elegantly framed with violet velvet drapes, and the focal point is the central oval mahogany and marble bar, frequently mobbed with local politicos and patrons of the arts (the symphony hall and opera house are across the street). Appetizers are Des Jardins's strong point, especially the flavor-packed lobster, leek, and chanterelle strudel and the delicate kabocha squash ravioli with chestnuts and sage brown butter. Some of her best entrees thus far have included the crisp chicken with chanterelles and applewood-smoked bacon, herbed lamb loin with cranberry beans and tomato confit, and pan-roasted salmon with lentils, celery root salad, and red-wine sauce. After your meal, consider the chef's selection of domestic and imported cheeses, which are visible in the temperature-controlled cheese room on the main floor. The live entertainment makes this restaurant ideal for a special night on the town. *$$$; AE, DC, DIS, MC, V; no checks; lunch Mon–Fri, dinner, late-night menu every day; full bar; reservations recommended; jardin1997@aol.com; map:L4* ♿

Kabuto Sushi / ★★½

5116 GEARY BLVD; 415/752-5652

In a town where hip sushi clubs are all the rage, Kabuto is something of a dinosaur. In fact, most people would never guess that this rather drab, unpretentious Japanese restaurant is run by one of the most talented and revered sushi chefs in the city: Sachio Kojima, San Francisco's godfather of sushi. It's a joy to sit at the small, semicircular sushi bar and watch his smooth yet swift technique as he prepares the standard seafood-and-rice delicacies—unagi, toro, spicy tuna roll, and such—in a whir of knives and bamboo rollers. But for the adventurous diner, the real fun begins when you say, "Mr. Kojima, surprise us!" and give him free rein to prepare some of his off-menu specialties that have made him so famous. Regardless of how much you order or how busy he is, Kojima usually finds time to sneak you a complimentary delicacy that never fails to amaze. If raw fish isn't your gig, classic tempura, teriyaki, and sukiyaki dinners are served in the adjoining dining room. Tip: If you prefer your wasabi deadly hot, ask for the stronger stuff Kojima serves on request. *$$; MC, V; no checks; dinner Tues–Sat; full bar; reservations recommended; map:G4* &

Kan Zaman / ★★

1793 HAIGHT ST; 415/751-9656

Glass-beaded curtains lead into Kan Zaman, a favorite destination for grunge types who populate the Haight. Shed your shoes and gather around knee-high tables under a canopy tent—or snag the premier window seat—and recline on pillows while sampling the tasty, inexpensive hot and cold Middle Eastern meze (appetizers). Before long, you'll think you've been transported to (as Kan Zaman literally translates) "a long time ago." Traditional menu items include hummus, baba ghanouj, kibbee (cracked wheat with spiced lamb) meat pies, and various kebabs. Sample platters offering tastes of a little bit of everything are ideal for large parties. For a novel and truly exotic finish, puff on an *argeeleh* (hookah pipe) filled with fruity honey or apricot tobacco. Wine, beer, and spiced wine round out the beverage offerings. Another plus: Kan Zaman serves till midnight—a real find in this town. *$; MC, V; no checks; lunch, dinner every day; beer and wine; reservations recommended; map:I5* &

Kate's Kitchen / ★

471 HAIGHT ST; 415/626-3984

It's almost standard procedure these days: go to brunch on a weekend and wait an hour for a table. But at Kate's, which serves one of the best brunches in the Haight, the wait is well worth it. Perhaps no other restaurant in town serves Flanched Flarney Garney, a dish featuring delicious flaky biscuits topped with eggs. The ginger-peach pancakes are another favorite and can easily serve as your only meal of the day. The simple, rustic decor isn't much to look at, but once you've settled in with your newspaper and ordered a hot cup of coffee, the only thing you'll want to see is the giant omelet (try the one with red peppers and pesto) on your plate. *$; MC, V; local checks only; breakfast, lunch Mon–Fri, brunch Sat–Sun; no alcohol; reservations not accepted; map:K5*

Khan Toke Thai House / ★★★

5937 GEARY BLVD; 415/668-6654

If you're in the mood for an exotic dining experience (or you just want to impress the heck out of your date), dine at the Khan Toke Thai House, the loveliest Thai restaurant in San Francisco. Following Thai tradition, you'll be asked to remove your shoes at the entrance, so be sure to wear clean (and hole-free) socks. You'll then be escorted through the lavishly decorated dining room—replete with carved teak, Thai statues, and hand-woven Thai tapestries—and seated on large pillows at one of the many sunken tables (or, if you prefer, at a table in the garden out back). Start with the appetizing *tom yam gong*, lemongrass shrimp with mushroom, tomato, and cilantro soup. Other delicious dishes include the prawns with hot chilies, mint leaves, lime juice, lemongrass, and onions; the chicken with cashew nuts, crispy chilies, and onions; and the ground pork with fresh ginger, green onion, peanuts, and lemon juice. For those dining family style, be sure to order the exquisite deep-fried pompano topped with sautéed ginger, onions, peppers, pickled garlic, and yellow-bean sauce. And if the vast menu has you bewildered, opt for the multicourse dinner: appetizer, soup, salad, two main courses, dessert, and coffee. And if you're feeling frivolous after sipping a Singha beer or two, you might want to engage your tablemate in a game of shoeless footsie—after all, how often do you get a chance to do that in public? *$$; AE, MC, V; no checks; dinner every day; beer and wine; reservations recommended; map:F4*

Kokkari Estiatorio / ★★★

200 JACKSON ST; 415/981-0983

Kokkari's owners have done their best to invent a new category—upscale Greek with a California twist. And why not? It worked for Italian food. Indeed, Kokkari works on many levels: it's a beautiful, lavishly decorated restaurant (a $5 million investment) with a ritzy country-house ambience, thanks to the fire crackling in the oversize fireplace, the ornate rugs and plush chairs suitable for royalty, and the large windows and sun-bleached walls. This is a place to relax, soak up the atmosphere, and revel in California-style contemporary Hellenic cuisine. The front dining room feels the most luxurious. There's a second, larger dining room with an open kitchen, and cushy booths line a walkway between the two dining areas. The usual Greek suspects play well here: avgolemono, the lemony egg, rice, and chicken soup; moussaka, the divinely spiced casserole of eggplant, lamb, and potato; and the quintessential Greek salad—no lettuce, just tomato, olive, red onion, and cucumber. Presentations are stunning, and the flavors are fresh and bright. The grilled lamb chops with fried potatoes are classic. Thick Greek coffee is made in a multiple-step process that involves an elaborate urn of sand (you can even ask the wait staff for a demo). And be sure to leave room for dessert, in particular the luscious yogurt-granita duo (a dense chocolate cake with nougatine) or the rice pudding with a poached pear and black-currant sauce. *$$$; AE, DC, MC, V; no checks; lunch Mon–Fri, dinner Mon–Sat; full bar; reservations recommended; map:N2* &

Kuleto's / ★★

221 POWELL ST; 415/397-7720

If you're shopping in the Union Square area and you want to experience a classic high-energy San Francisco trattoria, follow the cable car down Powell Street to Kuleto's. Hanging prosciuttos, dried herbs, and peppers add a rustic note to an otherwise sleek, modern black-marble-and-mahogany hot spot where both tourists and locals squeeze in to be a part of the lively scene. Our usual modus operandi when dining here is to scout out the antipasto bar for some vacant stools, order a glass of chianti, nosh on antipasti and appetizers, and chat with the friendly wait staff. If you're hungry enough for a full meal, there's a wide array of main courses as well. A few of our favorites include the penne pasta drenched in a tangy lamb-sausage marinara sauce, the clam linguine packed with fresh clams, or any of the fresh fish specials grilled over hardwoods. This isn't groundbreaking Italian cuisine, but it's not supposed to be; it's good, hearty Italian comfort food served in a beautiful, boisterous setting that has become a San Francisco institution. *$$; AE, CB, DC, DIS, MC, V; no checks; breakfast, lunch, dinner every day; full bar; reservations recommended; map:N3* &

Kyo-ya / ★★★

2 NEW MONTGOMERY ST (PALACE HOTEL); 415/392-8600

This elegantly austere restaurant in the Palace Hotel serves some of the best sushi and sashimi in town. Catering to well-heeled business execs visiting from the other side of the Rim, Kyo-ya's food is fresh, authentic, and delicious. Sit at the sushi bar or settle into one of the dining room's black-lacquered chairs flanked by a glossy wood table set with a simple arrangement of fresh flowers. Order a decanter of sake (there are more than a dozen to choose from) and some toro (tuna belly), ebi (shrimp), hotate (scallops), or anything else on Kyo-ya's extensive list of sushi offerings-it's sure to be some of the finest you've ever had. While the sushi and *nabemono* (one-pot dishes cooked tableside) are undeniably expensive, several other dishes, including wonderful appetizers like steamed clams in sake and complete tempura and teriyaki dinners, are more reasonably priced. *$$$; AE, DC, DIS, MC, V; no checks; lunch Tues–Fri, dinner Tues–Sat; full bar; reservations recommended; toshi_matsumura@ ittsheraton.com; map:N3* &

La Folie / ★★★★

2316 POLK ST; 415/776-5577

After a stingy San Francisco restaurateur fired him for spending too much on ingredients and serving overly generous portions, French-born chef Roland Passot decided to open his own restaurant where he could spend as much as he liked to make the food perfect. The paradisiacal result is the charming, small, family-run La Folie, now glistening after a much-needed interior refurbishing completed in the summer of '97. The intimate, whimsical, theatrical dining room with white puffy clouds painted on the sky-blue ceiling now has red-patterned carpeting, new chairs, a colorful stained-glass entryway, and even marionettes from Lyon dangling from the wall—an appropriate stage for Passot's creative, exuberant, but disciplined menu. His Roquefort soufflé with grapes, herbs, and walnut bread alone is worthy of four stars. Other memorable starters are the wonderful foie gras dishes; the potato blinis with golden osetra caviar, salmon, asparagus, and crème fraîche; the rabbit loin stuffed with exquisitely fresh vegetables and roasted garlic; the velvety corn-and-leek soup; the parsley and garlic soup with snails and shiitake mushrooms; and the lobster consommé. For an entree, choose whatever meat or fish suits your fancy, for it surely will be exquisitely prepared. To accommodate vegetarians, Passot has thoughtfully included a separate Vegetable Lovers' menu. And for those who can't make up their minds, there's a discovery menu that allows you to choose five courses à la carte (though it's pricey). For dessert, indulge in clafouti with chocolate sauce or croquettes of chocolate with orange zest sauce. The wine list is extensive but the prices are steep. *$$$; AE, DC, DIS, MC, V; no checks; dinner Mon–Sat; full bar; reservations recommended; map:L2* &

La Taqueria / ★★

2889 MISSION ST; 415/285-7117

Among colorful fruit stands, thrift shops, and greasy panhandlers lining bustling Mission Street sits La Taqueria, the Bay Area's best burrito factory. Its lackluster interior is brightened only by a vibrant mural depicting south-of-the-border scenes and a shiny CD jukebox pumping out merry Mexican music, all of which could mean only one thing: people come here for the food. Don't expect a wide variety, for the folks behind the counter just churn out what they do best: burritos, tacos, and quesadillas. It's all fresh, delicious, and guaranteed to fill you up—for little more than pocket change. The moist, meaty fillings include grilled beef, pork, sausage, beef tongue, and chicken (you won't find any rice in these burritos); and the *bebidas* vary from beer and soda to cantaloupe juice and even horchata (a sweet rice drink). Stand in line to place your order and pay, then take a seat at one of the shared, long wooden tables and wait for someone to bellow out your number (somehow they just know whether to say it in Spanish or English). *$; no credit cards; local checks only; lunch, dinner every day; beer only; reservations not accepted; map:L7* &

La Villa Poppi / ★

3234 22ND ST; 415/642-5044
Don't walk by too fast or you might miss this undiscovered gem wedged in among the lively Mission District restaurants and nightspots. La Villa Poppi is a cozy, tiny, but entirely charming spot. And the rustic Italian fare is delicious, if just a bit simplistic. The menu changes weekly, offering the characteristic pastas, soups, and salads as well as an antipasto plate. The house-baked breads are a tasty starter. You'll be hard pressed to find a wine on the list that costs more than $20. *$; AE, DC, MC, V; no checks; dinner every day; beer and wine; reservations recommended; map:L7*

Laghi / ★

2101 SUTTER ST; 415/931-3774
Just around the corner from the thriving heart of Pacific Heights is this cozy little outpost serving sophisticated, Italian-influenced fare. Surprisingly few locals have discovered it, but those who have experienced owner-chef Gino Laghi's expertise keep coming back for more. In fact, many regulars now make the trek here since the restaurant moved from its original location in the Richmond District. The new Laghi is elegant and charming, with an open kitchen along one side and beautiful Asian antiques here and there. Almost everything is good here—from the daily-changing soups and salads to the house-made pastas. The daily risotto specials are also recommended. *$; AE, CB, DC, MC, V; no checks; dinner Tues–Sun; full bar; reservations recommended; map:K3* &

Le Charm / ★★

315 5TH ST; 415/546-6128
This classic, stylish, intimate French bistro south of Market Street offers some of the best values in French cuisine in the city. There aren't many places where you can find a three-course, expertly prepared, professionally served prix-fixe menu for about $24. The appetizers might include fricasee d'escargot, roasted quail stuffed with mustard greens, or a perfect French onion soup. For the entree, your options might include duck confit, pan-roasted halibut, or the enormous leg of lamb. Desserts, which must be ordered in advance, are superb. The tarte Tatin and the chocolate roulade with coconut are showstoppers. Outdoor seating is available, making this a great place to enjoy a sophisticated lunch on a warm summer afternoon. *$; AE, MC, V; no checks; lunch Mon–Fri, dinner Mon–Sat; full bar; reservations recommended; map:N4* &

Le Colonial / ★★☆

20 COSMO PL; 415/931-3600
The once-popular Trader Vic's restaurant thrived for many years on this tiny, tucked-away side street near the Tenderloin and Union Square.

Today this hideaway is the home of Le Colonial, which serves excellent Vietnamese food that is much more expensive than what you'll find at the usual Asian restaurants around town. But this is no typical Asian restaurant. It's a place to be seen, to dress up, and to pose (and jackets are required for men). Fashioned after a 1920s Vietnamese plantation, complete with wicker, fans, and rich wood, Le Colonial offers a blend of French and Vietnamese cooking. Upstairs in the lounge, relax with a drink and choose from an extensive list of appetizers. The dinner menu also offers a wide selection, and most dishes are a tantalizing blend of sweet, spicy, sour, and aromatic flavors. Dishes can be ordered individually as entrees or served family style. Some good choices include the coconut curry prawns with mango and eggplant, wok-seared beef tenderloin with watercress and onion salad, cold beef salad with tender chunks marinated in lime, ginger roast duck, and steamed sea bass wrapped in a banana leaf. *$$$; AE, DC, MC, V; no checks; dinner every day; full bar; reservations recommended; map:M3* &

Lhasa Moon / ★

2420 LOMBARD ST; 415/674-9898

If you can't hike the Himalayas, you can at least trek to the Marina district to experience the food of Tibet. This is San Francisco's only Tibetan restaurant and one of the few on the West Coast. Restaurant creator Tsering Wangmo, Tibetan born and raised in a Tibetan refugee settlement in South India, revives the dishes she learned to cook from her mother. She's eager to introduce people to both the cuisine and the culture from whence it came. The menu is curious and amazing, with such dishes as *churul* (a pungent cheese and minced beef soup) and *phing alla* (a crepe filled with bean thread, vegetables, and mushrooms). A highlight is the *momo*, a dim sum–like array of juicy dumplings filled with anything from chopped beef to mint-flavored vegetables. Among the intriguing and flavorful main dishes, the *kongpo shaptak* (spicy cheese-flavored beef and chili peppers) and *jhasha shamdeh* (curry-marinated chicken in yogurt and herbs) are two standouts. Several vegetarian dishes are available as well. *$; AE, MC, V; no checks; lunch Thurs–Fri, dinner Tues–Sun; beer and wine; reservations recommended; map:J1* &

Liberty Cafe / ★★

410 CORTLAND AVE; 415/695-8777

The neighborhood of Bernal Heights is fast becoming known as the last bastion of affordable housing in the city. And as residents move in, the restaurants are springing up to feed them. The Liberty Cafe is the best one so far. The big draw is its traditional (though pricey) chicken potpie, with lots of juicy chicken, potatoes, carrots, pearl onions, and other tasty treats. The seasonally changing menu often has a pleasant surprise or two, including a fantastic tamale dish on a recent visit. The desserts, anchored by juicy, delicious fruit pies, get their own space in a cottage next door. The bakery/wine bar has a couple dozen more seats; here you can have an appetizer while you wait for your table. Reservations are not accepted, and the wait can sometimes be long. *$$; AE, MC, V; no checks; lunch Tues–Fri, dinner Tues–Sun, brunch Sat–Sun; beer and wine; reservations not accepted; map:L8* ⅙

L'Osteria del Forno / ★★☆

519 COLUMBUS AVE; 415/982-1124

Don't let the touristy Columbus Avenue location fool you: This small eight-table cafe attracts legions of locals who brave lousy parking for anything that comes out of the brick-lined oven, such as fantastic focaccia sandwiches, freshly made pizzas and pastas, kick-butt cipolline, and a wondrously succulent roast pork braised in milk (everyone's all-time favorite). Small baskets of warm focaccia bread and Italian wine served by the glass tide you over until the entree arrives. The kitchen is run by two charming Italian women who have combined good food with a homey Italian-bistro atmosphere. Ergo, expect a warm welcome and authentic Italian food at low prices. Darn good espresso, too. *$–$$; cash only; lunch, dinner Wed–Mon; beer and wine; reservations not accepted; map:M2* ⅙

LuLu / ★★☆

816 FOLSOM ST; 415/495-5775

LuLu may not enjoy the legendary status it once commanded, but it's still one of the most energetic and popular restaurants in San Francisco and yet another feather in the chef's cap of Reed Hearon (who has since gone on to fry bigger fish). It's easy to see why LuLu was and remains a hit. As soon as you enter you're pleasantly assaulted with divine aromas emanating from the massive open kitchen, which overlooks the cavernous yet stylish dining room where a hundred or more diners are feasting family style and creating such a din that the kitchen staff has to wear two-way headsets (it's quite a scene). The sine qua non starter is the sputtering iron skillet–roasted mussels served with drawn butter. Essentially everything that comes from the twin wood-burning ovens is superb, particularly the pork loin rubbed with fennel, garlic, and olive oil and served with mashed potatoes; the rosemary-infused chicken and warm potato salad; and the thin, crisp pizzas topped with first-rate prosciutto, pancetta, and other savory toppings. Everything is served on a large platter to facilitate sharing. For dessert go for the gooey chocolate cake served with a scoop of gourmet ice cream. *$$; AE, DC, MC, V; no checks; lunch, dinner every day; full bar; reservations recommended; map:N4* ⅙

Manora's Thai Cuisine / ★★☆

1600 FOLSOM ST; 415/861-6224
There are dozens of Thai restaurants in the city, but this SoMa institution has always managed to stand out as one of the best. That explains the crowded seating arrangement, the noisy atmosphere, and the guaranteed wait during the peak dining hours, but the food is so incredibly flavorful and reasonably priced that no one sweats these little things. Be sure to start the feast with the chicken satay, followed by the fresh stuffed mint rolls (divine). The menu has a vast array of Thai-style curries, tangy soups, meats, and vegetarian plates, but it's the seafood dishes that really shine, particularly the exotic deep-fried crab shell stuffed with fresh pork, shrimp, crab, herbs, vegetables, and spices. If you plan on going out after dinner, finish the meal with Manora's addictively sweet, caffeine-laden Thai iced tea or coffee. *$–$$; MC, V; no checks; lunch Mon–Fri, dinner every day; full bar; reservations recommended; map:N4* &

Marcello's Pizza / ★☆

420 CASTRO ST; 415/863-3900
Every neighborhood has to have one: a late-night pizza-by-the-slice old standby that's always there for you when you leave the party bombed and starving. In the Castro that place is Marcello's, which must make a small fortune serving a wide array of slices to a *very* eclectic crowd until 1am Sunday through Thursday, and until 2am Friday and Saturday. Both thick- and thin-crust pizzas with a wide array of toppings are enticingly set behind the glass counter, and it usually takes only one big slice to do the trick. Chicken wings, calzones, salads, and sandwiches are also available, but most everyone sticks with the thick, gooey, God-this-tastes-good pizza. Beer and wine are available as well. There are only about half a dozen stools in the cramped and narrow pizzeria, but the crowd moves quickly. *$; cash only; lunch, dinner every day; beer and wine; reservations not accepted; map:K6* &

Mario's Bohemian Cigar Store / ★★

566 COLUMBUS AVE; 415/362-0536
2209 POLK ST; 415/776-8226
You can't consider yourself a San Franciscan unless you've had a focaccia-bread sandwich at this classic century-old North Beach Italian institution that, in a previous incarnation, really was a cigar store. It's an adorable little low-key cafe in a prime location at the corner of Columbus and Union across from Washington Square. Both tourists and locals squeeze themselves into the well-worn bar or at a windowside table overlooking the park, order a cappuccino or a glass of chianti, watch the foot traffic, and ponder the old black-and-white photos of longtime regulars. There are several kinds of sandwiches to choose from, but the best are the hot meatball and the eggplant, both topped with melted Swiss cheese

and cut into triangles for easy pickings. Note: There's also a much newer and larger Mario's on Polk Street between Green and Vallejo. It offers live jazz Wednesday and Sunday nights, but it doesn't have half the classic charm of the original. *$; cash only; lunch, dinner every day; beer and wine; reservations not accepted; map:M2, L2* ♿

Masa's / ★★★★

648 BUSH ST; 415/989-7154

No one just drops in for dinner at Masa's. Not only do you have to make a reservation at least three weeks in advance, but it may take that long to arrange the financing: this is probably San Francisco's most expensive restaurant. That said, the prices accurately reflect the precious ingredients, generous portions, stunning presentations, and labor-intensive nature of the elegant French-California cuisine invented by the late Masataka Kobayashi and was carried on flawlessly by Julian Serrano since 1985. In August of 1998, however, Serrano passed the chef's cap on to his protégé Chad Callahan—who has been with Masa's for nearly a decade—and opened the Picasso restaurant in Las Vegas, leaving many to wonder if Masa's four-star legacy had finally come to an end. Not the case. By all accounts Masa's continues to impress its cultivated clientele with its inviting atmosphere (neither glitzy nor snobbish), professional service (never intimidating), and unremittingly stellar cuisine. To get a hint of Masa's idea of indulgence, take a gander at the offerings from a typical prix-fixe ménu dégustation: warm lobster salad with crispy leeks and truffle vinaigrette; sautéed snapper with red wine sauce; foie gras with Madeira truffle sauce; a choice of either medallions of fallow deer with caramelized apples and zinfandel sauce or mignon of veal rôti; and for dessert, a choice of rum- and lime-sautéed bananas with coconut milk ice cream and toasted macadamias or Valrhona bittersweet chocolate terrine with raspberry sorbet. The excellent wines are even more exorbitantly priced than the food; moreover, if you want to bring a special bottle of your own, you should know that the corkage fee is equal to the retail value of a top-flight chardonnay. The dining room remains as elegant as ever with its works of modern art, luxuriously upholstered chairs, and walls covered in red Italian silk. Two seatings are available nightly (and only two fixed-price menus are offered), and gentlemen are requested to wear a jacket and tie. *$$$ AE, DC, DIS, MC, V; checks OK; dinner Tues–Sat; full bar; reservations required; map:M3*

Maya San Francisco / ★

303 2ND ST; 415/543-6709

When Maya opened here, many San Franciscans wondered how anyone could show us something in Mexican cuisine we hadn't seen before. After all, we live in a Mexican food mecca, and a West Coast version of a popular New York–based restaurant would seem to offer nothing new. Judging by the crowds in this place, however, there was plenty we hadn't seen. The food here is something of a gourmet spin on traditional Mexican dishes, prepared with regional touches and presented with unprecedented flair. What's more, there are many dishes that simply are not served in most local Mexican restaurants. The corn soup is delicious—and probably impossible to find short of inviting yourself into a Mexican family's home. Other highlights include the chile relleno, pan-roasted Chilean sea bass, and grilled pork tenderloin. The sauces are a specialty in themselves. The dining room makes the most of its windswept, mall-like location with warm, earth-toned walls and subtle ambient lighting. *$; AE, DC, MC, V; no checks; lunch Mon–Fri, dinner every day; full bar; reservations recommended; map:O3* &

MC² / ★★★
470 PACIFIC AVE; 415/956-0666
One of the best-looking restaurants in the city, this sleek, modern establishment has earned awards and acclaim as much for its architecture as for its food. Built into a historic brick warehouse from the Barbary Coast era, the room features wood ceilings, brick walls, and exposed beams, a stylish aesthetic that threatens to make the meals here a second act. Luckily, chef Yoshi Kojima is behind the stoves in the exhibition kitchen, and his light, flavorful contemporary California-French cuisine is among the best in town. Kojima's Japanese heritage is evident in some of the better dishes, such as the appetizer of seared tuna and tuna tartare with shiitake mushrooms or the dinner entrees of roasted day-boat scallops and shiitake-crusted filet of beef with root vegetables. The Sonoma duck breast with caramelized turnip tart and foie gras sauce is also outstanding. The massive wine list can be a bit daunting, but the sommelier is friendly and quick with a perfect recommendation. Service is generally flawless but can be distant. *$$$; AE, DC, MC, V; no checks; lunch Mon–Fri, dinner Mon–Sat; full bar; reservations recommended; map:N2*

Mecca / ★★☆
2029 MARKET ST; 415/621-7000
Mecca is a magnet for those who want an abundance of atmosphere with hearty American bistro fare—and this sexy, silver supper club lined with chocolate-brown velvet drapes delivers. Start with one of the sassy cocktails (how about She's-a-Bad-Girl-Mecca-rita with Cuervo, Cointreau, and lime?) at the slick, zinc-topped bar inset with multicolored fiber-optic lights, and enjoy the moody music, which is often provided by live jazz and R&B ensembles on the small stage. Chef Lynn Sheehan, former sous chef at Rubicon and a graduate of Madeleine Kamman's School for American Chefs, creates wonderful appetizers, including a Caesar salad topped with shavings of Parmigiano-Reggiano, a warm Catalan spinach salad with toasted pine nuts and chicken confit, and a roasted beet and

goat-cheese tart with mizuma, walnuts, and beet chips. Sheehan's wood-burning oven turns out great cornmeal-crust pizzas, and although some entrees have been more successful than others, the fish dishes are delicious, including seared salmon with a French lentil vinaigrette and boneless Idaho trout with roasted tomatoes and hazelnuts in a sherry-vinegar browned butter. Unlike most San Francisco restaurants, the glamorous Mecca serves dinner until midnight Thursday through Saturday. *$$$; AE, DC, MC, V; no checks; dinner every day; full bar; reservations recommended; www.sfmecca.com; map:K5* &

The Meetinghouse / ★★★

1701 OCTAVIA ST; 415/922-6733

Without the forest-green awning jutting from its Victorian facade, the Meetinghouse could easily be mistaken for a residence. Luckily for lovers of good American food, it's not one. In 1996 owner-chefs John Bryant Snell and Joanna Karlinsky converted an old apothecary space into one of the very best restaurants in San Francisco. Custard-yellow walls, dark green trim, wood ceiling fans, and hardwood floors make this warm, intimate space utterly inviting. To add to the charm, one entire wall still boasts the remnants of an earlier identity—hundreds of tiny built-in drawers that formerly held medicinal potions. This dinner-only establishment offers superb seasonal American cuisine served by an exceptionally professional staff. Baskets of warm biscuits and homemade breads arrive at your table immediately. A small seasonal menu typically boasts no more than five enticing entrees. A fall offering included a marvelous rock shrimp and scallion johnnycake appetizer with a sweet-pepper relish, and an exquisite tomato salad drizzled with a lightly sweetened balsamic vinaigrette and toasted pine nuts. Unforgettable entrees have included a grilled pork loin chop with applesauce served with braised baby greens; a pan-seared Chilean sea bass in a sumptuous red-wine jus; and braised short ribs smothered in a sweet barbecue sauce. For dessert, try the utterly delectable strawberry shortcake with sweet berries nestled in a cloud of whipped cream atop a strawberry and wine purée. A carefully selected, reasonably priced list of primarily California wines is perfectly matched with the extraordinary American cuisine. *$$$; AE, DC, MC, V; checks OK; dinner Mon–Sat, brunch Sat–Sun; beer and wine; reservations recommended; map:L3* &

Mel's Diner / ★★☆

2165 LOMBARD ST; 415/921-3039
3355 GEARY BLVD; 415/387-2244

When you're in the mood for a cheeseburger, greasy fries, and a chocolate shake, there's no place that does it better than Mel's. Modeled after an *American Graffiti*–style '50s diner, the place is replete with glimmering stainless steel, large comfy booths, and even nickel jukeboxes at each table. Some toe-tappin' hit from the '50s or '60s is bound to be playing, and the staff even dresses for effect in spotless short-sleeve white shirts and hats. Along with the diner standards—hot dogs, cheese sandwiches, hot fudge sundaes—are a half-dozen "blue-plate specials" such as a turkey dinner complete with stuffing and mashed potatoes, and meat loaf just like Mom (or somebody's Mom) used to make. A classic American breakfast is served each morning as well. Mel's two best attributes, however, are that it's open late (till 3am Sunday through Thursday and 24 hours Friday and Saturday) and it's one of the few restaurants in the city that caters to kids and teens. *$; cash only; breakfast, lunch, dinner every day; beer and wine; reservations not accepted; map:K2, I4* &

Mifune / ★

1737 POST ST; 415/922-0337

"It's OK to slurp your noodles," says a note on Mifune's menu. And that's a good thing, because you are likely to do just that at this spartan restaurant in the Upper Fillmore area. When a noodle fix is what you require, there is no better place than Mifune. Choose either an udon (broad, flat) or a soba (thin, buckwheat) base, then select from more than 50 toppings. Whether it's beef, chicken, tempura, or plain old miso, you won't be disappointed. The lunch special, with noodles, sushi, salad, and tea for less than about $7, is a real bargain. You'll also find a few tempura and sushi selections, but don't waste your time. Noodles are the order here. Just raise the bowl to your chin, shovel in the goodies with your chopsticks, and slurp, slurp, slurp! *$; AE, DC, DIS, MC, V; no checks; lunch, dinner Mon–Sat; beer and wine; reservations recommended; map:K3* &

Millennium / ★★

246 MCALLISTER ST; 415/487-9800

When Millennium opened a few years back, it seemed as if it wouldn't live to see the new century, simply because upscale vegetarian/vegan restaurants rarely do well. But chef Eric Tucker has proved the critics wrong with his wonderfully creative and inventive meatless menu (if you've ever tried cooking for a vegan, you know how difficult it can be). Set in a narrow Parisian bistro–style dining room within the Abigail Hotel in the city's Civic Center district, Millennium enjoys a strong repeat clientele. They come for Tucker's egg-, butter-, and dairy-free dishes, which even meat and dairy eaters concede are delicious (most of the time). One of our favorite main courses from the weekly-revised menu is the ragout of wild mushrooms, leeks, and butternut squash inside a flaky filo purse. The sautéed portobello mushrooms and rosemary polenta are also quite good, and Tucker's meat substitutes made with seitan are astonishingly similar to the real thing. Occasionally Tucker can really muddle some daily specials, so be sure to query the friendly wait staff for a recommendation. *$$; DC, MC, V; no checks; dinner every day; beer and wine; reservations recommended; map:M4* ♿

Miss Millie's / ★★☆

4123 24TH ST; 415/285-5598

When you want comfort in Noe Valley, stop by to see Miss Millie. The welcoming, 1930ish diner first opened as a strictly vegetarian restaurant, but has evolved into one of the best places in the area for brunch. The brunch menu is huge, with flavorful takes on recognizable favorites. Try the lemon-ricotta pancakes with blueberry syrup or the spinach and goat-cheese omelet for something you won't soon forget. Dinners are also a treat. The roasted chicken risotto and the grilled red snapper are terrific. The menu is still heavily vegetarian, but the fare is so hearty that carnivores will feel right at home. And that's the whole point at Miss Millie's: to make everyone feel at home. *$; MC, V; no checks; dinner Tues–Sun, brunch Sat–Sun; beer and wine; reservations not accepted; map:K7* ♿

Moki Sushi and Pacific Grill / ★

830 CORTLAND AVE; 415/970-9336

Everyone in town has a favorite sushi spot, and everyone argues over which is the best. People's opinions tend to be influenced by whatever sushi bar is located near their homes. The folks in Bernal Heights have argued in favor of Moki since the day it opened. While the sushi here is actually not quite on a par with that of several other popular places in town (not yet, anyway), this place excels where the others try and fail: with selections from the grill. Try the Thai-style crab cakes in red curry sauce or the Vietnamese-style rice paper rolls stuffed with shrimp and avocado and you'll see what we mean. On the sushi side, the Ecstasy Roll is the specialty, with white and red tuna, avocado, tobiko, and green onions (whether or not it inspires its namesake state of being will depend on the sushi eater). The Outrigger Roll with tempura shrimp and creamy avocado is another good choice. *$; DC, MC, V; no checks; dinner every day; beer and wine; reservations recommended; map:L8* ♿

Mom Is Cooking / ★★

1166 GENEVA AVE; 415/586-7000

For three decades this friendly family-style restaurant has provided the Excelsior district with some of the best, most authentic Mexican food in San Francisco. Mom is Abigail Murillo, who hails from Mexico City and spends most of her time in the kitchen. That's good for us, because Mom's cooking is mouthwateringly delicious and well worth making the trip to the outskirts of the city to enjoy. The tamales are second to none, and no matter which enchilada you choose (succulent pork, juicy chicken) you won't be disappointed. The breakfasts are also worth getting up early for. *Huevos* (eggs) come in some 10 variations, and the breakfast burritos are gigantic. Most everything is made from scratch—and the mole sauce is unbelievable! On top of all this, it seems as if the prices haven't gone up since the place opened. At the bar, tequila reigns, with countless varieties available for sipping or mixing into a zesty margarita. *$; cash only; breakfast, lunch, dinner every day; full bar; reservations recommended; map:JJ5* &

Momo's / ★★

760 2ND ST; 415/227-8660

When plans for San Francisco's new baseball stadium were announced, business owners in the surrounding South of Market area licked their chops in anticipation of the commercial windfall to follow. The spacious, modern-looking Momo's was first to pounce, and those who promptly made it a hit have been licking their chops for a different reason. Chef Tricia Tracey is expert at utilizing the wood-fired grill in her enormous, spotless kitchen. The classic dishes—from ribs to roast to chicken to great pizzas—are served in large portions, and each bursts with flavor. Tracey and her kitchen hit nothing out of the park here, but they're a solid team and surprisingly consistent given the giant size of the dining room. Desserts are another plus, especially the delicious banana bread pudding. Heated outdoor patio seating is available, and there's another patio in front where after-work revelers jostle for cocktails every night of the week. But beware: This place will be a zoo during baseball season. *$$; AE, MC, V; no checks; lunch, dinner every day; full bar; reservations recommended; map:O4* &

Montage / ★

101 4TH ST, 2ND LEVEL (METREON); 415/369-6111

Sony's massive Metreon, a high-tech mall and futuristic wonderland, contains about half a dozen options for dining. The anchor of these is Montage, a handsome space set in a sleek, curving room affixed with monitors displaying images of the artwork on view at the San Francisco Museum of Modern Art and Yerba Buena Center for the Arts across the way. Art as entertainment is the theme here, and the dishes angle to be sculptural in presentation. At times they look better than they taste, but more often than not this place serves above-average American-California fare. Chef Jennifer Cox visits local farms and bakeries for her ingredients, so her dishes are nothing if not fresh. The Atkins Ranch lamb sirloin and the pan-seared local sand dabs are two of the menu's best offerings, and there's a big selection of salads and sandwiches. The desserts—whimsically created concoctions that don't skimp on flavor or size—may become the Montage calling card. One is a chocolate cake fashioned to look like a popcorn bag, with caramel popcorn spilling out into scoops of surrounding peanut ice cream. The kids are sure to love it.

$$; AE, MC, V; no checks; lunch, dinner every day; full bar; reservations recommended; map:N3 &

Moose's / ★★

1652 STOCKTON ST; 415/989-7800 OR 800/28-MOOSE

Every major city has a place where the prime movers-and-shakers hang out, and ours is Moose's. Run by well-respected San Francisco restaurateur Ed Moose, the lively, ever-so-friendly establishment facing Washington Square in San Francisco's North Beach district is abuzz every night with lawyers, politicians, and local celebrities who come to sup and schmooze within the spacious, high-energy dining room. Chef Brian Whitmer runs the exhibition kitchen, offering a monthly changing menu of upscale American dishes that have garnered many a favorable review. The most recommended dishes are anything that's cooked in the wood-burning oven, particularly the famous tender grilled veal chop served with a potato galette. When in doubt, stick with the legendary Caesar salad and juicy Mooseburger combo, washed down with a glass of spicy zinfandel. There's always a jazz combo playing nightly, and the adjacent bar—separated from the main dining room by a frosted-glass partition—stays busy long after the kitchen closes. Moose's hosts a popular weekend brunch as well. *$$–$$$; AE, CB, DC, JCB, MC, V; no checks; lunch Thurs–Fri, dinner every day, brunch Sat–Sun; full bar; reservations recommended; www.mooses.com; map:M2* &

North Beach Restaurant / ★★

1512 STOCKTON ST; 415/392-1700

For a traditional taste of Northern Italian cooking, you can't do much better than North Beach Restaurant. A staple of the largely Italian neighborhood for two decades, this place is elegant, classic, and refined. The kitchen doesn't toil in trends, offering instead straightforward interpretations of such dishes as eggplant Parmesan, veal scaloppine, and calamari. The cioppino, a house specialty, comes shelled so you don't have to make a mess to enjoy it. The sand dabs are also highly recommended. Everything here is well executed, and the service follows suit. If you don't see anything you like on the menu, the kitchen takes requests—but allow some extra time if you opt for that route. All desserts are made on the premises, and the tiramisu and cheesecake are presented in classic large and unfettered form. North Beach Restaurant also has one of the best wine cellars in town, with nearly 100 cabernets as well as some 75 grappas and 25 California white wines, not to mention vintages from 20 regions of Italy. For an unforgettable North Beach experience, this is the place. *$$$; AE, MC, V; no checks; lunch, dinner every day; full bar; reservations recommended; map:M2* &

North Star / ★

288 CONNECTICUT ST; 415/551-9840

A while ago a restaurant called Aurora's opened in this up-and-coming Potrero Hill neighborhood, and the locals gave it rave reviews. But no sooner did it get up and running than it shut its doors, giving way to North Star, a beacon to which residents flocked with some trepidation. Soon, however, it became the talk of the street, then the area, then the city. The opening chef left and his substitute, Ricardo Cabrera, took over and made the place shine. At lunch, the multimedia types who work in the area populate the chic, comfortable room. Dinners are a relaxed affair, with casual, friendly service and lively conversation. The menu is rooted largely in American classics, from meat loaf in wild mushroom gravy to barbecued pork chops to tasty fried chicken. A few unusual items set this place apart from the usual glorified diner, such as deep-fried maki tempura. The desserts come from the Little Dipper Bakery next door—and be sure to save room, because they're a true highlight. *$; MC, V; no checks; lunch every day, dinner Tues–Sun; beer and wine; reservations recommended; map:N6* &

One Market / ★★

1 MARKET ST; 415/777-5577

Celebrity chef Bradley Ogden became a household name among Bay Area gastronomes when he opened San Francisco's chichi Campton Place restaurant in 1983, serving the fanciest versions of American food many people had ever seen. Then in 1989 he opened the more affordable and less pretentious Lark Creek Inn in the suburbs of Marin County. Spurred by that success, Ogden decided to branch out, coming back to the city in 1993 with One Market—a much larger venue for his fresh-from-the-farm–style cooking. From the start, the fare at One Market was surprisingly inconsistent, bringing both bravos and boos from major restaurant critics. So the enterprising (and overextended) Ogden made the wise decision to hire chef George Morrone (of Aqua fame) to rule over the kitchen, and now the food is prepared much more consistently. One Market's seasonal menus are still influenced by Ogden's midwestern roots, but it's Morrone's contemporary American fare—especially his excellent fish dishes—that dominates. On the list of starters you'll likely see George's Signature Sonoma Quail prepared with smoked bacon truffle jus, as well as Bradley's Caesar Salad tossed with garlic-Parmesan croutons. Main courses might include a delightful potato-crusted rainbow trout, rack of pork (for two) with a pomegranate glaze, and Prince Edward Island mussels steamed with garlic and andouille sausage. The made-from-scratch dessert menu features Tahitian vanilla-bean ice cream served with a trio of warm sauces (caramel, hot fudge, and strawberry) and Ogden's signature dessert, chocolate brioche custard bread pudding with chocolate-bourbon sabayon. The 500-bottle American wine list is one of the city's best, and live jazz piano music filters through the cavernous dining room every evening. *$$$; AE, DC, MC, V; no checks; lunch Mon–Fri, dinner Mon–Sat; full bar; reservations recommended; map:O2* &

Oritalia / ★★★

586 BUSH ST; 415/782-8122
Oritalia is an amalgamation of "oriental" and "Italian," which is precisely what the menu delivers at this plush and popular downtown restaurant. Actually, the flavors of Italy, China, Korea, France, and Southeast Asia are all represented in various combinations on the sophisticated menu, often with outstanding results. The restaurant's decor—silk chandeliers, Oriental rugs, curtained booths—offers both artistry and intimacy, but the most attractive items are on the dinner plate, such as the heavenly satsuma potato gnocchi made with sautéed Maine lobster, asparagus, and lime beurre blanc. Other dishes that are simply incredible are the sake-steamed sea bass with Chinese black-bean sauce, and the five-spice duck confit and frisée salad. End the world tour with a slice of dreamy passion-fruit cheesecake. Even restaurant-jaded San Franciscans are consistently surprised and impressed with what Oritalia has to offer. *$$–$$$; AE, CB, DC, MC, V; no checks; dinner every day; full bar; reservations recommended; map:N3* &

Pacific / ★★★

500 POST ST (PAN PACIFIC HOTEL); 415/771-8600
Ensconced within the Pan Pacific Hotel is one of San Francisco's best and least-known haute cuisine restaurants. Perhaps its lack of an off-street entrance is the reason it hasn't quite caught on, but anyone who samples chef Erik Oberholtzer's terrine of fresh Sonoma foie gras will become a die-hard fan of this immensely talented chef. The beautiful mezzanine-level dining room, stellar wine list, and professional yet unpretentious service are certainly appreciated, but it's Oberholtzer's mastery with seasonally-inspired dishes that brings us back again and again. Dishes we strongly recommend include the sweet potato gnocchi with foraged mushrooms and pineapple sage, roasted beef tenderloin on braised leeks, and mashed potatoes with a crispy oxtail and root vegetable strudel. Tip: The hotel offers free four-hour valet parking for diners. *$$$; AE, DC, MC, V; no checks; breakfast, lunch, dinner every day; full bar; reservations recommended; map:M3* &

Pane e Vino / ★★★

3011 STEINER ST; 415/346-2111
Well hidden on the outskirts of posh Pacific Heights, this dark-wood–trimmed trattoria framed by a cream-colored awning is a local favorite. The two tiny, simply furnished dining rooms with small white-

clothed tables fill up fast, and as waiters spouting rapid-fire Italian dart back and forth between the kitchen and their customers, folks waiting for a table are often left frantically searching for a place to stand out of the way. It's all enchantingly reminiscent of the real ristorante scene in Italy, which is perhaps one of the reasons people keep coming back. Newcomers unaccustomed to the hustle and bustle may be a bit disconcerted at first, but after a sip or two of wine and a bite of rustic Italian fare everything becomes rather entertaining. Do yourself a favor and indulge in the amazing chilled artichoke appetizer, stuffed with bread and tomatoes and served with a vinaigrette—it's divine! Follow that lead with one of the perfectly prepared pastas, ranging from the simple but savory capellini tossed with fresh tomatoes, basil, garlic, and extra-virgin olive oil to the zesty bucatini (hollow straw pasta) smothered with pancetta, hot peppers, and tomato sauce. The excellent entrees vary from rack of lamb marinated in sage and rosemary to the whole roasted fresh fish of the day. Before you raise your napkin to your lips for the last time, dive into the delightful *dolci*: a luscious crème caramel, assorted gelati, and a terrific tiramisu are the standouts. *$$; AE, MC, V; no checks; lunch Mon–Sat, dinner every day; beer and wine; reservations recommended; map:K2* &

Park Chow / ★★

1240 9TH AVE; 415/665-9912

There just aren't enough good things to say about Park Chow, one of our all-time favorite places to eat in the city. First of all, it's cheap (you get hefty servings of quality food for around $10 to $13), it's consistently good, the service is fast and friendly, the atmosphere is lively and fun, and you always leave feeling satisfied. The restaurant, which is fashioned after a rustic ski lodge, is located in the Inner Sunset District near Golden Gate Park and caters mostly to a local clientele. Sample Park Chow's outstanding braised short ribs served with fresh greens and mashed potatoes, the giant portobello mushroom cap served with creamy polenta, and the linguine with calamari, mussels, clams, and shrimp. Burgers, chicken, salads, and a reasonably good wine-by-the-glass list are on the menu as well. While you're waiting for a table (they're always busy and don't take reservations), order a glass of wine from the bar and snuggle with your honey by the fireplace. On sunny days, request a table in the roof garden. Brunch is served until 2:30pm on weekends. If you're in the Castro, check out the sister restaurant, Chow (see review). *$–$$; MC, V; no checks; lunch, dinner every day, brunch Sat–Sun; beer and wine; reservations not accepted; map:H5* &

Pastis / ★★

1015 BATTERY ST; 415/391-2555

Named after the anise-flavored apéritif, Pastis continues co-owner Gerald Hirigoyen's tradition of hearty brasserie fare at reasonable prices.

Like Fringale (see review), his other top-flight San Francisco restaurant, this is a classy little bistro. Inside, there's an industrial feel, with tile floors, hardwood banquettes, brick walls, a beamed ceiling, and a curved concrete bar. The French-American fusion fare comes across as sophisticated and European. For starters, try the tender spinach salad with crisp pieces of bacon and hard-cooked eggs; generous slices of crisp foie gras with grapes and *verjus* (a tart grape juice); or prawns marinated in pastis, garlic, and thyme. Entrees might include a tender rack of lamb served in a soup plate over a bed of meaty beans mixed with a tomato broth, a steak with Roquefort and basil butter, and baked halibut with quinoa risotto and papaya. End your meal with the sophisticated warm chocolate tart topped with purple-basil ice cream. Portions are moderate, as they are in Paris, but you'll get value for your dollar and you'll dine in style. *$$; AE, MC, V; checks OK; lunch Mon–Fri, dinner Mon–Sat; full bar; reservations recommended; map:N2* &

Pauline's Pizza / ★★

260 VALENCIA ST; 415/552-2050
The pizza debate in San Francisco is a never-ending affair. It seems everyone is an expert, eager to offer his or her opinion on whose fire-baked dough with cheese on top is tops. Meanwhile, Pauline's has been quietly churning out what very well could be the "chosen pizza" for years. The bright yellow building on Valencia Street is as unassuming as the restaurant's reputation. But patrons come from around the city to sit and enjoy the basic meal: pizza and salad. Don't bother looking for anything else, because you won't find it—and you won't want it. There's plenty to hold your interest on the toppings menu, from French goat cheese to spiced pork shoulder to house-spiced chicken. It all goes on Pauline's handmade thin-crust dough. The eclectic salads are prepared from certified organic, hand-picked lettuces and vegetables, accented with herbs from the restaurant's own local gardens. Also, the service here always comes with a welcoming smile. *$; MC, V; checks OK; dinner Tues–Sat; beer and wine; reservations recommended; map:L5*

Pintxos / ★

557 VALENCIA ST; 415/565-0207
The heart of the Mission District pulsates with small, interesting restaurants, so when Pintxos (pronounced PEEN-chos) moved in, locals were nonplussed. That changed quickly once people got wind of the traditional Spanish tapas prepared with Basque influences served in this rustic, colorful, often noisy dining room. The name is Spanish for "appetizers or small plates," and dining here is like a journey through an endless, adventurous starter menu. Those familiar with tapas will feel at home, but will also be surprised to find some lesser-known specialties such as *exqueeixada* (salt cod with grated tomato and garlic) or sautéed sweet-

breads with wild mushrooms. The full-fledged entrees are prepared ably and in some cases with whimsical touches. Try the chicken *guisado*, made with beer, prunes, and pine nuts, or the monkfish with saffron and honey sauce. The wine list features the requisite Napa and Sonoma labels, but be bold and choose one of the excellent Spanish varietals. *$; AE, MC, V; no checks; lunch, dinner every day; full bar; reservations required for parties of 6 or more; map:L6* &

PJ's Oysterbed / ★★☆

737 IRVING ST; 415/566-7775
For a taste of Mardi Gras, just head to PJ's. Step into this perennially packed, festively decorated hot spot, feel the loud rhythms of zydeco music, breathe the intoxicating smells of spicy Cajun cookin', and get ready to take it all in. Bring your appetite for the plentiful portions chef Pachi Calvo y Perez whips up. The all-you-can-eat crawfish is a favorite, and hearty plates of spicy jambalaya or shrimp gumbo are some of the best San Francisco has to offer. Several exotic offerings for the adventurous diner include alligator eggs or double-trouble alligator nuggets. Either sit in the bustling dining room or at the oyster bar, which provides an entertaining view of the kitchen. Or if you've come without a reservation, order a drink or two from PJ's well-stocked full bar and enjoy the festivities while you wait. *$$$; AE, DC, DIS, MC, V; checks OK; lunch Mon–Fri, dinner every day, brunch Sat–Sun; full bar; reservations recommended; map:H6* &

Plouf / ★★

40 BELDEN ST; 415/986-6491
Walk down the chichi little alley called Belden in the Financial District, and you'll swear you'd just stepped into a Parisian street full of curbside cafes. Forbidden to cars, Belden Street is filled with umbrella-topped outdoor tables and folks who come for the European ambience and cuisine. One of the restaurants gracing the alley is Plouf, which is onomatopoeic for "splash." It's a hybrid California-French seafood bistro specializing in mussels. An oversize steel door leads to a fun, Euro-modern interior with a long steel bar and booths of polished wood. The French wait staff wears jaunty striped T-shirts. Don't pass up the huge bowl of mussels served with your choice of seven sauces (ranging from escargot butter to a bold crayfish and tomato sauce), designed to be sopped up with bread. If you like fries, order a bowlful—they're salty and crisp here. The main courses are stylish as well as delicious: monkfish with cabbage, pearl onions, and bacon; tuna with black pepper, served over ratatouille; sea bass with fennel and a ginger-port sauce; steamed salmon with braised leeks and mushrooms and a mustard-tarragon sauce. There are also pork, chicken, lamb, and steak entrees for non-seafood-lovers. *$$; AE, DC,*

MC, V; no checks; lunch Mon–Fri, dinner Mon–Sat; full bar; reservations recommended; map:N3 &

PlumpJack Cafe / ★★★

3127 FILLMORE ST; 415/563-4755

Co-owned by Bill Getty (son of billionaire Gordon Getty) and wine-connoisseur-cum-politician Gavin Newsom, this exotic California-Mediterranean bistro is one of San Francisco's leading restaurants, with consistently excellent food and (thanks to its companion wine store a few doors away) a surprisingly extensive wine list featuring fine bottles offered at near-retail prices. The appetizers are often the highlight of the menu, particularly the bruschetta, topped with roasted beets, goat cheese, and garlic one night, and eggplant, sweet peppers, and chèvre the next. Don't miss the remarkable risottos, richly flavored with artichokes, applewood-smoked bacon, and goat cheese, or perhaps smoked salmon and shiitake mushrooms. Other recommended dishes include the superbly executed roast herb chicken breast with foie gras, hedgehog mushrooms, and spinach and the roast duck breast and leg confit with French green lentils, barley, parsnip chips, and a sour cherry jus. While the restaurant's highly stylized, handcrafted interior design is unique—gold-leafed lights, chairs with medieval-shield–shaped backs, curved metal screens at the windows—the taupe and olive color scheme ensures that what really stands out is the food. *$$$; AE, MC, V; no checks; lunch Mon–Fri, dinner Mon–Sat; full bar; reservations recommended; map:K2* &

Postrio / ★★★

545 POST ST; 415/776-7825

Owned by Southern California superstar chef Wolfgang Puck and the Kimpton Hotel & Restaurant Group, Postrio is a splashy slice of Hollywood set in the heart of San Francisco, with superglitzy decor à la restaurant designer Pat Kuleto, delightful culinary combinations, and the perpetual hope of catching sight of some celeb at the next table. One enters through a spiffy street-level bar that serves tapas and little Puckish pizzas to the unreserving; from there a grand sculpted-iron and copper staircase—on which everybody can at least play a star—descends dramatically into a crowded, pink-lighted dining room ringed with paintings and plants. It's a lovely, sophisticated setting for some terrific food, prepared by Mitchell and Steven Rosenthal, who proved themselves capable successors when founding chefs Anne and David Gingrass jumped ship to open Hawthorne Lane in '95. Working closely with Puck, the brothers Rosenthal have crafted an exciting hybrid of California-Asian-Mediterranean cuisine that includes such creations as grilled quail accompanied by spinach and a soft egg ravioli with port wine glaze; sautéed salmon with plum glaze, wasabi mashed potatoes, and miso vinaigrette; Chinese duck with mango sauce; and roasted leg of lamb with garlic potato purée and niçoise olives. Tempting choices, indeed, but the dessert menu has its own array of showstoppers—from the potato-pecan pie to the caramel pear tart with Grand Marnier crème fraîche. The wine list is excellent, the service professional, and reservations are essential—make them several weeks in advance. *$$$; AE, DC, DIS, MC, V; no checks; breakfast, lunch Mon–Fri, dinner every day, brunch Sat–Sun; full bar; reservations recommended; www.postrio.com; map:M3* &

Potrero Brewing Co. / ★

535 FLORIDA ST; 415/552-1967
These days it seems so many places are brewing their own beer. The microbrew restaurant trend has been good to San Francisco, but this one may be the best so far. Built into an old mayonnaise plant in the newly trendy section between the Mission District and Potrero Hill, the Potrero Brewing Co. restaurant retains its industrial charm, right down to the two gigantic brewing tanks out front. Inside, the huge place unspools before you as if you're on a factory tour. From the front downstairs bar, packed with the high-tech after-work crowd, move upstairs, grab a pint, and shoot a game on one of the three pool tables. Beyond that is a massive outdoor patio with tables warmed by heat lamps. The outstanding beers include a crispy pale ale, a robust porter, a rich stout, an authentic ESB, a tangy IPA, and a flavorful wheat. They also make seasonal brews and handcraft their own sodas. And when you get hungry? The risotto cakes, crispy calamari, and pan-roasted clams are good starters. Among the dinner selections, the braised brisket with spinach and green onion mashed potatoes is a perfect complement to the beer. Other menu highlights include the fried lemon buttermilk chicken and the enormous double-cut pork chop, served with horseradish mashed potatoes. Clearly, this is well beyond your typical pub grub. *$$; AE, DC, MC, V; no checks; dinner every day; full bar; reservations recommended; map:M6*

R&G Lounge / ★

631-B KEARNY ST; 415/982-7877
Situated in limbo between the edge of Chinatown and the edge of the Financial District, the R&G Lounge attracts a mixed crowd of tourists, businesspeople, and local Chinese residents. The restaurant has a loyal following of diners who champion the fresh Cantonese seafood dishes and good prices. The main downstairs dining room has all the charm of a cafeteria, with glaring fluorescent lights and Formica tables. It's harder to get a table in the formal upstairs dining room, where the lighting is a little easier on the eyes. Each dining room offers the same menu, half in English, half in Chinese. Not everything is on both menus, so ask your server for recommendations. Usually, he or she will happily oblige. *$; AE, DC, MC, V; no checks; lunch, dinner every day; full bar; reservations not accepted; map:N2*

Red Herring / ★

155 STEUART ST; 415/495-6500

Fittingly located near the city's Embarcadero with some spectacular bay views, Red Herring serves what it calls New American seafood. That's not to say all the fish is American or even exactly local, but the waterfront makes for a scenic backdrop while you're enjoying the fresh and imaginative fare. The restaurant, long, narrow (a bit dark in the middle section), and relatively new, reels in the finicky locals with a "Bait Bar," which serves oysters on the half shell, cracked crab, and the like. The menu features a delightful lobster and mango salad and a decadent Dungeness crab chop—a crab cake fashioned to resemble a pork chop. Chef James Ormsby's interpretation of surf-and-turf is oxtail and prawn. If you'd rather get "out of the water," the spit-roasted chicken or dry-aged New York strip are good choices. *$$; AE, DC, MC, V; no checks; lunch Mon–Fri, dinner every day; full bar; reservations recommended; map:D2* &

Ristorante Ecco / ★★½

101 SOUTH PARK; 415/495-3291

Ristorante Ecco offers a quiet yet sophisticated oasis among the bustling new-media businesses surrounding the South Park area. Amid large windows overlooking the tree-lined park, you can sit in the earth-toned dining room and actually have a conversation without raising your voice. The rustic Italian-California fare is ample and lively, updated with an urbane twist. Lunch offerings include an ahi tuna salad with green beans, arugula, fennel, potatoes, beets, and olives; thin-crust pizzas; and panini, with such ingredients as artichokes, roasted garlic, and fontina. At dinner, pasta dishes range from bow-ties in artichoke purée with olives, capers, and bread crumbs to the signature pasta dish: linguine with pears, pecans, Gorgonzola, and Parmesan. The main courses take a hearty bent, such as the tender New York steak with tangy olive butter and fennel mashed potatoes, or the salmon served with salsa verde, zucchini, eggplant, and fingerling potatoes. The wine list is as smart as the surroundings, and the rich array of desserts is a treat. *$$–$$$; AE, DC, MC, V; local checks only; lunch Mon–Fri, dinner Mon–Sat; full bar; reservations recommended; map:O4* &

Rose Pistola / ★★★

532 COLUMBUS AVE; 415/399-0499

A star has been born in North Beach, and her name is Rose Pistola. The brainchild of Midas-like chef-restaurateur Reed Hearon (who launched the reputations of LuLu and Cafe Marimba), this sleek and sexy addition to the Columbus Avenue promenade is as pleasing to behold as it is to dine in (it's actually named after a popular octogenarian North Beach restaurateur). If you prefer to oversee the preparation of your meal, sit at the counter overlooking the grill; however the family-style meals are best enjoyed in the large dining room's comfy booths (and tables on the sidewalk offer an alfresco option). The food is rustic Italian with a California flair (less fats, more flavors) inspired by the cuisine of Liguria: roast rabbit with fresh shell-bean ragout and polenta, pumpkin-filled ravioli, or roast pork chop with panzanella, an Italian bread salad infused with onions, basil, and tomatoes. The pastas, wood-fired pizzas, and antipasti are also very well prepared, but the fish dishes (particularly the whole roasted fish) are Hearon's specialty. A late-night menu is served until 1am on weekends. *$$–$$$; AE, DC, MC, V; no checks; lunch, dinner every day; full bar; reservations recommended; map:M2* &

Rotunda / ★

150 STOCKTON ST; 415/362-4777
Popular with the ladies who lunch, the Rotunda is a sophisticated respite from the throngs of shoppers below on Union Square. This restaurant within the Neiman Marcus department store, which anchors one corner of the square, is a light, comfortable room with natural light streaming through a historic stained-glass dome overhead. Specialties are the lobster club sandwich, the fresh pastas, fish, and salads, and the popular house-made popovers with berry-flavored butter. The room's circular design makes for lots of privacy, and the mood always seems quiet. It's just what you need to send you back out into the square, where shopping is a competitive sport. A formal tea service is offered each afternoon. *$$; AE, DC, Neiman Marcus store cards; local checks only; lunch Mon–Sat, brunch Sun; beer and wine; reservations recommended; map:N3*

Rubicon / ★★★

558 SACRAMENTO ST; 415/434-4100
Thanks to Rubicon's star-studded cast of financial backers—Robert De Niro, Robin Williams, and Francis Ford Coppola—this Financial District restaurant received so much advance publicity that San Franciscans were setting dates to eat here long before the seismic reinforcements were bolted to the floorboards. Chances are slim that you'll see any Tinseltown talent at the table next to you, but if you want to catch a rising star, keep an eye out for Rubicon's young chef, Scott Newman. A native New Yorker who once studied acting, Newman swapped Broadway aspirations for the culinary stage. After graduating from the California Culinary Academy, he worked with famed chef Julian Serrano and Rubicon's founding chef, Traci Des Jardins, who left to launch her own restaurant, Jardinière (see review). Newman's superb starters have included pan-seared rouget (a mild, pink-fleshed French fish) with ratatouille vegetables in a lobster broth, and a luscious lobster ravioli with spinach and chervil butter. Main courses on the French-inspired menu may include a crispy polenta cake with wild mushrooms, roasted pork loin with black-eyed peas, and halibut

with chanterelles and cranberry beans. There's also a pair of prix-fixe menus and a tasting menu. The excellent, extensive, and expensive wine list is presented by Larry Stone, one of the nation's premier sommeliers. *$$$; AE, DC, MC, V; no checks; lunch Mon–Fri, dinner Mon–Sat; full bar; reservations recommended; www.cuisine.com; map:N2* &

Rumpus / ★★☆

I TILLMAN PLACE; 415/421-2300
Located in a small cul-de-sac off Grant Avenue near Union Square, Rumpus is well known among San Francisco's cognoscenti for serving upscale California-bistro fare in an attractive, modern, and fuss-free setting. It's very popular among weekend shoppers, who stop in for lunch or dinner before heading home; many a business lunch takes place here as well. The menu offers a reasonably priced array of high-quality dishes ranging from crispy pan-roasted chicken atop fluffy mashed potatoes to a thick cut of New York steak, smoked chicken ravioli, and seasonal fresh fish. However, the most popular menu item is the puddinglike chocolate brioche cake (in fact, it's worth dining here just for the brioche). If you're a connoisseur of wine, you'll enjoy sifting through Rumpus's award-winning wine list. The only caveat is the noise level, which can get bothersome when the restaurant is full. *$$; AE, DC, MC, V; no checks; lunch Mon–Sat, dinner every day; full bar; reservations recommended; map:N3* &

Sam's Grill & Seafood Restaurant / ★

374 BUSH ST; 415/421-0594
If you want to take a trip back in time to an old-school San Francisco dining institution, head to Sam's Grill, one of the last remaining steak and seafood houses in the city. It's everything you would expect from a Raymond Chandler novel: oodles of polished mahogany, dark wood wainscoting, velvet, brass, and high-backed booths with privacy curtains and buzzers for summoning the appropriately brusque waiters. It's hugely popular with Financial District heavies, who have been coming here to conduct power lunches since 1967. Eschewing all that fancy-shmancy fusion stuff, the kitchen sticks to the same basics it's been serving for more than three decades: charbroiled fish, thick-cut steaks, fresh shellfish, and stiff pours of single-malt scotch. Start with a bowl of clam chowder followed with the sole or sand dabs, a side of creamed spinach, and for dessert, French pancakes anisette. If you're not a fan of heavy sauces, ask for yours on the side. *$$; AE, CB, DC, MC, V; no checks; lunch, dinner Mon–Fri; full bar; reservations recommended; map:N3* &

Sapporo-ya / ★

1581 WEBSTER ST; 415/563-7400

Located at one end of the Japantown shopping center, Sapporo-ya is a great place for a big, heaping bowl of soba or ramen on a Saturday afternoon. The charming little room does noodles and they do them right: the ancient noodle-making machine on display at the entrance pays homage to the house specialty. Some 10 versions of ramen are available, served with lots of tasty additions, including fresh vegetables, barbecued pork, and tempura. The noodles come in large clay bowls, piping hot and swimming with bamboo shoots, carrots, egg, and spinach. Given the quick, efficient service, you might want to stop here before taking in a movie at the Kabuki movie complex on Japantown's opposite end. *$; AE, MC, V; no checks; lunch, dinner every day; beer and wine; reservations not accepted; map:K3* &

Scala's Bistro / ★★

432 POWELL ST; 415/395-8555

Opened in 1995, Scala's Bistro immediately won an enthusiastic following by offering exceptional rustic Italian and country French cooking in a lovely, welcoming setting. Co-owners Donna and Giovanni Scala, who operate Napa's Bistro Don Giovanni, installed a golden bas-relief ceiling, amber walls, and lead-pane windows, along with brass wall sconces and Craftsman-type chandeliers that cast a warm glow reminiscent of a Mediterranean sunset. (A remarkable transformation indeed, considering this spot in the Sir Francis Drake Hotel used to be a dingy sports bar with the singularly unappetizing name of Crusty's.) Standout appetizers include grilled portobello mushrooms, crispy calamari, and sautéed veal sweetbreads. Pastas range from a dynamite persillade tagliatelle with artichokes, wild mushrooms, and truffle oil to rigatoni with veal meatballs in an oregano and tomato sauce. The seared salmon fillet with buttermilk mashed potatoes and the grilled pork loin with Yukon Gold mashed potatoes and rosemary oil are two excellent entrees; risottos, salads, and pizzas round out the menu. Portions are generous, but do try to save room for dessert such as the Chocolate I.V. (layers of chocolate ice-cream cake and mousse encased in a toasted butter-pecan crust) and the Bostini cream pie (creamy vanilla custard topped with orange chiffon cake and a warm chocolate glaze). *$$; AE, DC, DIS, MC, V; no checks; breakfast, lunch, dinner every day; full bar; reservations recommended; map:M3* &

Sears Fine Food / ★★

439 POWELL ST; 415/986-1160

Sears is your classic San Francisco–American coffee shop, where the decor and the staff haven't changed since the Nixon administration. Story has it that Sears first opened in 1938 when Ben the Clown decided to retire from the circus and open his own restaurant. His Swedish wife, Hilbur, chipped in her family's secret recipe (still a secret to this day) for Swedish pancakes (18 silver dollars to a serving), and there's been a line out the door every weekend morning ever since. Some might call it tacky, but there's something comforting about the matronly waitresses in their pink uniforms serving classic American food and the booths covered with pink vinyl tablecloths. If pancakes aren't your thing, try the crispy dark-brown waffles or sourdough French toast. The fresh fruit cup marinated in orange juice is also quite popular. Lunch is served as well, but it's the classic breakfast experience that makes Sears worth the wait. *$; cash only; breakfast, lunch Thurs–Mon; no alcohol; reservations accepted; map:M3* &

Shalimar / ★

532 JONES ST; 415/928-0333

If you're searching for truly authentic Indian fare, and you don't mind venturing into an area that is a bit beyond unsavory, Shalimar is for you. It's located right in the heart of the Tenderloin, and that may be the only reason it hasn't been overrun by yuppies. Because when it comes to tandoori lamb and chicken and beef skewers, Shalimar does it with a skill that can only be learned from the homeland. The flatbreads are warm and delicious. But the place really is all about the food: linoleum and glaring lights dominate the decor, and service is strictly from the counter. Yet from the minute you step inside, the aroma will be your reward for braving the neighborhood. And what they save on interior design, they pass on to you: some items are less than $3! *$; cash only; lunch, dinner every day; no alcohol; reservations not accepted; map:M3*

Shanghai 1930 / ★★

133 STEUART ST; 415/896-5600

Experience the cosmopolitan and exotic lifestyle of pre–Communist China at Shanghai 1930. A deco entrance leads to this below-street-level restaurant. You'll walk past a packed bar with a live jazz band; behind the bar is a dazzling 40-foot backlit aquamarine mirror, with rows of silhouetted bottles. This classy restaurant serves upscale Chinese food in beautiful presentations: minced duck in lettuce with water chestnuts, celery, mushrooms, and (a Mediterranean twist) kalamata olives in plum sauce; stacked baskets of dim sum—little pillows of pork, chopped scallops, and shrimp, with three dipping sauces; rock cod garnished with fresh red grapes and a red-wine-and-soy reduction sauce; chicken breast stir-fried with fresh lily bulbs in a black-bean sauce; and pretty prawns cooked in a bright red-bean chili sauce. Decadent desserts are both Western- and Chinese-style—from warm chocolate cake to fried banana flambé—and change seasonally. Owner George Chen also started Betelnut (see review), a popular pan-Asian beer house on Union Street, and the Long Life Noodle Co. & Jook Joint in the Soma area. Shanghai 1930 is his most glamorous restaurant so far, with service and cuisine to match. *$$$; AE, MC, V; no checks; dinner every day; full bar; reservations recommended; map:O3* &

The Slanted Door / ★★★

584 VALENCIA ST; 415/861-8032

Thank goodness chef Charles Phan abandoned his original plan to build a crepe stand in San Francisco, because otherwise we never would have had the opportunity to sink our teeth into his superb green papaya salad or stir-fried caramelized shrimp. When Phan and his large extended family discovered a vacant (and affordable) space on a slightly run-down stretch of Valencia Street, they ditched the crepery plan in late 1995 and transformed the high-ceilinged room into a small, bilevel restaurant specializing in country Vietnamese food. Phan's design talents (he's a former UC Berkeley architecture student) are evident from the moment you enter the stylish, narrow dining room and take a seat at one of his green-stained wood tables. But even more impressive is Phan's unique fare, which attracts droves of people for lunch and dinner. The dinner menu changes weekly to reflect the market's offerings, but look for the favored spring rolls stuffed with fresh shrimp and pork; crab and asparagus soup; caramelized shrimp; curried chicken cooked with yams; "shaking" beef sautéed with onion and garlic; any of the terrific clay pot dishes; and, of course, Phan's special Vietnamese crepes. When business is booming the service gets slow, but if you order a pinot gris from the very good wine list, you won't mind so much. For dessert, the hands-down favorite is the all-American chocolate cake. Go figure. *$-$$; MC, V; no checks; lunch, dinner Tues–Sun; beer and wine; reservations recommended; eat@slanteddoor.com; map:L6* &

Slow Club / ★★☆

2501 MARIPOSA ST; 415/241-9390

Hidden away in the city's happening Multimedia Gulch is the hard-to-find Slow Club. Though small, this sleek restaurant with its cool cement floors, metal railings, and stark design exudes urban chic. And this isn't the only thing that draws a loyal following: the California cuisine is top-notch. Lunch and dinner are equally good. During the day the juicy Niman Ranch burgers and oven-roasted potatoes served with aioli are favorites. Even the crisp Caesar salad hits the mark. You can also choose from an ever-changing selection of consistently fresh and tasty tapaslike small plates. Prices at dinner are higher, but the food remains impeccably fresh and well prepared. Various roasted chicken dishes, succulent pork chops served with seasonal ingredients, and rosemary-infused leg of lamb might be typical fall offerings on the daily-changing menu. This still-hip neighborhood spot is well worth a visit, even if only for a cocktail and appetizers at the small bar. *$$; MC, V; no checks; lunch Mon–Fri, dinner Tues–Sat, brunch Sat–Sun; full bar; reservations not accepted; map:M6* &

South Park Cafe / ★★☆

108 SOUTH PARK; 415/495-7275

If you're fond of Parisian-style cafes you'll adore the South Park Cafe, one of our favorite lunch spots in the city. Located on the north side of South Park—a small patch of grass in the heart of SoMa's Internet community—this popular cafe with its pale yellow walls, French-accented wait staff, copper-lined bar, and assortment of French newspapers hanging on racks has a distinct European ambience to complement the authentic French cuisine. Popular dishes range from steamed mussels sautéed in white wine to roasted duck breast with lavender sauce, grilled steak served with thin pommes frites, and (but of course) grilled rabbit—all at moderate prices. One caveat: The noisy lunch crowd gets rather thick from about 12:30–2pm. *$$; AE, MC, V; no checks; breakfast, lunch Mon–Fri, dinner Mon–Sat; full bar; reservations recommended; map:O4* &

Stars / ★★

555 GOLDEN GATE AVE; 415/861-7827

Celebrity chef Jeremiah Tower opened this restaurant years ago and saw that it lived up to its name. The local luminati—politicos, movie stars, socialites—packed the place. The star faded, however, and Tower left for more glamorous pastures. But he left the restaurant's name behind, and the new owners have been quick to capitalize on that, giving the place a sleek, modern update, with clean lines and low-slung fixtures that provide great sight lines. The bar (purportedly the longest in the city) is once again a high-profile gathering spot, and the restaurant is also regaining its luster. New chef Christopher Fernandez makes fine use of the massive open kitchen, turning out rustic, Italian-inspired dishes from the wood-burning grill, rotisserie, and oven. The menu changes seasonally, but usually features good spit-roasted chicken and pork loin and a delicious grilled fish of the day. The soups, pastas, and small plates (including an excellent duck confit) are a good bet as well. The wine list is lengthy and well arranged; several selections are offered by the glass. *$; AE, DC, MC, V; no checks; lunch, dinner every day; full bar; reservations recommended; map:L4* &

Stinking Rose / ★

325 COLUMBUS AVE; 415/781-7673

"We season our garlic with food," boasts the menu at the Stinking Rose, one of the most popular tourist restaurants in North Beach. Everything, from the ice cream to soup to pizzas, salads, pastas, and meats, is given a healthy infusion of garlic. It's a high-energy, festive place decorated with black-and-white checkered floors, large windows overlooking the street, and lots of hanging strands of garlic. Actually, you can smell the Stinking Rose before you can see it: the garlicky aroma wafting down Columbus Avenue has become a North Beach fixture. As with most theme restaurants, the cuisine doesn't strive for greatness, but we have ferreted out a few favorites, including the garlic-steamed clams and mussels, the garlic pizza, the 40-clove garlic chicken, and the Stinking Special, braised rabbit served with garlic mashed potatoes (naturally). If you're into this sort of dining experience, you'll love the place; if not, then head down the road to L'Osteria del Forno (see review). *$$; AE, DC, JCB, MC, V; no checks; lunch, dinner every day; full bar; reservations recommended; map:N2* &

Straits Cafe / ★★

3300 GEARY BLVD; 415/668-1783

There are a handful of restaurants worth venturing all the way out to the Richmond District for, and Straits is definitely one of them. Owner-chef Chris Yeo delivers a knockout combination of authentic and fantastic Singaporean dishes (a combination of Indian, Malaysian, Indonesian, and Chinese cuisines) in a kitschy yet clever setting that resembles a Singapore village. Burlap palm trees, pastel-painted murals, faux balconies, and clotheslines strung across the walls set the stage for Yeo's multicultural meal. It takes several trips to Straits to become even remotely familiar with the menu, but the white-jacketed wait staff is adept at deducing your culinary tolerance. A recommended starter is the *murtabak* (Indian bread stuffed with spiced onion and beef), and if you like it hot and spicy then try the *ikan pangang* (fish stuffed with a chili paste) or the even-hotter *sambal udang* (prawns sautéed in chili-shallot sambal sauce). Other popular dishes are the salmon wrapped in banana leaves and the fried rice with prawns and mixed vegetables. Start the feast with a tropical drink and end it with the *sago* tapioca pudding or the *bo bo cha cha* (taro root and sweet potato in sweetened coconut milk). *$$; AE, DC, MC, V; no checks; lunch, dinner every day; full bar; reservations recommended; map:I4* &

Suppenkuche / ★★

601 HAYES ST; 415/252-9289

 Come here hungry and thirsty. Smack in the middle of the hip and trendy Hayes Valley is a little slice of Deutschland, a German *wursthaus* whose authenticity runs from the bratwurst to the beers to the volume level.

Everything here is large and hearty. Favorites include the potato soup and the potato pancakes to start, then the Wiener schnitzel and the *Gebratene Rehmedaillions* (venison medallions in red-wine plum sauce). Brunches are very popular and include massive omelets with a plateful of potatoes and roast pork sausages in an egg scramble. But the biggest draw has to be the beer, served in giant-size steins and running the gamut from Hefe (three kinds) to Pils (four varieties) to bock (two types). It's all served on tap, and there are also a couple of Belgian and English brands just to keep things even. *$; AE, MC, V; no checks; dinner every day, brunch Sat–Sun; full bar; reservations recommended; map:L4*

Sushi Groove / ★

1916 HYDE ST; 415/440-1905

It's hard to decide which looks better: the restaurant or the clientele. Whatever the case, this handsome sushi spot is populated by an attractive (and sizable) crowd. Small, chic, modern, and well lit, the room fits in perfectly with its Russian Hill surroundings. Good music usually permeates the air. And while you might think a place that takes its appearance so seriously could never follow through on substance, the sushi is fresh, well cut, and nicely presented. All the requisite rolls and pieces are on the menu; a few good variations do exist, however, such as the jungle roll (yellowtail tuna and papaya) and the monkey roll (sea urchin with eel and avocado). A nice selection of fine sakes is available, too. Service is friendly, welcoming, and typically as good-looking as the clientele. *$$; AE, CB, DC, MC, V; no checks; dinner every day; full bar; reservations not accepted; map:L2* &

Swan Oyster Depot / ★★☆

1517 POLK ST; 415/673-1101

You won't find white linen tablecloths at this oyster bar—in fact, you won't even find any tables. Since 1912, patrons have balanced themselves on the 19 hard, rickety stools lining the long, narrow marble counter cluttered with bowls of oyster crackers, fresh-cut lemons, napkin holders, Tabasco sauce, and other seasonings. On the opposite side stands a quick-shucking team of some of the most congenial men in town, always ready and eager to serve. Lunch specialties include Boston clam chowder, sizable salads (crab, shrimp, prawn, or a combo), seafood cocktails, cracked Dungeness crab, lobster, and smoked salmon and trout. If you want to take home some fish for supper, take a gander at all the fresh offerings in the display case: salmon, swordfish, delta crawfish, red snapper, trout, shrimp, lingcod, and whatever else the boat brought in that day. *$$; no credit cards; checks OK; lunch Mon–Sat (open 8am–5:30pm); beer and wine; reservations not accepted; map:L3* &

Tadich Grill / ★★

240 CALIFORNIA ST; 415/391-1849

The Tadich Grill is one of the most venerated and venerable seafood restaurants in California and, along with Sam's Grill & Seafood Restaurant (see review), one of the last "old San Francisco" restaurants left in the city. It's supposedly been open in one form or another since 1849 and claims to be the very first to have broiled seafood over mesquite charcoal, back in the early 1920s. The original mahogany bar still remains, as do the classic private booths, dim lighting, and crusty old white-jacketed waiters (expect brusque service—that's their job). It's hugely popular with both tourists and Financial District heavies, and is a refreshing change from all the trendy restaurants that surround it. The best dishes are the ones that forgo the heavy sauces, such as the shrimp or prawn Louis salad, the seafood cioppino, or the best-selling charcoal-broiled petrale sole with butter sauce. If you're not counting calories, feast on the baked casserole of stuffed turbot with crab and shrimp à la Newburg. Most dishes come with a side of fried potatoes and, you guessed it, sourdough bread. *$$; MC, V; no checks; lunch, dinner Mon–Sat; full bar; reservations not accepted; map:N2* &

Taqueria Cancun / ★

3211 MISSION ST; 415/550-1414

In spite of itself, this taqueria has a huge loyal following. It does little to keep people coming back other than offer incredibly flavorful Mexican dishes à la carte and at bargain-basement prices. Its location, on a decidedly unseemly stretch of Mission Street, makes for some unusual characters coming through the doors. But that's part of the Cancun experience, second only to the incredible *carne asada* burritos and tacos and the hot, fresh-made salsas. The *carnitas* are another reason it's worth putting up with the occasional dining-room argument that can ignite in this place. *$; cash only; breakfast, lunch, dinner every day; beer only; reservations not accepted; map:L6*

Tavolino / ★★

401 COLUMBUS AVE; 415/392-1472

Tavolino, the latest from the husband-and-wife team behind Enrico's (see review) and US Restaurant, is ideal for people-watching through the large floor-to-ceiling windows on bustling Columbus Avenue. The dark-oak trim, terra-cotta floors, and warm yellow walls create an airy and visually stunning space. Start with a cocktail at the handsome oak bar or ask the professional and attentive wait staff for a recommendation from the list of well-priced Italian varietals. Tavolino brings the Italian equivalent of tapas to North Beach. The menu features almost 40 intriguing *cicchetti* (pronounced chee-KET-tee, it means "savory little tastes"). But with the exception of a flavorful amarone-braised duck with creamy polenta, many of the hot plates fall short. You'll fare better with the cold selections. An altogether original pickled salmon is worth a try, a colorful and refreshing corn-and-tomato medley hits the spot, and a well balanced spinach, endive, and pancetta preparation is pretty tasty, too. The Venetian *tramezzini* (little sandwiches) are also good bets. For dessert, an absolutely decadent chocolate espresso torte more than satisfies any chocoholic's cravings, or try the richly satisfying zabaglione paired with perfectly ripe fruit. *$$; AE, DC, MC, V; no checks; lunch, dinner every day; full bar; reservations recommended; map:N2* &

Terra Brazilis / ★★

602 HAYES ST; 415/241-1900

At this contemporary restaurant that sits beneath a senior citizens center, chef-owner Alberto Petrolino endeavors to take Brazilian cuisine to tastier, healthier heights. The small place, bound on two sides by huge windows, its walls hung with original work by local artists, has become enormously popular in its relatively short existence. This is mostly due to Petrolino's skill at such dishes as curried shellfish stew with prawns and baby clams, as well as his use of *vatapa* sauce, a Brazilian mainstay made with peanuts and curry spices. But Petrolino hasn't really shown us anything new—rather, he's made his restaurant popular with his no-nonsense approach, his nutrition-conscious preparations, and his flavor combinations. The wine list is excellent, with lots of Spanish varietals, and the wait staff is knowledgeable enough to make informed recommendations. There is a full bar, though it seats only three at a time. *$$; AE, MC, V; no checks; dinner Tues–Sun; full bar; reservations recommended; map:L4*

Thai House / ★
Thai House Bar and Cafe / ★

151 NOE ST; 415/863-0374
2200 MARKET ST; 415/864-5006

The very popular Thai House restaurant has a loyal following in its Noe Valley neighborhood. The atmosphere is friendly and while the fare is a bit predictable, it's also predictably good: the kitchen regularly turns out tasty spicy shrimp rolls, a savory sirloin served with spinach and peanut sauce, excellent chicken satay, and delicious pan-fried shrimp. A satellite outlet, the Thai House Bar and Cafe on Market Street in the Castro district, offers the same menu with less consistency but in a more sociable environment. *$; MC, V; no checks; dinner every day (Noe St); lunch, dinner every day (Market St); beer and wine (Noe St); full bar (Market St); reservations not accepted; map:K6, K5*

Thep Phanom / ★★★

400 WALLER ST; 415/431-2526

Thailand's complex, spicy, cosmopolitan cuisine has always been adaptive, incorporating flavors from India, China, Burma, Malaysia, and, more recently, the West. San Francisco boasts dozens of Thai restaurants; virtually all of them are good, and many (including Khan Toke Thai House and Manora's Thai Cuisine) are excellent. Why, then, does Thep Phanom alone have a permanent line out its front door even though it takes reservations? At this restaurant, a creative touch of California enters the cultural mix, resulting in sophisticated preparations that have a special sparkle. The signature dish, *ped swan*, is a boneless duck in a light honey sauce served on a bed of spinach—and it ranks with the city's greatest entrees. Tart, minty, spicy *yum plamuk* (calamari salad), *larb ped* (minced duck salad), coconut chicken soup, and the velvety basil-spiked seafood curry served on banana leaves (available Wednesday and Thursday only) are superb choices, too. Service is charming and efficient; the tasteful decor, informal atmosphere, eclectic crowd, and discerning wine list are all very San Francisco. *$$; AE, DC, DIS, MC, V; no checks; dinner every day; beer and wine; reservations recommended; map:K5* &

Thirsty Bear Brewing Company / ★★

661 HOWARD ST; 415/974-0905

Stupid name, yes, but great house-made microbrews and authentic Spanish tapas have made Thirsty Bear one of SoMa's most popular after-work hangouts for the late 20- to 30-something crowd of artists, techies, and brokers. The split-level restaurant/brewery is housed in a high-ceilinged brick warehouse that's been given an industrial-chic makeover with little regard to sound dampening (during happy hour it can get really noisy in here). Our preference is to sit at the bar and order from the dinner menu, though we always know what we want well ahead of time: the paella Valenciana, a sizzling combo of chicken, shrimp, sausage, shellfish, and saffron-laden rice served in a cast-iron skillet, and a *tortilla de patatas* appetizer to tide us over. Other recommended dishes emanating from the open kitchen are the *escalivada* (roasted vegetables served at room temperature), the *espinacas à la Catalana* (spinach sautéed with garlic, pine nuts, and raisins), and the fish cheeks. If you're visiting the San Francisco Museum of Modern Art, we highly recommend you walk around the corner and stop in here for a light meal and a tall, cool glass of India Pale Ale. *$$; AE, DC, MC, V; no checks; lunch Mon–Sat, dinner every day; full bar; reservations recommended; map:N3* &

Ti Couz / ★★☆

3108 16TH ST; 415/252-7373

Other restaurants offer crepes, but none compare to what this popular Mission District establishment does with the beloved French pancake.

The now-expanded Ti Couz serves delectable, Brittany-style sweet and savory crepes in a homey setting that feels very much like an old French inn. Don't be overwhelmed by the menu: though countless ingredients are listed so you can create your own, the menu (in French and English) lists several suggestions. Entree recommendations include ham and cheese, mushroom-almond, and much more. A ratatouille-and-cheese creation bursts with flavor, and a hearty sausage-filled pancake won't disappoint. But be forewarned: the large buckwheat crepes are *très énormes*! And you must leave room for dessert. The sweet wheat-flour crepes, fluffier than the savory buckwheat versions, are ideal for luscious fillings such as apple, ice cream, and caramel, or fresh berries à la mode. Complete the meal with a choice of several hard ciders served in bowls— the fruity flavors complement this unique and tasty fare like nothing else. You can also choose from a list of French wines or Celtic beers. *$; MC, V; no checks; lunch, dinner every day; full bar; reservations not accepted; map:L6* ⅏

Timo's / ★★☆

842 VALENCIA ST; 415/647-0558

Tapas bars are plentiful these days, but despite the growing competition, Timo's remains one of San Francisco's best. The exuberant food matches the vibrancy of the purple-and-orange-painted walls, and the happenin' Valencia Street location draws a varied crowd, from Mission hipsters to Marina-ites. These "little plates" of food go especially well with Timo's popular sangría, or you can choose from a small list of Spanish wines. Start with a sampling of both hot and cold plates and be sure to try Spain's best-known tapa, the *tortilla espagnola*, a simple dish of layered potatoes and onions. A delicious Catalán-style spinach tapa brimming with pine nuts, raisins, and apricots combines incredible flavors and textures. The mushroom preparations are always enjoyable, especially the hot grilled mushroom plate with a hearty dose of garlic. Other favorites include potato decadence—creamy Yukon Gold potatoes layered with earthy mushrooms—and ahi ceviche with avocado. A flamenco guitarist adds a festive note on Thursday evenings to this already lively hot spot. *$$; AE, MC, V; no checks; dinner every day; full bar; reservations recommended; map:L6* ⅏

Tommaso Ristorante Italiano / ★

1042 KEARNY ST; 415/398-9696

It's just off the main Broadway strip, sandwiched in between "adult entertainment" arcades. So it's at first surprising to find that Tommaso's comes highly recommended for family dining. The small, cozy place with wooden booths and no windows regularly has folks lining up at the door. The restaurant has endeared itself to locals by consistently turning out amazingly delicious traditional-style pizzas, available with any of 19 different toppings and baked in an oak-burning brick oven—all at rock-bottom prices. While pizzas are the main draw, the hearty Italian classics such as chicken cacciatore and a super-cheesy lasagne should not be overlooked. Order a bottle of chianti for the table and you're in business. Service is quick, efficient, and downright neighborly. A true San Francisco treasure. *$; AE, DC, MC, V; local checks only; dinner Tues–Sun; full bar; reservations not accepted; map:N2*

Tommy Toy's / ★★★

655 MONTGOMERY ST; 415/397-4888

Tommy Toy's is so lavish in every manner that it's almost surreal. It's sort of a cross between a plush men's club, a fancy Chinese restaurant, and a four-star French restaurant. The $1.5 million dining room was fashioned after a 19th-century empress dowager's reading room, complete with dimly lit candelabras, museum-quality artwork, and oodles of opulence. The stellar service is equally impressive, but of course such niceties don't come cheap. Expect to pay about $50 per person for Tommy's signature dinner: a prix-fixe, six-course, French-Chinese fusion feast of minced squab in lettuce leaves, lobster bisque served in a coconut shell and topped with puffed pastry, a whole lobster sautéed with peanuts and mushrooms, duck served with plum sauce, medallions of beef, and a coup de grâce dessert of peach mousse. Dining at Tommy's isn't something one does with regularity, but it's certainly worth a visit if only to experience that rarest of the rare—haute Chinese. *$$$; AE, DC, DIS, JCB, MC, V; no checks; lunch Mon–Fri, dinner every day; full bar; reservations recommended; map:N2* &

Tokyo Go Go / ★★

3174 16TH ST; 415/864-2288

The owner of Ace Wasabi's in the Marina district figured the success he's had there could surely be duplicated in the Mission. So he opened Tokyo Go Go and gave it a retro-futuristic look, with quirky fixtures and smooth surfaces. His Marina loyalists followed, but they quickly gave way to residents of the area, who now populate this fun, lively spot. Fun is the order of the day here. The sushi is fresh and flavorful and you'll find all the standard selections. But the kitchen likes to cut loose, too, and if you are willing to experiment, you'll find some surprises. The Go Go Roll places cooked shrimp over a roll of cucumber that wraps a garlic crouton. The Tuscan Roll features salmon, cucumber, sun-dried tomatoes, basil, and capers rolled with rice in a cone of seaweed—hard to imagine, easy to eat. Or try the Flying Kamikaze: spicy tuna and asparagus topped by albacore tuna and ponzu sauce. The bar serves premium sakes in martini glasses garnished with cucumber slices. This is certainly not your typical sushi joint. *$; MC, V; no checks; dinner Tues–Sun; full bar; reservations recommended; map:L6*

Ton Kiang / ★★

5821 GEARY BLVD; 415/387-8273

Ton Kiang has established a solid reputation in San Francisco as one of the best Chinese restaurants in the city, particularly when it comes to dim sum and Hakka cuisine (a mixture of Chinese cuisines, sometimes referred to as "China's soul food," developed by a nomadic Chinese tribe). Ton Kiang's dim sum is phenomenal—fresh, flavorful, and not the least bit greasy (tip: on weekends ask for a table by the kitchen door to get first dibs from the dim sum carts). Other proven dishes on the regular menu are the ethereal steamed dumplings, chicken wonton soup, house special beef and fish-ball soup (better than it sounds), fried spring rolls, steamed salt-baked chicken with a scallion and ginger sauce (a famous though quite salty Hakka dish), and any of the stuffed tofu or clay pot dishes (a.k.a. Hakka casseroles). *$$; AE, DC, MC, V; no checks; lunch, dinner every day; beer and wine; reservations recommended; map:G4* &

Tu Lan / ★☆

8 6TH ST; 415/626-0927

If you're a fan of hole-in-the-wall ethnic dives in seedy locations that serve top-notch food at bargain prices, have we got a gem for you. Located in one of the sketchiest and foulest-smelling parts of the city, Tu Lan is a greasy, grimy little Vietnamese diner that, unless you are hip to the secret, you would neither find nor frequent. Which makes it all the more bewildering that a drawing of Julia Child's unmistakable face graces the cover of the greasy menus, but apparently she's one of Tu Lan's biggest fans. And once you try the light, fresh imperial rolls served on a bed of rice noodles, lettuce, peanuts, and mint, you'll become one too. Other recommended dishes include the lemon beef salad, the fried fish in ginger sauce, and the pork kebabs, though pointing at whatever looks good on the Formica counter works just as well. Note: The faint-of-heart may want to order to go, and definitely *do not* use the upstairs bathroom (that's a dare, of course). *$; cash only; lunch, dinner Mon–Sat; beer and wine; reservations not accepted; map:M4*

2223 Restaurant and Bar / ★★☆

2223 MARKET ST; 415/431-0692

Also known as the No Name, this popular Castro district spot has been packing in the crowds because it's one of the first upscale restaurants in the area that offers serious food, friendly and professional service, and a terrific bar scene. You'll see only the restaurant's address on the outside of the building, so look for a red exterior and a lively crowd visible through large storefront windows. A long bar flanked by a mural dominates one side of the restaurant. You'll probably end up waiting there for a table, which will give you time to enjoy the great cosmopolitans and martinis. Across the room, the narrow dining area has wood tables, bistro chairs, and cushioned banquettes. The menu is as eclectic as the crowd—mostly American-Mediterranean, with Southwestern and Southeast Asian touches. The romaine salad is a great Caesar variation, with capers, thinly sliced cornichons, and smoky onions. Try one of the pizzas, such as the pancetta, onion confit, Teleme cheese, marjoram, and sun-dried tomato pesto version. For entrees, the kitchen serves generous portions of comfort food: juicy pan-roasted chicken with garlic mashed potatoes, grilled salmon with lemon-caviar fondue, and sliced lamb sirloin fanned on a ragout of fava beans and fresh artichoke hearts. Indulge in the Louisiana crème brûlée with pecan pralines for dessert. Despite the noise from the bar, 2223 Market is a terrific neighborhood spot—especially if you can find a nearby parking place. *$$; AE, DC, MC, V; local checks OK; dinner every day, brunch Sun; full bar; reservations recommended; map:K5* &

Universal Cafe / ★★★

2814 19TH ST; 415/821-4608
The Universal Cafe is the kind of place you would kill to have on your block. First off, the industrial-art decor is extremely sleek, suave, and chic and the staff is refreshingly sans attitude. Second, you can actually find parking in this quiet section of the Inner Mission. And third, the food is both fantastic and reasonably priced. Truly, this is one of those out-of-the-way gems that either you discover by accident or someone sends you to. For lunch, try the salmon sandwich on focaccia (outstanding), gourmet thin-crust pizza, or one of the wickedly good salads. Dinner gets more serious: braised duck leg on a bed of creamy polenta; sea bass served with risotto, spinach, and caramelized onions; pot roast with lumpy mashed potatoes and fresh veggies; pan-roasted filet mignon. If your dish doesn't come with it, ask for a side of the addictive mashed potatoes. Trust us—if you're anywhere near the Mission or Potrero Hill, seek this place out and join the converted. *$$; AE, MC, V; no checks; breakfast, lunch, dinner every day; beer and wine; reservations recommended; map:L6* &

The Waterfront Restaurant & Cafe / ★★☆

PIER 7 (ON THE EMBARCADERO NEAR BROADWAY); 415/391-2696
In a city that has some of the most spectacular vistas in the world, it's surprising how few restaurants there are with grand views of the bay. Let's rephrase that: how few *good* restaurants there are with grand views of the bay. In its previous life the Waterfront was just another lousy tourist restaurant, but after a $3 million-plus makeover in 1997 and a new menu, it's now one of the darlings of the restaurant scene. The combination of Bay Bridge views, sunny patio, and handsome high-ceilinged dining room is the perfect setting for a romantic evening. The lunch menu, served at the adjoining cafe, offers a wide selection of choices:

excellent salads and pizzas, wood-fired grill items, Maine blue crab cakes, grilled apricot-glazed quail, and house favorites such as falafel-crusted sea bass and sautéed chicken breast with herbed polenta and rosemary pan sauce. The dinner menu is equally impressive: Kasu-marinated filet of beef with taro gnocchi, tatsoi and shiitake relish, and soy consommé; roasted squab with potato and wild rice galette and Bing cherry chutney; and Sonoma lamb carpaccio. Be sure to arrive before sunset to admire the view. *$$$; AE, DC, MC, V; no checks; lunch Mon–Fri (cafe every day), dinner every day; full bar; reservations recommended; map:N2* &

Woodward's Garden / ★★★

1700 MISSION ST; 415/621-7122
In what is arguably one of the least desired commercial spaces in the city stands what is certainly one of the Bay Area's best restaurants. Woodward's Garden is tucked under a busy highway overpass on a gritty, windy, noisy corner of Mission Street at Duboce Avenue. But that doesn't deter those who reserve one of the diminutive restaurant's 11 tables at least a couple of weeks in advance for a weekend night (there are four seatings per night). To say Woodward's Garden has an open kitchen is putting it mildly—the kitchen takes up at least half the room and the handful of tables are lined up around it. Not only can you see and smell your food being prepared, but you can feel the heat of the flames! Chef-owners Margie Conard (from Postrio) and Dana Tommasino (from Greens) offer an American/Mediterranean–influenced menu featuring five appetizers and five entrees. The menu changes weekly; a recent visit started with a savory sweet-potato–ginger soup with a dollop of crème fraîche, smoked trout bruschetta with Romesco sauce and arugula, and perfectly sautéed scallops served with endive, Meyer lemon beurre blanc, and caviar. The entrees were equally delightful: a fork-tender lamb shank braised with fennel and orange was nestled on a bed of saffron risotto with asparagus and Reggiano, and a duck breast was roasted to perfection and paired with grilled polenta, a cherry-onion marmalade, and braised chard. Bravo! *$$$; MC, V; checks OK; dinner every day; beer and wine; reservations required; map:L5* &

XYZ / ★

181 3RD ST; 415/817-7836
The W Hotel was the first ground-up hotel to open in San Francisco in more than a decade. The restaurant inside, cleverly named XYZ, has been wildly popular with visitors and locals alike, all of whom seem to resemble characters from whatever urban-setting sitcom is currently tops in the ratings. The place itself is adequately chic and stylish, and the service is never as austere as you'd expect given the rarefied surroundings. Chef Alison Richman was stolen from the kitchen at Jardinière, and here

she excels at preparing light, flavorful dishes with French and Asian accents. Good dinner choices might include the peppered ahi on mushroom potatoes and the broiled sea bass. The entree selection is a bit limited, however, so you may opt to order from among the many excellent soups, salads, and pastas instead. If you're staying at the W, order breakfast here—which actually offers the best menu of the three meals. *$$; AE, CB, DC, DIS, MC, V; no checks; breakfast, lunch, dinner every day; full bar; reservations recommended; map:N3* &

Yank Sing / ★★★

427 BATTERY ST; 415/781-1111 OR 415/362-1640
49 STEVENSON ST; 415/541-4949

Living on the edge of the Pacific Rim has its advantages. For example, the best dim sum in the United States is probably served in the Bay Area. Yank Sing's fare is as good as any dim sum you'll get in Hong Kong, and the prices (and service) are much better than in nearby Harbor Village Restaurant (see review). Numerous servers wander past your table with carts bearing steamer baskets, bowls, and tureens. If you want some, just nod. Yank Sing serves more than 90 varieties of dim sum, including such standards as pot stickers, spring rolls, plump shrimp, crab, fried eggplant, and bao (steamed buns stuffed with aromatically seasoned minced meat). The barbecued chicken is a house specialty, although some find it too sweet; other favorites are Peking duck (served by the slice), minced squab in lettuce cups, and soft-shell crab. Make reservations or prepare to wait and wait and wait, especially for a weekend brunch. Takeout is available, too, and it costs much less. Another (though less popular) branch of Yank Sing is located in the SoMa district. *$$; AE, DC, MC, V; no checks; lunch every day, brunch Sat–Sun; beer and wine; reservations recommended; www.yanksing.com; map:N2, N3* &

Zarzuela / ★★★

2000 HYDE ST; 415/346-0800

You can't miss it—nobody passes the huge yellow awning out front without noticing. You also can't park here: the crowded Hyde Street location means nobody should even try to drive to Zarzuela. But this excellent tapas spot atop Russian Hill has been popular since day one. Drenched in soothing colors, this is an elegant, sophisticated spot for well-priced Spanish cuisine. Fresh bread and Spanish olives are whisked to your table as soon as you sit down. And from there the noshing begins. The tapas recipes are not extraordinarily original, but they are prepared with fresh ingredients and a liberal use of seasonings that sets them apart from the usual tapas fare. The paella is excellent, arguably the best in town; it's available only for two or more and requires a 30-minute wait—but it's more than worth it. Zarzuela takes its name from one of the menu's dishes, a traditional seafood stew that has become this restaurant's trademark. *$; DC, MC, V; no checks; dinner Tues–Sat; full bar; reservations not accepted; map:M2* &

Zax / ★★☆

2330 TAYLOR ST; 415/563-6266

If you're a lover of fresh and stylish food, you'll rejoice over many of the creations at Zax, a sophisticated California-Mediterranean restaurant tucked away in North Beach. Owned by husband-and-wife duo Barbara Mulas and Mark Drazek, who met at the California Culinary Academy, Zax offers a chic but understated interior and a charming blend of casual, often excellent cuisine. The small, seasonal menu changes monthly, but it's always healthy and well balanced, with an emphasis on quality and flavor as opposed to heavy sauces. The house specialty appetizer is the warm, puffy, and golden-brown twice-baked goat-cheese soufflé. Don't miss it. The simple but savory salads range from tomato, feta, and olives with oregano-flecked olive oil to romaine leaves dressed with anchovies, lemon, garlic, and Romano cheese. The half-dozen main courses might include lamb stew with grilled rosemary polenta and roasted tomatoes, sweet roasted Sonoma duck breast with a grilled-fig vinaigrette, and spicy short ribs with horseradish mashed potatoes. *$$$; MC, V; no checks; dinner Tues–Sun; beer and wine; reservations recommended; map:M1* &

Zazie / ★★

941 COLE ST; 415/564-5332

As the Cole Valley neighborhood's popularity grows with the 20-something crowd, so do the lines for Sunday brunch at Zazie. In fact, on weekend mornings the wait for a table on the cozy patio can take as long as an hour. Catherine Opoix's cheery French bistro, with its inviting dining room, checkerboard floors, and light and airy ambience, serves tasty (if somewhat inconsistent) fare. Breakfast is served daily until 2:30pm; a reliable favorite is the gingerbread pancakes served with roasted pears and a tangy lemon curd. The egg dishes, though decent, sound better than they taste; they range from eggs valence (fried eggs served atop grilled eggplant and chèvre) to a changing omelet option, accompanied by slightly bland potatoes. Lunch features such simple *plats du jour* as a grilled tuna sandwich, salade niçoise, or a tomato-fennel soup. Dinner specialties include a Provençal fish soup of mussels and snapper topped with Gruyère cheese; a hearty coq au vin; and pork medallions with honey-braised cabbage and fresh plum sauce. To add to Zazie's European-style charm, opera singers and jazz musicians perform on Sunday evenings. In temperate weather, the patio offers some of the best outdoor dining in the city. *$$; MC, V; no checks; breakfast Mon–Sat, lunch Mon–Fri, dinner every day, brunch Sat–Sun; beer and wine; reservations not accepted; map:I5*

Zinzino / ★★★

2355 CHESTNUT ST; 415/346-6623

Owner Zen Zankel took a huge gamble opening up yet another trendy Italian restaurant in the Marina district, but there's no better recipe for success than exceptional food and reasonable prices, and that's exactly what Zankel and chef Andrea Rappaport have accomplished. The long, narrow trattoria is smartly arranged for such a small space (it used to be a laundromat). At the entrance is a small wine bar where you'll often find Zankel greeting customers, followed by the main dining room, the exhibition kitchen, and a cute little heated patio in the back. Though the menu changes seasonally, there are a few dishes that we hope they'll never take off the menu, such as the crispy calamari with a choice of herbed aioli or tomato sauce, the shaved-fennel-and-mint salad, and the roasted jumbo prawns wrapped in crisp pancetta and bathed in a tangy balsamic reduction sauce. Rappaport puts her wood-fired oven to good use; her roasted half chicken is one of the most tender and flavorful we've ever tasted, and the accompanying goat-cheese salad and potato frisée are the perfect touch. Rappaport also offers weekly rotating specials such as her oven-roasted half lobster, roasted shellfish platter, and baby lamb chops. *$$; AE, DC, MC, V; no checks; dinner every day; beer and wine; reservations recommended; map:J1* ⅃

Zodiac Club / ★

718 14TH ST; 415/626-7827

Get lost in space at this trendy restaurant and nightspot in the Upper Market/Duboce triangle area. Living up to its name, the club has a celestial theme, and many of the folks who frequent it certainly do look like stars. The California-inspired menu changes with each astrological phase, and each sign gets its own dish (on one visit, the Libra special was grilled skewers of scallops and beef). The food is generally good if just a bit fussy and far-reaching (do we really need to see paella and linguine on the same menu?). But the main attraction is the atmosphere, dark and textural, with a nightly crowd of see-and-be-seen types who come for late-night suppers and to sip such inventive cocktails as the Leo Drop (Absolut Citron, fresh lemon juice, and lemon-zest sugar) and the Scorpion (Meyer's Platinum Rum, brandy, fresh fruit, juices, and a hint of almonds). But beware: Cocktail prices are similarly stratospheric—the Scorpion is $8! *$$; MC, V; no checks; dinner every day; full bar; reservations recommended; map:K5*

Zuni Cafe / ★★★

1658 MARKET ST; 415/552-2522

Before it got famous, Zuni was a tiny Southwestern-style lunch spot in a low-class neighborhood. When Chez Panisse alumna Judy Rodgers came on board as chef and co-owner, the cafe became so popular it had to more than double its size. Today, with its roaring copper-topped bar, grand piano, and exposed-brick dining room, it's nearly as quintessential a San Francisco institution as Dungeness crab and sourdough bread, though many loyal patrons miss the days when it was little more than a hole in the wall. It wouldn't be stretching the truth to say that one reason the neighborhood started improving was Zuni's Mediterranean-influenced upscale food, as divinely simple as only the supremely sophisticated can be. Picture a plate of mild, house-cured anchovies sprinkled with olives, celery, and Parmesan cheese; polenta with delicate mascarpone; a terrific Caesar salad; a small, perfectly roasted chicken for two on a delicious bed of Tuscan bread salad; a grilled rib-eye steak accompanied by sweet white corn seasoned with fresh basil. At lunchtime and after 10pm, you can get some of the best burgers in town here, too, served on focaccia with aioli and house pickles (and be sure to order a side of the great shoe-string potatoes). Service is first-rate for regulars and those who resemble them. *$$; AE, MC, V; no checks; lunch, dinner, late dinner Tues–Sun; full bar; reservations recommended; map:L5* &

LODGINGS

LODGINGS

Campton Place Hotel / ★★★★

340 STOCKTON ST; 415/781-5555 OR 800/235-4300
Almost as soon as Campton Place reopened after an extensive restoration in 1984, its posh surroundings, stunning objets d'art, superlative service, and elegant accommodations began swaying the patrons of the carriage trade away from traditional San Francisco hotels. The lobby, reminiscent of a gallery with its domed ceiling, miles of marble, crystal chandeliers, and striking Asian art, alone is worth the price of admission. The 110 guest rooms are very comfortable, and the Henredon armoires, custom-built chairs, and handsome desks help create a pervasive air of luxury. The travertine-marble bathrooms are equipped with telephones, terry-cloth robes, hair dryers, French-milled soaps, and bath scales. For the best views, ask for one of the larger double deluxe corner rooms on the upper floors. The view from room 1501, which overlooks Union Square, is particularly stunning. For help with your laundry, dry cleaning, a shoe shine, or even baby-sitting, just pick up the phone and you'll be accommodated, *tout de suite*. The concierge will make any and all of your arrangements (a reservation for the hotel's limo, perhaps?), and 24-hour room service will deliver whatever you're craving from the menu at the well-regarded Campton Place restaurant, one of the city's prettiest—and priciest—dining establishments (see review in the Restaurants chapter). *$$$; AE, DC, MC, V; checks OK (for lodgings only); breakfast, lunch Mon–Sat, dinner every day, brunch Sun; full bar; reserve@ campton.com; www.camptonplace.com; map:M3* &

Clift Hotel / ★★★

495 GEARY ST; 415/775-4700 OR 800/65-CLIFT
San Francisco's turn-of-the-century opulence is beautifully preserved at this resplendent 17-story mansion. The vast gilded lobby is replete with sparkling chandeliers and fine Oriental carpets, but the Clift's crowning jewel is the Redwood Room. Built entirely from a single 2,000-year-old Northern California coastal redwood, this romantic, dimly lit retreat is considered by many the most beautiful cocktail lounge in the city, with carved redwood panels polished to a high gloss, art deco lamps, and gorgeous reproductions of Gustav Klimt paintings adorning the walls. This isn't the only lavishly appointed room in the house: each of the 326 individually designed guest rooms has luxurious hardwood furnishings, an abundance of Brunschwig & Fils fabric, attractive armoires that conceal TVs (and VCRs on request), marble bathrooms complete with plush robes and hair dryers, and well-stocked honor bars. You'll find all the usual high-class perks at the Clift: 24-hour room service, a complimentary limo

SAN FRANCISCO RESERVATION SERVICES

If you're having trouble finding a vacancy in a San Francisco lodging (a common problem during the summer months), you might want to try one of the city's reservation services. Two recommended services include:

San Francisco Reservations (22 2nd St, San Francisco, CA 94105; 800/677-1500 or 415/227-1500) can make a reservation for you at any one of more than 300 San Francisco hotels, often at discounted rates. They also offer event and hotel packages that include discount admissions to various San Francisco museums. Their Web site (www.hotelres.com) allows you to make your reservations online.

Bed-and-Breakfast California (12711 McCartysville Pl, Saratoga, CA 95070; 800/872-4500 or 408/867-9662; fax 408/867-0907; info@bbintl.com; www.bbintl.com) can set you up with a selection of San Francisco B&Bs whose rates are from $80 to $150 per night, with a two-night minimum stay. Accommodations range from single rooms in private homes to luxurious, full-service mansions and Victorian homes.

to transport you to the Financial District, overnight shoe shines, a concierge, a fitness center, and an exemplary business center. Families will appreciate the Clift's VIK (Very Important Kids) program, which offers younger guests (and their grateful parents) a staggering array of services and supplies ranging from pacifiers, strollers, and diapers to Disney movies, video and board games, and activities for older children. This is also one of the few hotels in the city that allows pets. Note: Hotelier Ian Schrager, creator of such ultrahip hotels as New York's Paramount, Los Angeles's Mondrian, and Miami's Delano, purchased the Clift three years ago, but has yet to make any major changes. *$$$; AE, DC, MC, V; checks OK; map:M3* ♿

Commodore International Hotel / ★★

825 SUTTER ST; 415/923-6800 OR 800/338-6848

The 113-room Commodore International Hotel is a surprisingly fun and affordable hostelry. The management actually helps guests explore the city by offering a free staff-created tour book highlighting San Francisco's top insider attractions; if after reading it you're still baffled about what to do next in this city of plenty, spin the gimmicky but fun Wheel of Fortune located in the hotel's sexy lobby and let it choose an only-in-San-Francisco activity for you. The hotel's lower Sutter Street location means that all the hot tourist spots—Chinatown, Union Square, the Financial District—are within walking distance. And after a day of exploring, you can cool your tired dogs here at the wickedly hip Red Room, a dazzling bar and cocktail lounge that reflects no other spectrum of light but ruby red. Also adjoining the lobby is an art deco–style diner serving inexpensive buckwheat griddle cakes, big burgers, tofu sandwiches, and similar fare. If you're on a tight budget, stick with the plain but pleasant rooms on the first four floors; otherwise, break out an extra Jackson and live it up near the top, where the interiors echo the neo-deco theme. All guest rooms feature a large walk-in closet, a tub and shower, cable TV, and a phone with a data port. There's also access to a full-service health club, room service via Waiters on Wheels (a company that delivers from numerous restaurants in the city), and nearby parking for an extra fee. $$; AE, DC, MC, V; no checks; www.joiedevivre-sf.com; map:M3

Golden Gate Hotel / ★★☆

775 BUSH ST; 415/392-3702 OR 800/835-1118

The Union Square area has a slew of small, reasonably priced European-style hotels housed in turn-of-the-century buildings, and the Golden Gate Hotel is one of the best. It's a family-run affair, owned by John and Renate Kenaston and managed by their daughter, and these kind folks will bend over backwards to make sure you have an enjoyable stay. The guest rooms are individually decorated with antique and wicker furnishings, quilted bedspreads, and sweet-smelling fresh flowers; all have phones and TVs as well. If you like a good soak, request a room with a claw-footed tub. A complimentary afternoon tea is served daily from 4–7pm, a good time to chat with the Kenastons. You'll like the location as well—2 blocks from Union Square and Nob Hill, and a stone's throw from the cable car stop for Fisherman's Wharf and Chinatown. $; AE, CB, DC, MC, V; no checks; map:M3

Grand Hyatt San Francisco on Union Square / ★★★

345 STOCKTON ST; 415/398-1234 OR 800/233-1234

Union Square exudes big-city excitement, and right in the thick of it is the Grand Hyatt, the alpha mother of San Francisco's three Hyatt hotels. She's a big one, too: 693 rooms within 36 floors of steel, marble, and glass, and surrounded by some of the best shopping and restaurants on terra firma. Waltz past the doorman into the gilded lobby with its museum-quality Asian objets d'art and take the speedy elevator to your high-rise room with its stunning view of the city. Okay, so decor-wise it's not the Ritz-Carlton (though it's just as expensive), but the recently renovated rooms are pleasantly decorated and spacious and come with such luxury amenities as TVs in the bathroom, telephones with computer hookups, and access to the hotel's extensive health club. For a reasonable fee you can upgrade to the Regency rooms, which are slightly larger and include continental breakfast and evening hors d'oeuvres, or the Business Plan rooms, which come with a private fax machine and 24-hour access to a host of business services. The new 36th-floor Grandviews Restaurant (appropriately named) serves breakfast, lunch, and dinner daily and features live jazz most evenings. $$$; AE, DC, DIS, JCB, MC, V; checks OK; map:N3 ᕱ

Hotel Diva / ★★★

440 GEARY ST; 415/885-0200 OR 800/553-1900

Ever since it opened in 1985, Hotel Diva has been the prima donna of San Francisco's modern hotels, winning Best Hotel Design from *Interiors* magazine for its suave, ultramodern design. The hotel's facade is still a veritable work of art, a fashionable fusion of cement, steel, and glass that is *très chic*. But the high style doesn't stop here: even the 111 guest rooms are works of art, decorated with handsome Italian modern furnishings. Standard luxury amenities in each room include an individually controlled air conditioner, a remote-control television with interactive multimedia and VCR, two telephones with extra-long cords, a data port, voice mail, and a personal safe. Guest services include a complimentary breakfast of fresh fruit, breads, yogurt, coffee, and orange juice delivered to your boudoir, as well as room service, a concierge, a 24-hour fitness center, and a business center offering free use of computers, software, and a laser printer. Best of all, the Diva is in a prime location, just around the corner from Union Square. Insider tip: Reserve one of the rooms ending in "09," which have extra-large bathrooms with vanity mirrors and makeup tables. *$$$; AE, DC, DIS, MC, V; checks OK; map:M3* ⅍

Hotel Monaco / ★★★★

501 GEARY ST, SAN FRANCISCO; 415/292-0100 OR 800/214-4220

"Wow!" is a common exclamation among first-time guests at Hotel Monaco, one of the hottest new hotels in a city brimming with top-notch accommodations. After a $24 million renovation, Monaco opened in June 1995 and has received nothing but kudos for its sumptuous, stunning decor. Expect a melding of modern European fashion with flourishes of the American Beaux Arts era—the trademark of award-winning designer Cheryl Rowley, who envisioned the 201-room hotel as a "great ship traveling to the farthest reaches of the world, collecting exotic, precious treasures and antiquities." Hence the guest rooms replete with canopy beds, Chinese-inspired armoires, bamboo writing desks, old-fashioned decorative luggage, and a profusion of bold stripes and vibrant colors. The entire hotel is truly a feast for the eyes, particularly the Grand Café with its 30-foot ceilings, cascading chandeliers, plethora of stately columns, and many art nouveau frills—all vestiges of its former incarnation as the hotel's grand ballroom. A chic see-and-be-seen crowd typically fills the impressive dining room, noshing on trendy California-French cuisine (see review in the Restaurants chapter). And of course, there are the requisite hotel toys (health club, steam room, whirlpool spa, sauna), services (massages, manicures, valet parking, business and room service), and complimentary perks (newspaper delivery, morning coffee, evening wine reception). You'll like the location as well: in the heart of San Francisco's theater district, a mere two blocks from Union Square and the cable cars. *$$$; AE, DC, DIS, MC, V; no checks; breakfast, lunch, dinner every day; map:M3* &

Hotel Rex / ★★★

562 SUTTER ST; 415/433-4434 OR 800/433-4434

The Joie de Vivre hotel company has created another winner with the 94-room Hotel Rex, the latest addition to its cadre of fashionable yet affordable accommodations. The hotel's sophisticated and sensuous lobby lounge is cleverly modeled after a 1920s library, meant to create a stylish sanctuary for San Francisco's arts and literary community (hence the adjoining antiquarian bookstore). To keep costs—and rates—down, many of the site's former Orchard Hotel's imported furnishings have been retained, which adds a bit of authenticity to the European boutique hotel–style ambience. All of the spacious (for a downtown hotel) and newly renovated rooms feature CD players, two-line telephones with voice mail and data port, and an electronic key-card system. The rooms in the back are not only quieter, they also overlook a tranquil, shaded courtyard. Perks include room service, same-day laundry/dry cleaning, complimentary newspaper, an evening wine hour, concierge service, and morning car service to the Financial District. The hotel is in a key location as well, within walking distance of Union Square and surrounded by first-rate galleries, theaters, and restaurants. *$$$; AE, DC, MC, V; no checks; map:M3*

Hotel Triton / ★★★

342 GRANT AVE; 415/394-0500 OR 800/433-6611

The Hotel Triton has been described as modern, whimsical, sophisticated, chic, vogue, neo-baroque, ultrahip, and retro-futuristic—but words just don't do justice to this unique hostelry-cum-art-gallery that you'll simply have to see to appreciate. The entire hotel, from the bellhop's inverted pyramid–shaped podium to the iridescent throw pillows on the beds and the ashtrays ringed with faux pearls, is the original work of four imaginative (some might say wacky) San Francisco artisans. For a preview of what's behind the bedroom doors, peek into the lobby, where you'll see curvaceous chairs shimmering in gold silk taffeta, an imposing duo of floor-to-ceiling pillars sheathed in teal, purple, and gold leaf, and a pastel mural portraying mythic images of sea life, triton shells, and human figures—all that's missing are Dorothy, Toto, and the ruby slippers. Add to this visual extravaganza all the amenities you'd find in any luxury hotel, including a concierge, valet parking (essential in this part of town), room service, complimentary wine and coffee, business and limousine services, and even a fitness center. The 147 rooms and designer suites (designed by such celebs as Carlos Santana, Joe Boxer, and the late Jerry Garcia) continue the modern wonderland theme: walls are splashed with giant, hand-painted yellow and blue diamonds, king-size beds feature navy-and-khaki-striped camelback headboards, and armoires that hide remote-control TVs are topped with golden crowns. The tree-hugger in all of us can embrace the EcoFloor, the Triton's environmentally conscious seventh floor where almost everything is made from recycled, biodegradable, or organically grown materials, and the air and water is passed through fancy filtration systems. Heck, the Triton is so utterly hip, even the elevator swings to Thelonious Monk. *$$$; AE, DC, DIS, MC, V; checks OK; www.hotel-tritonsf.com; map:N3* &

Pan Pacific / ★★★☆

500 POST ST; 415/771-8600 OR 800/533-6465
While most other Union Square hotels are bending to the winds of fashion, the Pan Pacific remains a cornerstone of class, style, and awe-inspiring architecture. Even if you're not staying here, it's worth a few minutes of your time to take a ride up the glass elevator to marvel at the sky-rise's 18-story atrium-style interior, a marvel of engineering and architectural art. The lobby is located on the third floor, as is the cozy piano lounge and highly recommended Pacific restaurant—note the rather risqué marble fountain with the four nude dancing figures (see review in the Restaurants chapter). The 329 spacious, immaculate guest rooms seem rather ordinary at first, but it doesn't take long to appreciate the quality of the fabrics and furnishings and the soothing shades of sage and brown. All the usual first-class offerings are here, including big marble-laden bathrooms with mini-TVs, three phones with voice mail, plush bathrobes, in-room safes, and fax machines. Of course luxury hotel services are also available, including baby-sitting, a health club, a business center, secretarial services, complimentary Rolls-Royce transportation in the city, newspaper delivery, and in-room massage. The Pan Pacific may not be fashionable, but it's still one of our favorites. *$$$; AE, DC, DIS, JCB, MC, V; no checks; map:M3* &

Petite Auberge / ★★

863 BUSH ST; 415/928-6000
Located a few blocks from Union Square, the Petite Auberge is a romanticized version of a French country inn with terra-cotta tile floors, Pierre Deux fabrics, oak furniture, lace curtains, and dried floral wreaths adorning the walls. You'll also see lots of teddy bears on parade, vintage children's toys on shelves and mantels, and a carousel horse cantering in the lobby—not everyone's taste, for sure. In truth, the 26 rooms are small but sweet, with inviting window seats; most have fireplaces. (Rooms on the upper floors toward the back tend to be the quietest.) Honeymooners should splurge on the Petite Suite, which has its own private entrance, deck, and spa tub. Guests are supplied with terry-cloth robes, and shoes are shined overnight and delivered with the morning paper; nightly turndown service includes the proverbial chocolate on the pillow. A generous buffet breakfast is served downstairs in a quaint breakfast room with

French doors that open onto a small garden. In the afternoon, you may sip tea or wine and snack on hors d'oeuvres in a lounge where a horde of teddy bears on gingham-checked couches face off with a row of rabbits in front of the fireplace. Guests who need to work may use the business services at the White Swan Inn (owned by the same people), just two doors away. *$$$; AE, DC, MC, V; checks OK; map:M3*

The Prescott Hotel / ★★★

545 POST ST; 415/563-0303 OR 800/283-7322
Opened in 1989 by San Francisco hotel magnate Bill Kimpton, the Prescott has put pressure on Union Square's neighboring luxury hotels by offering first-rate accommodations at a fairly reasonable price. This, combined with dining privileges at one of the city's most popular restaurants (the adjoining Postrio; see review in the Restaurants chapter), superlative service from an intelligent, youthful staff, and a prime location in the heart of San Francisco, places the Prescott at the top of the Union Square hotel list. The rooms, decorated with custom-made cherrywood furnishings, black-granite–topped nightstands and dressers, and silk wallpaper, have rich color schemes of hunter green, deep purple, cerise, taupe, and gold. The Prescott offers 164 rooms, including numerous suites and a wildly posh penthouse complete with a grand piano, a rooftop Jacuzzi, a formal dining room, and twin fireplaces. For an additional $30 per night, you may gain "Club Concierge Level" status, which grants you access to a plush lounge (complete with a complimentary premium bar), an hors d'oeuvres reception, and a continental breakfast, as well as a host of other privileges—not a bad investment for 30 bones. Standard perks include limo service to the Financial District, overnight shoe shine, valet parking, laundry service, a daily newspaper delivered to your room, and access to the adjacent fitness facility. *$$$; AE, DC, DIS, MC, V; checks OK (for lodgings only); breakfast, lunch Mon-Fri, dinner every day, brunch Sat–Sun; map:M3* ఈ

Savoy Hotel / ★★

580 GEARY ST; 415/441-2700 OR 800/227-4223
Originally built in 1913 for the Panama-Pacific International Exposition, this seven-story hotel is a posh French country-style inn with a gorgeous facade of richly veined black marble, beveled glass, mahogany, and polished brass. It's ideally located in the center of the theater district, just 2½ blocks from Union Square. The 83 guest rooms and suites are small but beautifully appointed, with reams of toile de Jouy fabrics, heavy French cotton bedspreads, imported Provençal furnishings, plump feather beds, goose-down pillows, two-line telephones with modem jacks, and minibars. A few of the suites come with Jacuzzi tubs. The most tranquil rooms are on the northeast corner (farthest from the traffic noise) facing a rear courtyard. Guests are nurtured with a continental breakfast and afternoon

THE CHAIN GANG

San Francisco has some of the most unique and fashionable hotels and B&Bs in the nation, but for some people there's nothing better than a good ol' reliable chain hotel, where the rates are reasonable and there are no unwanted surprises. Here is a list of San Francisco's chain gang, all of which have hotels either in the downtown area or nearby.

Best Western 800/528-1234	**La Quinta Motor Inns** 800/531-5900
Comfort Inn 800/228-5150	**MOTEL6** 800/466-8356
Days Inn 800/325-2525	**Ramada** 800/2-RAMADA
Doubletree Hotels 800/222-TREE	**Rodeway Inns** 800/228-2000
Econo Lodges 800/55-ECONO	**SUPER8** 800/800-8000
Holiday Inn 800/HOLIDAY	**Travelodge** 800/255-3050
Howard Johnson 800/654-2000	**Vagabond Inns** 800/522-1555

tea and sherry; a full breakfast is also available. Additional amenities include an overnight shoe shine and room service from the hotel's popular Brasserie Savoy (see review in the Restaurants chapter). This restaurant is a replica of an authentic French brasserie, right down to the zinc bar, black-and-white marble floors, comfy banquettes, woven-leather chairs, and a staff clad in long, starched white aprons. Its air of casual sophistication, reasonable prices, and generally very good food—pâté de foie gras, filet mignon with truffle sauce, crispy sweetbreads, duck confit—make it a reliable bet, especially for a meal before show time (ask about the well-priced three-course dinner special offered from 5–8pm daily). $$; AE, DC, DIS, MC, V; no checks; breakfast, dinner every day; www.masteryellowpages.com; map:M3 &

Sir Francis Drake Hotel / ★★☆

450 POWELL ST; 415/392-7755 OR 800/227-5480

While nowhere near as resplendent as the nearby Westin St. Francis, the 21-story Sir Francis Drake gives us ordinary folks a reasonably priced opportunity to stay in one of San Francisco's grande dames. A recent $5 million renovation has spruced up the 417 rooms a bit, but there's still a little wear around the edges. No matter—it's the experience of listening to the sounds of Union Square wafting through your window that makes staying here an enjoyable experience. Then there's Tom Sweeny, the legendary and ever-jovial Beefeater doorman who has graced more snapshots than any other San Franciscan; and the top-floor Harry Denton's Starlight Room, one of the most fun and fashionable cocktail-dance lounges in the city; and Scala's Bistro on the lower level, an upscale yet affordable restaurant we guarantee you'll enjoy (see review in the Restaurants chapter); and all the requisite big-hotel services such as room service, newspaper delivery, business services, baby-sitting, in-room massage, and laundry. So considering that you can get a standard room here for about half the price of rooms at the St. Francis—and with far better eating, drinking, and dancing—the Drake is definitely worth looking into. *$$$; AE, DC, DIS, MC, V; no checks; breakfast, lunch, dinner every day; reservations recommended; map:M3* &

Westin St. Francis / ★★★½

335 POWELL ST; 415/397-7000 OR 800/228-3000
San Francisco's first world-class hotel still attracts a legion of admirers; most of them can't afford the steep room rates but are content with lounging in the lobby just to soak up the heady, majestic aura of this historic hotel. The who's who of the world have all checked in at one time or another, including Queen Elizabeth II, Mother Teresa, Emperor Hirohito, the Shah of Iran, King Juan Carlos of Spain, and all the U.S. presidents since Taft. Just strolling through the vast, ornate lobby with its century-old hand-carved redwood paneling is a treat in itself. To keep up with the times, the adjacent 32-story Tower was added in 1972, which doubled the capacity (1,189 rooms total) and provided the requisite banquet and conference centers. The older rooms of the main building vary in size, but have more old-world charm than the newer rooms. The Tower rooms, however, have better views of the city from the 18th floor and above. In 1999 the Westin dumped a staggering $60 million into renovations, replacing the furniture, carpeting, and bedding in every guest room, as well as enhancing the lobby and restoring the façade. A $2 million fitness center has been added too. And if there's one thing you must do while visiting San Francisco, it's high tea (3–5pm) at the hotel's Compass Rose cafe and lounge, one of San Francisco's most enduring and pleasurable traditions. *$$$; AE, DC, DIS, JCB, MC, V; checks OK; map:M3* &

White Swan Inn / ★★

845 BUSH ST; 415/775-1755 OR 800/999-9570
Perhaps the only hotel in San Francisco more adorable than the White Swan is its nearby sister inn, Petite Auberge. The theme here also harks back to a cozy English-garden bed-and-breakfast, embellished with teddy bears piled on steps, shelves, and couches, as well as a colorful carousel horse in the small lobby. The 1903 building with curved bay windows has 26 rooms with fireplaces and private bathrooms, and each chamber is charmingly decorated with colorful prints, comfy armchairs, antiques, and floral-print wallpaper. Some rooms have inviting bay windows where you can sit and read or gaze out at the garden, and each has a refrigerator, TV, phone, and wet bar. For peace and quiet, ask for a room

in the back overlooking the sunny, tree-lined courtyard. If you have business matters to tend to, data ports, a fax machine, and a conference room with audio/video machines are available. Guests are treated to a big breakfast, morning newspaper, afternoon tea, and home-baked cookies. The cozy library, often warmed by a roaring fire, is an ideal spot to curl up and read a novel in the company of—surprise!—more teddy bears. *$$$; AE, DC, MC, V; checks OK; map:M3*

Financial District

Mandarin Oriental / ★★★

222 SANSOME ST; 415/276-9888 OR 800/622-0404
The rooms at the award-winning Mandarin Oriental offer some of the most remarkable views in the city. Because it's perched high in the sky (on the top 11 floors of the 48-story First Interstate Building, San Francisco's third-tallest skyscraper), you're not only guaranteed a bird's-eye view of the city, you'll be gazing at the entire Bay Area. The 158 rooms are comfortable and deceptively austere. Well hidden among the simple blond-wood furniture and fine Asian artwork are all the latest deluxe amenities: three two-line speakerphones with fax hookups, remote-control televisions with access to videos, and fully stocked minibars and refrigerators, as well as jumbo marble bathrooms with stall showers and extra-deep soaking tubs (you can even admire the city's skyline from some of the bathtubs). Once settled in your room, you'll be treated to jasmine tea and Thai silk slippers. Contrary to the policy of many other hotels, the room rates at the Mandarin don't vary according to scenery, so request one of the corner rooms (numbers ending with 6 or 11) for the best views. Additional perks include access to numerous business services, valet parking, a continental breakfast served in the lounge, shoe shines, 24-hour room service, and a state-of-the-art fitness center. The hotel's award-winning restaurant, Silks, may be the Maytag repairman of luxury restaurants: it's all gussied up and anxious to serve, but a tad lonely and underappreciated. Regardless, chances are you won't be disappointed if you choose to dine here. *$$$; AE, DC, DIS, MC, V; checks OK (for lodgings only); breakfast, lunch, dinner every day; mosfo@aol. com; www.mandarin-oriental.com; map:N2* &

Palace Hotel / ★★★

2 NEW MONTGOMERY ST; 415/512-1111 OR 800/325-3535 (RESERVATIONS ONLY)
 Reminiscent of more romantic times, this opulent hotel built in 1875 has housed such luminaries as Thomas Edison, D. H. Lawrence, Amelia Earhart, and Winston Churchill, as well as 10 American presidents and numerous aristocrats and royalty from around the world. Hoping to

attract a similarly high-class clientele in the future, the management closed the Palace in 1989 for 27 months and poured $170 million into restoring it to its original splendor. And splendid it is. The downstairs decor is truly breathtaking, from the multiple sparkling Austrian-crystal chandeliers, the double row of white Italian marble Ionic columns, and the 80,000-pane stained-glass dome of the Garden Court, to the three grand ballrooms and early 19th-century French tapestry gracing the walls. Unfortunately, all this impressive glitz comes to a screeching halt when you open the door to one of the 550 guest rooms. Although comfortable and attractive, the rooms are more akin to gussied-up generic hotel rooms than to any palace chamber. However, this place does offer all the perks you'd look for in a luxury hotel, including a concierge, 24-hour room service, valet parking, and an elaborate business center, plus a new, palm-embellished health club with an exercise room, co-ed sauna, whirlpool, and stunning white-tiled lap pool capped by a dome of clear glass. Restaurants include the Garden Court, famous for its elaborate breakfast buffet and elegant afternoon tea (see review in the Restaurants chapter); Kyo-ya, a rather austere Japanese dining room serving the best (and most expensive) sushi and sashimi in town; and the Pied Piper Bar, which is dominated by a stunning, $2.5 million, 1909 Maxfield Parrish painting of the Pied Piper of Hamelin leading a band of 27 children. Even if you don't have the resources to recline or dine here, this place, like most palaces, is worth a self-guided tour. *$$$; AE, DC, DIS, MC, V; checks OK (for lodgings only); breakfast, lunch, dinner every day; www.sheraton.com; map:N3* &

Park Hyatt San Francisco / ★★★⯪

333 BATTERY ST; 415/392-1234 OR 800/HYATT-CA
It may not look it from the outside, but this is one of San Francisco's best first-class business hotels. Located in the heart of San Francisco's Financial District, the 26-story Park Hyatt (which is about half the size of Hyatt's typical megahotels) has a rather ordinary exterior, but the interior is all class: Australian lacewood paneling, handmade custom carpets from China, polished Italian granite, and opalescent Spanish alabaster chandeliers adorn the gilded lobby. The 360 rooms are more understated but equally impressive. Each comes loaded with Italian wood furnishings, wondrously comfortable beds, large bathrooms, and extraordinary views of the city. If it's on the company's tab, request one of the corner suites on the upper floors, which also come with outdoor balconies or a Jacuzzi tub—a tough choice. Complimentary exercise cycles and rowing machines can be delivered to your room, or you can use the on-site health center. Other pluses include complimentary service via the house Mercedes-Benz to anywhere within the downtown area, and every business service you could possibly need. The hotel's restaurant, the Park Grill, serves

California-Continental cuisine in an elegant setting; more casual alfresco dining is available on the Outdoor Terrace. Be sure to check out the sexy sake bar as well. *$$$; AE, DC, JCB, MC, V; checks OK; map:N2* &

SoMa (South of Market Street)

Harbor Court Hotel / ★★★

165 STEUART ST; 415/882-1300 OR 800/346-0555

On the southwest edge of the Financial District, this low-key, high-style hotel caters mainly to business travelers, but will equally impress the weekend vacationer. It's larger and less expensive than the adjacent Hotel Griffon (see below), and it was once a YMCA, but don't let that dissuade you: the high-quality accommodations, gorgeous views of the bay, and complimentary use of the adjoining fitness club—complete with indoor Olympic-size swimming pool—add up to one sweet deal. Guest rooms are nicely equipped with soundproof windows, half-canopy beds, large armoires, and writing desks. Amenities range from limited room service to secretarial services, laundry and dry cleaning, newspaper delivery, valet service, and car service to the Financial District. When the sun drops, slip on down to the bar at Boulevard and mingle with the swinging yuppie singles (see review in the Restaurants chapter). *$$$; AE, DC, MC, V; no checks; map:O2* &

Hotel Griffon / ★★★

155 STEUART ST; 415/495-2100 OR 800/321-2201

This is one of our favorite small luxury hotels, a 62-room sleeper that does a brisk repeat-customer business. It's in an ideal location, on the south end of the Embarcadero at the foot of San Francisco's historic waterfront. The guest rooms are beautifully decorated with whitewashed brick walls, contemporary cherry-wood furnishings, marble vanities, high ceilings, window seats, and art-deco–style lamps. You have to pay extra for the beautiful Bay Bridge view, but it's definitely worth it (believe it or not, it used to be a view of a freeway overpass). And for a small hotel, the Griffin offers a lot of big-hotel amenities, including room service, secretarial services, concierge, in-room massage, free access to a nearby health center, and complimentary town car service to the Financial District. The new adjacent restaurant, Red Herring (see review in the Restaurants chapter), is receiving favorable reviews as well. *$$$; AE, DC, DIS, MC, V; no checks; map:O2* &

San Francisco Marriott / ★★☆

55 4TH ST; 415/896-1600 OR 800/228-9290

It's your call: either an architectural masterpiece or the world's biggest parking meter. Opinions sway both ways about the San Francisco Marriott, one of the largest buildings in the city and a definite eye-catcher with its numerous fantails and thousands of glimmering windows. The massive hotel, completed in 1989, does a brisk convention business (the Moscone Convention Center is two blocks away), but hundreds of visitors pass through daily simply to gape at the panoramic view of the city and bay from the Atrium Lounge on the 39th floor (best seen when the fog rolls in from below). For a corporate citadel, its 1,500 rooms are surprisingly attractive and cozy, with extra-large bathrooms, big comfy beds, and—of course—extraordinary views (ask for a room overlooking Yerba Buena Gardens). Somewhere within the hotel are an indoor pool, spa, and health club (complimentary use, of course), as well as a Japanese teppanyaki restaurant and sushi bar (Kinoko), the Garden Terrace restaurant, and two cocktail lounges on the top floor where live entertainment plays nightly. *$$$; AE, DC, JCB, MC, V; checks OK; map:N3* &

W Hotel / ★★★

181 3RD ST; 415/777-5300 OR 877/W-HOTELS
Hip hotels are all the rage now, and the Westin hotel corporation has capitalized on the craze with a San Francisco addition to its popular W hotel in New York. Art, technology, service, and sex appeal are all applied in force from the moment you walk into the lobby. In fact, you don't even know you're in a hotel at first, because the first person to greet you is the bartender (brilliant). To your right is a gaggle of hip, young, beautiful people lounging in the ever-so-chic lobby, and to the left is XYZ, the latest SoMa restaurant hot spot (see review in the Restaurants chapter). The room decor mimics the overall theme—bold colors, soft fabrics, sensual curves—almost enough to make you not notice how small they are. No matter: dive onto the thick, luscious goose-down comforter and you won't ever want to leave. High-tech toys include a 27-inch TV, CD player, and modem jacks for your laptop. The location is fantastic as well, smack-dab in the smoking-hot SoMa district and literally sharing real estate with the beautiful San Francisco Museum of Modern Art and Yerba Buena Gardens. The verdict? If you want to play with San Francisco's in crowd, W is the place to be (at least for now). *$$$; AE, DC, JCB, MC, V; checks OK; www.whotels.com; map:N3* &

Nob Hill

Fairmont Hotel & Tower / ★★★

950 MASON ST; 415/772-5000 OR 800/527-4727
The Fairmont is another one of San Francisco's grand old hotels that are part hotel, part tourist attraction. Few hotels in the world have such a fabulous entrance: massive Corinthian columns of solid marble, vaulted

ceilings, velvet smoking chairs, enormous gilded mirrors, and a colossal wraparound staircase. Heck, they even have a harpist posted near the entrance. All that's lacking is your top hat and coattails. Unfortunately, the opulent decor isn't applied to the guest rooms, which are rather conservative compared to the public areas (though, to be fair, they're a hard act to follow). The luxury is there, however: rooms offer such niceties as goose-down pillows, large walk-in closets, multiline phones with private voice mail, and electric shoe buffers. Hefty room rates help pay for the 24-hour concierge and room service, complimentary morning limousine to the Financial District, free shoe shine, business center, and baby-sitting services. Within the hotel there's a beauty salon, barbershop, shopping arcade, and even a pharmacy (yes, this place is *big*). There are several restaurants and bars as well, including the famous Polynesian-style Tonga Room bar and restaurant, fine dining at Masons, and the top-floor Crown Room restaurant and bar, which has a spectacular panoramic view of the city. *$$$; AE, CB, DC, DIS, MC, V; checks OK; map:M3* &

Huntington Hotel / ★★★

1075 CALIFORNIA ST; 415/474-5400 OR 800/652-1539 (IN CALIFORNIA) AND 800/227-4683 (OUTSIDE CALIFORNIA)
The small, modest lobby of this imposing Nob Hill landmark belies its lavish interiors. The Huntington is graced with a remarkable array of antiques, plush sofas, and museum-quality objets d'art; the doorman is subdued and genteel but always seems delighted to see you; the staff maintains a professional attitude and at the same time treats you like a favored guest. These things—along with superb security—explain why the Huntington has long been a favorite of many of San Francisco's visiting dignitaries and celebrities, from Archbishop Desmond Tutu to Robert Redford. The 12-story hotel's 140 rooms are spacious and lavish, with imported silks, 17th-century paintings, and stunning views of the city and the bay. The rooms are individually decorated, and some are so handsome they have been featured in *Architectural Digest*. Several flaunt gold velvet sofas and fringed, tufted hassocks surrounded by antiques, while others boast modern leather couches, faux-leopard-skin hassocks, and marble bars. Guests are treated to a formal afternoon tea and complimentary sherry, nightly turndown service, and a morning paper. Valet parking and room service are also available, along with a full range of business services and access to the Nob Hill Club, a top-of-the-line fitness center one block away. Yes, Virginia, it's expensive, but offers such as the Romance Package (including free champagne, sherry, and limousine service) make the Huntington worth considering for that special occasion. *$$$; AE, DC, DIS, MC, V; checks OK; map:M3*

Nob Hill Inn / ★★

1000 PINE ST; 415/673-6080
Any well-appointed bed-and-breakfast ought to have a resident ghost or two. This elegant establishment—housed in a four-story Edwardian mansion built in 1907—has three: a wispy woman who likes to linger in room 12, a well-bred gentleman in room 21, and a winsome lass who wanders through the inn's Louis XIV– and Louis XV–style decor at whim. Take the etched-glass English elevator upstairs to the 21 rose-and-pink, antique-filled guest rooms, which have TVs tucked inside wardrobes and armoires. The low-end rooms are quite small, so splurge on a spacious suite. Downstairs, ceiling fans turn slowly above the wicker furniture in the parlor and dining nook, where a continental breakfast is served. You may sip wine or sherry among the racks in the atmospheric wine cellar or lounge on the sun deck or in the hot tub on the roof. Add to this an afternoon tea and nightly turndown service, and it's little wonder that even the ghosts don't want to leave. *$$–$$$; AE, DC, MC, V; checks OK; nobhill@nbn.com; www.nobhill.com; map:M3*

The Ritz-Carlton, San Francisco / ★★★★

600 STOCKTON ST; 415/296-7465 OR 800/241-3333
In 1991, after a four-year, multimillion-dollar renovation, this 1909 17-columned neoclassical beauty—formerly the Metropolitan Life Insurance Company building—reopened as the Ritz-Carlton hotel. Since then, it's been stacking up heady accolades, including a seventh-place ranking in *Condé Nast Traveler*'s 1997 list of the top 25 hotels in North America. The hotel's lobby is breathtaking, with a series of enormous, high-ceilinged lounges, gigantic floral arrangements, an abundance of museum-quality paintings and antiques, and crystal chandeliers at every turn. The spectacular Lobby Lounge is the place to mingle over an afternoon tea or sushi, and live piano performances perk up the scene every day. The 336 guest rooms are also luxury personified, though we find the decor rather staid, to say the least: people looking for a more artistic ambience might want to try Hotel Monaco or W Hotel. Regardless, the rooms are sinfully plush and loaded with high-society amenities such as spiffy marble bathrooms, fully stocked honor bars, thick terry-cloth robes, in-room safes, phones, and remote-control TVs. Some (though not many) have wonderful views of the city and the bay, but your best bets are the quieter rooms overlooking the landscaped courtyard. The hotel's ritzy fitness center has an indoor lap pool, whirlpool, sauna, fully equipped training room, and massage services. Two restaurants are located in the hotel: the formal Dining Room at the Ritz-Carlton, one of the top restaurants in the city (see review in the Restaurants chapter), and the more casual Terrace, serving excellent Mediterranean fare and sensational desserts in a pleasant dining room adorned with handsome oil paintings. *$$$; AE, DC, DIS, MC, V; no checks; Terrace: breakfast, lunch, dinner every day, jazz brunch Sun; www.ritzcarlton.com; map:N2* &

North Beach

Hotel Bohème / ★★

444 COLUMBUS AVE; 415/433-9111

Hopelessly chic is perhaps the best way to describe the Hotel Bohème, one of the sexiest small hotels in the city and a favorite retreat of visiting writers and poets. Hovering two stories above Columbus Avenue—the Boulevard Saint-Michel of San Francisco streets—the Bohème artfully reflects North Beach's bohemian flair dating from the late 1950s and early '60s. The time trip starts with a gallery of moody black-and-white photographs lining the hallways and segues into the 15 guest rooms decorated in soothing shades of sage green, cantaloupe, lavender, and black. The rooms feature handmade light fixtures crafted from glazed collages of jazz sheet music, Ginsberg poetry, and old menus and headlines, as well as black iron beds with sheer canopies, European armoires, bistro tables, wicker chairs, and Picasso and Matisse prints. Modern amenities abound, including private baths, remote-control cable TV, and telephones with modem jacks. A couple of minor caveats: most rooms are quite small, and those facing Columbus Avenue aren't kind to light sleepers (though views of the ever-bustling cafes and shops are entrancing). Otherwise, Hotel Bohème's engaging amalgamation of art, poetry, and hospitality will forever turn you away from America's cookie-cutter corporate hotels. *$$; AE, DC, DIS, MC, V; no checks; AK@hotelboheme.com; www.hotelboheme.com; map:M2*

San Remo Hotel / ★

2237 MASON ST; 415/776-8688 OR 800/352-REMO

Hidden in a quiet North Beach neighborhood between bustling Washington Square and Fisherman's Wharf, the San Remo is within easy walking distance of San Francisco's main attractions, including Chinatown, the Embarcadero, Pier 39, and one of the main cable car stations. Combine the locale with an inexpensive price tag, and you have one of the best room bargains in the city. This well-preserved, charming three-story Italianate Victorian building originally served as a boardinghouse for dockworkers displaced by the great fire of 1906. Space was at a premium, so the hotel's 63 rooms are rather small, the bathrooms are shared, and the walls are thin. If you can live with these minor inconveniences, however, you're in for a treat. The rooms are reminiscent of a European pensione, modestly decorated with brass or iron beds, pedestal sinks, wicker furniture, and oak, maple, or pine armoires; most have ceiling fans. Rooms 42 and 43, which overlook Mason Street, are the favorites. The old-fashioned bathrooms, spotlessly clean and restored to their original luster, have brass pull-chain toilets with oak tanks, showers, and claw-footed tubs. The penthouse suite, one of the best deals in town, offers a private bath, a small deck, and a 360-degree view of the city. The hotel's lobby and hallways are awash with antiques, leaded-glass windows, and plants bathed by sunlight filtering through stained-glass skylights. You can count on the friendly, city-savvy staff to help you plan your day touring San Francisco's abundant attractions. *$; AE, DC, DIS, MC, V; checks OK; info@sanremohotel.com; map:M1*

The Washington Square Inn / ★★

1660 STOCKTON ST; 415/981-4220 OR 800/388-0220
The Washington Square Inn's prime location in the middle of the historic North Beach district—just a short walk from Fisherman's Wharf, Ghirardelli Square, the Embarcadero, and Chinatown—is its best asset. And behind the inn's plain, inconspicuous facade is a delightful European-style bed-and-breakfast. The 15 comfortable, modest rooms are furnished with European antiques, bright flower-print drapes and matching bedspreads, and vases of fresh flowers. The least expensive rooms share a bath; the priciest units are the larger corner rooms with private baths and bay windows where you can sit and watch the hustle and bustle in the tree-lined square. In the morning you'll find a local newspaper and your freshly polished shoes waiting outside your door. The expanded continental breakfast can be served in your room or in front of the lobby fireplace, although you may want to stroll over to one of the many nearby Italian cafes for a frothy cappuccino or latte instead. Guests are treated to crisp cucumber sandwiches, freshly baked cookies, and tea every afternoon, as well as wine and hors d'oeuvres in the evening. Parking in North Beach is virtually impossible, so take advantage of the hotel's valet parking services. *$$$; AE, DC, DIS, MC, V; checks OK; map:M2*

Fisherman's Wharf

Sheraton Fisherman's Wharf / ★☆

2500 MASON ST; 415/362-5500 OR 800/325-3535
If there's no room at the Tuscan Inn, your second-best option for Fisherman's Wharf lodging is the Sheraton Fisherman's Wharf. It's a rather unsightly, boxy, brown three-story building (notice that its facade doesn't appear on the brochure), built in the mid-'70s and completely renovated in 1999. The rooms are exactly as you'd expect them to be—clean, comfortable, and boring—but at least there are no unpleasant surprises. Which is just as well, because if you're looking for lodging near Fisherman's Wharf, it's probably because you have the kids along (we recommend that you stay somewhere with more authentic San Francisco appeal, such as North Beach or Pacific Heights). All the usual big-chain amenities are available, such as 24-hour room service, evening turndown, access to a nearby health club, a business center, a car-rental desk, dry

cleaning and laundry, and newspaper delivery. There's also Chanen's Restaurant, serving standard American fare for breakfast, lunch, and dinner daily. One of the best perks about the Sheraton (and why we recommend it for families) is that it's one of the few reasonably priced hotels in the city that has an outdoor heated swimming pool. Tip: Another good Fisherman's Wharf family-friendly hotel is The Wharf Inn (2601 Mason St; 415/673-7411 or 800/548-9918), which offers quality rooms starting at $100 and has free parking as well. *$$$; AE, DC, DIS, MC, V; checks OK; map:M1* &

Tuscan Inn / ★★

425 N POINT ST; 415/561-1100 OR 800/648-4626

With its location in the heart of Fisherman's Wharf, just a skip away from Ghirardelli Square, the Embarcadero, and the cable car lines, it's no wonder the low-key Tuscan Inn is the favored hideout of many of Hollywood's actors and producers. You won't find the glitz of San Francisco's downtown hostelries or even a terrific view here, but the Tuscan's 221 attractive guest rooms (including 12 deluxe suites) offer every creature comfort one could need. Burgundy floral-print bedspreads, armchairs, writing desks, honor bars, remote-control TVs, direct-dial phones, and private bathrooms are standard features of every room. And as is typical of a hotelier Bill Kimpton enterprise, a room at the Tuscan comes with a plethora of complimentary services: a concierge, coffee and biscotti served in the lobby every morning, weekday limousine service to the Financial District and the Moscone Convention Center, an evening wine reception, room service, valet parking, and same-day laundry service. The Tuscan also offers guest privileges at several popular San Francisco fitness centers, including a 24 Hour Nautilus just a block away. Adjoining the hotel is the glittering Cafe Pescatore, a classic Italian trattoria serving very good fresh fish and pasta dishes as well as a variety of pizzas baked in a wood-fired oven. When weather permits, the Pescatore opens its floor-to-ceiling windows to allow for prime people-watching and quasi-alfresco dining. *$$$; AE, DC, DIS, MC, V; checks OK; breakfast, lunch, dinner every day; map:M1* &

Civic Center and Japantown

The Archbishop's Mansion / ★★★

1000 FULTON ST; 415/563-7872 OR 800/543-5820

This stately Belle Epoque mansion, built in 1904 for San Francisco's archbishop, is an exercise in Victorian splendor and excess: a three-story staircase winds beneath a gorgeous, 16-foot-tall stained-glass dome, and the surrounding redwood Corinthian columns, crystal chandeliers, Oriental carpets, and gorgeous antiques create an aura of almost papal splendor. The 15 large rooms and suites, each named after a famous opera, are decorated with lush fabrics, embroidered linens, and 19th-century antiques. All have partial canopied beds and private baths with stacks of plush towels and French-milled soaps. Many rooms have a fireplace, a Jacuzzi tub, and a view of Alamo Park, and some have a parlor and sitting area. The posh, rose-colored Carmen Suite has a claw-footed bathtub in front of a fireplace, a comfortable sitting room with yet another fireplace, and another pretty park view. The ultra-luxurious Don Giovanni Suite boasts a cherub-encrusted antique four-poster bed imported from a French castle, as well as a parlor with a palatial fireplace and a lavish seven-head shower in the bathroom. You may breakfast in bed on scones and croissants; then, after spending the day strolling through the park admiring the neighborhood's cherished Victorian homes, return in the afternoon for wine in the French parlor, which is graced by a grand piano that once belonged to Noël Coward. *$$$; AE, DC, MC, V; checks OK; www.sftrips.com; map:K4*

Hotel Majestic / ★★

1500 SUTTER ST; 415/441-1100 OR 800/869-8966
An orgy of Victorian grandeur, this five-story Edwardian building, located in a residential neighborhood near Japantown, was one of San Francisco's earliest grand hotels. Marble steps and ornate beveled-glass doors open onto a magnificent, cozy lobby featuring dark green marble pillars, black-and-burgundy floral carpeting, plush rose-colored sofas, chairs and pillows cloaked in silk-tasseled brocades, a white marble fireplace topped with a precious 19th-century bronze clock, and numerous antique fixtures. Upstairs, the 60 guest rooms and luxury suites are individually decorated with a mixture of French Empire and English antiques and custom-made matching furniture (including large, hand-painted, four-poster canopied beds), as well as modern amenities such as televisions, private baths, direct-dial phones, and individually controlled thermostats. For maximum charm, request a deluxe room or suite; these rooms have wonderful semicircular bay windows as well as fireplaces and queen-size beds. Concierge services, business facilities, valet service, a limousine, and valet parking are also available. The adjacent Cafe Majestic, one of the city's more romantic restaurants, serves very good California-Asian dishes ranging from sautéed coho salmon with fresh peach salsa to a mixed grill of lamb chop, quail, and sausage with polenta. After dinner, sip a digestif at the handsome 19th-century French mahogany bar and note the fascinating framed butterfly collection displayed on the dark turquoise walls. *$$$; AE, DC, MC, V; no checks; breakfast, dinner Tues–Sat; map:L3* &

Phoenix Hotel / ★★

601 EDDY ST; 415/776-1380 OR 800/248-9466

What do the Red Hot Chili Peppers, Johnny Depp, Ziggy Marley, Pearl Jam, Linda Ronstadt, and Arlo Guthrie have in common? At one time or another they've all checked into the Phoenix Hotel. Why? Because it's cool. Not hip, mind you, or lavish or discreet or exclusive. In fact, at a first glance you wouldn't think much of it, except for the heated outdoor pool with its paisley mural by artist Francis Forlenza and the modern-sculpture garden surrounding it. And you definitely won't think highly of the seedy Tenderloin location. But this retro 1950s-style hotel is the primo pick of visiting rock bands, writers, filmmakers, and celebrities, partly because the Phoenix is the best thing San Francisco has to offer for Southern Californians seeking a Palm Springs–style hotel. The 44 bungalow-style guest rooms are uniquely decorated with bamboo furnishings, an assortment of tropical plants, and original local artwork. VCRs and movies are available on request, as well as an on-call massage therapist. Heck, there's even free parking (if the limos and tour buses haven't hogged the lot). Adjoining the hotel is Backflip, an aqua-blue cocktail lounge serving tapas and Caribbean-style appetizers to a young, hip crowd (see review in the Restaurants chapter). *$$; AE, DC, MC, V; no checks; map:L4*

Queen Anne Hotel / ★★★

1590 SUTTER ST; 415/441-2828 OR 800/227-3970

The Queen Anne is one classy hotel. In fact, it was once a grooming school for upper-class young women, and has since been converted into a fabulous re-creation of San Francisco's turn-of-the-century inns. The "Grand Salon" lobby, for example, is draped with rich burgundy fabrics and replete with English oak paneling and period antiques. The rooms are equally opulent, each decorated with marble-top dressers, beautiful armoires, and a various assortment of Victorian-era antiques. They also have a wide array of niceties: some have a separate parlor area with a wet bar, while others have corner turret bay windows, reading nooks, and fireplaces. All rooms have two telephones (one's in the bathroom) and a television. Guests can also retire to the parlor with its fluted columns and floor-to-ceiling fireplace, or in the hotel's library. Luxury amenities include morning newspaper delivery, complimentary continental breakfast and afternoon tea and sherry, room service, and access to an off-premises health club with a lap pool. *$$$; AE, DC, DIS, MC, V; checks OK (in advance); www.queenanne.com; map:L3* &

Pacific Heights

The Bed and Breakfast Inn / ★★

4 CHARLTON CT; 415/921-9784

San Francisco's first bed-and-breakfast maintains the convincing illusion that it's a charming old English inn in a picturesque mews somewhere in Cornwall. The main difference, of course, is that you're not surrounded by verdant countryside dotted with horses and sheep munching on grassy meadows and wildflowers. Instead, this B&B tucked into a cul-de-sac is just steps away from the popular boutiques, bars, and restaurants lining Union Street, one of the city's most popular shopping areas. The three adjoining green Victorian buildings—graced with twining ivy, window boxes bursting with bright red geraniums, and a birdhouse bobbing from a tree out front—offer 13 enchanting guest rooms, each individually decorated with family antiques, floral prints, and appealing personal touches (ask for a room that opens directly onto the alluring back garden). The least expensive rooms have shared baths. Of the two sunny penthouses, the Mayfair offers a living room, kitchen, latticed balcony, and spiral staircase leading to a bedroom loft with a king-size bed; the Garden Suite, popular with groups of four, has a king-size bed in the master bedroom, a double bed in the loft, a fully stocked kitchen, a living room with a fireplace, two bathrooms (one with a Jacuzzi tub), and French doors leading to a private atrium and garden. You may enjoy your simple continental breakfast in your room, the garden, or the diminutive English tearoom. *$$; AE, CB, DC, DIS, MC, V; checks OK; map:K2*

Edward II Inn & Pub / ★★

3155 SCOTT ST; 415/922-3000 OR 800/473-2846

The best part about this three-story faux English country inn is that it has a guest room to match most anyone's budget, ranging from one of the pensione-style rooms with shared bathrooms (starting at $75) to one of the $225-a-night luxury suites complete with living room, kitchen, and whirlpool bathtub. The inn was originally built to house visitors to the 1915 Panama-Pacific International Exposition, and now it's the pride and joy of innkeepers Denise and Bob Holland, a friendly couple who have put together a fine hotel that does a lot of repeat business. Regardless of the rate, all the guest rooms are spotlessly clean and comfortably appointed with antique furnishings. Light sleepers will want to request a room that doesn't face busy Lombard Street; the hotel is also close to a wealth of great shops and restaurants along Union and Chestnut Streets. Perks include a complimentary breakfast and evening apéritifs, served in the adjoining pub (naturally). *$–$$$; AE, MC, V; no checks; map:J1*

El Drisco / ★★★

2901 PACIFIC AVE; 415/346-2880 OR 800/634-7277
If you're a fan of San Francisco's Ritz-Carlton, you'll adore El Drisco. The six-story structure, perched on one of the most coveted blocks in the city, was built in 1903 as a boardinghouse for neighborhood servants. After surviving the great fire of 1906, it was converted into a hotel in the mid-'20s but eventually fell into major disrepair. Combining the financial might of hotelier Tom Callinan (Meadowood, the Inn at Southbridge) and the interior design skills of Glenn Texeira (Ritz-Carlton, Manila), El Drisco's proprietors transformed years of blood, sweat, and greenbacks into one of the finest small hotels in the city. The 24 rooms and 19 suites are bathed in soothing shades of alabaster, celadon, and buttercup yellow and feature rich fabrics, quality antiques, and superior mattresses. Standard amenities include a two-line phone with a modem hookup, a CD player, a discreetly hidden TV with a VCR, and a minibar; suites include a handsome sofa bed, an additional phone and TV, and terrific views. The spacious marble-clad bathrooms are equipped with hair dryers, plush robes, and (in most units) bathtubs. Room 304A—a corner suite with an extraordinary view of Pacific Heights mansions and the surrounding bay—is a favorite. An extended continental breakfast is served in one of the three quiet, comfortable common rooms. *$$$; AE, DC, DIS, MC, V; no checks; map:J2* ⴲ

Jackson Court / ★★

2198 JACKSON ST; 415/929-7670
Tucked away behind a brick archway and a white-trellised garden courtyard, this three-story brownstone is set in the heart of the exclusive Pacific Heights residential neighborhood. The living room of the sedate manse is comfortably grand, with Oriental carpeting, gilt-framed mirrors, and a striking, oversize fireplace adorned with figures of wind sprites and storm gods. All 10 blissfully quiet guest rooms have handsome architectural details, pleasantly spare high-quality antiques, telephones, cable television, and private baths; two rooms have fireplaces. Particularly noteworthy is the luxurious Garden Court suite, originally the mansion's dining room, which boasts handcrafted wood paneling and cabinets, an antique chandelier, period furnishings, a king-size bed, and a private garden patio. After dining downstairs on the expanded continental breakfast, spend the day browsing the numerous boutiques along bustling Union Street, and return in time for the late afternoon tea served in the living room. *$$$; AE, MC, V; checks OK; map:K2*

Marina Inn / ★★✫

3110 OCTAVIA ST; 415/928-1000 OR 800/274-1420
 If you don't really care where you stay in San Francisco and you want the most for your money, book a room here; we checked out all the

inexpensive lodgings in the city and none have come close to offering as good a deal. The building, located on busy Lombard Street (the *only* caveat), is a handsome 1924 four-story Victorian, and the guest rooms are equally impressive: four-poster beds with cozy comforters and mattresses, rustic pine-wood furnishings, attractive wallpaper, and a pleasant color scheme of rose, hunter green, and pale yellow. You'll especially appreciate the high-class touches that even many of the city's expensive hotels don't include, such as full bathtubs with showers, remote-control televisions discreetly hidden in pine cabinetry, and nightly turndown service à la chocolates on your pillow. How much for all these creature comforts? As little as $65 a night, and that includes complimentary continental breakfast and afternoon sherry. It's in a good location as well—within easy walking distance of the shops and restaurants along Chestnut and Union Streets, and right on the bus route to downtown. *$–$$; AE, MC, V; no checks; map:L1* &

The Sherman House / ★★★★

2160 GREEN ST; 415/563-3600 OR 800/424-5777
Once the home of musical-instrument magnate and opera buff Leander Sherman, this 1876 Victorian mansion has housed such luminaries as Lillian Russell and Enrico Caruso, who sang to privileged guests in the house's private three-story recital hall. The stunning decor is based on a French Second Empire motif, with fine antiques and choice custom replicas, richly upholstered sofas and chairs, and gorgeous carpets covering polished hardwood floors. The huge, sky-lit recital hall still has a grand piano, but now the room serves as a luxurious lobby guarded by a bevy of musically minded finches. Most of the eight guest rooms and the six one-bedroom suites feature gilded bronze chandeliers, brocaded bed hangings, rich tapestries, and beautifully crafted wainscoting. A few rooms even have such extras as a private garden, bay view, and rooftop deck, and all but one have a wood-burning marble fireplace (ask for one of the upstairs rooms, which have broad bay windows, plush window seats, and views of the bay). If you prefer more contemporary surroundings, the Carriage House contains three luxury suites decorated with silk floral fabrics and French country furnishings. The concierge, butler, valet parking, and 24-hour room service are superb. Guests are also given exclusive seating at the Sherman House Restaurant—a grand dining establishment that, unfortunately, is closed to nonguests. *$$$; AE, DC, MC, V; checks OK; breakfast, lunch, dinner every day for guests only (reservations required); www.integra.fr/relaischateaux/sherman; map:K2*

Union Street Inn / ★

2229 UNION ST; 415/346-0424
Owners Jane Bertorelli and David Coyle have lent such a pleasant personal touch to the period decor, and the staff is so convivial, that this

delightful bed-and-breakfast wins a prize for overall ambiance. Although the two-story Edwardian mansion is situated amid the bustle of trendy Union Street, it's set high above the traffic at the top of a steep set of stairs. The five large guest rooms and a deluxe carriage house across the garden have private baths (some feature Jacuzzis), king- or queen-size beds, telephones, terry-cloth robes, fresh cut flowers, and televisions (for those who can't survive the Edwardian era without one). Each room has its own theme and color scheme, enhanced by bay windows, patterned wallpaper, Oriental carpets, antiques, and comforters. The best rooms, such as the Wildrose, face the flourishing back garden. The parlor downstairs is furnished with a fireplace, a beguiling range of period finds, and a 24-hour coffee/tea/buffet station. Start your day with a full breakfast in the beautiful English garden, in the parlor, or in bed; spend the afternoon strolling through Union Street's ever-popular boutiques, bars, and cafes; then return by 5pm for a predinner snack of wine and cheese. *$$; AE, MC, V; checks OK; www.unionstreetinn.com; map:K2*

Haight-Ashbury

The Herb 'n Inn / ★★

525 ASHBURY ST; 415/553-8542

If you really want a true only-in-San Francisco experience, reserve a room at the Herb 'n Inn, one of our favorite B&Bs in the city. It's run by sister-brother duo Pam and Bruce Brennan, an immensely likable pair who know the highlights and history of the Haight better than anyone. Four cozy guest rooms are housed in a big, classic Victorian home situated a half-block from the famed intersection of Haight and Ashbury Streets. Since the rates are very reasonable, spend a few extra bucks on the Cilantro Room, the largest room and the only one with a private bathroom (as well as a view of the sunny back garden). The large Coriander Room, which faces the streets, is popular as well, while the Tarragon Room has two small beds and its own private deck (perfect for smokers, who aren't allowed to fire up inside the house). You'll love Bruce's breakfasts, featuring heaping mounds of potato pancakes, waffles, crepes, popovers, and such, served in the big, inviting country-style kitchen. Bruce also offers tours of his Psychedelic History Museum (formerly the living room) as well as personal tours of the city. The Brennans also offer basic office services (for example, you can have your email forwarded here) and unlimited advice on the best places to go in the city. Children and gay couples are always welcome. *$; MC, V; no checks; map:J4*

Red Victorian Bed, Breakfast & Art / ★★☆

1665 HAIGHT ST; 415/864-1978

The Red Vic, located smack-dab on an exciting stretch of Haight Street, is one of the most eclectic and groovy lodgings in the city. You'll have the quintessential Haight-Ashbury experience staying in any of the 18 colorfully decorated rooms, each with its own Summer of Love theme. For example, the Flower Child room has rainbow-colored walls, a mural of the sun on the ceiling, and a hand-crocheted shawl on the bed's headboard. The Peacock Suite features psychedelic, multicolored patterns, hanging beads, and a canopy bed. Four of the guest rooms have private baths, while the remaining rooms share four bathrooms down the hall. A complimentary continental breakfast is served family style, offering an opportunity to meet the other guests (and what an interesting lot it is). Former flower child Sami Sunchild owns and runs this one-of-a-kind tribute to the '60s, and you couldn't dream up a more perfect, gracious host. So c'mon, inject a little peace, love, and happiness into your vacation and give Ms. Sunchild a call. *$–$$$; AE, DIS, MC, V; checks OK; map:I5*

Stanyan Park Hotel / ★★

750 STANYAN ST; 415/751-1000

If you're interested in the historic Haight-Ashbury area but aren't willing to forgo the creature comforts you've grown accustomed to over the years, you'll appreciate what the Stanyan Park Hotel has to offer. The stately three-story Victorian has been in operation since 1904, long enough to put it on the National Register of Historic Places. Hence the Victorian theme throughout: Victorian furnishings, bedding, wallpaper, curtains, and carpets, all tastefully done. You'll like the bathrooms as well: each has a tub-shower with a massaging showerhead and scented soaps. Standard guest rooms start at about $110. The hotel also has a bevy of suites starting at $250 that include full kitchen, dining room, and living room and can comfortably sleep up to six. A complimentary continental breakfast is included, as is a tea service each afternoon and evening. *$$–$$$; AE, DC, DIS, MC, V; no checks; map:I5* ♿

The Castro

Dolores Park Inn / ★★

3641 17TH ST; 415/621-0482

Rumor has it that celebrities such as Robert Downey Jr. and Tom Cruise stay at this beautiful 1874 Victorian inn to avoid their fans. Either that, or they just like staying here, which is easy to understand. First off, it's in a great location—adjacent to popular Dolores Park and just a short stroll to the numerous Castro district shops, cafes, and clubs. The guest rooms are appealing as well, each individually decorated with beautiful antiques and queen-size beds. The two most popular rooms are the Suite, which has a 20-foot sun deck overlooking Twin Peaks as well as a four-poster bed and kitchen, and the deluxe Carriage House with its Jacuzzi tub, fireplace, heated marble floor, kitchen, and washer-dryer. A two-night minimum stay is required (four nights in the Carriage House), though we guarantee you'll want to stay longer. *$$; MC, V; checks OK; map:L6*

Inn on Castro / ★☆

321 CASTRO ST; 415/861-0321

This convivial bed-and-breakfast, catering to the gay and lesbian community for nearly two decades, has developed an ardent following—hence the intriguing collection of more than 100 heart-shaped boxes on the sideboard in the hallway, trinkets left behind by a legion of wistful patrons who can say they left their hearts in San Francisco. The restored Edwardian exterior is painted in a pleasing medley of blue, rose, and green, with gilded details and dentils. The interior is equally festive, with contemporary furnishings, original modern art, exotic plants, and elaborate flower arrangements. There are eight individually decorated guest rooms ranging from a small single to a suite with a deck; every room has a private bath and a direct-dial phone. Avoid the sunny but noisy rooms facing Castro Street. TVs are available (though noses tend to wrinkle if you ask for one). An elaborate breakfast, served in the dining room, may feature a fresh fruit salad, house-made muffins, fruit juice, and scrambled eggs, French toast, or pancakes. After your repast, relax in the cozy living room with its fireplace and deeply tufted Italian couches, or head out for a stroll in the colorful, ever-bustling Castro. *$$; MC, V; checks OK; www. innoncastro.com; map:K6*

Airport Area

Comfort Suites / ★

121 E GRAND AVE, SOUTH SAN FRANCISCO; 650/589-7100 OR 800/228-5150

The midpriced Comfort Suites is recommended for families who want to be well situated for an early departure. There's the outdoor hot tub for Mom and Dad to relax in while the kids duke it out on the Nintendo game system or watch one of the pay-cable channels. As the name says, each room is a suite, and comes with a king bed, queen sleeper sofa for the kids, microwave, and a refrigerator, as well as a hair dryer, iron and board, and the requisite coffeemaker. The rooms are clean, comfortable, and ordinary—exactly what you'd expect. It's the free perks that make this hotel attractive, such as complimentary continental breakfast, evening soup-and-bread bar, and airport shuttle service. *$$; AE, DC, DIS, MC, V; no checks; map:KK5* &

Embassy Suites / ★★☆

250 GATEWAY BLVD, SOUTH SAN FRANCISCO; 650/589-3400 OR 800/362-2779

Your best pick—and most expensive—of the airport chain hotels is Embassy Suites, which does its darnedest to make you forget you're in the middle of dreary, industrial South San Francisco. It's almost as if you're in Las Vegas, what with the spewing fountains, numerous palm trees, and indoor pool, whirlpool, and sauna. The guest rooms are all two-room suites and come with all the standard deluxe amenities such as two TVs, two phones, microwave, fridge, wet bar, coffeemaker, hair dryer, iron, and so on. A cooked-to-order breakfast (delivered to your door upon request) is included in the room rate. Shuttle service to SFO is complimentary as well. *$$$; AE, DC, MC, V; checks OK; map:KK5* &

Holiday Inn (San Francisco Airport North) / ★

275 S AIRPORT BLVD, SOUTH SAN FRANCISCO; 650/873-3550 OR 800/HOLIDAY

If you prefer to go with who you know, there's the Holiday Inn next to the airport. The guest rooms are Holiday Inn standard: spotless, inoffensively decorated, with all the usual amenities such as minibars, coffeemakers, hair dryers, movie channels, and such. There's also a health spa (sauna, gym, Jacuzzi, and tanning bed) to keep you entertained until your flight leaves, as well as a gift shop, full business services, and Rookie's Sports Bar & Grill and the City Cafe, which serves American-style breakfast, lunch, and dinner daily. The rates are surprisingly reasonable for all the perks included, starting at only $85 per night. *$$–$$$; AE, DC, DIS, MC, V; no checks; map:KK5* &

San Francisco Airport North Travelodge / ★

326 S AIRPORT BLVD, SOUTH SAN FRANCISCO; 650/583-9600 OR 800/578-7878

If you've got kids in tow and a limited budget, the Travelodge near SFO is your best choice for a quick morning departure. All of the rooms are at or under $100, but the real clincher is the hotel's large heated pool, where the kids can play Marco Polo all day while the parents relax in the typically warm South San Francisco weather. The list of free amenities includes a complimentary copy of *USA Today*, in-room coffee and tea, free HBO, and voice mail. There's a so-so American-style restaurant adjacent to the hotel, though we recommend you walk to Rookie's Sports Bar & Grill at the Holiday Inn down the street. The hotel's 24-hour complimentary shuttle will get you to SFO in about 5 minutes. *$$; AE, DC, DIS, MC, V; no checks; map:KK5*

EXPLORING

EXPLORING

Top 25 Attractions

1) ALCATRAZ ISLAND

Access from Pier 41; 415/705-5555 This tiny land mass in the middle of the San Francisco Bay was first "discovered" in 1775 by Spaniard Juan Manuel Ayala, who named it after *los alcatrazes* (the pelicans) that populated this coastal area. After the United States annexed California, the island served as a military post for 80 years. The first lighthouse on the West Coast was built here in 1854, and in the 1860s the island held prisoners from the Civil War. From 1870 to 1890, during the western Indian Wars, captured Native Americans were held on the island as well.

But Alcatraz is undoubtedly most famous as a federal penitentiary that harbored the 20th century's most villainous gangsters. From 1934 to 1963, "the Rock" was home away from home for the likes of Al Capone, Machine Gun Kelly, and legendary "birdman" Robert Stroud. The icy waters of the bay made escaping alive all but impossible. Frank Morris and the Anglin brothers, whose attempt to do so was turned into the Clint Eastwood blockbuster *Escape from Alcatraz*, did manage to leave the island, but whether they made it across the frigid bay is still the subject of debate. In 1963, shortly after their departure, the prison was closed permanently (though primarily for financial, not security, reasons). The masks they used as decoys to trick the guards are on display at the Maritime Museum (see Attraction number 25).

In 1972 the island was made part of the Golden Gate National Recreation Area, and it has since become one of San Francisco's must-see tourist spots. But Alcatraz isn't for everyone. The park can get extremely crowded during summer months and weekends, so it's not recommended for those averse to sharing their day with a pack of strangers. If the crowds don't deter you, then perhaps the steep quarter-mile climb to the prison or the chilly bay winds will. For those eager to see the Rock firsthand, warm clothing and comfortable shoes are strongly recommended, as are advance tickets. Reservations during peak season are mandatory, and if you don't plan your tour early, you may be shut out.

Self-guided tours let you wander at your own pace, while the excellent audio tours (narrated by actual former prisoners) offer a fantastic account of what it was like being a prisoner here—definitely worth the small additional fee. Park rangers lead crowds off the ferry and up the hill, recounting colorful stories about the island's former residents and critiques of Hollywood's various attempts to translate prison life to the silver screen. The Blue and Gold Fleet also offers evening tours of the island, which include a sunset view of the city (fog permitting). *Admis-*

TOP 25 ATTRACTIONS

1) Alcatraz Island
2) Cable cars
3) Fisherman's Wharf
4) Pier 39
5) Union Square
6) Golden Gate Bridge
7) Lombard Street
8) Golden Gate Park
9) Coit Tower
10) The Presidio
11) Ghirardelli Square and The Cannery
12) The Exploratorium and the Palace of Fine Arts
13) San Francisco Museum of Modern Art
14) Yerba Buena Gardens
15) Golden Gate National Recreation Area
16) Embarcadero Center
17) Alamo Square Historical District
18) Grace Cathedral
19) California Palace of the Legion of Honor
20) Cliff House
21) Fort Mason
22) Mission Dolores
23) Yerba Buena Center for the Arts and Metreon
24) City Hall
25) San Francisco Maritime National Historical Park–Hyde Street Pier–Aquatic Park

sion charge for adults and children 5 and older. Summer, every day 9:15am–4:15pm; winter, every day 9:30am–2:15pm. Ferries depart every half hour at 15 and 45 minutes after the hour on weekends, and every 45 minutes Mon–Fri. Arrive at least 20 minutes before departure time; map:K1 (ferry) &

2) CABLE CARS

Hyde-Powell and Powell-Mason cable car lines begin at Powell and Market Sts; the California line begins at Market and Drumm Sts The once-extensive network of cable cars that traversed San Francisco's steep streets was the brainchild of Andrew Smith Hallidie, a London-born mechanic turned entrepreneur. Like so many others, he came to California in 1852 to make his fortune. Instead of digging for gold, however, he developed a transport system for gold mining, and his patented wire ropes were soon hauling more than nuggets.

With an eye on San Francisco's peaks and valleys, Hallidie thought to use his cable system to carry passengers up Nob Hill (then, as now, one of the most prestigious pieces of real estate in the town). Many people who lived along the hill's steep inclines welcomed the idea of a cable car in their neighborhood and invested in Hallidie's Clay Street Hill Railroad. On August 1, 1873, the first cable car cruised down Clay Street from Jones to Kearny and miraculously made it back up again. A San Francisco icon was born.

Skeptics ridiculed the engineless invention, but slowly the cable car was embraced by the city as a much-improved—not to mention cleaner—alternative to horse-drawn cars (particularly since horses were often injured trying to climb the brutally steep hills). Soon there were eight lines running in Pacific Heights, the Castro, Russian Hill, and Nob Hill. Popular as they were, however, their star was soon eclipsed by the electric trolley. By 1893 many cable car lines were already being replaced. In the 20th century, buses and budget concerns meant the elimination of several more lines. Concerned citizens fought hard to preserve the California, Hyde-Powell, and Powell-Mason lines and, in 1964, they were added to the National Register of Historic Places. Such landmark status ensures that the 6-ton cars will run—always at a steady 9½ miles an hour—well into the 21st century.

The cars are so popular with tourists that the Hyde-Powell and Powell-Mason lines are almost impossible to get on unless you wait in the unbelievably long line near the bottom of Powell at Market or at the Hyde Street Pier. Locals, however, still use the California line to commute to and from the Financial District. This less-popular trip offers great views with less waiting time. Tip: If you're an early riser, the lines are usually quite short during the first run, which is often the most beautiful. *Map:M3 (Hyde-Powell and Powell-Mason), N2 (California)*

3) FISHERMAN'S WHARF

Jefferson St between Grant and Van Ness Aves Fisherman's Wharf, one of the most popular tourist destinations in the world, has had a long and varied history. During the heady Gold Rush years, this bustling waterfront area—known then as Meigg's Wharf—was a major shipping port. Around the turn of the century, however, construction of new, larger port facilities along the Embarcadero forced the city's Italian immigrant fishermen to move their fleet here from east of Telegraph Hill.

And so Fisherman's Wharf remained a bastion for San Francisco's fishing fleet until, in the late '50s and '60s, two concurrent forces changed the face of this bustling waterfront for better or worse: a boom in tourism and a drop in commercial fishing. Cost Plus Imports opened in 1958 while waterfront real estate was still within affordable reach. The **GHI-RARDELLI SQUARE** shopping complex rose like a phoenix in 1968, the same year **THE CANNERY** overhaul was completed (see Attraction number 11). Pier 39 opened to the public in 1978. As with many of San Francisco's historic districts, tourism forever changed the look and feel of this once working-class neighborhood. But remnants of San Francisco's commercial fishing industry can still be found—arrive in the early morning hours to see the fishing fleet at the foot of Taylor Street bring their catch onto the docks.

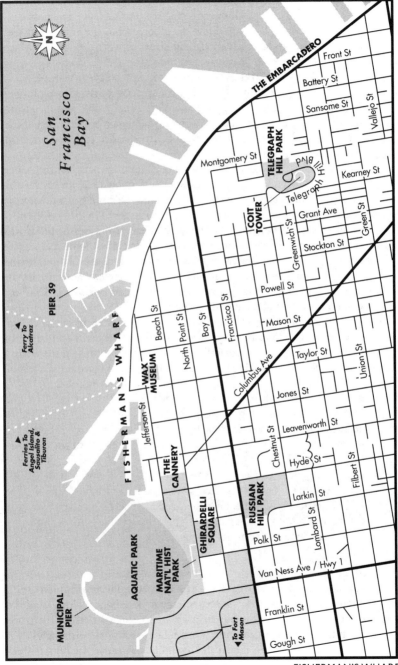

San Francisco Bay

THE EMBARCADERO

Front St

Battery St

Sansome St

Vallejo St

Montgomery St

TELEGRAPH HILL PARK

Hill Blvd

Kearney St

Telegraph

COIT TOWER

Greenwich St

Grant Ave

Green St

Stockton St

Powell St

Francisco St

PIER 39

Beach St

North Point St

Bay St

Mason St

FISHERMAN'S WHARF

Ferry To Alcatraz

WAX MUSEUM

Columbus Ave

Taylor St

Union St

Jones St

Jefferson St

Ferries To Angel Island, Sausalito & Tiburon

Chestnut St

Leavenworth St

THE CANNERY

Hyde St

Filbert St

RUSSIAN HILL PARK

Larkin St

GHIRARDELLI SQUARE

Lombard St

AQUATIC PARK

Polk St

MARITIME NAT'L HIST PARK

Van Ness Ave / Hwy 1

MUNICIPAL PIER

To Fort Mason

Franklin St

Gough St

FISHERMAN'S WHARF

Today, sidewalk stalls that once served up fish stew to local fishermen now sell cooked Dungeness crabs to tourists from Tallahassee and Tokyo. It's not a place you'll find many locals, but the amusement-park atmosphere that dominates Jefferson Street between Taylor and Mason attracts millions each year from around the world.

After 30 years, **RIPLEY'S BELIEVE IT OR NOT! MUSEUM** (415/771-6188; www.ripleysf.com) still draws the curious tourist looking for jaw-dropping proof that the world is full of the unbelievable and the bizarre. Robert LeRoy Ripley made his career assembling a museum full of oddities, such as a shrunken human torso, a two-headed calf, and other outlandish freaks of nature.

Where else would the likes of Fidel Castro, Michael Jackson, Count Dracula, Marilyn Monroe, and George Bush mingle but within the walls of a wax museum? In the style of Madame Tussaud's more notorious London venture, San Francisco's **WAX MUSEUM** (415/202-0400) offers an up-close and personal experience with the likenesses of the world's most famous people, monsters, and Republicans. Some 250 figures already crowd the waterfront, with recent favorites like Leonardo DiCaprio and Will Smith regularly being added. The museum has expanded to engulf the Haunted Goldmine next door, and the $15 million renovation will include shops and dining.

Of course, there are numerous restaurants catering to the crowds; most are Italian, offering moderately priced pasta and seafood (all served with sourdough bread, naturally). The oldest restaurant on the wharf is **ALIOTO'S** (415/673-0183), said to be the premier place for the famous seafood stew that's a city favorite, cioppino **A. SABELLA'S** (415/711-6775) at 2766 Taylor Street was founded in 1920 by the Sabella family, Sicilian immigrants. Eighty years and three generations later, they've added a touch of Asian to their Italian seafood dishes (see review in the Restaurants chapter). After dinner, try **LOU'S PIER 47 CLUB** (415/771-0377) at 300 Jefferson, which offers live music nightly. For a touch of history, slip into the **BUENA VISTA CAFE** (415/474-5044) at 2765 Hyde Street, where the first Irish coffee was served in the United States in 1952.

Fisherman's Wharf is open year-round. There's no charge for wandering around, but the surrounding parking lots fill quickly and charge a small fortune, so consider taking public transportation. *Every day; map:L1* &

4) PIER 39

The Embarcadero at Beach St; 415/981-7437 The goal behind the creation of Pier 39 was to re-create the genteel boardwalk culture of the last century. It opened to the public in 1978, offering more than 100 stores, 10 restaurants, an arcade, and beautiful bay views. But although Pier 39 is certainly a spectacle, it bears no resemblance to anything remotely genteel. Then again, it's hard to get an overall impression of the architecture while elbowing through throngs of people. Reportedly the third most-visited tourist site in the *world* (Walt Disney can claim the first two), this place is not recommended for the claustrophobic.

The Pier's restaurants are known for fun atmosphere rather than phenomenal food, and the shops are more kitsch than classic, but with so many wares and attractions, it endeavors to offer something for everyone, particularly families. **PUPPETS ON THE PIER**, the **NFL SHOP, SF TEA & COFFEE COMPANY**, and **VICTORIAN SHOPPE** are among the stores vying for tourist dollars. Restaurants include **BUBBA GUMP SHRIMP CO.** (415/781-4867), **NEPTUNE'S PALACE** (415/434-2260), and **YET WAH** (415/434-4430). The 707,000-gallon, $38 million **UNDERWATER WORLD** wows visitors with a menagerie of finned creatures including sharks and stingrays. And the **CINEMAX THEATER** provides visitors with an informative 35-minute movie about San Francisco, perfect for first-timers.

There are countless places for you to drop your cash (and credit) at Pier 39, but the best attraction is free: the boisterous California **SEA LIONS** that call the actual pier home. Since the winter of 1990, hundreds of the barking pinnipeds have claimed the marina for their own, much to the annoyance of the property owners, who would prefer to rent the space to paying customers. Safeguarded by the Federal Marine Mammal Protection Act, the sea lions are here to stay—at least until they decide to find other digs. On the weekends from 11am to 5pm, volunteers from the Marine Mammal Center give informative talks about the sea lions. The noisy herd summers in the Channel Islands, so if you're visiting anytime from June to August you may miss out. *Free; every day 10:30am–8:30pm; map:M1* &

5) UNION SQUARE

Bounded by Geary, Post, Stockton, and Powell Sts The area around Union Square was once home to fashionable turn-of-the century houses, synagogues, and churches. In 1847, civil engineer Jasper O'Farrell designed a spacious open square as a refuge in the growing city. During the American Civil War, San Franciscans—influenced by the elegant oratory of preacher Thomas Starr King—took a decidedly pro-Union stance, a momentous decision that eventually swayed the entire state. The square was named to commemorate this historic position. At the center of the square a bronze statue of Victory stands atop a granite Corinthian column, commemorating Admiral Dewey's exploits in the Spanish-American War. (The model for *Victory* was a young art student named Alma de Bretteville, who went on to marry the heir to the Spreckels sugar fortune. Decades later, she would help fund the creation of the California Palace of the Legion of Honor.)

Union Square was soon surrounded with the by-product of San Francisco's economic boom: businesses and stores blossomed in the decades following the Gold Rush and statehood. In 1876, I. Magnin opened its doors at the corner of Geary and Stockton (sadly, the store has since closed). In 1896, the City of Paris (now Neiman Marcus) went up across the street. The famed St. Francis Hotel (now the Westin St. Francis) was not far behind, bursting on the scene in 1904. Soon after, the great earthquake and fire struck, leveling the entire area.

Undaunted by Mother Nature, San Franciscans continued their building boom and the square was soon in business again. Only a few of the older establishments, such as **BULLOCK & JONES** and **SHREVE & COMPANY**, remain. Most of the postquake buildings have been either demolished or taken over by newer, trendier tenants such as Niketown, Macy's, and Saks Fifth Avenue. Gone are the days of crinoline-clad ladies promenading with parasols to protect themselves from the sun, but Union Square, like New York's Fifth Avenue, is still the historic heart of San Francisco shopping. A major renovation of the square is purportedly in the works, but it will be years before it's completed. *Map:M3*

6) GOLDEN GATE BRIDGE

Hwys I/101, between San Francisco and Marin County; 415/921-5858 The happy marriage of engineering, design, and necessity has transformed the highway bridge linking San Francisco and Marin County into one of the most recognizable—and the most photographed—landmarks in the world. Designed by engineer Joseph P. Strauss and architect Irving F. Morrow, the mile-long Golden Gate Bridge was built by a crew of hundreds, a number of whom gave the ultimate sacrifice. The 887,000-ton bridge, which opened in 1937, took a mere 52 months to complete, but cost a then-riveting $35 million. The toll booths, designed by Donald MacDonald to complement the original art deco feel, were added in 1982; the charge is now $3 for southbound traffic.

Though it's more than 60 years old, the Golden Gate Bridge's numbers are still impressive. The art deco twin towers rise 746 feet into the sky like a ladder—each rung a slightly different dimension—narrowing as the eye rises. The daring 4,200-foot span between the two towers held the record for the longest span of a suspension bridge for over 20 years. The bridge boasts 7,650 feet of cables from anchorage to anchorage; the maximum side sway of the center span is 27.7 feet.

But don't take our word for it, because if there's one thing everyone should do at least once in their life, it's to walk across the world-famous Golden Gate Bridge. Simply driving across won't work; to feel the bridge swaying under your feet as you peer 260 feet down to certain death—now that's living. It's a 1¼-mile stroll across and takes about an hour round-trip. Pedestrians and bicyclists must use the path on the east side of the bridge, which is open daily from 5am to 9pm (bicyclists have to use the west side on weekends). Free parking is available at both ends of the bridge, though the lots usually fill up fast on summer weekends (late arrivals will have to park in the Presidio and walk). The vista point on the Marin side provides a perfect place to stop and reflect on the sheer beauty of this architectural and engineering wonder. Be sure to dress warmly or you'll be sorry: the weather is windy and cold most of the year. *Map:G1*

7) LOMBARD STREET

1000 block of Lombard St One curvaceous block of Lombard between Hyde and Leavenworth has given the street the title "the Crookedest Street in the World." In actuality, the majority of Lombard is wide and straight and filled with cheap motels. But this little Russian Hill block with its eight switchbacks is certainly circuitous. What it isn't, however, is San Francisco's crookedest, let alone the world's. Vermont Street on Potrero Hill takes the honor for curves, but tourists still flock to Lombard in droves to wend their way down the world-renowned one-way street.

Perhaps it's the terraced gardens filled with hydrangeas, the beautiful brick-lined road, or the carefully manicured picturesque hedges that attract such attention. What is certain is that block-long lines of cars queue up to witness this urban wonder during the summer weekends, causing some major congestion in a once-peaceful neighborhood (and boy do the neighbors complain—but to no avail). While the best photo opportunities are from the bottom of the hill, most people linger at the top to take in the stunning vistas to the east. The view of the bay from this spot is truly breathtaking.

Lombard used to be a simple cobblestone street back in the early part of the century. The hill's steep 27 percent grade led one inventive resident to propose a series of curves to make the area accessible to the increasingly popular automobile. Engineer Clyde Healy designed the present configuration, which transformed the steep grade to a mere 16 percent. The city paid for the initial work, but the residents chipped in for the fancy brick-work and agreed to tend their gardens. Talk of privatizing the street has been heard on and off for years, but city funds keep the site open to tourists.

Unfortunately for residents and tourists alike, this small stretch of Lombard simply can't handle all the traffic it attracts. If you plan to drive it, expect long lines and potential overheating as you crawl up the steep incline that leads to the crooked block. All for a few seconds of fun. *Map:L1*

8) GOLDEN GATE PARK

Bounded by Stanyan St and the Great Hwy, Fulton St and Lincoln Wy; 415/831-2700 Encompassing 1,017 acres of beautiful, lush grounds dotted with magnificent museums, lakes, and ponds, San Francisco's beloved Golden Gate Park is a masterpiece of park design. For a good

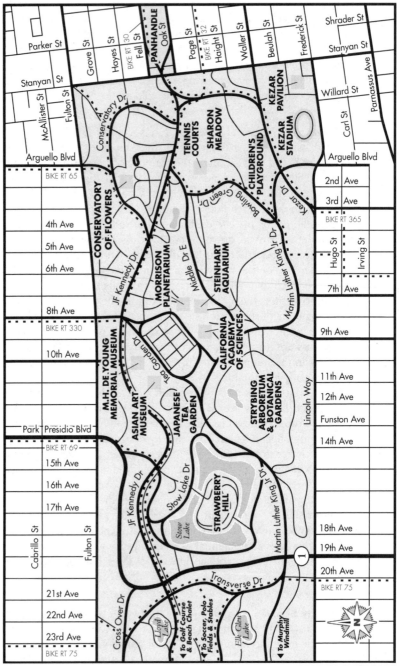

GOLDEN GATE PARK

introduction to the park's attractions, join one of the **FREE GUIDED WALKING TOURS** held every weekend from May through October; call the Friends of Recreation and Parks (415/263-0991 or 415/750-5105) for more information. Park highlights include the **STRYBING ARBORETUM AND BOTANICAL GARDENS** (near 9th Ave and Lincoln Wy; 415/661-1316), home to 7,500 plant and tree varieties. Nearby is the spectacular **CONSERVATORY OF FLOWERS** (John F. Kennedy Dr near Conservatory Dr; 415/641-7978), an 1879 Victorian fairyland hothouse that was full of tropical flora until massive storms destroyed most of its glass-paneled glory in 1995. It's still an architectural beauty worth admiring from the outside, but is closed until enough money can be acquired to pay the lofty repair bill.

West of the conservatory is lovely **STOW LAKE**, where you can rent rowboats, paddleboats, and electric boats and circle the 430-foot-high artificial island known as Strawberry Hill, the highest peak in the park. Highlights include the hill's waterfall and Chinese moon-watching pavilion, as well as the numerous turtles and ducks that live on the serene lake; call 415/752-0347 for boat rental information.

The oldest Japanese-style park in the United States, the **JAPANESE TEA GARDEN** (415/752-1171) attracts crowds, particularly when the cherry blossoms and azaleas bloom in late March and April. Weekdays and rainy afternoons are ideal times to visit. The garden first opened its gates in 1894. The story goes that the original curators, the Hagiwara family, invented the fortune cookie to be served here with tea (though the Golden Gate Fortune Cookies factory makes the same claim). It's located off Martin Luther King Jr. Drive in Golden Gate Park (between Strybing Arboretum and the Asian Art Museum).

If you have youngsters in tow, don't skip the **CHILDREN'S PLAYGROUND**, which has a dazzling, restored 1912 carousel (the oldest one in a public park) that's guaranteed to make every child's heart go pitter-patter, located at the intersection of Martin Luther King Jr. and Kezar Drives.

Every Sunday, Golden Gate Park's main drag is closed to auto traffic so skaters and joggers can let loose on the tree-lined street. Skate rentals are readily available on Fulton Street and on Haight Street. *Map:D5-I5*

9) COIT TOWER

I Telegraph Hill Blvd; 415/362-0808 A childhood rescue from a fiery blaze left Lillie Hitchcock forever fascinated with firefighting and firemen. Legendary for her saucy behavior, this 19th-century socialite liked to hang out at the Engine Company Number 5 and, according to legend, often dressed in firemen's uniforms. (It was the undressing that made society cringe.)

In spite of her brazen past, she married Howard Coit, a wealthy businessman, and when she died in 1929 she left $125,000 to the city "to be expended in an appropriate manner for the purpose of adding to the beauty of the city which I have always loved." The Coit Advisory Committee, after much haranguing, settled on a memorial tower. In 1933 a 180-foot fluted pillar was erected high atop a hill amid the trees of Pioneer Park, one of the city's oldest parks. Designed by architect Arthur Brown Jr. of City Hall fame, this still-controversial tower is said to resemble a fire hose. Off-color comparisons have also been made over the years, but the tower remains a landmark on the city's skyline nonetheless.

In 1934 President Franklin Roosevelt's Works Progress Administration provided funding for local artists to embellish the tower lobby with a series of frescoes that pay homage to the men and women who labored to make California great. Twenty-five master artists and 19 apprentices worked on the murals for 8½ months; each received $94 a month for their efforts. Ray Boynton's *Animal Force and Machine Force* juxtaposes fishermen pulling their catch in from the sea with a hydroelectric dam. *California*, by Maxine Albro, highlights the importance of agriculture to the state. One of the most controversial murals is by John Langley Howard: his *California Industrial Scenes* depicts the harsh reality of the country's laboring poor—migrant workers, miners, and construction workers toiling in dangerous, stressful conditions for little pay.

Today, Coit Tower houses a tacky gift shop and a seemingly permanent "roach coach," but it also affords some of the most spectacular views of the North Bay, including the Golden Gate Bridge, and of the hills of Contra Costa County to the east. Stroll up at sunset on a clear San Francisco day and be rewarded by the sight of the magical lights of the skyscrapers, bridges, and the sailboats floating on the bay. *Admission charge for adults and children 5 and older; every day 10am–7pm; map:N1*

10) THE PRESIDIO

Entrances via Lombard St, Marina Blvd, Arguello Blvd, Presidio Ave, and Lincoln Blvd; 415/561-4323 For more than 200 years the Presidio served as San Francisco's principal military outpost, originally commandeered for its strategic importance and later retained for its private golf course. Founded in 1776 by Spaniard Jose Joaquin Moraga, it was occupied from 1822 to 1835 by the Mexican government when the region was known as Alta California. When California's gold-filled upper half was annexed by the United States, the Presidio remained a military base. During the rough-and-tumble Gold Rush years, added fortifications were built to protect the city. At the turn of the last century, the Presidio proved strategically important as the United States stretched its interests west across the Pacific to Hawaii and beyond.

Crissy Army Airfield, the first of its kind on the West Coast, was established in the 1920s. After the attack on Pearl Harbor and the ensuing U.S. involvement in World War II, more than a million soldiers passed through the Presidio on their way to war. The base hospital served 72,000 sick and wounded during that era.

In 1972 sections of the 1,480-acre installation were turned over to the Golden Gate National Recreation Area (GGNRA) and opened to the public as part of the largest network of urban parkland in the world. In 1989 the military left for good, and the entire area—consisting of coastal scrub, prairie grasslands, sand dunes, a variety of rare plants, and more than 150 species of birds—became part of the GGNRA (though many army officers' homes and barracks still remain). With miles of biking and hiking trails and a first-class golf course, the Presidio remains a verdant oasis in the urban jungle.

As you drive through the Presidio, you'll see numerous signs of its military past, including dozens of recessed bunkers and many **WAR MEMORIALS**. One of the most poignant is the tribute to the men of the USS *San Francisco*. Sections of the actual bridge of the warship—riddled with enormous holes from enemy gunfire—flank a series of bronze plaques depicting the sad, heroic story of the 107 men lost in one of the fiercest close-quarter battles in naval history. The shrine is located at the end of El Camino del Mar, one block up from the Cliff House Restaurant and gift shop. The **PRESIDIO ARMY MUSEUM** at Lincoln Boulevard and Funston Avenue (Wed–Sun noon–5pm) offers detailed exhibitions on the rich history of the park and features a complete model of the 1915 Panama-Pacific International Exposition, which gave the city the Palace of Fine Arts.

To inquire about a wide array of **FREE GUIDED TOURS** of the Presidio's highlights—everything from bike rides to pier crabbing and cemetery walks—call the Presidio **VISITOR CENTER** (415/561-4323). The top tour pick is **FORT POINT**, where park rangers clad in authentic Civil War garb play soldier, loading and firing a smoothbore cannon from within the pre–Civil War brick fortress (open Wed–Sun, 10am–5pm). After the tour, take a bayside walk along the **GOLDEN GATE PROMENADE**, the most popular and scenic jogging route in the city. The 4-mile path, which starts (or ends) at Fort Point, leads past the wind surfers off Crissy Field, around the Yacht Harbor, and along the Marina Green toward Fort Mason and Aquatic Park.

Note: Navigating your way into, through, and out of the Presidio is almost comically confusing. Even locals get temporarily turned around as they attempt to negotiate the maze of winding roads, dead ends, and maddening loops, so don't even attempt the trip without a map. The smartest approach is to head due west on Geary Boulevard to the end, stop by the **GGNRA VISITORS CENTER** behind the Cliff House Restaurant, and plunk down $2.50 for *The Official Map & Guide to the Presidio. Every day 10am–5pm; 415/556-8642; map:G1-3–J1-3*

11) GHIRARDELLI SQUARE AND THE CANNERY

900 North Point St, between Polk and Larkin Sts, 415/775-5500 ■
2801 Leavenworth St, 415/771-3112 Domenico Ghirardelli, the Italian-born founder of San Francisco's signature chocolate company, came to California in 1849 to search for gold, but he had better luck selling sweets. He set up shop in Jackson Square and was so successful that his sons later expanded the business. In 1893 they purchased land in a then-remote northern district of the city for a new factory. The Ghirardelli family hired architect William Mooser Sr., an important player in the development of turn-of-the-century San Francisco, to design a modern complex that would span an entire block of the waterfront. The famous Clock Tower office building, a derivation of the French Château de Blois, was the final edifice to go up.

Along with the glowing Ghirardelli sign that lit the harbor at night, the Clock Tower became a treasured jewel in the skyline. When the plant could not keep up with technology and was abandoned for a newer, sleeker East Bay property, fear grew that the landmark would be demolished. Enter another San Francisco entrepreneur, William Roth, heir to the Matson shipping fortune. In order to preserve the city's now-famous waterfront silhouette, he bought the property and decided to transform it.

His vision was not some staid museum, but a 10-level shopping complex with 50 stores and 20 eateries of various stripes. Dozens of architects and artists worked on the project, which attempted to capture the spirit of the old factory while offering a modern touch. Today it is one of the more tasteful spots in the frenetic maze of consumerism that has overwhelmed the wharf.

From July to September, **HISTORIC WALKING TOURS** of the square are offered by guides dressed in period costume. The 20-minute tour includes historic information about Domingo Ghirardelli and his family, his chocolate empire, the eight buildings within Ghirardelli Square, and *Andrea*, the controversial mermaid fountain sculpture. Guests receive chocolate treats at the end of the tour.

Dozens of boutiques make Ghirardelli Square a fun destination for shopping enthusiasts. **CARLO BARON LEATHER** features a good selection of leather fashions. **GORDON BENNETT** specializes in furnishings for home and garden. The **HAT GENERATION** has a collection of unique headgear, both playful and serious. The nationally known **NATURE COMPANY** sells gifts, books, music, and toys with an environmental focus. A wide array of glass art and decorative items are available at **THE GLASS SCULPTORS. PEARL OF THE ORIENT** offers a fine collection of pearl jewelry.

Three art galleries call Ghirardelli home. The **MARK REUBEN GALLERY**, on the first floor of the Cocoa Building, focuses on sports-related works and history legends. Works by contemporary American artists fill the **MUD, WIND, AND FIRE** gallery on the first floor of the Mustard Building. The Woolen Mill Building is home to the **WHITE BUF-FALO GALLERY**, which specializes in American Indian art and jewelry. Several fine restaurants are located in the complex. **THE MANDARIN RESTAURANT** (415/673-8812), in the Woolen Mill Building, has long offered one of San Francisco's finest Peking-Sichuan dining experiences. **MCCORMICK & KULETO'S** (415/929-1730), in the Wurster Building, features classic seafood dishes with a spectacular view of the bay. The city's most elegant Indian food can be found at **GAYLORD INDIA RESTAURANT** (415/771-8822), on the third and fourth floors of the historic Chocolate Building. Recently opened in the spot formerly held by Long Bar is **ANA MARANDA** (415/771-6800). Located in the Power House Building, this French-Vietnamese restaurant is owned in part by Don Johnson and sometimes appears on his show *Nash Bridges*. *Free; every day 10am–9pm summer, 10am–6pm winter; map:L1*

The brick facade is all that remains of architect William M. Mooser Sr.'s 1907 fruit canning plant, affectionately known as **THE CANNERY** (2801 Leavenworth St; 415/771-3112). The building's entrails were completely gutted in the late 1960s when enterprising developers converted it into a mall with more than 50 different shops on three floors. For stability, a reinforced concrete structure was carefully inserted into the existing brick building. The result is a whimsical blend of old and new, where hundred-year-old olive trees mingle with modern cafes and trendy vendors in a central courtyard.

On the top floor, **JACK'S CANNERY BAR** (415/931-6400) boasts more than 110 beers on tap, a national record. Also on the third floor, the **MUSEUM OF THE CITY OF SAN FRANCISCO** (415/928-0289; Wed–Sun 10am–4pm) features maps, photographs, and other memorabilia from the city's colorful past. Special exhibitions highlight the 1906 earthquake and fire, San Francisco's role in international affairs, and the city's rich ethnic and cultural heritage. *Free; every day 10am–9pm summer, 10am–6pm winter; www.thecannery.com; map:L1* ⅙

12) THE EXPLORATORIUM AND THE PALACE OF FINE ARTS

3301 Lyon St (at Bay St); 415/563-6504 Architect Bernard Maybeck's mock-Roman ruin and reflecting pool, an ode to classical art and architecture, is all that remains of the Panama-Pacific International Exposition, held along San Francisco's marina in 1915. The event was more than an international fair; it was a chance for San Francisco to celebrate its renaissance after the devastation of the recent earthquake and fire. In a spirited show of decadence, a mile-long stretch of the marina was lined with neoclassical buildings to form a mock classical city, with the Palace of Fine Arts its glowing centerpiece. Since officially the party was meant to celebrate the opening of the Panama Canal, the Tower of Jewels re-created that engineering feat, complete with movable parts and electric lights.

The party lasted 288 days, and when it was over many locals didn't want the fabulous centerpiece destroyed. Maybeck's design was saved and used as a recreation area. Later it housed ammunition during World War II. After the war the building fell into ruin (actual this time, not re-created). In 1962 Walter Johnson, a wealthy Marina district resident, offered to help refurbish the Beaux Arts structure. With matching funds from the government in hand, William Merchant was enlisted to bring the beauty back to life. It took 13 years and $7 million, but the central rotunda with its sea of rosy Corinthian columns now resides permanently at the corner of Lyon and Bay Streets. The swan-filled waters and ver-dant grounds provide an ideal setting for picnicking, strolling, and the ever-popular wedding photos.

Part of the city-owned space has been converted into a theater. Orig-inally built for ballet performances, the **PALACE OF FINE ARTS THEATRE** boasts a 75-foot-wide stage. Today it houses not only stage productions but film festivals, concerts, local graduation ceremonies—and, when he's in town, the antics of David Letterman's *Late Show*.

Founded by Frank Oppenheimer, brother of the inventor of the A-bomb, the **EXPLORATORIUM** (3601 Lyon St at Marina Blvd; 415/563-7337 or 415/561-0360 for recorded information) has been called the finest science museum in the United States by *Scientific American* maga-zine. But to call it a museum is misleading. While more than 100,000 square feet of science-related objects are on display, visitors aren't expected to look from a distance: touching is definitely encouraged. The Explorato-rium offers 400 hands-on displays where children and adults alike can create fog, experience a face-morphing screen, design bubbles, or step inside an optical illusion. Visitors are invited to explore the wondrous world of science through displays that explain the phenomena behind light, electricity, motion, sound, and weather.

A visit to the **TACTILE DOME**—a series of lightproof, soundproof chambers that visitors navigate using only their sense of touch—requires making reservations. **PLAYSQUARE** offers younger children (accompa-nied by an adult) the chance to use their imaginations as they try out motor skills and social skills.

The Exploratorium's unique appeal draws visitors from all over the globe, including such notables as President Bill Clinton and science author Oliver Sacks. The gift shop, stuffed with educational tools and toys, is well worth a visit (great for educational stocking stuffers). Parking is free. *Admission charge for adults and children 3 and older; free on the first Wed of each month. Memorial Day–Labor Day and holidays: Mon–Tues and Thurs–Sun 10am–6pm, Wed 10am–9pm. Rest of the year: Tues and Thurs–Sun 10am–5pm; Wed 10am–9pm; map:J1* &

13) SAN FRANCISCO MUSEUM OF MODERN ART

151 3rd St between Mission and Howard Sts; 415/357-4000 The San Francisco Museum of Modern Art (SFMOMA), now housed in a new modernist building designed by internationally acclaimed Swiss architect Mario Botta, offers more than 17,000 works of art, including gems by Picasso, Matisse, O'Keeffe, Rivera, Pollock, Warhol, Klee, De Forest, and Liechtenstein, to name just a few. Some contend that the museum's exhibition space plays second fiddle to the dramatic black-and-white central tower that climbs out of Botta's impressive sienna brick building. The interior architecture is equally impressive. Natural light falls through the circular skylight, illuminating the central atrium and a few of the nearby galleries. A catwalk stretches high above the atrium, offering museum-goers a touch of adventure along with their culture.

After whisking David Ross away from his position at the helm of New York's Whitney Museum, SFMOMA went on a buying spree, acquiring 23 new works by leading 20th-century artists, including Louise Bourgeois, Marcel Duchamp, Alberto Giacometti, Anselm Kiefer, Brice Marden, Piet Mondrian, Robert Motherwell, Barnett Newman, Robert Rauschenberg, and Wayne Thiebaud. Newly installed are 14 key works by Rauschenberg, Duchamp's *Fountain*, Giacometti's *Head*, and Bourgeois's *The Nest*.

In addition to its growing permanent collection, the museum has become the West Coast stop for many ambitious traveling shows. Exhibitions run the gamut from shows highlighting Jasper Johns and René Magritte to exhibitions on contemporary Japanese textiles and 19th-century landscape photographer Carleton Watkins. The museum also offers an excellent bookstore and cafe. *Admission charge for adults and children 13 and older; Mon, Tues, Fri–Sun 11am-6pm, Thurs 11am–9pm; map:N3* &

14) YERBA BUENA GARDENS

3rd and Mission Sts; 415/543-1275 In the heart of the city, across from the San Francisco Museum of Modern Art, is Yerba Buena Gardens. This five-acre park in the middle of the growing South of Market (SoMa) district features an Esplanade Garden with restaurants and cafes, a sculpture garden, and inviting stretches of wide open space. A beautiful memorial to Martin Luther King Jr. sits partially hidden behind a glistening waterfall. The memorial's multiple panels feature odes to peace and tolerance written in a number of languages. Bands play regularly during lunch, making this a popular spot for a noontime picnic.

Newly added is the $56 million **ROOFTOP AT YERBA BUENA**, devoted to youth recreation; the highlight is a 93-year-old hand-carved **CAROUSEL**. Originally from San Francisco's infamous Playland-at-the-Beach, the carousel returns to the city after spending 20 years in Southern

California. Also at the Rooftop is a NHL-regulation-size **HOCKEY RINK**, which serves hockey teams and figure skaters and boasts a breathtaking view of the San Francisco skyline. The rink is the home of former Olympian Brian Boitano's Youth Skate, which provides free ice time and skating lessons to area kids. Children can also enjoy a 12-lane **BOWLING ALLEY**, a technology and arts center called **ZEUM**, and a garden for and by kids.

Tours of Yerba Buena Gardens are available by appointment for a nominal fee; for more details, call 415/541-0312. *Map:N3*

15) GOLDEN GATE NATIONAL RECREATION AREA

415/556-0560 The Golden Gate National Recreation Area (GGNRA) encompasses some of the Bay Area's (and Northern California's) most beautiful real estate. At nearly 80,000 acres, it is twice the size of San Francisco itself, and welcomes 20 million visitors each year. The late San Francisco Congressman Philip Burton, an early environmentalist, was responsible for drafting the legislation that preserves lands vacated by the military for public use. The National Park Service protects these lands against developers, whose mouths must salivate at the thought of all the potential million-dollar lots that line the coast.

While the GGNRA is the modern protector of this vast land, it is really the military we have to thank for the preservation of so much open space. Even before statehood, the Marin Headlands and San Francisco coast were sequestered for strategic military installations; their presence has long kept developers at bay. Today these now-decommissioned installations provide some of the most beautiful views found anywhere in the world.

In San Francisco, the GGNRA consists of the **PRESIDIO, FORT POINT, CRISSY FIELD,** the **SAN FRANCISCO MARITIME NATIONAL HISTORICAL PARK, OCEAN BEACH , BAKER BEACH, CHINA BEACH,** and **LAND'S END,** along with the shoreline between Fort Mason and the Golden Gate Bridge. **ALCATRAZ** falls under GGNRA jurisdiction as well. The paths and trails leading from Fort Mason to Fort Point are ideal for walking, jogging, or cycling, and you can even do in-line skating along some stretches.

Across the bay in Marin, the GGNRA oversees still more land. The **MARIN HEADLANDS** provide sanity to many San Franciscans. A mere bridge away from the hustle of urban life, the headlands are a verdant paradise for hikers, bikers, and horseback riders. Spend a day hiking around Mount Tamalpais or soaking up the sun on Tennessee Beach. At Rodeo Beach, stop by the **MARIN HEADLANDS VISITORS CENTER,** housed in another decommissioned army base, for maps and information on this amazing area. Back in the city at Fort Mason, the GGNRA official headquarters is the place to go for maps, information, and a free copy of the quarterly publication *Park Events,* listing GGNRA activities and events.

16) EMBARCADERO CENTER

Bordered by Drumm, Sacramento, Clay, and Battery Sts; 415/772-0500 Developer David Rockefeller and architect John C. Portman Jr. turned a 10-acre downtown area into a modern shopping complex filled with a number of fabulous works of art, including Louise Nevelson's *Sky Tree* and Jean Dubuffet's *La Chiffonniere.* With more than 120 shops, this three-level, four-block outdoor shopping complex endeavors to provide a happy compromise between the San Francisco Shopping Centre's enclosed mall world and the genteel shops along Post and Geary in Union Square. Bordered by Battery and Drumm west to east and Clay and Sacramento north to south, the busy center offers office workers a convenient place to shop during the lunch hour and also attracts tourists from all over the world. They come for the popular names in fashion like **BANANA REPUBLIC, TALBOT'S, GAP, VICTORIA'S SECRET, ANN TAYLOR,** and **ENZO ANGIOLINI** and housewares giants like **WILLIAMS-SONOMA** and **POTTERY BARN.** But there are also a number of smaller boutiques with an indie feel, like **EDWARD'S LUGGAGE** and **EARTH'S SAKE.**

Small soup-and-sandwich cafes cater to the eat-and-run crowd, while tried-and-true favorites like **CHEVY'S** (415/391-2323) and **PIZZERIA UNO** (415/397-8667) provide a more festive dining atmosphere. For a more elegant meal try **SCOTT'S SEAFOOD** (415/981-0622), **HARBOR VILLAGE** (415/781-8833), or **SPLENDIDO** (415/986-3222).

A welcome new addition to the complex is the **EMBARCADERO CENTER CINEMA** (415/352-0810). The five screens occasionally show blockbuster titles, but the focus is definitely on foreign and independent features. *Map:N2*

17) ALAMO SQUARE HISTORICAL DISTRICT

Hayes and Steiner Sts; 415/292-2009 Alamo Square, named for the poplar trees that lined the area in the 1860s (*alamo* is Spanish for "poplar"), is a quiet hilltop park bounded by Steiner, Fulton, Webster, and Grove Streets. Home to San Francisco's famous Victorians known as the Painted Ladies, the park is one of the most visited and photographed spots in the city. Built between 1892 and 1896 by Irish-born carpenter Matthew Cavanaugh, the seven Queen Anne–style homes lining Steiner Street feature similar three-story design with bay windows, decorative wood trim, and steeply angled roofs. Cavanaugh lived in number 722 with his family, but he built the others as spec houses. Most people pass through on their way to Japantown or the Haight, taking a few snapshots of the colorful houses and continuing on their way. But the park deserves a longer look. A leisurely picnic allows time to admire the views of the renovated City Hall down Fulton Street and reflect on the turn-of-the-century elegance of the surrounding Victorian homes (a handful have been turned into bed-and-breakfasts).

The **ARCHBISHOP'S MANSION** (1000 Fulton St), which opened as a bed-and-breakfast in 1982, was built in 1904 as the residence for the Catholic Archbishop of San Francisco. In 1980, Jonathan Shannon and Jeffrey Ross began renovating the Second Empire–style mansion. After the walls and woodworking were overhauled, furnishings were gathered from sources around the world in an attempt to capture the feeling of the 19th-century French Belle Epoque. From the foyer, a three-story staircase sweeps upward to the guest rooms and suites, named after leading characters in famous operas. A 16-foot-wide stained-glass dome miraculously survived the 1906 earthquake. It's open to the public, so feel free to pop in and take a look.

Built in 1865 by the Baum family, the **ALAMO SQUARE BED & BREAKFAST** (719 Scott St; 415/922-2055) is a 15-room mansion designed by German-born architects Kenitzer and Barth. From a transitional period in San Francisco architecture, the Baum house incorporates three different styles: Queen Anne, neoclassical, and Colonial revival. The roofline and cantilevered circular corner bay window are Queen Anne style, while the exterior ornamentation and oval window are neoclassical. The interior architecture boasts 12-foot ceilings and floors made of quarter-sawn oak. Also part of the Alamo Square Bed & Breakfast is the Tudor-revival house next door. Constructed in 1896 by the firm of Knox and Cook, the building features elaborate half-timbering along its stucco finish. The interior of the home boasts its original unpainted redwood paneling with butterfly joints as well as built-in window seats, cabinetry, and bookcases.

A third restored treasure is **CHATEAU TIVOLI** (1057 Steiner St; 415/776-5462). Built in 1892 by architect William H. Armitage, it was restored a century later at a cost of more than a million dollars. Today the 22-room historic landmark is a bed-and-breakfast. *Map:K4*

18) GRACE CATHEDRAL

1100 California St at Taylor St; 415/749-6310 The former site of railroad tycoon Charles Crocker's mansion is now the seat of the Episcopal Church in San Francisco. The Crocker family donated their block of real estate to the church after the fire of 1906 demolished their homes. Inspired by the Gothic architecture of Notre Dame in Paris, this neo-Gothic edifice was designed by Lewis Hobart in the late 1920s; it took 53 years to complete. Ralph Adams Cram added to Hobart's original plan, and the building was finally consecrated in 1964.

In a thoroughly 20th-century fashion, the cathedral pays tribute to various artistic styles. The many stained-glass windows are fairly modern creations, but they recall the medieval mastery of Saint-Chapelle in Paris. The heavy bronze doors are copies of Lorenzo Ghiberti's Renaissance masterpiece *Gates of Paradise* in Florence. A modern black and bronze stone sculpture of St. Francis by Beniamino Bufano welcomes visitors with outstretched arms.

Grace is perhaps most renowned for its brilliant rose window, a 25-foot-wide stained-glass wonder made in Chartres, France, at the Gabriel Loire studios in 1964. The design depicts St. Francis of Assisi's 13th-century *Canticle of the Sun*. Featured at the center is Brother Sun. Surrounding the sun are Chi Rho (Greek symbols for Christ), Sister Moon, Sister Earth, Sister Death, Sister Water, Brother Fire, and Brother Wind.

Another popular attraction is the re-creation of a 13th-century labyrinth at Chartres. A purple and beige carpet sits near the entrance to the church past the baptismal font. Take your shoes off and join the silent walkers as they meditate through the quarter-mile maze. A similar labyrinth sits in the cathedral's outer courtyard. In 1995, an AIDS Interfaith Chapel was opened as a memorial to the countless lives lost to the disease. A Keith Haring sculpture and panels from the AIDS Memorial Quilt comfort those who have lost loved ones.

Soaring architecture and room for 1,300 people make Grace an ideal spot for concerts. From uplifting church choirs and organ recitals by John Fenstermaker (the cathedral's organist and choir master) to jazz jam sessions, music is frequently heard within these walls. Other cultural events held here include weekly forums on spiritual, social, and political issues, as well as silent films.

The Grace Cathedral Gift Shop sells mugs, T-shirts, religious books, and artistically rendered copies of religious icons. There's also a small cafe. *Free; Sun–Fri 7am–6pm, Sat 8am–6pm; map:M2*

19) CALIFORNIA PALACE OF THE LEGION OF HONOR

Legion of Honor Dr at 34th Ave and Clement St; 415/863-3330
Perched on a hilltop along San Francisco's rugged coast is one of the world's most dramatically situated museums. Closed for three years for seismic work and general renovation (which unearthed the bones of more than 1,000 pioneers buried in what was the old Golden Gate Cemetery), the museum reopened on November 11, 1997. Founded in 1924 by Alma de Bretteville Spreckels (wife of the sugar magnate) and Adolph Bernard, the California Palace of the Legion of Honor stands as a monument to the soldiers who fell in France during World War I. The museum's neoclassical style and the triumphal arch were designed by George Applegarth and modeled after the Legion of Honor in Paris.

The Legion is home to one of the finest collections of **RODIN SCULPTURES** outside Paris. Several imposing statues fill the grounds as well; these include equestrian bronzes of El Cid and Joan of Arc, and one of only five original castings of Rodin's *The Thinker*. One of the most controversial works of art on the lawn is George Segal's *The Holocaust*. White plaster figures writhe on the ground while a solitary figure watches from behind a barbed-wire fence. The juxtaposition of this intense suffering with the natural beauty of the surrounding landscape renders the artwork even more disturbing—as was intended.

The Legion was originally devoted exclusively to French art but recently expanded its collection. Today the museum's holdings span 4,000 years of art. The 20 galleries on the museum's upper level are devoted to European art from the 14th to 20th centuries. Key artists include El Greco, Rubens, Cellini, Rembrandt, Manet, Rodin, Monet, and Cézanne. Period rooms feature furniture and decorative arts from various eras, and include a dramatic Mudejar ceiling from medieval Spain. The lower level houses English and European porcelain and ancient Assyrian, Greek, Roman, and Egyptian art. Also on the lower level is the collection of the Achenbach Foundation for Graphic Arts, which has the largest holdings of graphic art in the West. The museum's collection of 70,000 works on paper has been digitized to make these fragile pieces available to the public.

The Legion Cafe has a garden terrace with a spectacular view of the Golden Gate Bridge. Parking here is limited, so be prepared to walk up the hill from the surrounding streets. *Admission charge for adults and children 12 and older; Tues, Thurs–Sun 9:30am–5pm, Wed 9:30am–9pm (last admission at 8pm); map:E4*

20) CLIFF HOUSE

1090 Point Lobos Ave (at Upper Great Hwy); 415/386-3330 If 19th-century photographs of this shoreline establishment have lured you out to Ocean Beach, prepare to be disappointed. The famous seven-story structure built by Adolph Sutro in 1896 was actually the second incarnation of the Cliff House; the original, built in 1863, was destroyed in a fire in 1894. Sutro seized the opportunity to create something truly extraordinary. His architectural wonder, designed by C. J. Colley and F. S. Lemme, was lavish even by Victorian standards. Often compared to a gingerbread house, the building, sadly, was destroyed in a fire in 1907, though it lives on in photographs, postcards, and the memories of those who were alive at the turn of the century.

The present Cliff House, the fifth incarnation, is a sad shadow of its former self. What used to be an architectural treat is now a boring box—albeit a box with great views. Design aside, the lack of truly spectacular waterfront dining in this city by the bay ensures that the Cliff House will draw crowds for decades to come. In what feels like an attempt to make up for the sub-par exterior, visitors can choose from no less than three dining options. The most casual atmosphere is on the bottom level at **PHINEAS T. BARNACLE** (or PTB), where soups, sandwiches, and bar-food favorites like nachos and deep-fried calamari are available (along with magnificent ocean views in the fireside cocktail lounge next door).

The **SEAFOOD & BEVERAGE COMPANY** features oysters on the half shell, crab cakes, and a long list of fresh fillets and shellfish along with its beautiful view. A more elegant atmosphere is available at **UPSTAIRS AT THE CLIFF HOUSE,** where brunch is served on Sundays and traditional Continental cuisine—lobster, rack of lamb, and pasta—is dished up nightly. The ocean view and candles add a bit of romance to the otherwise unremarkable meal.

If there was ever a museum that was truly "fun for all ages," it's the **MUSÉE MÉCANIQUE,** a glorious old trove of antique mechanical amusement machines that actually work (providing you have a pocket full of quarters). Watch the children cower in fear as Laughing "Fat Lady" Sal— of San Francisco's Playland-at-the-Beach fame—gives her infamous cackle of a greeting, or see what Grandmother the Fortune Teller has to say about your future. Most older kids congregate around the far less imaginative video games in back. Behind the arcade museum is the **CAMERA OBSCURA,** a replica of Leonardo da Vinci's invention that reflects and magnifies an image of nearby Seal Rocks and Ocean Beach on a giant parabolic mirror. Both are located directly below the Cliff House Restaurant at 1090 Point Lobos Avenue, and are open daily 11am to 7pm (open earlier on weekends); 415/386-1170.

If you're feeling adventurous, consider a tour through the ruins of the **SUTRO BATHS**—the famous bathing area that once drew hundreds to the shore. In 1886, Adolph Sutro completed the baths at a cost of $250,000. The complex spread over three acres and included fresh- and saltwater tanks, three restaurants, history exhibits, art galleries, and an amphitheater. Phenomenally popular in its early years, the bath complex was struggling financially by the 1930s. A skating rink was attempted, but that too failed. In 1966 the site was sold to land developers, but before their high-rise apartments were completed a fire destroyed the property. Today the ruins of the baths are part of the Golden Gate National Recreation Area. *Map:C4*

21) FORT MASON

Marina Blvd and Buchanan St; 415/441-3400 The city of San Francisco has benefited time and time again from obsolete military real estate, and Fort Mason is perhaps the most inventive case. An important western command post for the U.S. Army in the second half of the 1800s and later a major military depot during World War II, Fort Mason Center is now part of the Golden Gate National Recreation Area (GGNRA). Since 1977 the vast complex of waterfront warehouses has housed more than 50 nonprofit arts, advocacy, and environmental groups.

Fort Mason's military history spans two centuries. In 1797 Spanish soldiers built a small fortification here and called it Bateria San Jose. When the Yankees claimed the area in the mid-1800s, they inherited the existing battery and renamed it Black Point. In 1863, during the Presidency of Millard Fillmore, the fort became a major army headquarters in the ongoing Indian wars. In 1882 the name was changed to Fort Mason in honor of Colonel Mason, the military governor of California from 1847 to 1849. During World War II, more than 1.5 million U.S. soldiers embarked for the Pacific theater from Fort Mason.

Today the focus is on culture. The center publishes a free monthly paper, *Fort Mason Center*, to keep locals and visitors abreast of the myriad events, exhibitions, and classes offered here. A number of museums and galleries bring the art world to the waterfront. The **MEXICAN MUSEUM** (presently in Building D, but scheduled to move to the South of Market area in 2002) was the first museum in the country to focus on the arts of Mexico and Mexican Americans. **MUSEO ITALO-AMERICANO** is devoted to contemporary works by Italian and Italian-American artists. The **SAN FRANCISCO CRAFT AND FOLK ART MUSEUM** exhibits handicrafts from around the world and offers many distinctive items for sale. The **AFRICAN-AMERICAN HISTORICAL AND CULTURAL SOCIETY** features a library, gallery, and exhibitions of African art.

The Center's five theaters include **LIFE ON THE WATER THEATRE** (Building B), the family-oriented **YOUNG PERFORMERS THEATRE**, the **MAGIC THEATRE** (Building D), which has premiered works by such playwrights as Sam Shepard, and **COWELL THEATER** (Pier 2), which hosts larger productions and the weekly radio program *West Coast Live*. International art exhibitions, crafts shows, and music events like the Celtic Music & Dance Festival are featured here throughout the year. Greens restaurant (Building A; 415/771-6222) offers brilliant bay views along with its award-winning vegetarian cuisine.

A fairly demanding stairway leads from the waterfront to upper Fort Mason, where the **GREAT MEADOW** offers hours of recreation. This wide stretch of rolling green is perfect for picnics, Frisbee, or a nap in the sun (or fog!). Alongside the meadow, former officers' quarters now house a youth hostel and the headquarters for the GGNRA, which provides information about its extensive park system. *Map:K1*

22) MISSION DOLORES

3321 16th St at Dolores St; 415/621-8203 Mission San Francisco de Assis (better known as Mission Dolores) is the sixth of Father Junípero Serra's 21 California missions, as well as the oldest standing structure in San Francisco. The adobe building, designed by Father Francisco Palou, was begun in 1782 and completed in 1791. Miraculously, the edifice survived a period of neglect during the middle of the 19th century and then two major earthquakes, one in 1868 and the infamous one in 1906. Architect Willis Polk began the restoration of the site in 1918.

The original mission is a compact structure standing a mere 22 feet wide and 114 feet long. The original four-foot-thick adobe walls have since been coated with cement to protect them from erosion, but several original details remain untouched. A trio of bronze bells brought from Mexico in the early 1800s decorate the chapel's interior. The hand-wrought ironwork along the font and altar is also original. Various statues and paintings record the rich Spanish Baroque tradition brought over to the New World by the conquistadores and later absorbed by Mexico.

The purpose for the many missions that run up and down the Camino Real from San Diego to Sonoma was to Christianize the Native Americans of the California frontier. The basket-weave designs of converted Costanoan Indians decorate the ceiling of the 175-seat chapel, where mass is still held at 7:30am on weekdays and 5pm on Saturdays.

For a $2 admission fee, visitors can wander leisurely through the chapel and into the neighboring museum, which is filled with religious artifacts from Spanish America, including gifts to the mission from Father Serra. Also on display is a glass window that provides an interesting look at the building's underlying adobe.

One of the mission's best features is its cemetery (old movie buffs may recognize the spot from Hitchcock's *Vertigo*). Gravestones from three centuries fill this small parcel of land, but what you can't see are the markers for the more than 5,000 Costanoans who are reportedly buried here. Prominent figures from the days when Mexico ruled the land rest in peace here—among them Francisco de Haro, the first mayor of San Francisco, and Captain Luis Antonio Arguello, the first Mexican governor of Alta California. Not far away is the grave of mission architect Father Palou.

The larger, multidomed basilica next to the chapel was built in 1913. It can accommodate up to 1,100 parishioners and is used for three masses on Sunday as well as numerous weddings. *Every day 9am–4:30pm; map:K5* &

23) YERBA BUENA CENTER FOR THE ARTS AND METREON

701 Mission St at 3rd St, 415/978-2787 ■ 4th and Mission Sts at Yerba Buena Gardens; 415/537-3400 After 20-plus years of politics, Yerba Buena Center for the Arts opened in 1993 and instantly provided a welcome addition to the burgeoning South of Market district. Across Third Street from the San Francisco Museum of Modern Art, and set amid a peaceful park, the center hosts artists from the worlds of theater, dance, plastic arts, and performance art. Unlike most museums, Yerba Buena has no permanent collection, but strives instead to offer exhibition opportunities to a broad range of artists.

Built by the San Francisco Redevelopment Agency, the center fills two buildings: a theater and a visual arts space. The **GALLERIES AND FORUM**, designed by Japanese architect Fumihiko Maki, features works by local, national, and international artists. Recent exhibitions include *Nothing but Ways* by filmmakers Lynn Kirby and Trinh T. Minh-Ha, and new ceramic works by Robert Hudson and Richard Shaw. The theater space, designed by James Stewart Polshek, features a 45-foot-deep stage and a 44-foot proscenium and seats 755 people. The space is rented out to dance and theater companies. *Admission charge for adults and children 6 and older; Tues–Sun 11am–6pm (until 8pm on first Thurs of each month); map:xxx* &

METREON—a South of Market megaplex entertainment center—is billed as one of the most forward-looking play/shop environments in existence. It certainly blows the movie competition out of the water, with 3,900 stadium-style seats and "the most advanced digital cinema sound in the world today." The **IMAX THEATRE**—with the largest screen in North America—features 3-D headsets that bring the screen action "into" the audience.

Metreon also offers a number of shops to peruse before or after the show. **MICROSOFT SF** and **SONYSTYLE** sell a predictable array of their own gadgets. More interesting is the **DISCOVERY CHANNEL STORE**, sure to be a hit with devotees of animal documentaries. At **WILD THINGS**, kids are encouraged to make up and perform in their own adventures with a crew of creative monsters modeled after Maurice Sendak's book. The Metreon Gateway hosts a lively marketplace that aims for a street-fair feel. Local artists sell original art, clothing, and gift items.

A few new dining venues endeavor to draw picky San Franciscans to the complex. **JILLIAN'S** claims to be the ultimate in entertainment with food, drinks, pool tables, videos, live music, and a DJ. **MONTAGE** (415/369-6111; see review in the Restaurants chapter) cooks up California cuisine with an emphasis on fresh seafood. You can order movie tickets while you dine, and they will be brought to your table. And a cantina in a garage?? That's **MALVINA'S**, tucked into the bizarre world of Jean "Moebius" Giraud's fictional work *The Airtight Garage*. Maurice Sendak is on display here, too; his artistry is the inspiration for this diner-style restaurant. Don't expect a crew of hovering waiters, though—this is a do-it-yourself spot.

In addition to new eateries, there are also spin-offs from five of the city's favorites: SoMa's **LONG LIFE NOODLE CO. & JOOK JOINT** offers unique and inexpensive Asian cuisine; the Castro's **FIREWOOD CAFE** features salads and pizza; Marin's venerable **BUCKHORN** specializes in grilled meats; **SANRAKU** re-creates the Japanese favorites popular at its lower Nob Hill location; and **LUNA LOCA** offers south-of-the-border fare. And of course, there's the ever-present Starbucks. *Map:N3*

24) CITY HALL

I Dr. Carlton B. Goodlett Pl at Polk St; 415/554-4858 San Francisco earthquakes have certainly taken their toll on City Hall. The old City Hall was devastated by the catastrophic events of 1906. In a drive to rebuild the city, newly elected Mayor "Sunny Jim" Rolph called for architects to bid on the new project. The front-runner was Chicago architect Daniel Burnham, who envisioned a complete overhaul of the entire Civic Center. The idea appealed to many in government who wanted to bring the city back to its prequake stature. Surprisingly, the job went to the local firm of Bakewell and Brown, with Arthur Brown Jr. in charge of designing the building. (Brown also designed the Opera House, Coit Tower, and Berkeley's City Hall.)

The striking Beaux Arts design was favored by Americans educated at the Ecole des Beaux Arts in Paris. The granite-and-marble edifice was topped by a massive dome (the world's fifth tallest), modeled after St. Peter's in Rome and the Capitol building in Washington, D.C. At 307 feet, it actually stands taller than the latter (which measures 287 feet). Over the Polk Street entrance, Renaissance-style sculptures by Henri Crenier symbolize Labor, Industry, Truth, Learning, Wisdom, and the Arts.

The doors to the 83-year-old City Hall reopened to the public in January 1999 after a four-year, $300 million renovation. The money was used to repair damage done by the 1989 Loma Prieta earthquake. In order to be completely retrofitted, the building was lifted off its base and placed on top of 600 vulcanized rubber and stainless steel base isolators, designed to insulate against tremors. About 1,200 tons of steel near the top of the dome were intended to help it sway in the event of another quake. Other renovations were more cosmetic, like the dome's $400,000 gold-leaf detailing and the enlarged atrium that accommodates more visitors.

The glory of City Hall is still the rotunda and the vast, fanning marble staircase. To the north is the City Store, filled with San Francisco memorabilia; a coffee bar is open during the week from 11am to 5pm. To the south is *Icons of San Francisco*, an exhibition filled with historical artifacts and tchotchkes. The second floor holds the offices of Mayor Willie Brown and the board of supervisors, the sheriff, and other officials. The massive building, which spans two full city blocks, serves a workforce of more than 1,000 people. Free docent tours are available seven days a week. *Free; Mon–Fri 8am–8pm, Sat–Sun noon–4pm; map:M4* ♿

25) SAN FRANCISCO MARITIME NATIONAL HISTORICAL PARK—HYDE STREET PIER—AQUATIC PARK

Beach St at Polk St; 415/556-3002 Before the completion of the Golden Gate Bridge, the **HYDE STREET PIER** served as a terminal for ferry service to Marin County and Berkeley. Today it draws crowds of cable car riders and historical ship enthusiasts. Among the vessels of yesteryear are the

193

Balclutha, a 256-foot square-rigger and one of the last great 19th-century sailing ships; the *C. A. Thayer*, a 156-foot schooner once used to transport Pacific coast lumber; the *Eureka*, a 300-foot ferry that carried passengers between San Francisco and Sausalito in the 1800s; the *Hercules*, a 135-foot steam tug; the *Alma*, a 59-foot, flat-bottomed cargo-carrying sailboat; and a 100-foot paddle tug called the *Eppleton Hall*, built in 1914. *Every day 10am–6pm; the museum closes at 5pm. Admission charge for adults and children ages 12 to 17; free for seniors over 62.*

Developed in the 1930s as part of the Works Progress Administration, **AQUATIC PARK** today houses the **MARITIME MUSEUM**. This white, ship-shaped building boasts one of the finest collections of maritime artifacts and memorabilia in the world. On display are figureheads, nautical instruments, and minutely detailed model ships. Photographs and naval memorabilia pay tribute to the history of the seafaring vessels around the world. For bibliophiles, the Porter Shaw Library has more than 14,000 volumes, back issues of some 500 periodicals, and an extensive bibliographic file on maritime-related works. The oral history collection preserves more than 400 interviews with salty sailors and some 100 sea chantey recordings. The library offers classes in oar-making and chantey singing. *Every day 10am–5pm. Admission charge for adults and children ages 12 to 17; free for seniors over 62.*

Also at the park is the **U.S.S. PAMPANITO**, located at Pier 45. This veteran submarine, built in 1943, sank five Japanese ships in the Pacific during World War II. Now a National Landmark, it has been restored and is open to the public. Don't forget to duck as you explore the sub's torpedo room, control room, crew's quarters, and fully operational galley. World War II submarine captain Edward Beach narrates the self-guided audio tour, providing an insider's perspective on the underwater world of war (415/775-1943). *Sun–Thurs 9am–6pm, Fri–Sat 9am–8pm. Admission charge for adults and children ages 6 and older. Map:L1*

Neighborhood Districts

FINANCIAL DISTRICT

More than 200,000 people make the pilgrimage to the Financial District—a sea of glass and steel skyscrapers bordered by Washington Street, Market Street, Montgomery Street, and the bay—every Monday through Friday to work, work, work. They come from as far away as Sacramento and Sebastopol and arrive by bridge, BART, Muni, ferry, train, bike, or on foot. From seven in the morning to six at night the streets are filled with people, cars, and buses, and the air is filled with a cacophony of horns, the clanging of construction equipment, and the tell-tale bells of

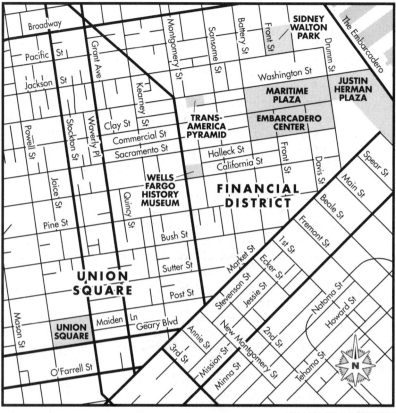

FINANCIAL DISTRICT

the cable cars. In fact, the only people who aren't in perpetual motion are the newspaper vendors and the homeless.

It wasn't always thus. The Financial District, like the Marina, is built on landfill. Over a century ago, before the city went mad with the news of gold, the waters of Yerba Buena Cove rose and fell at the foot of Rincon, Telegraph, and Nob Hills. There was no flat, gentle entryway into the city; rather, it was hilly and inhospitable. But then the Gold Rush began. Once a simple bayside beach town, San Francisco was soon transformed into a bustling metropolis. The influx of fortune seekers, and of savvy businessmen ready to make money off them, was unprecedented.

But the men who made the most money weren't panning for gold; they were sitting behind the desks at fledgling banks that supported the city's rapid growth. A. P. Giannini founded the Bank of Italy primarily to help newly arrived immigrants like his parents, who could not get loans from more established banks. During the early hours of the 1906 earthquake and subsequent fire, Giannini personally secured his holdings and was among the first to lend money to rebuild the city. Several years later, he also helped back the building of the Golden Gate Bridge, an adventure considered foolhardy by many. By then his company had been renamed Bank of America to coincide with the institution's growing power and Giannini's phenomenal wealth.

Today, two little-known downtown museums celebrate the city's chaotic growth during the 19th century. They are the **WELLS FARGO HISTORY ROOM** (415/396-7152) at 420 Montgomery Street and the **MUSEUM OF THE MONEY OF THE AMERICAN WEST** in the Bank of California at 400 California Street.

Nowadays, firms specializing in banking, telecommunications, power, engineering, insurance, and oil make their headquarters here in the neighborhood's massive skyscrapers. The most distinct of the Financial District's many high-rises is the quartz-aggregate **TRANSAMERICA PYRAMID**. Designed by William Pereira and Associates, and built from 1970 to 1972, this 853-foot-tall structure is the highest office building in the city. Adjacent to the Pyramid is **REDWOOD PARK**, a lush, tranquil oasis amid the downtown hubbub planted with 80 redwood trees imported from the Santa Cruz Mountains.

One of the most striking buildings on the San Francisco skyline is the **BANK OF AMERICA WORLD HEADQUARTERS** on California Street. Carved in dark granite, it stands 779 feet tall in A. P. Giannini Plaza before Masayuki Nagare's *Transcendence*, a black granite sculpture affectionately nicknamed "the Banker's Heart." Other buildings that stand out: aglow with a cluster of bright lights during the winter holiday season, the four high-rises of **EMBARCADERO CENTER** offer hundreds of shops to peruse in a modern, multilevel complex. For spectacular views, try the **CARNELIAN ROOM** on the 52nd floor of the BofA building.

Along the actual Embarcadero, the **FERRY BUILDING**, built in 1903, survived the quake and fire thanks to the heroic efforts of many. In its heyday, before bridges linked San Francisco to the mainland, it was the second-busiest transportation terminal in the world. More than 150 ferries carried commuters across the bay and back each day. Today the Ferry Building holds no such records, but stands as a landmark welcoming visitors nonetheless. Recently, Pier 7 received a face-lift; decked out with new benches and fancy lampposts, it is now a popular public promenade and a great place to watch the day draw to a close.

JACKSON SQUARE, in the Financial District's northwest corner, was once smack in the middle of the infamous Barbary Coast. Today it's a protected historical district filled with antique shops and restaurants. As legend has it, this was the place to go during the city's uncivilized boom years for drinking, dancing, gambling, and whoring. Even murder was commonplace along these streets (though there were patches of respectability). Ghirardelli Chocolate had offices here in the late 1800s before it moved to Jefferson Street. Anson Parsons Hotaling ran a liquor and real estate business along the 400 block of Jackson. Mickey Finn, a chemist who worked in the area, apparently sold a powerful drug used to knock out the unsuspecting—a devilish trick that later bore his name. After the disastrous events of 1906, one poet quipped: "If, as they say, God spanked the town for being over-frisky, Why did He burn the churches and spare Hotaling's whiskey?"

Several Financial District eating establishments from the city's early years are still around today: **JACK'S** (615 Sacramento St; 415/421-7355), **SAM'S GRILL & SEAFOOD RESTAURANT** (374 Bush St; 415/421-0594), and the state's oldest restaurant, the **TADICH GRILL** (at a different location—now at 240 California St; 415/391-1849), established in 1849. For a more modern culinary experience, join the downtown power brokers as they lunch on cutting-edge cuisine at **AQUA** (252 California St; 415/956-9662) and **SILKS** (222 Sansome St; 415/986-2020). (For reviews of Sam's Grill & Seafood Restaurant, Tadich Grill, and Aqua, see the Restaurants chapter.)

Before you leave the Financial District, be sure to visit the lively **FARMERS MARKET** held along the Embarcadero on Saturday mornings. Local restaurants offer breakfast treats, snacks, and coffee, but the real stars here are the Northern California farmers and ranchers who fill the market with fabulous fresh produce, organic meats, local oysters, and olive oils. *Map:N2-O3*

SOMA (SOUTH OF MARKET STREET)

The area south of Market Street, known by the acronym SoMa, is many things to many people: cutting-edge arts mecca, "Multimedia Gulch," club-hopping heaven, and—as of recently—overdevelopment hell. The multiple-personality syndrome is not surprising, considering that SoMa encompasses a huge amount of real estate that continues to become more expensive as the Internet economy heats up.

Until just recently, much of SoMa had long been a bastion of affordable—albeit ramshackle—housing; even in the early days of the Gold Rush, it was home to a tent city of newly arrived immigrant forty-niners. As San Franciscans prospered on Gold Rush fever, the area around South Park—now the heart of Multimedia Gulch—evolved into a gated community surrounded by opulent mansions. Though the mansions have since vanished, a bit of old-world charm remains: at 615 Third Street, a plaque marks the site where Jack London was born in 1876 (the original structure was destroyed in the 1906 quake).

When the city rebuilt after the devastation, industrialists took hold of the area, putting up warehouses, factories, and train yards. All that remains of SoMa's affluent patches are the historic **WPA MURALS** at the

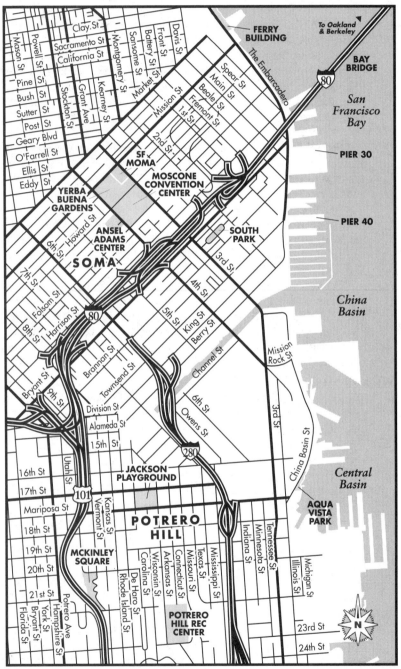

SOMA/POTRERO HILL

former Rincon Hill post office (now Rincon Center, 99 Mission St). A gem from the more recent past is the **PACIFIC BELL TELEPHONE BUILDING**, a 1925 skyscraper that provides a dramatic backdrop to the San Francisco Museum of Modern Art.

In the last century, SoMa was known as South of the Slot, because of the cable car slots that ran down Market Street. Eventually SoMa became the transportation hub of San Francisco, and remains so today. The CalTrain station, the Southern Pacific train depot, the Greyhound bus terminal, and the Transbay Terminal are all located here. The intercity system known as BART tunnels beneath the waters of the bay, delivering throngs of passengers daily to four underground stations along Market Street. The Bay Bridge (Interstate 80/101), connecting San Francisco and Oakland, shovels thousands of cars into the area each day.

All this mass traffic, of course, deterred all but the most intrepid from settling in the noisy neighborhood. Then, in the 1960s, a controversial plan to revitalize the area was proposed. Mayor George Moscone was strongly opposed to it, particularly the construction of Yerba Buena Center for the Arts (yes, it was 20 years in the making), because it called for the destruction of several blocks of cheap hotels that housed many of the city's indigents, pensioners, and other elderly. One of only two people on the board of supervisors to vote against the project, Moscone lost this 1965 battle, though it would still be years before the plan bore fruit.

Ironically, it was **MOSCONE CONVENTION CENTER**—completed in 1981 and named after the city leader, who was slain in 1978—that brought the first injection of tourist money into the area. Since then, numerous apartment complexes have sprung up along the waterfront, along with dozens of high-tech work lofts. For many older businesses, this urban renewal is a mixed blessing. Many of SoMa's outlet stores are closing as rents continue to rise. Cheap hotels along Third and Fourth Streets were razed to make room for the new buildings. And parking? Forget about it, particularly with the PacBell baseball stadium in place.

It was the unveiling of Swiss architect Mario Botta's **SAN FRANCISCO MUSEUM OF MODERN ART** in 1995 that solidified SoMa's reputation as the artistic heart of the city, attracting visitors from all over the world. On the heels of the museum's completion came the **YERBA BUENA CENTER FOR THE ARTS**, which hosts diverse exhibitions ranging from avant-garde video and installation art to the more conventional *Impressionists in Winter*. Surrounding the center is **YERBA BUENA GARDEN**, a five-acre public oasis that includes a Martin Luther King, Jr., Memorial—etched glass panels displayed behind a long, shimmering cascade of water—as well as other sculptures.

SoMa is also a destination for serious diners. **BIZOU** (598 4th St; 415/543-2222) offers a comforting Mediterranean menu; **FRINGALE** (570 4th St; 415/543-0573) is hugely popular for its classic French bistro food (for reviews of both, see the Restaurants chapter). One of the more interesting additions to the SoMa dining scene is **ASIA SF** (201 9th St; 415/255-2742). This is more than your basic Asian fusion place; here your food is served by drag queens who also lip-synch to the likes of Donna Summer.

Museums and restaurants may be the focus for much of the day, but around midnight, the club scene takes center stage. Hip clubs continue to come and go. Eleventh Street, with **SLIM'S** (333 11th St; 415/522-0333), **PARADISE LOUNGE** (1501 Folsom St; 415/861-6906), and **TWENTY TANK BREWERY** (316 11th St; 415/255-9455), is the center of mainstream nightlife, but alternatives exist in abundance. Depending on the night of the week, your favorite club could be something entirely unexpected. The **END UP** (401 6th St; 415/357-0827) becomes "The Fag" on Fridays, with beautiful boys dancing into the wee hours, but on Thursdays it's the "Kit Kat Club" and caters to both gay and straight night owls. "Bondage a Go-Go" happens at the **CAT CLUB** (1190 Folsom St; 415/431-3332) on Wednesday nights. Come in your fetish gear and get a discount at the door. On Fridays, Latin tunes, funk, and soul fill the Cat Club as it morphs into Ibiza. On Fridays, **THE STUD** (399 9th St; 415/863-6623), normally a gay bar, becomes the Dollhouse, a meeting place for lesbians looking for a wild night out. The Stud's Saturday incarnation is more inclusive; it becomes Sugar and welcomes the ultrahip het set as well as the usual gay crowd. In short, whatever it is you're into, chances are it's taking place South of Market. *Map:M3-O4*

CHINATOWN

Chinatown has long been a blend of tacky and traditional. As early as 1893, Baedeker's *Guide to the United States* was advising travelers that "the Chinese Quarter is one of the most interesting and characteristic features of San Francisco and no one should leave the city without visiting it." In the early 1900s, when the city was recovering from the quake and fire, there was a movement afoot to rebuild the neighborhood with its original "ethnic" attributes. (Even back then, it seems, Chinatown was good for tourism.) At the turn of the century, after the 1906 earthquake, Anglo architects designed Edwardian buildings and then added chinoiserie detailing to the architecture to give the area an Asian feel. One prime example is the elaborate facade at 745 Grant Avenue, built in 1920—the result bore no resemblance to the architecture of Asia yet became a distinctly San Francisco phenomenon.

The Chinese who first settled into this cramped neighborhood in the early 1800s hailed from two main regions in China. The wealthier, more prosperous immigrants came from the province of Guangzhou. They learned English and succeeded as city merchants and cultural ambassadors to the predominantly European city. The majority of Chinese, how-

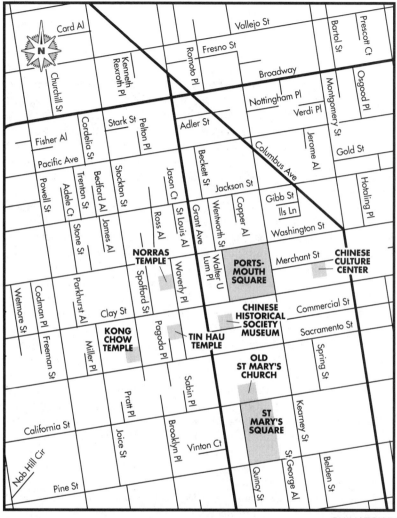

CHINATOWN

ever, were neither well educated nor wealthy. Rather, they were laborers who hailed from Toishan County and spoke a Chinese dialect unintelligible to their more affluent neighbors. They had no desire to learn the local language or customs; most intended to stay only long enough to make a small fortune and return to China.

The Chinatown of the Gold Rush years was predominantly male. Because of growing prejudice, the Chinese Exclusion Act of 1882 was passed, which outlawed immigration for 10 years and restricted it until

1943. Hence, there was little chance of the area becoming a family-oriented neighborhood. Lonely, isolated men were forced to remain in the city, as few were able to pay for their return voyage to China. Opium dens helped many locals cope with their loneliness and the growing racism of the outside world.

Today, Chinatown spreads from Union Square toward North Beach and the Financial District. It's one of the most densely packed neighborhoods in the country—second only to Harlem—and its boundaries are generally regarded as Broadway, Taylor, Bush, and Montgomery Streets. The popular dragon-crowned portal at Bush and Grant welcomes visitors into another world. Grant Avenue has changed since Chinatown's early days, when it was known as Dupont Street and catered to an underworld culture of gambling and drugs. Today, kitsch shops prevail (if you spend more than $10 for three T-shirts, you're paying too much). Stores crammed full of poorly made luggage and trinkets rub elbows with those selling elegant jade jewelry. The schlock shops last for blocks unless you turn into one of the more interesting streets, like Sacramento or Clay.

A more authentic Chinatown experience can be had along Stockton Street. The sidewalks are crammed full of tourists and locals alike, all moving at a snail's pace past lively fishmongers and produce markets bursting with durian, Asian pears, lychees, Chinese broccoli, and baby bok choy. Other markets specialize in packaged goods like dried shiitake mushrooms, jasmine tea, and crispy rice snacks. Herbalists trained in the art of Chinese medicine sell bulk curatives to faithful customers who prefer the old ways to Western medicine. Stop by a shop and watch as a merchant measures out the gnarled ginseng root or haggles over fresh armadillo meat. Though not on Stockton Street, another must-see is the **GOLDEN GATE FORTUNE COOKIES** factory (56 Ross Alley; 415/781-3956), which sits amid cloistered sweatshops on Ross Alley. Said to be the birthplace of the fortune cookie, the factory is open to tourists.

As crass and commercial as the area may seem to some, it also has a spiritual side. Dedicated in 1854, **OLD SAINT MARY'S CHURCH** (660 California St) towered above the fledgling city. It survived 1906 with little damage, only to be threatened by the wrecking ball decades later. A grassroots campaign to save the historic building seems to have succeeded. More in keeping with the traditional Chinese culture are the neighborhood's many Buddhist temples. Lanterns, incense, and burnt offerings await visitors to the **TIN HAU TEMPLE**, on the fourth floor of a nondescript building on Waverly Place. A few doors down sits the **NORRAS TEMPLE**, run by the Buddhist Association of America. Chanting monks and the gentle tinkle of bells lend a sense of calm to the building, which also houses Chinese cultural associations. The oldest Buddhist temple in the country, the **KONG CHOW TEMPLE**, is located at

FAMILY ATTRACTIONS

With its incredible selection of restaurants, bars, and museums, San Francisco is a great playground for adults, but it also has a number of kid-friendly venues. Top among them is the **Exploratorium** (415/563-7337 or 415/561-0360). Located at the Palace of Fine Arts in the Marina District, the Exploratorium offers youngsters a chance to experience science firsthand—literally. There are dozens of fun and fascinating exhibitions kids can touch and play with and experiments they can take part in. Other family favorites include the **San Francisco Zoo** (Sloat Blvd at 45th Ave; 415/753-7080) which may not rank among the nation's biggest, but the koalas, gorillas, and lions are certainly a hit with children. Younger kids will love the Children's Zoo—a four-acre park featuring the Insect Zoo and barnyard area, where kids can feed the animals. The herd of bison that makes **Golden Gate Park** its home offers a rare chance for kids and adults to see this historic beast up close. One of the neatest sites in the city for kids is the recently opened **Rooftop at Yerba Buena Gardens** at Fourth and Howard Streets. With a skating rink, children's museum, bowling alley, and kid-run garden to explore, your young ones can spend hours at this downtown oasis.

855 Stockton Street above a post office. The modernized exterior offers little hint of the carved, gilded altars and elaborate furnishings within. Another religious enclave in this bustling neighborhood is the GOLD MOUNTAIN MONASTERY at 800 Sacramento Street.

PORTSMOUTH SQUARE (Washington and Kearny Sts) was the town square of San Francisco's original Spanish settlement, known as Yerba Buena. Back in the 18th century the surf swelled up onto Montgomery Street—once the shoreline of that fledgling village before the shallow waters were filled in to make room for the growing Financial District. Today this seemingly forgotten square serves as a gathering spot for many elderly Chinese. In the morning, large groups congregate to practice the ancient art of tai chi; checkers is a popular afternoon activity.

After immigration restrictions were relaxed in the 1960s, recently arrived Chinese immigrants didn't settle in Chinatown, but instead moved out into the city's more spacious western neighborhoods. New Chinatowns have sprung up along Clement Street in the Richmond District and Taraval Street in the Sunset District. But the downtown neighborhood is still the key to the past for many second- and third-generation Chinese Americans. The CHINESE HISTORICAL SOCIETY MUSEUM (415/391-1188) on Commercial Street and the CHINESE CULTURE CENTER (415/986-1822) on Kearny Street both feature regular exhibitions celebrating the cultural heritage of the area. Photos and artifacts from the Gold Rush era speak of the important role the Chinese community played in the growth of San Francisco and the state.

Food is one of the highlights of any Chinatown visit, and the number of dining options seems endless. Cantonese food is the local specialty, but Sichuan, Hunan, and Mandarin restaurants are also easy to find. A fun alternative to a standard Chinese meal is dim sum. These tiny dumplings filled with pork, shrimp, scallops, and vegetables are ordered in plates of three and four and arrive at the table in bamboo baskets. Pork spare ribs, roast duck, and a variety of vegetable dishes also feature prominently in any dim sum service. Neighborhood eateries fill to capacity with locals during the weekend lunch hour, the traditional time to eat dim sum, attesting to the popularity of this delightful dining experience.

One of the most festive times to visit the neighborhood is in February during **CHINESE NEW YEAR**. This colorful three-week celebration features street fairs with traditional opera and dance, the Miss Chinatown USA Pageant and Fashion Show, displays of elaborate silk lanterns, giant puppets, art exhibits, folk dances, and martial arts demonstrations. In preparation for the event, vendors sell bundles of quince blossoms (a Bay Area stand-in for traditional peach blossoms), a symbol of immortality. During the first week of the festivities, Chinatown restaurants serve elaborate (and expensive) multicourse banquets with popular New Year's dishes like lobster in a special sauce, Peking duck, and shark's-fin soup. The grand finale is marked by the three-hour parade that winds though Chinatown. Highlights include elaborately decorated floats, Chinese acrobats, stilt walkers, lion dancing, and the 160-foot Golden Dragon. The joyful explosion of more than 600,000 firecrackers tops off the evening. *Map:M2-N3*

NOB HILL

The staggering wealth of railroad and silver barons had a significant impact on the history and development of San Francisco. The Big Four, as they were called, left their personal mark all over the city in the last half of the 1800s, particularly on the city peak called Nob Hill. Sacramento power brokers Leland Stanford, Collis Huntington, Charles Crocker, and Mark Hopkins joined forces to create the Central Pacific Railroad, which connected the rest of the country to California. These "nabobs" (Urdu for "very rich men") amassed an amazing fortune in the bustling days before the earthquake and fire, and they sank their money into ostentatious mansions high atop Nob Hill. Only the **FLOOD MANSION** (1000 California St at Mason), now the exclusive Pacific Union Club, remains. For a look back into the past, visit the Big Four Restaurant in the Huntington Hotel (415/771-1140), which showcases memorabilia and photography from the era.

Even though the original architecture was destroyed in 1906, the summit of Nob Hill still reflects that golden era of unbridled wealth. The **FAIRMONT, MARK HOPKINS,** and **HUNTINGTON** hotels are bastions of antique opulence. The manicured lawns, sandbox, swings, and central Tortoise Fountain attract tourists and locals alike to **HUNTINGTON PARK,** donated to the city in 1915 by the widow of Collis Huntington. **GRACE CATHEDRAL**'s 20th-century Gothic architecture creates an impressive profile on the corner of California and Taylor. With its popular meditative labyrinth, stained-glass windows, quilt panels from the AIDS-related Names Project, and formidable bronze doors, this house of worship offers something for even the most ardent atheist.

No exclusive neighborhood is complete without an exclusive eatery or two. For today's elite it's **CHARLES NOB HILL** (1250 Jones St; 415/771-5400). Home to an award-winning chef and charming atmosphere, this

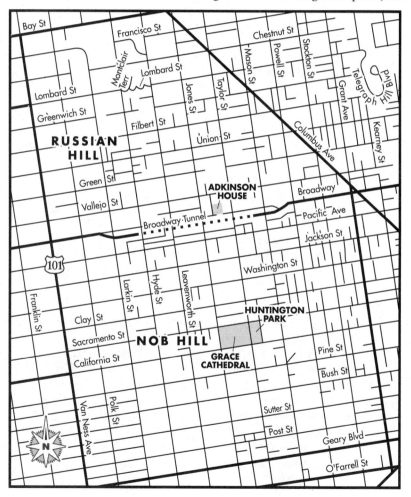

NOB HILL/RUSSIAN HILL

cousin to downtown Aqua is well worth the splurge. Also catering to the upper crust, The **DINING ROOM AT THE RITZ-CARLTON** (600 Stockton St; 415/773-6198) boasts the best cheese cart in the city (for reviews of both, see the Restaurants chapter). **GRAMERCY GRILL** (1177 California St; 415/885-3300) and **VENTICELLO** (1257 Taylor St; 415/922-2545) offer fine dining in a less formal atmosphere.

Though not known for its nightlife, Nob Hill does offer a few places to let your hair down. The Fairmont Hotel's ode to the South Seas, the **TONGA ROOM** (950 Mason St), is the perfect spot for a campy night out. For more civilized drinking, **JOHN BARLEYCORN** (1415 Larkin St) serves up Bass and Guinness and has a cozy fireplace. On a clear day, the newly redecorated **TOP OF THE MARK** (999 California St; 415/392-3434) offers beautiful sunset views and live music in the evening.

The summit of Nob Hill may be ritzy, but the surrounding neighborhood is home to a more diverse community. Some high-priced apartment buildings do cater to the city's trust-fund babies, but the majority have been divided into studios and one-bedrooms whose tenants work in the Financial District, a convenient walk down the hill. With Chinatown bursting at the seams, many Asian families have also migrated up the hill and settled in apartments along Sacramento, Clay, and Washington Streets.

In addition to majestic hotels, Nob Hill also offers architectural indulgences for residents. In 1907, Julia Morgan, the architect of Hearst's San Simeon castle, redesigned the circa-1881 brick structure at 920 Sacramento Street, now the **DONALDINA CAMERON HOUSE**. She also drew up the plans for the shingle-and-stucco building at 1202–1206 Leavenworth. Prominent San Francisco architect Willis Polk lent his architectural talent to the row of town houses along Mason Street (numbers 831 to 849). The impressive 1924 Brocklebank Apartments at 1000 Mason Street may look familiar to *Vertigo* fans—Kim Novak's character lived here. *Map:M2*

RUSSIAN HILL

To the north of Nob Hill lies Russian Hill, another sought-after address and one where it's uncommonly hard to find a parking space. The neighborhood earned its name from the Russian explorers and trappers who arrived in the early 1800s to trade with the Spanish and Native Americans in the San Francisco Bay. The rough voyage from Fort Ross up north and exposure to the New World diseases proved too much for many sailors, who did not live to make the journey back home. They were buried high atop the hill that overlooked the harbor, their graves marked by black crosses with Russian inscriptions. For years the gravestones were all that distinguished this uninhabited hill.

As the city grew, so did the demand for a room with a view. Cable car lines made living in this uphill district possible. Soon the summit of what came to be called Russian Hill—the neighborhood between Van Ness and Columbus Avenues, Broadway and Fisherman's Wharf—drew businessmen, architects, and the literati. Mark Twain, Frank Norris, Jack London, Robert Louis Stevenson, and Ambrose Bierce all belonged to Russian Hill's literary circles. Photographers Dorothea Lange and Imogen Cunningham lived and worked here as well. Decades later, Jack Kerouac also drew inspiration from the neighborhood's slopes and magnificent views while crashing at Neal Cassady's tiny attic on Russell Place. Most recently, Macondray Lane has been immortalized in Armistead Maupin's *Tales of the City*.

Head to Nob Hill and Pacific Heights for grand Victorian mansions, but for historic architecture on a more livable scale, Russian Hill is second to none. The **ADKINSON HOUSE** at 1032 Broadway between Jones and Taylor is the oldest house on Russian Hill. An example of Italianate architecture, it was designed by William H. Ranlett in 1853. In 1893, Willis Polk did significant work on the interior. In the neighborhood's more bohemian days, Kate Adkinson, daughter of the original owner, opened her house as a salon for artists, architects, and writers. The house was granted San Francisco Landmark status in 1977. The Reverend Joseph Worcester, an amateur architect, was the creative force behind the Bay Area shingle style; his creations at 1034 and 1036 Vallejo are the oldest remaining examples in the area. High atop the summit at 1023 Vallejo sits a 1917 Julia Morgan–designed home done in the Bay Area shingle-style tradition popular in the early 1900s. Morgan reworked the 1866 Italianate home at 1055 Green Street into a Beaux Arts wonder. A few doors down at 1067 Green stands another San Francisco landmark, the **FEUSIER OCTAGON HOUSE**, built from 1857 to 1859 for George Kenny (a friend of Leland Stanford and Mark Twain); the mansard roof and cupola were added in the late 1880s. Willis Polk's Spanish Revival houses, built around 1916, sit at 1, 3, 5, and 7 Russian Hill Place.

Shops along Russian Hill's busy stretch of Polk Street come and go, but **ROSE PAOLI'S CITY DISCOUNT** (2436 Polk St) has been around for decades. Come to this little-known gem for ramekins, cast-iron skillets, mammoth jars of marinated artichoke hearts, and olive oil. At 1903 Hyde Street, up away from the Polk Street melee, is **ATELIER DES MODISTES** (415/775-0545), a fashionable boutique for women. Ice cream lovers shouldn't miss the original **SWENSEN'S** (415/775-6818) at the corner of Union and Hyde. This old-time parlor has been family owned since 1948.

Russian Hill boasts some excellent restaurants. One of the city's best is **LA FOLIE** (2316 Polk St; 415/776-5577), where elegant French-inspired food is served in an intimate setting; **ZARZUELA** (415/346-0800) on Hyde and Union comes closer than any other San Francisco restaurant to recreating the true taste of Spanish tapas. (For reviews of both, see the Restaurants chapter.) At the corner of Polk and Broadway, **LITTLE THAI** (415/771-5544) dishes up delicious Thai food at reasonable prices. Across the street, there's **SHANGHAI KELLY'S** (415/771-3300) for a rowdy night of drinking and shouting to your neighbor. For a more relaxed nightcap, head to the **ROYAL OAK** (415/928-2303) at Polk and Vallejo. Filled with relics from the Victorian era, this charming bar offers the perfect way to end a tour of Russian Hill. *Map:L1*

CIVIC CENTER

Politics, highbrow culture, and homelessness all mingle at the Civic Center. The mayor's office and the board of supervisors' chambers are housed in the beautiful Beaux Arts **CITY HALL** (see Top 25 Attractions in this chapter) designed in 1916 by Arthur Brown. Its magnificent dome measures 308 feet, a full 16 feet higher than the Capitol dome in Washington, D.C., and is a visible landmark from many points in the city.

The Civic Center borders the city's infamous red-light district, the Tenderloin, where many homeless live. While this has long been a neighborhood to avoid, an influx of Vietnamese, Laotian, and Cambodian families has changed the neighborhood over the years. And while it's still not for the faint-hearted, it now has a number of good ethnic markets and many excellent—though bare-bones—eateries. If you're looking for kaffir lime leaves or galangal (and who isn't?), this is the place to come.

In the Civic Center area itself, the newly remodeled City Hall and cultural buildings are well worth the visit. The **WAR MEMORIAL OPERA HOUSE**—another Arthur Brown design—stretches along Van Ness Avenue, the city's widest thoroughfare. The site where the United States and Japan signed their peace treaty after World War II, today it hosts San Francisco's ballet and opera seasons, which run from January to May and September to July, respectively. Built in 1932 to honor the soldiers of World War I, the **VETERAN'S BUILDING** contains the Herbst Theatre, home to the City Arts and Lectures series, which has welcomed such noted writers as Saul Bellow, Stephen King, Jane Smiley, and Frank McCourt, as well as San Francisco Performances, which highlights classical soloists, duets, trios, and quartets.

LOUISE M. DAVIES SYMPHONY HALL, built in 1981 on the corner of Van Ness Avenue and Gough Street, boasts the largest concert-hall organ in North America. The instrument's 9,235 pipes are played with the aid of a computer. The symphony season runs from September through May. Also of note is the **SAN FRANCISCO PERFORMING ARTS LIBRARY AND MUSEUM** at the corner of Grove and Gough Streets. Devoted to the local arts scene, this building houses more than 4,000 books on theater, dance, opera, and music from the city's beginnings to the present, as well as a wealth of theater posters, playbills, and newspaper clippings.

The old Main Library, which closed in 1995, was replaced by a brand-new building right across the street. (The old building is set to be home to the Asian Art Museum, currently in Golden Gate Park.) The new **SAN FRANCISCO PUBLIC LIBRARY** (100 Larkin St; 415/557-4257) opened in 1996 to mostly rave reviews and more than a few boos for its less-than-inviting exterior. The Beaux Arts architecture of the government buildings is complemented by the library's entrance on Larkin and Fulton Streets. The Grove and Hyde Street facades offer a dramatically modern design. The highlight of the equally modern interior is a five-story-high atrium that fills much of the building with natural light. Three large-scale art installations add drama to the interior. Mounted on the wall behind the grand staircase is Nayland Blake's *Constellation*, a collection of 160 illuminated glass ovals bearing the names of authors among the library's holdings. Alice Aycock's *Fantasy Stair* and *Cyclone Fragment* hang between the fifth and sixth floors. Hundreds of old catalog cards, scribbled on by book lovers, come together in Ann Hamilton and Ann Chamberlain's installation, which covers an entire wall. Other inside attractions include the Book Arts and Special Collections Center, the James C. Hormel Gay and Lesbian Center, the Wallace Stegner Environmental Center, and the African American Center.

On Grove Street across from the Main Library, the **BILL GRAHAM CIVIC AUDITORIUM**, named after the late rock impresario, is used as a convention hall and music venue. Also part of the civic hub is the American Automobile Association (AAA) building on Van Ness Avenue, offering free maps for members, a travel agency, traveler's checks, and car-related information.

On Market Street between Seventh and Ninth Streets, the **UNITED NATIONS PLAZA** commemorates the charter meeting of the organization, held in June 1945 at the War Memorial Opera House. Today it is the site of a twice-weekly farmers market. Fulton and Market Streets bustle on Wednesdays and Sundays with predominantly Asian purveyors whose tables overflow with fresh fruits and vegetables at reasonable prices.

The **CALIFORNIA CULINARY ACADEMY** (625 Polk St; 415/771-3500) is a training ground for many of the city's chefs. The school offers a 16-month course for those interested in a career in the kitchen, as well as continuing education for the less dedicated gourmet. The Academy opens its doors to the general public at the **CAR'ME ROOM** (415/771-3536), a restaurant with glass walls that provide views of the students preparing your food in the kitchen. Another restaurant downstairs, the **ACADEMY GRILL** (415/771-3536), offers reasonably priced burgers and blue-plate specials. *Map:L4*

UNION SQUARE

See Top 25 Attractions in this chapter.

FISHERMAN'S WHARF

See Top 25 Attractions in this chapter.

NORTH BEACH

Long a neighborhood of immigrants, today North Beach is famous for its Italian food and sidewalk cafes. So charming is the area—bordered by Columbus Avenue, Washington and Beach Streets, and the Embarcadero—that few notice that there isn't even a beach here. There was one about a hundred years ago, until it was filled in to make room for factories and waterfront activity. During the Gold Rush years, immigrants from all over the globe flocked here to live near the wharves and factories. They worked as fishermen and toiled in canneries along the then-industrial waterfront. Over the years the Italian community grew and soon outnumbered other ethnic groups. By the early 1930s more than 50,000 Italian Americans were living and working in North Beach, and five Italian-language newspapers were published locally.

Tourism keeps the Italian community here employed, but the Little Italy portion of North Beach is shrinking as Chinatown continues to expand. The citywide rise in rents and real estate prices has made it difficult for many small, family-owned businesses to stay afloat. Many area merchants have joined together to protest the arrival of chain stores like Starbucks and Rite Aid that would take away the historic look and feel of the neighborhood. So far they have succeeded in keeping the chains at bay, but it may be only a matter of years before the area's charm is lost forever.

Plenty of old-world charm can still be found in places like **MOLINARI'S DELICATESSEN** (415/421-2337) on Columbus Avenue and **PANELLI BROTHERS** (415/421-2544) on Stockton. Drop in for prosciutto di Parma, Gorgonzola, cured olives, and a loaf of crusty bread—the perfect North Beach picnic. **FIOR D'ITALIA** (415/986-1886) on Union Street, established in 1886, claims to be the oldest Italian restaurant in the United States and still caters to a coterie of neighborhood insiders. Family-style meals are still served up hot at **CAPP'S CORNER** (415/989-2589) on Powell Street and the **GOLDEN SPIKE** (415/421-4591) on Columbus, but younger crowds flock to places like **MICHELANGELO** (415/986-4058), **MARIO'S BOHEMIAN CIGAR STORE** (415/362-0536), and **ROSE PISTOLA** (415/399-0499), all on Columbus. (For reviews of the latter two, see the Restaurants chapter.)

At the corner of Columbus and Union Street is **WASHINGTON SQUARE PARK**, a haven for tai chi practitioners and sunbathers, painters, and panhandlers. At the north end of the park stands the **SAINTS PETER AND PAUL ROMAN CATHOLIC CHURCH**. Designed in 1922 by Charles

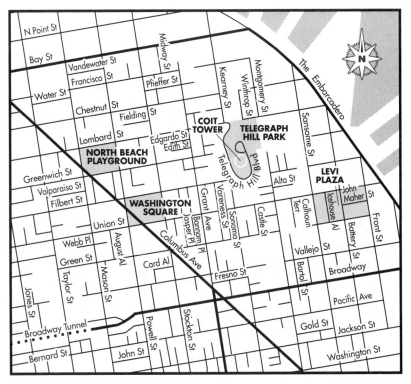

NORTH BEACH

Fantoni, this Romanesque building, with its distinctive twin spires and animal statuary, provides a picturesque backdrop for a Sunday picnic or impromptu soccer game. It's also known as the church of the fishermen, and processions depart from here each October for the annual blessing of the fleet. Once an Italian-language church, it now also offers services in English.

In the late 1950s a group of young artists and writers made North Beach their late-night hangout and changed the path of American culture. Legendary Bay Area columnist Herb Caen called them beatniks, but for many fans they will forever be known as founders of the Beat movement. Allen Ginsberg, Lawrence Ferlinghetti, Jack Kerouac, and their coterie of poet and writer friends haunted the bars and cafes of North Beach, holding poetry readings and drinking late into the night. For lovers of this area's bohemian heritage, a visit to **CITY LIGHTS BOOK-STORE** (415/362-8193) on Columbus is a must. Ferlinghetti, poet, publisher, and champion of free speech, opened the store in 1953. Famous for publishing poet Ginsberg's controversial work, it was also the first store in America to feature paperback books. Ferlinghetti, still the proprietor, is alive and well and is often spotted in and around the shop. To relive the Beat years, visit **VESUVIO CAFE** (415/362-3370) or **TOSCA CAFE** (415/986-9651) on Columbus below Broadway, where not much has changed since Jack Kerouac drank here. In the evening this quaint neighborhood is transformed into a boisterous block party where entertainment options abound. Postprandial coffee can be had at one of the numerous cafes along Columbus. Or head to **CLUB FUGAZI** (415/421-4222) for a raucous good time at a performance of the city's famous *Beach Blanket Babylon*, a cabaret show that spoofs current politics and pop culture. Listen to music at **GRANT & GREEN BLUE CLUB** (415/693-9565) or swing dance at the **HI-BALL LOUNGE** (415/397-9464). If it's X-rated fun you're looking for, the neon lights along Broadway east of Columbus advertise a seemingly endless array of topless bars and "adult" clubs and shops. *Map:N1*

TELEGRAPH HILL

Back in the pre-boom 1800s, living high atop San Francisco's hills was considered a curse, not a sign of wealth and success. After all, what's a "million-dollar" view when you have to schlep your aching body back up the hill each night? As a result, fishermen and their families were once the primary residents of now-exclusive Telegraph Hill.

This neighborhood, which got its name from a nearby Morse code signal station, is best known as the home of **COIT TOWER** (see Top 25 Attractions in this chapter). The 1934 monument was named after its benefactor, Lillie Hitchcock Coit, a 19th-century socialite who left money to the city to memorialize her beloved firefighter friends. Designed by Arthur Brown of City Hall fame, the narrow tower affords amazing views of the city and also houses some fine murals documenting Depression-era San Francisco.

The completion of Coit Tower gave Telegraph Hill a new, spiffed-up image around town. Most of the rough-and-tumble cottages gave way to fancy new houses and elegant new apartment buildings. Gentrification brought better streets and garbage service and meant increased rents for many dockworkers. As cottages were razed to make way for architectural dream homes, some San Franciscans foresaw the end to a piece of the city's history. A concerned group of residents formed the Telegraph Hill Historic District in 1986 to ensure preservation of the existing cottages.

Today, a hike up the **FILBERT STEPS** is rewarded with a peek at these time capsules from another era, as well as numerous weathered benches, plush gardens, and amazing views. Some of the gems along the way include 228 Filbert Street, a Gothic Revival cottage built in 1873. At 10 Napier Lane stands an Italianate house from 1875. Down the lane at number 21 is an 1885 cottage that epitomizes the simple working-class housing that covered the hillside before it was home to the well heeled. Another set of still-steeper steps leads down to Greenwich Street and the waterfront area below. A walk along Montgomery Street offers another pair of architectural treats. Bogie and Bacall's *Dark Passage* was filmed at 1360 Montgomery, a splendid example of art deco design built in 1936 by Irving Goldstine. Down the street at 1541 sits **JULIUS' CASTLE** (415/392-2222); its crenellated edifice was built in 1921 by Italian architect Louis Mastropasqua. The restaurant's tight location proved so difficult to drive in and out of that a turntable was installed back in the 1920s to enable large cars to come and go (they now provide valet parking). *Map:N1*

PACIFIC HEIGHTS

Pacific Heights, one of San Francisco's most exclusive neighborhoods, is bordered by Van Ness Avenue, Broadway, and Divisadero and Pine Streets. When transportation extended to the outer districts of the city, the elite moved west, away from the noise of downtown. They sought quiet streets and bigger lots on which to build their grand mansions. Many of those still stand today; a few are even open to the public.

The **HAAS-LILIENTHAL HOUSE** (2007 Franklin St; 415/441-3000) is one of them. While much of the surrounding architecture burned in the 1906 blaze, this jewel, designed by Peter Schmidt in 1886 with a Queen Anne circular tower and bay windows, survived. A bigger threat was the subsequent bulldozing of single-family houses to make way for large apartment buildings. But the owners preserved their home as a testament to the glory of Victorian San Francisco. The house, now a museum run by the Foundation for San Francisco's Architectural Heritage, has been furnished with period pieces, many from the Haas-Lilienthal family.

For another look at the grand homes of Victorian and Edwardian San Francisco, visit the **WHITTIER MANSION** at 2090 Jackson. Once the director of the present-day Pacific Gas and Electric Company (PG&E), Whittier came to California from Maine in 1854. After making his fortune, he built a state-of-the-art San Francisco home complete with steel-reinforced brick walls, hydraulic elevator, and central heating. Accordingly, the house survived the events of 1906. Now run by the California Historical Society, this 1896 mansion, designed by Edward Swain, is open to the public for visits and tours. Lavish interiors are paneled with rich mahogany, birch, and oak and filled with late-19th-century furnishings. Another symbol of fin de siècle decadence is the Turkish smoking room, complete with a built-in humidor. Separate galleries feature exhibits on California history and a collection of early California landscapes.

The **JAMES FLOOD MANSION**, designed in 1913 by Bliss and Faville, is now one of three impressive buildings that constitute the Convent and Schools of the Sacred Heart, which educate the city's elite. Built with

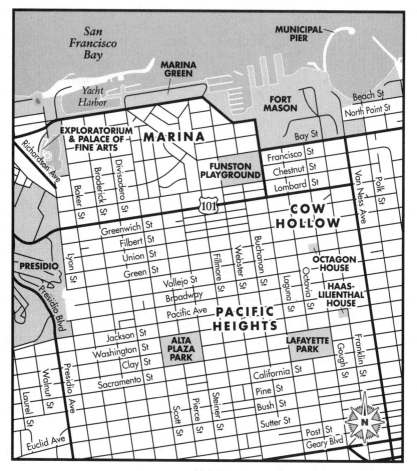

San Francisco Bay

MUNICIPAL PIER

MARINA GREEN

Yacht Harbor

FORT MASON

Beach St

North Point St

EXPLORATORIUM & PALACE OF FINE ARTS

M·A·R·I·N·A

Bay St

Richardson Ave

Baker St

Broderick St

Divisadero St

FUNSTON PLAYGROUND

Francisco St

Chestnut St

Lombard St

Van Ness Ave

Polk St

101

C·O·W H·O·L·L·O·W

PRESIDIO

Lyon St

Greenwich St

Filbert St

Union St

Green St

Fillmore St

Webster St

Buchanan St

Laguna St

Octavia St

OCTAGON HOUSE

HAAS- LILIENTHAL HOUSE

Presidio Blvd

Vallejo St

Broadway

Pacific Ave

P·A·C·I·F·I·C H·E·I·G·H·T·S

Jackson St

Washington St

Clay St

Sacramento St

ALTA PLAZA PARK

LAFAYETTE PARK

Franklin St

Gough St

Walnut St

Laurel St

Presidio Ave

Scott St

Pierce St

Steiner St

California St

Pine St

Bush St

Sutter St

Euclid Ave

Post St

Geary Blvd

N

PACIFIC HEIGHTS/MARINA/COW HOLLOW

an unlimited budget, the mansion resembles a hotel in scale and accommodations. Located at 2222 Broadway at Webster, the magnificent red brick mansion features the finest stonework in San Francisco. Spiraled Corinthian columns and Tennessee marble add to the majesty of this palatial estate. Also among the buildings of the Sacred Heart are the 1910 **JOSEPH DONOHOE GRANT MANSION** at 2200 Broadway and the 1905 **ANDREW HAMMOND MANSION** at 2252 Broadway.

Other fine buildings worth a look are the **SPRECKELS MANSION** (now home to romance novelist Danielle Steel) on Washington Street, designed by George Applegarth, better known as the architect of the California Palace of the Legion of Honor, and the **BOURN MANSION** at 2250 Webster Street. Designed by Willis Polk for mining baron William Bourn in 1896, this building features a unique tunnel entrance. Two luxury apartment buildings of note are 2006 Washington Street, a 10-story salmon-colored building, and 2000 Washington, a 7-story Beaux Arts building, both designed by C. A. Meussdorffer in 1925 and 1922, respectively.

No architectural tour of Pacific Heights would be complete without a look at two of the area's distinctive houses of worship: The **TEMPLE EMANU-EL** on Arguello Boulevard and Lake Street and the **SWEDEN-BORGIAN CHURCH** on Lyon and Washington Streets. The temple, Northern California's largest synagogue, was designed by Arthur Brown after Union Square construction swallowed up the original downtown structure. Its magnificent 150-foot dome was influenced by the Haggia Sophia in Istanbul. In 1927, a year after its completion, Temple Emanu-El was selected as the finest piece of architecture in Northern California by the American Institute of Architects. The Swedenborgian Church, originally called the Church of New Jerusalem, stands in stark contrast to the opulence of neighboring mansions with its refined rustic interior and fireplace. Built in 1894 by a group of architects and artists committed to the American Craftsman movement, the church features carved wooden beams, stained-glass windows, handcrafted chairs, and a wood-burning fireplace.

Two beautiful parks offer greenery in this otherwise cramped neighborhood. Landscape architect John McLaren, who designed Golden Gate Park, also left his mark on **ALTA PLAZA PARK**, a small patch of land bordered by Clay, Steiner, Jackson, and Scott Streets. The park's terraced landscape was modeled after the Grand Casino in Monte Carlo. The uppermost level affords spectacular vistas in all directions. A few blocks to the east, **LAFAYETTE PARK** sits at the corner of Laguna and Sacramento Streets. The four square blocks of open space offer views of Twin Peaks and the bay to the north.

The commercial heart of Pacific Heights is upper Fillmore Street. Upscale shops, fashionable restaurants, and a surprising number of thrift stores attract patrons from all over the city. Step into **MRS. DEWSON'S** (2050 Fillmore St; 415/346-1600) for hats—Mayor Willie Brown does. **MIKE FURNITURE** (415/567-2700) on the corner of Fillmore and Pine is filled with beautiful designs for your dream home. **BEBE** (415/563-6895), **ZOE LIMITED** (416/929-0441), and **GIMME SHOES** (415/864-0691) offer chic women's fashions and footwear for the neighborhood's upscale clientele. The **CLAY THEATRE** shows art-house films that draw movie-goers from all over town.

Even though people flock to Fillmore Street from across the city, the area's restaurants manage to retain a cozy neighborhood feeling. Up away from the action, **JACKSON FILLMORE** (2506 Fillmore St; 415/346-5288) has won over the locals with its rustic Italian fare. **CAFE KATI**

(1963 Sutter St; 415/775-7313) has been open for years and still gets rave reviews. Newer to the neighborhood is **FLORIO'S** (1915 Fillmore St; 415/775-4300), which cooks up classic bistro food in a very Parisian setting. (For reviews of all three, see the Restaurants chapter.) *Map:K2-L3*

TWIN PEAKS

When the Spaniards arrived in San Francisco in the 1700s, they set up a mission, fortified the area, and began naming the countryside's geographical points of interest. This pair of hills in the center of the city was named Los Pechos de la Choca, or "Breasts of the Indian Maiden," a name that testifies to the loneliness of frontier life. Many of San Francisco's place names have survived from that earlier period but, for obvious reasons, Breasts of the Indian Maiden didn't cut it with the Victorians. Ergo, the more PC moniker Twin Peaks.

Though Mount Davidson at 928 feet is the highest point in the city, it's Twin Peaks that draws the visitors. On a clear day, tourists flock here for truly spectacular panoramic views of the city, the bridges, the East Bay, and beyond. Marin's Mount Tamalpais and the Campanile clock tower at UC Berkeley are both visible, weather permitting. Much of the hillside is undeveloped, making it a perfect venue for urban naturalists. Challenging terrain and clusters of wildflowers reward those willing to tackle Twin Peaks on foot.

It wasn't until the 1920s that daring developers decided to have a go at the area. Even then, steep hillsides and limited public transportation deterred many from snatching up the new housing. Boring, boxy apartment buildings make up much of the east side of the neighborhood, but attractive, affluent areas can be found in the sections of Clarendon Heights, Forest Knolls, Miraloma Park, and Parnassus Heights. Today more than 10,000 people reside along the steep, circuitous streets of Twin Peaks. It has become a desirable area for both gay and straight couples as well as a few families.

Though stunning views abound here, many locals must also live in the shadow of the controversial Sutro Tower. Visible from most points in the city, this enormous red-and-white-striped television antenna is a familiar San Francisco landmark (and a godsend for anyone without cable), but so far it hasn't won over locals as Coit Tower and the Transamerica Pyramid did.

One neighborhood gem is **TOWER MARKET** (415/664-1600) at Portola Drive and Woodside Avenue. Beautiful produce, a fine deli, and a wide selection of affordable wines attract more than just the locals. Another attraction is the **RANDALL MUSEUM** (415/554-9600). Hidden at the top of Roosevelt and Masonic Streets, this fantastic children's museum offers hands-on nature exhibits, an activity center with ceramics and woodworking classes, and a small art gallery. *Map:J7*

THE MARINA

With spectacular views of the Golden Gate Bridge, Alcatraz, and the bay, the Marina (see map on page 214) is desirable real estate for the young and affluent. A middle-class Italian neighborhood until the 1960s, the Marina now houses some of that community's wealthiest families, who live in the elegant homes that line the waterfront. Cozy art deco flats and stucco houses with Mediterranean-tiled roofs sit on quiet streets only steps away from waterfront activities.

At the turn of the century, the Marina was virtually underwater. The marshland was filled in when it was chosen as the site of the 1915 Panama-Pacific International Exposition, which celebrated the opening of the Panama Canal. Today, the Palace of Fine Arts building, located at Baker and Beach Streets, serves as a beautiful reminder of that festive event (see Top 25 Attractions in this chapter).

Within a few blocks of home, Marina residents can find the **EXPLOR-ATORIUM** and **PALACE OF FINE ARTS**, the historic **PRESIDIO**, and the **MARINA GREEN**, popular with joggers, in-line skaters, sunbathers, kite flyers, and outdoor sports enthusiasts of all kinds. **FORT MASON** (Marina Blvd and Buchanan St), a former military outpost turned into a cultural center, houses the Mexican Museum, the Museo Italo-Americano, the San Francisco Craft and Folk Art Museum, and a number of theaters and nonprofits. On Saturdays, Sedge Thomson's radio show *West Coast Live* is taped before a live audience at the Cowell Theater. For a picnic lunch, pop into the Marina Safeway, a legendary pickup spot for local singles. (For more information on these sites, see Top 25 Attractions in this chapter.)

The heart of the Marina is **CHESTNUT STREET** between Fillmore and Divisadero Streets. Once a quaint shopping district, Chestnut was permanently altered by the 1989 earthquake. Extensive damage forced a number of small businesses to close. It was only a matter of months before big-name chains and high-end boutiques set up shop (an unwelcome citywide trend that sticks in the gullet of most every San Franciscan). Today it's a yuppie shopping haven, complete with Gap Kids, Pottery Barn, and Williams-Sonoma. One welcome newcomer is **HEAVEN DAY-SPA & CENTER FOR WELLNESS** (2209 Chestnut St; 415/749-6414), which offers body wraps, acupuncture, yoga, and full salon services.

Restaurants come and go on fickle Chestnut Street, but the choices are always diverse. **ZINZINO** (2355 Chestnut St; 415/346-6623) serves rustic Italian food in a lively atmosphere. For gourmet hamburgers, head to **BARNEY'S MARINA** (3344 Steiner St; 415/563-0307). **ZAO NOODLE CLUB** (2031 Chestnut St; 415/563-7048) stirs up innovative Asian food. Fort Mason is home to **GREENS** (415/771-6222), one of the city's finest vegetarian restaurants. (For reviews of Zinzino and Greens, see the Restaurants chapter.) *Map:J1-K2*

COW HOLLOW

In the 19th century numerous dairies populated the rural valley between Pacific Heights and the Marina. Springs gurgled up from underground and provided farmers with natural irrigation for their acres of grazing pasture. Bucolic as that sounds, the dairies were banned in the 1880s when the board of health declared that cows were a health risk to the growing population. In 1891 the animals that gave Cow Hollow its name were shipped off to farms and slaughterhouses.

Bordered by Broadway, Lyon, and Lombard Streets and Van Ness Avenue (see map on page 214), Cow Hollow is one of the city's most attractive neighborhoods—for those able to pay the expensive rents. Single, white-collar professionals and double-income families settle here to enjoy the nearby shops, Marina Green, and the Presidio.

Nearby attractions include **OCTAGON HOUSE** (2645 Gough St; 415/441-7512), one of only two remaining eight-sided houses in the city. Built in the mid-19th century when such houses were considered good luck, it is now open as a museum filled with antiques and decorative arts from the colonial and Federal periods. Among the many treasures is a collection of autographs by the signers of the Declaration of Independence.

UNION STREET, especially between Van Ness Avenue and Steiner Street, is Cow Hollow's most obvious claim to fame. Every day thousands of locals and tourists visit its numerous restaurants, bars, cafes, boutiques, and galleries. Big names like Bebe, Armani Exchange, and Kenneth Cole share the sidewalks with independent boutiques. **FUMIKI** (2001 Union St; 415/922-0573) sells fine Asian art, antiques, and some furniture. **GIRLFRIENDS** (1824 Union St; 415/673-9544) caters to women who want youthful fashions. **CASA COLLECTION** (3108 Fillmore St; 415/346-5008) offers an eclectic collection of armoires, chairs, chests, and tables.

Both Union and Fillmore Streets offer varied dining options. **BETELNUT** (2030 Union St; 415/929-8855) re-creates the feel of an Asian beer house and serves up myriad pan-Asian dishes. **ROSE'S CAFE** (2298 Union St; 415/775-2200) is yet another popular restaurant of chef Reed Hearon, though with a lower profile than some of his hot spots. In spite of the city's love-hate relationship with the Getty family, **PLUMP-JACK CAFE** (3127 Fillmore St; 415/563-4755), co-owned by Bill Getty, has won over the public with its inexpensive wine list, and the Mediterranean-style food isn't bad either. (For reviews of all three, see the Restaurants chapter.) The new kid on the block is **EASTSIDE WEST RESTAURANT & RAW BAR** (3154 Fillmore St; 415/885-4000). The confusing name derives from Manhattan, not the Orient—hence the clubby, upscale New York feel of the place.

Cow Hollow has also earned a reputation for its raucous bar scene and is known as a prime pickup spot for young singles. Back in the '80s the **BALBOA CAFE** (415/921-3944), the **CITY TAVERN** (415/567-0918), and the former **BAJA CANTINA** (415/885-2252) formed what was once a sort of Bermuda Triangle, from which on any given Friday or Saturday night you probably didn't make it home alone or remotely sober. It's still quite the singles scene, but today's crowds are somewhat better dressed and behaved. Another boisterous spot is the **UNION ALE HOUSE** (415/921-0300), located on Union Street in a restored Victorian and featuring 19 microbrews on tap. Down the street a bit, the **BUS STOP** (1901 Union St; 415/567-6905) offers sports fans a friendly place to sip a beer, watch a ball game, and shoot some pool. *Map:J1-L2*

JAPANTOWN

Located in what is variously known as the Western Addition and lower Pacific Heights, Japantown disappoints many tourists who come expecting to find a Japanese version of Chinatown. In truth this small neighborhood enclosed by Geary Boulevard and Sutter, Laguna, and Fillmore Streets is more a monument to the cultural and historical importance of San Francisco's Japanese community than a true ethnic neighborhood. Like their Chinese-American neighbors, Japanese Americans live in many different districts throughout San Francisco. Japantown is what remains of a postquake community torn apart by racism and war.

Japanese immigration to San Francisco was minimal during much of the 1800s. It was only after enforcement of the Chinese Exclusion Act of 1882 that the Japanese arrived in greater numbers. They mainly were employed in agriculture and proved to be hardworking and successful farmers. Many saved and bought land of their own. Japanese immigrants settled in Chinatown alongside the Chinese and also in the industrial area south of Market Street. After the 1906 earthquake and fire, the Chinese were encouraged to rebuild Chinatown because it had become a tourist attraction, but many Japanese could not afford to rebuild and instead took to the outer reaches of the city west of Van Ness Avenue, settling in what is now known as Japantown. By 1940 the area had spread to 30 blocks.

The Japanese community was growing and thriving, but soon a number of racist, protectionist policies would hamper that prosperity. In 1913 the Alien Land Law was passed, which deprived Japanese Americans of the right to buy farmland. The only way Japanese immigrants could hold on to their property was to turn the title over to their nisei, or American-born children. But with the bombing of Pearl Harbor, even that tactic was no longer viable. During World War II Japanese-American bank accounts were frozen. With the signing of Executive Order 9066, 112,000 Japanese Americans, "aliens and citizens alike," were taken from their homes and sent to camps in California, Utah, and Idaho. For a brief period Japantown became a ghost town; then its houses, apartments, and stores were occupied by a new wave of immigrants—Southern blacks.

When the Japanese Americans were released from internment camps in 1945, they returned to find that their old neighborhood had moved on without them. Many tried to reestablish businesses and pick up the pieces of their former lives, but most resettled in the avenues of the Richmond and Sunset Districts.

Today, Japantown is most famous for the five-tiered **PEACE PAGODA** at the heart of the Japan Center shopping mall, as well as the myriad sushi and noodle restaurants crammed into a six-block area. For traditional Japanese ceramics, rice steamers, and sushi knives, visit **SOKO HARDWARE** (415/931-5510) across from the Miyako Hotel at Post and Buchanan Streets. Another reason to visit is the **KABUKI SPRINGS AND SPA** (1750 Geary Blvd; 415/922-6002), a traditional Japanese public bathhouse open to men and women on alternate days of the week; on Tuesdays it's co-ed. *Map:K3*

HAIGHT-ASHBURY

The Summer of Love lasted a mere three months, but 30 years later tourists and nostalgic San Franciscans still flock to the Haight to experience the flavor of the late '60s. Once home to Janis Joplin, the Grateful Dead, and myriad hippies, Haight-Ashbury has long since lost the uplifting spirit of that infamous summer, but drugs, alcohol, and tie-dye remain. As old-timers from several nearby rehabilitation centers struggle to overcome their drug-filled past, a new generation of street urchins zones out along the storefronts of the neighborhood, playing guitars, stringing beads, boldly demanding "Spare a buck for a beer?" or mumbling "Kind bud" (Translation: "Want to buy some pot?") to random passersby.

Bordered by Stanyan, Fulton, Divisadero, and Waller Streets, the Haight went through several ups and downs in the years before it became world famous. Once part of the far-reaching Outside Lands, a 17,000-acre sand dune west of Divisadero, this was a desolate area home only to a squadron of squatters hired by local businessmen with designs on developing the area. The lands lay in limbo until an 1865 Supreme Court decision ruled that the City of San Francisco was the legitimate heir to the area acquired from the Yerba Buena pueblo settled by the Mexican government. Frank McCoppin, a city supervisor, represented the area that included the Outside Lands. His grand plan for the area included a massive public park. In 1866, he became mayor and decided to secure his plan by organizing the claimants and negotiating a deal. Eventually all parties agreed to an arrangement whereby claimants would cede some 10 percent of their stake to the city in return for official rights to develop their remaining land. The protected 10 percent would soon become Golden Gate Park, while the remaining 90 percent was developed and became Haight-Ashbury and later the avenues. Neighborhood streets are named after city supervisors Haight, Ashbury, Cole, Clayton, Stanyan, and Shrader.

STANYAN PARK HOTEL (415/751-1000) at Stanyan and Waller Streets, built in 1904, dates back to the days of early development, when an amusement park and baseball field brought tourists out to this area. The events of 1906 further spurred a building boom. Displaced by the earthquake and fire, up-and-coming immigrants flocked to the area. They included Germans, Irish, Swedes, Jews, Scots, French, and Japanese. A large number of African Americans also settled here. The postquake development brought a wealth of Queen Anne homes to the neighborhood; many still stand today.

This once-prosperous enclave took a turn for the worse two decades later. In 1928, a tunnel was built through Buena Vista Park that carried middle-class residents from downtown out to the Sunset District, bypassing Haight-Ashbury completely. The Depression of the 1930s brought still more decline. The grand homes were simply too big to heat and maintain, and subdivision soon followed. Today, large single-family dwellings are few and far between, and most of the opulent Victorians have been converted to flats and apartments.

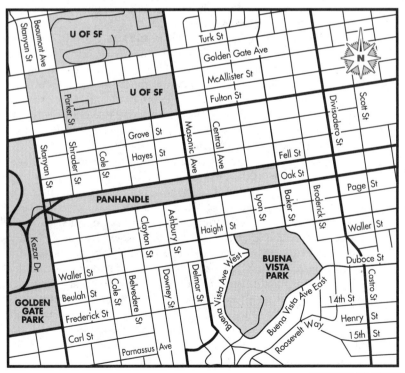

HAIGHT-ASHBURY

Economically, Haight-Ashbury, or the Upper Haight, as it is also known, has cashed in on its illustrious past. Commerce has replaced free love: stores dedicated to the hippie legacy sell tie-dyed shirts, psychedelic posters, incense, pot paraphernalia, and used records. The **RED VICTORIAN BED, BREAKFAST & ART** (1665 Haight St; 415/864-1978) dedicates its entire lower level to '60s and '70s memorabilia. Tattoo parlors and pipe shops draw alternative crowds, but the majority of people parading down Haight Street are tourists. Hundreds flock here each day to witness the nonstop freak show this street has become. When Jerry Garcia died in 1995, the neighborhood became a meeting place for the bereaved. His former home at 710 Ashbury has long been part of the Haight pilgrimage.

As a sign of the times, the Gap now holds down the fort at the infamous corner of Haight and Ashbury; across the street is the hippie-capitalist bastion Ben & Jerry's. Trendy boutiques selling space-age shoe designs and retro fashions line the street from Masonic to Stanyan, along with a plethora of used clothing shops and an Army-Navy surplus store.

Haight-Ashbury has long been a fun place for cheap eats. Years after opening, **CHA CHA CHA** (1801 Haight St; (415/386-5758) still has people lining up out the door for its funky decor and inventive tapas-style Caribbean food. **MASSAWA** (1538 Haight St; 415/621-4129) serves up spicy Eritrean (think Ethiopian) fare. The **CITRUS CLUB** (1790 Haight St; 415/387-6366) is riding the popular pan-Asian wave with cheap noodle dishes and hearty soups. One of the hippest fusion (read upscale) restaurants is around the corner in a quiet area known as Cole Valley. **EOS** (901 Cole St; 415/566-3063) features haute California cuisine with a decidedly Asian flair. Around the corner is **EOS WINE BAR**, one of the city's best places to improve your wine knowledge. (For reviews of Cha Cha Cha and Eos, see the Restaurants chapter.)

For residents, one of the main draws of the neighborhood is its proximity to so many parks. The city's gargantuan **GOLDEN GATE PARK** begins at Stanyan Street, a short walk from the heart of the Haight, and extends to the ocean, providing acres of "backyard" space to cramped apartment dwellers. Closer still, the eight-block Panhandle is a popular playground for adults and children, though many homeless live here as well; on the weekends locals can be found walking babies and dogs, practicing tai chi, or just lying in the sun. Little-known **BUENA VISTA PARK**, located high above the Haight at the end of Frederick Street, offers challenging hiking trails and breathtaking views of the Pacific, Golden Gate Bridge, Marin Headlands, and the spires of St. Ignatius. The park has a reputation as a place to buy drugs or pick up men, but during the day it is a peaceful refuge filled with dog walkers and nature lovers. Like the Panhandle, it is not a particularly safe place to stroll after dark. *Map:I4-J5*

THE CASTRO

Once part of the 4,000-acre ranch belonging to Jose de Jesus Noe, former alcalde of Mexican San Francisco, the Castro area underwent a huge transformation when the Yankees moved into town. In 1854, John Horner bought the undeveloped stretch of ranch land and planned a neighborhood along a rigid grid pattern that didn't take into account the area's steep grades. Originally called Eureka Valley, the land was parceled out in the 1860s, though few were adventurous enough to set up house here, as it was isolated from the downtown area.

Around the turn of the century, the Market Street Cable Railway was extended to Castro Street, opening the area to middle-class families. The 1920s were boom years for the newly developed neighborhood. Built in 1922, the Castro Theatre stood as the elegant centerpiece of this growing community (and still does). Eureka Valley remained a peaceful lower- and middle-class neighborhood for about 50 years; then the dynamic area we know today began to take shape.

In the 1970s, a large number of gay men moved into the area, renovated weathered Victorians, and gave the neighborhood a general facelift. The Castro came alive again, this time as the epicenter of gay pride. The neighborhood rejoiced in 1977 when local camera store owner Harvey Milk was elected to the city council, becoming the nation's first openly gay elected city official. A year later, the community suffered a devastating blow when Supervisor Milk and Mayor George Moscone were gunned down in City Hall by former supervisor Dan White. Today, Harvey Milk Plaza at Castro and Market Streets is a popular meeting place for marches and political rallies. The dozens of rainbow-striped flags gracing the neighborhood attest to its current status as the capital of gay America.

AIDS, understandably, is one of the neighborhood's most uniting causes. Hospices and crisis centers have sprung up to support the sick and their caregivers. The Names Project office, anchored at Castro and Market Streets, houses the famous **NAMES QUILT**, a powerful array of more than 30,000 panels, each representing a casualty of AIDS.

The Spanish Renaissance–style **CASTRO THEATRE** (429 Castro St; 415/621-6120) draws crowds for its innovative and retro movie offerings as well as its landmark architecture. Another added plus is the restored Wurlitzer on which an organist plays "San Francisco, Open Your Golden Gate" before each show (it then sinks into the floor by way of a hydraulic lift). Also unique to the neighborhood are the painted vintage streetcars that run through here from lower Market Street. A fairly recent addition to Muni's old-time F line, these trains were imported from faraway cities like Beijing, Milan, Lisbon, and Baltimore. It was such a costly endeavor that there was talk of reverting to the standard

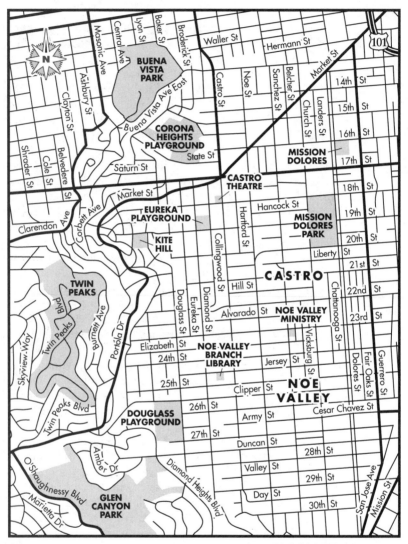

THE CASTRO/NOE VALLEY

trains, but these little gems had become so popular that huge protests squashed the proposal.

The neighborhood's main shopping areas are on Market, Castro, and 18th Streets. **DOES YOUR FATHER KNOW** (548 Castro St; 415/241-9865), or DYFK, sells gay-themed greeting cards. **A DIFFERENT LIGHT BOOKSTORE** (489 Castro St; 415/431-0891) stocks a large collection of books by, for, and about gays and lesbians. **JOSEPH SCHMIDT CON-FECTIONS** (415/861-8682) gourmet chocolates can be found at high-end stores around the city, but he started in the Castro—chocolate lovers shouldn't miss his store at 3489 16th Street.

The Castro has a dynamic restaurant scene ranging from burgers and fries to duck confit. The restaurant at 2223 Market Street remained nameless for months until it became known simply as **2223 RESTAU-RANT AND BAR** (415/431-0692), where upscale cuisine is served in a swanky setting. Industrial chic is the theme at **MECCA** (2029 Market St; 415/621-7000), a popular meeting place for food and drink. On a sunny day the patio at **CAFE FLORE** (2298 Market St; 415/621-8579) is packed with gays and hets alike who come for the tasty salads, sandwiches, specials, and scene. (For reviews of the former two, see the Restaurants chapter.)

For after-dinner drinks and a chance to soak up the local color, head toward **METRO** (3600 16th St; 415/703-9750), where you can watch the locals stroll by from the wraparound balcony. If you're feeling more adventurous and aren't intimidated by male meat markets, a drink at **DETOUR** (2348 Market St; 415/861-6053) comes complete with go-go dancers. An eclectic crowd flocks to **CAFE DU NORD** (2170 Market St; 415/861-5016) for live salsa, swing, jazz, and blues. Dance classes are offered before some shows. *Map:K6*

NOE VALLEY

Long before 24th Street was lined with fashionable shops and cruised by young parents pushing strollers, the sunny patch of land known as Noe Valley was home to San Francisco's last Mexican mayor, Jose de Jesus Noe. Noe built a ranch on the 4,443 acres given to him in 1834 by Spanish governor Pio Pico. His holdings extended from Twin Peaks to Daly City, but today only a street and this quiet neighborhood, bounded by 22nd and 30th and Dolores and Castro Streets, bear his name. When Alta California was annexed by the United States, the land was purchased and developed by John Horner, who mapped out a grid of blocks that stretched from Castro to Valencia and from 18th to 30th Streets. Today many streets are still named after prominent Mexican ranchers from the alcalde's era.

In the early 1900s, improved public transit opened the neighborhood to working-class families, who flocked here for the quiet streets and warm weather. Noe Valley and the Mission District were collectively known as the Emerald Enclave when the Irish began to settle here in large numbers. German, Scandinavian, and Mexican Americans flocked to the valley as well. Before the housing crunch of the 1990s, it was one of the city's last bastions of affordable housing because while it offers some sweeping hilltop panoramas, it lacks those sought-after bay views.

Twenty-Fourth Street was an active commercial district even before the turn of the century. The 1906 earthquake and fire stopped at 20th and Church Streets, sparing most of Noe Valley. Today it's a bustling community with a large commercial street and an amazing number of beautifully maintained houses.

A plethora of interesting shops and good cafes line 24th Street from Castro to Church Streets. **COMMON SCENTS SOAPS AND LOTIONS** (3920-A 24th St; 415/826-1019) is a popular store, as is **ASTRIDS RABAT** (3909 24th St; 415/282-7400), which sells shoes and accessories. For the little one in your life, **SMALL FRYS** (4066 24th St; 415/648-3954) offers a selection of baby things. If you're in the mood for a picnic, **REAL FOOD COMPANY** (3939 24th St; 415/282-9500) sells organic veggies and bulk items.

Dining options run the gamut from contemporary American and Japanese to family-owned cafes and gourmet hamburger joints. The stoves at **FIREFLY** (4288 24th St; 415/821-7652; see review in the Restaurants chapter) cook up contemporary California favorites. At 3919 24th Street, **SAVOR** (415/282-0344) adds an international accent to its menu. **DIAMOND CORNER CAFE** (415/282-9551) at the corner of Diamond and 24th is the perfect spot for a weekend lunch break.

In addition to the shops and charming homes, other attractions include the **NOE VALLEY MINISTRY** (1021 Sanchez St), a Stick-style church designed by Canadian Charles Geddes and completed in 1889. Restored in the late 1970s, it today serves not only as a place of worship but as a community center offering day care, senior programs, lectures, and exercise classes. Another worthwhile stop is the **NOE VALLEY BRANCH LIBRARY** (415 Jersey St; 415/695-5095), built in 1916 with money from Andrew Carnegie. *Map:K7*

MISSION DISTRICT

Known as one of the sunniest and most diverse neighborhoods in the city, the Mission District stretches across a huge swath of land roughly bounded by Market, Cesar Chavez (Army), and Dolores Streets and Potrero Avenue. The site of San Francisco's original Spanish settlement, Mission Dolores, the Mission District owes much to the Mexican ranchers who bought up large tracts of land during the pre–Gold Rush days when Alta California belonged to Mexico.

During the early 1900s, a large number of immigrants settled here. The first wave of immigration included Irish, Germans, Scandinavians, and Jews. During the second half of this century the majority of new faces have been Latino and Asian. But the Mission isn't merely a home to recent arrivals. For decades artists, students, and blue-collar workers of all stripes have flocked here for sunshine and affordable housing. Today, a large lesbian population vies for housing with Silicon Valley transplants and first- and second-generation Mexican and Salvadoran immigrants.

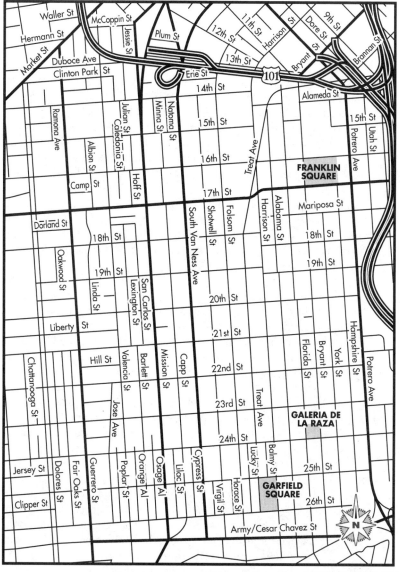

MISSION DISTRICT

To experience the heart of the Mission's Latino culture, head to 24th Street between Guerrero and Van Ness; you may just see a wandering mariachi band on your way there. **CASA LUCAS** (415/334-9747) at 24th and Alabama sells delicious sweet-corn tamales along with scores of Latin American staples. **GALERIA DE LA RAZA** at 24th and Bryant

227

honors the neighborhood's cultural heritage with exhibitions, movies, and classes. Off 24th and Harrison, the murals along Balmy Alley draw visitors from all over the world.

The Mission is known more for its lively energy than its architectural wonders, but it has a number of historical buildings. Head to **LIBERTY STREET** at Dolores for a look at 40 years of architectural design. Styles include Italianate (#159), Craftsman (#151–153), Queen Anne (#123), and Stick-style Victorian (#121–121A, 117–119, and 111–115).

The streets are filled with shopping opportunities. Bookstores and thrift shops abound, and recently the area has attracted a slew of home furnishings stores. The Irish-owned **HARRINGTON BROS. ANTIQUES** (599 Valencia St; 415/861-7300) is one of the oldest neighborhood businesses. Located on the corner of 17th and Valencia, it sits on what has recently become prime real estate. **THERAPY** (415/861-6213) has stores at 545 and 1051 Valencia where you can find vintage furniture and collectibles as well as clothing. **RAYON VERT** (3187 16th St; 415/861-3516) carries furniture as well as decorative items like lamps, dishware, and candles.

If you're hungry, the stretch of Mission between 21st and 24th Streets bursts with produce stands selling inexpensive fruits and vegetables, including hard-to-find ethnic items like plantains, yucca, and nopales. **LUCCA RAVIOLI COMPANY** (1100 Valencia St; 415/647-5581) sells delicious fresh pasta and sauces. A few blocks down at 548 Valencia Street is **BOMBAY BAZAR** (415/621-1717), an Indian market filled with imported spices, groceries, and yummy ice cream.

The Mission draws crowds nightly to its multitude of cheap taquerias, where the $4 burrito is king and more ambitious eats abound. Amid a sea of newcomers, the **FLYING SAUCER** (1000 Guerrero St; 415/641-9955) still stands as one of the best and most interesting restaurants in the Mission. Chef-owner Albert Tordjman, a surly Frenchman, puts a Gallic twist on what he calls world cuisine. Another relative old-timer is **TI COUZ** (3108 16th St; 415/252-7373), a Breton crepery. It's always Christmas at **LA RONDALLA** (901 Valencia; 415/647-7474), a quirkily decorated Mexican restaurant in the heart of the Valencia corridor. The food's not memorable, but the restive late-night atmosphere and potent margaritas make for an enjoyable pre- or post-clubbing spot. New and notable restaurants include **THE SLANTED DOOR** (584 Valencia St; 415/861-8032), specializing in innovative Vietnamese cuisine, and **VINERIA** (3228 16th St; 415/552-3889), a quaint spot for rustic Italian fare. (For reviews of Flying Saucer, Ti Couz, and The Slanted Door, see the Restaurants chapter.)

A growing number of businesses have settled in the once-dangerous neighborhood south of Mission Street near Potrero Hill. Today the area is home to a number of restaurants worth a visit, including the **UNIVERSAL CAFE** (2814 19th St; 415/821-4608), **GORDON'S HOUSE OF FINE EATS** (500 Florida St; 415/861-8900), **BLOWFISH SUSHI TO DIE FOR** (2170 Bryant St; 415/285-3848), and **SLOW CLUB** (2501 Mariposa St; 415/241-9390); for reviews of all four, see the Restaurants chapter.

Nightlife in the Mission is as varied as the people who live here. The **ELBO ROOM** (415/552-7788) on Valencia has long been a hot spot for live music. An older crowd flocks to the **LONE PALM** (415/648-0109) for occasional live jazz and a comfortable ambience. Nightly drag shows at **ESTE NOCHE** (415/861-5757), a Latino gay bar, bring the Castro crowd down to the Mission. Lesbians have made a place for themselves at the **LEXINGTON CLUB** (415/863-2052) on 19th Street.

The heart of experimental, cutting-edge culture in the city, the Mission offers a wealth of options for an evening's entertainment. Located at 1062 Valencia Street, **THE MARSH** (415/641-0235) showcases new and offbeat performance work; Mondays offer an opportunity for aspiring actors, comedians, and playwrights to hone their craft. The **ROXIE CINEMA** (415/863-1087), a slightly ramshackle but well-loved 275-seat repertory theater at 16th and Valencia Streets, features offbeat feature films and documentaries. **INTERSECTION FOR THE ARTS** (415/626-2787), with its cement walls and bleacher seats, is located in an unsavory part of the Mission, but has long been a prime venue for performance artists, dancers, writers, and dramatic artists. For up-and-coming bands, head to the **SWEAT SHOP** (415/487-1903) at Mission and 16th Streets, but bring your own beverages and refreshments—this barebones establishment places music at center stage.

One of the most memorable times to experience the sights and sounds of the Mission is during one of the Latino holidays such as the Day of the Dead, Cinco de Mayo, or Carnaval. These special events reveal the true soul of this dynamic community. *Map:L5-N7*

POTRERO HILL

The area south of 16th Street between Potrero Avenue, Highway 280, and Cesar Chavez Boulevard (see map on page 198), Potrero Hill is a quiet, sunny neighborhood with views of the downtown skyline, the industrial side of the bay, and Daly City. Once called Goat Hill, this former home to grazing herds is now an up-and-coming residential area. Infamous for its low-income housing known as "the projects" (O. J. Simpson grew up here), the sunny hillside was once one of the last bastions of affordable housing in the city. Word has since got out and it's affordable no longer (though patches of sketchy neighborhoods definitely remain, so be aware). Local architecture varies from modern condos and airy lofts to Victorian and Edwardian remodels and nondescript stucco buildings.

MCKINLEY SQUARE, bounded by Vermont, 20th, and San Bruno Streets, offers great views and a fantastic playground for kids. The portion of Vermont Street leading down to 22nd Street is as crooked as the famous stretch of Lombard Street. **POTRERO HILL RECREATION CENTER** (415/753-7001) at 22nd and Arkansas Streets may be a small city park, but it has big, big views. It also offers facilities for baseball, tennis, and barbecues.

Over the years a cadre of design firms and antique shops has grown in the area around 16th and Division Streets on the border of SoMa, but for the most part Potrero is still a quiet neighborhood for shopping. Also known as the Teddy Bear Factory, **BASIC BROWN BEAR FACTORY** (444 De Haro St; 415/626-0781 or 800/554-1910) manufactures 30 different styles of bears, and you can even stuff your own. Tours are offered daily by reservation; prices start at $12 for stuff-your-own bears. Connoisseurs of fresh seafood should head down by the water to **NIKKO FISH CO.** (699 Illinois St; 415/864-5261), where glistening slabs of fresh ahi tuna sit waiting to be sliced into sushi and fresh oysters can be had for a song. Beer lovers shouldn't miss the tour at the **ANCHOR BREWING CO.** (1705 Mariposa St; 415/863-8350)—the only brewery in the country hand-crafting quality steam beers. Free weekday tours cover the company's history and brewing techniques and also offer the chance to sample each of Anchor's seven brews. Reservations are difficult to obtain, however, so be sure to call as far in advance as possible.

Potrero Hill is home to a growing number of fun dining spots. Nibble on a chicken topped with preserved lemon, or spinach and ricotta tortellini with pistachio, pancetta and sun-dried tomato, at **APERTO** (1434 18th St; 415/252-1625). Across the street at 1457 18th Street, **ELIZA'S** (415/648-9999) sizzles with California-influenced Hunan and Mandarin food. **CONNECTICUT YANKEE** (415/552-4440) at 100 Connecticut Street offers East Coast seafood favorites with a Boston accent. The menu features New England clam chowder, Carl Ripken crab cakes, and fresh Maine lobster. At 300 Connecticut Street, **GOAT HILL PIZZA** (415/641-1440) dishes up tasty pies and also features the work of local artists on its wall and live music on Thursday, Friday, and Saturday nights. (For reviews of the former two, see the Restaurants chapter.)

Potrero's eclectic nightlife offers something for everyone. The **BOTTOM OF THE HILL** (415/621-4455) nightclub at 17th and Texas Streets draws crowds from all over the city to listen to its up-and-coming musical lineup. Once you get past the surly barkeeps at **BLOOM'S SALOON** (415/861-9467) at 1318 18th Street at Texas Street, head to the back deck where a spectacular view of the city awaits. Located at 1830 17th Street at DeHaro, the **METRONOME BALLROOM** (415/252-9000) offers a variety of dance classes and also opens as a nightclub on Friday,

Saturday, and Sunday nights from 7:30pm to midnight. New to the neighborhood is the LI-LO LOUNGE (415/643-5678), a tiki bar at 1469 18th Street that grooves with salsa and reggae tunes. Hawaiian for "lost," Li-Lo adds a shot of campy fun to the area with its fig-leaf ceiling fans, bamboo mats, wicker chairs, and palm trees. *Map:N5-O7*

RICHMOND AND SUNSET

The Richmond and Sunset neighborhoods, which sit at the western end of the city and stretch from Arguello Boulevard out to the ocean, are collectively known as "the avenues" (as opposed to SoMa and the Mission District, which are referred to as "the streets"). This area first became popular at the end of the last century when Adolph Sutro created two crowd-pleasing attractions in the city's western reaches. The first and foremost in the city's memory was the seven-story Victorian masterpiece called the CLIFF HOUSE (Sutro was responsible for its second and most splendid incarnation). The second was the ambitious SUTRO BATHS, a compilation of a half-dozen indoor ocean-water swimming pools. Sadly, neither attraction remains standing today—at least not as conceived by Sutro—but in their heyday they helped to bring the growing city out west.

Many present-day landmarks still draw tourists and San Franciscans alike to the RICHMOND DISTRICT. Perhaps the most dramatic are the rocky cliffs that loom over the pounding surf at Land's End. At the end of Clement Street and 34th Avenue, Lincoln Park is home to the CALIFORNIA PALACE OF THE LEGION OF HONOR (see Top 25 Attractions in this chapter) art museum and the 18-hole LINCOLN PARK GOLF COURSE, which skirts the Golden Gate. One of the Richmond's unique sites is the Neptune Society's COLUMBARIUM (415/752-7892). The only remnant of the old Odd Fellows cemetery, this neoclassical edifice was built in 1898 and houses urns and ashes of prominent San Franciscans. Located on Loraine Court off Anza, the building is open weekdays from 9am to 5pm and weekends from 10am to 2pm.

In recent decades, thousands of Russian, Irish, and Chinese immigrants have landed in the Richmond. They've settled in the bland stucco-covered houses that stretch from just past Pacific Heights to the Pacific Ocean, making this one of the most international neighborhoods in the city. Although the neighborhood is located miles from the city center, Geary Boulevard and 19th Avenue provide easy links to the rest of the city. The parallel commercial streets of Geary and Clement provide locals with most major conveniences.

The Richmond is gaining a reputation among the adventurous as a place to go for great inexpensive food, and the neighborhood's cuisine is as much of a melting pot as its citizens would suggest. In the Inner Richmond on Geary near Arguello, STRAITS CAFE (3300 Geary Blvd; 415/668-1783; see review in the Restaurants chapter) serves up authentic

Singaporean cuisine in a casual setting. One block north is Clement Street, which stretches from Arguello to the ocean and is home to a number of great Asian markets, restaurants, and the landmark **GREEN APPLE BOOKS** (506 Clement St; 415/387-2272). **BISTRO CHAPEAU** (1408 Clement St; 415/750-9787) offers traditional French bistro food amid a sea of Asian eateries. Down at the western end of Geary, a number of wonderful ethnic restaurants congregate in the shadow of **ST. MARY THE VIRGIN IN EXILE**, a Russian Orthodox Church whose gold domes can be seen from several blocks. **KHAN TOKE THAI HOUSE** (5937 Geary Blvd; 415/668-6654) treats diners to an elegant and traditional ambience as well as flavorful regional cuisine. The weekend lines outside of **TON KIANG** (5821 Geary Blvd; 415/387-8273), a stone's throw away, attest to the fact that this two-level restaurant dishes up some of the best dim sum in the city. (For reviews of both, see the Restaurants chapter.) Across the street, **LA VIE** (5830 Geary Blvd; 415/668-8080) is a good spot for casual Vietnamese food.

San Francisco's ever-present Irish community also has a strong presence in the Richmond. The **IRISH CULTURAL CENTER** is located at 2700 45th Avenue (415/661-2700). **PAT O'SHEA'S MAD HATTER** (3848 Geary Blvd; 415/752-3148) and the **PLOUGH & STARS** (116 Clement St; 415/751-1122) are among a number of Irish pubs that make the neighborhood a busy area for evening revelry (and the place to be on St. Patrick's Day).

The **SUNSET DISTRICT** is the neighborhood that runs south of Golden Gate Park to Sloat Boulevard, and west from Stanyan Street to Ocean Beach. The broad streets slope gently toward the sea and are lined with Mediterranean-style stucco homes. These ubiquitous, boxy tunnel houses (two-bedroom homes with bay window over the garage) sprang up after World War II when the economy mandated smaller lots and simple architecture.

The neighborhood is divided into the Inner Sunset, the area just east of 19th Avenue, and the Outer Sunset, the area past 19th toward the ocean. The Sunset has long frightened away newcomers due to its infamous fog, but proximity to the beach is still a strong draw for many. On Friday and Saturday nights, bonfires light up the coast of Ocean Beach (burning permits are not required). **STERN GROVE, LAKE MERCED**, and the **SAN FRANCISCO ZOO** are other nearby attractions.

Predominantly working class with lots of families, the Sunset is ethnically split between whites and Asians. The presence of the **UNIVERSITY OF CALIFORNIA MEDICAL CENTER** on Parnassus Street has brought many students to the neighborhood, as has **SAN FRANCISCO STATE UNIVERSITY**, located in the southwestern end of the city past Sloat Boulevard.

The area is really many small neighborhoods lumped together under one name. The district's major commercial streets include Irving, Judah, Noriega, Taraval, and Sloat Boulevard. Like the ethnically diverse Richmond, the Sunset offers a wealth of dining opportunities for those willing to travel to the outer reaches of the city. Innovative Mexican food can be found at **CASA AGUILA** (1240 Noriega St; 415/661-5593). In the Inner Sunset, two old standbys are **PJ'S OYSTERBED** (737 Irving St; 415/566-7775), a great spot for fresh seafood with a Cajun twist, and **EBISU** (1283 9th Ave; 415/566-1770) for excellent sushi. (For reviews of all three, see the Restaurants chapter.) *Map:C3-I5 (Richmond), C5-H7 (Sunset)*

Museums

Note: Galleries for established San Francisco artists are located primarily on lower Grant Avenue and near Union Square, while up-and-coming artists tend to exhibit in the SoMa (South of Market Street) area. For current art and gallery listings, check the *San Francisco Chronicle*'s "Datebook" in the Sunday paper, or log onto www.bayarea.citysearch.com and click on "The Arts" link.

ANSEL ADAMS CENTER FOR PHOTOGRAPHY / 250 4th St, between Howard and Folsom Sts; 415/495-7000 Photography buffs can marvel at the work of the master himself, as well as that of Imogen Cunningham, Dorothea Lange, and many other notable contemporary and historical photographers. The photos are showcased in the center's five exhibition galleries, one of which is dedicated solely to displaying the works and exploring the legacy of Ansel Adams. *Admission is $5 for adults, $3 for students, $2 for seniors and children 13–17, free for children 12 and under; every day; map:N3*

ASIAN ART MUSEUM / Tea Garden Dr, Golden Gate Park; 415/668-8921 Within Golden Gate Park is the Asian Art Museum, one of the largest museums in the Western world devoted exclusively to Asian art, with many masterpieces from the Avery Brundage collection. World-class artworks on exhibit include sculptures, ceramics, paintings, bronzes, and decorative objects spanning 6,000 years of history from more than 40 Asian countries. The museum's free daily guided tours are highly recommended as well; call for times. (Note: the museum will move to the former San Francisco Main Library building in the Civic Center in the year 2001.) *Admission is $7 for adults, $5 for seniors 65 and over, $4 for youths 12–17, free for children 11 and under; free the 1st Wed of each month; Tues–Sun; map:G5*

BAY AREA DISCOVERY MUSEUM / Fort Baker; 415/487-4398 Located on the other side of the Golden Gate Bridge in Sausalito, the Bay Area Discovery Museum is a wonderland of hands-on science, art, and multi-media exhibits designed for kids from toddlers on up. To get there, head north across the bridge, exit at Alexander Avenue, and follow the signs to East Fort Baker and the museum. *Admission is $7 for adults, $6 for children 1–18; Tues–Sun; www.badm.org; map:FF6*

CALIFORNIA ACADEMY OF SCIENCES / Golden Gate Park, off Middle Dr E, between John F. Kennedy and Martin Luther King Jr. Drs; 415/750-7145 While tourists flock to Fisherman's Wharf and Pier 39, locals often head in the other direction to the extraordinary California Academy of Sciences, where under one roof you'll find: the **NATURAL HISTORY MUSEUM**, which traces the course of 3½ billion years of evolution from the earliest life forms to the present day via dozens of fantastic exhibits; the **MORRISON PLANETARIUM**, offering guided tours through the universe via its 65-foot domed ceiling (with such evocative titles as "The Universe Unveiled" and "Star Death: The Birth of Black Holes"); the **LASERIUM**, a venue for trippy laser-light shows; and the superb **STEINHART AQUARIUM**, which contains one of the most diverse collections of aquatic life in the world—about 14,500 specimens, including seals, dolphins, and alligators. *Admission to Aquarium and Natural History Museum is $8.50 for adults, $5.50 for students 12–17 and seniors 65 and over, $2 for children 4–11, free for children under 4, free the 1st Wed of each month; Planetarium/Laserium shows are $2.50 for adults and $1.25 for children under 18 and seniors 65 and over; every day; map:H5*

CALIFORNIA PALACE OF THE LEGION OF HONOR / Legion of Honor Dr at 34th Ave and Clement; 415/863-3330 Witness the finest collections of Rodin sculptures outside Paris and other works of art at this beautiful neo-classical monument. See Top 25 Attractions in this chapter for more information. *Map:E4*

COIT TOWER FRESCOES / 1 Telegraph Hill Blvd; 415/362-0808 Inside the base of the tower are a series of murals titled *Life in California, 1934*, which were completed by more than 25 artists—many of whom studied under Mexican muralist Diego Rivera—as part of the New Deal. See Top 25 Attractions in this chapter for more information. *Map:N1*

EXPLORATORIUM / 3601 Lyon St (at Marina Blvd) in the Palace of Fine Arts; 415/563-7337 or 415/561-0360 for recorded information Don't miss what *Scientific American* calls "the best science museum in the world." See Top 25 Attractions in this chapter for more information. *Map:J1*

HAAS-LILIENTHAL HOUSE / 2007 Franklin St, between Washington and Jackson; 415/441-3000 Built in 1886, this Queen Anne Victorian housed the Haas-Lilienthal family from 1886 until 1972. Peter Schmidt's lavish design for the 24-room mansion cost $18,500 to build. The interior architecture features a yellow Sienna marble fireplace and a red Namidian marble hearth, redwood paneling, and oak wainscoting. A 1920s update by Gardner Daily brought modern conveniences such as a stove and elevator. What's the story? It all has to do with Alice Haas-Lilienthal, who grew up and passed away in this historic house. While much of the neighboring area was being sold to developers eager to build profitable apartment buildings, she held on to her family legacy and lived there until her death in 1972. In 1974, her heirs donated the house to the Foundation for San Francisco's Architectural Heritage. This nonprofit organization decided to open the doors of this amazing landmark to the public. It's a one-of-a-kind opportunity to glimpse the pristine interior of one of San Francisco's world-famous Victorians. *Admission ranges from $3 to $5. Tours are offered Wed noon–3pm and Sun 11am–4pm; map:L1*

THE JEWISH MUSEUM SAN FRANCISCO / 121 Steuart St, between Mission and Howard Sts; 415/543-8880 This museum houses hundreds of photographs, paintings, and sculptures—along with rotating exhibits—that focus on immigration, assimilation, and identity of the Jewish community in the United States and around the world. (Note: In 2000 the museum began renovations on a new location at Jessie and Mission Streets, but the move isn't scheduled until 2002.) *Admission is $5 for adults, $2.50 for students and seniors; free the 1st Mon of each month. Sun–Thurs; map:O2*

MARITIME MUSEUM / Beach St at Polk St; 415/556-3002 Peruse the dignified array of spectacular photos, ship models, and displays at this world-class museum dedicated to the ships of yesteryear. See San Francisco Maritime National Historical Park in Top 25 Attractions in this chapter for more information. *Map:L1*

MEXICAN MUSEUM / Bldg D, Fort Mason, Marina Blvd at Laguna St; 415/441-0404 The city has several terrific folk-art museums, most notably the Mexican Museum—the first museum in the country to focus on the arts of Mexico and Mexican Americans. Revolving shows cover pre-Hispanic, colonial, folk, Mexican fine art, and Chicano/Mexican-American art, including such exhibits as the art of New Mexican women and Mexican surrealism. (Note: The museum is expected to relocate to the Yerba Buena neighborhood at the end of 2000.) *Admission is $3 for adults, $2 for children; free the 1st Wed of each month. Wed–Sun; map:K1*

M. H. DE YOUNG MEMORIAL MUSEUM / Golden Gate Park, off John F. Kennedy Dr; 415/863-3330 The de Young Museum normally showcases

American art from colonial times to the 20th century, but the hugely popular museum was damaged by the 1989 earthquake and declared unsafe. De Young supporters are searching for a new home for the museum, and in the meantime all of its upcoming international exhibitions will be transferred to the California Palace of the Legion of Honor (see Top 25 Attractions in this chapter). *Map:G5*

MISSION DOLORES / 3321 16th St at Dolores St; 415/621-8203 Ponder the old tombstones and religious artifacts from Spanish America at this authentic Spanish mission. See Top 25 Attractions in this chapter for more information. *Map:K5*

MUSÉE MÉCANIQUE / Cliff House, 1090 Point Lobos Ave at Upper Great Hwy; 415/386-3330 You'll marvel at this collection of antique mechanical amusement machines that actually work. See Cliff House in Top 25 Attractions in this chapter for more information. *Map:C3*

MUSEUM OF THE CITY OF SAN FRANCISCO / 2801 Leavenworth St, on the third floor of the Cannery; 415/928-0289 The only museum dedicated to San Francisco's colorful history. See Ghirardelli Square and The Cannery in Top 25 Attractions in this chapter for more information. *Map:L1*

OCTAGON HOUSE / 2645 Gough St at Union St; 415/441-7512 Maintained by the National Society of Colonial Dames of America, this eight-sided, cupola-topped house dates from 1861 and is now a small museum displaying Early American antiques—furniture, ceramics, portraits—and historic documents such as signatures of 54 of the 56 signers of the Declaration of Independence. The architectural features are extraordinary as well. *Admission is free. Open only on the 2nd Sun and 2nd and 4th Thurs of each month from noon–3pm (closed Jan); map:L2*

PRECITA EYES MURAL ARTS CENTER / 2981 24th St at Harrison St; 415/285-2287 Fantastic murals decorate many public spaces in the city, particularly in the Mission District, the city's vibrant, primarily Hispanic neighborhood. At the Precita Eyes Mural Arts Center, you can pick up maps outlining self-guided walks, or opt for their very informative two-hour guided tour. If you don't have time for a tour, at least stroll down narrow Balmy Alley (near Harrison and 25th Streets), which is lined with about 30 incredibly colorful murals and is the birthplace of mural painting in San Francisco. *Admission to the center is free; call for tour rates and times. Every day; map:M7*

PRESIDIO ARMY MUSEUM / Lincoln Blvd and Funston Ave, The Presidio; 415/561-4323 At this small museum ensconced in an old army building you'll find detailed accounts of the Presidio's long and storied history, including dioramas of the city in the early 1900s and a complete model of the 1915 Panama-Pacific International Exposition. *Admission is free. Wed–Sun; map:I1*

RIPLEY'S BELIEVE IT OR NOT! MUSEUM / 175 Jefferson St at Fisherman's Wharf; 415/771-6188 Witness freaks of nature that stymie our perception of reality (that, and get totally grossed out). See Fisherman's Wharf in Top 25 Attractions in this chapter for more information. *www.ripleysf.com; map:M1*

SAN FRANCISCO CABLE CAR MUSEUM / 1201 Mason St; 415/474-1887 Housed in a brick building at the corner of Mason and Washington, the San Francisco Cable Car Museum is well worth a visit. The familiar hum of the cables moving underfoot should be your first clue that this is not merely a memorial to the past. It still serves as the powerhouse for the entire cable car system. A 1984 addition to the museum cleverly allows visitors to actually watch the sheaves—giant iron wheels—that power and regulate the cables. An amazingly simple feat of engineering propels the cars a consistent 9.5 miles per hour around town. If you can pull yourself away from the gears and pulleys, the museum also features vintage photographs and cable car memorabilia, including a cross section of cable. (You may not want to ride the cars again once you find out all that's holding you up!) Placards explain that the cables last between 100 and 300 days depending on which line they serve, the Powell-Mason line being the most demanding. A dummy car explains how the gripman and brakeman control the cars. Traditionally bells are used to communicate. One of the highlights is Car No. 8 from Andrew Hallidie's original 1873 Clay Street cable car. Saved from the 1906 fire because it was on loan to the city of Baltimore for an exhibition in 1905, the car has been restored and, along with two 1876 cars from the old Sutter Street line, stands as a monument to one of the city's best-loved legacies. A gift shop sells postcards, key chains, and coffee cups. *Admission is free; every day; map:M2*

SAN FRANCISCO MUSEUM OF MODERN ART / 151 3rd St, between Mission and Howard Sts; 415/357-4000 More than 17,000 works are housed in this $62 million monument to modern art. See Top 25 Attractions in this chapter for more information. *Map:N3*

WAX MUSEUM / 145 Jefferson St at Fisherman's Wharf; 415/202-0400 Sure, it's a cheesy, kitschy tourist trap, but it's still loads of creepy fun for both kids and adults. See Fisherman's Wharf in Top 25 Attractions in this chapter for more information. *Map:M1*

YERBA BUENA CENTER FOR THE ARTS / 701 Mission St at 3rd St; 415/978-2787 Witness cutting-edge multimedia shows and computer art at this stylish high-tech art center. See Top 25 Attractions in this chapter for more information. *Map:N3*

Parks and Beaches

Scenic spots abound in San Francisco, and views can be had all over the city. Some wonderful parks include **GLEN CANYON PARK**, which has a playground, on Bosworth Street and O'Shaughnessy Boulevard (map:J8); the lush **STERN GROVE**, on Sloat Boulevard at 19th Avenue (map:G9); and **LAKE MERCED**, where you can rent a rowboat, canoe, or paddleboat and fish for trout, located off Harding Road between Highway 35 and Sloat Boulevard, near the zoo (map:E9). Call 415/753-1101 for information on Lake Merced boat rentals.

Riptide-ridden and blustery **OCEAN BEACH**, a long, sandy stretch located off the Great Highway, is a haven for seasoned surfers as well as for families, dog-walkers, joggers, and strolling lovers (map:D2-9). On warm days, sun worshippers prefer to bask at **BAKER BEACH** while gazing at the stupendous view of the Golden Gate (as at most of the city's beaches, however, swimming is unsafe here). The east side of the beach is a popular gay hangout, where sunbathers bare all; take 25th Avenue west to the end, bear right, then look for signs to Baker Beach (map:F1-2).

In the southwest corner of the city, near the ocean and Lake Merced, is the popular **SAN FRANCISCO ZOO** (45th Ave and Sloat Blvd; 415/753-7061; map:D9). Don't miss the famed **PRIMATE DISCOVERY CENTER**, where several species of apes and monkeys live in glass-walled condos. The zoo also has rare Sumatran and Siberian tigers, African lions (visit during their mealtimes), a children's petting zoo, and even an insect zoo. On the other side of the Golden Gate Bridge, in Sausalito, is the **BAY AREA DISCOVERY MUSEUM** (415/289-7268; map:FF6), a wonderland of hands-on science, art, and multimedia exhibits designed for kids from toddlers on up; head north across the bridge, exit at Alexander Avenue, and follow the signs to East Fort Baker and the museum.

If you want to get out on the bay, but Alcatraz isn't your cup of tea, head to **ANGEL ISLAND**, a 740-acre state park with a few interesting sights and a lot of hiking and biking trails (map:FF5). Before the Spaniards "discovered" the island, it was a fishing and hunting spot for the local Miwok Indians. For almost 100 years, from the Civil War to the cold war, the island housed a variety of military installations. It also played a major role in the settlement of the West, serving as both a Public Health Service quarantine station and an immigration station. State park volunteers lead **TOURS** of Angel Island's historical immigration station, Camp Reynolds, and Fort McDowell on the weekends between 10am and 4pm, and by appointment during the week. Tours and admission to the park are free, though donations are accepted. Ferries land at Ayala Cove, the perfect site for a family picnic. Call the Blue & Gold Fleet

(415/773-1188; recorded information, 415/435-1915) for ferry service and rates from San Francisco.

For a fun morning of shopping with the added bonus of gorgeous city views, head to the **TREASURE ISLAND FLEA MARKET** (415/255-1923; map:GG4) on Sunday. It starts at 6am, but vendors will still be there if you sleep in a bit. Admission is free, but parking will cost you a few dollars. The food court offers good ethnic and American fare.

Organized Tours

GRAY LINE (415/558-9400) offers several ways to see San Francisco. Its **DELUXE CITY TOUR** wheels past the Civic Center, old Mission Dolores, Twin Peaks, Golden Gate Park, Cliff House, Vista Point North, and Golden Gate Bridge. The 3½-hour tour concludes at Fisherman's Wharf. Adult fare is $31, children (ages 5–11) pay $15.50. Tours run daily: 9am, 10am, 11am, 1:30pm, 2:30pm (3:30pm seasonal). Gray Line also offers this tour with a bay cruise option for an additional $12. An added trip to Alcatraz Island runs an extra $15.

A number of **FREE WALKING TOURS** are organized by City Guides, an affiliate of the San Francisco Library. Themed tours include Chinatown, Alamo Square, Downtown Deco, Old South Park, and Brothels, Boardinghouses, and Bawds. Call 415/557-4266 for schedules, or pick up a self-guided itinerary at the San Francisco Visitor Information Center on the lower level of Hallidie Plaza (900 Market St at Powell St; 415/391-2000; map:N3), or at any San Francisco Public Library.

For an expert tour of Chinatown, try **WOK WIZ CHINATOWN WALKING TOURS** (654 Commercial St; 415/981-5588). Shirley Fong-Torres leads a number of culinary tours throughout the neighborhood; one option even includes lunch. Rates run $25–$65 per person.

Literary walks through North Beach, led by **FOOTNOTES LITERARY WALK HIGHLIGHTS** (800/820-2220), include Jack Kerouac's favorite restaurant and the club where Maya Angelou was once an exotic dancer. Tuesday through Sunday 10am–1:30pm; $35 per person.

Rachel Heller leads a guided promenade through the psychedelic past of the **UPPER HAIGHT**. This tour covers the Haight's rich history, including, of course, the Summer of Love. Tuesdays at 9:30am and Saturdays at 9:30am; $15 per person; 415/221-8442.

For a different perspective on the city, try **SAN FRANCISCO FIRE ENGINE TOURS & ADVENTURES** (415/333-7077). One-hour tours cover the Golden Gate Bridge, the Presidio, and Union Street; or Fisherman's Wharf, the Embarcadero, and North Beach. The fire engine can also be chartered for a custom tour.

The **VICTORIAN AND EDWARDIAN PACIFIC HEIGHTS WALK** (415/441-3000) is led by guides from the Foundation for San Francisco's Architectural Heritage. The two-hour stroll covers the area's many turn-of-the-century mansions, family homes, and row houses. Tours meet daily at 2007 Franklin Street (map:L3). **SAINTS AND SINNERS** (415/922-7181), led by Footprints on the Pavement, is a tour through the Victorian mansions, row houses, churches, and hotels of the Cathedral Hill area. Cost is $35 per person and includes lunch.

PRECITA EYES MURAL ARTS CENTER (2981 24th Street; 415/285-2287; map:N7) offers walking tours to view the Mission District's many murals. Tours meet every Saturday and Sunday at Precita Eyes at 1:30pm and include an informative slide show. Adults $5, seniors $4, children and students (under 18) $1. For a three-hour tour of more than 100 murals take **EL VOLADO**, a colorful Mexican bus. Each tour is guided by a mural expert and includes traditional Mexican refreshments. Third Sunday of every month at 12:30pm (except December); adults $16, children 12 and under $12.

For a closer look at the exciting Castro neighborhood, **CRUISIN' THE CASTRO** (400 Castro St; 415/550-8110; map:K6) takes off from Harvey Milk Plaza and includes brunch at Caffe Luna Piena. Tours begin at 10am Tuesday through Saturday and most holidays. $35 per person includes tour and brunch.

SHOPPING

SHOPPING

Neighborhoods, Districts, and Malls

UNION SQUARE

Of all the great shopping destinations in San Francisco, none matches the high-energy sophistication of **UNION SQUARE**. Named for Union supporters who gathered here before the Civil War, this area at the turn of the century was a favorite with white-gloved society ladies who lunched at the St. Francis Hotel. The first Union Square department store opened in 1896. Today the newly expanded Macy's, genteel Saks Fifth Avenue, and luxe Neiman Marcus anchor the area, with retail theaters such as Niketown and Disney adding a glitzy '90s twist. New York–based Bloomingdale's opens in late 2001.

Just off the square is the Parisianstyle alleyway known as **MAIDEN LANE**. Originally called Morton Street and lined with bordellos, it got a name change (and started attracting a different clientele) in 1922. These days you'll find chic couturieres such as Chanel and Jil Sander commingling with fine home and accessory shops. Take a short walk east down Post Street to the beautiful **CROCKER GALLERIA** (50 Post St; Mon–Fri 10am–6pm, Sat 10am–5pm), modeled after Milan's Galleria Vittorio Emmanuelle. This elegant glass-domed pavilion features three tiers of shops, including big names like Nicole Miller, Versace, and Polo Ralph Lauren, with plenty of cafes and tea shops for a pleasant mid-shopping break. Go west down Market Street and you'll come to the skylit, nine-story **SAN FRANCISCO SHOPPING CENTRE** (865 Market St; Mon–Sat 9:30am–8pm, Sun 11am–6pm), one of a handful of vertical malls in the nation, with more than 100 shops including Abercrombie & Fitch, Enzo Angiolini, Club Monaco, and J. Crew. The unique spiral escalator circles all the way up to Nordstrom's fourth floor. If you can't find what you're looking for there, head back east toward the bay to the **EMBARCADERO CENTER** (bordered by Battery and Drumm Sts, Sacramento and Clay Sts; Mon–Fri 10am–7pm, Sat 10am–6pm, Sun noon–5pm). Here amid the towers of the Financial District is a four-tower complex with restaurants, award-winning gardens, and more than 130 shops and restaurants, from Pottery Barn and Crabtree & Evelyn to the Gap, Banana Republic, Liz Claiborne, and much more.

FISHERMAN'S WHARF

Yes, it's touristy, but there's more retail to this area than T-shirt shops. The three-level red-brick **CANNERY** (Leavenworth and Beach Sts; Mon–Fri 10am–6pm, Sun 11am–6pm), built at the turn of the century as a Del Monte fruit-packing plant, now holds a variety of restaurants, outdoor vendors, and stores purveying kitchenware, shoes, and fine local food and wine. The Museum of the City of San Francisco is on the third floor, and from the walkways and balconies you can look down to a tree-shaded courtyard where performers entertain daily. A stone's throw away is **GHIRARDELLI SQUARE** (900 North Point St; Mon–Sat 10am–9pm, Sun 10am–6pm), site of a former mill and chocolate factory; nowadays retailers such as Ann Taylor, Benetton, The Sharper Image, a shoe store, and an architectural bookstore coexist cheek by jowl with the famous chocolate shop. Another restoration success is **PIER 39** (The Embarcadero at Beach St; open every day), a converted pier lined with more than 100 restaurants and novelty shops. One of the novelties, decidedly nonretail, gives locals as well as visitors a kick: several years ago a large population of sea lions happened by and decided to stay. Today, officially accommodated by the management (displacing a marina full of pleasure boats in the bargain), the mammals are Pier 39's most famous waterside attraction, along with, of course, the spectacular views of Alcatraz and the Golden Gate Bridge (see Pier 39 under Top 25 Attractions in the Exploring chapter).

NEIGHBORHOODS

San Francisco's neighborhoods are rewarding retail therapy in themselves. Near the Marina district is an area known as **COW HOLLOW**, named after the cattle that grazed freely in this area in the mid-1800s; these days shoppers consider it good grazing for trend-setting clothing and home decor. Apparel stores on **UNION STREET** (between Van Ness Ave and Steiner St) tend toward European designs or the sporty, casual look; many shops and restaurants are housed in old Victorians or tucked down picturesque courtyards and alleys. **CHESTNUT STREET** (between Laguna and Lombard Sts) is the Marina's main artery; on weekends, in-line skaters and baby-boomers-with-strollers share the sidewalks, stopping at everything from old-fashioned delis and edgy boutiques to chain stores such as Williams-Sonoma and the Gap. Another upscale/hip enclave of high-end antiques, furnishings, and more can be found on **FILLMORE STREET** (from Pine St to Jackson St) in Pacific Heights; here you'll rub elbows with the city's elite, many of whom live in huge mansions a few blocks away. A dozen or so blocks down Fillmore Street on **SACRAMENTO STREET** (near Presidio Ave), amid a peaceful residential neighborhood of tree-shaded Edwardians, the antique dealers share the sidewalks with chic clothing boutiques such as Sarah Shaw and decorator treasure trove Sue Fisher King.

Across town, between Douglas and Dolores Streets, is 24th Street, **NOE VALLEY**'s version of the Chestnut Street shopping area in the Marina, only with a cozier flavor. Here you'll find lots of family-run retailers purveying toys, children's apparel, handicrafts, and books, plus loads of cafes and bakeries where you can nourish yourself after taking

SAN FRANCISCO'S STREET FAIRS

Combine balmy weather; a wide variety of neighborhoods, each with a different character and feel; and the tendency of San Franciscans to party at the drop of a hat, and you've got a full season of street fairs to choose from, according to your tastes in music, food, and cultural expression. The fair season runs from late spring, when the weather starts warming up, to the middle of fall. In between, here are the biggies:

The Summer of Love may be a long-gone if fondly recalled memory, but the **Haight Street Fair** annually attempts a resuscitation each June, right at the fabled intersection of Haight and Ashbury Streets. The art for sale tends toward the psychedelic, the T-shirts toward tie-dye, and wandering artists offer face-painting to some of the fair's 80,000 to 100,000 attendees at a reasonable price. Just like in the old days, there's music in the streets: ex–Grateful Dead crony Merle Sanders traditionally closes out the two days of festivities on the main stage at Haight and Stanyan Streets, while up-and-comers—from guitar-toting singer-songwriters to jug bands to eclectic unclassifiables—show off their chops at the smaller stage at Haight and Masonic Streets. More than 20 food booths help hold the munchies at bay: standbys such as burritos, pizza, and cheese steaks share the stalls with delicacies of China, Thailand, and Ghana in West Africa (try the yummy fried bananas). The merchandise for sale at all the city's street fairs is of a handcrafted, individually manufactured sort—no ready-mades.

Another two days in June brings the **North Beach Street Fair**, which usually draws 60,000 to 70,000 people to the still heavily Italian neighborhood that is also proud to proclaim itself the home of the Beat generation (Allen Ginsberg began working on his groundbreaking *Howl* at 1010 Montgomery Street, above Broadway). In keeping with finger-snapping '50s cool, there's a strong jazz current on at least two musical stages, but North Beach has over the years also become something of a home to the blues. Three blues-oriented bars (the Grant & Green Blue Club, the Lost and Found, and the Saloon) showcase a rotating talent roster, from the downhome acoustic to the slick-and-swinging-with-a-horn section. Along with food booths, the neighborhood's cafes and trattorias offer their delicious specialties on paper plates, best enjoyed during a leisurely tour on foot.

In the heavily Roman Catholic cultures of Latin America, the traditional Carnaval is pegged to Lent as a final burst of indulgence in all the things the devout are soon going to be expected to give up. Judging from the annual **Carnaval Parade and Festival**, a massive one-day street party at the end of May, this includes some of the skimpiest costumes this side of an arrest for indecent exposure—which may explain why attendance has been known to reach several hundred thousand. In recent years the palette of the festival has broadened to include tastes and sounds not strictly Latin. There are two big musical stages—one devoted to salsa, mariachi, and other more traditional forms, the other featuring the eclectic sounds of world beat—and several smaller stages showcasing a dizzying variety of musical styles. The same is true of the food— in addition to tacos and pupusas and mouthwatering roasted corn, you can feast on Caribbean-style jerk chicken and Cajun sausage, Thai and Chinese foods, gyros and gumbo. There are more than 50 crafts booths to choose from, with merchandise ranging from art to handbags, and a children's area.

Commemorating the defeat of the French at the Battle of Puebla on May 5, 1862, which forever spelled the end of French designs on Mexico, the **Cinco de Mayo Festival** is an expression of national pride. Three music stages feature sounds from the traditional *norteñas* and *rancheros, conjuntos,* and *corridas* to the hip-hop favored by the up-and-coming. The food from the 20-or-so booths similarly runs the gamut, from tasty tacos to Thai noodles. The 30-plus crafts booths offer clothing, jewelry, candles, paintings, and religious artifacts (the Virgin of Guadalupe is a major figure in Mexican folklore). One folk art form unique to Cinco de Mayo is the low-rider: after working on them all year, Chicano car clubs parade and exhibit beautifully detailed examples of the golden age of the American automobile, tricked out and accessorized in ways Detroit could only dream of. Attendance for this one-day event generally tops out at 50,000 to 60,000.

In the market for a studded dog collar for your significant other? Then head on down to the fetish-heavy **Folsom Street Fair**, thrown during the last week in September. The leather scene that once called Folsom Street its home is slowly waning (mostly due to skyrocketing real-estate rates), but once a year the faithful gather for a celebration of their highly ritualized vision of bearded, burly masculinity. There are 20 or so food booths—falafel, gyros, barbecue—and two stages featuring live music of a most cutting-edge variety. But the real attraction here is the crafts booths, if for no other reason than that you don't often find a good pair of leather chaps at other street fairs. This is probably not the best fair to take the kids to, and not just because there's no children's area—it might be tough to explain why the teddy bears for sale are dressed in metal. On a more serious note: all proceeds from this fair go to fund AIDS research and to provide support for those with AIDS.

The first Sunday in October brings revelers, on average more than 100,000 of them, to the **Castro Street Fair** to bid farewell to the last of the great summer weather. Jammed but mellow, the fair features some 30 food booths, with fare such as falafel, ice cream, and barbecue as well as beer and wine; more than 50 craft booths, where you can get outfitted in anything from shirts to sandals and see real men having serious discussions about their earrings; and a huge music stage at the corner of Castro and Market Streets, where DJs keep the beat going between live acts. Hope you like techno.

it all in. Martha's is a favorite morning commuters' stop and weekend hangout. A short drive away down Castro Street is **THE CASTRO**, the heart of the gay community, always packed with shoppers checking out the mainstream and offbeat (sometimes downright risqué) clothing and novelty shops, along with the historic Castro Theatre.

If it's ultra-ultra-hip you want, head toward the Civic Center area to **HAYES STREET**, which was a run-down strip of bars and liquor stores before forward-thinking merchants moved in. Today you'll find a pedestrian-friendly setting to browse for avant-garde clothes, shoes, books, and funky furniture finds.

Some neighborhoods are worth shopping just for their ethnic or subcultural flavor. **CLEMENT STREET**, chockablock with every imaginable Asian restaurant and produce market, also boasts terrific consignment shops and bookstores. **HAIGHT STREET**, even more threadbare these days but still with its heart in the '60s, has loads of stores hawking vintage clothing, Grateful Dead posters, and tie-dyed T-shirts. And **JAPAN-TOWN** (between Post and Buchanan Sts) is the place to go for imported Japanese textiles, ceramics, and silk.

HISTORIC DISTRICTS

It's hard to believe picturesque **JACKSON SQUARE** (between Columbus Ave and Sansome St) was once part of San Francisco's rough-and-tumble Barbary Coast. The Depression of the '30s closed the saloons and brothels, leaving vacant buildings; in the '50s, interior decorators and architects moved in. Today it's a delightful enclave of gaslamp-lit alleys and Victorian storefronts housing antique shops with superb European, Continental, and Asian furniture and decorative arts.

Follow Jackson Street to Columbus Avenue and you'll reach **NORTH BEACH**, the old Italian neighborhood that the Beat generation made famous. Bookstores and clothing shops still cater to bohemian (and upscale) tastes, and the area around Filbert Street holds Italian craft shops, delis, and bakeries galore.

And finally, there's **CHINATOWN**, with its big green metal dragon- and lion-flanked Grant Avenue gate. Home to one of the largest Asian populations in the world, it's a fun place to pick up kitschy imported trinkets, porcelains, and silks. Or join locals haggling over already bargain-priced produce, poultry, and meats.

SOUTH OF MARKET AREA (SOMA)

This former industrial warehouse district is now a hot spot for hip restaurants, nightclubs, and bargain and discount stores. Most of the action takes place on Brannan, Second, Third, Howard, and Townsend Streets. Though markdown outlets come and go, Burlington Coat Factory (899 Howard St; 415/495-7234)—carrying more than coats—is one of the stalwarts. The San Francisco Flower Mart is another great destination, where early risers can pick up well-priced fresh and dried flowers from wholesale merchants who also sell to the public. A newcomer to SoMa is Metreon (150 4th St; every day 10am–11pm). Inside are four floors of retail spectacle, including a Maurice Sendak–themed restaurant, a movie multiplex with an IMAX theater, a Discovery Channel store, a Microsoft store, a shop called Sony Style, a marketplace devoted to works by local retailers and artists, and more.

OUTLYING MALL

South down 19th Avenue in the foggy Sunset District is Stonestown Galleria (3251 20th Ave; 415/759-2626; Mon–Sat 10am–9pm, Sun 11am–6pm; map:G9)—a bit of a trek, but worth it for the terrific selection of stores under one roof. Besides Nordstrom and Macy's, there's Eddie Bauer, the Gap, Banana Republic, and lots of small jewelry, shoe, and accessory boutiques, plus an enormous sunlit food court and—hooray!—plenty of parking.

DEPARTMENT STORES

MACY'S UNION SQUARE / 170 O'Farrell St; 415/397-3333 ■ 3251 20th Ave (Stonestown Galleria); 415/759-2626 After a major remodel and expansion, Macy's Union Square is now the third-largest department store in the world (following Harrod's of London and Macy's New York): 700,000 square feet, including the separate men's store across the street. The refurbished eight-story building includes a six-story glass window overlooking the square. Inside you'll find departments representing mid- to high-end apparel, accessories, cosmetics, and housewares. "Shoes on Two" is the biggest footwear department on the West Coast, and the sportswear floors stock more than 80,000 pairs of jeans from all major makers. There's a terrific selection of furniture, kitchenware, bedding, and linen, including designer sheets and accents. Edibles sold in the Cellar range from healthy snacks at Jamba Juice to gourmet deli entrees by celebrity chef Wolfgang Puck. *Mon–Sat 10am–8pm, Sun 11am–7pm; map:N3, G9*

NEIMAN MARCUS / 150 Stockton St; 415/362-3900 The elegant Dallas-headquartered department store with its Philip Johnson–designed facade boasts a giant atrium with a stunning stained-glass ceiling—all that remains of the historic City of Paris store that once occupied the site. Thierry Mugler, Escada, and St. John are some of the high-end designers represented in the haute-couture boutiques. The main level boasts an excellent selection of fragrances and cosmetics. The accessories and gourmet food departments are also superb. During the holidays, shoppers flock to Neiman's to see its gaily decorated three-story tree. *Mon–Sat 10am–7pm, Thurs 10am–8pm, Sun noon–6pm; map:N3*

NORDSTROM / 865 Market St; 415/243-8500 ■ 3251 20th Ave (Stones-town Galleria); 415/759-2626 What started as a family-run Seattle shoe store has become one of the most popular shopping destinations in the West. In the San Francisco Centre store, Nordstrom's different levels are accessed by a spiral escalator—one of only two in the country. In addition to more than 100,000 pairs of shoes, you'll find fine jewelry, gift items, cosmetics, and high-end fashion from Oscar de la Renta, Valentino, and others. Services include a beauty spa, four restaurants, personal shoppers, a concierge, live piano music while you shop—and even valet parking (at the Fifth Street entrance). *Mon–Sat 9:30am–9pm, Sun 10am–7pm; map:M4, G9*

SAKS FIFTH AVENUE / 384 Post St; 415/986-4300 The West Coast branch of this New York–based retailer is renowned for its designer boutiques and high-end cosmetics and jewelry. Five floors are linked by a central escalator, and there's a cafe on the top floor overlooking the square. *Mon–Wed, Fri 10am–7pm; Thurs 10am–8pm; Sat 10am–7pm; Sun noon–7pm; map:N3*

SAKS FIFTH AVENUE MEN'S STORE / 220 Post St; 415/986-4300 Art deco detailing, wood paneling, a fireplace, and a bar in the fitting room add up to one of the classiest men's shopping destinations in town. Five floors feature sportswear, accessories, and traditional and contemporary attire. The fourth floor is modeled after a New York City penthouse to showcase fashions from Armani, Gucci, Prada, and others. *Mon–Wed, Fri 10am–7pm; Thurs 10am–8pm; Sun noon–7pm; map:N3*

Shops from A to Z

ANTIQUES

ARGENTUM–THE LEOPARD / 414 Jackson St; 415/296-7757 If you're looking for that elegant trinket to spruce up the table, then this is the place. Taking up the second floor of a historic building, Argentum specializes in English, Scottish, Irish, and American silver from the early 18th to late 19th century. The selection is dazzling, from flatware and trivets to knife rests and platters. Most items are food related: urns, soup tureens, sauceboats, salvers (small servants' trays used to hold drinks), and more. The array of silver wine accoutrements is one of the best in the country. If you're a serious collector, don't miss Paul Storr's creations or the coffee services and tea caddies by Hester Batemen, one of the first female silversmiths. *Mon–Fri 9am–5pm, Sat 10am–4pm; map:N2*

THE BUTLER & THE CHEF / 1011 25th St; 415/642-6440 Former French baker George Blum keeps clients well stocked with decorative and functional antique French kitchen and bar furniture from his homeland.

Besides pewter and marble-top tables, Blum carries lots of bars, sinks, farm tables, and fixtures from old French country estates. Other gems include French enamel signs, old-fashioned gaslamps, and authentic baker's racks used to cool baguettes and ficelles. Just browsing here feels like a trip back to 18th-century Provence. *Mon–Sat 11am–5pm; www. thebutlerandthechef.com; map:O7*

BUTTERFIELD & BUTTERFIELD / 220 San Bruno Ave; 415/861-7500 What was founded as a clearinghouse for surplus goods has become one of the most successful auction houses in the world. Established in 1865 on the site of the Transamerica Pyramid, the company moved to larger quarters south of Market Street when it expanded to represent antiques, fine art, and furnishings. Estate sales are held monthly, and the main gallery auctions are on Sundays. Catalogs are available for a fee. Absentee bids can be made by telephone, by mail, or online at www.butterfields. com. *Mon–Fri 8:30am–5pm; map:N5*

COLLECTIVE ANTIQUES / 212 Utah St; 415/621-3800 Housed in an old brick building just footsteps from the San Francisco Design Center, Collective Antiques is a 12,000-square-foot space with more than 40 dealers (many decorators) showcasing higher-end American and Oriental artifacts. Merchandise must be pre-1950 and in excellent condition. A full-time designer oversees the displays, which are arranged so you can see how the antiques might look in your home. The decorative elements alone are worth the trip; they run the gamut from French magazine stands and Victorian laptop desks to fabulous old lanterns and globes. *Mon–Sat 10am–5pm, Sun noon–5pm; map:N5*

DANIEL STEIN ANTIQUES / 458 Jackson St; 415/956-5620 A lawyer-turned-antiques-dealer owns this shop, which specializes in 18th- and 19th-century English furnishings and art, along with scientific instruments such as telescopes, barometers, and celestial and terrestrial globes. There are lots of library furnishings (what else from a lawyer?), including writing tables, bookcases, and elaborate desks. *Mon–Fri 9am–5pm, Sat 11am–3pm; map:N2*

DILLINGHAM & COMPANY / 700 Sansome St; 415/989-8777 Gaylord Dillingham is a dealer in the old-fashioned sense. He specializes in one area: authentic English and Continental furniture from the 17th to the 19th century. With more than 25 years of experience and a degree from the Victoria & Albert Museum in London, Dillingham keeps his gallery well furnished with authentic Chippendale, William & Mary, and Regency pieces, most found on his buying trips to Europe. *Mon–Fri 9am–5pm, Sat 11am–3pm; map:N2*

DRUM & COMPANY / 151 Vermont St; 415/551-1538 Though John Drum first opened his shop on historic Jackson Square, he moved to larger quarters near the San Francisco Design Center to better showcase his expanded selection of furnishings and decorative items. The commodes, painted screens, antique lamps, and tables are especially worth a visit. *Mon–Fri 9am–5pm; map:N5*

ED HARDY ANTIQUES / 188 Henry Adams St; 415/626-6300 A longtime veteran of San Francisco's antiques community, Ed Hardy had his business in the heart of downtown before building this gorgeous Palladian-style building with 15-foot ceilings, a Renaissance stone fireplace, and 16th-century Italian red marble columns. The merchandise, as elegant and eclectic as the surroundings, includes 16th- to 20th-century decorative items from Italy, England, and France. A fountain courtyard showcases antique garden furniture and statuary. Can't find what you're looking for? Ask the staff. Chances are it's hidden in one of the numerous nooks or crannies. *Mon–Fri 8:30am–5pm; www.edhardysf.com; map:N5*

EVELYN'S ANTIQUE CHINESE FURNITURE / 381 Hayes St; 415/255-1815 Disney executive Michael Eisner is one of the many celebrities whose home is decorated with antiques from this shop. Evelyn's is the largest importer of pre-1850 Chinese antiques in the nation, and it's been a well-kept secret of designers and collectors since it opened in 1987. The selection appears small at first glance (the Chinese custom is to show a little at a time), but in the back are a storeroom and restoration workshop jam-packed with Ming chairs, lohan beds (designed for Buddhist sages), altar tables, baskets, and pots. *Mon–Sat 11am–6pm; map:L4*

FOSTER-GWIN, INC. / 38 Hotaling Place; 415/397-4986 Bring money. Lots of money. Foster-Gwin caters to the well-heeled, who make frequent pilgrimages to the gallery for its splendid furnishings from the Renaissance to the early 19th century. Located on an alley named for a distiller and real-estate baron, the space served as a livery in days gone by. Stairs to the second floor were horse ramps to the stalls, though the feed troughs have long been replaced with ornate consoles and tapestries from 17th-century Belgium and France. *Mon–Fri 9am–5pm; map:N2*

INTERIEUR PERDU / 340 Bryant St; 415/543-1616 This is one of our favorite destinations for the country French look. The owners scour small villages and old farmhouses to keep the warehouse filled with rustic hutches, bistro tables and chairs, and antique daybeds and cribs. Adorable wooden goat carts are ideal for filling with pots of geraniums or ivy and placing next to Parisian park benches in your garden. You'll also find old farm tables, wire egg baskets, and enamel coffeepots and cups. *Mon–Sat 11am–6pm; map:O3*

INTERIOR PERSPECTIVES ANTIQUES / 3461 Sacramento St; 415/292-5962 This lovely shop specializes in 18th-, 19th-, and early 20th-century antiques from Europe and the Far East. Furnishings are attractively displayed in vignettes, and the designers offer suggestions on how furnishings will work in your living room or parlor. *Mon–Fri 11:30am–5:30pm, Sat 11:30am–5pm; map:J3*

JOHN DOUGHTY ANTIQUES, INC. / **619 Sansome St; 415/398-6849** Those looking for fine 18th- and 19th-century furniture, oil paintings, and decorative accessories need look no further than John Doughty, who purchases most of his inventory on buying trips to his native England. The shop was founded in 1963 and still serves many of its original clients. *Mon–Fri 9:30am–5pm; map:N2*

LA SALLE GALLERY / **1525 Union St; 415/931-9200** Now in its 30th year, La Salle Gallery holds regular auctions for everything from antiques and estate sale pieces to automobiles and household goods. Auctions take place on Tuesdays, with previews the previous Saturday and Sunday. Payment is in American dollars or with MasterCard, Visa, or American Express. Call for a schedule. *Mon–Fri 9am–5pm; www.lasallegallery.com; map:L2*

MURETA'S ANTIQUES / **2418 Fillmore St; 415/922-5652** Lifetime collector Gary Mureta runs this neighborhood shop in posh Pacific Heights, where society matrons allow him access to estate sales before other dealers. Mureta keeps the place pleasantly cluttered with silver, crystal, and china that befits a mansion as well as more humble abodes. *Tues–Sat noon–6pm; map:K2*

ROBERT DOMERGUE & CO. / **560 Jackson St; 415/781-4034** For 20 years Robert Domergue has kept collectors well-sated with 17th- and 18th-century French and Continental furniture and accessories. Besides Louis XVI–style *bergères* and benches, there are bureaus, sofas, giltwood chairs, and dining room tables. Accents run the gamut from Chinese screens and mirrors to sconces and lamps. *Mon–Fri 9am–5pm, Sat 10am–3pm; map:N2*

THOMAS LIVINGSTON / **414 Jackson St; 415/296-8150** What was once a tram barn for storing streetcars is now home to a shop specializing in 18th- and 19th-century English and American antiques. Former University of California at Berkeley professor Thomas Livingston switched to dealing antiques more than 25 years ago and has developed a stunning array of fine Georgian and Regency pieces, in addition to wonderful decorative items such as delftware, clocks, lamps, and chandeliers. *Mon–Fri 9am–5pm, Sat 10am–4pm; map:N2*

W. GRAHAM ARADER III / **435 Jackson St; 415/788-5115** Arader is world-renowned for its antique maps and prints, especially the works of Belgian-born Pierre Joseph Redoute, court artist to Napoleon and Josephine and considered the "Raphael of flowers." On a back wall are

251

original Redoute paintings of the emperor's garden. Audubon etchings dating to the early 1800s are another reason to stop by, including the popular California turtledove. There are also architectural prints from the 16th century and rare maps by Ortelius and Blaeu. *Mon–Fri 10am–6pm, Sat 11am–5pm; map:N2*

APPAREL

A/X ARMANI EXCHANGE / 2090 Union St; 415/749-0891 This branch of the nationwide chain, a casual, more affordable arm of Armani, carries sportswear and work wear geared to the chic but casual California lifestyle. You'll find a great selection of jeans, trousers, shirts, sweaters, jackets, skirts, and dresses at prices that won't cost a month's pay. Also look for leather totes, hats, and socks. *Mon–Sat 10am–8pm, Sun 11am–6pm; map:L2*

AMERICAN EAGLE OUTFITTERS / 865 Market St; 415/543-4550 Ever since this retailer outfitted the cast of the TV show *Dawson's Creek*, the college and 20-something crowd has been flocking to AE for its easygoing plaid shirts, boots, cargo pants, and weathered dungarees (the AE name is on almost everything, though, so logo-haters beware). Outdoor gear and equipment are also carried. *Mon–Sat 9:30am–8pm; Sun 11am–6pm; www.ae.com; map:M4*

ANN TAYLOR / 240 Post St (and branches); 415/788-0716 Ann Taylor is a big favorite with career women, who love its selections of well-made suits, silk blouses, evening dresses, and sweaters, as well as the Taylor accessory line of jewelry, scarves, fragrances, belts, and shoes. You'll see a few trendier touches among the sportswear knits and denims. Other branches include the San Francisco Shopping Centre (415/543-2487), 3 Embarcadero Center (415/989-5355), and Ghirardelli Square (415/775-2872). *Mon–Sat 10am–7pm, Sun 11am–8pm; map:N3*

BANANA REPUBLIC / 256 Grant Ave (and branches); 415/788-3087 The flagship store of this hip national chain takes up an entire city block. Inside are several levels of casual men's and women's slacks, shorts, T-shirts, and dresses in de rigueur black, white, and khaki, plus whatever other colors are in this season. Fabrics lean toward linen, wool, cotton, cashmere, velvet, suede, and silk. Other branches include 2 Embarcadero Center (415/986-5076) and the Stonestown Galleria (415/759-2626). *Mon–Sat 9:30am–9pm, Sun 11am–8pm; www.bananarepublic.com; map:N3*

BARCELINO / 498 Post St; 415/781-5777 If you're looking for impeccable Italian-made men's suits and apparel, this is the place. Catering to the fashion-conscious male, Barcelino features sport jackets, ties, shirts, shoes, hats, and ascots—all adding up to that dapper, well-polished look. *Mon–Sat 10am–7pm, Thurs 10am–8pm, Sun 11am–6pm; map:N3*

BEBE / 21 Grant Ave (and branches); 415/781-2323 Don't expect bows or ruffles at Bebe: this boutique chain attracts younger career women who go for the drop-dead sleek and snug European fit. Clothes are trendy, but stylish enough to go straight from the office to dinner. Expect lots of black, olive, and brown, with the occasional flash of burgundy or hot pink. Other branches include the San Francisco Shopping Centre (415/543-2323) and 2133 Fillmore Street (415/563-6895). *Mon–Sat 10:30am–5pm; map:N3*

BROOKS BROTHERS / 201 Post St; 415/397-4500 The 180-year-old New York–founded clothier still specializes in traditional button-downs and pinstripes as well as classic sweaters and accessories for both women and men. Though known for the ultraconservative Ivy League look, Brooks now has a trendier collection of sportswear and weekend wear. *Mon–Sat 9:30am–6pm, Sun noon–5pm; map:N3*

BULLOCK & JONES / 340 Post St; 415/392-4243 Since 1853, Bullock & Jones has dressed fashion-conscious San Francisco men who prefer the staid white-collar image. The store carries an extensive selection of jackets, suits, and shirts, as well as Pringle cashmere sweaters and Ferragamo and Cole-Haan shoes. An in-house hairstyling salon keeps shoppers well coifed. *Mon–Fri 9:30am–6pm, Sat 9:30am–5:30pm; map:N3*

BURBERRYS / 225 Post St; 415/392-2200 It made its name with the quintessential trench coat, but this English-based retailer also sells distinctive men's and women's clothes. Three levels showcase tailored shirts, sweaters, blazers, suits, and sportswear. *Mon–Fri 10am–6:30pm, Sat 9:30am–6pm, Sun noon–6pm; map:N3*

CAROL DODA'S CHAMPAGNE & LACE LINGERIE BOUTIQUE / 1850 Union St, #1; 415/776-6900 Legendary North Beach topless star Carol Doda, former queen of the Condor club, owns and operates this sliver of a shop featuring unique bras, panties, chemises, teddies, bustiers, and other not-so-basic "foundations" not often found in department stores. Most are sexy, slinky, and ultratransparent. Bridal corsets and garments in hard-to-find sizes are another reason to visit. There are also silk thongs and boxers for men. Ooh la la! *Every day 12:30pm–6:30pm; www.citysearch.com/sfo/champagnelace; map:L2*

CELINE PARIS BOUTIQUE / 216 Stockton St; 415/397-1140 This is one of only four Celine boutiques in the nation carrying the complete line of women's ready-to-wear clothing and accessories from design superstar Michael Kors. Heavy on gray, black, white, and red, Kors sportswear uses luxe fabrics such as silk, suede, cashmere, and fur. *Mon–Sat 10am–6pm; map:N3*

CHANEL / 55 Maiden Ln; 415/981-1550 Coco would be proud to know the little black dress still reigns supreme at her namesake boutique. Today Chanel fashions come under the Karl Lagerfeld label in a variety of fabrics, including tweeds and silks. The store also sells the signature quilted handbags, costume jewelry, and wraparound glasses. *Mon–Sat 10am–6pm, Sun noon–5pm; map:N3*

CIELO / 2225 Fillmore St; 415/776-0641 This Euro-boutique, the sister store of L'Uomo, imports avant-garde fashions for women. Miu Miu is one of the popular labels. Colors tend toward neutral beiges, blacks, and browns, and there are accessories to complement separates or ensembles. *Mon–Sat 11am–7pm, Sun noon–6pm; map:K3*

DAVID STEPHEN MEN'S / 50 Maiden Ln; 415/982-1611 One of the oldest men's stores in the city, David Stephen specializes in high-end, hand-tailored suits and sportswear from Italian designers such as Pal Zileri, Canali, and Ermenegildo Zegna. Along with jackets and shirts, you'll find sports coats, exquisite handmade cashmere sweaters and robes, and accessories. On-site tailoring is available, and there's a good selection of men's grooming products. *Mon–Sat 10am–5:30pm; map:N3*

DIESEL / 101 Post St; 415/982-7077 Diesel's West Coast flagship store is packed with trendy denim fashions. Browse for Italian-made jeans, sportswear, and a huge selection of denim skirts, vests, and jackets. More than 3,000 pairs of the signature boot-cut denims are in stock, as well as sunglasses and accessories. *Mon–Fri 10am–8pm, Sat 10am–7pm, Sun noon–6pm; map:N3*

EDDIE BAUER / 250 Post St; 415/986-7600 ■ 3251 20th Ave (Stonestown Galleria); 415/759-2626 The canoes hanging from the ceiling are a big tip-off: this huge three-level store for men and women stocks stylish but functional outdoor and leisure wear. The emphasis is on well-made shirts, T-shirts, casual pants, shorts, and outerwear, in traditional colors. There's also a line of dress sportswear called AKA Eddie Bauer and an Eddie Bauer Home collection. *Mon–Fri 10am–8pm, Sat 10am– 7pm, Sun 11am–6pm; map:N3, G9*

EMPORIO ARMANI / I Grant Ave; 415/677-9400 The elegant marble setting is the perfect showcase for Armani's suits, sportswear, formal wear, and accessories. The style is professional and classy, yet more affordable than other big-name boutiques. Some home furnishings are available. For a break from shopping, have an espresso or lunch at the classy cafe. *Mon–Fri 10am–7pm, Sat 10am–6pm, Sun noon–6pm; map:N3*

GAP / 890 Market St (and branches); 415/788-5907 The flagship store of the San Francisco–based nationwide chain purveys all the hallmark "Gap casual" slacks, skirts, dresses, sports coats, T-shirts, sweaters, accessories, and more. Designs are stylish bordering on hip, yet classic enough to wear to the office or a special event. The palette changes a few times each season. Prices are incredibly reasonable, as is the liberal return policy. Other branches throughout the city include 2159 Chestnut Street (415/929-1744) and 3 Embarcadero Center (415/391-8826). *Mon–Sat 9:30am–8pm, Sun 10am–6pm; www.gap.com; map:M4*

JESSICA MCCLINTOCK / 180 Geary St; 415/398-9008 Ever since San Francisco designer Jessica McClintock introduced her demure country-print Gunne Sax dresses in the early 1960s, young girls have been flocking to her boutiques in search of the romantic, feminine look. This shop is heavy on elegant wedding gowns and bridesmaid's dresses, plus luxurious long dresses for formal occasions. Purses and shoes are available to complete the ensemble. *Mon–Wed 10am–6pm, Thurs–Sat 10am–7pm, Sun 11am–5pm; map:N3*

LEVI STRAUSS / 300 Post St; 415/501-0100 Where else can you sit in a shrink-to-fit tub? Levi's latest gimmick in its new 24,000-square-foot store is a two-person tub, where shoppers can take a quick dip into the water while wearing a new pair of pants; the pants are quickly dried so the wearers can make sure the pants really fit. Baby boomers can get jeans adorned with flower-power and other '60s touches. Besides jeans, there are khaki and cargo pants, shirts, belts, and jackets. *Every day 10am–8pm; map:N3*

L'UOMO / 352 Sutter St; 415/397-3633 ■ 2120 Fillmore St; 415/776-0669 Look for Vestimenta, Luciano Barbera, Gravati, and Ferragamo at this Union Square atelier, which imports fine Italian fashions and accessories for men. In-house tailoring is complimentary and finished in two days. *Mon–Sat 10am–6pm, Sun noon–5pm; map:N3*

METIER / 355 Sutter St; 415/989-5395 Locals love this boutique for its California and international labels from designers such as Peter Cohen, Rebecca Taylor, Souchi, and Alberto Biani. The store offers classic career apparel and separates, as well as contemporary evening dresses and coordinating accessories. Don't miss Cathy Waterman's jewelry. *Mon–Sat 10am–6pm; map:N3*

MIO / 2035 Fillmore St; 415/931-5620 A neighborhood shop popular for its suits, linen dresses, sweaters, tunics, and skirts from Harari, Issey Miyake, Longchamps, and others. Coordinating bags, hats, belts, and jewelry complete the look. *Mon–Sat 10:30am–6:30pm, Sun noon–6pm; map:K3*

SARAH SHAW / 3095 Sacramento St; 415/929-2990 Designer Sarah Shaw's Pacific Heights shop is a welcome change from your basic sterile, minimalist '90s boutique. Fresh flowers and shabby-chic chairs set the mood for leisurely browsing through racks of apparel from top designers such as Trina Turk and Michael Kors. The look is hip, yet classic enough to wear to work. Some cocktail gowns and dresses are sold, too. *Mon–Sat 11am–7pm, Sun noon–5pm; map:J3*

SUSAN / 3685 Sacramento St; 415/922-3685 Yohji Yamamoto, Dolce & Gabbana, and Helmut Lang are a few of the designers carried in this high-end shop. Susan's capricious sister, The Grocery Store (3615 Sacramento St; 415/928-3615), features second-label casual and contemporary clothing, including T-shirts and informal suits. *Mon–Sat 10:30am–6:30pm; map:I3*

TOUJOURS / 2484 Sacramento St; 415/346-3988 or 888/621-9397 Owner Beverly Weinkauf keeps this tidy boutique packed with romantic lingerie from high-end names such as Calida and Wolff. She also carries Wolford's deluxe hosiery. For the bride-to-be, there are bustiers and merry widows to wear under the gown, plus lacy leg garters for the ceremonial postnuptial toss. Toujours also has a mail-order catalog. *Mon–Sat 11am–6pm, Sun noon–5pm; www.toujourslingerie.com; map:K3*

WILKES BASHFORD / 375 Sutter St; 415/986-4380 Local haberdasher Wilkes Bashford has dressed three generations of San Franciscans, including such prominent politicos as Willie Brown, in fine Italian suits, sportswear, cashmere sweaters, and imported leather shoes. The six-level shop features top designers Brioni, Gautier, and Wilson & Dean, among others. *Mon–Sat 10am–6pm, Thurs 10am–8pm; map:N3*

BAKERIES

THE BAGELRY / 2139 Polk St; 415/441-3003 Located on a rapidly gentrifying stretch of Polk Street, the 25-year-old Bagelry produces what are quite possibly the best bagels in the city. Boiled before they are baked, in the authentic New York style, the bagels come out lightly crusted with a dense, chewy center. Flavors are mostly traditional: sesame, onion, garlic, poppy, plain, and salt, plus cinnamon-raisin, along with onion bialys and seeded bagel sticks. A refrigerator stocks cream cheese, lox, and other accoutrements to round out your nosh. *Mon–Sat 6:30am–5pm, Wed 6:30am–noon, Sun 7am–4pm; map:L2*

BOUDIN SOURDOUGH BAKERY & CAFÉ / Fisherman's Wharf, 156 Jefferson St (and branches); 415/928-1849 This place put sourdough bread on the San Francisco food lover's map. In 1849, French refugee Isidore Boudin combined sourdough starter with the French bread-making technique and opened the French Bread Bakery where, as legend has it, locals and panhandlers lined up each morning for a loaf of her famous sourdough bread. Today you can still see the bakers at work through a rear window in the bakery's Fisherman's Wharf location. For the holidays, Boudin (nowadays pronounced bow-DEEN) creates whimsical sourdough Christmas trees, stockings, turkeys, and plump snowmen with quirky bow ties. Panettone, the traditional Italian holiday dessert, is available year-round. Though the breads can be delivered by mail (call 800/992-1849 for details), there's nothing like the taste of sourdough bread fresh from the oven. Each bakery has an adjoining cafe dishing up fresh soups, salads, and specialty sandwiches. Tops on this list are the turkey havarti and the "turkey berry," the latter a Dagwood-size creation piled high with cranberry sauce, onion, mayo, and white turkey on sliced sourdough or sourdough roll. The house-made clam chowder is served in a mini–gold miner's loaf. There are more than 40 Boudins throughout the city, including at 2223 Chestnut Street (415/440-3003), 120 O'Farrell Street (415/296-7372), and 67 Fifth Street (415/543-8304). *Sun–Fri 7:30am–10pm, Sat 7:30am–11pm; map:M1*

CITIZEN CAKE / 399 Grove St; 415/861-2228 Former pastry chef Elizabeth Falkner whips up innovative sweets and baked goods with unusual shapes at this artisan bakery in Hayes Valley, an ultrahip shopping district near the Civic Center and Davies Symphony Hall. Signature desserts include the After Midnight devil's food cake, made with a moist buttermilk base and Scharffen Berger chocolate mousse and ganache filling, and the Rosebud brûlée tart. Also don't miss the Retro Tropical Shag, made with creamy passion-fruit mousse layered between a buttery genoise and slathered with a rum buttercream frosting. Falkner also makes melt-in-your-mouth Mexican wedding cookies and chewy date-pecan tartlets. Afternoon tea is served daily with assorted savories and a choice of tea or champagne. See also the review in the Restaurants chapter. *Mon–Fri 7am–7pm, Sat–Sun 9am–7pm; map:L4*

EPPLER'S / Laurel Village Shopping Center, 3465 California St (and branches); 415/752-0825 Every neighborhood should have an Eppler's, and in San Francisco, almost every one does. From first thing in the morning to closing, customers keep the staff busy ordering the European-style pastries, coffee cake, breads, and delicate cookies made with rich creamery butter. Scones come laden with apricots, raspberries, raisins, or blueberries. The cakes are artfully crafted and include lemon, cheesecake, cappuccino, chocolate raspberry, and pudding; the sacher tortes are created from an old Austrian recipe. The immaculate setting is a perfect place to indulge in a cup of fresh-brewed coffee and a napoleon or custard eclair. *Mon–Fri 6am–7pm, Sat 6am–5pm, Sun 7am–3pm; map:J3*

IL FORNAIO / 1265 Battery St (Levi Plaza); 415/986-0100 This award-winning bakery, related to the chain of the same name in Italy, produces the regional Italian breads and pastries served at the popular Il Fornaio restaurants; you can also buy the baked goods at a handful of restaurant locations in the western states. Besides the ever-popular ciabatta (a crusty elongated bread whose name translates to "slipper" in Italian), you can pick up filone, pane noci (whole wheat–walnut), pane pugliese, and doughy breads made with potatoes and olives. The grissini (bread sticks) come plain or with seeds. On weekdays, fans of the Italian roast coffee line up early for their fix and a pastry or cookie to take to the office. See also the review in the Restaurants chapter. *Mon–Fri 6:30am–9pm, Sat–Sun 8am–9pm; map:N2*

I LOVE CHOCOLATE / 397 Arguello Blvd; 415/750-9460 Locals have been queuing up for pastries at this neighborhood bakery since it opened seven years ago. Owner Mary Brinkmann studied cooking in Paris and makes everything from scratch. Sure, there are the usual cookies and muffins, but the real lure is the blow-your-diet I Love Chocolate Cake with its famous white and semisweet chocolate mousse filling and chocolate truffle frosting. A close second is the Cookies 'n' Cream cake, oozing with vanilla buttercream and a crushed Oreo cookie center. Mary's croissant recipe comes from the cooking school where she studied in Paris. *Every day 6:30am–6pm; map:I3*

JUST DESSERTS / 3735 Buchanan St (and branches); 415/922-8675 Everything really is just right at Just Desserts. Founded in 1974 by Elliott Hoffman to market his rich homemade cheesecake, the popular cafe has expanded to offer chocolate mousse cake, carrot cake, fudge cake, triple lemon cake, and the beloved chocolate Weekend Cake with chocolate butter-cream frosting. All items are made from scratch daily. Muffins and coffee cake are available for early-bird patrons. Other branches are at 248 Church Street (415/626-5774) and 3 Embarcadero Center (415/421-1609). *Mon–Thurs 7am–8pm, Fri 7am–10pm, Sat 8am–10pm, Sun 8am–8pm; map:K1*

LA NOUVELLE PATISSERIE / 2184 Union St; 415/931-7655 ■ 865 Market St (San Francisco Centre); 415/979-0553 Forget counting calories when you shop at this tidy bakery, owned by a Frenchman who crafts rich French-style pastries he calls edible Van Goghs. Specialties include fresh fruit tarts (apple, pear, raspberry, and plum) and a variety of cakes: chocolate charlotte cake, opera cake, napoleons, and a three-mousse cake with white, dark, and milk chocolate smushed between chocolate sponge layers. The President's Cake alternates layers of rich hazelnut buttercream and chocolate hazelnut cake. *2184 Union St: Mon–Thurs 6:30am–8pm, Fri–Sat 6:30am–11pm, Sun 8am–7pm. 865 Market St: Mon–Sat 9:30am–6pm, Sun 11am–6pm; www.nouvelle patisserie.com; map:K2, M4*

GOLDEN GATE BRIDGE BY THE NUMBERS

Length: 8,981 feet

Span: 6,450 feet

Cost: $35 million

Completion date: May 28, 1937

Date paid in full: July 1971

Engineer: Joseph B. Strauss

Road height: 260 feet

Tower height: 746 feet

Swing span: 27 feet

Deepest foundation:
   110 feet under water

Cable thickness: 36½ inches

Cable length: 7,650 feet

Steel used: 83,000 pounds

Concrete used: 389,000 cubic yards

Miles of wire cable: 80,000

Gallons of paint annually: 10,000

Color: International Orange

Rise, in cold weather: 5 feet

Drop, in hot weather: 10 feet

Traffic: 3 million vehicles per month

Toll: $3 (southbound only)

LIGURIA BAKERY / 1700 Stockton St; 415/421-3786 You'll be hard-pressed to find a better focaccia than what comes out of this North Beach institution. Known as Ligurian pizza bread, the focaccia is slowly baked night to morning in an old-fashioned Italian brick oven dating back to 1911. The focaccia comes plain, topped with raisins, or sprinkled with olive oil and salt. Come early and buy a large slab; the bread always sells out soon after it comes out of the oven. *Mon–Fri 8am–5pm, Sat 7am–5pm, Sun 7am–noon; map:N1*

STELLA PASTRY & CAFFE / 446 Columbus Ave; 415/986-2914 This North Beach landmark is known for its *sacripantina* (sponge cake with maraschino liqueur and zabaglione), cannoli, tiramisu, and Italian rum cake. But Stella's also makes delicious butter cookies and biscotti, ideal for dunking in a good strong espresso from one of the neighboring cafes. *Mon–Thurs 7:30am–10pm, Fri–Sat 8:30am–midnight; map:N2*

VICTORIA PASTRY CO. / 1362 Stockton St; 415/781-2015 Yes, the St. Honoré cake is the most popular, but others vying for top honors include the fedora (a sponge cake with chocolate custard and whipped-cream filling), chocolate truffle, mocha butter, lemon custard, and *gâteau Antoinette* (devil's food with whipped-cream filling and fudge topping). Don't miss the cookies; there are dozens to choose from. Pick up extras to freeze and serve when your great-aunt comes to tea. *Mon–Sat 7am–6pm, Sun 8am–5pm; map:N2*

BODY CARE

**BARE ESCENTUALS / 3 Embarcadero Center (and branches);
415/391-2830** Started 25 years ago in a San Francisco suburb, this
family-run purveyor of custom-blended scents has grown to 20 outlets
nationwide. While the all-natural body products are still a big draw, the
makeup line is fast gaining favor and has even made the fashion magazines. Employees give complimentary makeovers, then show patrons
how to mix and match on their own. A mail-order department will keep
you well stocked if there isn't a store in your town. Other San Francisco
branches include Pier 39 (415/781-0631) and 2101 Chestnut Street
(415/441-8348). *Mon–Fri 10am–7pm, Sat 10am–6pm, Sun noon–5pm;
map:N2*

THE BODY SHOP / 865 Market St (and branches); 415/281-3760 This
British import is easy to spot by its green apothecary-style facade. Once
inside, you'll find shelves brimming with environmentally correct beauty
care items, with a host of scents ranging from herbal to citrus. There are
also full product lines for men, babies, and sensitive skin. Branches
include stores at 100 Powell Street (415/399-1802); 2106 Chestnut Street
(415/202-0112); 506 Castro Street (415/431-8860); and the San Francisco airport (650/794-9160). *Mon–Sat 9:30–8:30pm, Sun 11am–
6:30pm; www.the-body-shop.com; map:M4*

BODY TIME / 2072 Union St (and branches); 415/922-4076 Founded
30 years ago in Berkeley, Body Time is legendary for dye- and perfume-
free products packaged in reusable containers to minimize waste. More
than 80 perfume oils are available for blending. Other branches include
1932 Fillmore Street in the Marina (415/771-2432) and 1465 Haight
Street (415/551-1070). *Mon–Sat 10:30am–7pm, Sun 11am–6pm;
www.bodytime.com; map:K2*

**ELIZABETH ARDEN RED DOOR SALON & SPA / 126 Post St; 415/989-
4888** Most people come here for the legendary day of pampering and
beauty treatments—makeovers, facials, massage, and the famous Red
Door Manicure—but you can also buy the complete line of skin-care
products and cosmetics. *Sun–Mon 9am–6pm, Tues–Wed 9am–7pm,
Thurs–Fri 9am–8pm, Sat 8am–7pm; map:N3*

JACQUELINE PERFUMERY / 103 Geary St; 415/981-0858 One of the
first boutiques devoted exclusively to perfume, this place now has a loyal
clientele from around the world. Its incredible selection includes many
hard-to-find scents. Crystal atomizers and gift items are also for sale,
along with a small array of European skin-care products, including Sten-
dahl. Refills by mail or by phone. *Mon–Sat 9:30am–6pm, Sun noon–5pm;
map:N3*

MISTER LEE / 834 Jones St; 415/474-6002 This downtown sanctuary has been indulging the city's elite for more than three decades. Have your hair restyled, or relax in a hydrojet tub. Everything from shampoos to bath oil is custom made for the shop and available for purchase. *Mon–Fri 7:30am–6pm, Sat 7:30am–6pm; map:M3*

SEPHORA / 1 Stockton St; 415/392-1545 It was just a matter of time before hands-on shopping hit the beauty biz, and who better than Europe's largest cosmetic company to take on this turf? Shopping is self-service, and the innovative displays include a fragrance wall and a lipstick rainbow with one shade for each day of the year. Besides carrying well-known French labels from Dior, Guerlain, and Yves St. Laurent, Sephora also stocks lesser-known brands such as Stila and Club Monaco. *Mon–Sat 10am–9pm, Sun 11am–7pm; map:N3*

77 MAIDEN LANE SALON & SPA / 77 Maiden Ln, 2nd floor; 415/391-7777 Celebs who have frequented this joint include Hillary Rodham Clinton, Sharon Stone, Sean Connery, and Nicolas Cage. Though famous for its hair coloring, the salon also offers manicures and massages, plus a full line of eco-friendly hair and skin care. *Mon–Sat 9am–6pm, Thurs 9am–8pm, Sun 10am–6pm; map:N3*

SPA NORDSTROM / San Francisco Centre, 865 Market St; 415/977-5102 Whoever coined the phrase "shop till you drop" probably imagined dropping at a place like this. Try an individual treatment or indulge in the whole caboodle with a half-day Spa Package. The spa lotions and oils for sale at the counter were developed by a Beverly Hills dermatologist with ingredients derived from sea extracts and natural clays. Make reservations far in advance—especially for massages. *Mon–Sat 10am–9pm, Sun 10am–7pm; map:M4*

BOOKS AND MAGAZINES

BARNES & NOBLE / 2550 Taylor St; 415/292-6762 One of the now ubiquitous breeds of megabookstores, Barnes & Noble stocks more than 170,000 titles on everything from psychology and tai chi to cooking and gardens. The wood-and-brick interior makes this branch feel cozier than others, and you can peruse your potential purchase over a snack in the literary cafe. *Every day 9am–11pm; www.barnesandnoble.com; map:M1*

BOOKS INC. / Laurel Village Shopping Center, 3515 California St (and branches); 415/221-3666 This place feels like one of those old-fashioned neighborhood bookstores where you can while away an afternoon browsing for a good mystery or novel. There are three branches in the city, but the Laurel Village branch has especially good sections for children and travelers. Don't miss the sale table, always piled high with great deals on last season's best and worst sellers. Other branches include 2251 Chestnut Street (415/931-3633) and 864 Market Street (415/864-6777), which devotes a large area to gay-and-lesbian literature. *Every day 9am–7pm; map:I3*

BORDERS BOOKS & MUSIC / 400 Post St; 415/399-1633 A bibliophile's Eden, stocking more than 200,000 titles, plus a dazzling array of music and videos. The espresso bar and cafe overlooks Union Square and is a pleasant place to have coffee and a snack while you browse. *Mon–Wed 9am–11pm, Thurs–Sat 9am–midnight, Sun 9am–9pm; www.borders. com; map:N3*

CAFE DE LA PRESSE / 352 Grant Ave; 415/398-2680 Located across from the Chinatown gate, this Euro-cafe attracts an international crowd with its fabulous array of European magazines and periodicals. Sip an espresso or *bière* while catching up on *Le Monde*, the *International Herald Tribune*, or the *London Times*. You'll feel like you're in Paris. *Every day 7am–11pm; map:N3*

CALIFORNIA HISTORICAL SOCIETY / 678 Mission St; 415/357-1860 Quite simply, this is one of the best places to find authoritative books on local and western history. Housed inside the new California Historical Society near the Yerba Buena Center for the Arts, this well-organized bookstore features topics that run from wild women of the West to the Gold Rush and the Barbary Coast. Paintings, cards, and photographs are also for sale, and lectures are occasionally held. *Tues–Sat 11am–5pm; map:N3*

CITY LIGHTS BOOKSTORE / 261 Columbus Ave; 415/362-8193 If Allen Ginsberg were alive, he'd still be hanging out at this North Beach landmark opened in 1953 by Lawrence Ferlinghetti. Once a mecca for Beat poets and writers, who scrawled their stuff at nearby cafes, the store now attracts book lovers who peruse works on art, philosophy, politics, and fiction, including some by Kerouac and other icons of that bohemian age. *Every day 10am–midnight; www.citylights.com; map:N2*

A CLEAN, WELL-LIGHTED PLACE FOR BOOKS / 601 Van Ness Ave; 415/441-6670 This is literally a clean, well-lighted place to shop for books, located in Opera Plaza near the Civic Center. The shop's name is taken from an Ernest Hemingway short story; inside you'll find shelves filled with his works, as well as other classic and general fiction and nonfiction. The staff is knowledgeable and helpful, and author signings are regularly scheduled. *Mon–Sat 10am–11pm, Sun 10am–9pm; www.bookstore.com; map:L4*

GREEN APPLE BOOKS / 506 Clement St; 415/387-2272 You'll find the largest used book selection in the city at this neighborhood gem, which has more than 100,000 used titles as well as 60,000 new books. The entire stock of used fiction, along with music CDs, is housed in an annex a few doors down. One employee is an authority on graphic novels and comics, another specialty of the store. You can bypass a visit by buying online, but half the fun of Green Apple is sharing good reads with fellow bookworms and the knowledgeable staff. *Sun–Thurs 10am–10:30pm, Fri–Sat 10am–11:30pm; www.greenapplebooks.com; map:H3*

HAROLD'S NEWSSTAND / 524 Geary St; 415/441-2665 Harold's old-fashioned newsstand offers an incredible array of national and international newspapers and magazines. *Every day 7am–11pm; map:M3*

MODERN TIMES / 888 Valencia St; 415/282-9246 Alternative and not-so-alternative thinkers flock to this Mission District bookstore, voted the Best Independent Bookstore by locals for its comprehensive selection of literary reviews and magazines. Books in Spanish are well represented, along with general fiction, women's studies, and books on anarchism and other social issues. Author readings and cultural events are held weekly. *Mon–Sat 10am–10pm, Sun 11am–6pm; www.mtbs.com; map:L6*

RAND MCNALLY MAP & TRAVEL STORE / 595 Market St; 415/777-3131 A must-stop for the inquisitive traveler in search of a tremendous selection of travel guides, maps, globes, atlases, language tapes, and videos. *Mon–Fri 9am–6:30pm, Sat 10am–6pm, Sun 11am–5pm; www.randmcnallystore.com; map:N3*

RICHARD HILKERT BOOKSELLER / 333 Hayes St; 415/863-3339 This delightful jewel is reminiscent of those old-fashioned bookstores you find on a side street of London. Classical music plays in the background, and floor-to-ceiling shelves are jam-packed with tomes on gardening, interior design, art, and music. Hilkert, the son of an Ohio haberdasher and music teacher, is a bespectacled charmer who welcomes each customer personally, believing that the shop is an extension of his home. *Mon–Fri 9am–5:30pm, Sat 11am–5pm; map:L4*

RIZZOLI / 117 Post St; 415/984-0225 A stunning Union Square setting for perusing fine books from the popular New York–based publisher. The first floor is devoted to literature, the second floor has the famous architecture and coffee-table books, and the third level stocks music and CDs. An extensive selection of libris Italia pays tribute to the Italian owner and founder. *Mon–Sat 10am–7pm, Sun 10:30am–6pm; map:N3*

STACEY'S / 581 Market St; 415/421-4687 The city's oldest and largest independent bookstore is a mecca for professionals seeking reference books on computers, medicine, management, finance, and other technical subjects. A broad range of general books and fiction also draws customers in. *Mon–Fri 8:30am–7pm, Sat 10am–7pm, Sun 10am–6pm; www.staceys.com; map:N3*

THOMAS BROS. MAPS & BOOKS / 550 Jackson St; 415/981-7520 The retail outlet for the famed mapmaker stocks possibly the best selection of maps in the city. Look for atlases, travel guides, and local and international hiking and street maps, which will take you from San Francisco to Sydney. *Mon–Fri 9:30am–5:30pm; map:N2*

WILLIAM K. STOUT ARCHITECTURAL BOOKS / 804 Montgomery St; 415/391-6757 Explore the granddaddy of architectural bookstores, housing more than 20,000 titles in a 1,500-square-foot space. Stout, an architect, started collecting early in his career, but when his collection numbered in the thousands he opened the shop. Today there are more than 20,000 titles covering architecture, interior design, and modern art, plus rare and out-of-print books. A must-see for lovers of design and architecture tomes. *Mon–Sat 10am–5:30pm, Thurs 10am–9pm; map:N2*

CANDY AND CHOCOLATES

CHOCOLATE COVERED / 3977 24th St; 415/641-8123 "Anything good is better covered with chocolate" is the slogan at this tiny shop, which packs an incredible assortment of sweets into 200 square feet. Owner Jack Epstein looks for emerging and undiscovered candy makers with superior products. A favorite is Richard Donnelly, who crafts French chocolate bars, then adds coconut, hazelnut toffee, or macadamia nuts double-dipped with white chocolate. DeGroot is another small confectioner who makes gorgeous Belgian chocolate truffles with tequila, Rémy Martin, or Jack Daniel's fillings. Epstein custom-packages the chocolates in appealing hand-covered tins, which he designs and fabricates himself. Hours are "as early as we can make it, as late as we can take it," but generally from 11:30am to 7pm. *Every day 11:30am–7pm; map:K7*

CHOCOLATE HEAVEN / Pier 39; The Embarcadero; 415/421-1789 The name says it all. Buy in bulk or pick up souvenir gift boxes with San Francisco icons such as cable cars on the wrappers. The store also carries hard-to-find Guylian, and novelty shapes like Band-Aids, motorcycles, and miniature bottles of Kahlua. *Every day 9:30am–10pm; map:M1*

CONFETTI LE CHOCOLATIER / 525 Market St (and branches); 415/543-2885 A family-owned gem of a place to indulge in old-fashioned caramels and gooey nut clusters, plus chocolates from Neuhaus, Joseph Schmidt, Ghirardelli, and Gaston. Other branches are at 4 Embarcadero Center (415/362-1706); The Cannery, 2801 Leavenworth Street (415/474-7377); and in Macy's, 120 O'Farrell Street (415/296-4228). *Market St: Mon–Thurs 10am–7pm, Fri–Sun 10am–8pm; other branches: Mon–Sat 7am–5:30pm; map:N3*

GHIRARDELLI CHOCOLATE SHOP / 900 North Point St (Ghirardelli Square); 415/474-3938 ■ 44 Stockton St; 415/395-3615 This San Francisco institution has supplied locals and visitors with sweets since it was founded by Domingo Ghirardelli in 1861. The headquarters is at Fisherman's Wharf, where visitors are treated to an old-fashioned soda fountain selling the famous Ghirardelli hot-fudge sundae. Don't miss the small chocolate factory, which still uses the original equipment. A retail shop carries the full line of chocoholic products. *Ghirardelli Square: Mon–Thurs 9am–11pm, Fri–Sat 9am–midnight; Stockton St: Sun–Wed 9am–6pm, Thurs–Sat 9am–7pm; map:L1, N3*

GODIVA / San Francisco Centre, 865 Market St; 415/543-8910 Can you imagine: a shop devoted just to Godiva! Fillings include Key lime, nuts, buttery caramel, and nougat. Gift baskets can be custom made to fit individual budgets and tastes. *Mon–Sat 9:30am–8pm, Sun 11am–6pm; map:M4*

JOSEPH SCHMIDT CONFECTIONS / 3489 16th St; 415/861-8682 Former pastry chefs Joseph Schmidt and Audrey Ryan hand-sculpt Belgian chocolate into Transamerica buildings, windmills, tulips, and cable cars (including a five-foot car made for Queen Elizabeth on her last visit). During the holidays you'll find adorable nutcrackers, toy soldiers, Santas, and sleds, and at Easter there are chocolate bunnies and eggs. Year-round, shelves are always well stocked with at least 20 varieties of truffles, including Grand Marnier and Earl Grey tea. The chocolate teddy bears are enormously popular as gifts. *Mon–Sat 10am–6:30pm; map:K6*

NUTS ABOUT YOU / 325 Hayes St; 415/864-6887 This old-fashioned Victorian candy store has kept candy lovers well sated with gummy bears, premium nuts, brittle, and European caramels for nearly two decades. Besides more than 20 flavors of licorice from Finland, Italy, Holland, and Italy, there is a special house-made toffee packed with butter, dark chocolate, and almonds. German marzipan is another sweet worth the trip, and this is one of the few places carrying Lake Champlain and Lyla's handmade chocolates. Custom gift packages are a specialty. Enjoy an espresso in the adjoining cafe while you wait. *Mon–Fri 10am–8pm, Sat noon–8pm; map:L4*

CHILDREN'S CLOTHING

DOTTIE DOLITTLE / 3680 Sacramento St; 415/563-3244 For more than two decades Dottie Dolittle has dressed little girls and boys for birthdays, baptisms, weddings, and holidays. Sizes range from infant to preteen, with apparel made of satin, linen, cotton, and tulle. Play attire, swimwear, nighties, and blankets are also for sale, plus charming shoes, purses, and jewelry. *Mon–Sat 9:30am–6pm, Sun noon–5pm; map:I3*

KINDER SPORT / 3566 Sacramento St; 415/563-7778 Bring your aspiring Chris Evert to this children's sportswear shop for the ultimate in chic tennis wear and gear, including tennis skirts, shorts, rackets, and shoes for newborns to preteens. Come winter, skiwear takes over the rounders, with complete lines and separates from names such as Spider, Marker, Balance, and Snowbird. Kinder Sport is also a must-visit for its pint-size sleeping bags, rain gear, snorkeling equipment, and hats. *Mon–Sat 10am–5pm, Sun noon–5pm; www.kindersport.com; map:I3*

MUDPIE / 1694 Union St; 415/771-9262 Grandmothers love shopping at this Union Street boutique, packed with dainty white lace gowns and matching straw bonnets. In addition, there are rompers, jumpsuits, and overalls in solids and prints, as well as colorful galoshes, toys, and games. A Mudpie furniture store at 1750 Union Street (415/673-8060) carries bunk beds, rockers, high chairs, and chests. *Mon–Sat 10am–6pm, Sun 11am–5pm; map:L2*

SMALL FRYS / 4066 24th St; 415/648-3954 Owned by a former Levi Strauss marketing manager, this place is chock-full of fun T-shirts, shorts, and dresses, as well as OshKosh overalls and, of course, loads of Levi jeans and jackets to fit babies and small children. Besides apparel, you'll find whimsical stuffed animals, baby dishes, quilts, and sandbox toys tucked away in corners and on shelves. *Mon–Sat 10am–6pm, Sun 11am–5:30pm; map:K7*

YOUNTVILLE / 2416 Fillmore St; 415/922-5050 Where else can you buy children's cashmere sweaters and silk blouses than Yountville, a Pacific Heights boutique catering to local society matrons and their young brood? Labels include Elle, Victoria's Kids, and Malina—and expect to pay top dollar for such name brands. In addition to stylish dresses and little boys' suits, you'll find jammies in storybook prints. Cards, books, and glassware round out the stock. *Mon–Sat 11am–5:30pm, Sun noon– 4pm; map:K2*

COFFEE AND TEA

COFFEE ROASTERY / 950 Battery St; 415/956-9772 ■ 2331 Chestnut St; 415/931-5282 This local roastery has kept neighborhood mugs topped off with its full-flavored coffee since it opened in 1979. There are more than 30 varieties to choose from, including the signature Plantation, a blend of four types of beans. A full espresso bar offers desserts, fresh pastries, and house-roasted peanuts and granola. Lunch is also served in some locations, featuring tasty focaccia sandwiches, quiches, soups, salads, and daily pizzas by the slice. *Mon–Fri 5:30am–6pm, Sat 9am–6pm; map:N2, J1*

GRAFFEO COFFEE ROASTING CO. / **733 or 735 Columbus Ave;** **415/986-2429 or 415/986-2420** You'll know you've arrived when you smell the beans. Graffeo is a North Beach institution purveying some of the best coffee in the city. Beans are roasted daily in four styles: Italian light, dark, light-and-dark blend, and a Swiss water–process decaf. While it mainly sells wholesale to restaurants, the shop accommodates walk-ins (though it doesn't serve coffee) and does a large mail-order business. *Mon–Fri 9am–6pm, Sat 9am–5pm; map:M1*

PEET'S COFFEE & TEA / **1156 Chestnut St (and branches); 415/931-8302** This favorite San Francisco gourmet roastery is known for its very intense European-style coffee developed by Alfred Peet, who grew up in the business in Europe and learned firsthand how to buy and roast beans. Peet introduced his blends to San Francisco in 1966. Today there are more than 30 roasts, including the ever-popular Major Dickason's, developed 27 years ago by a retired Army officer and longtime Peet's fan. Seasonal and organic beans are also for sale. In addition to coffee you'll find premium tea, espresso makers, mugs, and teakettles. Other branches include 2197 Fillmore Street (415/563-9930) and 235 Montgomery Street (415/421-8420). *Mon–Sat 6am–8pm, Sun 6am–7pm; mailorder@ peets.com; www.peets.com; map:J1*

STARBUCKS / **2222 Fillmore St (and branches); 415/673-3171** You'll find the ubiquitous green sign of this Seattle-based roastery in just about every neighborhood of the city—there's even one at the Fifth and Mission Parking Garage and a few Wells Fargo banks. Most locations offer assorted pastries and baked goods; a few sell small pizzas and sandwiches for lunch. *Mon–Sat 5:30am–9pm, Sun 6am–8pm; www.starbucks.com; map:K3*

TEA AND COMPANY / **2207 Fillmore St; 415/929-8327** A pleasant neighborhood shop for imbibing a cup or a pot of freshly brewed tea. Choose from more than 60 blends, using green, black, flavored, or herb leaves. Eight varieties are available in bags. Assorted savories and pastries can be purchased to enjoy with your cuppa. *Mon–Thurs 9am–10:30pm, Fri–Sat 9am–11pm, Sun 10am–9:30pm; map:K2*

TEN REN TEA CO. / **949 Grant Ave; 415/362-0656** Located in the heart of Chinatown, this shop stocks 50 imported teas, mostly from China and Taiwan. Guests are offered a cup to sip while browsing the shelves, which also feature ginseng, herbs, and tea accoutrements, including pots and infusers. Mail-order is available if you get hooked on a favorite. *Every day 9am–9pm; map:N2*

TORREFAZIONE ITALIA / **161 Montgomery St; 415/834-0368** This city newcomer makes rich, full-bodied Italian roast coffee developed by Umberto Bizzarri, who learned the craft from his Perugian father. There are eight blends of coffee based on old family recipes brought over from his homeland. Specialty espressos include espresso with chocolate, just like the baristas make in old-world Italian cafes. Gift sampler kits are for sale. *Mon–Fri 5:30am–6:pm, Sat 7:30am–3pm; www.titalia.com; map:N3*

TULLY'S / 3955 24th St (and branches); 415/550-7416 What was once San Francisco's own Spinelli Coffee Company has been converted to Tully's, a fast-growing chain based in the Northwest. Though the name has changed, Tully's continues to use the same Spinelli roaster and warehouse and serves many of the same blends, including Bambino, Dutchman's, and Mrs. D's (now called Viennese). Beans are mountain-grown arabica, roasted three times a week to ensure freshness. Sweets and gift items are also for sale. Other branches include 919 Cole Street (415/753-2287) and 504 Castro Street (415/241-9447). *Every day 7am–9pm; map:K7*

CONSIGNMENT AND DISCOUNT

ESPRIT OUTLET STORE / 499 Illinois St; 415/957-2550 This popular Esprit store is located in a warehouse setting and offers great bargains on seconds and discontinued apparel from the youthfully hip San Francisco-based label. You'll find loads of shoes, belts, and accessories at up to 70 percent off retail. Call for details on future special promotions and sales. Note: There's a retail Esprit store in the Stonestown Galleria (415/759-2626). *Mon–Fri 10am–8pm, Sat 10am–7pm, Sun 11am–6pm; map:O6*

GOODBYES / 3464 Sacramento St; 415/346-6388 Bargain hunters love this consignment shop for its incredible finds on men's and women's styles from Donna Karan, Armani, Polo/Ralph Lauren, and more. You'll find accessories and accents, too, and all are in excellent condition. *Mon–Sat 10am–6pm, Thurs 10am–8pm, Sun 11am–5pm; map:J3*

JOANIE CHAR / 404 Sutter St; 415/399-9867 Local designer Joanie Char built her fashion empire in the 1970s, when her clothes were carried at high-end stores nationwide. Now she sells her silk, wool, cotton, and rayon creations exclusively at this store. Prices are close to wholesale, and lower for off-season styles. *Mon–Sat 10am–6:30pm, Sun 11am–6pm; map:N3*

LOEHMANN'S / 222 Sutter St; 415/982-3215 The granddaddy of discount fashion stores, Loehmann's still offers great prices on designer lines, plus career apparel, shoes, lingerie, hosiery, fragrances, accessories, and swimwear. Labels are removed, so you're buying for quality and style (not brand names). Personal shopping service is available, too. *Mon–Fri 9am–8pm, Sat 9:30am–8pm, Sun 11am–6pm; map:N3*

THE NORTH FACE OUTLET / 1325 Howard St; 415/626-6444 This South of Market outlet gets a supply of surplus goods from the North Face factory and sells them at a substantial discount of 20 to 70 percent. Inventory changes quickly, but outerwear and daypacks are almost always in stock. Sometimes you'll also find tents, backpacks, and sleeping bags. Their retail store stocks current goods and equipment (see the Sports and Outdoor Gear section). *Mon–Wed 10am–6pm, Thurs–Sat 10am–7pm, Sun 11am–5pm; www.thenorthface.com; map:M4*

ETHNIC AND SPECIALTY FOODS

A. G. FERRARI / 468 Castro St; 415/255-6590 ■ 820 Irving St; 415/242-8800 A third-generation Italian family runs these upscale gourmet stores, well-stocked with goodies inspired by old family recipes. The Castro branch is an especially warm setting to browse for homemade pesto as well as sauces, porcini mushrooms, and a huge array of pastas, tortas, frittatas, and bite-size arancini (ricotta balls). *Spiedini* (skewered chicken), *tramezzini* (finger sandwiches), and *formaggi* (cheese and grissini) are other customer favorites. The sliced meats and cheeses are ideal for picnics or casual dinners. *Mon–Fri 11am–8:30pm, Sat 11am–8pm, Sun 11am–6pm; map:K6, H5*

ANDREW ROTHSTEIN FINE FOODS / 2238 Polk St; 415/447-4094 Until a few years ago, caterer Andrew Rothstein made his name supplying gourmet shops with his innovative salads. These days his namesake store features at least 18 of his signature creations, all tastefully displayed in clean, modern cases. Favorite salads are the wonton salad, Russian potato, brussels sprouts with almonds, Roman chicken, and roasted-vegetable ravioli. Ask for a free sample. Want something hot? There's salmon en croute, stuffed rolled turkey breast, or fruited pork loin in Madeira. Mashed celeriac potatoes, pumpkin soup, and balsamic glazed beets are some of the mouthwatering sides. For dessert, try the lemon tart or tiramisu. *Mon–Sat 11am–7pm; map:L2*

BOMBAY BAZAR / 548 Valencia St; 415/621-1717 Stock up on everything you need to cook an Indian dinner. Besides dals and freshly ground spices, Bombay Bazaar has chutneys, fresh ginger, and an amazing array of kari leaves, basmati rice, and teas. Everything is neatly arranged on shelves or in bins. This is also a good destination for traditional thali plates and Indian cookware. *Tues–Sun 10am–7pm; map:L6*

BRYAN'S / 3473 California St; 415/752-3430 Founded by Bryan Flannery in 1963, this neighborhood butcher shop, now run by his son Terry, is renowned for its superb meat, all-natural poultry, and excellent fish selection. Most of the beef comes from the Midwest, where old-timers still take pride in how the cattle is raised, though Bryan's is one of the few local butchers carrying flavorful Kobe beef from Japan ($125 a pound).

The fish is hand picked from the dock or shipped fresh from Fiji or Hawaii. Look for ono, opa, onaga, swordfish, and ahi tuna, among others. The California lamb is another big draw. *Mon–Fri 8am–7pm, Sun 8am–6pm; map:I3*

LA PALMA MEXICATESSEN / 2884 24th St; 415/647-1500 Hand-patted corn tortillas are the big draw at this 20-year-old Mission District shop—or you can pick up some fresh-ground masa to make your own. You'll also find an arsenal of chilies, chili powder, home-fried chips, tamale leaves, and authentic Mexican vanilla for baking cookies and flan. Hot tacos and burritos are made daily and ready to eat. *Mon–Sat 8am–6pm, Sun 8am–5pm; map:M7*

LITTLE CITY MEATS / 1400 Stockton St; 415/986-2601 Savvy cooks make the trek to this North Beach butcher for the superb locally raised veal. Buy it cut as scaloppini or thick chops, or as shanks to make osso buco. Rolled breast of veal comes ready to stuff. Flavorful Kansas-raised beef and pork ribs for grilling are another reason to visit. *Mon–Fri 8am–6pm, Sat 8am–5:30pm; map:M2*

LUCCA DELICATESSEN / 2120 Chestnut St; 415/921-7873 The Bosco family has been carrying on the family business since their Lucchesi grandfather opened this Marina district deli in 1929. Be prepared for a wait: the queue starts early as locals pop in for a succulent Lucca chicken, handmade ravioli, or freshly made sandwich. Shop shelves are jam-packed with Italian olive oil, condiments, and other imported goodies, along with Berkeley's incomparable Acme bread. *Mon–Fri 9am–6:30pm, Sat–Sun 9am–6pm; map:K2*

MOLINARI DELICATESSEN / 373 Columbus Ave; 415/421-2337 Opened in 1896, this North Beach fixture is one of the few remaining old-fashioned Italian delis in town. It carries the requisite Italian meats and sausages as well as homemade ravioli, tortellini, semolina, arborio rice, and Italian cheeses, including fresh mozzarella. Complete the meal with a bottle of Italian wine, loaf of bread, and fine Tuscan olive oil. *Mon–Sat 8am–6pm; map:N2*

NEIMAN MARCUS EPICURE DEPARTMENT / 150 Stockton St; 415/362-3900 This is one of the few places in the world selling true Petrossian Russian caviar from the Caspian Sea, shipped fresh two to three times a week (expect to pay $40 to $200 for the luxury). Pâtés, imported cheeses, and smoked salmon are also in stock. Top quality and imported candy are also on hand; truffles are flown in weekly from France. The selection of chilled French champagne is one of the best in the city and includes Ayala and Dom Perignon. *Mon–Sat 10am–7pm, Thurs 10am–8pm, Sun noon–6pm; map:N3*

SAY CHEESE / 856 Cole St; 415/665-5020 Though known for its French regional chèvres, this Cole Valley treasure carries more than 200 other cheeses, including the hard-to-find Brillat-Savarin (a triple-cream cheese named for an 18th-century food writer) and a rare Italian sheep's-milk cheese with porcini mushrooms and black truffles. Caviar and tortes are a must-buy for the gourmet, as are the 12 kinds of pâtés including venison and pheasant. *Mon–Sat 10am–7pm, Sun 10am–5pm; map:I5*

TSAR NICOULAI CAVIAR / 144 King St; 800/952-2842 The Tsar offers a no-frills setting in a no-frills neighborhood where you can stock up on mega-sizes of imported Russian caviar. There's beluga, osetra, American sturgeon, and salmon; the Tsar line of beluga is popular for its rich, robust flavor. This is also one of the few places you'll find California-farmed osetra, which tastes just like the imported version but is organically raised. *Mon–Fri 8:30am–5:30pm; map:O4*

24TH STREET CHEESE CO. / 3893 24th St; 415/821-6658 It's hard to believe, but there are close to 400 cheeses in this tiny Noe Valley shop. You'll find at least 20 goat cheeses, plus fresh Camembert from Normandy, cheddars, imported Goudas, and cheese for grating. It's one-stop shopping if you also need bread and wine. *Mon–Fri 10am–7pm, Sat 10am–6pm, Sun 10am–5pm; map:K7*

VIVANDE PORTA VIA / 2125 Fillmore St; 415/346-4430 Squeezed in between an apartment complex and a cafe on a bustling, upscale stretch of Fillmore Street, this neighborhood institution is owned by superchef Carlo Middione, who prepares mouthwatering dishes either for sit-down dining or to go. Try the signature eggplant sandwiches and chicken hand pies or daily pastas and fresh broasted meats. The terrines, homemade sausages, and tortas are other good bets. *Every day 10am–7pm; map:K3*

FLOWERS AND PLANTS

FIORDELLA / 1920 Polk St; 415/775-4065 San Franciscans pay dearly for Fiordella's innovative creations—and the arrangements are worth it. Custom work is a specialty, and the designers use unusual and hard-to-find flowers. The store also sells accents, furnishings, and trinkets in case you need to pick up a gift. *Mon–Fri 9am–6pm, Sat 10am–6pm; map:L2*

FIORI / 2314 Chestnut St; 415/346-1100 Specializing in lush English garden–style arrangements, this neighborhood shop uses only high-quality flowers—no mums, gladiolas, carnations, or baby's breath. Choose from hydrangeas, dahlias, lilacs, or whatever is in season. Worldwide shipping is available. *Mon–Sat 8am–7pm, Sun 9:30–5:30pm; map:J1*

FRENCH TULIP / 3903 24th St; 415/647-8661 ■ 1 Market St; 415/764-4916 This Noe Valley flower stand could have been plucked from a side street of Paris. The specialty is European-style bouquets, loosely wrapped as if just picked from the garden. Arrange in a white porcelain pitcher or jug and you have a fetching centerpiece for the table. The Market Street location has staff designers who can craft more sophisticated arrangements. *Mon–Sat 8am–8pm, Sun 9am–7pm; www.frenchtulip. com; map:K7, O2*

HOOGASIAN FLORIST / 1674 Lombard St; 800/229-2732 (800/BAY-AREA) For 25 years this neighborhood florist has kept local homes and offices looking pretty with fresh-cut arrangements and bouquets. Buy single flowers, or have a cluster professionally assembled. Hard-to-find blooms such as sterling silver roses are another reason to visit. *Mon–Sat 8am–6pm, Sun 10am–3pm; www.hoogasian.com; map:L1*

LIVING GREEN / 3 Henry Adams; 415/864-2251 This jewel of a garden and interior landscape shop is filled with a jungle of exotic palms, bushy ferns, and towering ficus artfully displayed around antiques from Indonesia, Greece, China, and the Philippines. Smaller plants are tucked in corners and around tables. The staff is a joy to deal with and happily shares tips on caring for your purchase. *Mon–Fri 9am–5pm, Sat 11am–5pm; map:N5*

PODESTA BALDOCCHI / 508 4th St; 415/346-1300 One of the city's best-known florists creates simple and artistic arrangements, from fairytale centerpieces for weddings to themed creations for Christmas, Easter, or Halloween. *Mon–Sat 7am–6pm, Sun 7am–4pm; map:N4*

SMEDLEY HERRERA / 511 Laguna St; 415/864-2506 Smedley Herrera is known for its wild and bountiful Parisian-style bouquets. The flower selection includes lavender, roses, and gladiolas, among others. Locals pop in for colorful arrangements to brighten up the workplace or home. *Wed–Sat 11am–6pm, Sun noon–4pm; map:L4*

FURNITURE

HARVEST INTERIORS / 3349 Sacramento St; 415/922-3622 Baby boomers love the American Country furnishings at this Pacific Heights shop. The cozy showroom is chock-full of end tables, dining tables, armoires, and hutches, available in more than 30 wood finishes. Spiff up existing dressers and bureaus with the old-fashioned door pulls and hardware. With the reasonable prices, you get a lot of style for your dollar. *Mon–Sat 10am–6pm, Sun 11am–5pm; map:I3*

LIMN / 290 Townsend St; 415/543-5466 Sleek, modern furniture from more than 900 vendors, including Cappellini, Cassina, B&B Italia, and Herman Miller, can be found at this cavernous gallery. High-end Bulthaup kitchens from Germany come complete with cabinetry, islands, and all the appliances. Agape does the same for the bath. Accents are fashioned from a cutting-edge mold, and there's a complete lighting gallery with obscure lamp shades shaped as umbrellas and asymmetrical globes. The Limn Art Gallery showcases modern works from a variety of artists. *Mon–Fri 9:30am–5:30pm, Sat–Sun 11am–5:30pm; www.limn. com; map:O3*

THE MAGAZINE / 528 Folsom St; 415/777-4707 A glass-walled loft is home to this atelier showcasing modernist reproductions from Le Corbusier, Mies van de Rohe, and other designers. Most furnishings are chrome, glass, or upholstered leather in vibrant reds, blues, and yellows. A reproduction Eames chair made of molded plywood is one of the big sellers. *Mon–Sat 10am–6pm, Sun noon–4pm; www.themagazine.org; map:O3*

MIKE FURNITURE / 2142 Fillmore St; 415/567-2700 Michael Moore takes designs by legends such as Billy Baldwin, Michael Taylor, and Jean-Michael Frank and gives them a contemporary twist. His Chanel sofa is the living-room couch on the TV series *Frasier*. There are dozens of living- and dining-room sets, plus armchairs and ottomans available in a slew of fabrics and patterns. Pieces are custom made in the factory, including lamps, pillows, and decorative items. *Mon–Sat 10am–6pm, Sun noon–5pm; www.surfmike.com; map:K3*

THOS. MOSER CABINETMAKERS / 3395 Sacramento St; 415/931-8131 This is the only West Coast outlet for this master woodworker, who fashions rockers, cabinets, chairs, and tables as tomorrow's antiques. His handcrafted goods have the simplicity of Shaker furnishings, but are custom made to order in his Maine workshop out of cherry, walnut, or maple and a wide variety of finishes. *Mon–Sat 10am–6pm; map:I3*

ZONAL / 568 Hayes St; 415/255-9307 ■ 2139 Polk St; 415/563-2220 Walking into Zonal is like taking a trip back in time to your great-grandmother's farm. Two floors hold a panoply of painted pie safes, jelly cupboards, and old porch gliders with the original weathered patina. Owner Russell Prithard scours the Midwest to keep the store well stocked, and he's recently added armchairs upholstered in leather as well as faded florals to fit an old-fashioned parlor. Antique linens from France are in a back nook, along with Bella Notte's beautiful velvet shams and duvets to dress up that vintage four-poster bed. *Mon–Sat 11am–6pm, Sun noon–5pm; map:L4*

GIFT AND SPECIALTY SHOPS

ARCH / 407 Jackson St; 415/433-2724 Arch is stocked to the rafters with high-quality supplies for the architecture trade, as well as portfolios, photo albums, and loads of first-rate vellums in funky patterns and colors. You'll also find spiral paper clips, unusual pens, classy clocks, designer paperweights, clever cards, toys, and other intriguing small treasures ideal for gift-giving or that occasional splurge. *Mon–Fri 9am–6pm, Sat noon–5pm; map:N2*

BELL'OCCHIO / 8 Brady St; 415/864-4048 Tucked down an alleylike street just off Franklin and Market Streets, Bell'occhio ("beautiful eye" in Italian) is a charming place to browse for imported linens, ribbons, and trimmings, including 18th-century "point de beauvais" needlepoint and heavy silk bands for decorating purses, garters, and hats. The store's black-and-white ribbon graced Kate Winslet's gloves in *Titanic*. Don't miss the private-label lotions and makeup, pretty French pottery, jewelry, handmade boxes, and prints. *Tues–Sat 11am–5pm; map:L4*

BRITEX / 146 Geary St; 415/392-2910 Family-owned and -operated since 1952, Britex is a New York–style fabric store with six floors of well-organized textiles and trimmings. Expect to find every fabric imaginable, from English men's suiting to imported woolens, chiffons, and couture designs. A home decorating department has an array of upholstery and sheers for slipcovers and curtains. The third floor is popular with bargain hunters for its discounted remnants. There are also dozens of trims and collars and more than 30,000 new and antique buttons. The knowledgeable staff collectively speaks more than 18 languages, including Chinese and Persian. *Mon–Wed 9:30am–6pm, Thurs 9:30am–8pm, Fri–Sat 9:30am–7pm; map:N3*

CANDELIER / 33 Maiden Ln; 415/989-8600 Candelier is a pleasant place to purchase all manner of candles, including long-burning paraffin and hand-dipped beeswax. There's an assortment of holders, plus gift frames, pillows, vases, and porcelain. The coffee-table books are other good bets. *Mon–Sat 10am–6pm; map:N3*

DANDELION / 55 Potrero Ave; 415/436-9500 Dandelion is an all-time favorite stop for its lovely interior setting and selection of accents and gifts. Furnishings range from Japanese tansus edged in leather to pottery and ceramics. You'll also find an appealing array of barware, books, and toys. The Zen-like second floor has slate tabletop fountains, bamboo place mats, and screens. *Tues–Sat 10am–6pm; map:M5*

DE VERA / 580 Sutter St (and branches); 415/989-0988 Designer Federico de Vera travels the world in search of antique and contemporary decorative wares. Vividly colored vases, goblets, and bowls, many from Italy, Austria, and other European countries, fill the shelves, with art and artifacts mixed in. Look for sleek Japanese lacquer, jewelry, and other museum-quality items, plus de Vera's own exquisite creations. Other branches are at 384 Hayes Street (415/861-8480) and 29 Maiden Lane (415/788-0828). *Mon–Sat 10am–6pm; map:M3*

FLAX ART & DESIGN / 1699 Market St; 415/552-2355 More than 20,000 square feet of handmade papers, custom stationery, artist's tools, and blank journals keep people rolling into this 60-year-old store. There are literally thousands of graphic supplies for kids of all ages. The Flax Gallery showcases work by local artists, and a gift department includes Venetian masks, vases, Zen fountains, handsome picture frames, and desk accents. Flax also has a mail-order catalog. *Mon–Sat 9:30am–6pm; map:L5*

GUMP'S / 135 Post St; 415/982-1616 No trip to San Francisco would be complete without a visit to this premier destination for antiques and objets d'art. Founded in 1861 by Solomon Gump as a mirror and framing shop, Gump's is now housed in a light, airy building down the street from its original site. Jade, Baccarat, Steuben crystal, and antiques are still specialties of the house; you'll also find contemporary crafts, bedding and towels, and garden ornaments and accessories. Another big draw is the artistic glass from Italian-born Lino Tagliapietra, known for his playful spiral shapes. Traditional glassware and china comes in some 400 patterns. *Mon–Sat 10am–6pm; map:N3*

JAPONESQUE / 824 Montgomery St; 415/391-8860 This handsome gallery of Asian arts, crafts, and antiques stocks a good supply of ricepaper books, stone sculptures, porcelain bowls, and other treats from the East. Well-heeled New Yorkers often stop by in between business meetings when they feel the urge to splurge on a new treasure for the home or office. *Tues–Fri 10:30am–5:30pm, Sat 11am–5pm; map:N2*

MUSEUM STORE AT SAN FRANCISCO MUSEUM OF MODERN ART / 151 3rd St; 415/357-4035 Locals as well as tourists flock here for the incredible selection of contemporary gifts. Perennial favorites are Finnish architect Alvar Aalto's fine glass angular vases and the specially designed MOMA dinnerware. Then, of course, there's the huge selection of art and architecture books, including a sale nook with markdowns of up to 70 percent. *Mon–Wed, Thurs 10am–9:30pm, Fri–Sun 10am–6:30pm; map:N3*

PAXTON GATE / 824 Valencia St; 415/824-1872 One glance inside and you'll know this is not your average garden gift shop. Landscape designer Sean Quigley keeps the tiny barnlike space filled with quirky pots, handmade garden tools, flower-arranging supplies, and decorative ornaments for the yard. Vintage hardware and mounted insects, fossils, scarab beetles, and obscure science supplies are other house specials. *Tues–Sat 11am–6pm, Sun noon–5pm; map:L6*

ZINC DETAILS / 1905 Fillmore St; 415/776-2100 This charming little shop is filled with contemporary interpretations of minimalist '50s designs, including beech consoles that double as dining tables, birch chests, rice-paper lamps, colorful dishware, and glasses mouth-blown by local artists. The famous Zinc bud vase is still available in a full palette of colors. *Mon–Sat 11am–7pm, Sun noon–6pm; map:K3*

HARDWARE STORES

BAUERWARE CABINET HARDWARE / 3886 17th St; 415/864-3886 This hardware boutique specializes in decorative knobs, drawer pulls, and handles. Owned by San Francisco interior designer Lou Ann Bauer, the shop features three walls of galvanized bins brimming with traditional and contemporary styles, from deco-era knobs to custom art-glass pulls at $1,500 a pair. You'll also find handmade ceramic and wood handles, plus pantry pulls crafted out of billiard balls and old mah-jongg game pieces. *Mon–Sat 10am–6pm; www.bauerware.com; map:K6*

CLIFF'S HARDWARE / 479 Castro St (at 18th St); 415/431-5365 A clean, well-organized megastore housing 6,000 square feet of hardware and supplies. The electrical department has everything you need to rewire or add circuits, and there's a full paint section with Fuller O'Brien paints, brushes, scrapers, and rollers. The experienced staff can cut and thread pipes or glaze windows. A spacious annex next door stocks housewares, including towels, drapes, blenders, and toasters. There's even a toy section to keep youngsters happy while Mom and Dad shop. *Mon–Sat 9:30am–8pm; Annex Mon–Sat 10am–7pm; map:K6*

FREDERICKSEN HARDWARE / 3029 Fillmore St; 415/567-3970 Easily the best hardware store in the city, 103-year-old Fredericksen is jam-packed with every gadget and tool imaginable, plus a staff that knows how to use it all. Half the store is devoted to top-quality hardware to keep your house running. The other half has domestic goodies: gourmet cookware, juicers, food mills, and other functional items. Decorative accents such as table linens and glassware are also available. Planning an outdoor party? Fredericksen stocks barbecue equipment and accoutrements, including aprons and mitts. A great place to browse. *Mon–Sat 9am–6pm, Sun 10am–5pm; map:K2*

HARDWARE UNLIMITED / 3326 Sacramento St; 415/931-9133 Sandwiched between posh Pacific Heights and prosperous Laurel Heights, Hardware Unlimited has what you need for basic repairs. Besides the ubiquitous paint, light bulbs, and nuts and bolts, there are storage bins and containers to organize your garage, closet, or pantry. Keys are also duplicated and cut. *Mon–Sat 9am–6pm, Sun 11am–5pm; map:I3*

LAKESIDE HARDWARE & LUMBER CO. / 3401 Taraval Ave (at 44th Ave); 415/731-5252 This is one of those old-fashioned neighborhood stores where your father or grandfather might have hung out on Saturday mornings and talked bits and drills with other do-it-yourselfers. The well-edited merchandise includes hard-to-find stuff for your Tim Allen wannabe, as well as the usual hammers, nails, and sundries. A small lumberyard in back is piled high with plywood and pine. Locals consistently vote this best local hardware store for its friendly, no-rush service. Owner George Zlatunich, whose father and uncle opened the store in 1947, manages the business with partner Gary Bucchianeri, and though it's located in the outer reaches of the Sunset District, this place is well worth the trek. *Mon-Sat 8am–6pm, Sun 9am–1pm; citysearch.com/sfo/lakesidehrdware.com; map:D8*

SOKO HARDWARE / 1698 Post St; 415/931-5510 A two-story building in Japantown is home to Soko Hardware, run by the grandson of the original owner. What sets this place apart is its amazing array of Japanese-made gardening tools such as ikebana shears, pots, bonsai clippers, and pruners. The store also carries an extensive selection of Japanese cookware and dishes, including miso kettles and sushi plates and rollers. A rack of Japanese seeds will get you started on your own Oriental garden. *Mon–Sat 9am–5:30pm; map:K3*

HEALTH-FOOD STORES

RAINBOW GROCERY / 1745 Folsom St; 415/863-0620 This health-food supermarket has a dazzling array of natural baked goods, organic produce, herbs, spices, and aromatherapy bath and body care products. No meats are sold here, but you'll find a good selection of hormone-free milk, butter, and cheese, including fresh goat's- and sheep's-milk ricotta and imports from Africa and France. A good source for hard-to-find items such as chestnut flour, organic linguine, seaweed, and masa harina. *Mon–Sat 9am–9pm, Sun 10am–9pm; map:M6*

THE REAL FOOD COMPANY / 2140 Polk St; 415/673-7420 ■ 3060 Fillmore St; 415/567-6900 These neighborhood health-food stores stock bulk grains and flours, pesticide-free fruits and veggies, dairy products, and fresh bread from top bakers. The small butcher counter in back has hormone-free poultry and meats. Vitamins, supplements, and skin-care products are well represented upstairs in the Polk Street store's "vitaloft." *Every day 9am–9pm; map:L2, K2*

WHOLE FOODS MARKET / 1765 California St; 415/674-0500 Whole Foods is one-stop shopping for everything from eco-friendly paper products and all-natural pet food to fresh fish, meat, vitamins, and supplements, not to mention healthy takeout fare. One section is devoted to bins of bulk nuts, grains, and dried fruits; another has organic and nonorganic produce. The deli is staffed by California Culinary Academy graduates, who whip up seared ahi, citrus salmon, and chicken Mirabella, to name just a few treats. Vegans will find black-bean polenta torte, dolmas, risotto cakes, and Thai black rice and noodles, and the vegetarian platter comes with grilled barbecued seitan, yam millet patties, and teriyaki tofu. *Mon–Fri 9am–10pm, Sat–Sun 8am–8pm; map:L3*

HOME ACCESSORIES

BROWN DIRT COWBOY / 2406 Polk St; 415/922-9065 Named for an Elton John song, this shop with a picturesque entry resides in a restored Victorian on Russian Hill. Brown Dirt Cowboy started out selling refurbished wood armoires, chests, and decorative items, but has expanded to include reupholstered chairs from the '20s and '30s and a line of custom children's furniture painted with whimsical storybook characters. Colorful pots, ceramic tiles, unique kitchen gadgets, and towels are other treasures to check out. *Mon–Sat noon–7pm, Sun noon–6pm; map:L2*

CITY DISCOUNT / 2436 Polk St; 415/771-4649 This tidy neighborhood shop has kept cooks well supplied with discounted pots, pans, and culinary gadgets for more than a decade. In addition to loads of mashers and basters, there are pie tins, pans, steamers, and griddles galore. One section is devoted entirely to barware and stacks of the white plates and platters used in French restaurants and bistros. Another features gourmet goodies from around the world. *Mon–Sat 10am–6pm, Sun 11am–7pm; map:L2*

COOKIN' / 339 Divisadero St; 415/861-1854 Cookin' is a funky little gem crammed to the rafters with recycled and obscure gourmet trinkets and tools. Look for Jell-O molds, cast-iron skillets, roasters, and old-fashioned casseroles for making macaroni and cheese. French pastry bags, measuring cups, and rolling pins are also for sale. Most of the secondhand goods are in excellent condition and bring back warm memories of watching Grandma or Grandpa make breakfast or Thanksgiving dinner. *Tues–Sat noon–6:30pm, Sun 1pm–5pm; map:K6*

CRATE & BARREL / 125 Grant Ave; 415/986-4000 Crate & Barrel is a popular purveyor of affordable domestic chic, and this light, airy, three-level Union Square branch has an especially good selection of glassware and barware. You'll also find trays, wooden tables, chairs, rugs, lamps, and storage bins here. One level showcases cookware, including copper pots, griddles, and souffle pans. (Psst . . . a Crate & Barrel discount outlet is located on the other side of the Bay Bridge at 1785 Fourth Street in Berkeley; 510/528-5500.) *Mon–Fri 10am–7pm, Sat 10am–6pm, Sun noon–5pm; map:N3*

FILLAMENTO / 2185 Fillmore St; 415/931-2224 There are imitators, but few stores of its kind can rival Fillamento for quality and style. Housed in a restored three-level Edwardian, this gallery of chic domesticity stocks everything from contemporary dinnerware and goblets to traditional Limoges platters and old-fashioned tassels. The table linens and textiles are top quality and include Ann Gish's exquisite handmade pillows. A bath department stocks luxe towels and accents, and there's a huge array of furniture for living areas and the home office. *Mon–Sat 11am–7pm, Sun noon–6pm; map:K2*

GORDON BENNETT / 900 North Point St (Ghirardelli Square); 415/929-1172 English expatriate Ian Johnson scours his native countryside to keep Gordon Bennett a treasure trove of unusual knickknacks and gifts. Antique pots, terra-cotta urns, birdhouses, and French metal buckets are scattered about. The staff will help you track down that perfect accent or trinket. If you're buying for the gardener, ask about the custom-made grab bags, which come with colorful rubber gloves, Farmer's Friend hand salve, miniature soaps, and a tiny garden trowel. *Every day 10am–9pm; map:L1*

HOMECHEF / 3527 California St; 415/688-3191 What started as a cooking school in owner Judith Ets Hokin's kitchen has grown to one of the city's most popular kitchenware stores. Shelves are neatly arranged with well-edited essentials, along with entertaining accessories and gourmet foods. Familiar brands include Emile Henry, All-Clad, and Calphalon, plus the HomeChef house label. Still part cooking school, HomeChef also hosts classes and workshops led by well-known industry professionals. *Mon–Sat 9:30am–6:30pm, Sun 11am–5pm; map:I3*

MA MAISON HOME ACCENTS / 400 Brannan St; 415/777-5370 Owners John and Isabelle Karatzas import direct to keep prices down on their objets d'art from South Africa and France. In addition to champagne flutes, pewter cutlery, and Limoges porcelain, the store features Italian cast-metal culinary tools, handmade frames, velvet pillows, and bedding. *Mon–Fri 10am–5pm, Sat 11am–5pm; www.ma-maison.com; map:O4*

MAISON D'ETRE / 92 South Park; 415/357-1747 This tiny boutique near pretty, leafy South Park specializes in French-style antiques. Look for rusty garden chairs with spring-metal seats, weathered wooden benches, hutches, tables, and decorative pieces such as iron platters, glassware, tasseled pillows, and French milk jugs and urns. *Mon–Sat 11am–6pm; map:O4*

NEST / 2300 Fillmore St; 415/292-6199 Nest is a charming place to poke around for reproduction European antiques found at French flea markets in Paris and Provence. An old goat cart and rustic farm table evoke Marcel Proust, and fancy birdcages, tableware, vintage linens, and decorative treats abound. David Bowie and Anne Heche are among the celebs who have browsed here. *Mon–Sat 10:30am–6:30pm, Sun noon–6pm; map:K2*

SCHEUER LINENS / 140 Sutter St; 415/762-3950 Established in the 1930s, family-run Scheuer's is known for superb linens and table coverings imported from all over the world. What sets the store apart, however, is how the sales staff gives customers a hands-on education in the various weaves and thread counts. There are loads of colors and prints to choose from, and the selection of towels and gift items is worth a stop in itself. More than 40 kinds of soap from 40 countries are available, including Palais Royale's wildly popular triple-milled soap imported from Scotland. Embroidery and monogramming services are available. *Mon–Sat 9:30am–5:30pm; map:N3*

SUE FISHER KING / 375 Sutter St; 415/398-2894 ■ 3067 Sacramento St; 415/922-7276 This shop is a longtime favorite for elegant gifts, lamps, pillows, and imported sheets from Italy in creamy damasks or Egyptian cotton. The bath/spa boutique has fluffy white towels and plush mats and robes. King takes buying trips to Europe to keep the lineup fashionable and fresh. During the holidays she fills shelves with ornaments from more than 30 countries. *Mon–Sat 10am–6pm, Thurs 10am–8pm; map:N3*

SUR LA TABLE / 77 Maiden Ln; 415/732-7900 Founded in Seattle more than 25 years ago, Sur La Table features two floors jam-packed with everything a cook could need for a well-equipped kitchen. Fulfill any fantasy: Bakers will find dozens of cookie cutters in fanciful shapes as well as rosette molds to create doves, snowflakes, and roses. One area has place mats and napkins; another features teapots, teacups, and sushi-dipping bowls and trays. There's a slew of barbecue items, including sturdy mitts, aprons, and chips for the fire along with those hard-to-find gadgets such as cornichon slicers and claw-shaped lobster crackers. You'll also find hundreds of cookbooks on everything from vegan cooking to baking with figs. The lower level holds an 800-square-foot cooking school and demonstration kitchen. *Mon–Sat 10am–7pm, Sun noon–6pm; map:N3*

VICTORIAN INTERIORS / 575 Hayes St; 415/431-7191 Here's the destination for Victorian-era items, including moldings, cornices, and hard-to-find lace curtains based on original panels. The selection of wallpapers is the best in Northern California and includes Bradbury & Bradbury, Scalamandre, and Brunschwig & Fils. The staff will help you select a pattern. *Tues–Sat 11am–6pm, Sun noon–5pm; map:L4*

WILLIAMS-SONOMA GRANDE CUISINE / 150 Post St (and branches); 415/362-6904 The beautiful flagship store purveys the same upscale culinary equipment as the famous catalog. Two levels showcase furniture, appliances, and table accents, including Italian ceramics, olive-oil urns, and colorful linens. Gift items range from quaint aprons and fancy foods to the lavishly photographed Williams-Sonoma line of cookbooks, which are produced by a San Francisco–based publishing house. A tasting bar has samples and occasional cooking demonstrations. Other branches are at 2 Embarcadero Center (415/421-2033) and in the San Francisco Shopping Centre (415/546-0171). *Mon–Wed 9:30am–6pm, Thurs–Fri 9:30am–7pm, Sat 10am–6pm, Sun 11am–5pm; map:N3*

IMPORTED GOODS

ANOKHI / 1864 Union St; 415/922-4441 Beautiful hand-blocked cotton fabric from Rajasthan is turned into stylish women's apparel, table linens, and cozy bedroom fashions and sold in this Union Street boutique. Blouses, jackets, skirts, and pants in solids and prints can be mixed and matched for coordinated outfits. Robes, sarongs, fabric briefcases, and cosmetic bags are ideal as souvenirs or gifts. Quilts are a specialty. *Mon–Sat 11am–6pm, Sun noon–5pm; www.citysearch.com/sfo/anokhi; map:K2*

CANTON BAZAAR / 616 Grant Ave; 415/821-2465 Canton Bazaar showcases a wide assortment of arts and crafts from China and other Asian cultures. Antique treasures are hidden among ubiquitous Chinatown wares. This is a good place to browse for that quirky trinket or lovely jade amulet or bracelet. *Every day 11am–7pm; map:N2*

COST PLUS WORLD MARKET / 2552 Taylor St; 415/928-6200 The beaded curtains are long gone. The new, gentrified Cost Plus focuses on housewares, food, and furniture from around the world, including reasonably priced pine and beechwood kitchen tables, chairs, and stools from Italy and Thailand. The rustic wood bedroom furniture from Mexico is also worth a look. To round out your decorating project, there's a great selection of imported lamps, baskets, pillows, screens, and area rugs. And check out the extensive, well-priced wine section. *Every day 9am–9pm; www.costplusworldmarket.com; map:M1*

COTTAGE INDUSTRY / 3961½ 24th St; 415/206-0704 This basement shop specializes in gorgeous adult and children's clothing, bags, and purses made from Guatemalan cotton, which is also sold by the yard. Don't miss the rayon batiks from Indonesia and silver earrings from Nepal. Refurbished furniture from India is carried at a sister location at 4018 24th Street (415/821-2465). *Every day 11am–7pm; map:K7*

FOLK ART INTERNATIONAL–BORETTI AMBER–XANADU TRIBAL ARTS / 140 Maiden Ln; 415/392-9999 Housed in a historic Frank Lloyd Wright–designed building, this upscale gallery is actually three in one, each carrying museum-quality imported art and antiques. Works range from neolithic pots circa 3,000 B.C. to Panama basketry and hand-loomed wool from Kashmir. Check out the Bwami hats made of fiber, buttons, and elephant hair. *Mon–Sat 10am–6pm; www.folkartintl.com; map:N3*

MA-SHI'-KO FOLK CRAFT / Japan Center, 1581 Webster St, 2nd floor; 415/346-0748 Though its specialty is pottery from Ma-Shi'-Ko, the oldest pottery village in Japan, this shop also carries delicate handmade sake cups and teacups, Akita Masome cedar chopstick rests, and beautiful chestnut and cypress bowls and trays. *Mon–Sat 11am–6pm, Sun 11am–5pm; map:K3*

POLANCO / 393 Hayes St; 415/242-5753 Located in funky, upmarket Hayes Valley, this attractive gallery carries imported Mexican antiques and contemporary folk art, including religious icons from the 18th and 19th centuries, Day of the Dead figurines, and traditional "Tree of Life" ceramics. Lacquerware boxes, trays, and other Mexican handicrafts also abound. *Tues–Sat 11am–6pm, Sun 1pm–6pm; www.polanco.citysearch.com; map:L4*

SILKROUTE / 3119 Fillmore St; 415/563-4936 Step into Silkroute for its mammoth collection of more than 2,000 old and new floor coverings from around the world, including Oriental carpets, tribal rugs, and kilims from China, Turkey, Persia, Morocco, India, Pakistan, and Afghanistan. The shopkeepers also buy, trade, clean, and repair carpets. *Mon–Fri 11am–6:45pm, Sat 11am–6pm, Sun noon–6pm; map:K2*

TOUCH OF ASIA / 1784 Union St; 415/474-3115 Beautiful black lacquer cabinets and tansu chests are among the decorative items found in this upscale shop, dealing in both antiques and reproductions from China, Japan, Korea, and Thailand. Standouts include a gold satsuma fish bowl and a pair of custom cloisonne lamps. *Mon–Sat 11am–6pm, Sun noon– 5pm; map:L2*

XELA IMPORTS / 3925 24th St; 415/695-1323 The Italian owner of this small outlet imports rayons and cottons from Indonesia and India and turns them into stylish clothes. Hand-printed cotton T-shirts are especially popular with locals. Gift items include Sri Lanka moonstone jewelry, amber from Poland, Balinese mirrors, and gauze sarongs. *Every day 10:30am–7:30pm; map:K7*

JEWELRY AND ACCESSORIES

ALFRED DUNHILL / 250 Post St; 415/781-3368 The San Francisco outpost purveys the same high-quality accessories as its mother store in England (founded in London in 1893), including watches, cuff links, jewelry, and ties. A back room does a brisk business in humidors, pipes, tobacco, and imported cigars—despite the city's strict anti-smoking regulations. Personal services include monogramming, polishing, and wardrobe advice. *Mon–Sat 9:30am–6pm, Sun noon–5pm; map:N3*

AMIR H. MOZAFFARIAN / 155 Post St; 415/391-9995 A fourth-generation family of jewelers runs this elegant shop, first established in the late 1800s. Look for names like Fabergé, Piaget, and Harry Winston, whose designs fill the display cases and shelves. Along with opulent diamonds and sapphires, there are rubies, emeralds, and a stunning selection of gold bracelets and rings. *Mon–Sat 10am–5:30pm; map:N3*

BULGARI / 237 Post St; 415/399-9141 What started more than 300 years ago as a silversmith in Rome has become one of the world's most famous jewelers. Bulgari still handcrafts works out of gold, platinum, or a mix of gems and metals. Rings are hand-set on prongs in the time-honored tradition. Designs tend to be bold with lots of intricate detail, but understated enough to fit most occasions. *Mon–Sat 10am–5:30pm; www.bulgari.com; map:N3*

CARTIER / 231 Post St; 415/397-3180 This shop carries elegant jewelry from the famous French designer, including the hallmark Tank ring, bracelets, and earrings, plus luxury gift items such as scarves, leather accessories, pens, crystal, and perfume. *Mon–Sat 10am–5:30pm; map:N3*

COACH STORE / 190 Post St; 415/392-1772 This branch of the much-touted leather goods store proffers the famed well-made handbags, briefcases, wallets, and belts, plus leather jackets, most in traditional shades of mahogany, black, burgundy, and tan. A new line of Coach furniture, recently unveiled, can be found here as well. *Mon–Sat 10am–6pm, Sun noon–5pm; map:N3*

GHURKA / 170 Post St; 415/392-7267 Named for an old tanning process used by Nepalese soldiers, this New York wholesaler-turned-retailer is giving the Coach folks a run for their money. Prices are high, but so is the quality. Leather is processed with a vegetable-based dye so scratches come out easily and the color won't fade over time. Don't miss the leather slippers, alligator wallets, golf bags, and wine caddies. Scarves, jewelry, and home accessories round out the selection. *Mon–Sat 10am–6pm, Thurs 10am–7pm; map:N3*

GOING IN STYLE / 865 Market St; 415/512-9477 Finally, one-stop shopping for travel accessories and gadgets. Going in Style keeps shelves filled with an ambitious array of duffels, toiletries, fanny packs, and travel-size containers, plus travel alarms, luggage carts, and folding rain gear. The staff is knowledgeable and well versed in how the merchandise works and what's appropriate for your journey. *Mon–Sat 9:30am–8pm, Sun 11–6; www.goinginstyle.com; map:M4*

GUCCI / 200 Stockton St; 415/392-2808 Superbly crafted leather goods have been the hallmark of this Italian-based company for some 70 years. Look for shoes, handbags, and luggage to complement the chic Gucci line of ready-to-wear. Expect to pay dearly for that G on the label. *Mon–Sat 10am–6pm, Sun noon–5pm; map:N3*

LANG ANTIQUES AND ESTATE JEWELRY / 323 Sutter St; 415/982-2213 If you're looking for antique watch fobs or stickpins, here's the spot. Founded by Czech native Jarmilla Lang, the shop has an incredible selection of estate and hard-to-find jewelry, such as vintage bracelets, cuff links, and old-fashioned cameo pendants. Don't miss the window displays, which change daily to showcase the latest antique treasures. *Mon–Sat 10:30am–5:30pm; map:N3*

LOUIS VUITTON / 230 Post St; 415/391-6200 The signature LV on handbags and luggages has been a status symbol for years, but Louis Vuitton now features a full coterie of designs, including the trendy Monogram and Damier lines. *Mon–Sat 10am–6:30pm, Sun noon–6pm; map:N3*

MALM LUGGAGE / 50 Post St (Crocker Galleria); 415/391-5222 Malm manages to cram an incredible amount of luggage and travel accessories into one space. Started by a leather craftsman in 1856, the family-owned business carries labels from Hugo Bosca, Tumi, Boyt, and Hartmann. There's complimentary monogramming and gift wrap, along with luggage repair for most airline claims. *Mon–Fri 10am–6pm, Sat 10am– 5pm; www.malm-luggage.com; map:N3*

MRS. DEWSON'S HATS / 2050 Fillmore St; 415/346-1600 The colorful Ruth Dewson owns this funky little gem, brimming with sophisticated and fun hats for both sexes. For women, there are '40s-style cocktail hats trimmed in silk or rosettes. Men can choose from old-fashioned boaters, bowlers, Biltmores, and Panamas. The famous "Willie" fedora is named for a famously flamboyant San Francisco mayor, Willie Brown. Most hats are handmade and hand-dyed. *Mon–Sat 11am–6pm; map:K3*

PEARL EMPIRE / 127 Geary St; 415/362-0606 ■ 427 Post St (Westin St. Francis); 415/362-0608 The name says it all—this is a veritable empire of pearls in all colors, sizes, and shapes, which can be turned into rings, pendants, or pins. Burma jadeite—the finest in the world—is sold here as well. Many of the staff have worked in the store since it opened in 1957 and will help you develop a jewelry wardrobe to fit your budget and lifestyle. *Mon–Sat 9:30am–5:30pm; map:N3*

THE SAK / 334 Grant Ave; 415/433-3100 Local entrepreneurs Mark Talucci and Todd Elliott created this line of bags and backpacks using a handmade nylon weave called Tightweave, which gives the Sak its crocheted appearance. The bags were so popular that they launched their flagship Union Square store, where you can also pick up belts, luggage, and the new line of pillows, table linens, rugs, and throws. *Mon–Sat 10am–7pm; Sun 11am–6pm; www.thesak.com; map:N3*

SHREVE & CO. / 421 Post St; 415/421-2600 Founded in 1852, and one of the city's oldest retailers, Shreve is located in a historic building with a gorgeous marble-and-wood interior where its famous jewelry, silver, crystal, and gifts are showcased. There's a Mikimoto pearl boutique as well as a watch boutique carrying Patek Philippe and Chopard. *Mon–Sat 10am–6pm; map:M3*

SWATCH / Pier 39, The Embarcadero; 415/788-4543 A favorite destination for those searching for hip, sporty watches, including the Internet watch, electronic ski-lift watch, and AquaFun Swatch, which comes attached to an inflatable cuff that looks like the water wings you used in wading pools as a kid. Art watches are designed by artists such as Keith Haring, among others. *Every day 10am–10pm; map:M1*

TIFFANY & CO. / 350 Post St; 415/781-7000 Beautiful people shop at this beautiful store, established in 1837 in New York and immortalized by Audrey Hepburn in the movie *Breakfast at Tiffany's*. Along with designs from Jean Schlumberger, Elsa Peretti, and Paloma Picasso, there are scarves, crystal, silver, and the Tiffany perfume. All come wrapped in the signature blue box with white bow. *Mon–Sat 10am–5:30pm; map:N3*

UNION STREET GOLDSMITH / 1909 Union St; 415/776-8048 This is the place to buy custom jewelry made on-site by Bay Area designers. The specialty is rose, yellow, or white gold creations in 14, 18, and 22 karats. Display cases also feature designs from Italian, German, and other European jewelers. *Mon–Sat 11am–5:45pm, Sun noon–4:45pm; map:K2*

MATERNITY AND SPECIAL SIZES

THE COMPANY STORE / 1913 Fillmore St; 415/921-0365 For years Company Store owner Mary Lou Dowdy specialized exclusively in plus-size clothes for women. Now she carries clothes in standard women's sizes 6 to 20, but she still has an eye for loose, flowing styles flattering to any woman's figure. If something doesn't fit, the store's full-time seamstress will alter it for you. Many of the clothes are from local or California designers. The store also offers jewelry, scarves, hats, and a quirky collection of hand-painted reading glasses. *Mon–Sat 11am–7pm, Sun noon–6pm; map:K2*

HARPER GREER / 580 4th St; 415/543-4066 Harper Greer's own ultra-chic line of women's fashions in sizes 12 and larger is available exclusively at this designer-direct retail store. Carefully designed to flatter the larger figure, the garments are made with the finest imported and domestic fabrics. The emphasis is on career dressing, with a large selection of suits and related separates, all sold individually to ensure a perfect fit. Store services include an in-house tailor and worldwide shipping. *Mon–Sat 10am–6pm, Sun noon–5pm; www.harpergreer.com; map:N4*

JAPANESE WEEKEND / 500 Sutter St; 415/989-6667 This high-end maternity store is a must for fashion-conscious expectant mothers in search of sleek, sophisticated clothes for all occasions. Fabric quality and construction are top of the line. The store carries several signature products, including an expandable waistband that rests comfortably on the hips. *Mon–Sat 10am–6pm; www.japaneseweekend.com; map:N3*

A PEA IN THE POD / 290 Sutter St; 415/391-1400 Providing the newest and hippest styles for young mothers-to-be, A Pea in the Pod works with Laundry and other outside vendors, as well as with its own designers, to produce everything from evening wear to swimsuits to hosiery. Drawstrings, tummy panels, back-ties, and jacket clips leave room to grow. A relatively new line, French Fit, features form-fitting silhouettes for the woman who wants to show off her emerging new shape. *Sat–Mon 10am–6pm, Sun 11am–5pm; www.maternitymall.com; map:N3*

ROCHESTER BIG AND TALL / 700 Mission St; 415/982-6455 Established in San Francisco in 1906, Rochester Big and Tall now has 21 shops across the globe selling a broad selection of fine sportswear, footwear, and tailored clothing, including Versace, Fila, DKNY, Tommy Hilfiger, Levi, Cole-Haan, and Ferragamo. Clothes are available off the rack starting at sizes 46 regular, 46 long, and 46 extra-long; for those who don't fit this profile, Rochester offers an outstanding custom business. The chain's only discount outlet, called California Big and Tall, is located in San Francisco at 625 Howard Street (415/495-4484) and offers phenomenal discounts. *Store: Mon, Wed, Fri 9am–6:30pm, Thurs 9am–8pm, Sat 9am–6pm, Sun noon–5pm; Outlet: Tues–Sat 9am–5pm; www.2cataloguesite.com; map:N3*

THE SHORT SHOP / 49 Kearny St; 415/296-9744 The Short Shop, the nation's leading clothing outfitter for the shorter man, offers both dress clothing and casual wear. Suits, shirts, pants, coats, sweaters, ties, and even socks are correctly proportioned to the needs of the shorter fella. Shoes come in men's hard-to-find sizes ranging from 5 to 7. Designer labels include Gianni, Terzo Uomo, and Petrocelli. *Mon–Fri 9:30am–5:30pm; www.shortshop.com; map:N3*

MUSIC (CDS, RECORDS, AND TAPES)

AMOEBA MUSIC / 1855 Haight St; 415/831-1200 This bustling music emporium is as popular for people-watching as it is for buying, selling, or trading CDs, videos, and tapes. Located in the Haight-Ashbury district, the store is jammed with an eclectic mix of tattooed Gen-Xers and baby boomers browsing the 500,000 new and used discs. The store is well organized and represents every type of music imaginable, from hip-hop to rap to experimental. One section is devoted to old 45rpm records. *Mon–Sat 10:30am–10pm, Sun 11am–9pm; www.amoebamusic.com; map:I5*

GREEN APPLE BOOKS AND MUSIC / 520 Clement St; 415/386-6128 Louie, the house cat, watches over the scene as music fans buy, sell, and trade CDs, cassettes, and vinyls. You need to be at least 18 years old and have a driver's license or other reliable ID to sell or trade. LP specials go for $1. The music annex, opened only a few years ago, is connected to Green Apple Books (see the Books and Magazines section), a neighborhood landmark and one of the few remaining independent bookstores in town. *Sun–Thurs 10am–10:15pm, Fri–Sat 10am–11:15pm; www.green applebooks.com; map:H3*

HEAR MUSIC / 150 4th St (Metreon); 415/537-3400 This music boutique is adjacent to Sony Style in the new Metreon near Moscone Center. CD specialties are world music, jazz, and blues. There are lots of listening stations as well as interactive stations where you can scan the CD's bar code and learn more about the artist while you listen to the tunes. The shop also carries the new minidiscs. *Every day 10am–10pm; www. metreon.com; map:N3*

MEDIUM RARE RECORDS / 2310 Market St; 415/255-7273 This cozy music shop specializes in show tunes, lounge music, and pop stars from the past. You'll find vocals by Sophie Tucker, Bing Crosby, Doris Day, Judy Garland, Peggy Lee, Liza Minnelli, and many others. There are both CDs and LPs. The store also has a good selection of international film soundtracks. *Mon–Thurs 11am–7pm; Fri–Sat 11am–9pm, Sun noon–6pm; map:K6*

STAR CLASSICS / 425 Hayes St; 415/552-1110 Located near Davies Symphony Hall, Star Classics sells CDs, tapes, and videos for aficionados of classical music. You'll also find a smattering of international, Broadway, cabaret vocals, jazz, and Latin. The shop hosts free recitals at noon on Fridays, near the grand piano in back. *Mon–Sat 10am–8pm, Sun noon–7pm; www.star-classics.com; map:L4*

TOWER RECORDS / Bay and Columbus Sts (and branches); 415/885-0500 Tower Records is always hopping, partly due to its convenient (and free) parking lot. Fans of rock, soul, and country also gravitate to the store for its huge selection of CDs and cassettes. There's a splash of easy listening, pop vocals, soundtracks, Latin, blues, and New Age—even folk and gospel. Across the street is an annex catering to the classical set. Other branches are at Market and Noe Streets (415/61-0588) and in the Stonestown Galleria (415/759-2626). *Every day 9am–midnight; www. towerrecords.com; map:M1*

VIRGIN MEGASTORE / 2 Stockton St; 415/397-4525 With three levels of listening stations and music for just about every taste, Virgin is indeed a megastore. Cruise the racks for that perfect CD, cassette, or DVD. The store carries every genre, even film soundtracks and comedy. It's heaven for classical music lovers, who have a separate room to themselves. The store also has loads of magazines, books, and computer games focusing on music and musicians. Consider buying a cool Virgin T-shirt, sweatshirt, or jacket as a souvenir. *Mon–Thurs 9am–11pm, Fri–Sat 9am–midnight, Sun 10am–11pm; www.virginmega.com; map:N3*

SEAFOOD

NIKKO FISH CO. / 699 Illinois St; 415/864-5261 For more than a decade Tadanory Chiyo has run this unpretentious fish market, selling possibly the freshest fish in town. Oysters are available by the bag, and there are live crabs, giant prawns, halibut, salmon, and fresh tuna. Imported caviar is available by special request. *Mon–Sat 9am–6pm; map:O6*

SWAN OYSTER DEPOT / 1517 Polk St; 415/673-1101 Half oyster bar, half fish counter, Swan's is a neighborhood landmark, serving fresh oysters and shellfish since it opened in 1912. Four Danish brothers operated it for more than three decades before selling it in 1946 to Sal Sancimino, a fifth-generation fisherman whose five very friendly grandsons, Steve, Vince, Tom, Jim, and Phil, now run the counter. Locals make this place a regular pilgrimage for the convivial service and to pick up the day's catch for dinner. Don't miss the famous Boston clam chowder. *Mon–Sat 8am–5:30pm; map:L6*

YUM YUM / 2181 Irving St; 415/566-6433 The retail outlet for Nikko Fish Co. (see above), this tiny shop purveys fresh filleted fish, ranging from halibut and haddock to snapper and yellowfin tuna. The quality is consistent, and there's fresh sushi to go if you don't want to make it yourself. *Tues–Sun 10:30am–7:30pm; map:G6*

SHOES

THE ALDEN SHOP / 201 Kearny St; 415/421-6691 Opened in 1884, this is one of the nation's oldest men's shoe stores, carrying an incredible selection of well-made dress and casual footwear in a variety of styles and hard-to-find sizes. The oxfords, cap-toes, and loafers are especially popular with the white-collar crowd. *Mon–Sat 10am–6pm; www.aldenshoes.com; map:N3*

ARTHUR BEREN SHOES / 222 Stockton St; 415/397-8900 If you've been to Arthur Beren but not lately, you're in for a surprise. The ultra-conservative men's and women's footwear store has now given way to high-fashion designs from Robert Clergerie, YSL, Emanuel Ungaro, Stuart Weitzman, Arche, Bruno Magli, and others. Shoes are finely crafted from leather, stretch fabric, and an occasional exotic skin (a pair of crocodile loafers fetches $1,300). A must-stop if your feet are especially narrow or wide. *Mon–Wed 9:30am–6:30pm, Thurs–Fri 9:30am–7pm, Sat 9:30am– 6pm, Sun noon–5pm; map:N3*

BALLY OF SWITZERLAND / 238 Stockton St; 415/398-7463 The well-heeled are well-shod in the soft, supple styles of this century-old chasseur. Pumps, strappy '40s-style sandals, and slingbacks are some of the styles for women, while men can choose from two-tones, classic lace-ups, and the signature calfskin loafers with gold tassels. Prices are high, but so is the quality. *Mon–Sat 9:30am–7pm, Sat 10am–6pm, Sun noon–5pm; map:N3*

BIRKENSTOCK SAN FRANCISCO / 42 Stockton St; 415/989-2475 Once an icon for the fashionably unfashionable, Birkenstock now attracts mainstream buyers with its two floors of footwear in more than 350 colors and styles. You'll find the familiar hippie sandals sharing space with wedges, black patent flats, kids' shoes, and clogs. A new line of dressy footwear is ideal for business or that special occasion. *Mon–Sat 10am–6pm, Sun 11am–6pm; www.birkenstock.com; map:N3*

BULO MEN / 437-A Hayes St; 415/864-3244 ■ BULO WOMEN / 418 Hayes St; 415/255-4939 Bulo is Perugian for "hip," which describes the selection of shoes at these tiny Hayes Valley boutiques. Italian imports from OXS, Krizia, Roberto del Carlo, and Enzo Romanelli fill the shelves and include mules, platforms, slip-ons, and boots. Textures such as leather, canvas, and mesh keep changing with new shipments to keep the inventory fresh. *Mon–Sat 11:30am–6:30pm, Sun noon–6pm; www.buloshoes.com; map:L4*

CHURCH'S ENGLISH SHOES / 50 Post St; 415/433-5100 or 888/99-SHOES This branch of the century-old English shoemaker offers veddy proper gentlemen's shoes, such as wingtips, brogues, two-tones, and boots. Styles are featured in burgundy, black, and brown. *Mon–Fri 9:30am–6pm, Sat 10am–5pm; map:N3*

GIMME SHOES / 416 Hayes St; 415/864-0691 Shoppers who want to stay one step ahead of the trends make regular pilgrimages to this avant-garde salon to check out edgy footwear from European makers such as Dries Van Noten, Prada, Espace, and Miu Miu. Geared to the shoe hound who believes footwear makes a loud statement about the wearer, Gimme Shoes stocks everything from fur slip-ons to orange-and-white polka-dot pumps. *Mon–Sat 11am–6:30pm, Sun 11am–6pm; map:L4*

JOAN & DAVID / 172 Geary St; 415/397-1958 A longtime favorite of many shoe lovers, Joan & David was founded by a former Harvard professor and his wife who developed a footwear-designing fetish. Their award-winning styles range from boots and sandals to ballet shoes and pumps—all made of leather or leather crafted to look like velvet or flannel. Everything is limited edition; no two stores stock identical lines or displays. A second label caters to the cost-conscious shopper; yearly sales are held in February and July. *Mon–Wed and Sat 10am–7pm, Thurs–Fri 10am–7pm, Sun noon–5pm; map:N3*

KENNETH COLE / 865 Market St (and branches); 415/227-4536 Styles by this hip New York designer, who launched his career selling boots from a trailer, are now carried by major retailers as well as in his own boutiques. Most shoes—for men and women—have the familiar masculine square toe; many are modern remakes of classic leather loafers, oxfords, mules, and Mary Janes. He has expanded his line to include gorgeous leather and cashmere jackets, sweaters, handbags, belts, and eyewear. Other branches include a flagship store at 166 Grant Avenue (415/981-2653) and a smaller store at 2078 Union Street (415/346-2161). *Mon–Sat 9:30am–8pm, Sun 11–6pm; map:N3*

TUFFY'S HOPSCOTCH / 3307 Sacramento St; 415/440-7599 The pitter-patter of little feet is a familiar sound in this Sacramento Street shop, catering to tots with European footwear from Brakkies, Elefanten, Aster, and Mod 8. There's a wonderful array of colors and styles in play shoes and dressy styles for christenings, the first day of school, and other special occasions. *Mon–Sat 10am–6pm; map:J3*

SPORTS AND OUTDOOR GEAR

ANY MOUNTAIN–THE GREAT OUTDOOR STORE / 2598 Taylor St; 415/345-8080 Conveniently located at Fisherman's Wharf, Any Mountain provides hikers and campers with apparel, boots, and gear. The friendly and well-informed staff is quick to help in selecting the appropriate tent, sleeping bag, or other outdoor essentials. Swimsuits and water gear are for sale in summer, snowboards and skis in winter. In-line skates, Sundog photo bags, and Eagle Creek travel accessories are carried year-round. *Every day 9am–9pm; www.anymountaingear.com; map:M1*

COPELAND'S SPORTS / 901 Market St; 415/495-0928 ■ 3251 20th Ave (Stonestown Galleria); 415/759-2626 Copeland's is packed with apparel and gear for just about every sport: baseball, basketball, football, soccer, golf, tennis, running, skating, skiing, bicycling, swimming, skateboarding, bodyboarding, snowboarding—you name it. Fitness freaks will find a section devoted to exercise machines and weight-lifting equipment. Casual wear and men's and women's athletic and golf shoes are also in stock. *Mon–Fri 10am–8pm, Sat 10am–7pm, Sun 11am–6pm; map:M4*

DON SHERWOOD GOLF AND TENNIS WORLD / 320 Grant Ave; 415/989-5000 Established in 1961, this store is for the serious golf and tennis enthusiast. Merchandise is organized by floor: tennis rackets in the basement, men's and women's apparel and shoes on the lower level, and golf equipment on the two upper floors. The golf staff conducts a computer analysis of each golfer's swing before fitting him or her with a club shaft. Don't miss the tennis tunnel, where you can try out a racket before buying. *Mon–Sat 10am–6:30pm, Sun noon–5pm; www.citysearch.com/sfo/donsherwoodgolf; map:N3*

G&M SALES, THE GREAT OUTDOORS STORE / 1667 Market St; 415/863-2855 Highly regarded by locals, G&M carries an extensive selection of camping and backpacking supplies, including a large array of tents, sleeping bags, pads, backpacks, duffels, stoves, cook kits, coolers, freeze-dried foods, and fishing poles. Unbreakable wineglasses and enamel espresso cups are also for sale. This is where city slickers come for everything from a mosquito headnet to a "Luggable Loo." Plus, tents, bags, stoves, lanterns, coolers, and fishing poles are available to rent at reasonable rates. *Mon–Fri 10am–7pm, Sat 10am–5pm, Sun 11am–4pm; www.gmoutdoors.com; map:L4*

LOMBARDI SPORTS / 1600 Jackson St; 415/771-0600 This spacious store stocks a variety of sports apparel, shoes, and gear, and the specialty is backpacking and bicycling equipment, which takes up the second floor. There's a good array of water accessories, including suits, goggles, snorkels, and masks, plus in-line skates from Rollerblade, Soloman, Tecnica, and K2. Women runners and joggers will appreciate the large selection of running shoes and bras, including the Champion line. *Mon-Wed 10am–7pm, Thurs–Fri 10am–8pm, Sat 10am–6pm, Sun 11am–6pm; www.lombardisports.com; map:L2*

NIKETOWN / 278 Post St; 415/439-4656 Here's the very hip, very cool place to shop for the Nike brand of clothing and shoes. Goods are grouped by sport—basketball, soccer, running, tennis, golf, et cetera—with the exception of kids' wear, which has its own section. Videos and multimedia displays entertain you while you shop. *Mon–Fri 10am–8pm, Sat 10am–7pm, Sun 11am–6pm; www.nike.com; map:N3*

THE NORTH FACE / 180 Post St; 415/433-3223 "Never stop exploring" is the mantra of this top-notch climbing store. Whether the goal is scaling El Capitan, Mount Everest, or simply the nearest indoor climbing wall, North Face can outfit you with no-nonsense expedition apparel, tents, packs, backpacks, and sleeping bags. Subzero jackets, bodysuits, and layered outerwear are ideal for hard-core mountaineering enthusiasts, and rock climbers shouldn't miss the quick-drying and lightweight Tekware line. The store hosts monthly lectures and events about climbing. Their outlet in SoMa has great deals on their trademark goods and equipment (see the Consignment and Discount section). *Mon–Sat 10am–8pm, Sun 11am–6pm; www.thenorthface.com; map:N3*

PATAGONIA / 770 North Point St; 415/771-2050 Patagonia manufactures outdoor clothing for men, women, and children, including the well-known line of windbreakers and fleece jackets. The soft organic cotton knit and flannel shirts for men and women and the multipocket mesh vests for fishers and photographers are especially great finds, as is the Capilene underwear in pretty pastels and muted colors. Patagonia surfboards are sold here as well. *Mon–Wed 10am–6pm, Thurs–Fri 10am– 8pm, Sat 10am–6pm, Sun 11am–5pm; www.patagonia.com; map:L1*

TOYS

ARK / 3845 24th St; 415/821-1257 For nearly two decades this store has been selling high-quality European and American crafts and toys. Besides an incredible selection of musical instruments, including steel drums, accordions, tambourines, and kazoos, you'll find hand-carved ships, piggy banks, rideable trucks, and playful walking ducks with webbed feet. *Mon–Sat 11am–6pm; map:K7*

BASIC BROWN BEAR FACTORY / 444 De Haro St; 415/626-0781 or 800/554-1910 This is one of the few remaining stuffed-animal factories in the nation. Bears and bear-themed toys are designed by Merrilee Woods and handmade at the factory. Drop-in tours are held daily at 1pm and include behind-the-scenes demonstrations of how bears are designed and made. Then you get to stuff your own bear, dragon, bunny, or reindeer as a souvenir of your visit. *Mon–Sat 10am–5pm, Sun noon–5pm; www.basicbrownbear.com; map:N6*

DISNEY STORE / 400 Post St; 415/391-6866 The Disney store sells everything from oversize Mickey Mouses and Donald Ducks to cartoon clothing, backpacks, games, videos, and accessories. The helpful sales staff will steer you to merchandise commemorating your favorite Disney personality. And if that's not enough, a high-end gallery features art based on popular Disney cartoon figures, but expect to find five-figure price tags attached. *Mon–Fri 10am–7pm, Sat 10am–6pm, Sun 11am–5pm (extended summer and holiday hours); map:M3*

FAO SCHWARZ / 48 Stockton St; 415/394-8700 This three-story, upscale toy store was made famous by actor Tom Hanks when he danced on a giant toy piano in the popular movie *Big*. A small version of the now-famous piano is located on the third floor. Allow lots of time to linger here—kids of all ages love browsing through flamboyant Barbie World, oogling over the giant plush animals, and testing the flashy toy race cars and trains. *Mon–Sat 10am–7pm, Sun 11am–6pm; www.fao.com; map:N3*

IMAGINARIUM / 3535 California St; 415/387-9885 At Imaginarium, youngsters can play with many of the toys while you shop. Look for old favorites such as Gumby, as well as modern storybook characters, Raggedy Ann and Andy dolls, trains, educational books and cassettes, and the store's own entertaining line of learning games. *Mon–Fri 9:30am–7pm, Sat 9:30am–6pm, Sun 11am–6pm; map:I3*

JONATHAN KAYE / 3548 Sacramento St; 415/563-0773 A delightful emporium of tiny-tyke toys and games. Play with Babar, Madeline, Curious George, and other childhood pals; there's also a huge array of adorable handcrafted and painted furnishings. The rocking horses and puppet theaters are especially popular with kids, and the doll cradles can be custom ordered in pink or blue with fanciful moon and star designs. *Mon–Fri 10am–6pm, Sat 10am–5:30pm, Sun noon–5pm; map:I3*

VINTAGE CLOTHING

AARDVARK'S ODD ARK / 1501 Haight St; 415/621-3141 The atmosphere is more thrift store than boutique, but the sheer quantity of mostly '50s and '60s shirts, skirts, pants, and leather jackets makes Aardvark's, a Haight Street institution, one of San Francisco's most popular vintage clothing stores. The real treasures are buried in the back room, where intrepid shoppers will find perfectly preserved zoot suits and silk smoking jackets from the '30s and '40s. *Every day 11am–7pm; map:J5*

AMERICAN RAG COMPANY / 1305 Van Ness Ave; 415/474-5214 Located in a former auto showroom, this cavernous store offers both new and vintage clothing, shoes, and accessories for men and women. The new clothes, many from European designers, are cutting-edge trendy and expensive. The huge selection of vintage clothes, mostly from the '40s through the early '70s, seems to go on and on; it's a bit pricey, but in good condition. This is where you'll find the city's largest selection of little black dresses. *Mon–Sat 10am–9pm, Sun noon–7pm; map:L3*

DEPARTURES FROM THE PAST / 2028 Fillmore St; 415/885-3377 Owner Stephen "Spig" Spigolon aptly describes his filled-to-the-rafters store as a "wacky Woolworth's." The emphasis here is on '50s and '60s costumes, with all the accessories—wigs, hats, sunglasses, jewelry, purses, and shoes—to complete the look. Don't miss the knockout silk pajamas and other great vintage lingerie. The store also carries some new items patterned after vintage styles. *Mon–Sat 11am–7pm, Sun noon–6pm; map:K2*

GUYS AND DOLLS / 3789 24th St; 415/285-7174 Tucked away in Noe Valley, Guys and Dolls is a cheerful, well-lit shop purveying a young, hip look. Lounge music complements the '30s, '40s, and '50s fun day wear, which includes straight skirts, beaded sweaters, Hawaiian shirts, and swimsuits, all in good condition. The store also carries new sunglasses, jewelry, and other accessories in older styles, plus a few collectibles, such as Reglor lamps (around $500) and harlequin wall hangings. The friendly owners hand-select all items and change merchandise seasonally. *Mon–Fri 11am–7pm, Sat 11am–6pm, Sun noon–6pm; map:L7*

LA ROSA / 1711 Haight St; 415/668-3744 A thickly carpeted floor, soothing plum-colored walls, and votive candles floating in champagne glasses set the mood at La Rosa, one of the Bay Area's best high-end vintage clothing stores. Most of the merchandise dates back to the '40s and earlier, though there's a large selection of men's suits from the '50s and '60s. Items range from a spectacular rhinestone cowgirl outfit (boasting a $2,000 price tag) to gorgeous silk robes and old-fashioned doctors' satchels. A nice touch: each garment comes with a tag noting the approximate year it was manufactured, along with its fabric content, condition, and care instructions. *Mon–Sat 11am–7pm, Sun 11am–6pm; map:I5*

MARTINI MERCANTILE (THE HAIGHT) / 1773 Haight St; 415/362-1944 Hats off to this small, owner-operated store that stocks mostly vintage menswear from the '40s and '50s. The clothes are in good condition and fairly priced, but the specialty here is hats—numerous well-made vintage and vintage-style fedoras (in straw and felt), homburgs, bowlers, and even top hats. *Every day 11am–7pm; map:I5*

MARTINI MERCANTILE (NORTH BEACH) / 1453 Grant Ave; 415/362-1944 This high-quality, tastefully decorated shop in the heart of North Beach carries sophisticated vintage and vintage-style clothing for women, plus a few clothes for men. Most of the merchandise is from the '30s through the '60s, and all of it is in top condition. The store also has an appealing array of old perfume bottles, radios, and other collectibles. *Every day noon–8pm; map:N2*

THIRD HAND ROSE / 1839 Divisadero St; 415/567-7332 At the same address since 1967, Third Hand Rose is San Francisco's oldest vintage clothing store, and certainly one of its best. The merchandise will appeal not just to vintage aficionados but also to anyone who appreciates well-made, one-of-a-kind styles. From elegant Victorian gowns to early '70s "trash," this smallish store offers museum-quality items, including hard-to-find flapper dresses, exquisite lace blouses, sumptuous brocade jackets, and even dyed turkey feather vests. Specialties include well-priced bridal gowns (both antique and new) and vintage ethnic wear from the Middle East and Asia. *Mon–Sat noon–6pm; map:J3*

WASTELAND / 1660 Haight St; 415/863-3150 Located in a converted vaudeville and silent-movie palace, Wasteland is a vast emporium of clothes dating from the Victorian era to the present—8,000 items in 5,000 square feet. Prices are a bit inflated, but the store's colorful gargoyles, famously loud and obnoxious music, and outrageously attired salespeople add up to one of the best shows in town. *Every day 11am–8pm; map:I5*

WINE, BEER, AND SPIRITS

CALIFORNIA WINE MERCHANT / 3237 Pierce St; 415/567-0646 A 25-year-old neighborhood institution, California Wine Merchant offers hard- and not-so-hard-to-find West Coast wines. Though tiny, the shop packs floor-to-ceiling racks with well-edited bottles of boutique and esoteric wines, such as Lewis, Peter Michael, and Au Bon Climat. It leans slightly more toward reds in keeping with the trend; there's a good selection of California-style Rhônes. The knowledgeable staff can suggest a wine to fit any occasion. *Mon–Sat 11am–7pm, Sun noon–5pm; map:K1*

CANNERY WINE CELLARS / 2801 Leavenworth St; 415/673-0400 Here amid the touristy shops of Fisherman's Wharf is an incredibly sophisticated array of wines, beers (more than 300 labels), and liquor, including the West Coast's largest selection of single-malt scotch. The store ships all over the world, and offers one-stop shopping for wine gadgets and gifts. *Every day 10am–8pm; map:M1*

PLUMPJACK WINES / 3201 Fillmore St; 415/346-9870 Named for a Shakespearean character, this Marina district hot spot sells well-priced and well-edited California and imported wines, especially lesser-known labels. Service is a big reason customers make PlumpJack a repeat destination. *Mon–Sat 11am–8pm, Sun 11am–6pm; map:K1*

WINE CLUB / 953 Harrison St; 415/512-9086 or 800/966-7835 Serious wine connoisseurs peruse the Wine Club's shelves for bargain prices on more than 1,000 local and imported labels. Markups are just above wholesale, and most collectors buy in quantity to take advantage of the savings. Though heavy on burgundies, including rare vintages, the stock also includes loads of reds and whites from France, Italy, Germany, Spain, and Australia. Phone orders are shipped for a fee. *Mon–Sat 9am–7pm, Sun 11am–6pm; map:N4*

WINE IMPRESSIONS / 3461 California St; 415/221-9463 Three wine-buffs-cum-judges opened this place in 1990 and turned it into one of the city's penultimate destinations for fine wine, champagne, and port. One owner worked at the legendary Ashbury Market before going out on his own. There are more than 800 wines, with 130 priced at less than $11. You'll find loads of Belgian and microbrew beers, plus high-end spirits, including more than 50 bourbons and 40 tequilas. Imported cigars are also for sale. Daily tastings begin at noon. *Mon–Fri 10am–8pm, Sat 9am–8pm, Sun 10am–6pm; map:I3*

PERFORMING ARTS

PERFORMING ARTS

Theater

Purists lament that San Francisco lacks a theater scene worthy of the city's global acclaim. But in reality, the theater culture here is world class. Only a dreamer or a fool would compare it to the stages of London or New York. But as long as such lofty examples remain in sight, Bay Area producers and performers will continue to improve on what is already a polished, wide-ranging collection of offerings for the stage. Sure, a provincial texture persists, evident in the excitement generated whenever a major touring production from the Best of Broadway series arrives and unloads its trucks. But resident houses such as the beloved American Conservatory Theater, the Magic Theatre, and the New Conservatory Theatre Center routinely unleash a dramatic torrent that creates national waves. And it's in the work of these local houses—from mainstream repertory to leading-edge fringe, from traditional drama to lesbian-themed musicals—where the true flavor of San Francisco theater resides. The following are some of the best groups currently performing innovative theatrical works. Check the weekly tabloid-size *San Francisco Bay Guardian* and *SF Weekly* or the Datebook section of the Sunday *Chronicle and Examiner* for the complete up-to-date picture.

ACTOR'S THEATRE / 533 Sutter St; 415/296-9179 Tucked away on Sutter Street above Union Square, away from the main theater district, the Actor's Theatre produces high-quality productions on a minimal budget for appreciative audiences, many composed of fellow actors. The theater has fewer than 100 seats, and there's not really a bad one in the house. Much of the fare is chosen to show off the actors' abilities—so expect to see lots of Tennessee Williams and heavy American drama. *Map:M3*

AMERICAN CONSERVATORY THEATER (ACT) / Geary Theater, 415 Geary St (performances); 30 Grant Ave (office); 415/749-2228 ACT is one of the best established resident theater groups, not only in San Francisco but in the nation. From its home stage at the historic Geary Theater, the company presents polished interpretations of the classics as well as important contemporary U.S. and world premieres. ACT is known as much for its stage presentations as for its tradition of thespian teaching: it has earned Tony Awards for both outstanding theatrical performance and training. Actors the world over have studied here, and alums include Annette Bening, Denzel Washington, John Turturro, and Winona Ryder. The season runs from September to midsummer and is punctuated by lectures, audience discussions, and special student plays. A local favorite is the holiday production of Dickens's *A Christmas*

Carol. In spite of all its accomplishments and national renown, ACT is refreshingly unstuffy, making both veteran theatergoers and first-timers feel at home. *www.act-sfbay.org; map:M3*

BAY AREA PLAYWRIGHTS' FESTIVAL / 470 Florida St; 415/399-1809 or 415/263-3986 A regular in San Francisco's fall arts season, the Bay Area Playwrights' Festival was founded in 1976 as one of the nation's first writer-focused theater festivals. It has garnered national kudos, developing the work of such award-winning playwrights as Sam Shepard, Anna Deavere Smith, Holly Hughes, and David Henry Hwang. A creative haven for writers that stays out of the limelight most of the year, the festival usually opens its doors to the public in early September or late October to provide a glimpse of participants' new work. Recently, in its new home at A Traveling Jewish Theatre in the Mission District, the festival premiered Lillian Garrett-Groag's *Bones* and Alexander Woo's *Forbidden City Blues. Map:M6*

BAY AREA THEATRESPORTS / Bayfront Theater, Fort Mason Center, Bldg B, 3rd Floor, Marina Blvd at Buchanan St; 415/474-8935 When it comes to improv comedy, Bay Area Theatresports (BATS) does it so well it's like playing a game. In fact, it is a game. This company of actors and comedians produces a highly dynamic summer improv series, in which "teams" of performers compete on a stage, much to audiences' delight. It's one of the top improv festivals in the Bay Area. BATS also offers an assortment of fun and inventive acting classes for all skill levels. *www.lobstershell.com/bats; map:K1*

BERKELEY REPERTORY THEATRE / 2025 Addison St, Berkeley; 510/845-4700 (performances) or 510/204-8901 (information) Although a fairly small company, this dramatic magnet across the bay has a huge impact on national theater circles and won the 1997 Tony Award for outstanding regional theater. The Berkeley Rep, founded in a storefront amid the counterculture hubris of 1968, has grown to become a mature theater company, though no less socially or politically aware. Works range from inventive updates on the classics to premieres of specially commissioned pieces by top playwrights. The annual seven-play season begins in September and runs through midsummer. *www.berkeleyrep.org; map:FF2*

BRAVA THEATER CENTER / 2781 24th St; 415/641-7657 A few years ago, after operating on a shoestring budget, Brava for Women in the Arts purchased a dilapidated old movie house in a run-down part of the city's Mission District. A bold move, to be sure, but not out of character with the company's penchant for gutsy and aggressive theater. Brava's politically motivated and mostly feminist-, lesbian-, and Latina-oriented fare has earned it quite a following in San Francisco. Plays are usually small in scale, but always adventurous. The new space, which seats 250, may turn out to be a catalyst for the improvement of its new neighborhood. *www.brava.org; map:N7*

COWELL THEATER / Fort Mason Center, Bldg D (Marina Blvd at Buchanan St); 415/441-3687 One of a few charming theaters in the expansive Fort Mason Center, Cowell plays host to everything from new dance works by experimental ensembles to monologues by Spalding Gray to the annual season of San Francisco's New Pickle Circus. The high stage lends itself to big spectacles, although the moderate size (about 450 seats) keeps the feeling intimate. Another factor that makes it a favorite venue with San Franciscans: lots of free parking! *Map:K1*

CURRAN THEATRE / 445 Geary St; 415/551-2000 Many lose sight of the fact that this gorgeous 1,665-seat theater has hosted all manner of dramatic fare on its stage since 1922. That's because for six years starting in 1993 it was home to the wildly popular production of Andrew Lloyd Webber's *Phantom of the Opera*. Producers poured money into the place to accommodate the special theatrics, a renovation that restored the building's original grandeur and added modern lighting and technical updates. Since *Phantom*'s closing, the Curran has provided another great venue for several hit Broadway plays. *www.bestofbroadway-sf.com; map:M3*

EUREKA THEATRE / 215 Jackson St; 415/243-9899 or 415/392-4400 The Eureka Theatre was long known for its intimate staged readings, playwright development, and lively, socially relevant, community-based theater. Then in 1992, the company premiered Tony Kushner's *Angels in America*—and, willy-nilly, had to grow up with that play's skyrocketing success. Now in a beautiful new permanent home in a renovated old movie house, the Eureka continues to foster innovative theater under a more structured administration. The theater still hosts staged readings and works-in-progress, in addition to more fully developed productions by the likes of the multimedia performance group AWD. Another recent success was the audience-interactive, continuously developing, and increasingly wacky live soap opera performed by San Francisco's own Liquid Soap. *Map:N2*

42ND STREET MOON / New Conservatory Theatre Center, 25 Van Ness Ave; 415/861-8972 (performances) or 415/281-5868 (information) This is one of only a few theater companies in the nation devoted entirely to the revival of "lost" musicals. Founded in 1993, the company got its name from a 1920s song about the bright lights of Broadway. It focuses on lesser-known gems from the golden age of American musical theater—from Cole Porter and Gershwin to Rodgers and Hammerstein—and each year presents them anew in the intimate New Conservatory Theatre Center. Past seasons (beginning in October) have included *One*

COFFEEHOUSE CULTURE

Decades before there was a Starbucks on every American street corner, there was a coffeehouse culture in San Francisco. In the '50s a group of freethinkers descended on the North Beach area and created a social phenomenon centered around open expression, art, red wine, and, of course, coffee. The Beats, led by Allen Ginsberg, Neal Cassady, Lawrence Ferlinghetti, and Jack Kerouac, were drawn to San Francisco in general because it was known to be a cosmopolitan city, far from the social constraints of Middle America. And North Beach in particular was a desired destination because of its European atmosphere and abundance of coffeehouses and taverns with great entertainment.

San Francisco has been home to many alternative thinkers and takes great pride in being the supportive hot spot where these minds can flourish. So take a notebook or a sketch pad down to one of the many cafes on Columbus Avenue—Caffe Trieste, Vesuvio Cafe, Caffe Greco, Tosca Cafe—have a few shots of espresso, and feel your creative spirit emerge in a way it never would in the slick chrome confines of a franchise.

Touch of Venus, Let's Face It, Hollywood Pinafore, Once in a Blue Moon, and the U.S. premiere of Rodgers and Hammerstein's *Three Sisters. www.capybara.com/42ndStMoon; map:L4*

GOLDEN GATE THEATRE / I Taylor St (at Market St and Golden Gate Ave); 415/551-2000 Despite its proximity to one of the less attractive stretches of Market Street, the Golden Gate packs 'em in from all over town, usually showing the latest blockbuster from the Best of Broadway series. The large 1920s theater was once a two-screen movie house owned by RKO. It has been a stage theater since 1979, hosting such productions as *Chicago, Carousel*, and *Rent. map:M4*

MAGIC THEATRE / Fort Mason Center, Bldg D, 3rd Floor (Marina Blvd at Buchanan St); 415/441-8001 One of the best and most popular companies in San Francisco, the Magic once had a policy of staging only world-premiere works. It has since lightened up, but the quality is still evident in season after season of works by new and emerging American playwrights. Founded in 1968, the Magic is perhaps best known as the theatrical birthplace of Pulitzer Prize–winning playwright Sam Shepard, but has certainly earned notoriety beyond that, including its debut of the specially commissioned *Pieces of the Quilt*, an evening of AIDS-related one-acts by Tony Kushner and Lanford Wilson. Another Magic world premiere was Michelle Carter's *Hillary and Soon-Yi Shop for Ties*. The theater is divided into two spaces, one seating 156, the other 160. *Map:K1*

THE MARSH / 1062 Valencia St (between 21st and 22nd Sts); 415/641-0235 The Marsh bills itself as a "breeding ground for new performance" and does a pretty good job of living up to the claim. The company presents more than 300 performances a year in its three venues: the main stage, the Mock Cafe, and the Marsh Studio. Audience members, many from the Mission District neighborhood, like being surprised by the eclectic bill of fare. Various local acting, dance, and music ensembles perform here; works-in-progress are a common occurrence, as are solo shows and longer runs of full-fledged original plays. Tickets are usually cheap—well under $20. *Map:L6*

NEW CONSERVATORY THEATRE CENTER / 25 Van Ness Ave; 415/861-8972 The New Conservatory Theatre Center (NCTC) hosts the annual gay-themed Pride Season of original musicals, comedies, and dramatic plays. A recent season included the world premiere of the gay comedy *Key West* by Jack Heifer and Ed Decker. Another NCTC offering was Karen Finley's one-woman show *Shut Up and Love Me*, part of the theater's Celebrating Women Festival. The company also hosts a matinee series for kids on Tuesday and Saturday mornings, as well as productions by local ensembles. The NCTC is located in an office building near the Civic Center, and it's home to 42nd Street Moon's annual season of "lost musicals" (see 42nd Street Moon above). *Map:L4*

ORPHEUM THEATRE / 1192 Market St; 415/551-2000 With a whopping 2,200 seats and an enormous stage, the Orpheum may be the most grandiose theater space in the city. Accordingly, it gets to host the big shows. A massive remodel of the 1926 building brought the technical facilities into the 21st century, and they were used to full effect when the theater was home to the popular touring production of *Miss Saigon*. The Orpheum usually presents large-scale productions from the Best of Broadway series. *Map:M4*

SAN FRANCISCO FRINGE FESTIVAL / 156 Eddy St, and other venues; 415/673-3847 Started in 1991, this festival is a celebration of uncensored, uncurated, fly-by-the-seat-of-your pants theater. Held each September in various Union Square–area venues (primarily the Exit Theatre and the Exit Stage Left at 156 Eddy St), the Fringe features strange, offbeat, and obscure performances by actors, comedians, jugglers, poets, clowns, and experimentalists of all kinds. The 1999 festival featured about 250 performances over an 11-day period by 51 local, national, and international theater companies. Locals have elevated "fringing" to an art form, bouncing from performance to performance, taking in only what they like. It's easy to do, since most shows last less than an hour, and you can sometimes see five different performances within 30 minutes. *www.sffringe.org; map:M3*

SAN FRANCISCO MIME TROUPE / Various venues; 415/285-1717 Each summer in city parks, the renowned San Francisco Mime Troupe presents free shows that address burning political and social issues, ranging from neighborhood gentrification to racism to the ills of the information age. Alumni of the Tony Award–winning troupe include Peter Coyote, Sharon Lockwood, and Arthur Holden. *www.sffringe.org*

SAN FRANCISCO SHAKESPEARE FESTIVAL / Golden Gate Park, and other venues; 415/422-2222 or 800/978-PLAY Since 1983, this beloved theater group has been producing its annual Free Shakespeare in the Park series each September in Golden Gate Park and other locales. A performance is often apt to be a whimsical update of the Bard's classics, transplanted to such environs as 1950s Italy, a contemporary Maine fishing village, or the Roaring '20s. The festival is also known for its inventive youth theater programs, including Midnight Shakespeare. Be sure to bring a picnic lunch. *www.sfshakes.org; map:D5-H5*

THEATRE ON THE SQUARE (TOTS) / 450 Post St; 415/433-9500 In a 740-seat space originally built as a hotel ballroom, TOTS typically stages long-running, very popular productions of dance theater, musical revues, or small plays that earn big reviews. One of its longest runs was Steve Martin's *Picasso at the Lapin Agile*. *Map:N3*

THEATER RHINOCEROS / 2926 16th St; 415/861-5079 Its motto is "We're Here, We're Queer, We Do Plays," and indeed, this is the nation's oldest lesbian and gay theater. Founded in 1977, it still produces some of the most relevant and engaging fare in the genre. The productions endeavor not just to preach to the choir, however, but to gain a voice in the mainstream. As a result of the company's world renown, it has hosted many premieres and special commissions; a recent season included the West Coast premiere of the controversial play *Shopping and Fucking*, a hit on London's West End. *www.therhino.org; map:L5*

A TRAVELING JEWISH THEATRE / 470 Florida St; 415/399-1809 Although this acclaimed actor-led ensemble, true to its name, has traveled to perform in some 60 cities, it was happy to establish a permanent home in the Mission District not long ago. A Traveling Jewish Theatre is one of the city's most skilled and challenging theater groups. Founded in Los Angeles in 1978 (it moved here officially in 1982), the group produces Jewish-themed pieces that examine the condition of all humanity. In 1990 it was one of the first American theaters to tour post–Warsaw Pact Eastern Europe. Deep, thought-provoking, poignant, and funny, the original works are inspired by everything from the legends of Hasidism to Yiddish poetry. In late 1999, the group presented the Bay Area premiere of the off-Broadway play *The Memoirs of Glückel of Hameln* and a revival of founding member Naomi Newman's solo play, *Snake Talk: Urgent Messages from the Mother*. *www.atjt.com; map:M6*

303

Classical Music and Opera

San Franciscans take their classical music very seriously and enjoy it with fervor. The San Francisco Symphony, one of the world's top-notch orchestras, is led by the colorful Michael Tilson Thomas, one of the world's most touted and talented musical directors. Next door to the symphony is the world-renowned San Francisco Opera, the oldest continuously-running opera company in the United States. At the smaller end of the spectrum, groups like the Pocket Opera perform less traditional but no less significant fare. The **SAN FRANCISCO GAY MEN'S CHORUS** (415/863-4472) and the **LESBIAN/GAY CHORUS OF SAN FRANCISCO** (415/861-7067) are only two of the groups that harmoniously coexist on the choral music scene. Concerts at Grace Cathedral (415/749-6310) feature the popular Choir of Men and Boys as well as guest performers ranging from the Slavyanka Russian Chorus to pianist George Winston. And if it's festivals you want, you'll find plenty of those too, including the popular **MIDSUMMER MOZART** (415/954-0850). Here are some of the major music makers in town.

KRONOS QUARTET / Yerba Buena Center for the Arts, 701 Mission St; 415/978-2787 One of the world's leading-edge chamber ensembles, the Kronos Quartet has spent two and a half decades stretching, bending, and contorting the conventions of contemporary music for the string quartet. Ensemble members Jennifer Culp, Hank Dutt, John Sherba, and David Harrington are formally trained and firmly rooted in tradition. Kronos commissions several new works each season and performs more than 100 concerts a year, visiting an average of 15 countries and more than a dozen U.S. states. Since its inception in 1973, the quartet has performed more than 600 works and recorded about 30 albums. The list of composers who have created works especially for Kronos reads like a who's who of the music world: from John Adams, Peter Apfelbaum, and Frank Zappa to Mr. Bungle, John Coltrane, and Thelonious Monk. The home season usually begins in September. *www.kronosquartet.org; map:N3*

OLD FIRST CHURCH CONCERTS / 1751 Sacramento St; 415/776-5552 With a truly active congregation, this 1911 Romanesque church is known for its lively and warm Presbyterian prayer services as well as its impressive calendar of recitals and choral and chamber music concerts. The acoustics are outstanding. *www.oldfirst.org; map:L3*

PHILHARMONIA BAROQUE ORCHESTRA / Herbst Theatre, 401 Van Ness Ave, and other venues; 415/495-7445 Symphony director Michael Tilson Thomas may command the classical spotlight, but Nicolas McGegan, musical director of the Philharmonia Baroque, is a quiet powerhouse in his own right. The Cambridge- and Oxford-trained conductor is one of the world's foremost Handel interpreters. He and his 40-piece ensemble perform refined and perfectly balanced renditions of early music, from Handel to Bach to Vivaldi. The company started in 1987 with two concerts, and today performs more than 30 times per season throughout the Bay Area. In San Francisco it plays primarily in Herbst Theatre. The season, which usually includes a program of Handel's *Messiah* during the holidays, begins in October. *www.philharmonia.org; map:L4*

POCKET OPERA / Palace of the Legion of Honor, Lincoln Park, 34th Ave and Clement St, and other venues; 415/575-1102 Fear of the Viking-helmeted fat lady is all too common, but for anyone remotely curious about the grandeur of opera—especially young ones—Donald Pippin's Pocket Opera is a great place to start. Pippin, who leads the singers and chamber orchestra on piano, has said that "if you don't know the opera's story on the way to the theater, you won't know it on the way home either." With that in mind, he began creating translations of classic operas and presenting them in a North Beach bar; soon the show was so popular he took it on the road. Now the Pocket performs throughout the Bay Area with a regular season that runs from December till spring. Programs are sung in English (translated to convey the thrust of the story) and are scaled down with minimal costumes and usually no formal set. It's great fun for families. Some performances are adaptations of complete operas, such as *The Marriage of Figaro* or *La Traviata*; others are inventive originals by Mr. Pippin, like the local favorite *Alice in Operaland*. *www.pocketopera.org; map:E3*

SAN FRANCISCO BACH CHOIR / Various venues; 415/922-1645 (performances) or 415/441-4942 (information) The oldest community choir in the western states, this group has spent the past 63 years introducing Northern Californians to the works of J. S. Bach. Since 1981 it has been led by music scholar and accomplished concert organist David Babbitt. Performances are usually held from fall through late spring in churches and temples throughout the Bay Area. *www.sfbach.org*

SAN FRANCISCO CONSERVATORY OF MUSIC / 1201 Ortega St; 415/564-8086 Founded in 1917 as a piano school, the conservatory is now a world-renowned learning institution. The school is kept deliberately small; the study is intense, but less rigid than at many well-known European conservatories. In addition to academics, the school presents concerts by students, the Conservatory Orchestra, and distinguished visiting musicians. Most events are free or very low priced. Each Christmas the conservatory holds its *Sing-It-Yourself Messiah* at Davies Symphony Hall

(301 Van Ness Ave), an audience-participation sing-along to Handel's beloved masterwork. *www.sfcm.edu; map:G7*

SAN FRANCISCO CONTEMPORARY MUSIC PLAYERS / **Yerba Buena Center for the Arts, 701 Mission St; 415/978-2787 (performances) or 415/252-6235 (information)** The San Francisco Contemporary Music Players is the oldest contemporary chamber music ensemble on the West Coast and one of the top ensembles of its kind in the country. It's also a five-time winner of the national ASCAP/Chamber Music America Award for Adventurous Programming of Contemporary Music. Special commissions include works by such composers as John Adams, John Cage, Chen Yi, and Julia Wolfe. The six-concert season usually begins in September; formats vary from 6 to 18 performers. *www.sfcmp.org; map:N3*

SAN FRANCISCO OPERA / **War Memorial Opera House, 301 Van Ness Ave (performances); Ticket and Patron Services, 199 Grove St; 415/864-3330 (information)** San Francisco's opera company, currently the country's second largest, was founded in 1923; on September 26 of that year, locals were treated to a lively performance of *La Bohème* in the Civic Auditorium. The auditorium couldn't hold the burgeoning company for long, however, and in 1932 the opera moved into the opulent, Arthur Brown Jr.–designed, Beaux Arts–style War Memorial Opera House—the anchor of the city's performing-arts complex today. The building was christened with a performance of Puccini's *Tosca*—and 75 years later, reopened with yet another *Tosca* after an extensive $50 million retrofit (in the wake of the 1989 earthquake). The renovation not only restored the building to its original glory but added new 21st-century technical innovations. These days, the company is on an adventurous yet well-scripted path; the repertory season undertakes the classics (*Madama Butterfly, Carmen*) and new, often specially commissioned works, including André Previn and Philip Littell's acclaimed adaptation of *A Streetcar Named Desire*. For nearly a month in 1999, the company performed Wagner's massive *Der Ring des Nibelungen*, and it was the talk of the town. The season begins in September and lasts until late spring. Traditionally, the company follows opening night with a free concert in Golden Gate Park. Operas are performed in their native language and presented with English supertitles. The Merola Opera Program, one of the nation's top training grounds for young singers, performs in the summer. *www.sfopera.org; map:L4*

SAN FRANCISCO PERFORMANCES / **Various venues; 415/398-6449** This nonprofit group, founded in 1979 by a former administrator with the San Francisco Opera, is dedicated to the cultivation of the arts in San Francisco by presenting classical and chamber music, jazz, dance, and solo recitals in intimate settings (many shows are held at Herbst Theatre or at

Yerba Buena Center for the Arts). The repertoire has grown from seven to more than 180 programs, along with educational and community outreach activities. San Francisco Performances kicks off its season in October and features the likes of the Lincoln Center Jazz Orchestra or perhaps violinist Anne-Sophie Mutter. Your ticket to the show often includes a chance to meet the performers. *www.sfperf.org; map:M3*

SAN FRANCISCO SYMPHONY / Davies Symphony Hall, 201 Van Ness Ave; 415/864-6000 (performances) or 415/552-8000 (information)
San Franciscans are so fond of their symphony that even during the Great Depression, when hard times for all threatened to put an end to the music, citizens passed a bond measure to save it. Founded in 1911, the San Francisco Symphony quickly played its way into the hearts of locals and went on to capture kudos from critics and fans all over the world. It's since become one of the finest classical acts around, acclaimed for both its performances and its numerous Grammy Award–winning recordings. The distinguished list of music directors has included Henry Hadley, one of the top American composers of his era; Alfred Hertz, who led many important American premieres at the Metropolitan Opera; and Pierre Monteux, who introduced the world to *Le Sacre du Printemps*; as well as Josef Krips, Seiji Ozawa, and Herbert Blomstedt. Michael Tilson Thomas (also known as "MTT"), who took the helm in 1985, continues to lead the company into new and interesting terrain, with intensely eclectic programs that suit many tastes. A season schedule might include anything from a classic such as Prokofiev's *Romeo and Juliet* to Copland's *The Modernist*, with guest performers ranging from violinist Itzhak Perlman to soprano Lisa Vroman and guest conductors such as Sir Georg Solti. Concerts at the technically top-flight Louise M. Davies Symphony Hall are routinely packed, and the season opener each September is one of the city's biggest cultural fetes. Other highlights include the annual "Night in Old Vienna," a holiday-themed program of waltzes and operettas, and the Summer in the City pops series with such guest artists as Arlo Guthrie and Roberta Flack. The San Francisco Symphony Chorus, always a treat, performs several times a year. Community programs are another company focus, including performances in local schools, educational and outreach offerings for kids, the award-winning San Francisco Youth Symphony, frequent free open rehearsals, and occasional free outdoor concerts. In 1989, not long after the Loma Prieta earthquake ratttled nerves around the bay, the symphony gave a gratis performance of Beethoven's Ninth Symphony in Golden Gate Park; 20,000 people turned out to reaffirm their civic pride. *www.sfsymphony. org; map:L4*

FUN FOR FREE

San Francisco is one of the costliest cities in the country to visit (and live in), but that doesn't mean you can't get some of your kicks for free. Here are numerous top attractions that are gratis either all the time or at least once in a while:

City Guides There are over 20 different walking tours of San Francisco offered; tours start at various points throughout the city. Call for locations and times. *Free: always. Tours offered year-round; 415/557-4266; www.walking-tours.com/cityguides.*

Fort Point A National Historic Site under the south end of the Golden Gate Bridge; off Lincoln Blvd at Long Ave. *Free: always. Every day; 415/556-1373 or 415/556-1693.*

Golden Gate Park Main Entrance: Stanyan St at Fell St; maps are available at the San Francisco Visitor Information Center (415/391-2000) and at park headquarters in McLaren Lodge, Stanyan St at Fell St. *Free: always. Every day (park headquarters Mon–Fri 8am–5pm); 415/831-2700; www.civiccenter.ci.sf.ca.us/recpark/location.nsf.*

The Presidio In the northwest corner of the city, near the Marina district and the foot of the Golden Gate Bridge (also see the Presidio Museum below). *Free: always. Every day; 415/561-4323; www.nps.gov/prsf/.*

San Francisco Zoo At Sloat Blvd and 45th Ave. *Free: 1st Wed of the month. Every day; 415/753-7080.*

Sigmund Stern Grove Various music concerts are held outdoors throughout the summer; in Stern Grove, at Sloat Blvd and 19th Ave. *Free: always. Held on select summer weekends, rain or shine; 415/391-2000 (SF Visitors Bureau).*

California Academy of Sciences Steinhart Aquarium and Natural History Museum, on the Music Concourse at Golden Gate Park. *Free: 1st Wed of the month. Every day; 415/750-7145.*

California Palace of the Legion of Honor In Lincoln Park, 34th Ave and Clement St. *Free: 2nd Wed of the month. Tues–Sun; 415/750-3600.*

Cartoon Art Museum 814 Mission St, between 4th and 5th Sts. *Free: 1st Wed of the month. Tues–Sun; 415/CAR-TOON (227-8666).*

Exploratorium In the Palace of Fine Arts, 3601 Lyon St at Marina Blvd. *Free: 1st Wed of the month. Every day in the summer, Tues–Sun the rest of the year; 415/561-0360; www.exploratorium.edu.*

The Jewish Museum San Francisco 121 Steuart St, between Mission and Howard Sts. Note: The museum is expected to move to the Yerba Buena Center for the Arts area in 2002. *Free: 1st Mon of the month and Thurs 6pm–8pm. Sun–Thurs; 415/543-8880; www.jewishmuseumsf.org.*

Mexican Museum Fort Mason Center, Building D, Marina Blvd at Laguna St. Note: The museum is expected to move to the Yerba Buena Center for the Arts area in 2002. *Free: 1st Wednesday of the month. Wed–Sun; 415/441-0404.*

M. H. de Young Memorial Museum On the Music Concourse at Golden Gate Park. *Free: 1st Wed of the month. Tues–Sun; 415/750-3600.*

Presidio Army Museum In the Presidio, in the northwest corner of the city, near the Marina district. *Free: always. Wed–Sun; 415/561-4331; www.nps.gov/prsf.*

San Francisco Cable Car Museum 1201 Mason St at Washington St. *Free: always. Every day; 415/474-1887; www.cablecarmuseum.com.*

San Francisco Fire Department Museum 655 Presidio Ave at Bush St. *Free: always. Thurs–Sun 1pm–4pm; 415/558-3546 or 415/563-4630.*

Maritime Museum In Aquatic Park, at the northernmost end of Polk St. *Free: always. Every day; 415/556-3002.*

San Francisco Museum of Modern Art (SFMOMA) 151 3rd St, between Mission and Howard Sts. *Free: 1st Tues of the month. Thurs–Tues; 415/357-4000; www.sfmoma.org.*

Wells Fargo History Museum 420 Montgomery St, between California and Sacramento Sts. *Free: always. Mon–Fri; 415/396-2619.* **Yerba Buena Center for the Arts** 701 Mission St at 3rd St. *Free: 1st Thurs of the month 5pm–8pm. Tues–Sun; 415/978-2700; www.yerbabuenaarts.org.*

Yerba Buena Center for the Arts 701 Mission St at 3rd St. *Free: 1st Thurs of the month 5pm–8pm. Tues–Sun; 415/978-2700, www.yerbabuenaarts.org.*

THE WOMEN'S PHILHARMONIC / Yerba Buena Center for the Arts, 701 Mission St; 415/978-2787 (performances) or 415/437-0123 (information) Founded in 1981 to help boost the representation of women in the classical music world, the Women's Philharmonic is now known the world over and is the winner of several national music awards. It has presented the work of more than 150 female composers, including 35 specially commissioned pieces. Artistic director and conductor Apo Hsu, an accomplished musician, has worked with an impressive list of artists including Andre Watts, Gil Shaham, Sarah Chang, Tony Bennett, and Judy Collins. Programs usually feature newer works, with the occasional earlier composition by Amy Beach or Mabel Daniels. The season begins in October and continues through May. *www.womensphil.org; map:N3*

Dance

San Francisco enjoys a vibrant and varied dance community that includes the world-famous San Francisco Ballet as well as some of the nation's foremost modern dance troupes. The city is also home to numerous wonderful smaller groups, including the **MARGARET JENKINS DANCE COMPANY** (415/826-8399), the **STEPHEN PELTON DANCE THEATER** (415/241-0111), and a variety of ethnic dance troupes ranging from **ROSA MONTOYA'S ARGENTINIAN BAILES FLAMENCOS** (415/824-1960) to the **CHINESE FOLK DANCE ASSOCIATION** (415/834-1359).

ETHNIC DANCE FESTIVAL / Palace of Fine Arts, 3301 Lyon St; 415/474-3914 Presented annually by World Arts West for more than 20 years, the Ethnic Dance Festival is now a highly anticipated San Francisco cultural event. In fact, it's so popular that the auditions, held in January, now draw nearly as many people as the June festival itself. The festival features dance and music from Africa, Latin America, China, Japan, India, Ireland, Eastern Europe, and many other countries. World Arts West also puts on educational programs for children, low-income groups, and seniors, including a great puppet theater show and a summer dance workshop. *www.worldartswest.org; map:J1*

JOE GOODE PERFORMANCE GROUP / Yerba Buena Center for the Arts, 701 Mission St; 415/978-2787 (performances) or 415/646-4848 (information) Quirky, whimsical, and athletic—that's Joe Goode, a true Bay Area treasure and one of the nation's most intriguing modern choreographers. The city has turned out en masse to see his ensemble perform visually stunning works that are often multimedia performances, usually political, and always artistic and avant-garde. Headquartered in San Francisco since 1979, the Joe Goode Performance Group has also become a sensation on the road. A recent program, the critically acclaimed *Deeply There*, examined the unlikely relationships born within the shadow of the AIDS epidemic. The home season starts in June. *Map:N3*

LAWRENCE PECH DANCE COMPANY / Yerba Buena Center for the Arts, 701 Mission St; 415/978-2787 Worldwide patrons of ballet know the name Lawrence Pech. He studied under Mikhail Baryshnikov and has worked with such illustrious choreographers as George Balanchine, Martha Graham, Twyla Tharp, and Jerome Robbins. Now based in San Francisco, Pech works outside the confines of traditional ballet; his namesake ensemble, founded in 1995, has quickly established itself as an innovative force in the dance world. Pech has choreographed and premiered more than a dozen original ballets; most are rooted in classical movement, but have decidedly contemporary dramatic threads and scores. The two-part performance season usually takes place in the spring and fall. *Map:N3*

LINES CONTEMPORARY BALLET / Yerba Buena Center for the Arts, 701 Mission St; 415/978-2787 (performances) or 415/863-3040 (information) Alonzo King has a firm reputation as an innovator, challenging the conventions of traditional movement while crafting ballets that fall well within the framework of classical dance. He has created works for a wide range of companies, from the Dance Theater of Harlem to the Joffrey Ballet. In 1982 he established LINES Contemporary Ballet, a national touring company of 12 to 15 dancers, and turned it into an integral part of the national dance vernacular. He also helped transform the

San Francisco Dance Center, the company's home, into one of the largest training facilities on the West Coast. King's work mines the rich quarries of classical music as well as traditional African music and avant-jazz—it's one of the most eclectic repertoires in modern dance. The home season begins in May. *www.linesballet.org; map:N3*

ODC–SAN FRANCISCO / 3153 17th St; 415/863-6606 Its high-flying acrobatics and extraordinary energy set this ensemble well apart from the pack. With a well-deserved international reputation, ODC is one of the country's top modern dance companies, fueled by the tireless creativity and commitment of its three resident choreographers, Brenda Way, K. T. Nelson, and Kimi Okada. Way, who trained in New York under George Balanchine, founded the company in 1971; it moved to San Francisco in 1976 and became one of the first established modern dance companies to flourish outside the Big Apple. ODC was also the nation's first modern dance company to establish its own resident facility, where it now houses a dance school, theater, and gallery. The group performs its impressive original and collaborative repertoire to about 50,000 people a year. Programs are presented in the namesake facility, but one of the company's biggest events is Dancing Downtown, held each spring at Yerba Buena Center for the Arts. Another popular ODC work is the holiday production of *The Velveteen Rabbit. www.odcdance.org; map:L6*

ROBERT MOSES' KIN / Theatre Artaud, 450 Florida St, and other venues; 415/621-7797 or 415/586-1466 An excellent dance ensemble, Robert Moses' Kin is one of a select few in the city that's rooted in the African-American aesthetic. Founded in 1995 to explore such issues as race, class, and gender through dance, the company features more than 30 original works by artistic director Robert Moses, who also collaborates with such artists as jazz composer Marcus Shelby and the a cappella ensemble SoVoSo. The pieces are complex and provocative. Most performances are held at Theatre Artaud in the Mission District or at Yerba Buena Center for the Arts. *Map:M6*

SAN FRANCISCO BALLET / 455 Franklin St; 415/865-2000 (performances) or 415/861-5600 (information) Founded in 1933 as the San Francisco Opera Ballet, the city's ballet is the oldest, and now one of the three largest, professional ballet companies in the United States. It got off to an auspicious start by presenting America's first full-length productions of *Coppélia* and *Swan Lake*. And it wasn't long before the company, renamed the San Francisco Ballet, had established itself as a leading force in American dance. The ballet presented the national premiere of *The Nutcracker* in 1944, and in 1951, under artistic director Lew Christensen, the company began touring the world to international acclaim. In 1972 the ballet started staging its annual season in San Francisco's War

Memorial Opera House, where it still performs today. Not so long ago, the company fell on hard times, teetering toward financial failure. San Franciscans, of course, would have none of that, and a grassroots effort called Save Our Ballet managed to bring the company back from the brink. Helgi Tomasson, the company's artistic director since 1985, has taken it to new heights. With a roster of 65 dancers, the company presents its home season (usually about six programs) from January to May. Its training program, the San Francisco Ballet School, annually draws some 300 students from far and wide to the company's $13.8 million facility; graduates are now dancing in some of the world's best ballet companies. *www.sfballet.org; map:L4*

SMUIN BALLETS–SF / Yerba Buena Center for the Arts, 701 Mission St, and other venues; 415/665-2222 The company's namesake, Michael Smuin, is a former director of the San Francisco Ballet. Founded in 1994, this group quickly stirred the passions of local lovers of dance. Smuin, who has won a Tony Award and several Emmys, imbued his debut program, *Dances with Songs*, with languid, athletic movement and set it to the classic pop hits of Willie Nelson, Elvis Presley, and Nat King Cole. The following year he introduced the city to what would become its newest holiday tradition, *The Christmas Ballet*, a 180-degree departure from the traditional *Nutcracker* that includes a wild mix of traditional takes on J. S. Bach's *Magnificat* and obscure, whimsical pieces with titles like *Santa Got a DWI*. The group also premiered the world's first ballet set to mambo music, *Frankie and Johnny*. More recently it has taken to the road, performing in select U.S. cities. The home season starts in May; *The Christmas Ballet* is usually performed in early December. *Map:N3*

Film

San Francisco is one big film festival. If locals aren't stumbling over each other to attend a first-run documentary or an international premiere, they're stumbling over cables strewn across sidewalks by movie crews filming on location. These days, of course, the Bay Area is also a haven for independent filmmakers shunning the trappings of Tinseltown. And while the mighty multiplex has definitely reared its head here, there are still a few single-screen holdouts. At the **UNITED ARTISTS VOGUE** (3290 Sacramento St; 415/221-8183; map:J3), an intimate movie house with a postage stamp–size lobby, you can see first-run pictures produced by its parent company. The **UNITED ARTISTS CORONET** (3575 Geary Blvd; 415/752-4400; map:H3) may host a lot of blockbusters, but it's still a grand old stadium-style theater in the best moviegoing tradition. In the Marina district are two thriving throwbacks: **CINEMA 21** (2141 Chestnut St; 415/921-6720; map:J1), with its balcony and enormous curved screen, and the **PRESIDIO THEATER** (2340 Chestnut St; 415/922-1318; map:J1). In Pacific Heights, the **CLAY** (2261 Fillmore St; 415/352-0810; map:K3), built in 1910, is the oldest continuously operating movie house in town and, together with smaller complexes such as the Embarcadero and Opera Plaza Cinemas, is now owned by Landmark Theaters, the largest exhibitor of first-run international and art-house films in the country.

For a funkier repertory experience, the **ROXIE** (3117 16th St; 415/863-1087; map:L5) screens and distributes original works of all kinds, and it has one of the most eclectic lineups around. You never know what you'll find, but it's usually worth checking out—anything from a controversial documentary to the revival of Bruce Lee's *Enter the Dragon*. Another old chestnut is in the Mission District: the ornate 1908 **VICTORIA THEATRE** (2961 16th St; 415/863-7576; map:M6), with orchestra, mezzanine, and balcony seating. And then there's the king of all the San Francisco movie palaces, the gorgeous 1922 Timothy Pflueger–designed **CASTRO THEATRE** (469 Castro St; 415/621-6120; map:K6)—as vital today as it ever was, screening everything from special revivals and director's cuts to touring art-house flicks. To get the full effect of this place, arrive well before showtime to hear the organist pump out a rousing rendition of "San Francisco, Open Your Golden Gate" on the vintage pipe organ. For the really serious cinema hound, **YERBA BUENA CENTER FOR THE ARTS** (701 Mission St; 415/978-2787; www.yerbabuenaarts.org; map:N3) screens films geared to artistic, sociocultural, and academic perspectives—not snobbish symposia on dead French directors, but curated series on such esoteric themes as bizarre violence or women in prison.

Here's a look at the many annual film festivals held in San Francisco.

CINE ACCIÓN FESTIVAL / 346 9th St, 2nd floor; 415/553-8140 For a few days in September, San Francisco hosts one of the country's top celebrations of Latino cinema, highlighting full-length features, shorts, and other top-notch efforts from the United States, Latin America, and beyond. *www.cineaccion.com; map:N3*

FILM ARTS FOUNDATION FESTIVAL OF INDEPENDENT CINEMA / 346 9th St, and other venues; 415/552-8760 "Where independent film is still independent" is the motto of the Film Arts Foundation, and this event, held in November, lives up to the claim. It's a treasure trove of new, inventive, and locally grown cinema, presented by a nonprofit organization for Bay Area film- and video-makers. Since its inception the festival has launched such films as the Oscar-nominated *Complaints of a Dutiful Daughter*, *For Better or for Worse*, and *Waldo Salt*. Screenings are often held at the Roxie and Victoria theaters. The Film Arts Foundation of Independent Cinema also offers film- and video-related seminars and workshops, and an excellent magazine. *www.filmarts.com; map:N3*

SAN FRANCISCO ASIAN AMERICAN FILM FESTIVAL / 346 9th St, and other venues; 415/863-0814 Presented in early March by the National Asian American Telecommunications Association (NAATA), this event in the past 18 years has become the largest of its kind. More than 100 films and videos from more than a dozen countries are screened, from North America, the Pacific, and all Asian areas of the globe. Among the many works that have premiered here are the Academy Award–winning feature documentary *Maya Lin: A Strong Clear Vision*, Deepa Mehta's *Fire*, and Kayo Hatta's *Picture Bride*. Throughout the year, NAATA also presents several sneak previews, including local premieres of films such as *Shanghai Triad*, *The Wedding Banquet*, and *Farewell My Concubine*. *www.naatanet.org/festival; map:N3*

SAN FRANCISCO INTERNATIONAL FILM FESTIVAL / 1521 Eddy St, and other venues; 415/561-5000 This 43-year-old salute to cinema, presented by the prestigious San Francisco Film Society each April and May at the Kabuki, the Castro, and other Bay Area locations, is one of the best on the film-festival circuit. The opening gala is a star-studded event, bringing out such locally based luminaries as Sean Penn, Francis Ford Coppola, and Nicolas Cage, as well as Steven Spielberg or any other industry bigwigs who happen to be in town. Featured are new films by both well-known and up-and-coming filmmakers from around the world. The enormous list of works that have debuted here include *A Hard Day's Night*, *Gigi*, and *Scarface*. Special screenings of Bay Area–made films are a regular highlight and have unearthed such gems as the Oscar-nominated Vietnam documentary by Barbara Sonneborn, *Regret to Inform*. Each event features special tributes to actors and directors, many of whom accept the honor in person and discuss their work. *www.sfiff.org; map:K4*

SAN FRANCISCO INTERNATIONAL GAY & LESBIAN FILM FESTIVAL / 346 9th St, and other venues; 415/703-8650 The world's oldest, largest, and best festival of its kind celebrated its 24th year in 2000. Each year it screens more than 200 films, videos, and documentaries at the Castro, Roxie, and Victoria theaters. The event is one of the most talked about in the city; selections shown here often win national and international acclaim. Notable films from the 23rd festival included Jim Fall's hit comedy *Trick* and the U.S. premiere of the Swedish lesbian love story *Show Me Love*. Special appearances by directors and stars are always part of the fun. The festival promotes environmentally friendly modes of transportation and even offers valet-parking services for your bicycle if you ride it to a screening. *www.frameline.org; map:N3*

SAN FRANCISCO JEWISH FILM FESTIVAL / 346 9th St, and other venues; 415/552-3378 Each July and August in the Bay Area, the San Francisco Jewish Film Festival screens a diverse range of films that address the subjects of Jewish identity and history—some but not all of them by Jewish filmmakers. At about 20 years old, it's the longest-running celebration of Semitic cinema in the country. A typical lineup includes approximately 40 works, from Russian- and German-language films to heartrending documentaries to French features such as *Mina Tannenbaum. www.sfjff.org; map:N3*

Literature

There's much more to San Francisco's literary legacy than Danielle Steel. This is a decidedly writerly town, home to scribblers famous and unknown, highbrow, lowbrow, and everything in between. *Maltese Falcon* author Dashiell Hammett, who wrote most of his grittier mysteries here, put the city on the book lover's map when he placed Sam Spade's Continental Detective Agency in the Flood Building on Market Street (where Hammett worked a part-time day job at Pinkerton's Detective Agency in real life). The city returned the favor by naming a street after him—an honor it also bestowed on many other literary native sons and daughters. Cruising the city's streets, you'll come across signs bearing the names of Jack London, Mark Twain, Ambrose Bierce, Frank Norris, William Saroyan, and, of course, Kerouac and Ferlinghetti of Beat generation and City Lights Bookstore fame. The bookstore lives on in North Beach, as do former Beat hangouts like Vesuvio Cafe.

The bohemian trappings have changed, but today's San Francisco is still home to author readings, signings, and literary happenings galore. Several cafes hold scheduled or spontaneous poetry slams, and you'll find a full literary lineup at all the major (and most smaller) chain and independent bookstores in town, including **STACEY'S** (581 Market St; 415/421-4687; map:N3), the city's largest independent bookstore; the **BOOKSMITH** (1644 Haight St; 415/863-8688; map:I5) in the Haight-Ashbury neighborhood; and **MODERN TIMES BOOKSTORE** (888 Valencia St; 415/282-9246; map:L6) in the Mission District, which showcases local, socially conscious writers and young poets from California schools. And once a year, you can get it all in one place: every July, the Northern California Independent Booksellers Association (415/927-3937) presents **BOOKS BY THE BAY**, an outdoor festival with publishers' booths, author readings and signings, poetry-fests, and activities for kids. Year-round, here's where to look for other literary events.

CITY ARTS & LECTURES / Herbst Theatre; 401 Van Ness Ave (events); 180 Redwood Alley (information); 415/392-4400 Discussing everything from literature and criticism to science and performing arts, stellar intellects conduct enlightened conversations and monologues on the Herbst Theatre stage. Recent guests have included Jane Smiley, Stephen King,

Jamaica Kincaid, Saul Bellow, and Richard Price—all in the span of a month. Many programs benefit nonprofits such as the California Academy of Sciences, Friends of the San Francisco Public Library, and California Poets in the Schools. *Map:L4*

CITY LIGHTS BOOKSTORE / 261 Columbus Ave; 415/362-8193 The Beat goes on here, with poet-proprietor Lawrence Ferlinghetti still leading the charge. In the '50s, Ferlinghetti started a small press at this Columbus Avenue address to publish the works of comrades Allen Ginsberg, Jack Kerouac, and others. Today the shop has virtually everything ever written by those folks, along with an incredibly large selection of poetry and local writers' works. While you're not likely to stumble across any impromptu *Howls*, the store holds occasional signings and readings and is probably the best-known and best-loved bookstore in town. *www.citylights.com; map:N2*

A CLEAN WELL-LIGHTED PLACE FOR BOOKS / 601 Van Ness Ave; 415/441-6670 A favorite writers' hangout, this bookstore has shelf after shelf of literary journals, plus excellent fiction and nonfiction sections; many of the featured authors appear for book signings and discussions. *Map:L4*

A DIFFERENT LIGHT BOOKSTORE / 489 Castro St; 415/431-0891 The inventory here is entirely "by, about, or of interest to" gays and lesbians, the proprietors say. The small shop, run by a friendly staff, has a patio with a garden where readings are held. *Map:K6*

SAN FRANCISCO BAY AREA BOOK FESTIVAL / 415/487-4541 Presented by the Bay Area Book Council, the San Francisco Bay Area Book Festival is both a celebration of the written word and a resource for aspiring writers. Usually held over a weekend in October, it's a literary wonderland with writers new and old milling about; you're apt to stumble on inspired conversation, music, readings, poetry workshops, storytelling, panel discussions, and more. Local celebs from politicians to chefs turn out to give speeches or cooking demonstrations, promote a new book, or just browse. Would-be authors can attend seminars on how to get published or build confidence to present new work. *www.sfbook.org.*

NIGHTLIFE

Nightlife by Feature

ALTERNATIVE
Bottom of the Hill
Elbo Room
The Fillmore
Great American Music Hall
Make-Out Room
Paradise Lounge
Slim's
Warfield Theatre

BLUES
Bimbo's 365 Club
Biscuits & Blues
Blue Lamp
The Fillmore
Grant & Green Blue Club
Great American Music Hall
Harry's on Fillmore
John Lee Hooker's Boom
    Boom Room
Pier 23 Cafe
San Francisco Brewing
    Company
Warfield Theatre

CABARET
Beach Blanket Babylon–
    Club Fugazi
Cafe du Nord
Finocchio's
Paradise Lounge

CELTIC
An Bodhran
Fiddler's Green
Harrington's Bar and Grill
Irish Bank Bar and Grill
O'Reilly's Irish Bar
Plough & Stars

COCKTAIL LOUNGES
Backflip
Bimbo's 365 Club
Bix Restaurant
Bubble Lounge
Cafe du Nord
Cafe Mars
Club Deluxe
15 Romolo
Harry's on Fillmore
Hi-Ball Lounge
Julie's Supper Club
Marina Lounge
Martuni's

Mercury
Royal Oak
330 Ritch Street
Tosca Cafe

COMEDY
Cobb's Comedy Club
Punchline Comedy Club

DANCING/
DANCE FLOORS
Bimbo's 365 Club
Bottom of the Hill
The Cafe
Cafe du Nord
The Cat Club
Club Deluxe
Elbo Room
The End Up
Fiddler's Green
The Fillmore
Grant & Green Blue Club
Great American Music Hall
Hi-Ball Lounge
John Lee Hooker's Boom
    Boom Room
Make-Out Room
Mercury
Nickie's BBQ
Paradise Lounge
Pier 23 Cafe
Polly Esther's
Six
Slim's
Sound Factory
Storyville
The Stud
1015 Folsom
330 Ritch Street
The Top
Warfield Theatre

DRINKS WITH A VIEW
Buena Vista Cafe
Equinox
Pier 23 Cafe

FOLK/ACOUSTIC
An Bodhran
Fiddler's Green
Plough & Stars

GAY/LESBIAN BARS
The Cafe
The Eagle Tavern

The End Up
Lexington Club
The Stud
Twin Peaks Tavern

JAZZ
Bimbo's 365 Club
Bix
Blue Bar
Cafe du Nord
Club Deluxe
Enrico's
Gold Dust
Harry's on Fillmore
Jazz at Pearl's
    Restaurant & Bar
Rasselas Jazz Club and
    Ethiopian Cuisine
San Francisco Brewing
    Company
Storyville
Up & Down Club

OUTDOOR SEATING
Backflip
Blondie's
Bottom of the Hill
The Cafe
Cafe Mars
The Eagle Tavern
The End Up
Enrico's
Fiddler's Green
Harrington's Bar and Grill
Irish Bank Bar and Grill
O'Reilly's Irish Bar
Pier 23 Cafe
San Francisco Brewing
    Company

PIANO BARS
Gold Dust
Lone Palm
Martuni's

POOL TABLES/
BILLIARDS
Blondie's Bar and No Grill
Blue Lamp
Bus Stop
Cafe du Nord
Cafe Mars
Crow Bar
The Eagle Tavern

Elbo Room
The End Up
Fiddler's Green
Greens Sports Bar
Marina Lounge
Nickie's BBQ
Paradise Lounge
Plough & Stars
Sound Factory
The Stud
Thirsty Bear Brewing
    Company
330 Ritch Street
The Top

PUBS/ALE HOUSES

An Bodhran
Fiddler's Green
Gordon Biersch Brewery
    Restaurant
Harrington's Bar and Grill
Irish Bank Bar and Grill
O'Reilly's Irish Bar
Plough & Stars
San Francisco Brewing
    Company
Thirsty Bear Brewing
    Company
Toronado
Twenty Tank Brewery

REGGAE/SKA/ WORLD BEAT

Elbo Room
The End Up
Great American Music Hall
Nickie's BBQ
Paradise Lounge
Pier 23 Cafe
Warfield Theatre

ROCK

Bimbo's 365 Club
Blue Lamp
Bottom of the Hill
Elbo Room
The Fillmore
Grant & Green Blue Club
Great American Music Hall
John Lee Hooker's Boom
    Boom Room
Make-Out Room
Paradise Lounge
Pier 23 Cafe
Slim's
Warfield Theatre

ROMANTIC

Absinthe Brasserie and Bar
Bimbo's 365 Club
Enrico's
Hayes and Vine Wine Bar

Jazz at Pearl's
    Restaurant & Bar
Lone Palm
Martuni's
Rasselas Jazz Club and
    Ethiopian Cuisine

SPORTS BARS

Bus Stop
Greens Sports Bar

SWING

Bimbo's 365 Club
Cafe du Nord
Club Deluxe
Harry's on Fillmore
Hi-Ball Lounge
330 Ritch Street

UNDERAGE/ NO ALCOHOL

Beach Blanket Babylon–
    Club Fugazi
Cobb's Comedy Club
The Fillmore
Great American Music Hall
Punchline Comedy Club
Slim's
Warfield Theatre

Nightlife by Neighborhood

CASTRO
The Cafe
Cafe du Nord
Cafe Flore
Twin Peaks Tavern

CHINATOWN
Li Po

FINANCIAL DISTRICT
Bix
Bubble Lounge
Harrington's Bar and Grill
Irish Bank Bar and Grill
London Wine Bar
Pier 23 Cafe
Punchline Comedy Club

FISHERMAN'S WHARF
Buena Vista Cafe
Cobb's Comedy Club
Fiddler's Green

LOWER HAIGHT
An Bodhran
Nickie's BBQ
Storyville
The Top
Toronado

UPPER HAIGHT
Club Deluxe
Jammin' Java Coffee House
Persian Aub Zam Zam

HAYES VALLEY
Absinthe Brasserie and Bar
Hayes and Vine Wine Bar
Mad Magda's Russian Tea
    Room and Mystic Cafe

MARINA/COW HOLLOW
Balboa Cafe
Bepples Pie Shop

Bus Stop
Coffee Time
Comet Club
Marina Lounge

MISSION DISTRICT
Beauty Bar
Blondie's
Dalva
Elbo Room
Lexington Club
Lone Palm
Make-Out Room
Martuni's
Muddy Waters Coffee House
Skylark

NORTH BEACH
Beach Blanket Babylon–
    Club Fugazi
Bimbo's 365 Club
Blue Bar

NIGHTLIFE

Bubble Lounge
Caffe Greco
Caffe Puccini
Caffe Trieste
Crow Bar
Enrico's
15 Romolo
Finocchio's
Grant & Green Blue Club
Hi-Ball Lounge
Jazz at Pearl's Restaurant & Bar
The North End
O'Reilly's Irish Bar
The Saloon
San Francisco Brewing Company
Specs' Twelve Adler Museum Cafe
Steps of Rome
Tosca Cafe
Vesuvio Cafe
Zero Degrees

PACIFIC HEIGHTS
The Fillmore

Harry's on Fillmore
John Lee Hooker's Boom Boom Room
Rasselas Jazz Club and Ethiopian Cuisine

POTRERO HILL
Bottom of the Hill

RICHMOND DISTRICT
Joe's Ice Cream
Plough & Stars
Toy Boat Dessert Cafe
Trad'r Sam

RUSSIAN HILL
Greens Sports Bar
Royal Oak

SOUTH OF MARKET (SOMA)
Cafe Mars
The Cat Club
The Eagle Tavern
The End Up
Infusion Bar & Restaurant
Julie's Supper Club

Mercury
Paradise Lounge
Six
Slim's
Sound Factory
The Stud
1015 Folsom
Thirsty Bear Brewing Company
330 Ritch Street
Twenty Tank Brewery
Up & Down Club

TENDERLOIN
Backflip
Blue Lamp
Great American Music Hall
Polly Esther's

UNION SQUARE AND DOWNTOWN
Biscuits & Blues
Gold Dust
Warfield Theatre

NIGHTLIFE

Music and Clubs

Because San Francisco is such a cosmopolitan city, a lot of the club trends surface here before the rest of the country gets wind of them (well, aside from New York). Recently the sound reverberating through many of the hottest clubs was "drum and bass," but who knows when the next wave is going to hit? Most of the dance clubs are in the South of Market area (that's SoMa for you out-of-towners) and in the Mission District. Don't be surprised if you walk into a club that someone told you was just your kind of scene and you find it's completely not. Most of the clubs change the style of the party every night. For example, a club might be gay on Thursday, a rave on Friday, techno on Saturday . . . well, you get the point. If there's a particular club you're set on visiting, call first and find out what's doing that night.

For more information on what's going on in the city, you can also check the entertainment listings in the tabloid-size *San Francisco Bay Guardian* or *SF Weekly*. Both are free weeklies that come out every Wednesday and can be found all over the city in newspaper racks or coffeehouses. A good online resource is San Francisco CitySearch (www.bay area.citysearch.com). For even more up-to-the-minute info you just can't get in the papers, call the **BE-AT LINE** (415/626-4087) and listen to a recording of daily updates on the hip-hop, house, and acid jazz scene; **HOUSE-WARES** (415/281-0125) for the rave and techno action; or the **CLUB LINE** (415/339-8686) for the more mainstream dance clubs. The following is a list of venues and clubs that will most likely be around for your next night on the town, but definitely phone before you go to make sure.

Note: San Francisco has officially banned smoking in all bars, clubs, and restaurants, though not all bars enforce the controversial law.

BACKFLIP / 601 Eddy St; 415/771-3547 The Phoenix Hotel houses this ultracool, aqua-blue cocktail lounge that's supposed to resemble a swimming pool, complete with a deep end (a few shots helps the illusion—though there is a pool off the courtyard). In the middle of the seedy Tenderloin neighborhood, it's an oasis of trendy nightlife. On the weekends the hiply dressed crowd of twentysomethings waits in line to drink and pseudo-dance (it's too crowded to let loose) to anything from ambient to techno music spun by an international set of visiting DJs. There is a menu of "small plates" of cocktail-type food. On a rare warm night you'll want to sit out by the real pool, which was designed by Andy Warhol. *Full bar; AE, MC, V; no checks; Tues–Sun; map:M4*

BEACH BLANKET BABYLON–CLUB FUGAZI / 678 Green St; 415/421-4222 North Beach's Club Fugazi is the exclusive home to this campy and very San Francisco cabaret extravaganza, which has been playing to sold-out audiences for more than 25 years. In the early '70s Steve Silver created a show of fantastic characters with kooky costumes and stage sets. Silver died in 1994, but his everlasting freak show parties on. The main story of the comedic musical revue remains the same, but it gets a periodic shot in the arm with updated spoofs on whatever happens to be in the news at the moment, so it's a little different every time you go. The performers can really belt out the tunes, but the real showstoppers are the phenomenal hats, which can weigh up to 100 pounds and are engineered to pull off some amazing special effects. This show is extremely popular with locals and tourists, so advance ticket purchase is highly recommended. Tickets designate seating in a certain area, but within that area seats are first-come, first-served, so line up early with the rest of the crowd to get a good spot. Drinks are served at all but the Sunday matinee performances, where patrons under 21 are allowed. A photo ID is required for the evening shows. Call for box office hours and show times. *Full bar; MC, V; no checks; Wed–Sun; map:N2*

BIMBO'S 365 CLUB / 1025 Columbus Ave; 415/474-0365 No, this isn't a great place to pick up empty-headed, silicone-implanted babes. Bimbo's has been owned by the same family since it opened in 1931 and is named after the family patriarch. Through the years and ever-changing styles this North Beach club has kept its swanky interior intact. The naughty paintings of large-busted mermaids and the nude girl riding the giant goldfish on your cocktail napkin remind you of a simpler, less politically correct time. The powder room attendant makes even a '90s woman feel like Holly Golightly. The kind of crowd varies with the live entertainment for the evening, and that could be anything—country, rock, jazz, R&B—you name it. Call for the schedule. *Full bar; no credit cards, no checks; dates depend on shows; www.bimbos365club.com; map:M1* &

BISCUITS & BLUES / 401 Mason St; 415/292-2583 Just off Union Square you'll find this underground supper club serving good Southern food and live blues. Some of the best local and national blues players perform here nightly. Chances are whatever night you come, you're in for a good show. The dim candlelit tables and the New Orleans speakeasy theme set the mood. When things get cooking here it gets loud and conversations stop, so order up some fried chicken and sit back and listen. *Full bar; AE, MC, V; no checks; every day; map:M3*

BLUE BAR / 501 Broadway; 415/981-2233 Downstairs from Reed Hearon's Black Cat Restaurant is a small, dark, cozy little jazz club. The plush decor of crushed velvet and a blue backlit bar make this a swanky little stop for the "in" 30- to 40-something crowd. North Beach used to be famous for its jazz; the music scene is now having a renaissance with new clubs opening all over. The Blue Bar even hosts some jazz and poetry nights (Jack Kerouac's rolling in his grave). You can order from the club menu (a shortened version of the restaurant's pricey offerings) until 1am. *Full bar; AE, MC, V; no checks; every day; map:N2*

BLUE LAMP / 561 Geary St; 415/885-1464 It's small, dark, and dusty and it's covered in red-velvet-flocked wallpaper—how much cooler can a place get? It also has a great bar, a pool table, and a foosball table, and it rocks every night with loud live music. The neighborhood is a weird mix of the Tenderloin homeless and hoity-toity theatergoers, but once you're inside the bar the crowd is mostly music-and-beer-loving locals. Weekends are usually for rock bands, with a special blues jam session on Sundays. *Full bar; no credit cards; no checks; every day; map:M3* &

BOTTOM OF THE HILL / 1233 17th St; 415/621-4455 This Potrero Hill live music venue is out of the way but worth the trip. There's not much else out in these parts, but once you get into the club for a good night of local indie music there's no reason to leave. You've probably never heard of the bands that play here—it's a small place, and once a band makes it big it moves on to larger clubs, so this is a great opportunity to listen to the newest cutting-edge music. There's an outside patio area to get a breath of fresh air and give your ears a rest, as well as a pool table. Most Sundays there's an incredibly cheap all-you-can-eat barbecue with the music included. *Full bar; MC, V; no checks; every day; map:O6* &

THE CAFE / 2367 Market St; 415/861-3846 This Castro-area gay and lesbian dance club is all about having a good time. There's no cover, and the place gets packed and sweaty as the mostly young, hip crowd shimmies their booties off to the extremely danceable sounds of techno, house, '80s, and disco. There's a patio outside to take a breather and a few tables near the back. Earlier in the evening locals come by for a more mellow scene of beer drinking and pool playing. But when the music starts, the party begins, and goes on and on until last call. Even then the fun continues with everybody spilling out into the street, where the pickup scene is at its spiciest. *Full bar; no credit cards; no checks; every day; map:K6*

CAFE DU NORD / 2170 Market St; 415/861-5016 When you know you're in a club that used to be a speakeasy, it just makes you feel a little naughtier. Cafe du Nord has been a hot spot for a few years now and attracts a young, chic crowd. The place does serve dinner, but most of the people are here for the nightlife. The front area consists of a beautiful, long carved-wood bar and a dining room where the club patrons take over when dinner hours are through. The back room is the cabaret area, where musicians play swing, jazz, or salsa to a packed house. Sunday evenings there are free dance lessons. *Full bar; AE, DC, MC, V; no checks; every day; www.cafedunord.com; map:K6*

THE CAT CLUB / 1190 Folsom St; 415/431-3332 The newly remodeled Cat Club caters to a mixed crowd, and everyone's welcome here regardless of sexual (or any other) orientation. There are two dance floors; DJs spinning from up above the masses turn up anything from techno to funk. The Cat Club's most famous night is Bondage a Go-Go, a fun techno-driven fetish fest every Wednesday that even the bridge-and-tunnel crowd can appreciate (that means it won't scare the pants off you unless you're a major prude). *Full bar; AE, MC, V; no checks; every day; map:N4* &

CLUB DELUXE / 1511 Haight St; 415/552-6949 Many people say the '90s cocktail-lounge craze started here at the Deluxe. It sounds right, when you first walk up to the silver metal exterior and through that art deco door. It hits home even harder when you hear owner Jay Johnson crooning away in his special tribute to the Chairman himself on Frank Sinatra Night. This small Haight Street bar gets packed every weekend, with swingers and their dolls at every table and lining the bar in their slick duds. During the week it's still popular but a little mellower. The only drawback: there's no space to really dance to the hot tunes of the live bands. Oh well, just throw back another Manhattan and tap those toes to the swingin' beat. *Full bar; no credit cards; no checks; every day; map:I5* &

COBB'S COMEDY CLUB / 2801 Leavenworth St; 415/928-4320 Housed in the Cannery building near Fisherman's Wharf, this club features mostly mainstream comedians. With its wharf location, it caters to a largely tourist crowd; ergo, the comics usually make jokes about different nationalities and San Franciscans. The place is windowless yet intimate, and when a good comedian is onstage that intimacy can really work (hence all the couples on first and second dates). Tip: If you don't want to get picked on by the comic, sit in the back. There's a two-drink minimum and some bar-type food available (chicken wings and the like). *Full bar; MC, V; no checks; every day; map:M1* &

ELBO ROOM / 647 Valencia St; 415/552-7788 This bohemian joint in the Mission houses a comfortable bar with pool tables, a jukebox downstairs, and a kind of rec-room live music bar upstairs. It's purposely dim and moody and caters to a young, casual crowd. The live music ranges from jazz to hip-hop to funk. Both the upstairs and downstairs bars have some good beers and pour a strong drink. Check out the photo booth and get a few snaps of yourself and a buddy. *Full bar; no credit cards; no checks; every day; www.elbo.com; map:L6*

THE BARBARY COAST

In 1849 San Francisco boomed as thousands of people headed west to find gold. What was once a small town of about 1,000 soon became an international port city of nearly 100,000. Those who came to find their fortunes were named forty-niners after the year they arrived (a few months after gold was discovered in the Sierra foothills). Most of the arrivals weren't what you'd call proper gentlemen, and with so many of these unsavory characters descending upon the city a district was soon formed to cater to their carousing. That area—where parts of the Embarcadero, Chinatown, and North Beach neighborhoods now exist—was called the Barbary Coast after the infamous region of the same name in North Africa.

The Barbary Coast remained the seedy nightlife epicenter of San Francisco for close to 70 years, evolving from the raucous haunts of miners and prostitutes to the more refined—yet still illegal—speakeasies of Prohibition. It was this underground legacy that drew the social misfits of the '50s—the Beats and their followers, the beatniks—to North Beach. While there are still some strip clubs along the main drag of Broadway, most of the area shows little sign of its bawdy past—unless you look closely.

Some of the bars in North Beach pay homage to the denizens of the Barbary Coast. Stop in at the **San Francisco Brewing Company** (155 Columbus Ave; 415/434-3344) and ask for an Emperor Norton brew, named after the self-proclaimed emperor whose eccentricities endeared him to San Franciscans. This microbrewery is housed in what is believed to be one of the last standing Barbary Coast saloons. Look down at the tiled trough running along the base of the bar, which once funneled off tobacco spit . . . and *other* liquids. (These troughs are present in some other area bars, but are usually covered with a wood plank.)

Other small glimpses of the past can be had at the **Saloon** (1232 Grant Ave; 415/989-7666), one of the oldest bars in the city. While mostly a local hangout, it's still a good place for visitors to stop for a drink and see what a Barbary Coast saloon looked like in its heyday (there's that trough again). Off Columbus Avenue near Broadway, down a tiny alley, you'll find **Specs' Twelve Adler Museum Cafe** (12 Saroyan Pl; 415/421-4112). Specs' has gone through many transformations since its inception as a bordello, and proudly displays artifacts of all its past lives—including a certain whale appendage. It may have been a century and a half ago, but it takes just a moment in one of these haunts to feel the presence of the revelers of the old Barbary Coast.

THE END UP / 401 6th St; 415/357-0827 This hard-core club is mainly for the after-hours set and not for the faint of heart. The DJ music scene changes nightly but mostly caters to the gay club crowd. On Mondays and Wednesdays the End Up houses Club Dread, a mellow reggae club;

on Saturdays the lesbian crowd takes over for G-Spot. On Sunday at about 5:30am gay clubbers come from all the other late-night spots to "end up" at the Sunday T Dance, which lasts until 2 Monday morning. Needless to say, the crowd here looks like the slightly warmed-over living dead at certain times. *Full bar; no credit cards; no checks; every day; map:N4* &

FIDDLER'S GREEN / 1333 Columbus Ave; 415/441-9758 This Irish pub in the wharf area on the outskirts of North Beach is of two minds. There's the downstairs bar where most of the crowd is throwing back pints and listening to a guitar player sing Irish folk songs and U2 covers, and then there's the upstairs bar, which packs in a crowd of European tourists and a few locals dancing to the DJs spinning Euro-cool rave and house tunes. It's a young bunch upstairs, especially in summer when the college kids come over with their student visas. Downstairs is a mixed bag, where the locals grudgingly share the bar with the lowly tourists and by the end of the night everyone has become friends. Ah, the power of a few pints of Guinness. Fiddler's also sports a great pub menu. *Full bar; MC, V; no checks; every day; map:N2*

THE FILLMORE / 1805 Geary Blvd; 415/346-6000 The historic Fillmore started out its life as a dance hall in the early 1900s, but became world famous when promoter Bill Graham turned the space into the epicenter of live music concerts in the late '60s. Jimi Hendrix, Janis Joplin, the Grateful Dead, and every other important band of that era played here at one time or another. The Fillmore still hosts most of the big-name acts that come into the city, and even though the capacity is about 1,000, it still feels intimate when you go to a show. Check out the poster room upstairs for a psychedelic journey through the days of flower power. On your way out grab a free apple, a tradition started by Graham in the '60s that survives to this day. *Full bar; AE, MC, V; call for show dates; www.thefillmore.com; map:K3* &

FINOCCHIO'S / 506 Broadway; 415/982-9388 This family-owned female impersonators' cabaret has been a North Beach institution for over 60 years. The grande dames do three shows a night and will surprise you with their resemblance to such stars as Madonna, Carmen Miranda, and Tina Turner. A couple of the veterans do a little shtick in between numbers to keep you interested, and they'll often incorporate the audience into the act. Try to sit up front and get a good look at these talented men—er, ladies. There is no dress code, but it's much more fun to get all dolled up and really immerse yourself in the scene. Although the crowd is mixed socially, this place is only for 21 and older. *Full bar; no credit cards; no checks; Thurs–Sat; map:N2*

GRANT & GREEN BLUE CLUB / 1371 Grant Ave; 415/693-9565 This medium-size joint in the heart of North Beach presents local blues acts every night. The dress and attitude is casual and the crowd is a strange mix of cool locals, red-nosed old-timers, and the occasional overdressed couple from the burbs. The blues bands rock *loudly,* and the noise reverberating down the block is what draws all these different types in—it just sounds like there's too much fun going on in there. *Full bar; no credit cards; no checks; every day; map:N2*

GREAT AMERICAN MUSIC HALL / 859 O'Farrell St; 415/885-0750 This ornate Victorian beauty once housed a bordello and restaurant in the early 1900s. Now it's a live music venue, and fortunately no one ever tried to change the decor over the years. You can't help but marvel at the marble columns holding up the massive balcony below the elaborately frescoed ceiling. It's one of the coolest San Francisco experiences to sit and listen to some band that you really dig in the middle of this amazing old building where the city's finest illicit night-lifers once reigned. But besides being a historic treasure, it also books some great music acts running the gamut from alternative to rock to country. *Full bar; MC, V; no checks; every day; www.musichallsf.com; map:L3* &

HARRY'S ON FILLMORE / 2020 Fillmore St; 415/921-1000 Located on a quiet section of Fillmore Street, Harry's is a comfortable and classy place to have a meal and a few drinks while listening to some hot jazz or cool funk. This is San Francisco bon vivant Harry Denton's first bar. The crowd can vary from old-timers to college kids. It's a nice place for a laid-back evening. *Full bar; AE, DC, MC, V; no checks; every day; map:K3* &

HI-BALL LOUNGE / 473 Broadway; 415/397-9464 When you look up retro in the dictionary, the caption should read "see Hi-Ball Lounge." It's a small space but smartly arranged, with comfy booths lining the walls and intimate tables in between. There's a small dance floor in front of a red-velvet-draped stage where local and visiting bands play to the young swingers. Some nights the dancers are out-of-control hot, but most of the time you won't feel too stupid joining them. There are lessons early in the evening on certain nights; call to find out when. *Full bar; MC, V; no checks; every day; www.hiball.com; map:N2* &

JAZZ AT PEARL'S RESTAURANT & BAR / 256 Columbus Ave; 415/291-8255 Pearl's is an elegant, old-time North Beach jazz club with exposed brick walls hung with old pictures of jazz legends. This is the place to go in San Francisco to hear the local talent, which plays every night of the week. The intimate tables are a great place for couples to gaze into each other's eyes. While there is no cover, there's a two-drink minimum and the bar specializes in froufrou-type drinks. *Full bar; AE, MC, V; no checks; every day (call for Sun); map:N2*

JOHN LEE HOOKER'S BOOM BOOM ROOM / 1601 Fillmore St; 415/673-8000 John Lee Hooker bought this neighborhood hangout a couple of years back, and he and partner Alex Andreas have renovated it into one of the best blues clubs in the city. When a big-name act plays here it can get cramped and steamy, just like a blues club should. It's a great place to grab a few drinks before a show at the Fillmore (see above), then come back after a show lets out early. Last time the Rolling Stones were in town they came here for a jam session unannounced. You never know who might show up. *Full bar; no credit cards; no checks; every day; boomboomblues.com; map:K3* &

MAKE-OUT ROOM / 3225 22nd St; 415/647-2888 Right now this Mission District spot is a hipster haven, but by the time you finish reading this sentence who knows if it still will be. Either way, it's a cool dive with an even cooler name, although there's not as much spit-swapping as you'd expect with that moniker. It's basically a large room with a huge oak bar and a couple of booths, decorated with some deer heads. Local indie bands play on the small stage a couple of times a month, and it can get crowded on the weekends. *Full bar; no credit cards; no checks; every day; map:L6* &

MERCURY / 540 Howard St; 415/777-1419 Club master Dr. Winkie just opened his latest club/restaurant, and already the restaurant part has closed. Hopefully the club will be around for a while because it's simply too fabulous. Every detail is done up to the extremes—even the staff wears ultramodern uniforms. There are three different bar scenes inside: the Feather Lounge, decorated in black and white and located downstairs; the Pearl Bar, all pearlized and pretty; and the Mirror Bar, covered with small mirrors with a spectacle of a rhinestone deer head glinting in the lights. No, we're not making this up. The DJs spin a variety of tunes and, depending on where you are in the club, you can be mellow and ambient, groove to the techno dance, or drink up to some lounge-style tunes. *Full bar; AE, DC, MC, V; no checks; Mon–Sat; map:N3* &

NICKIE'S BBQ / 460 Haight St; 415/621-6508 If you like your dance clubs small, intimate, and sweaty, then Nickie's is your place. A young and pretty crowd comes to this Lower Haight club to get down and man, do they ever. The small dance area is packed every night and each night is a different DJ scene, from Grateful Dead Jam early in the week warming up to funk and disco by the weekend. Be careful when coming in and out of Nickie's since the neighborhood is a little sketchy. *Full bar; no credit cards; no checks; Thurs–Tues; www.nickies.com; map:L5*

PARADISE LOUNGE / 1501 Folsom St; 415/861-6906 Live music is the focus for this SoMa club. It's a huge industrial structure that has four different stages and multiple bars. The Blue Room is the main venue with its dance floor, elevated stage, and balcony seating. Adjacent is the lounge, where lesser-known bands strive to be heard, and upstairs is Above Paradise, where acoustic bands play and a pool room shares space with the bar. Next door the Transmission Theater hosts indie bands in an old garage that is attached to Paradise through a side door. The age range can be from early 20s to late 40s depending on the entertainment that evening, and the crowd tends to be pretty casual and laid back. *Full bar; MC, V; no checks; every day; map:M5* &

PIER 23 CAFE / Pier 23, The Embarcadero; 415/362-5125 This is where postcollegiate overgrown frat boys and the girls who love them go to get lucky. Pier 23 is prime property with its heated deck right on the water and great views of the Bay Bridge. When a good reggae, Latin, or soul band plays, the crowd really heats up on the small dance floor. Expect to wait in line on the weekends. The Long Island Iced Tea is frickin' expensive but hoo-boy good. *Full bar; MC, V; no checks; every day; map:N1* &

POLLY ESTHER'S / 181 Eddy St; 415/885-1977 When a hip New York club chain tries to take over the world, the result is Polly Esther's. It's a theme-based amusement center for those who grew up in the '70s and '80s. The upstairs is decorated in '70s kitsch, Twister boards, smiley faces, and wooden cutouts of the Brady Bunch. The downstairs does the same thing with '80s memorabilia and is called the "Culture Club." The DJs in both parts of the club play music that matches the era—disco, new wave, and so on. The bar makes some sticky specialty drinks with catchy names that are better left alone. Basically, it's good clean fun for overgrown kids. Careful when heading out—the Tenderloin area is kind of seedy. *Full bar; AE, CB, DC, DIS, MC, V; no checks; Thurs–Sat; www.pollyesthers.com; map:M3* &

PUNCHLINE COMEDY CLUB / 444 Battery St; 415/397-7573 This downtown comedy club is usually packed on the weekends and—believe it or not—is a great place to meet people. The tables seat four people, and if you come with a friend you'll be seated with another twosome. Top names in comedy perform here, and there are also nights devoted to local rising stars. It's a small, intimate theater where almost all the seats have a good view of the stage. Most shows are for ages 18 and over and require a two-drink minimum (nonalcoholic for those under 21, of course). FYI, local hero Robin Williams got his start here. *Full bar; AE, MC, V; no checks; Tues–Sun; map:N2* &

RASSELAS JAZZ CLUB AND ETHIOPIAN CUISINE / 2801 California St; 415/567-5010 Rasselas is a casually comfortable jazz club consisting of small tables and overstuffed couches occupied by people looking to hear local jazz bands. It's not pretentious or trying to be anything it's not. Rather, it's local San Franciscans hanging out and listening to some cool tunes. Mellow, baby. The bands that play here aren't usually famous, but they are quality musicians and always entertaining. The dining room next door serves up authentic Ethiopian meals. *Full bar; AE, CB, DC, MC, V; no checks; every day; map:J3* &

SIX / 60 6th St; 415/863-1221 This is the newest and most happening of the city's hard-core dance clubs for those brave enough to head into its rough neighborhood. Inside, the dance floor is big, and as word gets out it's getting more and more crowded on the weekends. The DJs spin techno and house for the young single crowd. Upstairs is a multicolored chill zone for taking it easy between dance sessions. Be careful in this area when walking to and from your car, and don't travel alone. *Full bar; no credit cards; no checks; Fri–Sat; map:M4*

SLIM'S / 333 11th St; 415/522-0333 One of the best local venues for live music, Slim's brings in some of the finest rock and alternative bands. The combination of a smokin' sound system, big dance floor, high ceilings, and expansive bar makes this a great place to enjoy good music. The crowd is usually casually dressed and friendly, and ranges in age depending on the entertainment. There's a pretty good pub menu for those who arrive early and can manage to get a table. *Full bar; MC, V; no checks; call for show dates; map:M5* &

SOUND FACTORY / 525 Harrison St; 415/339-8686 With new clubs opening all the time, it's amazing that people are still lining up to get into the aging Sound Factory, but they are. It's a gigantic behemoth of a club that's been divided into a bunch of different miniclubs, with something for everyone—live music, DJs, techno, drum and bass, and more. There's one giant main dance area, another smaller (but still pretty big) dance area called the Conga Room, and yet another dance floor called the Blue Room. Scattered throughout are busy bars selling overpriced water and drinks. There's also a pool room and a sky lounge (where you can look down on the dancers), and little rooms here and there to chill out and people-watch. *Full bar; no credit cards; no checks; Fri–Sat; map:N3* &

STORYVILLE / 1751 Fulton St; 415/441-1751 Storyville started out a couple of years ago as a classic jazz club but has loosened its description to include some other varieties such as acid jazz, drum and bass, and ambient sounds. It's a dark place with a mostly local crowd in front listening to live jazz or blues. In back the bigger names play, or DJs come in to spin for a dancing crowd. There's no cover, but there is a two-drink minimum of well-poured cocktails. *Full bar; AE, CB, DC, DIS, MC, V; no checks; Tues–Sat; map:J4* &

THE STUD / 399 9th St; 415/863-6623 This famous gay and lesbian hangout has been around for over 30 years. A laid-back crowd plays pool and pinball or dances to DJ music while the cute bartenders keep the liquor flowing. There are always some people standing around outside waiting to get in, but it's usually not long before you're in the door. The welcoming atmosphere and the casual clientele make this bar great for first-timers to the gay bar scene. "Trannyshack" is one of the most popular nights due to the amateur drag show. *Full bar; no credit cards; no checks; every day; map:M4*

1015 FOLSOM / 1015 Folsom St; 415/431-1200 1015 (say "ten-fifteen") is a SoMa after-hours dance club mainstay. Its popularity comes and goes with the local clubbers, but on weekends it's always packed. The three-story multiroom structure houses one of the city's largest dance floors, with international DJs spinning techno and house. There are smaller rooms with music ranging from light and danceable to mellow and ambient; the basement hosts the more experimental DJs. There are six bars, so it's easy to refresh yourself between sweaty dance sessions. Every Sunday (except the first one of the month) it's home to Spundae, the infamous techno party for those who just can't let their weekend end. Note: As of press time the club and the cops had been on less-than-amiable terms, so it might close down. *Full bar; no credit cards; no checks; Wed–Sun; www.1015.com; map:N4* &

330 RITCH STREET / 330 Ritch St; 415/522-9558 Hip techies known as the digerati frequent this SoMa supper club. The neighborhood has been called Multimedia Gulch because it's home to a lot of the Internet start-up companies, and 330 Ritch capitalizes on entertaining these young and newly rich. There is a different scene every night, so call first for the schedule: Wednesday is Swing and Lounge night with free dance lessons, and Friday there's no cover charge. There are pool tables in the back and comfy booths for dining on fusion cuisine and throwing back a few pints (they have a great beer selection). *Full bar; AE, MC, V; no checks; Wed–Sun; www.sf-nite.com; map:O4* &

THE TOP / 424 Haight St; 415/864-7386 This is not a place to bring a date or anyone else you are interested in talking to. This is a place to shut up and dance to the superloud sounds of the DJ-spun techno, house, and disco music on a crowded dance floor of young ravers. It's cheap, it's fun, and it's loud. They also have pool tables, but you've got to play early, before the crowds show up. It's a great singles scene, although you'd have to actually leave the club to hear your new friend's name. Did we mention it's loud? *Full bar; no credit cards; no checks; every day; map:L5*

UP & DOWN CLUB / 1151 Folsom St; 415/626-8862 A trendy, professional crowd hangs out at this small, popular SoMa jazz and supper club. The style of jazz veers toward newer styles of acid and fusion. It gets really crowded in here, so your best bet is to try to get in for dinner and stay for the show. If you hang at the bar you'll be able to hear the music but may not be able to see the performers. *Full bar; AE, V; no checks; Mon, Wed–Sat; map:M5*

WARFIELD THEATRE / 982 Market St; 415/775-7722 This old-time theater was built in the 1920s, but big-name rock acts have played in the opulent space since the early '70s. Although it holds about 2,250 people, it somehow has the feel of an intimate club. The downstairs has a large dance floor in front of the elevated stage and an area for standing right behind the dance floor near the conveniently located bars. Toward the back are tables that can be reserved. Upstairs the balcony has theater seating. Depending on the show you can choose which area you want to be in. The Warfield brings in all types of major artists from the rock, rap, country, and alternative scenes. *Full bar; AE, MC, V; no checks; call for show dates; map:M4* &

Bars, Pubs, and Taverns

San Francisco is teeming with bars in every neighborhood. The following is a sampling of some of the best. Keep in mind, though, that it's exploring the unknown that makes a trip an adventure. This is a good guide to start your journey, but go out and find some new places on your own.

ABSINTHE BRASSERIE AND BAR / 398 Hayes St; 415/551-1590 This stylish French brasserie doesn't serve up the illicit beverage absinthe, but makes up for it with its menu of deadly cocktails. The sexy-sounding drinks go down smooth, but don't let the good taste fool you—they'll kick your butt if you don't sip slowly. Hang out in the lovely 1920s-style bar for a couple of hours nursing a tasty concoction and nibbling on a cheese plate or a decadent dessert. The crowd is hip, well dressed, and somewhat sophisticated. The bar is a fun place to sit and flirt, and the little tables are nice for couples. See also the review in the Restaurants chapter. *Full bar; AE, DC, DIS, MC, V; no checks; Tues–Sun; map:L4* &

AN BODHRAN / 668 Haight St; 415/431-4724 Pronounced BOW-rahn (a traditional Irish drum), this very Celtic Lower Haight bar has become popular with a good-looking crowd of Irish emigrés. The front of the bar has a few tables for conversational clusters, and the more open back room is usually crowded with young people drinking Guinness and talking over the loud *Trainspotting*-type soundtrack. On Sundays there's a traditional Irish music jam session that shouldn't be missed. *Full bar; AE, MC, V; no checks; every day; map:K5* &

BALBOA CAFE / 3199 Fillmore St; 415/921-3944 The city's beautiful, single, and overpaid pack themselves into this Marina pickup bar. Boys smoke cigars (yes, some jokers are still doing that) and girls look appropriately sexy. It's a classic old-school bar with the requisite brass and wood. Expect a stiff drink, a great burger, and a phone number by the end of the evening. *Full bar; AE, DC, MC, V; no checks; every day; map:K2* &

BEAUTY BAR / 2299 Mission St; 415/285-0323 Don't be thrown off by the chrome-domed hair dryers or the manicurist who's actually doing someone's nails—this is really a bar. The owners of this Mission District hot spot transported an entire vintage beauty salon from Long Island to create the magic that is the Beauty Bar. It's already worked in New York, and this place just keeps getting more popular here. It's a young, hip crowd that digs the novelty but stays for the laid-back atmosphere. *Full bar; no credit cards; no checks; every day; map:L7*

BIX / 56 Gold St; 415/433-6300 Named after jazz legend Bix Beiderbecke, this 1930s-style supper club attracts a professional cocktail-sipping crowd (the Bix cocktail is a San Francisco staple). It's a sophisticated scene with white-jacketed bartenders pouring strong drinks and live jazz in the background. Local politicians and high powered business types rule this Financial District haunt. See also the review in the Restaurants chapter. *Full bar; AE, CB, DC, DIS, MC, V; no checks; every day; map:N2* &

BLONDIE'S BAR & NO GRILL / 540 Valencia St; 415/864-2419 Sometimes there's just nothing better than sitting outside and drinking a giant neon-blue martini. Blondie's packs in the fresh-faced cool crowd nightly to its open, airy space. There's a long martini menu, with the Blue Funk mentioned above as the specialty. The friendly bartenders always give you the shaker to refill your glass, so it's rare to order more than one martini per person. There are a couple of pool tables and live music on Saturday nights. *Full bar; no credit cards; no checks; every day; map:L6* &

BUBBLE LOUNGE / 714 Montgomery St; 415/434-4204 This super-chichi champagne bar is populated by the city's stylish and sophisticated, but is surprisingly comfortable and even fun. With over 300 types of champagne and sparkling wines, ordering can be a little intimidating, but the knowledgeable staff is helpful and friendly. If you prefer to forgo the bubbles, there's a full bar as well. The upstairs is more of a dig-me scene where people are checking each other out, but the downstairs Krug Room is intimate and laid back. There are also some equally extravagant treats to complement your bubbly, ranging from foie gras to caviar or something off the sushi cart. *Full bar; AE, DC, MC, V; no checks; Mon–Sat; map:N2* &

BUENA VISTA CAFE / 2765 Hyde St; 415/474-5044 Irish coffee. That's all that needs to be said about this San Francisco landmark. Located at the end of the Hyde Street cable car line, the Buena Vista was the first bar in the country to serve Irish coffee after a local journalist came back from a trip and described the concoction to his favorite bartender. The story is told in articles and stories posted all over the bar. Watch the bartenders line up the glasses and masterfully (or messily, depending on one's opinion) pour out the drinks. There's a large tourist crowd here because of the proximity to the wharf and cable car line. *Full bar; no credit cards; no checks; every day; map:M1* &

BUS STOP / 1901 Union St; 415/567-6905 If you want to watch 49er fans at their rowdiest, this is the place to go. This Cow Hollow sports bar fills up fast when a big game is on, so get here early to snag a seat. The Gap-clad patrons watch their favorite teams over some beers in a loud but laid-back scene. The bar's not very big, but it's split into different areas to help break the crowd up and have more walls to put TVs on. In the back are a couple of pool tables you can lean on to watch the game. *Full bar; no credit cards; no checks; every day; map:K2*

CAFE MARS / 798 Brannan St; 415/621-6277 The Jetsons decor, cool patio, strong drinks, and great music draws the 20- to 30-something urbanites to this popular SoMa hangout. It's a fun, festive atmosphere, and the friendly bartenders make a mean Martian martini. When Mars is really grooving, don't be surprised to see women dancing on the bar. There's also a bar menu of cosmic goodies. The heated patio is prime property, as is the pool room. The background music is jazzy and unobtrusive, but really starts pumping on weekend nights. This area is sketchy at night, so watch it on the way back to your car. *Full bar; AE, MC, V; no checks; every day; map:N5* &

COMET CLUB / 3111 Fillmore St; 415/567-5589 The Comet Club looks mighty weird from the outside—some sort of cosmic-themed funky metallic silver paint scheme—but it's a hopping singles scene inside with the Marina's prowling young ones checking each other out. It's a casual bar that can get crowded and loud as you try to talk over the pumping disco music. This is a good place to end your evening of debauchery along Union and Fillmore Streets. *Full bar; MC, V; no checks; Tues–Sat; map:K2* &

CROW BAR / 401 Broadway; 415/788-2769 People love this huge dark bar in North Beach because it makes no promises: it's just a bar. All types congregate here peacefully, from the after-work Financial District suit set to your basic pierced and tattooed pool shark. It's a supercasual place to throw back one of the many beers or scotches available and unwind from a hard day's whatever. There's a great jukebox with a mix of classic and cutting-edge music, as well as pool tables and darts. *Full bar; cash only; every day; map:N2* &

DALVA / 3121 16th St; 415/252-7740 This ultracool bar in the gentrified Mission District is usually full of cute young professionals sipping on margaritas, fine scotch, or the house sangría. Dalva also has an extensive menu of beers including some great Belgian ales. The bar is small but moody with red walls and dim lighting. There's a small back room that gets crowded on the weekends. Later in the evening DJs come in to spin ambient and drum-and-bass music as a background to intimate conversations. Here's a little secret: The hostess from the crepe restaurant across the street, Ti Couz, will come over and get you at Dalva when your table is ready. *Full bar; cash only; every day; www.dalva.com; map:L6* &

THE EAGLE TAVERN / 398 12th St; 415/626-0880 This is *the* premier gay biker bar for the leather-loving set. All ages, colors, and sizes are represented here, decked out in various macho ensembles of leather, denim, and steel (or nothing but combat boots, as we discovered one night). Tattoos and body piercings are de rigueur. The focus here is to check out, be checked out, and hook up; even nongays are welcome as long as they don't make a scene. There's a pool table, some pinball machines, and a back patio that holds the Sunday Beer Bust (a dance and drink party in the late afternoon). Be sure to try the fantastic Queer Beer. *Full bar; no credit cards; no checks; every day; map:M5* &

ENRICO'S / 504 Broadway; 415/982-6223 Among the neon-lit strip clubs and porn stores on this part of Broadway sits Enrico's, a Parisian-style sidewalk cafe catering to a mixed group of bohemians, tourists, and wannabes. The heated patio is the place to be, as the inner restaurant area can get too noisy when the live jazz band begins to play. Sit outside and people-watch while sipping a Mohito (a minty rum drink that goes down easy), their fantastic mint julep, or an imported ale. Enrico's serves a full menu of California-infused Mediterranean food until 12:30am on the weekends. See also the review in the Restaurants chapter. *Full bar; AE, DC, DIS, MC, V; no checks; every day; map:N2* &

15 ROMOLO / 15 Romolo Pl; 415/398-1359 You've got to know where you're going to find this little retro bar hidden on a secluded alley in North Beach (basically, bust a left at the porn store). The bar is part of the Basque Hotel, so you'll probably rub elbows with some international young tourists, but the main clientele is local youngish professionals relaxing after work. It's a laid-back type of place for mellowing out in one of the high-backed booths or comfy armchairs. This spot may be hidden away, but a lot of people have already found it and it can get crowded on the weekends. *Full bar; no credit cards; no checks; every day; map:N2*

GOLD DUST / 247 Powell St; 415/397-1695 You'd think the gold walls and red banquettes would be too garish and the Dixieland jazz music too cheesy, but for some reason this venerable Union Square joint still packs in the tourists and old-time locals. The Gold Dust has been around since the 1930s, and though its gilded glory has faded somewhat, it's still a fun spot to visit after shopping or the theater. You can sit around the piano and sing along as the band plays and make a new friend or two. It's all very San Francisco. *Full bar; no credit cards; no checks; every day; map:N3*

GREENS SPORTS BAR / 2239 Polk St; 415/775-4287 This popular Polk Street sports bar overflows onto the street when a big game is on, while passersby peer into the large open windows from the street to check the score. The crowd is loud and raucous, and there's always someone with a death wish who doesn't want the Niners to win. The walls are covered with old *Sports Illustrated* photos, autographed pictures, and the occasional girlie shot. When a game isn't on it's a pretty quiet locals' bar, where chances are a video of *Caddyshack* is playing on the TV and the pool table is open. *Full bar; no credit cards; no checks; every day; www.citysearch.com/sfo/greenssportsbar; map:L2* &

HARRINGTON'S BAR AND GRILL / 245 Front St; 415/392-7595 An after-work Financial District crowd has been unwinding at this Irish pub for over 60 years. There's a mix of old-timers and whippersnappers sharing the day's war stories over a pint in one of the two large bars inside. The small heated patio space is snatched up quickly. A pub menu of basic American grub is available. *Full bar; AE, MC, V; no checks; Mon–Sat; map:N2* &

HAYES AND VINE WINE BAR / 377 Hayes St; 415/626-5301 The best date place in the city! This stylish little wine bar in chic Hayes Valley caters to urbanites with a taste for the finer things. The attractive and knowledgeable staff is more than helpful when it comes to choosing your vintage. Try one of the flights, a four-glass sampling of certain wines. The vogue decor and tasty French-inspired snacks complete the picture in this cozy wine lover's haven. *Beer and wine; MC, V; no checks; every day; map:L4* &

INFUSION BAR & RESTAURANT / 555 2nd St; 415/543-2282 In SoMa's Multimedia Gulch, the young, cool, and techno-savvy digerati pack themselves into this unique bar and restaurant. Lined up behind the long bar are glass decanters full of cucumbers, chili peppers, berries, and et ceteras steeping in and infusing vodka that is then used to create a variety of cocktails. The best way to fully savor the Infusion experience is via a dry chilled martini, but Bloody Marys made with jalapeño vodka or a tart and tangy citrus vodka and soda are also good bets. Creativity is heartily welcome. The restaurant serves up an eclectic mix of imaginative dishes. See also the review in the Restaurants chapter. *Full bar; AE, DC, MC, V; no checks; every day; map:O3* &

SWANKY HOTEL BARS

Hotel bars aren't just for tourists anymore. Many of the nicer ones are frequented by locals who come for the great view, some campy fun, or just a stiff drink and good music. If that's what you're looking for, be sure to check out these choice hotel bars:

Equinox (5 Embarcadero Center; 415/788-1234) in the Hyatt Regency Hotel. The 360-degree view of the city is constantly changing in this rotating restaurant and bar. There are some happy-hour specials for the tourist and after-work crowd, but the view is the best reason to visit.

Harry Denton's Starlight Room (450 Powell St; 415/395-8595) in the Sir Francis Drake Hotel. The superswanky retro-style lounge atop this Union Square hotel is run by San Francisco's ultimate party maker. A mixed crowd of young and old enjoy the velvet booths and great bands performing big-band and swing.

The Pied Piper Bar (2 New Montgomery St; 415/392-8600) in the Palace Hotel. The Maxfield Parrish mural of the Pied Piper is the focal point of this historic bar in an exquisite downtown landmark. Try to come during a slow period (say, midafternoon) and take in how bloody cool this grand old hotel really is.

The Red Room (827 Sutter St; 415/346-7666) in the Commodore Hotel. Although not the hot spot it was a couple of years ago, this no-other-color-but-ruby-red lounge is still a sight to see. A crowd of 20- to 30-something hipsters hangs out here, but tourists are always popping in for a look.

The Redwood Room (495 Geary St; 415/775-4700) in the Clift Hotel. The Red-wood Room is a classic piano bar that's a step back in time. Its claim to fame is the beautifully paneled interior, which was created from a single, enormous, 2,000-year-old redwood tree. If you're in the area, stop in and take a look.

Tonga Room (950 Mason St; 415/772-5278) in the Fairmont Hotel. Tiki mania is the theme in this ultracampy Polynesian lounge. Have a tropical drink and some appetizers while listening to the island music. Be prepared for stormy weather—the indoor fountain shoots jets of water periodically.

Top of the Mark (999 California St; 415/392-3434) in the Mark Hopkins Inter-Continental Hotel. See the most famous and breathtaking hotel view in San Francisco from this newly remodeled and very classy bar atop Nob Hill. Swing bands play nightly, so call for the times and the cover charge.

View Lounge (55 4th St; 415/442-6127) in the San Francisco Marriott. OK, so this one feels like a hotel bar, but the view is incredible. But being a Marriott, it's not what you'd call full of San Francisco charm, so don't plan on spending a lot of time here drinking overpriced cocktails.

XYZ (181 3rd St; 415/777-5300) in the W Hotel. XYZ is on the cutting edge of hotel bars. It's in a great part of the South of Market area: close to the San Francisco Museum of Modern Art, so it draws a cool crowd that appreciates avant-garde art.

IRISH BANK BAR AND GRILL / 10 Mark Ln; 415/788-7152 Popular with the after-work crowd, this Irish pub gets crammed and uncomfortable inside from about 5–7pm on the weeknights, but there's usually plenty of room outside, where tables and a couple of benches have been set up in the alley. It's a fun crowd of professionals, and there are some Irish accents here and there, giving the place a little authenticity. The inside and outside are decorated with old Irish street signs, bottles, mirrors, and various other bits and pieces, along with some great black-and-white photos of Irish life. On the way to the back room you can sneak into an old confessional that's been converted into a booth. There's a pub menu of Irish specialties and you can order food in any part of the bar. *Full bar; MC, V; no checks; every day; map:N3*

JULIE'S SUPPER CLUB / 1123 Folsom St; 415/861-0707 Attractive, well-dressed urban dwellers have been making this '50s-style cocktail joint a SoMa favorite since the early '90s. The bartender serves stiff drinks to a fun-loving crowd that congregates for the yummy happy-hour food and drink specials. More often than not, however, that same crowd keeps partying into the night. It's got a swanky old-Hollywood feel with black-and-white photographs on the wall and a swing soundtrack in the background. *Full bar; AE, MC, V; no checks; every day; map:M4* &

LEXINGTON CLUB / 3464 19th St; 415/863-2052 Just around the corner from the many straight bars in the gentrified Valencia Corridor is this hip lesbian hangout, one of the only women-owned bars in the city. It offers a welcome respite from the busy Mission scene—the dark interior, moody lighting, and comfy booths make you settle right down. They have a great selection of beers and some good rock tunes on the jukebox. *Full bar; no credit cards; no checks; every day; map:L6* &

LI PO / 916 Grant Ave; 415/982-0072 Chinatown is full of strange little divey bars like this one, but for some reason people of all types and ages are drawn to the Li Po. It's mysterious, dimly lit, and kind of creepy (no big surprise, since it once was an opium den). The whole place is scarlet red, and the large ancient lantern hanging from the ceiling looks as if it could disintegrate at any moment. This is definitely a late-night hot spot, with a friendly staff who will try to creep you out with ghost stories of opium junkies come back from the dead. *Full bar; no credit cards; no checks; every day; map:N2*

LONDON WINE BAR / 415 Sansome St; 415/788-4811 With its exposed brick walls and wood paneling, this après-work destination feels like a European tasting room. A 50-page list of wines features some really good deals. There's a menu of snacks to accompany your glass, but most of the regulars munch on the complimentary little cheese cubes. This is a great place to meet up with friends and chat before your next destination. *Beer and wine; AE, CB, DC, DIS, MC, V; no checks; Mon–Fri; map:N2* &

LONE PALM / 3394 22nd St; 415/648-0109 Hidden among the crowded bars in the Mission District, this quiet and romantic piano bar is a convenient getaway. It's a great spot for couples to whisper sweet nothings in private at small candlelit tables. When there isn't someone playing the piano, the jukebox is belting out loungey background music. This is also a popular place for people who don't give a damn about San Francisco's no-smoking policy. *Full bar; no credit cards; no checks; every day; map:L6*

MARINA LOUNGE / 2138 Chestnut St; 415/922-1475 This retro locals' hangout is an oasis of originality on a street full of retail shops and chain restaurants. Come in from the craziness outside to this dark mahogany bar with Sinatra crooning in the background, grab yourself a drink, and reaffirm your belief that all is right with the world. The clientele is mostly an upscale cocktail-drinking crowd looking to unwind. There's a pool table in the back and several vantage points for people-watching. When you see something you like, it's perfectly OK to strike up a conversation. *Full bar; no credit cards; no checks; every day; map:K2*

MARTUNI'S / 4 Valencia St; 415/241-0205 It's kind of a strange place for a piano bar, but for some reason this offbeat location on Market and Valencia Streets has become San Francisco's new hot spot for stiff martinis and classic sing-alongs. As word gets around the various social circles, more and more people are showing up at Martuni's for a fun evening of show tunes and cocktails. All types of people congregate here, yet so far it has avoided being dominated by a chummy clique. It's a great place for couples and groups to get together and chat in the dark alcoves as the piano man entertains. *Full bar; MC, V; no checks; every day; map:L5*

O'REILLY'S IRISH BAR / 622 Green St; 415/989-6222 Literary types and serious drinkers (often one and the same) frequent this comfortable Irish pub in North Beach. On a nice night you'll want one of the outside tables, but more often than not it's like a wind tunnel and you'll need to take cover in the cozy interior. On the back wall there's a large mural of famous Irish authors (if you're having trouble naming them, look for the hints). At the bottom of the painting is a portrait of the owner's giant Irish wolfhound, who can sometimes be spotted blocking the door to the bathroom (don't worry, he's a real sweetie). They have a great Irish pub menu and pour a lovely Guinness. *Full bar; MC, V; no checks; every day; www.oreillysirish.citysearch.com; map:N1* ₖ

PERSIAN AUB ZAM ZAM / 1633 Haight St; 415/861-2545 If you like to drink something other than a martini, or hold hands with your date, or sit at a table instead of the bar, or talk to your mates, then this is not the bar for you. Why? Because the older man who owns this bar (and opens it up whenever he feels like it) rules here like a dictator, barking orders at the newbies who are unacquainted with Zam Zam's strict cocktail-ordering protocol. It's kind of fun and everyone wants to experience it at least once, and if you get booted there are plenty of friendly bars waiting for you on the rest of Haight Street. *Full bar (supposedly); cash only; no official hours; map:I5* &

PLOUGH & STARS / 116 Clement St; 415/751-1122 Irish bars are popular all over the world because they offer good drink, good music, and good *craic* (that's fun in Gaelic, pronounced "crack"), and the Plough & Stars is your typical fun-loving Irish pub. Whether it's packed or nearly vacant, it's always a good place to come and invariably meet people. The crowd is a mix of Irish immigrants who live in the neighborhood and other locals looking for a good time. There's a pool table and dartboard that are often in use. Guinness is creamy and well poured, and there's live Irish folk music many nights. *Full bar; AE, MC, V; no checks; every day; www.whatwasit.com/plough; map:I3* &

ROYAL OAK / 2201 Polk St; 415/928-2303 This popular Russian Hill hangout has cozy antique couches and chairs arranged in a variety of little conversation areas lit by the soft glow of Tiffany lamps. In contrast to the sedate decor, this place gets packed with local urbanites on weekends and can be pretty raucous, with disco blaring in the background but nowhere to dance. The wait staff is attentive and quick and, for some reason, 100 percent female. If you can't get one of the prime seats in the main room, the turnover at the bar is high. *Full bar; no credit cards; no checks; every day; map:L2*

SAN FRANCISCO BREWING COMPANY / 155 Columbus Ave; 415/434-3344 SF Brew Co. was one of the first microbreweries in the United States. It's a classic old beer joint, with loads of polished wood and brass (notice the large kettle brewing away through the window). The bar is housed in one of the last standing Barbary Coast saloons and is full of local history. Locals vie for outdoor seating on the sidewalk—great for people-watching—while quaffing $1 drafts at happy hour. There are usually about four to six different brews to choose from (you can have a cheap sample if you're not sure) and a good pub menu. A few nights a week a live jazz band plays. *Beer and wine; AE, MC, V; no checks; every day; www.sfbrewing.com; map:N2*

SKYLARK / 3089 16th St; 415/621-9294 Here is a dark, moody bar with no pretense in the midst of all the other bars in this area trying so hard to be hip. It is supremely hip for this very reason. Beautiful people huddle around the small candlelit tables in conversation while sipping cocktails, or crowd into the back and bar area on weekend nights when a DJ plays lounge and ambient music. Relax and take in some of the beautiful paintings, especially Skylark herself up on the ceiling. *Full bar; no credit cards; no checks; every day; map:L6* &

WHERE DO YOU WANT TO GO TONIGHT?

For a relatively small city (46 square miles), San Francisco is jam-packed with cool places to go and entertaining things to do. No matter what kind of action you're in the mood for, chances are you'll find it here. Following are general descriptions of some city neighborhoods and the kind of fun you may find there after the sun goes down:

North Beach: Something for everyone. Late-night cafes with outdoor seating, live music and dancing, cool old joints, hip new bars.

Mission District—Valencia Street: Young hipsters and poseurs, trendy but cool bars, and music spots in a not-quite-safe neighborhood. Gay, straight, and whatever mix it up.

Upper Haight—close to Golden Gate Park: Young, alternative, and hip crowd mixed in with some old hippies and young runaways on the street.

Lower Haight—away from Golden Gate Park: Young, edgy crowd in bars and dance spots in a somewhat dicey area.

Castro: Some of the world's best gay bars and hangouts.

South of Market (SoMa): Live music and dance club mecca in an industrial-type area. A mostly young crowd. Not entirely safe, but OK on weekend nights.

The Marina and Cow Hollow: Young urbanites and the postcollegiate set party hard in the many bars on Union and Chestnut Streets.

Pacific Heights: One of the more affluent neighborhoods, quiet but fun local bars, a couple of jazz clubs, and some sidewalk cafes for young and old alike.

Hayes Valley: Chic shops, restaurants, and wine bars in a working-class neighborhood. Getting trendier by the day.

Union Square and Downtown: Tourist central. The theaters and shops keep people coming to this area even though it borders on a seriously seedy part of town called the Tenderloin. A few cool old-school bars make the surroundings tolerable.

Yerba Buena: A hopping cultural center by day, but at night there isn't much besides chain restaurants catering to a conventioneer crowd.

Financial District: After-work business types belly up to one of the many bars for a few drinks before going home or on to another area. For the most part, very quiet after about 9pm.

Chinatown: Dive bars and late-night Chinese restaurants abound.

Fisherman's Wharf: Touristy, mostly chain-type sports bars, though there are a few places worth checking out.

Russian Hill: Young to middle-aged mellow crowd hangs at the neighborhood bars on Polk Street.

Nob Hill: Big hotels house some fancy, expensive bars with great views in this quiet area.

SPECS' TWELVE ADLER MUSEUM CAFE / 12 Saroyan Pl; 415/421-4112
Specs' has been around forever and constantly goes in and out of fashion with the fickle hipsters of the city. Little do they know that the regulars like it more when Specs' is out and you can always get a seat. Lately it's been in, especially on the weekends, when this historically bohemian hideaway gets jam-packed. If you can get a table, it's a great place to split some pitchers of Budweiser with friends and gab with people you've just met. Check out the giant wheel of cheese at the bar: for a nominal fee the bartender will cut you a chunk to have on saltine crackers. If you're lucky, Specs himself will come in and entertain you with stories of the old North Beach. *Full bar; no credit cards; no checks; every day; map:N2*

THIRSTY BEAR BREWING COMPANY / 661 Howard St; 415/974-0905
The excellent handcrafted microbrews at Thirsty Bear go well with the menu of authentic Spanish tapas. This cavernous SoMa space near the San Francisco Museum of Modern Art is frequented by museumgoers and the after-work multimedia crowd. Upstairs there are pool tables and another bar area, but most people hang downstairs at tables near the bar. See also the review in the Restaurants chapter. *Full bar; AE, DC, MC, V; no checks; every day; thirstybear.com; map:N3* &

TORONADO / 547 Haight St; 415/863-2276 This edgy neighborhood bar offers a mind-numbing number of draft and bottled beers (over 100). It's fairly small, dark, and narrow, and seating (if any) is mainly at the long bar. Serious beer drinkers of the tattooed and pierced ilk make up most of this Lower Haight hangout's clientele. It's a more relaxed alternative to the dance clubs down the block, but it can get a little loud on weekend nights when a DJ comes in. FYI, the Toronado hats make great San Francisco souvenirs. *Beer only; cash only; every day; www.toronado.com; map:K5*

TOSCA CAFE / 242 Columbus Ave; 415/986-9651 Tosca is as pure classic North Beach as you can get nowadays. The leather booths and long, dark bar—as well as the crisply dressed bartenders—conjure images of another time. The clientele is a mix of young locals and visitors, and the bar can get crowded on the weekends. If you can get a table in the back, settle in with a dry martini or a Tosca "cappuccino" (the house specialty, it contains no coffee—it's a frothy mix of brandy and hot chocolate) and soak up the atmosphere. The jukebox plays opera and big band–era tunes to accompany the hiss of the large brass espresso machines at either end of the bar. There is a secret back room reserved for friends of the owner (you may spot Nicolas Cage, Sean Penn, or Kevin Spacey heading back there on the occasional evening). *Full bar; no credit cards; no checks; every day; map:N2*

TRAD'R SAM / 6150 Geary Blvd; 415/221-0773 The last of the red-hot tiki bars is out of the way, but if you've got a group looking for a good time, this place is a ball. A menu of about 50 or so tropical drinks will get you in the party mood; one of them tastes just like a 50/50 bar—yum! Okay, so it's pretty cheesy, but the Polynesian charm is intoxicating, and before you know it you and your buddies are all hovering over a bowl of scorpions and sticking paper umbrellas in your hair. The jukebox plays good tunes, and people will tend to sing along to the oldies. It's a mostly youngish crowd; expect a line on the weekends. *Full bar; no credit cards, no checks; every day; map:F4*

TWENTY TANK BREWERY / 316 11th St; 415/255-9455 This large, casual bar in the middle of the live music scene on industrial 11th Street is a great place to meet up before going on to shows at Slim's and Paradise Lounge. The crowd is usually a mix of twenty- to thirtysomethings preparing to hit the clubs, so the scene changes a little depending on the lineup across the street. Twenty Tank brews its own beer on the premises, and many locals think it's the best around. If you can get a seat in this usually crowded bar, order up some pizzas or nachos to sustain you for the night. *Beer and wine; AE, MC, V; no checks; every day; map:M5* &

TWIN PEAKS TAVERN / 401 Castro St; 415/864-9470 This venerable San Francisco institution on the corner of Castro and Market Streets was the first openly gay bar in America. For almost 30 years the patrons of this comfortable, laid-back drinking establishment have looked out at the world through the large windows, and the wild world of the Castro has looked back. Now it's a mostly older crowd of gay men who live in the neighborhood. During the day it's very subdued, but in the evening it gets quite popular. As with most gay bars in the city, polite heteros are always welcome. *Full bar; no credit cards; no checks; every day; map:K6*

VESUVIO CAFE / 255 Columbus Ave; 415/362-3370 This Beat generation hangout has remained pretty much the same since it opened in 1948. Vesuvio's serves up alcohol to a mix of brooding writers, career drinkers, bohemian artists, North Beach hipsters, and tourists on the hunt for beatnik lore. It's a great place to people-watch or read about the past, as the walls are papered with poems and articles about the bar and the Beat era. Upstairs there's a cool balcony with additional seating. The bar gets crowded in the evenings and on weekends. *Full bar; no credit cards; no checks; every day; www.vesuvio@vesuvio.com; map:N2*

Coffee, Tea, and Dessert

ALFRED SCHILLING RESTAURANT, CHOCOLATE, AND PASTRY / 1695 Market St; 415/431-8447 Step back into the Egyptian-inspired dining room of this candy shop/restaurant and you'll feel like you're in some kind of surreal stage set, what with the desert (or is it dessert?) queen of the chocolate pyramids staring down at you from one of the exotic murals. If you're in an adventurous mood, gorge on the Willie Wonka Special, which is actually a full meal that includes chocolate in every course. You really can't go wrong with any of the outrageous sweet selections here—they are all amazingly decadent. Before you leave, pick up some of the pyramid-shaped truffles from the retail shop that made this candy maker famous. *Beer and wine; AE, MC, V; no checks; Mon–Sat; www.alfredschilling.com; map:L5*

BEPPLES PIE SHOP / 1934 Union St; 415/931-6225 The pies sitting in the window (à la *Leave It to Beaver*) will lure you in to Bepples for "just one piece." They carry a cornucopia of choices; you're bound to find your favorite on the menu. If you don't want sweets, there are savory selections, and if you don't like pie (what the hell is wrong with you?), they also have a great selection of huge muffins. Take a seat at the counter or a table in this homey cafe, a calming oasis in the midst of the Union Street shopfest. They'll treat you nice and you'll get a great slice of pie. *Beer and wine; no credit cards, checks OK; every day; map:K2* &

CAFE FLORE / 2298 Market St; 415/621-8579 Cafe Flore is a place for the predominantly gay, beautiful, and well-coifed Castro Street crowd to see and be seen. It's always packed, and on a sunny day the open-air patio is prime real estate. It's a popular place for younger men to strut their stuff and hang out with a cappuccino while checking out the other patrons. There is a nice light menu of California cuisine, but eating is not what the customers are passionate about. *Beer and wine; cash only; every day; map:K6* &

CAFFE GRECO / 423 Columbus Ave; 415/397-6261 Try to grab a sidewalk table or at least one by the large sliding windows open to Columbus Avenue, then sit back and people-watch while enjoying one of the best Italian coffee drinks this side of Roma. Small, intimate tables, Italian dessert specialties in the refrigerated case, and the sound of many languages being spoken by the cosmopolitan customers enhance the cafe's European ambience. It's a great place to linger over an Italian pastry and take in the North Beach experience. *Beer and wine; cash only; every day; map:M2* &

CAFFE PUCCINI / 411 Columbus Ave; 415/989-7033 This North Beach cafe is decorated to honor the famed Italian composer Giacomo Puccini, with a framed photo of the artist and posters from his operas. Sit back and enjoy one of the homemade desserts (the tortes are phenomenal), a foamy cappuccino, and the opera music softly playing in the background. You can also order a meal or antipasto plate full of Italian treats as you soak up the action on Columbus Avenue. *Beer and wine; no credit cards; checks OK; every day; map:M2*

CAFFE TRIESTE / 601 Vallejo St; 415/392-6739 This Beat generation hangout has been around since 1956, decades before the words "double decaf latte with nonfat milk and a twist" were ever uttered. You can sit here for hours, enjoying the rich, locally roasted Italian coffee and taking in the bohemian aura. The staff is curt and detached and that's how the locals like it, so know what you're going to order before you go to the counter. Trieste is a block off the main drag of Columbus so the foot traffic isn't as heavy here, except on Saturdays from 1:30 to 5 in the afternoon, when locals sing Italian operas and folk music for the cafe crowd. *Beer and wine; cash only; every day; www.caffeetrieste.com; map:M2* &

JAMMIN' JAVA COFFEE HOUSE / 701 Cole St; 415/668-5282 Just a few blocks from Haight Street, this bright coffeehouse is filled with a mix of old and young caffeine junkies sitting around the small tables listening to the loud tunes (hence the name Jammin' Java). They have great baked goods and superstrong coffee drinks. If you're not used to the real stuff, order a drink cut with milk or you'll be buzzing all the way into next week. *No alcohol; cash only; every day; map:I5* &

JOE'S ICE CREAM / 5351 Geary Blvd; 415/751-1950 A blast-from-the-past ice cream joint, Joe's has been around for over 50 years. Grab a seat at the old L-shaped counter for your trip back in time. Soda jerks serve up amazing house-made ice cream treats to neighborhood families and the occasional lucky visitor. Try the Joe's It, much better than the store-bought It's It, or any of the sodas, shakes, malteds, sundaes, and such made with Joe's delicious ice cream. The really great thing about Joe's: it's open until 11pm on weekends, so you can satisfy that late-night craving. *No alcohol; cash only; every day; map:G4* &

MAD MAGDA'S RUSSIAN TEA ROOM AND MYSTIC CAFE / 579 Hayes St; 415/864-7654 This kooky Hayes Valley spot is home to an ever-changing lineup of mystical fortune-tellers. Have your tarot cards read while noshing on a Russian delicacy like a piroshki and sipping one of a variety of teas. When you finish that tea you can practice reading your own tea leaves. The small garden patio is a relaxing spot to contemplate your fate. There's a great menu of sandwiches and Russian-inspired treats. *Beer and wine; no credit cards; checks OK; every day (closed early on Sun); map:L4* &

MAX'S OPERA CAFE / 601 Van Ness Ave; 415/771-7300 There are other Max's restaurants in the city, but this "Opera Cafe" location is special. Starting at about 7:30 the servers take turns belting out a variety of tunes for the patrons. Couple that with the jaw-dropping size of the delicious desserts and you've got a great late-night stop after the nearby opera, symphony, movie, or ballet. A favorite is the multilayered waterfall cake—a rich chocolate cake with white frosting and chocolate that cascades down the sides in a mouthwatering pattern. There is also a deli inside the restaurant where you can buy a cake or pastry to take home.

345

Full bar; AE, DC, DIS, MC, V; no checks; every day; www.maxs world.com; map:L4 ⛄

MUDDY WATERS COFFEE HOUSE / 521 Valencia St; 415/863-8006 In the midst of the ultracool Valencia corridor, this coffeehouse serves up some majorly caffeinated beverages. You can sit here all night listening to the ambient tunes or get a quick fix that'll keep you going late into the night at the surrounding bars. The crowd is a mixed bag of locals, while outside the door you'll find the regular Mission District druggies. It's a little rough around the edges on this block, so watch your back. *No alcohol; cash only; every day; map:L5* ⛄

THE NORTH END / 1402 Grant Ave; 415/956-3350 Away from busy Columbus Avenue and amid the cool boutiques and bars of Grant is the North End, the perfect place to relax and check out the stylish side of North Beach. Not only is the coffee great, they also carry sinfully good pastries from Victoria Pastry Co. (a North Beach institution). A fine selection of beers and some amazing sangría are available as well. While you're here, make a special trip to the bathroom and see the Elvis shrine—very cool. *Beer and wine; cash only; every day; map:N2* ⛄

STEPS OF ROME / 348 Columbus Ave; 415/397-0435 Charming, flirty Italian waiters and an ultracool European crowd make this place *the* hot spot on Columbus Avenue. The restaurant spills out onto the sidewalk, with the young and the beautiful crowding around tables to chain-smoke cigarettes. It's a fun, lively scene and, oh yeah, they serve food too. The gelato is fantastic, and the espresso drinks make an excellent accompaniment. But let's face it—it's the scene you come to Steps of Rome for, and you won't be disappointed. *Beer and wine; AE, CB, DC, DIS, MC, V; no checks; every day; map:N2* ⛄

TOY BOAT DESSERT CAFE / 401 Clement St; 415/751-7505 Kids rule at Toy Boat, and that includes the child within. The place is full of classic old toys that will bring back thoughts of your own childhood (all the old Saturday-morning stars are here, and for sale as well). When you're done perusing the toys, sit down for a slice of pie or the heavenly Fallen Angel cake—chocolate cake with a mousse center covered in shaved chocolate. They've also got great ice cream desserts and, as a healthier alternative, terrific smoothies. *No alcohol; MC, V; checks OK; every day; map:H3* ⛄

ZERO DEGREES / 490 Pacific Ave; 415/788-9376 The stark urban-chic decor of Zero Degrees doesn't make you feel like settling down with your coffee and book, but it is a great late-night destination on your way home from the bars and nearby restaurants (its parent restaurant, MC^2, is just down the block). You can get house-made ice creams in a variety of inventive flavors, as well as a selection of ports, champagnes, and scotches that make an elegant nightcap. *Full bar; MC, V; no checks; Mon–Sat; map:M2*

ITINERARIES

ITINERARIES

If we were going to spend our vacation in San Francisco, this is how we'd do it. Whether you're a first-time visitor or a San Francisco native, here are suggestions for spending a single day or an entire week enjoying some of the best that San Francisco has to offer.

More information on the places in boldface below can be found in other chapters throughout this book. If you're staying in the city, you won't need a car for Days One through Six; a car is necessary for Day Seven, however.

DAY ONE

Get your walking shoes on, because we're going to attempt to see the majority of San Francisco's most famous attractions in a single day.

MORNING: Start your day off in sumptuous style with breakfast at the **GARDEN COURT** within the Palace Hotel (2 New Montgomery St; 415/546-5010), one of the most elaborate and beautiful dining rooms ever built. Since you're in the neighborhood, it's time to do a little window shopping at **UNION SQUARE**, with a mandatory stop at **NEIMAN MARCUS** (150 Stockton St; 415/362-3900) to chuckle at the absurd price tags, and a stroll through the gilded lobby of the **WESTIN ST. FRANCIS**. Next, hop on either the Powell-Mason or Powell-Hyde cable car to **FISHERMAN'S WHARF**, and head to Pier 41 to catch the fantastic **ALCATRAZ ISLAND** tour (415/773-1188); be sure to make a reservation, and ask for the headphone tour.

AFTERNOON: After the prison tour, walk west along the water near Fisherman's Wharf to the intersection of Jefferson and Taylor Streets and buy a fresh Dungeness crab cocktail from the boisterous street vendors. Continue west along the wharf, making a few side trips to **THE CANNERY** (2801 Leavenworth St; 415/771-3112), **GHIRARDELLI SQUARE** (900 North Point St; 415/775-5500), and the **SAN FRANCISCO MARITIME NATIONAL HISTORICAL PARK** (foot of Polk St; 415/556-3002). You're probably in need of a picker-upper by now, so head for the intersection of Beach and Hyde Streets to have a world-famous Irish coffee at the **BUENA VISTA CAFE** (2765 Hyde St; 415/474-5044). If you don't mind the long but beautiful walk (if you do, take the number 28 or 29 bus, or hail a taxi), continue west along the shoreline, past Aquatic Park, along the Golden Gate Promenade to the **GOLDEN GATE BRIDGE** for an at-least-once-in-your-lifetime stroll across the world's most famous bridge.

EVENING: Okay, you've walked the bridge and now you're starving. Take a bus or taxi back to North Beach and head for **ENRICO'S** (504 Broadway; 415/982-6223). It's not the best restaurant in the city, but it has the best San Francisco vibe and live jazz nightly. Get a patio seat and order the

THE 49-MILE SCENIC DRIVE

Introduce yourself to San Francisco's splendor by cruising in your automobile along the 49-Mile Scenic Drive—a four-hour, self-guided journey on the city's prettiest streets and past its most scenic sites, including Union Square, North Beach, Chinatown, Nob Hill, and Fisherman's Wharf. The route is well marked by blue-and-white signs featuring a picture of a seagull—but don't follow the birdie during rush hour unless you also enjoy staring at lots of license plates. A detailed map outlining the course is available at the San Francisco Visitor Information Center (900 Market St at Powell St, near the Union Square cable car turntable; 415/391-2000).

burger and a mint julep. Afterwards, cruise northwest down Columbus Avenue, soaking in the sights and smells and stopping in at classic San Francisco haunts such as **SPECS' TWELVE ADLER MUSEUM CAFE** (12 Saroyan Pl; 415/421-4112), **VESUVIO CAFE** (255 Columbus Ave; 415/362-3370), and **CAFFE TRIESTE** (601 Vallejo St; 415/392-6739). By now it's probably time for the second showing of **BEACH BLANKET BABYLON** at Club Fugazi (678 Green St; 415/421-4222), San Francisco's best and longest-running comedic musical. If you're still up for more after the show, head back to Union Square to the Sir Francis Drake hotel and finish the night off with some drinking and dancing at the rooftop **HARRY DENTON'S STARLIGHT ROOM** (450 Powell St; 415/395-8595).

DAY TWO

More exploring of San Francisco attractions. You might want to pick up a bus map and purchase a day pass from a Muni driver because you'll be adventuring all over the city today.

MORNING: There are still plenty more quintessential San Francisco sights to see. Start off with a Swedish pancake breakfast at **SEARS FINE FOODS** (439 Powell St; 415/986-1160), a San Francisco classic. Next, spend a few hours wandering though world-famous Chinatown, exploring all the funky shops and back alleys; or take a guided **WOK WIZ CHINATOWN WALKING TOUR** (415/981-5588). This should work up enough of an appetite for lunch at **HOUSE OF NANKING** (919 Kearny St; 415/421-1429), another San Francisco landmark.

AFTERNOON: Now that you're refueled on pot stickers and Chinese greens, break out the map and head for **COIT TOWER** (415/362-0808) on the top of Telegraph Hill for a breathtaking view of the city (and some serious stair-climbing). Catch your breath, reload your camera, and head west to the world-famous winding block of **LOMBARD STREET** between Hyde and Leavenworth Streets (car or no car, it's still worth a visit). If you're towing kids around with you, they'd probably like to go play at

PIER 39 at this point. Or skip it altogether and head to the fantastic **SAN FRANCISCO CABLE CAR MUSEUM** (Washington and Mason Sts; 415/474-1887). Afterward, take the Powell-Mason or Powell-Hyde cable car back to Union Square.

EVENING: By now you're probably ready for some well-deserved R&R, so treat yourself to a blowout dinner at **FARALLON** (450 Post St; 415/956-6969), **POSTRIO** (545 Post St; 415/776-7825), or the **GRAND CAFÉ** (501 Geary St; 415/292-0101), three of the best "big-city" restaurants in San Francisco. Order a triple espresso for dessert and walk to **BISCUITS & BLUES** (401 Mason St; 415/292-2583) for some classic blues or, if you prefer a quieter evening, have a cocktail high above the city in the lounge of the **CARNELIAN ROOM** (555 California St; 415/433-7500).

DAY THREE

You've seen a lot of the big-name attractions; now it's time to do what you really came to San Francisco for—eat, drink, shop, and repeat.

MORNING: Sleep in late and have a very light breakfast because for lunch you'll be stuffing your face at **YANK SING** (427 Battery St; 415/781-1111), the most popular dim sum restaurant in the city (you can't go to San Francisco and not have a dim sum experience). Since you're already downtown, spend an hour shopping at **EMBARCADERO CENTER** (Drumm, Sacramento, Clay, and Battery Sts; 415/772-0500) or walking around the Financial District marveling at the numerous skyscrapers.

AFTERNOON: Now take a bus, taxi, or long walk to San Francisco's SoMa district. Three must-stops here are the **SAN FRANCISCO MUSEUM OF MODERN ART** (151 3rd St; 415/357-4000), the **YERBA BUENA GARDENS** (899 Howard Street; 415/543-1275), and, especially if you have kids tagging along, the new **METREON** mega-audiovisual complex (4th and Mission Sts; 415/537-3400)—all of which are right next to each other. This should take you well into the evening.

EVENING: Time for dinner. If you want small, intimate, and French, make a reservation right now for **FRINGALE** (570 4th St; 415/543-0573). If you prefer a high-energy, big city–style dining experience, then walk around the corner to **LULU** (816 Folsom St; 415/495-5775). Both restaurants are among our all-time favorites. When dinner is over, do something *really* romantic: hail a taxi and ask the driver to take you to the top of Twin Peaks for a breathtaking view of the city lights.

DAY FOUR

More sightseeing, this time at our favorite museums and the city's main playground, Golden Gate Park. Finish the day with a trip to our human zoo: the Haight-Ashbury district.

SAN FRANCISCO DAY BY DAY

There are some amazing events going on in San Francisco that happen only on certain days of the week. Here are a some local favorites:

Farmers market held every Saturday morning along the Embarcadero at the foot of Market Street.

A hand-clapping and foot-stomping praise to the Lord every Sunday at the **Glide Memorial Church** (330 Ellis St; 415/771-6300).

A sinfully sumptuous **Sunday brunch** at the Ritz-Carlton Hotel (600 Stockton St; 415/296-7465).

Operatic arias from 2–5pm every Saturday at Caffe Trieste (601 Vallejo St; 415/392-6739).

Thursday night art and music offerings at the **San Francisco Museum of Modern Art**, which stays open until 9pm and usually hosts live jazz and blues bands. It's quite popular with the locals.

Rent roller skates, in-line skates, or a tandem bicycle and cruise through **Golden Gate Park** on Sunday, when the main roads throughout the park are closed to auto traffic.

Sunset tours of **Alcatraz Island** Thursday through Sunday offer spectacular nighttime views of the city and an odd mix of romance and creepiness.

One of the best places to hear live rock in the city, **Bottom of the Hill**, also offers one of the best all-you-can-eat barbecues every Sunday from 4 to 7pm.

MORNING: Start the day with a gourmet breakfast at **DOIDGE'S** (2217 Union St; 415/921-2149), but be sure you have a reservation. Take some leftover bread with you and head toward the Palace of Fine Arts, which houses the **EXPLORATORIUM** (3601 Lyon St; 415/563-7337), the most amazing science museum in the world (the bread is for the ducks, geese, and swans that live at the pond outside).

AFTERNOON: Now it's time to explore **GOLDEN GATE PARK**. Stop by a deli to pick up some sandwiches, then plan to spend all of the afternoon here visiting the Steinhart Aquarium and Natural History Museum at the California Academy of Sciences (415/750-7145), as well as the Japanese Tea Garden (415/752-4227) and Stow Lake (415/752-0347), where you can rent paddleboats for a romantic trip around the lake. If you're feeling adventurous, it's also great fun to rent some in-line skates at **SKATES ON HAIGHT** (1818 Haight St; 415/752-8375) and skate along the park's wide roads (particularly on Sunday, when many of those roads are closed to vehicle traffic).

EVENING: Since you're already in the neighborhood, now is a good time to check out the famous Haight-Ashbury district. Start by putting your name on the waiting list at **CHA CHA CHA** (1801 Haight St; 415/386-5758), then explore the "upper Haight" on foot, browsing through the cornucopia of exotic shops and having an ice cream cone at the Ben & Jerry's on the corner of Haight and Ashbury Streets. After dinner, waddle over to **KAN ZAMAN** (1793 Haight St; 415/751-9656) to smoke from a hookah (trust us, it's a blast) and watch the belly dancers.

DAY FIVE

So little time and so much more to see and do. There are still a few famous San Francisco neighborhoods you need to explore—the Castro and the Mission—and more incredible restaurants to visit.

MORNING: First it's breakfast at **DOTTIE'S TRUE BLUE CAFÉ** (522 Jones St; 415/885-2767), then take a bus up Market Street to the Castro to check out one of the most renowned gay neighborhoods in the world. Besides just absorbing the positive energy flowing here, you can also do some serious shopping along Castro Street or, better yet, catch a classic flick at the incredible **CASTRO THEATRE** (429 Castro St; 415/621-6120). If you prefer a guided walking tour, make a reservation with Cruisin' the Castro (415/550-8110).

AFTERNOON: For a lesson in California's early history, head east on foot to **MISSION DOLORES** (3321 16th St; 415/621-8203), then continue east to the Mission District for a heavy dose of cross-cultures. Have a crepe for lunch at **TI COUZ** (3108 16th St; 415/252-7373), a burrito at **LA TAQUERIA** (2889 Mission St; 415/285-7117), or a Vietnamese feast at **THE SLANTED DOOR** (584 Valencia St; 415/861-8032), then browse the dozens of shops along Valencia and Mission Streets. You might also want to take a guided tour of the many colorful Mission District murals, given by the **PRECITA EYES MURAL ARTS CENTER** (348 Precita Ave; 415/285-2287).

EVENING: The Mission's not the friendliest place for tourists after dark, so before the sun sets take a bus or taxi to the foot of Mission Street at the Embarcadero to one of the top-ranked restaurants in the city (and one of our favorites as well): **BOULEVARD** (1 Mission St; 415/543-6084). End the night with a leisurely stroll down the Embarcadero—or grab a cab and head for **JOHN LEE HOOKER'S BOOM BOOM ROOM** (1601 Fillmore St; 415/673-8000) for some live rhythm and blues (and possibly an appearance by the man himself).

DAY SIX

Enough of the city—let's hop on a ferry and explore some of the surrounding Bay Area.

MORNING: Coffee and a pastry for breakfast at **CAFFE GRECO** (423 Columbus Ave; 415/397-6261) will get you going, then head down to Pier 41 at Fisherman's Wharf to catch the first ferry to **SAUSALITO**. Plan on spending a few hours here exploring the beautiful bayside community and having an early lunch at **HORIZONS** (558 Bridgeway; 415/331-3232), then take the ferry back to San Francisco and board another ferry to **ANGEL ISLAND** (believe us, the ferry rides are one of the best parts of the trip).

AFTERNOON: Spend the day hiking, mountain biking, and/or kayaking around Angel Island, then take the short ferry hop to **TIBURON** and bask in the sunshine (hopefully) at **SAM'S ANCHOR CAFE** (27 Main St; 415/435-4527), a local favorite on sunny summer days. You ain't driving, so have another margarita and relax.

EVENING: Take the evening ferry back to Pier 41, then take the Powell-Mason cable car toward Union Square, hop off in North Beach, and have dinner at **ROSE PISTOLA** (532 Columbus Ave; 415/399-0499). By this point you're probably wiped out, so let's end the evening with a leisurely stroll along Columbus Avenue to **BIX** (56 Gold St; 415/433-6300) for a martini nightcap and some cool jazz.

DAY SEVEN

Okay, it's time to rent a car and explore either the California coast or the Wine Country. If you have a love for wine and bucolic scenery, the Wine Country makes a wonderful day trip. If, on the other hand, you would rather see a gorgeous redwood forest and extraordinary coastal scenery along the Northern California coast, a trip to Point Reyes makes for an equally unforgettable excursion.

WINE COUNTRY

Cross the Golden Gate Bridge, head north on Highway 101, and follow the signs to **NAPA**. Since there are far too many wineries to see in a day (or a week, for that matter), pick just three or four of the best in Napa Valley to see and sample. (Sonoma Valley is beautiful as well, but it's impossible to do justice to both areas.) A few of our favorite **WINERIES** to visit: Beringer Vineyards, Clos Pegase, Domaine Chandon, the Hess Collection Winery, Schramsberg Vineyards, Neibaum-Coppola, and Sterling Vineyards. As for lunch and dinner, it's tough to choose. Great Napa Valley choices include Mustards, Pinot Blanc, Tra Vigne, Bistro Don Giovanni, Catahoula, French Laundry (if you can get in), and Terra. They are all fantastic, so the choice really comes down to where you plan to be and what you're in the mood for.

COASTAL TOUR

Get up early, cross the Golden Gate Bridge, and follow the signs to Stinson Beach (Hwy 1). Your first stop should be at **MUIR WOODS** to admire the pristine grove of redwoods that exists amazingly close to such a populated area. Next, continue along Highway 1 to **STINSON BEACH** for an early lunch at one of the outdoor cafes and perhaps a stroll along the beach. Continue up the coast to **POINT REYES NATIONAL SEASHORE** for some incredible hiking along the numerous seaside trails, or take a trip past the dairy farms to the Point Reyes Lighthouse. End the day with an early dinner at the **STATION HOUSE CAFE** in downtown Point Reyes Station (11180 Shoreline Hwy; 415/663-1515) before heading back to San Francisco.

DAY TRIPS

DAY TRIPS

Berkeley

10 miles northeast of San Francisco (approximately 15 to 20 minutes, traffic permitting). Cross the San Francisco–Oakland Bay Bridge, keep in the left lanes, take the Interstate 80 turnoff, then take the University Avenue exit; turn right onto University, which spills into the town of Berkeley.

You can still buy tie-dyed "Berserkley" T-shirts from vendors on Telegraph Avenue, but the wild days of this now middle-aged, upper-middle-class burg are gone. Although hot-button issues can still spark a march or two at the world-renowned University of California at Berkeley, these days most university students seem more interested in cramming for exams than in mounting a protest in People's Park. In some respects, the action has moved from the campus to City Hall, where the town's residents—many of them former hippies, student intellectuals, and peace activists—rage on against everything from Columbus Day (Berkeley celebrates Indigenous People's Day instead) to the opening of a large video store downtown (too lowbrow and tacky). The *San Francisco Chronicle* recently called Berkeley the "most contentious of cities," and it's a mantle most of its inhabitants wear with pride.

If you're a newcomer to Berkeley, start your tour of the town at the **UNIVERSITY OF CALIFORNIA AT BERKELEY** (also known as UC Berkeley or Cal), the oldest and second-largest of the nine campuses in the UC system. Driving through the campus is virtually impossible, so park on a side street or in a lot and set out on foot. The university isn't so huge that you'd get hopelessly lost if you wandered around on your own, but without guidance you might miss some of the highlights. Pick up a self-guided walking packet at the **UC BERKELEY VISITOR INFORMATION CENTER** (open Monday through Friday), or attend one of the free 90-minute tours (meet at the visitor center) offered Monday through Friday at 10am, Saturday at 10am, and Sunday at 1pm (meet in front of the Campanile clock tower in the heart of the campus for the weekend tours). The visitor center is at 2200 University Avenue at Oxford Street, University Hall, Room 101; 510/642-5215 (recording) or 510/642-INFO; www.berkeley.edu (click on the Visitor's Services link).

A few paces north of the intersection of Telegraph Avenue and Bancroft Way is the university's legendary **SPROUL PLAZA**, where the Free Speech Movement began in 1964. Walk up the famous steps of Sproul Hall, where many demonstrators stood (and still stand) to speak their piece; pass through the double doors, and just beyond the entrance you'll see a display of photos commemorating those exciting times. Several hundred feet north of Sproul Plaza is the pretty bronzed-metal and white-granite Sather Gate, originally the main campus entrance until the university was expanded in the '60s. If you head northeast toward the center of things you'll spot the **CAMPANILE** (officially named Sather Tower, though nobody calls it that), a 307-foot clock tower modeled after St. Mark's Campanile in Venice, Italy. Built in 1914, this is Cal's best-known landmark; for a small fee you can take the elevator to the top for a stunning view of the Bay Area. The only original building still standing on campus is just southwest of the Campanile: South Hall, built in 1873. Walk north past the tower and turn east on University Drive, and you'll eventually see, on your left, the Beaux Arts beauty known as the Hearst Mining Building. Continue east on University Drive, and at the top of the hill hidden in a eucalyptus grove is the **GREEK THEATRE**, which architect Julia Morgan (of Hearst Castle fame) modeled after the amphitheater in Epidaurus, Greece. The popular theater was presented in 1903 as a gift by newspaper publisher William Randolph Hearst.

A visit to Berkeley wouldn't be complete without a stroll down bustling Telegraph Avenue, still the haunt of students, street people, runaways, hipsters, professors, and tarot readers. If you want a cup of joe before you go, head east on Bancroft to **CAFFE STRADA** (2300 College Ave at Bancroft Wy, Berkeley; 510/843-5282) and nab a seat on the sunny patio, where all the architecture students get their caffeine blasts before disappearing inside the gray monstrosity across the street known as Wurster Hall. If you prefer classical music with your coffee, go to the nearby **MUSICAL OFFERING** (2430 Bancroft Wy, W of Telegraph Ave, Berkeley; 510/849-0211), which also sells sandwiches, soups, CDs, and tapes. Start your trek down Telegraph at the intersection with Bancroft (at the southernmost edge of UC Berkeley), and make a loop around all the friendly street vendors hawking everything from top-quality tie-dyed shirts, dresses, and boxer shorts to handmade earrings and hand-painted ties. Along this street are some great bookstores, most notably **CODY'S BOOKS** (2454 Telegraph Ave at Haste St, Berkeley; 510/845-7852; www.codysbooks.com) and **MOE'S BOOKS** (2476 Telegraph Ave, Berkeley; 510/849-2087; www.moesbooks.com), and numerous cafes, including the popular **CAFE INTERMEZZO** (2442 Telegraph Ave at Haste St, Berkeley; 510/849-4592), where you can get a salad the size of your head and freshly made pastries. Across the street is **CAFFE MEDITERRANEUM** (2475 Telegraph Ave, between Haste St and Dwight Wy, Berkeley; 510/549-1128), which made its film debut in *The Graduate*. "The Med" captures the bohemian flavor of Telegraph, and churns out good cappuccinos as well as burgers, pastas, and desserts.

On Dwight Way, between Telegraph Avenue and Bowditch Street, is People's Park, famous as a site of student riots, which first flared in 1969 when the university wanted to replace the park with a dormitory (then-governor Ronald Reagan decided to call in the National Guard). The dorm was never built, but in 1991 UC officials succeeded in placing a few sand volleyball courts and basketball courts in the park—and even that incited several protests.

Farther south in Berkeley, near the Berkeley-Oakland border, is the small Elmwood neighborhood shopping district, which stretches along College Avenue and crosses over Ashby Avenue. Poke your head into the tiny boutique **TAIL OF THE YAK** (2632 Ashby Ave, W of College Ave, Berkeley; 510/841-9891) for a look at the artsy displays of treasures from Central America and other regions, then stroll along College, where you can pet the lop-eared baby bunnies and squawk back at the beautiful parrots at **YOUR BASIC BIRD** (2940 College Ave, just N of Ashby Ave, Berkeley; 510/841-7617); dip into the huge candy jars at **SWEET DREAMS** (2901 College Ave at Russell St, Berkeley; 510/549-1211); munch on fantastic fresh-fruit cheese danish at **NABOLOM BAKERY** (2708 Russell St at College Ave, Berkeley; 510/845-BAKE); and shop for clothes at numerous boutiques. Has all that shopping made you peckish? Then try **A. G. FERRARI FOODS** (2905 College Ave, N of Ashby Ave, Berkeley; 510/849-2701) for fresh pasta salads and sandwiches, or visit **ESPRESSO ROMA** (2960 College Ave at Ashby Ave, Berkeley; 510/644-3773), where you can sip strong coffee drinks, teas (try a jolt of chai), fresh lemonade, beer on tap, or wine by the glass, and eat some great calzones and sandwiches. At the top of the hill just off Ashby Avenue is the terrific restaurant **RICK & ANN'S** (2922 Domingo Ave, in front of the Claremont Resort and Spa, Berkeley; 510/649-0869), which serves very good breakfasts, lunches, and dinners (don't miss the millet muffins).

On the opposite side of Berkeley, just northwest of the university on Shattuck Avenue, is the area well known as the Gourmet Ghetto, thanks to the international reputation of Chez Panisse and other great neighborhood restaurants. **CHEZ PANISSE** (1517 Shattuck Ave, between Cedar and Vine Sts, Berkeley; restaurant 510/548-5525, cafe 510/548-5049) is the most famous restaurant in Northern California—and one of the most famous in the nation, for that matter. Owner and chef Alice Waters has been at the forefront of the California cuisine revolution since 1971, when she started cooking simple French-influenced meals for groups of friends, then opened her legendary restaurant. Waters has never specialized in the showier, sometimes downright bizarre culinary creations that characterize so much of California cuisine these days. Instead, she concentrates on simple, exquisitely orchestrated meals using the finest natural ingredients available and has made Chez Panisse a major source of support for several small organic-food enterprises in Northern California (in fact, hers may be the only restaurant that pays a "forager" to find the best of everything). Chez Panisse is divided into a fantastic (albeit expensive) prix-fixe dining room downstairs and a lighthearted (and more reasonably priced) upstairs cafe.

Other favored dining establishments in this neighborhood are **CAMBODIANA'S** (2156 University Ave, between Shattuck Ave and Oxford St, Berkeley; 510/843-4630), a superb Cambodian restaurant open for lunch and dinner; **CHESTER'S CAFE** (1508-B Walnut Square, off Vine St, Berkeley; 510/849-9995), which serves breakfast all day, lunch, and weekend brunch—search for a seat on the upstairs deck, where you can look out at the bay and the Golden Gate; **SAUL'S** (1475 Shattuck Ave at Vine St, Berkeley; 510/848-DELI), an old-fashioned deli offering breakfast from sunrise to sunset as well as classic "regular or full-figured" sandwiches; and **CHA AM** (1543 Shattuck Ave at Cedar St, Berkeley; 510/848-9664), for good, reasonably priced Thai food served on a glassed-in patio under towering palms.

When Berkeley carnivores hear the call of the wild and nothing but a big, rare burger will do, they head for **FATAPPLES** (1346 Martin Luther King, Jr. Wy at Rose St, Berkeley; 510/526-2260), just a few blocks northwest of the famous Shattuck strip. A prime contender in the ongoing Berkeley burger wars, FatApples makes its burgers of exceptionally lean, high-quality ground beef and serves them on house-made wheat rolls. Don't miss the flaky olallieberry or pecan pie, the thick jumbo shakes, or the ethereal cheese puffs. For a hot dog and a good brewski, head south on Shattuck to the **TRIPLE ROCK BREWERY** (1920 Shattuck Ave at Hearst Ave, Berkeley; 510/843-2739) and order the specialty beer of the day, then go way up the hill on Hearst to **TOP DOG** (2503 Hearst Ave at Euclid St, Berkeley; 510/843-1241), a cheap, kinda grungy Berkeley institution that's been serving good hot dogs for years.

Tucked away near the bay in West Berkeley is the **FOURTH STREET SHOPPING AREA**. With its recent profusion of chichi stores and upscale outlets (Crate & Barrel Outlet Store, Dansk, Sur La Table, Pottery Barn, the Garden, Sweet Potatoes, et cetera), the Fourth Street area has become a shopping mecca—a somewhat ironic development considering the city's traditional disdain for conspicuous consumption. Get a bite to eat at **BETTE'S-TO-GO** (also known as BTG) or, better yet, plan on indulging in a big breakfast here at the adjoining **BETTE'S OCEANVIEW DINER** (1807 4th St, between Hearst Ave and Virginia St, Berkeley; 510/644-3230), a small, nouveau-'40s diner that doesn't have an ocean view (or any view, for that matter) but does have red booths, chrome stools, a checkerboard tile floor, a hip wait staff, the best jukebox around, and damn good breakfasts. On weekends, bring the newspaper or a good book and expect a 45-minute, stomach-growling wait, but consider the payoff: enormous, soufflé-style pancakes stuffed with pecans and ripe berries, farm-fresh eggs scrambled with prosciutto and Parmesan, outstanding omelets, corned beef hash, and the quintessential huevos rancheros. Nearby is the popular **CAFE ROUGE** (1782 4th St, Berkeley; 510/525-1440), where you'll find everything from duck braised in white wine to great grilled steaks for lunch and dinner. For less expensive fare or an inexpensive drink, belly up to the bar and hofbrau at **BRENNAN'S** (4th St and University Ave, under the overpass, Berkeley; 510/841-0960), a Berkeley landmark that's been serving hand-carved roasted-meat sandwiches with mashed potatoes and gravy since 1959. Brennan's handsome dark-wood bar serves great Irish coffee and beer.

A short drive away is another very popular breakfast and lunch spot, Alice Waters's (of Chez Panisse fame) diminutive **CAFE FANNY** (1603 San Pablo Ave, between Cedar and Virginia Sts, Berkeley; 510/524-5447). This corner cafe, nestled next to the famous **ACME BREAD COMPANY** (be sure to swing by and pick up a few loaves to go), can handle fewer than a dozen stand-up customers at once, but that doesn't deter anyone. On sunny weekend mornings the adjacent parking lot fills with the overflow, with the luckier customers snaring a seat at one of the few tiny outdoor tables. Named after Waters's daughter, this cafe recalls the neighborhood haunts so dear to the French. Breakfast on crunchy Cafe Fanny granola, jam-filled buckwheat crepes, or perfect soft-boiled eggs served on sourdough toast with a side of house-made jam, and sip a cafe au lait from a big, authentically French, handleless bowl. For lunch, order a small pizza or one of the seductive sandwiches. You won't get trencherman portions, but you'll love every crumb.

Where the northwest border of Berkeley meets the little town of Albany is Solano Avenue, a popular mile-long street lined with shops and cafes. Solano is also home to one of the East Bay's best pizza joints, **ZACHARY'S CHICAGO PIZZA** (1853 Solano Ave at Fresno St, Berkeley; 510/525-5950). For years Bay Area transplants from the East Coast complained about the wretched local pizza. Then along came Zachary's with its tasty rendition of Chicago-style deep-dish: a deep-bottom crust packed with a choice of fillings, covered with a thin second crust, and topped with tomato sauce (the bottom crust turns crisp in the oven; the top one melts into the filling).

In case you haven't heard, there is more to Berkeley than great food and shops. Several museums grace this little city, including the highly regarded **UC BERKELEY ART MUSEUM** (2626 Bancroft Way, between College Ave and Bowditch St, Berkeley; 510/642-0808), which has a small permanent collection of modern art and frequently hosts traveling exhibitions. The **JUDAH L. MAGNES MUSEUM** (2911 Russell St, off Claremont Ave, Berkeley; 510/849-2710), the third-largest Jewish museum in the West, offers numerous exhibitions of Jewish art and culture, and a vast array of anthropological artifacts is showcased at the **PHOEBE HEARST MUSEUM OF ANTHROPOLOGY** (in UC Berkeley's Kroeber Hall, at the corner of College Ave and Bancroft Wy, Berkeley; 510/643-7648). Hands-on exhibits exploring the world of lasers, holograms, and cutting-edge computers are featured at the **LAWRENCE HALL OF SCIENCE** (on Centennial Dr, near Grizzly Peak Blvd, Berkeley; 510/642-5133), and while you're there, duck outside to see (and hear) the giant, eerie wind chimes and take a peek at the Stonehenge-like solar observatory.

Theater lovers will appreciate the **BERKELEY REPERTORY THEATRE** (2025 Addison St; 510/845-4700), which has a national reputation for innovative new works and experimental productions of the classics and other plays. Every summer the **CALIFORNIA SHAKESPEARE FESTIVAL** (100 Gateway Blvd, off Hwy 24, Orinda; 510/548-3422, press 2; www.calshakes.org) performs in an outdoor theater (bundle up, 'cause it's usually quite cold) in the Berkeley hills near the city of Orinda. Movie mavens love the **UC THEATRE** (2036 University Ave, between Milvia St and Shattuck Ave, Berkeley; 510/843-3456, press 6), a revivalist movie house where the flicks change nightly, and the **PACIFIC FILM ARCHIVE** (2625 Durant Ave, in the University Art Museum, Berkeley; 510/642-1124), which shows underground and avant-garde movies as well as the classics. For up-to-date listings of cultural events, pick up a free copy of *The Express*, the East Bay's alternative weekly, available at cafes and newsstands throughout the city.

Berkeley has many musical offerings, including the **BERKELEY SYMPHONY**, which blends new and experimental music with the classics at Zellerbach Hall on the UC Berkeley campus (for tickets and directions, call 510/841-2800). Modern rock, blues, and funk are blasted at **BLAKE'S** (2367 Telegraph Ave, Berkeley; 510/848-0886), and if you're feeling a bit more mellow, take a seat at the **FREIGHT & SALVAGE COFFEEHOUSE** (1111 Addison St, Berkeley; 510/548-1761), a prime Euro-folkie hangout. Live rock, jazz, folk, reggae, and other concerts are frequently held at UC Berkeley's intimate, open-air **GREEK THEATRE** (on Gayley Rd off Hearst Ave, Berkeley; 510/642-9988), a particularly pleasant place for sitting beneath the stars and listening to music on warm summer nights. **CAL PERFORMANCES** presents up-and-coming and established artists of all kinds, from the Bulgarian Women's Chorus to superstar mezzo-soprano Cecilia Bartoli and rock star Sting; the concerts are held at various sites on the UC Berkeley campus (510/642-9988; www.calperfs.berkeley.edu).

When you're ready for more pastoral (not to mention free) diversions, stroll through the **BERKELEY ROSE GARDEN**, a terraced park with 3,000 rosebushes (250 varieties) and a stellar view of San Francisco, particularly at sunset (on Euclid Ave, between Bay View and Eunice, Berkeley), or walk through the 30-acre **UNIVERSITY OF CALIFORNIA**

BOTANICAL GARDEN (in Strawberry Canyon on Centennial Dr, Berkeley; 510/642-3343), where you'll see more than 12,000 plants, including a spectacular collection of cacti from around the world, a Mendocino pygmy forest, and a Miocene-era redwood grove; free guided tours are offered on weekends. The 2,065-acre TILDEN REGIONAL PARK (off Wildcat Canyon Rd, Berkeley; 510/562-PARK, press 7), set high in the hills above town, offers picnic sites, forests, open meadows, and miles of hiking trails, plus a steam train, a charming merry-go-round, pony rides, and a farm and nature area for kids. Tilden also boasts a beautiful botanical garden (510/841-8732) specializing in California native plants, and tours of the garden are offered regularly. For kite flying, Frisbee throwing, and the very popular Adventure Playground, drive to the west end of town to the BERKELEY MARINA, which extends 3,000 feet into the bay, providing a stunning view of the San Francisco skyline, the Bay Bridge, and the Golden Gate Bridge (at the foot of University Ave, just W of the Hwy 80 overpass, Berkeley; Adventure Playground is open weekends and holidays only, 510/644-8623).

If you're looking for a place to stay in Berkeley, some of the favored spots are the grand, gleaming white, 279-room CLAREMONT RESORT AND SPA (41 Tunnel Rd, at the intersection of Ashby and Domingo Aves, Berkeley; 510/843-3000 or 800/551-7266; www.claremontresort.com); THE ROSE GARDEN INN (2740 Telegraph Ave, between Ward and Stuart Sts, Berkeley; 510/549-2145), an attractive 40-room bed-and-breakfast surrounded by beautifully landscaped lawns; and the 18-room FRENCH HOTEL (1538 Shattuck Ave, between Cedar and Vine Sts, Berkeley; 510/548-9930), a simple, comfortable lodging in the heart of the Gourmet Ghetto. Berkeley is a college town, so bear in mind that just about every accommodation will be booked three to four months in advance for May graduations; this guaranteed booking period also prompts most lodgings to jack up their rates for that month. The rest of the year, you'll find that many of Berkeley's room rates are competitive with the ever-increasing rates of San Francisco's numerous hotels.

Wine Country

NAPA VALLEY: NAPA, YOUNTVILLE, OAKVILLE, ST. HELENA, AND CALISTOGA

55 miles north of San Francisco (approximately 1½ hours), traffic permitting. Take Highway 101 North across the Golden Gate Bridge, turn off at the Napa-Vallejo/Highway 37 exit, and follow the signs to Highway 121 and Napa.

Despite the plethora of nouveau châteaus, fake French barns, and gimcrack stores selling wine bottles full of cabernet-flavored jelly beans, the Napa Valley is still one of Northern California's most magical spots. In early spring, the hills are a vibrant green, bright-yellow mustard blossoms poke up between the grapevines, and stands of fruit trees burst into showy flower. In the summer, tourists flood the valley and its hundreds of wineries, cranking up the energy level a few notches and conferring a patina of glamour and excitement that some locals delight in and others deplore. Later, after the grape harvest, the vineyards turn a bright autumnal scarlet, and the region's quaint, Old West–style towns assume a more relaxed, homey atmosphere.

At any time of year, the Napa Valley is blessed with an abundance of excellent restaurants, scores of welcoming bed and breakfasts, a couple of ultraluxurious resorts, enough interesting shops to keep Gold cards flashing up and down the valley, and recreational opportunities galore: boating, biking, horseback riding, hot-air ballooning, gliding, hiking, soaking in mud baths or hot springs, and exploring historic sites. Diversity is the watchword here. You might grab a map of the region's numerous wineries and work on expanding the contents of your cellar (see Napa Valley Wineries and Sonoma Valley Wineries sidebars). Or engage in that ultimate food-to-go experience, the **NAPA VALLEY WINE TRAIN** (for information or reservations call 707/253-2111 or 800/427-4124), where passengers sip fine wines and sup on a meal while gazing out at the lush countryside on their cushy ride in a historically preserved vintage railcar. Winery maps and details about parks, hot-air balloon rides, and other recreational pastimes are readily available at many locations, including most hotels and the **NAPA VALLEY CONFERENCE AND VISITORS BUREAU** (open daily; 1310 Town Center Mall, off 1st St, Napa; 707/226-7459; www.napavalley.com).

The 35-mile-long Napa Valley is home to some of the most famous wineries in the world, and many of them are clustered along scenic Highway 29 and the verdant Silverado Trail, two parallel roads running the length of the region and through such quaint little towns as Yountville, Oakville, St. Helena, and Calistoga. The valley is a zoo on weekends—especially in summer and early fall, when traffic on narrow Highway 29 rivals rush hour in the Bay Area. Wise Wine Country visitors plan their trips here for weekdays, the misty months of winter, or early spring, when many room rates are lower and everything's less crowded, but the valley is no less spectacular.

At the southernmost end of Napa Valley is the pretty, sprawling town of **NAPA**, where about half of the county's 123,340 residents live. Although its name is synonymous with wine, most of the wineries are actually several miles north of town. The city, founded in 1848, is well

NAPA VALLEY WINERIES

Napa's wineries are mainly clustered along Highway 29 and the Silverado Trail, two parallel roads running the length of the valley. It's a busy place on weekends—expect backups in the summer and early fall, when Highway 29 traffic can be bumper-to-bumper. With the increasing numbers of visitors, most vintners now charge a small fee to taste their wines, and some require reservations for tours (don't let the latter deter you—the smaller establishments just need to control the number of visitors at any one time and make sure someone will be available to show you around). As you whiz along the highway and see the signs announcing some of the most famous wineries in the world, you'll be tempted to pull over and stop at every one. But do yourself a favor and follow a tip from veteran wine tasters: pick out the four or five wineries you're most interested in visiting over the weekend, and stick to your itinerary. Touring more than a couple of wineries a day will surely overwhelm and exhaust even the most intrepid wine connoisseur, although if you really want to see several wineries in a short period, skip the grand tours and just visit the tasting rooms. If you're new to the wine-touring scene, you'll be relieved to know you won't ever be pressured to buy any of the wines you've sampled—the vintners are just delighted to expose you to their line of products (besides, you'll often find much better prices at some of the good wine stores in town). Here's a roster of some Napa Valley's most popular wineries that offer tastings and/or tours of their facilities:

Beaulieu Vineyards Nicknamed "BV," this winery is housed in a historic estate and is famous for its cabernet sauvignon. *1960 St. Helena Hwy, Rutherford; 707/963-2411.*

Beringer Vineyards The Napa Valley's oldest continuously operating winery features a stately old Rhineland-style mansion and good tours of the vineyards and caves. It's well known for its chardonnay and cabernet. *2000 Main St, St. Helena; 707/963-7115.*

Château Montelena Winery This stunning French château-style winery, built of stone, is celebrated for its chardonnay. The beautiful setting includes a lake with two islands. *1429 Tubbs Ln, Calistoga; 707/942-5105.*

Clos Pegase Designed by architect Michael Graves, this stunning modern facility offers grand outdoor sculpture, a "Wine in Art" slide show every Saturday afternoon from February through November, and good guided tours of the winery, caves, and art collection. *1060 Dunaweal Ln, 2 miles south of Calistoga; 707/942-4982; www.clospegase.com.*

Domaine Chandon Good sparkling wines come from this winery's handsome building. There's a four-star dining room and fantastic guided tours, too. *1 California Dr, Yountville; 707/944-2280; www.dchandon.com.*

The Hess Collection Winery A stone winery in a remote, scenic location, the Hess Collection is well known for its cabernet sauvignon and chardonnay. Contemporary-American and European art is showcased in a dramatic building, part of the very good self-guided tour. *4411 Redwood Rd, Napa; 707/255-1144.*

Merryvale Vineyards Within Merryvale's historic stone building are daily tastings and, by appointment only, informative, thorough tasting classes on Saturday and Sunday mornings. The winery is best known for its chardonnay. *1000 Main St, St. Helena; 707/963-7777.*

Niebaum-Coppola Winery Filmmaker Francis Ford Coppola now owns this former Inglenook grand château, built in the 1880s. There's a good display on Coppola's film career and Inglenook's history, and a gift shop stocked with wine, pottery, books, T-shirts, and even Coppola's favorite cigars. Daily wine tastings are offered, and tours are by appointment. *1991 St. Helena Hwy, Rutherford; 707/963-9099.*

Opus One In a dramatic bermed neoclassical building, one daily tour with an expensive wine tasting ($25 per 4-ounce glass of wine) is offered by appointment at this extraordinary winery. *7900 St. Helena Hwy, Oakville; 707/944-9442.*

Robert Mondavi Winery This huge, world-famous winery, housed in a Mission-style building, offers excellent tours of the facilities. *7801 St. Helena Hwy, Oakville; 707/963-9611.*

Schramsberg Vineyards Schramsberg's first-rate sparkling wines are showcased in attractive, historic facilities and extensive caves. Interesting guided tours and tastings are available by appointment only. *1400 Schramsberg Rd, just south of Calistoga; 707/942-2414.*

Sterling Vineyards Sterling offers an excellent self-guided tour through its impressive white Mediterranean-style complex perched on a hill. Access is via an aerial sky tram offering splendid views, and there's a vast tasting room with panoramic vistas. *1111 Dunaweal Ln, 1 mile south of Calistoga; 707/942-3300.*

ZD Good tours of the winery are available by appointment. ZD produces fine barrel-fermented chardonnay and powerful reds. *8383 Silverado Trail, near Rutherford; 707/963-5188.*

known for its imposing Victorian structures, many of them in the downtown area near the Napa River. Introduce yourself by taking a self-guided walking tour of downtown Napa's architectural gems. A detailed map highlighting everything from a Victorian Gothic church to an art deco brewery and a Beaux Arts bank is available for free at the Napa Valley Conference and Visitors Bureau (see the contact information above), or you may choose from a half-dozen walking-tour maps sold for a nominal fee by **NAPA COUNTY LANDMARKS** (1026 1st St at Main St, in the Community Preservation Center, Napa, CA 94559; 707/255-1836; open Mon–Fri).

If you have time for only a quick tour, walk along Main Street, which crosses the river. At the south end of Main, adjacent to Veteran's Park on the river's west bank, is a handsome century-old building that's now home to **DOWNTOWN JOE'S RESTAURANT AND BREWERY** (902 Main St at 2nd St, Napa; 707/258-2337). Grab a table on the covered outdoor patio and sample a microbrew or two; Downtown Joe's even makes its own root beer and ginger ale. A couple of blocks north on Main, the locals kick back at the **NAPA VALLEY COFFEE ROASTING COMPANY** (948 Main St at 1st St, Napa; 707/224-2233), a great little spot for a cup of freshly brewed java. Across the street at **COPPERFIELD'S** (1303 1st St at Randolph St, Napa; 707/252-8002), you'll find new and used books at reasonable prices.

For terrific deli sandwiches, fresh vegetable juices, and smoothies, walk west on First Street to the **FIRST SQUEEZE DELI & JUICE BAR & CAFE** (1126 1st St at Coombs St, in the Clock Tower Plaza, Napa; 707/224-6762). You'll have to drive to get to the best deli in town, **GENOVA DELICATESSEN** (1550 Trancas St, W of Jefferson St, Napa; 707/253-8686), which makes great sandwiches, roasted chickens, and a variety of salads and sweets. You can even sit at the espresso bar and order an Italian soda, a gelato, or a great cup of joe. Another Napa favorite for a casual breakfast, lunch, or early dinner is the **ALEXIS BAKING COMPANY AND CAFE** (1517 3rd St at School St, Napa; 707/258-1827), which is also an ideal spot to pick up goodies-to-go such as chocolate-caramel cake and pumpkin-spice muffins. One of the town's best restaurants is the joyous **BISTRO DON GIOVANNI** (4110 St. Helena Hwy/Hwy 29, just N of Salvador Ave, Napa; 707/224-3300), a friendly Italian trattoria.

About nine miles north of Napa, right off Highway 29 where the hills are covered with grapevines, is the tiny town of **YOUNTVILLE**, home of Moet et Chandon's Napa Valley–based winery, Domaine Chandon. Yountville was founded in the mid-19th century by pioneer George Clavert Yount, reportedly the first American to settle in Napa Valley, and it's now the site of some of the best restaurants in the Wine Country, including chef Thomas Keller's **FRENCH LAUNDRY** (6640 Washington St at Creek St, Yountville; 707/944-2380), which also happens to be one of the nation's best restaurants, so reservations (usually months in advance) are essential. Other very popular restaurants are **DOMAINE CHANDON** (1 California Dr, at Domaine Chandon winery, Yountville; 707/944-2892), **MUSTARDS GRILL** (7399 St. Helena Hwy/Hwy 29, Yountville; 707/944-2424), and **THE DINER** (6476 Washington St, near Oak St, Yountville; 707/944-2626).

In the heart of Yountville is the beautiful brick complex now known as **VINTAGE 1870** (6525 Washington St, Yountville; 707/944-2451), a touristy mall with a few dozen shops and a handful of restaurants. The building was erected in 1870 as a winery, and now it's listed on the National Register of Historic Places.

Just up the highway from Yountville is the itsy-bitsy town of **OAKVILLE**, which produces some of the best cabernet sauvignon in the world (as does its little nearby twin town, Rutherford). For a snack or quick lunch, stop at the famous **OAKVILLE GROCERY CO.** (7856 St. Helena Hwy/Hwy 29, at the Oakville Cross Rd, Oakville; 707/944-8802), a gourmet deli disguised as an old-fashioned country grocery store with a striking "Drink Coca-Cola" sign painted on the wall outside. Inside you'll find a fine variety of local wines (including a good selection of splits), a small espresso bar tucked in the corner, and pricey but delicious picnic supplies ranging from pâté and caviar to turkey sandwiches and freshly made sweets.

If you continue north on this scenic stretch of Highway 29, you'll drive smack through the center of **ST. HELENA**, which has come a long way since its days as a rural Seventh Day Adventist village. On St. Helena's Victorian Main Street (a.k.a. Highway 29), farming-supply stores now sit stiffly next to chic women's clothing boutiques and upscale home furnishings stores. Just off the main drag you can find more earthy pleasures at such shops as the **NAPA VALLEY OLIVE OIL MANUFACTURING COMPANY** (Charter Oak and Allison Aves, St. Helena; 707/963-4173), an authentic Italian deli and general store stuffed to the rafters with goodies ranging from dried fruit and biscotti to salami and extra-virgin California olive oil. Take your Italian treats to **LYMAN PARK** (Main St, between Adams and Pine Sts, St. Helena) and picnic on the grass or in the beautiful little white gazebo, where bands sometimes set up for live summer concerts. The town's most popular restaurant is the lovely **RISTORANTE TRA VIGNE** (1050 Charter Oak Ave, off Main St, St. Helena; 707/963-4444), where you'll need a reservation to get a table for lunch or dinner, although you don't need to plan in advance to get a good lunch at the adjoining **CANTINETTA TRA VIGNE** (1050 Charter Oak Ave, St. Helena; 707/963-8888), which offers a beautiful patio for enjoying focaccia pizzas, Italian sandwiches, interesting soups and salads, pastas topped with smoked salmon and other delights, and a surfeit of sweets.

Leaving downtown St. Helena and heading north toward Calistoga, you'll pass under the Tunnel of the Elms (also called the Tree Tunnel), a fantastic row of dozens of elm trees arched across Main Street (Highway 29) in front of Beringer Vineyards. They were planted by the Beringer brothers more than 100 years ago, and their interlaced branches form a gorgeous canopy about a quarter of a mile long. Beyond Beringer are two parks popular for hiking and picnics. **BALE GRIST MILL STATE HISTORIC PARK** (3369 Hwy 29 at Bale Grist Mill Rd, 3 miles N of St. Helena; 707/963-2236) holds a historic flour mill built in 1846 by a British surgeon named Bale. The 36-foot wooden waterwheel still grinds grain into meal and flour on weekends; it also appeared in the 1960 film *Pollyanna*.

Next door is the 1,800-acre **BOTHE-NAPA VALLEY STATE PARK** (707/942-4575, 800/444-PARK reservations; www.reserveamerica.com), offering about 100 picnic spots with barbecues and tables, a swimming pool open from mid-June through Labor Day, and 50 campsites. You can hike from one park to the other by following the moderately strenuous 1.2-mile History Trail.

Water-sports enthusiasts and anglers in search of trout, bass, crappie, catfish, and silver salmon should make the long haul east to Napa County's **LAKE BERRYESSA** (on Berryessa Knoxville Rd, via Steel Canyon Rd or Pope Canyon Rd), the second-largest artificial lake in the state (after Shasta). The 21-mile-long, 3-mile-wide lake has boat launches, berths, picnic areas, campsites, 168 miles of shoreline, and marinas with boat and fishing rentals.

Mud baths, mineral pools, and massages are still the main attractions of **CALISTOGA**, a charming little spa town founded in the mid-19th century by California's first millionaire, Sam Brannan. Savvy Brannan made a bundle of cash selling supplies to miners in the Gold Rush and quickly recognized the value of Calistoga's mineral-rich hot springs. In 1859 he purchased 2,000 acres of the Wappo Indians' hot springs land, built a first-class hotel and spa, and named the region Calistoga (a combination of the words California and Saratoga). He then watched his fortunes grow as affluent San Franciscans paraded into town for a relaxing respite from city life.

Generations later, city slickers are still making the pilgrimage to this city of spas. These days, however, more than a dozen enterprises touting the magical restorative powers of mineral baths line the town's streets. You'll see an odd combo of stressed-out CEOs and earthier types shelling out dough for a chance to soak away their worries and get the kinks rubbed out of their necks. While Calistoga's spas and resorts are far from glamorous (you have to go to the Sonoma Mission Inn & Spa—see the Sonoma Valley section—for rubdowns in luxe surroundings), many offer body treatments and mud baths you won't find anywhere else in this part of the state. Among the most popular spas are **DR. WILKINSON'S HOT SPRINGS** (1507 Lincoln Ave, Calistoga; 707/942-4102; www.drwilkinson. com), where you can get a great massage and numerous other body treatments; **CALISTOGA SPA HOT SPRINGS** (1006 Washington St, Calistoga; 707/942-6269; www.calistogaspa.com), a favorite for families with young children, with four mineral pools in addition to several body-pampering services; **INDIAN SPRINGS RESORT AND SPA** (1712 Lincoln Ave, next to the Gliderport, Calistoga; 707/942-4913), for pricey spa treatments in a historic setting and the best (and largest) mineral pool in the area; and **LAVENDER HILL SPA** (1015 Foothill Blvd/Hwy 29, Calistoga; 707/942-4495; www.lavenderhillspa.com), which provides aromatherapy facials, seaweed wraps, mud baths, and other sybaritic delights in one of the most attractive settings in town.

After you've steamed or soaked away all your tensions, head over to the pretty outdoor patio of the **CALISTOGA INN RESTAURANT AND BREWERY** (1250 Lincoln Ave, Calistoga; 707/942-4101) for a tall, cool brewski. Try one of the house-brewed beers or ales, but save your appetite for one of the better restaurants in town (see below). Once you're rejuvenated, stroll down the main street and browse through the numerous quaint shops marketing everything from French soaps and antique armoires to silk-screened T-shirts and saltwater taffy. For a trip back in time to Calistoga's pioneer past, stop by the **SHARPSTEEN MUSEUM AND BRANNAN COTTAGE** (1311 Washington St, Calistoga; 707/942-5911); admission is free.

Along Calistoga's main drag are a number of restaurants and cafes. Walk south to north on Lincoln Avenue and you'll find California-style thin-crust pizza and calzone at **CHECKERS** (1414 Lincoln Ave, Calistoga; 707/942-9300), which also has an espresso bar and a children's menu. Or try the highly regarded **CATAHOULA RESTAURANT AND SALOON** (1457 Lincoln Ave, Calistoga; 707/942-2275) for gourmet pizza and chef-owner Jan Birnbaum's spirited brand of nouvelle Southern cuisine. Just off Lincoln Avenue is another very good restaurant serving a mix of cuisines for lunch and dinner: **WAPPO BAR & BISTRO** (1226-B Washington St, Calistoga; 707/942-4712). And at the north end of the town's shopping district, across from Nance's Hot Springs, is the **CALISTOGA ROASTERY** (1631 Lincoln Ave, Calistoga; 707/942-5757), a casual, cozy spot where you can get great coffee and iced-coffee drinks, as well as a simple breakfast of poached eggs on toast or a lunchtime sandwich; open daily at 6:30am.

A short drive outside of town is the famous **OLD FAITHFUL GEYSER** (1299 Tubbs Ln, 2 miles N of Calistoga; 707/942-6463; open every day), which faithfully shoots a plume of 350°F mineral water 60 feet into the air at regular intervals. Other natural wonders abound at the **PETRIFIED FOREST** (4100 Petrified Forest Rd, off Hwy 128, 6 miles N of Calistoga; 707/942-6667; www.petrifiedforest.org), where towering redwoods were turned to stone when Mount St. Helena erupted 3 million years ago; you can read about the fascinating event at the museum at the forest entrance. For a splendid view of the entire valley, hike through the beautiful redwood canyons and oak-madrone woodlands in Robert Louis Stevenson State Park to the top of **MOUNT ST. HELENA** (located off Hwy 29, 8 miles N of Calistoga; 707/942-4575).

The Napa Valley is rife with wonderful (albeit mostly pricey) lodgings. If money's no object, stay at either the gorgeous **AUBERGE DU SOLEIL** (180 Rutherford Hill Rd, Rutherford; 707/963-1211 or 800/348-5406), a 52-unit exclusive resort whose designers were inspired by the sunny architecture of southern France, or the impressive **MEADOWOOD RESORT** (900 Meadowood Ln, off the Silverado Trail, St. Helena; 707/963-3646 or 800/458-8080), a 256-acre New England–style Eden that's a mecca to golfers. For those with thinner but still healthy wallets, a couple of other popular choices are **LA RESIDENCE** (4066 St. Helena Hwy/Hwy 29, Napa; 707/253-0337), one of the valley's most luxurious bed-and-breakfasts, and the **INN AT SOUTHBRIDGE** (1020 Main St, between Charter Oak Ave and Pope St, St. Helena; 707/967-9400 or 800/520-6800), the Meadowood Resort's sister inn.

SONOMA VALLEY: SONOMA AND GLEN ELLEN

50 miles north of San Francisco (approximately 1½ hours), traffic permitting. Take Highway 101 North across the Golden Gate Bridge, turn off at the Napa-Vallejo/Highway 37 exit, and follow the signs to Highway 121 and Sonoma.

Many California enophiles would argue that when it comes to comparing the Sonoma Valley's wine country with Napa's, less is definitely more: Sonoma is less congested, less developed, less commercial, and less glitzy than its rival. Smitten with the bucolic charm of the region, Sonomaphiles delight in wandering the area's back roads, leisurely hopping from winery to winery and exploring the quaint towns along the way. Before setting out for this verdant vineyard-laced region, stop at the **SONOMA VALLEY VISITORS BUREAU** (453 1st St E, Sonoma; 707/996-1090) for lots of free, helpful information about the area's wineries, farmers markets, historic sites, walking tours, recreational facilities, and seasonal events. For a small fee you can also get the League for Historic Preservation's self-guided walking-tour map, which outlines a one-hour stroll to 59 historic plaza buildings.

Nestled between the Mayacama Mountains to the east and Sonoma Mountain to the west, the crescent-shaped Sonoma Valley is only 7 miles wide and 17 miles long. But what an impressive and historical stretch of land—after all, this is where California's world-renowned wine industry was born.

The town of **SONOMA**, designed by Mexican general Mariano Vallejo in 1834, is set up like a Mexican pueblo, with a massive tree-covered central plaza that's often hopping with fiestas and family gatherings. Several historic adobe buildings hug the perimeter of the plaza, most of them housing wine stores, specialty food shops, boutiques, and restaurants. The plaza's most famous structure is the Sonoma Mission, the last and northernmost California mission built by Father Junípero Serra.

One of the joys of exploring the small city of Sonoma is that you can park your car and spend the day touring the shops and sights on foot.

Begin your walk at the 8-acre Spanish-style **SONOMA PLAZA,** a National Historic Landmark and the largest town square in California. In the mid-1800s the square was a dusty training ground for General Vallejo's troops, and at the turn of the century a women's club transformed it into the lush park you see today, with more than 200 trees, rose gardens (look for the salmon-colored bloom called the Sonoma Rose), picnic tables and benches, a playground, and a pond swarming with ducks and their far-from-ugly ducklings. Sitting squarely in the center of the plaza is **SONOMA CITY HALL** (1 The Plaza, Sonoma; 707/938-3681) , a stone Mission Revival structure built by San Francisco architect A. C. Lutgens in 1908. Note that all four sides of it are identical—Lutgens didn't want to offend any of the plaza merchants, so he gave them all the same view of his building. The city hall should look familiar to fans of the former hit TV show *Falcon Crest,* which featured it as the Tuscany County Courthouse.

Many people come to Sonoma simply to browse the dozens of shops and galleries circling the plaza. A couple of notable establishments are **ROBIN'S NEST** (116 E Napa St, Sonoma; 707/996-4169), a small discount store that sells high-quality crockery and cooking utensils, and **READERS' BOOKS** (127 E Napa St, Sonoma; 707/939-1779), a strangely configured but pleasant bookstore that stocks many of its tomes in two hard-to-find rooms in the back. This is the place to shop for best-sellers, travel guides, and children's books. For used books, stroll south of the plaza to **CHANTICLEER BOOKS** (526 Broadway, Sonoma; 707/996-5364).

The town's beloved Mission San Francisco Solano de Sonoma, a.k.a. the **SONOMA MISSION** (114 E Spain St at 1st St E, Sonoma; 707/938-9560), sits on the northeast corner of the plaza, and for a nominal fee you can tour the interior of this early 19th-century adobe structure. Your ticket into the mission gives you access (provided you use it the same day) to the nearby **SONOMA BARRACKS** (1st St E and E Spain St, Sonoma), a two-story adobe structure built between 1836 and 1840 to house Mexican army troops; it also gets you into General Vallejo's well-preserved yellow-and-white Victorian home, known as **LACHRYMA MONTIS** (W Spain St at 2nd St W, Sonoma; 707/938-9559)—Latin for "tears of the mountain," a reference to a mineral spring on the property. Scattered locations notwithstanding, all of these historic structures are part of the Sonoma State Historic Park (707/938-1519).

The ever-popular **SEBASTIANI VINEYARDS** (389 4th St E, Sonoma; 707/938-5532 or 800/888-5532) is only four blocks from the Sonoma Plaza. After indulging in a few (or more) free sips of wine, walk or bicycle through the vineyards on the easy .75-mile paved path that leads to General Vallejo's home.

SONOMA VALLEY WINERIES

California's world-renowned wine industry was born in the Sonoma Valley. Franciscan fathers planted the state's first vineyards at the Mission San Francisco Solano de Sonoma in 1823 and harvested the grapes to make their sacramental wines. Thirty-four years later, California's first major vineyard was planted with European grape varietals by Hungarian Count Agoston Haraszthy at Sonoma's revered Buena Vista Winery. Little did the count know that one day he would become widely hailed as the father of California wine—wine that is consistently rated as some of the best in the world. Today more than 40 wineries dot the Sonoma Valley, most offering pretty picnic areas and free tours of their wine-making facilities. Here's a roundup of some of Sonoma's best:

Benziger Family Winery Tram ride tours take visitors through the vineyards here, and tastings are held in the wine shop. Home to good chardonnay and cabernet sauvignon. *1883 London Ranch Rd, Glen Ellen; 707/935-3000 or 800/989-8890.*

Buena Vista Winery California's oldest premium winery (founded in 1857) is a large estate set in a forest with picnic grounds. It offers tours of the stone winery and the hillside tunnels, wine tasting, and a gallery featuring locals' artwork and a gift shop. *18000 Old Winery Rd, Sonoma; 707/938-1266.*

Château St. Jean Follow the self-guided tour through this beautiful 250-acre estate with tastings in the mansion and stunning views from a faux medieval tower. There is also a picnic area. *8555 Sonoma Hwy (Hwy 12), Kenwood; 707/833-4134; www.chateaustjean.com.*

Ferrari-Carano Vineyards and Winery Ferrari-Carano offers good chardonnay, fumé blanc, and cabernet. A cutting-edge facility. *8761 Dry Creek Rd, Healdsburg; 707/433-6700; www.ferrari-carano.com.*

Geyser Peak Winery Established in 1880, this stone winery covered with ivy produces pleasant gewürztraminer, chardonnay, and shiraz. Group tours are offered and there are two small picnic areas. *22281 Chianti Rd, Geyserville; 707/857-9400 or 800/255-9463; www.peakwinesinternational.com.*

Gloria Ferrer Champagne Caves See interesting subterranean cellars on the excellent guided tour. Tastings are also offered. *23555 Hwy 121, Sonoma; 707/996-7256; www.gloriaferrer.com.*

Gundlach-Bundschu Winery This grand, historic building was established in 1858 and is set on impressive grounds. Gundlach-Bundschu is known primarily for its red wines. Picnic facilities and tastings are available at the winery. *2000 Denmark St, Sonoma; 707/938-5277; www.gunbun.com.*

Kenwood Vineyards Founded in 1970, Kenwood is renowned for its red wines and quaint wooden barns. There's a tasting room and the winery's Artist Series features a terrific collection of original art created especially for Kenwood wine labels. *9592 Sonoma Hwy (Hwy 12), Kenwood; 707/833-589; www.kenwoodvineyards.com.*

Korbel Champagne Cellars An ivy-covered brick building is set in a redwood forest with a view of the Russian River. Korbel hosts informative tours; the extensive and beautiful flower gardens are open for tours from May through September. *13250 River Rd, Guerneville; 707/887-2294; www.korbel.com.*

Kunde Estate Winery This century-old winery set on 2,000 gorgeous acres of rolling hills is one of Sonoma County's largest grape suppliers. It also boasts a good tasting room. *10155 Sonoma Hwy (Hwy 12), Kenwood; 707/833-5501; www.kunde.com.*

Matanzas Creek Winery A beautiful drive leads to this winery's attractive facilities. Matanzas offers outstanding chardonnay and merlot as well as guided tours, tastings, and picnic tables. *6097 Bennett Valley Rd, Santa Rosa; 707/528-6464 or 800/590-6464; www.matanzascreek.com.*

Sebastiani Vineyards Sonoma's largest premium-variety winery, Sebastiani Vineyards provides tours of its aging cellar, which includes an interesting collection of carved-oak cask heads. There's also a tasting room and picnic tables. *389 4th St E, Sonoma; 800/888-5532 ext. 3249; www.sebastiani.com.*

Viansa Winery and Marketplace These buildings and grounds modeled after a Tuscan village are owned by the Sebastiani family. Viansa produces good sauvignon blanc, chardonnay, and cabernet, plus gourmet Italian picnic fare and local delicacies perfect for the beautiful hillside picnic grounds. *25200 Hwy 121, Sonoma; 707/935-4700 or 800/995-4740; www.viansa.com.*

As you pound the pavement around the plaza, you'll pass many of the city's good restaurants and cafes. For a strong cup of coffee or an iced espresso shake and a quick bite to eat, head over to the **COFFEE GARDEN** (421 1st St W, Sonoma; 707/996-6645), then carry your purchase to the pretty vine-laced patio hidden in back, where you can relax to the sounds of classical music. Not far from the plaza, **THE GENERAL'S DAUGHTER** (400 W Spain St, Sonoma; 707/938-4004) dishes out good, moderately priced Continental cuisine in the beautifully remodeled Victorian home built in 1878 by General Vallejo's daughter, Natalia. Belly-bustin' deli sandwiches are slapped together at the **SONOMA CHEESE FACTORY** (2 W Spain St, Sonoma; 707/996-1931), where you can actually watch the factory workers make your cheese before they make your sandwich. Take your victuals to their covered patio or, even better, to a picnic table in the plaza. On the east side of the plaza, grab a stool at the handsome marble counter at the **BASQUE BOULANGERIE CAFE** (460 1st St E, Sonoma; 707/935-7687) and order one of several fine wines by the glass, a Caesar salad, and perhaps a French ham sandwich.

When you're ready to venture beyond the city limits, drive north a few miles to the tiny town of **BOYES HOT SPRINGS** (18140 Sonoma Hwy/Hwy 12 at Boyes Blvd, Boyes Hot Springs; 707/938-9000 or

800/862-4945), home of the ever-popular Sonoma Mission Inn & Spa, a great place to sleep and an even greater place for a massage in its deluxe European-style spa, where the likes of Barbra Streisand, Tom Cruise, and Harrison Ford come to get pampered.

A few more miles north is Jack London territory. There are more places and things named after Jack London in Sonoma County than there are women named María in Mexico, and this cult reaches its apex in **GLEN ELLEN**. This is where the author of *The Call of the Wild*, *The Sea Wolf*, and some 50 other books and numerous articles built his aptly named Beauty Ranch, an 800-acre spread now known as **JACK LONDON STATE HISTORIC PARK** (2400 London Ranch Rd, off Hwy 12 and Arnold Dr, Glen Ellen; 707/938-5216). London's vineyards, piggery, horse stalls, and other ranch buildings are here, as well as the cottage where he wrote (and where he died) and a beautiful stone house-turned-museum called the **HOUSE OF HAPPY WALLS**. Lining those walls are pieces from London's interesting and worldly art collection as well as personal mementos, including some of the 600 rejection letters he received from publishers (including a hotshot at the *San Francisco Chronicle*), who surely must have fallen over backwards in their cushy corporate chairs when London later became the highest-paid author of his time. There's a $5-per-car fee to enter the park (and it's worth spending an extra buck to get the informative park map), or you may hike or ride your bike or horse in for free. Your dog can come along, too (a $1 fee), though canines are restricted to certain trails.

The park is a pretty place for a picnic, with tables and barbecues set out under the oak and eucalyptus trees, a short walk from the parking lot. Carry your lunch to London's cottage to find the park's best table, next to a goldfish pond overlooking the grapevines. Hard-core hikers should plan to spend the day trekking to **BATHHOUSE LAKE** and up **SONOMA MOUNTAIN**'s steep slopes (carry water), which are blanketed with grassy meadows and forests of madrone, manzanita, redwood, and Douglas fir. Or consider letting the friendly folks at the Sonoma Cattle Company (707/996-8566), based in the park, saddle up a horse for you. Call for the lowdown on their guided horseback trips; reservations are required.

A ticket to Jack London Park allows you free entrance (on the same day only) to the spectacular 2,700-acre **SUGARLOAF RIDGE STATE PARK** (2605 Adobe Canyon Rd, 3 miles E of Hwy 12, Kenwood; camping reservations: 800/444-PARK; www.reserveamerica.com), a 20-minute drive north. Sugarloaf has 25 miles of hiking and horseback-riding trails (with great views from the ridge), guided horseback rides, 50 tent campsites, and a horse corral.

For lovely lodgings in the Sonoma Valley, check out **EL DORADO HOTEL** (405 1st St W, Sonoma; 707/996-3030 or 800/289-3031), offering moderately priced rooms that overlook the Sonoma Plaza; the palatial **SONOMA MISSION INN & SPA** (see the contact information above); or the posh 12-room **KENWOOD INN AND SPA** (10400 Sonoma Hwy/Hwy 12, 3 miles past Glen Ellen, Kenwood; 707/833-1293; www.sterba.com/kenwood/inn).

Marin County

Take Highway 1 North or Highway 101 North to the Golden Gate Bridge, get in the right lane, cross the bridge (this is the toll-free direction), and exit at Alexander Avenue; stay in the right lane and head east to Sausalito (approximately 15 to 20 minutes, traffic permitting).

SAUSALITO

Nestled on the east side of Marin County is the pretty little town of **SAUSALITO**, a former Portuguese fishing village that's now home to the well-heeled owners of spectacular hillside mansions. Once you exit the Golden Gate Bridge, stay on Alexander Avenue, which eventually turns into Bridgeway, the main drag through the center of town. Pricey boutiques and waterfront restaurants line this street, and a paved promenade offers a truly breathtaking, unobstructed view of Angel Island, Alcatraz, and the San Francisco skyline.

If you have kids in tow, be sure to spend an afternoon or a day at the **BAY AREA DISCOVERY MUSEUM** (Fort Baker, under the N end of the Golden Gate Bridge; 415/487-4398; www.badm.org), where children can sing and dance in the Discovery Theater, pretend to pump gas into a Model T in the Transportation Building, create a clay sculpture or paint a picture in the Art Sport Center, build a skyscraper in the Architecture & Design Building, dissect a squid in the Science Lab, and much more. This unique hands-on interactive learning center is designed for ages 1 through 10, and it's a guaranteed child-pleaser.

To best appreciate the town of Sausalito, park your car near Bridgeway (you may have to hit a municipal lot or a side street to find a spot) and walk along the promenade and through the tiny village. For the perfect perch on the bay, walk through the touristy restaurant **HORIZONS** (558 Bridgeway, Sausalito; 415/331-3232) and grab a seat on the wind-sheltered deck in back, where you can sip the spirit of your choice and wave at the yachters sailing just a few feet under your nose.

The **NO NAME BAR** (757 Bridgeway, Sausalito; 415/332-1392) is one of the few places on Bridgeway where you'll find a local resident. Don't try looking for the bar's name, because there's only a small, handsome wooden sign that says "Bar" in gold letters. The No Name's free jazz and R&B concerts (held Tuesday through Saturday night and Sunday afternoon) draw crowds. Stroll across the street and you'll see the pier, where you can catch a ferry to San Francisco. Nearby is the tiny **PLAZA VINA DEL MAR**, graced by a pair of elephant statues and a fountain from the Panama-Pacific International Exposition of 1915. One of the highlights of Sausalito is its gorgeous yachts—walk down the wooden planks and try to guess how many greenbacks it takes to own (and maintain) one of these glistening beauties.

The four-story **VILLAGE FAIR** (777 Bridgeway, Sausalito), on the west side of Bridgeway, is a quaint shopping mall honeycombed with shops and flowers and even a little waterfall. Don't expect to find any bargains here, but it's worth a quick look. You'll see many folks licking **LAPPERT'S ICE CREAM** in freshly made waffle cones, which is dished out in two shops on either side of Village Fair (689 Bridgeway, 415/332-2019; and 817 Bridgeway, Sausalito; 415/332-8175). One block west of Bridgeway is Caledonia Street, where the locals hang out. Cafes, shops, and a movie theater line this street, as well as **SUSHI RAN** (107 Caledonia St, next to the Marin Theater, Sausalito; 415/332-3620), a first-rate sushi bar and restaurant open for lunch and dinner.

At the north end of Sausalito is **FRED'S PLACE** (1917 Bridgeway, Sausalito; 415/332-4575), which has been making terrific French toast and other belly-packing breakfast fare since 1966. Eat a hearty breakfast, then head across the street and down the hill to the **BAY MODEL** (on Marinship Way, off the E side of Bridgeway, Sausalito; 415/332-3871), a gigantic working hydraulic model of the San Francisco Bay and the Delta region used by the U.S. Army Corps of Engineers to study the tides and various bay problems. The Bay Model also offers interactive exhibits and a World War II shipyard display; admission is free and it's open Tuesday through Saturday. Just before Bridgeway merges with Highway 101, you'll find Sausalito's community of houseboat dwellers. Take a gander at the floating homes, which vary from funky little wooden abodes covered with pots of bright flowers to swanky residences with helipads (park at the Waldo Point Harbor Houseboat Marina at the north end of Bridgeway).

Before you say so long to Sausalito, take a spin through the lush, landscaped hills, zigzagging your way from one end to the other to get a taste of how the rich really live. It's hard to get too lost—all the streets eventually wind down to Bridgeway—just don't get too distracted by the magnificent mansions as you navigate the narrow, twisting roads.

TIBURON

For a tour of tiny **TIBURON** and Belvedere, the waterfront towns that sit cheek by jowl directly across the bay, head north on Bridgeway until it hooks up with Highway 101, then follow the signs to Tiburon Boulevard and downtown Tiburon (about a 15-minute drive). Formerly a railroad town and until 1963 the terminus of the Northwestern Pacific Railroad, Tiburon (Spanish for "shark") is now a quaint New England–style coastal village. Its short Main Street is packed with expensive antique and specialty shops, as well as restaurants with incredible bay views. You can leave your car on the outskirts and walk to the village, or park in the large pay-lot off Main Street. (An even better way to get here is by bicycle or by taking the ferry from San Francisco; it drops off passengers at the edge of town.) At the tip of the Tiburon peninsula is a small grassy park with benches; on sunny days people flock here with picnics to admire the panoramic view of San Francisco and Angel Island.

For lunch or dinner, ask for a seat on the patio at **GUAYMAS** (5 Main St, at the ferry landing, Tiburon; 415/435-6300)—you'll likely need reservations on sunny days—and indulge in the restaurant's classic Mexican fare and a frothy margarita or one of the fine tequilas. You can get lesser-quality fare but equally spectacular views at the ever-popular **SAM'S ANCHOR CAFE** (27 Main St, Tiburon; 415/435-4527), where Bay Area residents crowd the huge outdoor deck in back on sunny weekends for beer, burgers, and big baskets of fries.

Stroll west on Main Street and you'll bump into the intimate **TIBURON DELI** (110 Main St, Tiburon; 415/435-4888), which offers Bud's ice cream, frozen yogurt, and healthy sandwiches. The deli is part of Tiburon's historic Ark Row, an assembly of charming 100-year-old restored arks that now houses several shops. Follow Main beyond the shops to Beach Road for another amazing view of the bay, one that includes the prized yachts docked in front of the members-only San Francisco Yacht Club.

BELVEDERE

This is where Tiburon blends into **BELVEDERE** (Italian for "beautiful view"), an ultra-exclusive community that makes Sausalito look like a poor cousin. The entire city consists of only half a square mile of land—but this is one tony piece of real estate. To get a better view of Belvedere, reclaim your car and drive up the tiny town's steep, narrow roads for a glimpse of the highly protected, well-shielded multimillion-dollar homes where international celebs such as Elton John have been known to hide out. After your hillside cruise, drive along San Rafael Avenue, which hugs Richardson Bay on the north side of Tiburon, for another great view of the water. You can't see it very well from the street, but behind a stretch of houses on the east side of San Rafael Avenue is Belvedere Lagoon, where residents sail, canoe, kayak, and mingle with their neighbors on their sunny waterside decks (you can get a peek at the lagoon just steps from the intersection of San Rafael Avenue and Windward Road).

MILL VALLEY

San Rafael Avenue winds its way north to Tiburon Boulevard, which leads back to Highway 101. If you stay on Tiburon Boulevard and follow it past the highway on-ramps, it turns into East Blithedale Avenue and leads directly into the heart of the lovely town of **MILL VALLEY**. This is where many millionaires have forsaken bayside plots of land for the highly coveted real estate nestled in the redwoods. Introduce yourself to the town by walking along Throckmorton Avenue, the main shopping strip off Blithedale. For more information on this city, contact the **MILL VALLEY CHAMBER OF COMMERCE** (85 Throckmorton Ave, next to the Depot Bookstore, Mill Valley; 415/388-9700, www.millvalley.org). For additional not-to-be-missed Marin County attractions, see the Marin Coast section.

Palo Alto

30 miles south of San Francisco (approximately 45 to 50 minutes, traffic permitting). Take Highway 101 South to Palo Alto.

The home of notable restaurants, fine-art galleries, foreign-movie houses, great bookstores, world-famous **STANFORD UNIVERSITY**, and some of the best shopping this side of heaven, Palo Alto is a beacon of cosmopolitan energy shining on the suburban sea. Much of the fuel for this cultural lighthouse comes, of course, from the university, which offers free tours of its attractive campus daily. Highlights of the university include the Main Quad, Hoover Tower (for a nominal fee you can get a great view from its observation platform), the huge Stanford bookstore, and gorgeous Memorial Church; call the **VISITORS INFORMATION SERVICES** (650/723-2560) for more tour information. If you'd like to try to glimpse some atom smashing, visit the nearby Stanford Linear Accelerator Center (650/926-3300, press 9 to arrange a tour).

If you didn't find the tome you were looking for at the university's bookstore, Palo Alto and its neighbors contain many other outlets for bibliophiles. **KEPLER'S BOOKS AND MAGAZINES** (1010 El Camino Real, Menlo Park; 650/324-4321) is a wonderland for serious bookworms; you'll also find a healthy selection of mind food at **PRINTER'S INC.** (310 California Ave, Palo Alto; 650/327-6500), **BORDERS BOOKS** (456 University Ave, Palo Alto; 650/326-3670), **STACEY'S** (219 University Ave, Palo Alto; 650/326-0681), and **BOOKS INC.** (Stanford Shopping Center, on El Camino Real near University Ave, Palo Alto; 650/321-0600). You'll probably need to follow up that literary excursion with a cup of joe. Some of the bookstores, such as Printer's Inc. and Borders, serve coffee and light snacks, but for authentic coffeehouse atmosphere and great espresso try **CAFFE VERONA** (236 Hamilton Ave, Palo Alto; 650/326-9942) or stop in to **CAFE BORRONE** (1010 El Camino Real, Menlo Park; 650/327-0830), located next to Kepler's.

Moviegoers have a broad range of choices. The beautifully restored **STANFORD THEATER** (221 University Ave, Palo Alto; 650/324-3700), which showcases classic flicks, is especially worth a visit. If you prefer your performances live, check out the local **THEATREWORKS** troupe (650/463-1950), the **LIVELY ARTS** (650/725-2787) series at Stanford University, or the top-name talents currently appearing at the **SHORE-LINE AMPHITHEATER** (1 Amphitheater Pkwy, Mountain View; 650/967-3000). If you have nothing to wear for the show (or, indeed, if you have any other shopping need), Palo Alto won't let you down. University Avenue and its side streets contain a plethora of interesting stores. The **STANFORD SHOPPING CENTER** (on El Camino Real, just N of downtown; 650/617-8585) is a sprawling, beautifully landscaped temple of consumerism, and includes such stores as Bloomingdale's, Macy's, Nordstrom, Ralph Lauren, the Gap, Crate & Barrel, the Disney Store, and many more. Good places to eat in this shopper's paradise include Bravo Fono and Max's Opera Cafe.

If you're looking for a good meal in town, Palo Alto offers many first-rate restaurants, including **BISTRO ELAN** (448 California Ave, just off El Camino Real, Palo Alto; 650/327-0284), which serves French fare with a California flair for lunch and dinner in a spare Parisian neighborhood bistro–style dining room; **EVVIA** (420 Emerson St, between Lytton and University Aves, Palo Alto; 650/326-0983), a warm and welcoming Greek restaurant with a sun-drenched, Mediterranean feel; **L'AMIE DONIA** (530 Bryant St, between University and Hamilton Aves, Palo Alto; 650/323-7614), an amiable, bustling French bistro and wine bar; and **MACARTHUR PARK** (27 University Ave, just off El Camino Real near the train depot, Palo Alto; 650/321-9990), in an attractive Julia Morgan–designed building, where crowds come for the lean, tender, oak-smoked ribs and first-rate mesquite-grilled steaks.

The favored lodging in Palo Alto is the modern, Mediterranean-style 62-room **GARDEN COURT HOTEL** (520 Cowper St, between University and Hamilton Aves, Palo Alto; 650/322-9000 or 800/824-9028), surrounded by Italianate architecture draped with arches and studded with colorful tile work and hand-wrought-iron fixtures. And just outside of Palo Alto is another great choice: **STANFORD PARK HOTEL** (100 El Camino Real, N of University Ave, Menlo Park; 650/322-1234 or 800/368-2468; www.woodsidehotels.com), a 163-room lodging near Stanford University with handsome English-style furniture, fireplaces, balconies, vaulted ceilings, and courtyard views.

Half Moon Bay

The fastest way to Half Moon Bay is to take the Highway 92 exit off Interstate 280, which leads straight into town. Far more scenic, however, is the drive along Highway 1, which, aside from the section known as Devil's Slide, moves right along at a 50mph clip. The entrance to Main Street is located about two blocks up Highway 92 from the Highway 1 intersection. Head toward the Shell station, then turn south onto Main Street until you cross a small bridge.

Most Bay Area families know Half Moon Bay as the pumpkin capital of the West, where thousands of pilgrims make their annual journey in search of the ultimate Halloween jack-o'-lantern. Since 1970 the Half Moon Bay Art & Pumpkin Festival has featured all manner of squash cuisine and crafts, as well as the Giant Pumpkin weigh-in contest, won recently by a 974-pound monster. A Great Pumpkin Parade, pumpkin-carving competitions, pie-eating contests, and piles of great food pretty much assure a good time for all; for more information call the Pumpkin Hotline at 650/726-9652.

Pumpkins aside, Half Moon Bay is a jewel of a town, saved from mediocrity by diverting its historic Main Street well away from the fast-food chains and gas stations of Highway 1. The locals are disarmingly friendly, actually bestowing greetings as you walk along the rows of small shops and restaurants. Then, of course, there are the 4 miles of golden crescent-shaped beach, one of the prettiest in all of California; bustling Pillar Point Harbor, launching point for whale-watching and deep-sea-fishing trips; and myriad hiking and biking trails along the coast and into the redwood forests. Combine this with an array of commendable accommodations and restaurants, and you have the perfect ingredients for a peaceful weekend getaway.

The best way to explore the small, flat town of Half Moon Bay and its beaches is on a mountain bike. Lucky for you, they're available for rent at the **BICYCLERY** (432 Main St, Half Moon Bay; 650/726-6000). Prices range from $6 an hour to $24 all day. Helmets—also for rent—are required. Be sure to ask one of the staffers about the best biking trails in the area, particularly the wonderful beach trail from Kelly Avenue to Pillar Point Harbor.

Once you have explored the town, take your mountain bike to **PURISIMA CREEK REDWOODS** (650/691-1200), a little-known sanctuary frequented mostly by locals. Located on the western slopes of the Santa Cruz Mountains, the preserve is filled with fern-lined creek banks, lush redwood forests, and fields of wildflowers and berries that are accessible to hikers, mountain bikers, and equestrians along miles of trails. From the Highway 1/Highway 92 intersection in Half Moon Bay, drive 1 mile south on Highway 1 to Higgins Purisima Creek Road and turn left, then continue 4.5 miles to a small gravel parking lot—that's the trailhead.

Another popular Half Moon Bay activity is deep-sea fishing. Even if you don't fish, it's worth a trip to Pillar Point Harbor to take in the pungent aroma of the sea; the rows of rusty trawlers and the salty men and women tending to endless chores evoke a sort of Hemingwayish sense of romance. **PILLAR POINT HARBOR** (4 miles north of Half Moon Bay off Highway 1) is just that sort of big ol' fishing harbor. Visitors are encouraged to walk along the pier and even partake in a fishing trip. Captain John's Fishing Trips (650/726-2913 or 800/391-8787) and Huck Finn Sportfishing (650/726-7133 or 800/572-2934) each charge around $55, including rod and reel, for a day's outing—a small price to pay for 60 pounds of fresh salmon. Between January and March, whale-watching trips also depart daily.

Near the harbor is one of the most infamous surf beaches in California: **MAVERICK BEACH**. If the name sounds familiar, that's because this local Half Moon Bay surf spot made national headlines as the site where famed Hawaiian surfer Mark Foo drowned in 1995 after being thrown from his board by a 20-foot wave. On calmer days, though, secluded Maverick Beach is still a good place to escape the weekend crowds because, although everyone's heard about the beach, few know where it is and you won't find it on any map. Here's the dope: From Capistrano Road at Pillar Point Harbor, turn left on Prospect Way, left on Broadway, right on Princeton, then right on Westpoint to the West Shoreline Access parking lot (on your left). Park here, then continue up Westpoint on foot toward the Pillar Point Satellite Tracking Station. Take about 77 steps, and on your right will be a trailhead leading to legendary Maverick Beach a short distance away.

If surfing isn't your thing, how about ocean kayaking? If you're one of those type A people who can't just lie on the beach and relax, **CALIFORNIA CANOE & KAYAK** (Pillar Point Harbor at the Half Moon Bay Yacht Club, Half Moon Bay; 650/728-1803) has the answer. For $89 they'll take you out on the bay for a 7-hour lesson in the fundamentals of the sea. Sure, it's expensive, but the rewards are priceless. Classes are usually held from 9am to 4pm Saturdays and Sundays, May through October (call to confirm); rentals are also available.

Back on land is the **ANDREOTTI FAMILY FARM** (227 Kelly Ave, halfway between Hwy 1 and the beach, Half Moon Bay; 650/726-9461). If you like vegetables, you'll love this place. Every Friday, Saturday, and Sunday one of the family members slides open the old barn door at 10am sharp to reveal a cornucopia of just-picked artichokes, peas, brussels sprouts, beans, strawberries, and just about whatever else is growing in their adjacent fields. The Andreotti enterprise has been in operation since 1926, so it's a sure bet they know their veggies. (Open till 6pm year-round.)

If you're a golfer, be sure to reserve a tee time at the oceanside 18-hole **HALF MOON BAY GOLF LINKS** (2000 Fairway Dr, next to the Half Moon Bay Lodge, Half Moon Bay; 650/726-6384). Designed by Arnold Palmer, it's rated among the top 100 courses in the country, as well as number one in the Bay Area, according to the *San Francisco Business Times*. Greens fees are a bit steep, however, ranging from $85 to $115. Reserve as far in advance as possible.

On your way out of town, be sure to stop at **OBESTER WINERY**'s Wine-Tasting and Sales Room (12341 San Mateo Rd, Half Moon Bay; 650/726-9463), which is only a few miles from Half Moon Bay up Highway 92. It's a pleasant drive—passing numerous fields of flowers, Christmas tree farms, and pumpkin patches—to this wood shack filled with award-winning grape juice. Behind the tasting room is a small picnic area that's perfect for an afternoon lunch break. (Open every day, 10am–5pm.)

Santa Cruz

The most scenic route to Santa Cruz is along Highway 1 from San Francisco, which you can cruise at a steady 50mph along the coast. Faster but far less romantic is Route 17, which is accessed near San Jose from I-280, I-880, or Highway 101 and literally ends at the foot of the boardwalk. The exception to this rule is on weekend mornings, when Route 17 tends to logjam with Bay Area beachgoers while Highway 1 remains relatively uncrowded.

For nearly a century, Santa Cruz has been synonymous with "beach and boardwalk," as if this seaside city of 50,000 exists solely to sustain what is now the only major beachside amusement park left on the Pacific Coast. Considering that the annual number of boardwalk visitors is 62 times greater than the city's population, it's no surprise that Santa Cruz's other highlights are all but ignored by the hordes of thrill-seekers who head straight for the waterfront each year.

Not that the **SANTA CRUZ BEACH BOARDWALK** (400 Beach St, Santa Cruz; 831/423-5590)—now a cement walk—isn't worthy of the limelight. Ranked among the top amusement parks in the nation, with a higher attendance than either Marine World–Africa USA or Paramount's Great America, the privately owned amusement park has cleaned up its once-tarnished act by pouring a pile of money into improvements and security; the boardwalk is truly safe and clean these days. Then, of course, there's the legendary Giant Dipper, considered by those-who-would-know to be the greatest roller coaster ever built, and the hand-carved horses of the Looff Carousel, the last bona fide brass ring merry-go-round in North America. These two rides alone are worth a walk down the boardwalk. Buy the reasonably priced day pass and stand in line for rides like Riptide and the Bermuda Triangle, and you won't be disappointed. If you're among the crowds here on a Friday night in the summer, don't miss the Boardwalk's free concerts, featuring the likes of the Shirelles, Chubby Checker, and Sha Na Na.

Yet even without its celebrated amusement park, Santa Cruz would still be one of California's top coastal destinations. Where else can you find a vibrant, cross-cultural college town (remember, this used to be the LSD capital of the world) perched on the edge of an immense bay teeming with marine life, ringed by miles of golden beaches, and backed by dense redwood forests? Remove those boardwalk blinders for a day and you'll find out that there's a whole lot more to Santa Cruz than cotton candy and arcades.

Beaches are Santa Cruz's second most popular attraction. At the western edge of the city, on the north end of West Cliff Drive, is **NATURAL BRIDGES STATE BEACH,** named after archways carved into the rock formations here by the ocean waves (only one of the three original arches still stands). The beach is popular with surfers, wind surfers, tide-pool trekkers, and sunbathers, as well as fans of the migrating monarch butterflies that roost in the nearby eucalyptus grove from late October through February. On the south end of West Cliff Drive is **LIGHTHOUSE FIELD STATE BEACH,** the reputed birthplace of American surfing. This beach has several benches for sitting and gazing, a jogging and bicycling path, and a park with picnic tables, showers, and even plastic-bag dispensers for cleaning up after your dog (it's one of the few public places in town where canines are allowed). The nearby brick lighthouse is now home to the tiny **SANTA CRUZ SURFING MUSEUM** (W Cliff Dr at Lighthouse Point, Santa Cruz; 831/429-3429)—the first of its kind in the world—which is chock-full of hang-ten memorabilia (admission is free).

Between the lighthouse and the boardwalk is that famous strip of the sea known as **STEAMERS LANE,** the summa cum laude of California surfing spots (savvy surfers say this—not Southern California—is the place to catch the best breaks in the state). Watch the dudes ride the gnarly waves, then head over to the marvelous (but often crowded) white-sand Santa Cruz Beach fronting the boardwalk. The breakers are tamer here, and free volleyball courts and barbecue pits make this a favorite spot for sunbathing, swimming, picnicking, and playing volleyball on the sand courts. In the center of the action is the 85-year-old **MUNICIPAL WHARF,** where you can drive your car out to the shops, fish markets, and seafood restaurants.

So maybe you can't surf, but surely you can paddle a stable sea kayak around the Santa Cruz coast. **VISION QUEST KAYAKING** (831/425-8445), located on the northeast end of the Santa Cruz Wharf, rents single-, double-, and triple-seater kayaks for exploring the nearby cliffs and kelp beds where a multitude of sea otters, seals, sea lions, and other marine animals congregate. No experience is necessary, and all ages are welcome. Guided tours are also available. And if kayaking is out of your league, you might want to rent a bike and tour the town. The pedal-friendly downtown area is flat and wide (ditto the wharf and boardwalk), and the shoreline bike path along West Cliff Drive is sensational. If you can't bring your own wheels, the **BICYCLE RENTAL & TOUR CENTER** (131 Center St, two blocks from the Municipal Wharf, Santa Cruz; 831/426-8687) rents touring, tandem, and mountain bikes at hourly, daily, and weekly rates, and even throws in free helmets, packs, maps, and locks.

The **PACIFIC GARDEN MALL** (a.k.a. Pacific Avenue) is Santa Cruz's main shopping district, and until the Loma Prieta earthquake hit in 1989, it was a charming amalgam of Victorian houses, street musicians, bag ladies and gentlemen, inexpensive restaurants, bookstores, antique shops, and New Age head shops. It's been recuperating slowly from the apocalypse (the earthquake's epicenter was only 10 miles away), but there's still plenty to gawk at. As you make your way down the mall, look for the Octagon Building, an ornate, eight-sided Victorian brick edifice built in 1882 that has survived numerous quakes. The building once served as the city's Hall of Records and is now part of the **MCPHERSON CENTER FOR ART AND HISTORY** (705 Front St at Cooper St, Santa Cruz; 831/429-1964), where museums showcase 10,000 years of the area's past as well as contemporary art of the Pacific Rim. Next door is the excellent **VISITOR'S INFORMATION CENTER** (701 Front St, Santa Cruz; 800/833-3494).

One good thing about a college town—it knows how to party. The Cruz's coolest blues are at **MOE'S ALLEY** (1535 Commercial Wy, Santa Cruz; 831/479-1854), featuring live music (and dancing) nightly. For traditional and modern jazz, it's the **KUUMBWA JAZZ CENTER** (320 Cedar St, Santa Cruz; 831/427-2227), a nonprofit (and nonsmoking) landmark that's been around for the past two decades. Local rock, reggae, blues, and world-beat bands mix it up at the **CATALYST** (1011 Pacific Ave, Santa Cruz; 831/423-1336), which occasionally pulls in some big names, too. Bluegrass, Hawaiian, and folk music finds a venue at cavernous **PALOOKAVILLE** (1133 Pacific Ave, Santa Cruz; 831/454-0600), which also has its share of rock and reggae.

The nearby **BOOKSHOP SANTA CRUZ** (1520 Pacific Ave, Santa Cruz; 831/423-0900) has an inventory worthy of any university town, with a particularly good children's section, an adjacent coffeehouse, and plenty of places to sit, sip, and peruse a bit of your prospective purchase. For great organically grown produce and other picnic-basket goodies, shop at the farmers market held Wednesday from 2:30pm to 6:30pm on

Lincoln Street, between Pacific Avenue and Cedar Street. Another town highlight is the small aquarium and marine exhibits at the **JOSEPH M. LONG MARINE LABORATORY** (100 Shaffer Rd, Santa Cruz; 831/459-4308; www.ucsc.edu/mb/lml/), where you can handle mollusks and other small sea creatures. You can also see scientists studying dolphins and sea lions in the lab's marine mammal pools.

For some serious hiking and mountain biking, drive about 23 miles north to the 18,000-acre **BIG BASIN REDWOODS STATE PARK**, California's first state park (established in 1902) and its second-largest redwood preserve. Big Basin is home to black-tailed deer and mountain lions, and 80 miles of trails wind past 300-foot-high redwoods and many waterfalls. Some trails even access the long golden strand of **WADDELL CREEK BEACH** (21600 Big Basin Wy, off Hwy 236, 9 miles N of Boulder Creek; 831/338-8860); call for recorded directions.

Locomotive lovers, kids, and fans of Mother Nature should hop aboard the historic narrow-gauge **ROARING CAMP TRAIN** (831/335-4400) for a 6-mile round-trip excursion up some of the steepest grades in North America. The steam-powered train winds through stately redwood groves to the summit of Bear Mountain. Another train, called the Big Trees Railroad, offers an 18-mile round-trip ride through mountain tunnels and along ridges with spectacular views of the San Lorenzo River before stopping at the Santa Cruz Beach Boardwalk. To reach the Roaring Camp and Big Trees Narrow-Gauge Railroad center, take Highway 17 to the Mount Herman Road exit, then turn on Graham Hill Road (near the town of Felton). Train schedules vary seasonally; call for more details.

Marin Coast

When you consider that the San Francisco Bay Area has more people than the entire state of Oregon, and that Marin County has the highest per capita income in the nation, you would expect its coastline to be lined with fancy lodgings and resorts. Truth is, you won't find even a Motel 6 along the entire Marin coast, due partly to public pressure but mostly to the inaccessibly rugged, heavily forested terrain (it may look like a 15-minute drive from San Francisco on the map, but 90 minutes later you'll probably still be negotiating hairpin curves down the side of Mount Tamalpais). In fact, the Marin coast is just short of Eden, a veritable organic playground for city-weary 9-to-5ers in search of a patch of green or a square of sand to call their own for a day.

MARIN HEADLANDS

Head north across the Golden Gate Bridge, take the Alexander Avenue exit, and make your first left onto Conzelman Road, which leads into the Marin Headlands.

On a sunny San Francisco day, there's no better place to spend time outdoors than in the Marin Headlands. For more than a century following the Civil War, this vast expanse of grass-covered hills and rocky shore was off-limits to the public, appropriated by the U.S. Army as a strategic base for defending the bay against invaders. Remnants of obsolete and untested defenses—dozens of thick concrete bunkers and batteries recessed into the bluffs—now serve as playground and picnic sites for the millions of tourists who visit each year.

There's a wealth of scheduled activities offered daily within the 15-square-mile **GOLDEN GATE NATIONAL RECREATION AREA**—birding clinics, bunker tours, wildflower hunts, geology hikes—but most visitors are satisfied with poking their heads into a bunker or two, snapping a photo of the San Francisco skyline, and driving home. For a more thorough approach, buy the handy "Marin Headlands Map and Guide to Sites, Trails and Wildlife" at the **INFORMATION CENTER AT FORT BARRY** (415/331-1540; follow the signs in the headlands), and plan your day from there. Free hiking, mountain biking, and pet-friendly trail maps are available, too. The center is open daily from 9:30am to 4:30pm.

A popular Marin Headlands attraction is the **MARINE MAMMAL CENTER** (415/289-SEAL), a volunteer-run hospital for injured and abandoned mammals-of-the-sea. It's virtually impossible not to melt at the sight of the cute sea lions and elephant and harbor seals as they lie in their pens (the center's staff, being no dummies, take donations right on the spot). Signs list each animal's adopted name, species, stranding site, and injury—the latter of which is usually human-caused. Located at the east end of Fort Cronkhite near Rodeo Lagoon, the Marine Mammal Center is open daily from 10am to 4pm and admission is free.

Closed to the public for several years due to storm damage, the precariously perched 1877 **POINT BONITA LIGHTHOUSE** (415/331-1540) is once again thrilling those tourists who are brave enough to traverse the long, dark tunnel and seven small footbridges leading to the beacon. (Because the cliffs along the passageway are so steep, one 19th-century lighthouse keeper rigged ropes around his children to prevent them from slipping into the raging sea below.) The reward for such bravery is, among other things, a rare and sensational view of the entrance to the bay. Call for tour times, and be sure to inquire about the full-moon tours, which take place twice a month by reservation only.

Also within the Marin Headlands is **HAWK HILL**, one of the most remarkable avian sites in the western United States and the biggest hawk lookout in western North America. Record count in 1992 was more than 20,000 birds, including 21 species of hawks. The best time to visit is during September and October, when thousands of birds of prey soar over the hill each day. The hill is located above Battery 129, where Conzelman Road becomes a one-way street. For a current schedule of the free ranger-led walks through the Marin Headlands—with topics ranging from bird-watching to wildflowers and war relics—call 415/331-1540.

MUIR WOODS–MUIR BEACH

Take the Stinson Beach/Highway 1 exit off Highway 101 just north of Sausalito and follow Highway 1 all the way to Muir Beach. A few miles before you reach the ocean, there's a fork in the road to the Muir Woods turnoff (you'll see the sign).

When you stand in the middle of **MUIR WOODS** (Muir Woods Rd and the Panoramic Hwy; 415/388-2595), surrounded by a canopy of ancient redwoods towering hundreds of feet skyward, it's hard to fathom that San Francisco is less than 6 miles away. It's a den of wooden giants; tourists speak in hushed tones as they crane their necks in disbelief, snapping photographs that don't begin to capture the immensity of these living titans.

Although Muir Woods can get absurdly crowded on summer weekends, you can usually circumvent the masses by hiking up the Ocean View Trail and returning via the Fern Creek Trail. Admission is free, but a donation box is prominently displayed to stoke your conscience. Picnicking is not allowed, although there is a snack bar (and gift shop) at the entrance. It's typically cool and damp here, so dress appropriately; open 8am to sunset.

Three miles west of Muir Woods, along Highway 1, is a small crescent-shaped cove called **MUIR BEACH**. Strewn with bits of driftwood and numerous tide pools, Muir Beach is a more sedate alternative to the beer-'n'-bikini crowds at the ever-popular Stinson Beach up north. If all you're looking for is a sandy, quiet place for some R&R, park your car right here and skip the trip to Stinson altogether (swimming, however, isn't allowed at Muir Beach because of the strong rip currents).

STINSON BEACH

Take the Stinson Beach/Highway 1 exit off Highway 101 just north of Sausalito, and follow Highway 1 all the way to Stinson Beach.

On those treasured weekend days when the fog has lifted and the sun is scorching the Northern California coast, blurry-eyed Bay Area residents grab their morning paper and beach chairs, pile into their Mazda Miatas and Jeeps, and scramble to the sandy shores of Stinson Beach—the North Coast's nice-try answer to the fabled beaches of Southern California.

SEE LIFE AT THE FARALLON ISLANDS

Several miles due west of San Francisco is the small gaggle of islets called the Farallon Islands. On a very clear day you can see them just off the horizon, but what you can't see with the naked eye is the teeming sea and bird life—puffins, albatrosses, terns, whales, dolphins, seals, sea lions, great white sharks, and more—that congregates on or around these barren, windswept refuges. For a closer look, you'll have to buy a ticket to board the nonprofit **Oceanic Society Expedition's** (415/474-3385; www. oceanic-society.org) 63-foot boat and take an all-day guided nature cruise to the islands. The exceptional tour, which lasts eight or nine hours and costs about $65 per person, departs from the Fort Mason area in San Francisco's Marina district at 8:30am on Saturdays, Sundays, and occasional Fridays. Shorter, less expensive excursions to see gray whales are available, too. Note: If you're prone to seasickness, be sure to take some Dramamine before you depart—it can get real choppy out there.

Stinson Beach is one of Northern California's most popular beaches, a 3.5-mile stretch of beige sand that offers enough elbow room for everyone to spread out beach blankets, picnic baskets, and toys. Swimming is allowed and lifeguards are on hand from May to mid-September, though notices about riptides (plus the sea's toe-numbing temperatures and the threat of sharks) tend to discourage folks from venturing too far into the water. For recorded weather and surf conditions at Stinson, call 415/868-1922. Joined at the hip with *la playa* is the town of Stinson Beach, which does a brisk summer business serving lunch alfresco at its numerous cafes.

There are plenty of adventurous things to do around Stinson. For example, Scott Tye, a kayak instructor for **OFF THE BEACH BOATS** (15 Calle del Mar, Stinson Beach; 415/868-9445) in downtown Stinson Beach next to the post office, offers 2-hour lessons on the basics of sea and surf kayaking. Rentals are surprisingly cheap (about $25 for 4 hours for surf kayaks), and they even rent a kayak that can hold an entire nuclear family.

A short drive north of Stinson Beach on Highway 1 leads to Bolinas Lagoon, a placid saltwater expanse that serves as a refuge for numerous shorebirds and harbor seals sprawled out on the sandbars. Across from the lagoon is the **AUDUBON CANYON RANCH'S BOLINAS LAGOON PRESERVE** (4900 Hwy 1, just N of Stinson Beach; 415/868-9244), a 1,014-acre wildlife sanctuary that supports a major heronry of great blue herons. This is the premier spot along the Pacific Coast to watch immense, graceful seabirds as they court, mate, and rear their young, all accomplished on the tops of towering redwoods. Admission is free, though donations are requested; open mid-March to mid-July on Saturdays, Sundays, and holidays, 10am to 4pm, and by appointment for groups.

And if you head back the other way, about a mile south of Stinson Beach off Highway 1 is **RED ROCK BEACH**, one of the few nude beaches on the Marin coast. It's easy to miss since you can't see it from the road; park at the first dirt pull-off on your right after leaving Stinson Beach and look for a steep trail leading down to the water.

BOLINAS

Take the Stinson Beach/Highway 1 exit off Highway 101 just north of Sausalito, and follow Highway 1 past Stinson Beach to Bolinas.

A sort of retirement community for aging rock stars, spent novelists, and former hippies, Bolinas is one of the most reclusive towns in Northern California. Residents regularly take down highway signs pointing the way to their rural enclave, an act that ironically has created more publicity for Bolinas than any road sign ever did. As a tourist, you don't have to worry about being chased out of town by a band of machete-wielding Bolinistas, but don't expect anyone to roll out the welcome mat either. The trick is to not look like a tourist, but more like a Bay Area resident who's only here to buy some peaches at the **PEOPLE'S STORE** (415/868-1433; open 8:30am–6:30pm every day).

What's the People's Store, you ask? It's a town landmark that's famous for its locally grown organic produce and exceptional service—the antithesis of the corporate supermarket. It's a little hard to find, hidden at the end of a gravel driveway next to the Bolinas Bakery (don't confuse it with the much larger general store down the street), but it's worth searching out just to see (and taste) the difference between Safeway and the Bolinas way.

Three side trips near Bolinas offer some adventurous exercise. Just before entering downtown Bolinas, turn right (west) on Mesa Road, left on Overlook Road, and right on Elm Road and you'll dead-end at the **DUXBURY REEF NATURE RESERVE**, a rocky outcropping with numerous tide pools harboring a healthy population of starfish, sea anemones, snails, sea urchins, and other creatures that kids go gaga over. If you continue west on Mesa Road you'll reach the **POINT REYES BIRD OBSERVATORY**, where ornithologists keep an eye on more than 400 feathered species—it's one of the few full-time ornithological research stations in the United States. Admission to the visitor center and nature trail is free, and visitors are welcome to observe the tricky process of catching and banding the birds Tuesday through Sunday mornings, weather permitting, from May through October. It's open every day, from 15 minutes after sunrise until sunset. Banding hours vary, so call 415/868-0655 for exact times and 415/868-1221, extension 40, for recorded general information. At the very end of Mesa Road is the **PALOMARIN TRAIL-HEAD**, a popular hiking trail that leads into the south entrance of Point Reyes National Seashore. The 6-mile round-trip trek—one of Point Reyes's prettiest hikes—passes several small lakes and meadows before it reaches Alamere Falls, a freshwater stream that cascades down a 40-foot bluff into Wildcat Beach.

Point Reyes National Seashore

The easiest route is via Sir Francis Drake Boulevard from Highway 101 at Larkspur. A much longer but more scenic route: take the Stinson Beach/Highway 1 exit off Highway 101 just north of Sausalito and follow Highway 1 west to the ocean, then due north.

Think of the Point Reyes National Seashore as Mother Nature's version of Disneyland, an outdoor-lover's playground with one doozy of a sandbox. Hiking, biking, swimming, sailing, wind surfing, sunbathing, camping, fishing, horseback riding, bird-watching, kayaking—all are fair game at this 71,000-acre sanctuary of forested hills, deep green pastures, and undisturbed beaches. Point Reyes is hardly a secret anymore—millions of visitors arrive each year—but the land is so vast and varied that finding your own space is never a problem. (As the old saying goes: if you want to be alone, walk up.)

As soon as you arrive at Point Reyes, stop at the **BEAR VALLEY VISITORS CENTER** (on Bear Valley Rd; 415/663-1092)—look for the small sign posted just north of Olema on Highway 1—and pick up a free Point Reyes trail map; open weekdays 9am to 5pm and weekends 8am to 5pm. On the westernmost tip of Point Reyes at the end of Sir Francis Drake Highway is the **POINT REYES LIGHTHOUSE** (415/669-1534), the park's most popular attraction. If you loathe lighthouse tours, go anyway. The drive alone is worth the trip, a 45-minute scenic excursion through windswept meadows and working dairy ranches (watch out for cows on the road). When the fog burns off, the lighthouse and the headlands provide a fantastic lookout point for spying gray whales and thousands of common murres that inundate the rocks below. Visitors have free access to the lighthouse via a thigh-burning 308-step staircase; open 10am to 4:30pm, Thursday through Monday, weather permitting.

That mighty pungent aroma you smell on the way to the Point Reyes Lighthouse is probably emanating from **JOHNSON'S OYSTER FARM**. It may not look like much—a cluster of trailer homes, shacks, and oyster tanks surrounded by huge piles of oyster shells—but that certainly doesn't detract from the taste of fresh-out-of-the-water oysters dipped in Johnson's special sauce. Eat 'em on the spot, or buy a bag for the road—either way, you're not likely to find California oysters as fresh or as cheap anywhere else. The oyster farm resides within **DRAKES ESTERO** (415/669-1149), a large saltwater lagoon on the Point Reyes peninsula that produces nearly 20 percent of California's commercial oyster yield. It's located off Sir Francis Drake Boulevard, about 6 miles west of Inverness, and is open 8am to 4pm Tuesday through Sunday.

A popular Point Reyes pastime is **OCEAN KAYAKING**. Don't worry, the kayaks are very stable and there are no waves to contend with because you'll be paddling through placid Tomales Bay, a haven for migrating birds and marine mammals. Rental prices at Tomales Bay Sea Kayaking (415/663-1743) start at about $35 for a half-day ($65 for a double-hulled kayak), and you can sign up for a guided day trip, a sunset cruise, or a romantic full-moon outing. Instruction, clinics, and boat delivery are available, and all ages and levels are welcome. The launching point is located on Highway 1 at the Marshall Boatworks in Marshall, 8 miles north of Point Reyes Station. It's open in the summer Friday through Sunday from 9am to 6pm and by appointment.

As most ardent Bay Area mountain bikers know, Point Reyes National Seashore also has some of the finest **MOUNTAIN-BIKE TRAILS** in the region. Narrow dirt paths wind through densely forested knolls and end with spectacular ocean views. A trail map is a must (available for free at the Bear Valley Visitors Center) since many of the park trails are off-limits to bikes, and fines are quite steep if you pedal up a bike-free path. If you didn't bring your own bicycle, you can rent a mountain bike at the Bear Valley Inn and Rental Shop (Bear Valley Rd and Hwy 1, Olema; 415/663-1958).

Angel Island State Park

One of the best adventures you can have in San Francisco is taking a ferry from Fisherman's Wharf out to Angel Island State Park, the largest of the San Francisco Bay's three islets (the other two being Yerba Buena and Alcatraz). Here you can hike, mountain bike, picnic, take guided tram tours of the uninhabited island, and even go on a guided ocean kayak trip around the island. Best of all, you don't need to bring anything along except some money and a light jacket (it can get a bit chilly out there); the bikes and kayaks are already here and available for rental, and there's even a cafe right next to the dock.

Angel Island has worn a lot of hats over the past few centuries. It's been a home for coast Miwok Indians and Spanish explorers, a cattle ranch, a World War II prison, a quarantine station, a missile base, and a popular site for duels between San Francisco's dandies. From 1910 to 1940 Angel Island was known as the dreaded "Ellis Island of the West"; army barracks were converted into holding cells for thousands of Chinese immigrants awaiting their citizenship papers. In fact, you can still see some faded Chinese characters on the walls of the barracks where the immigrants were held.

The island is now part of the state park system and hosts hundreds of visitors daily. Passengers disembark from the ferry at **AYALA COVE**, a small marina next to an inviting lawn area equipped with picnic tables, barbecue pits, and rest rooms. There's also a small store, cafe (with surprisingly good grub), gift shop, and mountain-bike rental shop (helmets included).

Surrounding Angel Island are about 12 miles of hiking and mountain-bike trails, though most visitors tend to stick to the **PERIMETER ROAD**, a partly paved path that circles the island. Along the way you'll see old troop barracks, former gun emplacements, and other military buildings. For a fantastic view of the surrounding bay, take one of the several trails that lead up to the top of **MOUNT LIVERMORE**, 776 feet above the bay. There are a limited number of campsites on the island as well, but reservations are required.

To take one of the **GUIDED SEA-KAYAK TOURS**, call Sea Trek (415/332-8494). The all-day trips run about $100 per person, which includes all the necessary equipment and a catered lunch. Both adults and kids can paddle the stable two- or three-person kayaks as a naturalist leads the group on a tour that encircles the island. The less adventurous can take a **GUIDED TRAM TOUR** around the island, which lasts about an hour and costs $10 for adults, $6 for children 9 to 12, and $9 for seniors; children under 9 are free.

The only **PUBLIC TRANSPORTATION** out to Angel Island is via the Blue & Gold Fleet ferries (415/705-5555), which depart several times daily from Pier 41 at Fisherman's Wharf and travel to both Angel Island and Tiburon. Since the ferries run on a seasonal schedule, you'll need to call for departure information. The round-trip fare is $10 to Angel Island, half price for kids 5 to 11, and free for kids under 5. For recorded information about Angel Island State Park, call 415/435-1915.

RECREATION

RECREATION

Blessed with a temperate climate and surrounded by ocean, bays, mountain ranges, and rolling hills, the San Francisco Bay Area is an excellent natural arena for all manner of outdoor sports, from surfing and ocean kayaking to mountain biking, sailing, in-line skating, hiking, golfing, tennis, and much more. Even in drizzly winter months weather is never severe enough to absolutely rule out a bit of fresh-air exercise—the sight of joggers splashing their way up and down the Embarcadero is not uncommon.

But for most of the year the sun beams down, the sky is blue, the weather mild, and the breezes refreshing even when brisk. And thanks to a slow-growth preservationist streak in its citizens, San Francisco and the surrounding Bay Area have plenty of wide-open space that's been kept in its natural condition and is open to the public.

The following is a comprehensive list of many of the recreational activities available to both the local and the visitor, most of them either free or relatively inexpensive. Best of all, it'll get you off your fanny, get your blood flowing, and get you into some of the most beautiful scenery on the California coast.

GYMS

Only a few decades ago it was rare to find a gym where a member of the general public could feel comfortable; most workout facilities were havens for dedicated if not fanatical weight lifters and competition-minded bodybuilders. Thanks to the fitness explosion, however, almost every neighborhood now has a gym where you don't have to look like Schwarzenegger to fit in.

The newly renovated **24 HOUR FITNESS TRAINING** (1200 Van Ness Ave at Post St; 415/776-2200; www.24hourfitness.com; map:L3) is one of seven franchise branches in San Francisco and Daly City. A day fee of $15 entitles you to use the wide range of machines (heavy on Nautilus) and free weights, step training, and cardiovascular cycles. Personalized training is available, and as the name states, they never close.

GOLD'S GYM (1001 Brannan St at 9th St and Division St; 415/552-4653; www.goldsgym.com; map:M5) has a day fee of $15, or $10 if you are the guest of a full-time member. Membership also includes classes in boxing, tai chi, and tai bo, among others; there are in-house as well as independent trainers. After using the wide selection of machines and free weights, enjoy the saunas and steam rooms. Hours are 5am to midnight, Monday through Thursday; 5am to 11pm Friday; 7am to 9pm Saturday; and 8am to 8pm Sunday.

Viewers of ESPN may know the Crunch chain from the TV show that originated in LA. San Francisco's **CRUNCH** (1000 Van Ness Ave at

O'Farrell St; 415/931-1100; www.crunchfitness.com; map:L3) offers, in addition to the usual array of free weights and cardiovascular equipment (Life Fitness, Star Track, Techno Gym), a dizzying array of classes, from the usual step and aerobics to more esoteric offerings—everything from kick-boxing to yoga, with firefighter and GI-type training in between. There's a steam room and sauna; the day rate is $22. Hours are 5:30am to 11pm, Monday through Thursday; 5:30am to 9:30pm Friday; 8am to 8pm Saturday; and 8am to 6pm Sunday.

A world away from the chains, with the feel of an unpretentious neighborhood gym (which is what it is), **VALENCIA STREET MUSCLE AND FITNESS** (333 Valencia St; 415/626-8360; www.valenciastreet-muscle.com; map:L5) operates on a low-key, work-at-your-own-pace philosophy that makes it one of the friendliest places in town. Operated by three-time Olympic coach Jim Schmitz, of the late and fondly remembered Sport Palace, it has a marvelously mixed clientele of all sizes, ages, weights, body types, and abilities. The staff is helpful but unintrusive: power lifter to stationary cyclist are all treated equally. A day pass is a bargain at $8; a no-time-limit 12-pack for $69 is an even better deal. Hours are 6am to 10pm, Monday through Friday; weekends 8am to 6pm.

ADVENTURE OUTFITTERS

OK, now you're a bit more toned up and ready to take on the world. But you'll have to get outfitted and pick up some pointers on your choice of new activities. Outdoors Unlimited and REI are good one-stop combination resources: not only can you buy or rent the gear you'll be needing, you'll find classes on the skills you'll need and groups of like-minded people to join up with for that kayaking expedition or bike tour. These organizations are much more than places to rent a tent or buy a new pair of shoes—they'll really help get you going.

OUTDOORS UNLIMITED (Box 0234-A, UCSF, San Francisco, CA 94143; 415/476-2078; www.outdoors.ucsf.edu/ou) is an expedition planning and outfitting group affiliated with the University of California at San Francisco, but it's also open to the public (which is invited to volunteer). It holds seminars in backwoods first aid, map and compass reading, and backpacking skills from basic to trip leader. OU also organizes its own excursions to locations that usually lie well outside the city limits (Yosemite, Mount Lassen, Death Valley); but the shorter bike trips sometimes originate from Golden Gate Park before heading out to Mount Tam or the Marin County town of Ross, and kayak training takes place on the bay. Autumn brings bonfires and volleyball at Ocean Beach and a sail through the Golden Gate on the square rigger the *Hawaiian Chieftain*. Visit the OU equipment rental facility at 550 Parnassus Avenue by Third Avenue (walk down the ramp leading under the campus library; map:H6) for a wide selection of tents, sleeping bags, lanterns and

THE TWO-WHEEL ROUTE: BICYCLING IN MARIN

The hilly, scenic bike trails of Marin are a magnet for amateur and professional cyclists alike. A favorite not-too-strenuous route takes you north across the Golden Gate Bridge, then follows the bike trail under the bridge and down a very steep hill to downtown Sausalito. The paved trail hugs Sausalito's waterfront, leading past floating homes and marshes to Bayfront Park in Mill Valley; this gorgeous ride takes about two to three hours for the average recreational biker (one-way). To avoid riding (or pushing) your bike uphill to the bridge for the return trip, coast onto a ferry in Sausalito or Tiburon and sail back to San Francisco's Fisherman's Wharf (call the Red & White Fleet for ferry info; 800/229-2784).

The Marin Headlands and Mount Tamalpais (also known as Mount Tam) are the bicycling hot spots for diehards, although you don't need Stallone-size thighs to make it up all the trails. Maps of the numerous bike paths are available at many Bay Area bike stores and bookstores, the Pan Toll Camp/Mount Tamalpais Ranger Station (415/388-2070), and the Marin Headlands Visitor Center (at the corner of Bunker and Field Rds, Sausalito; 415/331-1540). Mount Tam offers fantastic scenic trails for mountain bikers, but some trails are restricted to pedestrians only—and they're fiercely guarded. If you don't want to get slapped with a $200 fine for pedaling up the wrong path, be sure to look it up on a trail map first.

Recommended **bicycle rental shops** include American Rentals/Zapworld (2715 Hyde St, at Fisherman's Wharf; 415/931-0234); Marina Cyclery (3330 Steiner St; 415/929-7135); Blazing Saddles (1095 Columbus Ave; 415/202-1973); Wheel Escapes Bicycle Tours (30 Liberty Ship Wy, off the east side of Bridgeway, Sausalito; 415/332-0218); and Bike Sport (1735 Tiburon Blvd, Tiburon; 415/586-2377).

stoves, canoes, kayaks, wet suits, skis, and snowboards, to name just a few. OU members and volunteers receive an up to 40 percent discount on seminars, excursions, and gear rental.

REI (1338 San Pablo Ave, Berkeley; 510/527-4140; www.rei.com; map:FF2) is an outfitter that, in addition to offering a full line of clothing, shoes, sleeping bags, and tents, also presents in-store seminars and slide lectures on a wide range of topics: just one month, for instance, brought a talk on essentials in bike touring, lessons for beginning mountain climbers, and hints on how to travel safely through bear country. The store is of course open to the general public, but REI also offers a membership program that gives you discounts on merchandise and first crack at some of the training sessions and lectures. It's worth checking out: the cost is only $15 for a lifetime membership. REI has stores across the country, and the Web site is a good place to find mountaineering, hiking, and backpacking clubs nationwide as well as in one's own backyard.

ROCK CLIMBING (INDOOR)

Northern California is home to dozens of outdoor rock-climbing locations, from Yosemite National Park to the formations at Ocean Beach from which the Cliff House got its name. But for indoor climbing, whether you're a beginner just getting a taste or an experienced mountaineer limbering up El Capitan, everyone agrees the place to go is **MISSION CLIFFS ROCK-CLIMBING CENTER** (2295 Harrison St at 19th St; 415/550-0515; www.mission-cliffs.com; map:M6). They rent shoes and harnesses and offer basic, first climb, and kids' classes. But the main attraction is the center's massive simulated Matterhorn of a climbing wall, topping out at 55 feet, its 50 lead walls offering over 150 possible climbs (routes are changed regularly). Surface dimensions are 14,000 square feet, including 2,000 square feet of bouldering for the beginner. Designed by well-known climber Christian Griffiths, the surface is mostly vertical but features some overhangs as well as caves and crevasses. Prospective climbers are expected to pass a belay test (tying a figure-eight hitch and belaying another person) to obtain a card that allows them to start climbing; demonstrated mastery of belaying techniques waives the requirement, so you don't have to take the test each time you want to climb. The center is also available for parties and corporate events.

Outdoor Activities

BICYCLING / MOUNTAIN BIKING

First, it should be said that anyone riding a bike in everyday San Francisco traffic should remain extra-alert: even in this increasingly bike-friendly town, some drivers act as though they literally cannot see somebody on two wheels. In fact, raising the visibility of bicyclists is one of the goals of the monthly "bike-in" called Critical Mass (see below). *Always* wear a helmet and reflective gear, and remember that even if you have the right-of-way, the person who will come out on the short end of a car-bike collision will almost certainly be the one on the bike.

If you don't already have a bike, it's easy to rent one from a place conveniently located close to favored trails. For exploring the Presidio or crossing the Golden Gate Bridge to explore Marin, try **MARINA CYCLERY** (3300 Steiner St; 415/929-7135; www.marinacyclery.com; map:K1). Rates are $20 for 4 hours, $30 for 24 hours. There's also a $10 cleaning fee if your ride comes back caked with mud, so mountain bikers be forewarned.

Close to Golden Gate Park is **PARK CYCLERY** (1749 Waller St off Stanyan; 415/751-7368; www.parkcyclery.com; map:I5), where a driver's license and a credit card can get you a bike for $5 an hour, $25 for 24 hours. **GOLDEN GATE PARK SKATE AND BIKE** (see the Roller Skating and In-line Skating section) also has a selection of bikes for hire.

PLEASURE RIDES in the city suggest themselves from all sides. There are the perennial favorites, the Embarcadero and Golden Gate Park, or you might want to test yourself on one of the city's gut-busting hills. Many cyclists enjoy the northwestern edge of the city. Start out on the flat surface of the Marina Green, then explore the Presidio, with its many short, tree-lined roads. Or enter the Golden Gate National Recreational Area and follow the shore to reach ghostly Fort Point, a Civil War–era military outpost that protected California from the Confederates (who never bothered to show up). From here you can get on the Golden Gate Bridge for a 2-mile trip, then either continue into the Marin Headlands or turn back toward town.

MOUNTAIN BIKING in San Francisco is a more problematic matter. A mountain bike is useful for getting around the steeper parts of the Presidio or Golden Gate Park, but the city offers little in the way of the rugged terrain that mountain bikers seek; for that, you need to get out of town. The Parnassus Bike Club of **OUTDOORS UNLIMITED** (see the Adventure Outfitters section) frequently sponsors excursions to Marin. Also, several Web sites offer tips on good rides by region. Marin's Tennessee Valley is only one place discussed by Roger's Favorites at www. microweb.com/rogm/n-sf-bay-region.html. Those wishing to head south to check out the Peninsula and the Santa Cruz Mountains should go to www.members.cruzio.com/%7Ekrebsmap/M1.html. These are amateur sites put together by enthusiasts; surf around and you should be able to find a lot more free information.

Finally, any discussion of biking in the city would be fatally flawed without a mention of **CRITICAL MASS**, a leaderless, often traffic-stopping grassroots pedalfest that takes place on the last Friday of each month. Bike riders gather by the thousands at Justin Herman Plaza (map:O2) by the Embarcadero to agree on a route, and then bike home via major thoroughfares in an awe-inspiring caravan that is part political demonstration on behalf of heightened "bike consciousness" and part just a plain ol' party. City officials have been cooperative for the most part, though they frown on the occasional breakaway; if you don't want to risk arrest, stay with the group. (For the record, some irate drivers tried a "Critical Gas Car-in" once, but it fizzled.) Critical Mass has been a success not only by just continuing to exist but also by alerting the city to the needs of thousands of bike riders, resulting in more bike-only lanes on city streets.

GOLF

Golf is a sport in the midst of reinvention. Not only is Tiger Woods the new face of the pro game, but the makeup of the amateurs is changing too. You'll find a new kind of player on the links these days, from blue-collars to Gen-Xers, rubbing elbows with the more traditional practitioners in plaid slacks. This is particularly true at the municipally owned and operated courses.

The City and County of San Francisco maintains a **GOLF INFOR-MATION LINE** (415/750-4653), with a menu of detailed information on the city's five public courses. You can reserve a tee time, get directions to the courses, learn hours of operation, and get the rundown on greens fees, cart and club rentals, and lessons.

LINCOLN PARK GOLF COURSE (34th Ave and Clement St; 415/221-9911; map:E3), with 18 holes, is said to be the oldest of the municipal parks, featuring small greens and tricky traps as well as beautiful views of the Marin Headlands and the Golden Gate Bridge. There is no driving range. Pull carts are not available, but you can rent power carts. Clubs can be rented; call ahead to schedule lessons. Par is 68. Try to resist the temptation to drive a ball into the ocean from the hole that overlooks the Pacific. After all, it will cost you a stroke.

HARDING PARK GOLF COURSE AND JACK FLEMING GOLF COURSE (corner of Harding Rd and Skyline Blvd; 415/664-4690), near Lake Merced, is a two-in-one course totaling 27 holes. Harding Park is thick with pine and Monterey cypress trees as well as traps. Beginners or those seeking an easier, perhaps less aggravating game will prefer Jack Fleming, located inside the second nine of Harding Park. This course's surface is softer and flatter. There is a small driving range as well. Par is 72 for Harding, 32 for Jack Fleming.

GOLDEN GATE GOLF COURSE (47th Ave off Fulton St; 415/751-8987; map:D5) follows the same pattern as Harding Park (see above), with well-trapped short greens requiring tight maneuvering. All of its 9 holes are par three. Clubs are available to rent.

Those seeking a hitter's course should check out **SHARP PARK GOLF RANGE** (Fairway Dr west of Hwy 1; 650/355-0455; map:KK6), which the city operates in neighboring Pacifica. It's a long 18-hole course, flat and with the usual high number of traps; some players are put off by its occasionally marshy surface. There is no driving range; both power and pull carts, as well as clubs, are available for rental. Lessons are by appointment; call ahead.

Dating from the turn of the century, the **PRESIDIO GOLF COURSE** (Arguello Blvd and W Pacific Ave; 415/561-4653; map:H2), now operated by the Arnold Palmer Golf Management Company, is the oldest continuously operating golf course in the West. Originally used by officers on the army post that used to occupy this site, it served as temporary housing following the earthquake and fire of 1906. At 18 holes and par 72, with banked grass course, tree-lined fairway, and defined cut, it has hosted several pro tournaments. Equipment is available for rent; call ahead for lessons. A very nice driving range is here as well.

If bad weather or the dark of night is keeping you from a game, you can always head down to **MISSION BAY GOLF CENTER** (1200 6th St at Channel; 415/431-7888; map:O5) for two weatherproofed 300-yard driving ranges. You'll also find chipping and putting greens, target areas, and sand traps, as well as a fully stocked discount pro shop and a restaurant where you can contemplate your faults.

HIKING

Although nobody disputes the thrill of a good climb up Mount Tam, there are plenty of trails in the city for those in need of the tranquility and renewal a quick day hike can provide. On some of these paths you can even forget you're in a major urban area. Whole books have been published on the subject of adventuring in San Francisco on foot: you could spend a lifetime in Golden Gate Park alone. You can head out in practically any direction and find something of interest. So these are just suggestions: it's easy to design your own walks.

Warm up with a jaunt down **AQUATIC PARK'S MUNICIPAL PIER** (map: L1); admire the boats in the bay and marvel at the bravery of the fishers who are seemingly going to eat what they're catching. Continue west through the **MARINA GREEN**, dodging joggers and skaters and counting the kites that are legion on a windy-but-not-too-windy day. Following the **GOLDEN GATE PROMENADE**, a walking path just a few yards away from the water's edge, you can watch all manner of vessels, from sailboats to tankers. Keep going and you'll wind up at **FORT POINT**, where, as fans of Hitchcock's *Vertigo* will recall, Jimmy Stewart fished Kim Novak out of the drink. From here you can pick up the **COASTAL TRAIL** running under the toll plaza, near the abandoned artillery fortifications and then to the coast; you can follow the trail all the way to **BAKER BEACH**. Dress warmly.

In an opposite corner of the city, **BERNAL HEIGHTS PARK** (map: M8) offers a panoramic view from the top of what was once one of the early Spanish land grants on which San Francisco was founded. From Folsom and Ripley Streets, climb up the steep ascent of Bernal Heights Boulevard. People come from all over the city to walk dogs here, and there's a good deal of intercanine socializing. The dogs are generally friendly. Joggers enjoy the clear air and crisp breezes. There's also skateboard action—the downhill slopes are hard to resist if you want to see how fast you can get going. Keep an eye open, but don't be unduly worried: the kids usually post lookouts to make sure the coast is clear.

If you think hiking doesn't count unless it's done outside city limits, there are one or two organizations for you. One is **BAY TRAIL**, which can be reached at its Web site (www.abag.ca.gov/bayarea/baytrail/baytrail. hmtl). Bay Trail is both the name of the group and its goal, "an endeavor to encircle the San Francisco Bay." Sometime in the future, proponents hope, there will be a "ring around the Bay"—an unbroken corridor of park areas 400 miles long, so you can hopscotch from Marin to Mountain View and never leave a park. Until then, Bay Trail publicizes its program by organizing bike rides, hikes, and trail cleanups. Contact them if you want to be one of the 400 volunteers.

THE BEST VIEWS OF SAN FRANCISCO AND THE BAY

Few people forget seeing their first sunset at **Ocean Beach**. Whether viewed from the water's edge or over cocktails at the Cliff House or the Beach Chalet, the sight of the scarlet and purple tones slowly deepening into darkness as the sun slips below the horizon is something that resists adequate description. Check the weather section of the daily papers for the time the sun will be setting, and get there a little early for the full effect. It's easy to get to Ocean Beach: just take Geary Boulevard west all the way to the ocean. There's plenty of prime parking along the beach, and you can stay warm and dry in your car to watch the show.

The crest of **Dolores Park**, where the Mission gradually blends into Noe Valley, offers a breathtaking view of the city, with the downtown section in view and the hills of the East Bay glimmering in the distance. Sunny weekends find the park strewn with sunbathers, and some marriages are performed here with the city serving as a beautiful backdrop to the wedding photographs. It's located on Dolores Street (off upper Market Street) between 18th and 20th Streets.

But the sine qua non of grand San Francisco views is at **Twin Peaks**, the two rounded hills jutting out below the giant red-and-white-striped Sutro Tower on the southwest side of the city. A drive to this popular lookout area gives you a full 360-degree view that is particularly lovely as the fog drifts in, adding a hint of mystery and romance (particularly at night). It's reachable via Market Street—just keep heading southwest on Market until you reach the top of the hill (just past Clipper Street) and turn left on Twin Peaks Road, which leads to the top.

Other good viewpoints: the Golden Gate Bridge, Coit Tower, Angel Island, the Embarcadero just north of the Bay Bridge, the road to the Marin Headlands, and any of the top-floor high-rise cocktail lounges (see the "Swanky Hotel Bars" sidebar in the Nightlife chapter).

Since 1958 **GREENBELT ALLIANCE** (530 Bush St; 415/398-3730 or 800/543-GREEN; www.greenbelt.org; map:N3) has spread its land planning and conservation message by way of free fun outings open to the public, although you must call 415/255-3233 to reserve. They tour parks, lakes, and the Bay Area's forgotten farms; watch hawks; and visit the Wine Country. The outings are thoughtfully ranked according to degree of difficulty, from easy to "hard-core," factoring in miles and elevation gain.

HORSEBACK RIDING

Horses: some people like to ride them, others like to watch them. If you like to watch, then see the entry for Golden Gate Fields in the Spectator

Sports section. But if you want to hit the trail inside the city limits, the only place to go is **GOLDEN GATE PARK STABLES** (John F. Kennedy Dr at 36th Ave in Golden Gate Park; 415/668-7360; www.extendinc.com/ggps; map:E5), which offers rides and lessons. The guided rides take place every day, with the horses moving at a walk, and take about an hour, wending through the park to its western edge, by the tulip garden and the windmill, for a view of the Pacific (the horses do not go down to the beach, since the ocean has been known to overexcite them). Reservations are required, and the rides take place rain or shine; you may cancel if you don't want to ride in the rain, but be sure to do so far enough ahead that you don't get charged (no rain: call by noon the previous day; rain: call 2 hours before the ride). All riders must be under 230 pounds and over eight years old; of course minors must have the permission of a parent or legal guardian. Riding boots and helmets are both required and provided. Lessons at the stables begin with six- and eight-week introductory courses ($144 for six weeks, $192 for eight) and advance to all skill levels. Also offered are summer day camps (half-days for ages 5 to 8, full days for 8 and above) and pony-riding parties for the little ones. All prices are extremely reasonable.

KAYAKING / CANOEING

Kayaking opportunities in San Francisco are divided into two areas, the bay and the Pacific Ocean. Those just starting out might want to confine themselves to practice jaunts in the bay before taking on the stronger currents and higher swells of the Pacific.

To find like-minded people seeking to improve their Eskimo Rolls, check out **BAY AREA SEA KAYAKERS** (c/o Penny Wells, 229 Courtright Rd, San Rafael; 415/457-6094; www.bask.com) at its monthly general meeting (6:30 to 9:30pm on the last Wednesday of each month, usually in room 301 of the Health Sciences West Building at 513 Parnassus Street on the UCSF campus—check the Web site to confirm). Dues of $25 admit you to workshops and clinics, get you a subscription to the *Bay Currents* newsletter, and provide access to the club's weekly excursions. Alcatraz is a favorite destination, although the club organizes trips to test the kayaking as far away as Chile. (No, they don't row to get there.) BASK also sponsors an Annual Kayak Rodeo. The club has more than 500 members and is rather loosely organized—it doesn't take much more than a suggestion to get things going. The **DOLPHIN CLUB** (see the Rowing section) also offers kayak training several times a year.

Canoes are larger than kayaks, and usually somewhat slower unless in the hands of experts. Some consider this roominess, safety, and stability an acceptable trade-off for the adrenaline rush of kayaking—still, always wear a life jacket, whatever kind of boat you're using. Canoes may be rented from **OUTDOORS UNLIMITED** (see the Adventure Outfitters section) for $40 for a weekend; the rate is $28 for OU members. OU's policy is that you "must have experience" before they rent to you.

ROLLER SKATING / IN-LINE SKATING

Roller skating, once a weekend-only diversion, is now a day-to-day part of life. People are figuring out that they don't have to hang up their skates after childhood—and that skating can be a quick and clean way to get around in a crowded, traffic-jammed city. It's not uncommon to spot morning commuters takinge the "in-line" to work.

For a recreational roll the action is at **GOLDEN GATE PARK**, particularly on Sundays, when much of the park is closed to cars. John F. Kennedy Drive, in particular, offers slow easy curves and modest bumps that accelerate without pushing you out of control. Skaters like rolling along the **EMBARCADERO**—it's long and level with pleasant breezes and an enjoyable view of the bay—and the **MARINA GREEN**. Gregarious types should check out the informal mass "skate-in" down Market Street every Friday night. Assemble at the Ferry Building at the foot of Market Street in enough time to make the 8pm roll-out.

SKATES ON HAIGHT (1818 Haight St; 415/752-8375; www.skate. com; Mon–Fri 11am–7pm, Sat–Sun 10am–6pm; map:I5) is located half a block from Golden Gate Park. They rent both conventional and in-line skates for $6 per hour and $24 per day with a credit card. The store is known for its unannounced and unadvertised sales, so drop by and see if you can't pick up something on the sly.

GOLDEN GATE PARK SKATE AND BIKE (3038 Fulton St at 6th Ave; 415/668-1117; Mon–Fri 10am–6pm, Sat–Sun 10am–7pm; map:H4) rents conventional skates and Rollerblade-brand in-lines, by the hour or by the day. Rates are $4 per hour for conventional skates, $12 for 24 hours; in-lines are $6 an hour, $24 for 24 hours. San Francisco residents must present an up-to-date driver's license; out-of-towners will have to use a credit card. They also sell both kinds of skates. The store is across the street from a primo skating area much favored by locals; roll on over, especially on a weekend, and you'll soon be surrounded by fellow skaters, some of them performing fairly intricate choreography to music flowing from boom boxes.

ROWING

The type of rowing you'll be doing depends on whether you are rowing alone or in a team—in rowing jargon, if you are *sculling* or *sweep rowing*. Sculling involves one person alone in the shell (as the boat is called) with two oars; sweep rowing requires an even-numbered team of two to eight people. The power propelling the oars comes from not just the arm muscles but the whole body; the sliding boat seat allows rowers to add the power of the legs and torso to the stroke. You'll want to avoid "catching a crab"—digging the oar too deep into the water to make a good recovery—which can break the rowing rhythm of an individual or a team, and could lead to capsizing. You also need to consider water conditions: beginners, for instance, may want to practice on Lake Merced or Oakland's Lake Merritt, which are what is known as *flat water*, i.e., not as turbulent and windy. Some sections of the San Francisco Bay, especially those closer to the shore, are flat water; as one gets farther out in the bay, one begins to experience *open water*, which is choppier and more tricky. Novices might want to hug the shore until they build up their confidence.

The **SOUTH END ROWING CLUB** (500 Jefferson St; 415/776-7372; www.south-end.org; map:M1), next to the Hyde Street Pier, has been hitting the water since its founding in 1873. There you will be able to hook up with other rowers, and you'll find a dazzling collection of vessels to choose from: the club's fleet of 30 different crafts ranges from kayaks and single-person sculls to a fearsome Viking-style rowboat. The club's signature craft is the *South Ender*, a 1915-vintage six-person scull that's controlled by a coxswain (the coxswain manipulates the rudder and coaches the rowers, usually by yelling). The club is open to the public Tuesdays, Thursdays, and Saturdays, 10am to 5pm, for a day-use fee of $6.50. In addition to rowing, you can swim in the bay and return to the clubhouse for a sauna, a game of handball, or a workout in the gym. If you like what you see, $265.50 will cover your initiation fee ($100), key charge ($3), and first six months' dues ($162.50). The club participates in organized rowing competitions as well, including the Bridge to Bridge Regatta, in which teams race the 11.5 miles between the Bay and Golden Gate Bridges.

Literally next door to the South End, in a clubhouse built in 1896 and moved to its present location in 1938, you'll find the South End's friendly rivals, the **DOLPHIN CLUB** (foot of Hyde St at Jefferson St; 415/441-9329; www.dolphinclub.org; map:M1). Founded in 1877, the Dolphins began admitting women a mere 99 years later; women now make up about a third of the club's 900-person membership. Instructions in the art of kayaking are given several times a year; rowing training is offered once a month, with tips provided by former members of Olympic rowing teams and college champions. The club's fleet is less extensive than the South End's, comprised of 16 rowboats, four of them double-rower shells, and one six-oared barge. The club also has a boathouse at Lake Merced, for those who prefer flat water. Members keep tuned up by periodic jaunts to Tiburon and around Alameda Island; a particular favorite seems to be the trek down the southern edge of the waterfront to China Basin, where the Dolphins reward themselves with beers at the Ramp Restaurant, a favored hangout. These are mere practice runs, however, for the once-a-year trek up the Delta to Sacramento, which takes about a day and a half, with camping at selected checkpoints. The trip is timed to make the best use of the tides, which shift every six hours, but much of the journey is against the current, especially when the expedition finally reaches the Sacramento River. Dolphin Club dues are $246 for initiation fee and the first six months' membership, $31 per month subsequently. A day-use fee of $6.50 entitles a nonmember to use showers, sauna, lockers, and gym on Tuesdays, Thursdays, and Saturdays. The **PACIFIC ROWING CLUB** (PO Box 27548, San Francisco, CA 94127; 415/242-0252; www.PacificRC.org) plies the flat water of Lake Merced. Much of this club's emphasis is on cultivating the next generation of rowers through its high school programs, in which older adult rowers pass along lore and enthusiasm.

Finally, mention should be made of what might be the first gay rowing club, named, of course, the **SAN FRANCISCO BAY BLADES**—get it? Any same-sexers who want to get out on the water should contact Dean at 510/482-1362; the group's e-mail address is goblades@aol.com.

RUNNING

One of the advantages of running as a solitary sport is that it is uncomplicated: the runner really needs nothing more than a good pair of shoes and a fairly clear path. One of the advantages of running in San Francisco is the variety of terrain you can tackle. The **EMBARCADERO** is a long, even course of several miles from Berry Street to its terminus at Fisherman's Wharf, cooled by breezes all the way. It's a favorite jaunt for lunch-hour runners wanting to get back to the office for the afternoon, but is never too crowded. A run on the **GOLDEN GATE BRIDGE** is 2 miles each way, and it provides a giddy sense of elevation. (There is no pedestrian traffic of any kind allowed on the Bay Bridge.) Running in **GOLDEN GATE PARK** allows you to alternate between the flat paved surfaces of the main roads and the dirt paths you find when you detour into the brush. These paths take you over steeper and trickier ground. The **GOLDEN GATE NATIONAL RECREATION AREA** also has that mix of well-established and off-the-beaten trails. Or take BART or the Muni streetcar to Glen Park and enjoy its forestlike atmosphere. And some swear by (and during) a run up **NOB HILL**, along California Street from Market or up Taylor or Jones Street from either side. But be prepared to deal with traffic.

Let's say you don't want to run alone, that you like to test yourself in a crowd. Well, the biggest crowd in town is the one in the annual **BAY TO BREAKERS FOOT RACE**, held each May with tens of thousands of participants running the 7.5 miles from the Ferry Building to Ocean Beach. There are a number of serious runners who break away from the pack and actually compete for timed results, but the big draw here is the spectacle of silliness: people dressed as Elvis, as Brillo boxes, as animals, or sometimes in nothing at all. Call 415/777-7770 to register. Finishers who paid the entry fee (not required, however) get a T-shirt.

The **SAN FRANCISCO MARATHON**, sponsored by the *San Francisco Chronicle*, is a more serious event, drawing 6,000 to 7,000 runners in comparison to Bay to Breakers' 30,000 to 50,000. The course is the standard 26.2 miles, and begins and ends in Golden Gate Park. Call the *Chronicle*'s promotion department (415/777-7120) for details (note: internal business problems could put an end to the paper's sponsorship).

If you seek a smaller group, a regularly scheduled Wednesday night run originates from the **FLEET FEET** running-apparel store in the Marina district (2806 Chestnut St at Steiner St; 415/921-7188; www.fleetfeet.com; map:K1). It is open to all abilities, draws on average 50 participants, and lasts 7 to 9 miles. There is also a Thursday night women's run of 3 miles.

An invaluable resource for hooking up with running groups and events is the **RUNNER'S SCHEDULE** (80 Mitchell Blvd, San Rafael, CA 94903; 415/472-7223; www.theschedule.com), an exhaustive listing of running-culture resources in California and Nevada, which you can pick up at shoe stores, gyms, and even some supermarkets. In the back pages are lists of group trainings, averaging 50 to 80 per issue, and a calendar boasts over 400 listings for races, clinics, and other events. The schedule is published monthly.

SAILING

The San Francisco Bay has played a crucial role in making the city what it is: from Sir Francis Drake sailing *past* the Golden Gate (it seems he missed it in the fog), to entire ships' crews deserting their vessels to seek fortune in the Gold Rush, to the thriving waterfront that until recently served as the city's economic linchpin. Now, with most of the commercial shipping shifted across the bay to Oakland, the waterfront is primarily dedicated to amusement. On any sunny day the bay is festooned with dozens of watercraft carrying passengers enjoying water, wind, and landscape.

Although it is extremely pleasant, sailing the bay is also good training for conditions the seagoer will meet in other parts of the world. There is, for example, the infamous "Potato Patch" beneath the Golden Gate Bridge, also known as Four Fathom Bank, where the depth of the bay changes from several hundred feet to a few dozen, causing the water to rush turbulently upward as if it were boiling, making for a bumpy and sometimes treacherous ride.

At that point you may wish you had attended **SPINNAKER SAILING SCHOOL** (Pier 40, South Beach Harbor; 415/543-7333; www.spinnaker-sailing.com), which has trained tens of thousands of new sailors since its founding in 1978. Courses can last from a weekend to two weeks, ranging from tips for beginners to preparation for a cruise to Hawaii. All courses are American Sailing Association certified.

After that you might feel confident enough to take on one of the rentals available from Spinnaker's "Bare Boats" subsidiary. You can rent by the day, week, or month, skippering yourself if you complete the qualification procedure, or sailing with a captain provided by the school. For those more in the mood for sailing without the hassles of command, the Spinnaker location is also home to **RENDEZVOUS CHARTERS** (Pier 40, South Beach Harbor; 415/543-7333; www.rendezvouscharters.com), which provides skippered charters for day trips.

If you're going to have the boat for more than a few days, you'll need to stop somewhere for the night. You could try the **SAN FRANCISCO MARINA** (3950 Scott St; 415/292-2013; map:J1), home to the Golden Gate and St. Francis Yacht Clubs, but most of its 600-plus berths are spoken for by permanent guests, leaving only a few end-ties available. If you get in, though, you can avail yourself of a fuel dock that offers both gas and diesel, and pumphouse stations to clean out your stinky holding tanks. Laundry and restaurants are within walking distance.

You might have a better shot at **PIER 39 MARINA** (Pier 39 by Fisherman's Wharf; 415/705-5556; www.pier39marina.com; map:N1). It has more than 300 slips, but you should still call at least 24 hours ahead to reserve. Pier 39 does not offer fuel but does have pumphouse stations and laundry, and there are plenty of places to eat. It'll cost you about $35 to $50 to dock here overnight.

If still adrift, try **OYSTER POINT MARINA PARK** (95 Harbor Master Rd #1, South San Francisco; 650/952-0808; www.smharbors.com; map:KK5). With close to 600 berths, there's generally guest dockage available. Pumphouse stations and laundry facilities are available, as well as lodging if you don't feel like sleeping on board. Both you and your vessel may refuel—the boat with gas or diesel, you at one of the two restaurants on the premises. Cost is 40 cents per foot per night.

SWIMMING

Almost any time during the day one can find swimmers bobbing in the water off **AQUATIC PARK** (map:L1), the best place in San Francisco for swimming in open water. This cove is less affected by the sometimes dangerous tides that prevail farther offshore, and the surrounding land serves as a windbreak to reduce the water's choppiness. Beginners should start out at slack tide; tide information can be found in the weather section of the daily newspapers. Open-water swimming at other locations, such as Ocean Beach and Baker Beach, is strongly not advised, no matter how tempting. The currents are much stronger, the waves more turbulent, and shark attacks are not unknown. If you must tackle the Pacific, use a surfboard. The same caution should be exercised when swimming the bay: don't get too far out. Use the buoys as guidelines, and stay well inside them.

Another problem faced by the outdoor swimmer is the question of temperature. The bay is basically cold, averaging between 50°–60°F. And remember, that's the average: winter can bring temperatures of 40°F or below, guaranteed to induce hypothermia in even the hardiest if they stay in the water too long (which is why Alcatraz was so hard to escape from). The warmth of a summer day can vanish the second you step into the water. Nobody should think less of you for using a wet suit to keep warm (it also allows you to stay in the water longer). If you decide to swim bareback— i.e., without a wet suit—start out by swimming a quarter hour at a time until you get the feel of it. And if you begin to feel unusually tired, get out of the water as fast as you can—it could be the onset of hypothermia.

You might want to build up your swimming skills at a practice pool before braving the bay. The **SHEEHAN HOTEL** (620 Sutter St near Mason St; 415/775-6500; map:M3) has an indoor pool that's open to the public. It's 21 yards long, ranges in depth from 4 to 10 feet, and is kept at a comfortable 82°F. Hours are Monday through Friday 6am to 10pm, Saturday 6am to 8pm, and Sunday 6am to 6pm. Admission is $10 for a single visit. Passes are also available for extended use: $55 for 15 entries, $90 for 30, with no time limit. Paid admission to the pool also entitles you to use of the adjacent gym.

Not only can you swim at the **ANGELO ROSSI PLAYGROUND AND POOL** (Arguello Blvd and Anza St; 415/666-7014; map:I4), you can sign up kids for swimming lessons Wednesdays, Thursdays, and Fridays in the summer months. Cost is $1.50 per lesson. Rates for regular swims are 50 cents for kids 17 and under, $3 for those 18 and over, and $5 for a family of two adults and two kids. The pool is indoors, runs from 4 to 10 feet deep, and is kept at between 80° and 82°F.

After having built up your stamina and acclimated yourself to the conditions of the bay, it might be fun to join your fellow enthusiasts in a group swim. The **DOLPHIN CLUB** and the **SOUTH END ROWING CLUB** (see the Rowing section) sponsor regularly scheduled group swims. South End Rowing Club members swim together to Alcatraz twice a year— once in the summer and once on New Year's Day (brrr!). They also sponsor a group foray to the Golden Gate Bridge in the fall. All these swims embark from the club's headquarters at Aquatic Park. The Dolphin Club sponsors 20 group swims throughout the year, open to six-month members in good standing. Routes include the old favorites, the Golden Gate or Alcatraz, from Aquatic Park. The club's longest swim sets out from Fort Point and uses Aquatic Park as the finish line. For safety's sake, all group swims are accompanied by spotters in motorboats and on surfboards, ready to pluck out any swimmers whose enthusiasm turns out to be greater than their endurance.

The Dolphin Club also engages in mileage competitions, in which you are really competing against yourself—swimming 40 miles between December 21 and March 21 earns to the right to call yourself a Dolphin Club Polar Bear. There is also a mileage competition between June 1 and

October 31; not surprisingly, taking the warmer weather into account, you are expected to swim more to win this one—100 miles. Completing either competition earns you a nifty certificate.

For other opportunities to test your open-water swimming skills, you might contact the **SAN FRANCISCO BAY SWIMMING ASSOCIA- TION** (650/359-3773). This no-nonsense group declares itself "small on formality, organized coaching and rules . . . no T-shirts, timed results, awards ceremonies, or post-race refreshments." It holds an organized swim once a month, with participants offered .5-, 1-, or 2-mile options. The club specializes in out-of-town jaunts: when these guys swim to Alcatraz, it's in the context of a combined 2.4-mile swim/10-kilometer run biathlon. This is not an event, or a group, for beginners. If you think you've got what it takes, give them a call.

TENNIS

Unless it's simply pouring down rain (and even that won' t stop a fanatic), tennis enthusiasts can work on their backhands and net-rushing techniques at any of San Francisco's 153 municipal tennis courts, located at 69 sites throughout the city, including 21 courts at **GOLDEN GATE PARK'S TENNIS COMPLEX** (map:I5). If there are others waiting courtside, players at most municipal courts are expected to relinquish the court after a prescribed amount of play—five minutes of warm-up time and one set's worth for doubles or singles, or 30 minutes of rallying time for two players in lieu of a set. If there are no other players waiting you may, of course, go as long as you like (many of the courts, such as the ones at **DOLORES PARK**, are illuminated for night play; map:L6). There are no fees or reservations, but a set of rules is posted at each court; players count on good sportsmanship and common courtesy to see them observed. Call 415/753-7100 for a location near you.

The exception to all this is the Golden Gate Park Tennis Complex, where procedures are more, well, complex. Courts are available in 90-minute increments starting at 9am; the last set must start by 4:30pm on weekends, 6pm on weekday evenings. There are two ways to claim a court: walk-up or reservation. Rates are lower for walk-up, which is first-come, first-served (or, since it's tennis, first serving), but a reservation secures your court—it all depends on how badly you need to play. Walk-up rates Monday through Friday are $4 for 90 minutes for San Francisco residents; $6 for nonresidents; $2 for seniors 65 and over; no charge for ages 18 or under. Evenings after 6pm and weekends will cost the walk-up San Franciscan $5, the out-of-towner $6. Seniors will pay $5; those under 18, $2.

To make weekend and evening reservations for the forthcoming week, call 415/753-7101 or 415/753-7102 on Wednesday from 4pm to 6pm; Thursday 9am to 5pm; or Friday 9am to noon. After 1pm on Friday, call the complex itself at 415/753-7001; you might be able to sneak in under the wire. Advance rates are $6 for city dwellers, $8 for nonresidents, $6 for seniors, and $2 for players 18 and under.

Spectator Sports

Ticket availability fluctuates from team to team, from game to game, and according to a team's standing as the season progresses. Try the team's own box office first, although you may find slim pickings after the season ticket holders have staked their claims. Another useful source is **BASS TICKET SERVICE** (510/762-2277) in the East Bay, with charge-by-phone service. For a particularly sought-after seat, you may have to avail yourself of the services of the ticket brokerages that have armies of buyers purchasing the individual limit. The brokerages then turn around and resell the seats at a hefty markup. Grit your teeth and check the newspaper. You generally find tickets being hawked in the classifieds and in display ads; the yellow pages also has a section for Ticket Sales.

Five-time Super Bowl winners the **SAN FRANCISCO 49ERS** (415/468-2249; www.sf49ers.com) play their home games at 3Com Park at Candlestick Point, which awaits revamping following a narrow victory in a city referendum. Matters are further complicated by the squabbling of the team owners, the DeBartolos, providing family melodrama that's frequently as entertaining as anything taking place on the gridiron. Even worse, tickets are usually snapped up in blocks far in advance, sometimes for the entire season. Consult the classifieds in the newspapers for offers from ticket brokers. You get to the park by taking the 3Com exit off Highway 101 to Jamestown Avenue and Harney Way, but a highly recommended alternative is Muni's Ballpark Express—shuttle buses that get you to and from the game from a variety of locations at a price of $5 per round-trip. Call Muni at 415/673-6864 for stops and schedules. And for heaven's sake, bundle up: the wind from the bay whips into Candlestick Point something fierce—and then the fog sets in.

The **SAN FRANCISCO GIANTS** (415/467-8000; www.sfgiants.com; map:O4), apparently having had enough of Candlestick Point's frigid winds, debuted the brand new PacBell Park at China Basin on Opening Day 2000. The area of the stadium-to-be at Fourth and King Streets is already being served by Muni's N-Judah line; plans for other mass transit to this destination seem to be up in the air. Call Muni (see above) for late-breaking details. Most games at Candlestick did not sell out, but expect a flurry of interest at the beginning of the first season in a new home.

Those craving hoops action have to go across the bay to catch the **GOLDEN STATE WARRIORS** (510/986-2200 or 888/479-4667; www.warriors.com) at the Oakland Coliseum Arena. The easiest way to get out to see these three-time NBA Championship winners is to take BART to the Coliseum stop and follow the crowd. The fare is $2.75 one-way from downtown San Francisco, $3 from the farther-flung Balboa Park Station. The arena holds 19,500 spectators; seats are generally available.

GOLDEN GATE FIELDS (1100 East Shore Hwy, Albany; 510/559-7300; www.ggfields.com; map:FF3) in the East Bay is the place to go if you want to watch horse racing, both on the track in front of you and via satellite from other racetracks around the country. Golden Gate Fields' own schedule is divided into two seasons: spring, from the end of March to the middle of June, and winter, from mid-November to mid-January. The track is open Wednesdays through Sundays, presenting 9 or 10 races per day. Satellite racing is offered year-round. Admission is $2 for the Club House and $10 for entry into the Turf Club, a more elegant atmosphere with sit-down dining and a rigidly enforced dress code. The minimum bet is $1 with no upward limit for the races at the Fields and televised races taking place in California; some restrictions may apply for bets placed on races in other states.

CONFERENCES, MEETINGS, AND RECEPTIONS

CONFERENCES, MEETINGS, AND RECEPTIONS

Many hotels, restaurants, and museums featured in this book rent out some of their rooms or courtyards for conferences, meetings, receptions, and other special events. Here is a list of additional facilities favored for such occasions, including several not-so-obvious choices coveted by many city denizens.

ALCATRAZ ISLAND / 415/561-4300 or 415/561-4370 You won't find many former federal prisons in the United States that are open to the public, but Alcatraz is, and—despite its rather chilling history—has many interesting, one-of-a-kind places where you'd actually enjoy mingling with your friends. While there is no formal meeting space, the island and prison facility present several options for group gatherings of up to 2,000, ranging from tours of the cells to an incredibly scenic reception area outside the main cell block that overlooks the bay. Alcatraz is available for special events in the evening only, after 4:30pm in the winter, and after 6:30pm in the summer. For more information on Alcatraz, see the Top 25 Attractions in the Exploring chapter. *Map:GG5*

AMERICAN CONSERVATORY THEATER / 30 Grant Ave; 415/749-2228 When the American Conservatory Theater (ACT) is not busy presenting world-class stage productions, its Geary Theater is available for private meetings and receptions. Built in 1910, the beautiful building was refurbished in 1996 and fitted with state-of-the-art theatrical equipment as well as an expansive new lobby and bar area. The theater accommodates approximately 1,000 people on three seating levels. It's wheelchair accessible, and there is a listening system for the hearing impaired. For more information, see the American Conservatory Theater in the Performing Arts chapter. *Map:N3*

ANGEL ISLAND / 415/897-0715 Many don't know that Angel Island offers several unique options for private special events for small groups or gatherings of up to 1,000. Areas such as Ayala Cove, Fort McDowell, and Camp Reynolds are rustic alternatives to the traditional meeting hall, and food services are available from Angel Island Catering. Audio-enhanced historic tram tours, bike rentals, and sea kayaking also can be arranged. For more information, see Parks and Beaches in the Exploring chapter. *Map:FF5*

ANSEL ADAMS CENTER FOR PHOTOGRAPHY / 250 4th St; 415/495-7000 Founded and operated by the Friends of Photography, this 3,500-square-foot gallery accommodates up to 250 people for reception-style events. The gallery is divided into five exhibition spaces—four holding rotating shows, the fifth devoted to the work of its famous namesake. All the galleries are available to rent. For more information, see Museums in the Exploring chapter. *Map:N3*

BAY AREA DISCOVERY MUSEUM / East Fort Baker, 557 McReynolds Rd, Sausalito; 415/289-7275 or 415/487-4398 Located just off the north end of the Golden Gate Bridge (on the Marin County side), this museum is a kids' wonderland by day and provides fun, colorful surroundings for adult soirees by night. It accommodates banquets for up to 300 and receptions for as many as 2,000. The facility features adaptable interactive exhibit halls, a cafe with a kitchen, and areas for outdoor entertaining that provide stunning views of the San Francisco skyline. For more information, see Marin County in the Day Trips chapter. *Map:FF6*

BEACH BLANKET BABYLON / Club Fugazi, 678 Beach Blanket Babylon Blvd (commonly known as Green St); 415/421-4284 The nation's longest-running musical revue, famous for its satire of dubious personalities and its outrageous humongous hats, performs year-round in this handsome North Beach venue, but it will close on occasion for private functions. The club holds up to 400 people in a theater-style seating arrangement, and there's a small stage and kitchen. For more information, see Beach Blanket Babylon in the Nightlife chapter. *Map:N2*

BILL GRAHAM CIVIC AUDITORIUM / 99 Grove St; 415/974-4000 A cornerstone of San Francisco's Civic Center, "The Bill" is one of the city's most frequently used facilities for large conventions, trade shows, and corporate meetings. It also hosts concerts, sporting events, and various local celebrations. The auditorium seats up to 7,000 and has 22,000 square feet of meeting space, including 47 rooms, a portable stage, and 40-foot-high ceilings. In-house catering and bartending are available. *Map:M4*

BIMBO'S 365 CLUB / 1025 Columbus Ave; 415/474-0365 The city's oldest nightclub, opened in 1931, is still one of its best. Not much has changed about this art deco beauty, gussied up with red velvet walls, glowing table lamps, and big side booths. Bimbo's regularly hosts touring musical acts in its main show room, which can hold 600. The adjacent Continental Lounge accommodates 150 additional people. Kitchen services and valet parking are available. For more information, see Bimbo's 365 Club in the Nightlife chapter. *Map:M1*

CALIFORNIA ACADEMY OF SCIENCES / Golden Gate Park, Concourse Dr at 9th Ave; 415/750-7222 or 415/750-7145 The Academy of Sciences, which includes the Steinhart Aquarium and its vast, colorful family of fish, is available to rent after 5pm (after 6pm Memorial Day through Labor Day). The Academy's various halls provide interesting (not to mention stimulating and educational) backdrops for meetings of up to 2,000. There is also a 400-seat auditorium with a projection booth, as well as the 300-seat Morrison Planetarium. For more information, see Museums in the Exploring chapter. *Map:H5*

CALIFORNIA HISTORICAL SOCIETY / 678 Mission St; 415/357-1848 The California Historical Society presents exhibitions and lectures examining the state's legacy and offers a stimulating venue for private functions and banquets. Its events facility has a 2,000-square-foot reception area, which can be modified for a wide range of uses, from a grand wedding to a dinner party for 250. *Map:N3*

THE CANNERY / 2801 Leavenworth St; 415/771-3112 Built in 1906 near the edge of Fisherman's Wharf, this was once the world's largest fruit cannery. Today the three-level complex houses an eclectic assortment of shops, galleries, restaurants, a comedy club, and the small Museum of the City of San Francisco. Private events for up to 400 can be held in an open-air courtyard, and the museum and restaurants accommodate various group sizes. For more information, see Top 25 Attractions in the Exploring chapter. *Map:M1*

THE CITY CLUB / Stock Exchange Tower, 155 Sansome St; 415/362-2480 Many of San Francisco's elite have held wedding receptions in this opulent art deco club located downtown. The walls are adorned with an impressive collection of original art, including a Diego Rivera mural. The City Club offers a cafe lounge and bar on the 10th floor and a formal dining room on the 11th floor, which accommodates up to 200 for sit-down dinners or up to 800 for receptions. Six private dining rooms, seating up to 50 people each, are also available. *Map:N3*

COIT TOWER / 1 Telegraph Hill; 415/362-0808 This popular monument atop Telegraph Hill is available for meetings, receptions, and dinners for up to 75 people. For more information, see Top 25 Attractions in the Exploring chapter. *Map:N1*

CONCOURSE EXHIBITION CENTER AT SHOWPLACE SQUARE / San Francisco Design Center, 635 8th St at Brannan St; 415/490-5800 Encompassing 10 city blocks, the Concourse Center has 125,000 square feet of multiuse space, including a hall that accommodates 600 booths, a cafe, and banquet facilities for 1,000 to 6,800 people. *Map:N5*

COW PALACE / 2600 Geneva Ave off Hwy 280, Daly City; 415/469-6000 Located 15 minutes south of San Francisco, the Cow Palace is a multipurpose facility with 300,000 square feet of meeting and exhibition space. The main arena has permanent seating for 10,300 and a maximum capacity of 16,500. A full range of services is also available. *Map:II6*

THE EXPLORATORIUM / 3601 Lyon St; 415/561-0311 or 415/563-7337 Located within the gorgeous Beaux Arts–style, Bernard Maybeck–designed

Palace of Fine Arts, the Exploratorium provides numerous diversions for children and adults, making it a terrific venue for special events. The entire facility is available to rent for dinner and dancing for up to 300 people. For receptions, it accommodates 3,000. Plus, there's plenty of that rare San Francisco treat: on-site parking. For more information, see Top 25 Attractions in the Exploring chapter. *Map:J1*

FORT MASON / Marina Blvd at Buchanan St; 415/441-3400 A national historic landmark, this sprawling former military post is now part of the Golden Gate National Recreation Area. It is one of the most-used facilities in town, hosting myriad events, exhibitions, plays, and activities almost every day of the year. Options for private functions abound. The 30,000-square-foot Herbst Pavilion accommodates 3,000, and the 50,000-square-foot Festival Pavilion holds 4,500. Cowell Theater has fixed seating for 400, and Bayfront Theater is equipped with 200 seats. In addition, the Conference Center has three meeting rooms ranging in capacity from 20 to 350 people, and the Firehouse can accommodate up to 125. Fort Mason Center also offers more than 10 other meeting rooms in its various waterfront bungalows. For more information, see Top 25 Attractions in the Exploring chapter. *Map:K1*

GHIRARDELLI SQUARE / 900 North Point St; 415/775-5500 In the 19th century, this was a working chocolate manufactory turning out tons of the rich, decadent chocolate that made Domingo Ghirardelli a legend. Today, Ghirardelli Square is a vibrant complex of retail outlets and restaurants, many with great views of the bay. The facility's various courtyards offer intimate settings for receptions and other special events, and five restaurants are available to host catered gatherings for up to 2,000. For more information, see Top 25 Attractions in the Exploring chapter. *Map:L1*

HAAS-LILIENTHAL HOUSE / 2007 Franklin St; 415/441-3000 Situated near Pacific Heights, this beautiful, historic mansion is one of the finest examples of Victorian architecture in San Francisco. The 1,300-square-foot ballroom is a popular venue for wedding receptions with a regal flair. There's also a 900-square-foot main reception area and a banquet room for up to 90 guests. For more information, see Museums in the Exploring chapter. *Map:L2*

MOSCONE CONVENTION CENTER / 747 Howard St between 3rd and 4th Sts; 415/974-4000 The anchor among meeting and exhibition facilities in San Francisco, the Moscone is home to the city's largest and often most important conventions. It's composed of two major buildings: Moscone South encompasses approximately 261,000 square feet of primary space, augmented by 44,000 more square feet of meeting space in 34 rooms; Moscone North offers an additional 181,000 square feet in exhibition space and 116,000 square feet in meeting space. The lobby provides a generous pre-function area, plus there's a grand ballroom. A full range of services is available, including catering for up to 6,000 people. The convention center accommodates various group sizes ranging from 150 to nearly 10,000. Another perk: it's within walking distance of more than two-thirds of the city's hotel rooms. *Map:N3*

OLD FEDERAL RESERVE BUILDING / 400 Sansome St at Sacramento St; 415/772-0733 Once the nerve center of the West Coast's financial world, this magnificent classical-style building is now on the National Register of Historic Places. Refined and glamorous, it has interior walls and floors made from French and Italian marble; the doors are solid bronze; and ornate crystal chandeliers dangle from the ceiling. Two balconies are bordered by intricate balustrades. The main hall area is spacious enough for a sit-down dinner for 400 or a cocktail reception for 850. *Map:N2*

THE OLD FIREHOUSE / 117 Broad St; 415/333-7077 This 100-year-old Victorian-style firehouse pays homage to the fire departments that doused the great blaze of 1906. The large rooms, available for functions for as many as 250, are filled with interesting memorabilia and historic photographs. *Map:II6*

THE PALACE OF FINE ARTS / 3601 Lyon St; 415/563-6504 Architect Bernard Maybeck's masterpiece provides a beautiful environment for weddings, receptions, parties, and other events. The grass-covered grounds include a stunning rotunda that accommodates up to 400. Indoors are a theater and the Exploratorium (see above). For more information, see Top 25 Attractions in the Exploring chapter. *Map:J1*

RECREATION AND PARK DEPARTMENT, CITY AND COUNTY OF SAN FRANCISCO / Golden Gate Park, McLaren Lodge 17, Fell and Stanyan Sts; 415/831-2700 This city department manages about 4,000 acres of public land, and there are many great facilities within San Francisco's parks available for private functions of various sizes, including Coit Tower, Golden Gate Park, and the Palace of Fine Arts. Contact the department for more information on its numerous other venues. *Map:I5*

SAN FRANCISCO CABLE CAR MUSEUM / 1201 Mason St; 415/474-1887 What could be more quintessentially San Francisco than having your event at the Cable Car Museum? Housed within the Cable Car Barn and Powerhouse, this facility reveals the inner workings of the city's beloved cable car system: huge wheels and gears pulling and tugging at a network of steel cables. The museum has three vintage cable cars on display, as well as photos and other memorabilia. It accommodates up to 800 people for receptions, and about 400 for sit-down affairs. For more information, see Museums in the Exploring chapter. *Map:M2*

SAN FRANCISCO MARITIME NATIONAL HISTORICAL PARK / Jefferson St at Leavenworth St; 415/556-3002 This park celebrates San Francisco's seafaring history and regularly hosts special maritime-themed events. Its various facilities, including the Maritime Museum (offering excellent bay views) and the historic ships *Balclutha* (a classic square-rigger) and the *Eureka* (the last of the sidewheel-powered ferries to operate in the United States), are available for private parties and events for up to 50 people. For more information, see Top 25 Attractions in the Exploring chapter. *Map:M1*

SPECTRUM GALLERY / 511 Harrison St; 415/495-1111 A chic San Francisco favorite, this large, urban gallery boasts a view of the entire city skyline from its loft-style windows. A working art gallery, it is available for rent every day, 24 hours a day. It offers state-of-the-art lighting and sound equipment, a portable stage and dance floor, a 24-foot-high ceiling, and room for 450 for a sit-down meal or up to 600 for a reception. *Map:N3*

VORPAL GALLERY / 393 Grove St; 415/397-9200 A large, well-established art gallery near the Civic Center, Vorpal offers a 15,000-square-foot loft-style space with hardwood floors and exposed-beamed ceilings and is a popular venue for meetings and events. The gallery accommodates up to 250 for seated events and as many as 400 for standing affairs. *Map:L4*

YERBA BUENA CENTER FOR THE ARTS / 701 Mission St; 415/978-2700 The sleek, modern Yerba Buena Center is home to the city's most varied array of visual and performance art. There are many options for private facility rentals, including three galleries, a multipurpose room that seats up to 600, a 755-seat theater, a lobby reception area that holds more than 400, and a 96-seat screening room. The center is one block from the Moscone Center in the burgeoning South of Market area. For more information, see Top 25 Attractions in the Exploring chapter. *Map:N3*

Index

A

A. G. Ferrari Foods, 269, 358
A. Sabella's, 48, 172
A/X Armani Exchange, 252
Aardvark's Odd Ark, 293
Absinthe Brasserie and Bar, 48, 332
Ace Wasabi's, 49
Acme Bread Company, 360
Acquerello, 49
ACT (American Conservatory Theater), 298–99
   private gatherings, 414
Actor's Theatre, 298
Adventure outfitters, 395–96
African-American Historical and Cultural Society, 190
AIDS, information, 13
Air-BART Shuttle, 5
Airporter, 3
Airports
   Oakland International Airport (OAK), 4–5
   San Francisco International Airport, 2–4
Alamo Square Bed & Breakfast, 186
Alamo Square Historical District, 185–86
Alcatraz Island, 168–69, 184, 351
   private gatherings, 414
Alden Shop, The, 288
Ale houses, 319
   See also Microbreweries/brewpubs; Pubs; Taverns
Alexis Baking Company and Cafe, 366
Alfred Dunhill, 282
Alfred Schilling Restaurant, Chocolate, and Pastry, 343–44
Alice's Restaurant, 49
Alioto's, 172
"Amazing Grazing," 51
American Conservatory Theater (ACT), 298–99
   private gatherings, 414
American Eagle Outfitters, 252
American Rag Company, 293
Amir H. Mozaffarian, 282
Amoeba Music, 286
Amtrak, 5
An Bodhran, 332
Ana Maranda, 181
Anchor Brewing Co., 230
Andreotti Family Farm, 381–82
Andrew Rothstein Fine Foods, 269
Angel Island, 238–39, 353, 391–92
   private gatherings, 414
   tours, 392
   transportation to and from, 392
Angelo Rossi Playground and Pool, 408

Angkor Borei, 50
Ann Taylor, 185, 252
Anokhi, 281
Ansel Adams Center for Photography, 233
   private gatherings, 414–15
Antica Trattoria, 50
Antiques, 248–52
Any Mountain–The Great Outdoor Store, 290
Aperto, 51, 230
Apparel, 252–56
   children's, 265–66
   consignment and discount, 268–69
   maternity and special sizes, 285–86
   vintage, 293–94
   See also Clothing; Outdoor gear; Shoes
Aqua, 52, 197
Aquariums
   Joseph M. Long Marine Laboratory, 385
   Steinhart Aquarium, 234, 415–16
Aquatic Park, 193–94, 407
   Municipal Pier, 400
Arboretum
   Strybing Arboretum and Botanical Gardens, 177
   See also Gardens; Parks
Arch, 273–74
Archbishop's Mansion, The, 157, 186
Argentum–The Leopard, 248
Ark, 292
Art, public
   Coit Tower frescoes, 234
   El Volado, 240
   Precita Eyes Mural Arts Center, 236, 240
Art museums
   Ansel Adams Center for Photography, 233
   Asia Art Museum, 233
   California Palace of the Legion of Honor, 187–88, 234
   Cartoon Art Museum, 308
   free admission times, 308–9
   M. H. de Young Museum, 235–36
   San Francisco Museum of Modern Art, 183, 199, 237
   University of California at Berkeley Art Museum, 360
   Yerba Buena Center for the Arts, 237
Arthur Beren Shoes, 288
Asia Art Museum, 233
Asian American Film Festival, 314

Astrids Rabat, 226
Atelier des Modistes, 207
Auberge du Soleil, 369–70
Audubon Canyon Ranch's Bolinas Lagoon Preserve, 388–89
Auto Impound, 26–27
Avenue 9, 52
Azie, 53

B

Bacco Ristorante, 53
Backflip, 321
Bagelry, The, 256
Baja Cantina, 219
Baker Beach, 184, 238
Baker Street Bistro, 53
Bakeries, 70, 74–75, 92, 101–2, 256–59
   See also Dessert; individual entries
Balboa Cafe, 54, 219, 332–33
Bale Grist Mill State Historic Park, 367
Ballet, 310–12
   Lawrence Pech Dance Company, 310
   Lines Contemporary Ballet, 310–11
   San Francisco Ballet, 311–12
   Smuin Ballets–SF, 312
Bally of Switzerland, 288–89
Banana Republic, 185, 252
Bank of America, 29, 196
Banks, 28–29
"Barbary Coast, The," 325
Barcelino, 252
Barcelona, 54
Bare Escentuals, 260
Barnes & Noble, 35, 261
Barney's Marina, 217
Bars, 332–43
   hotel, 337
   See also individual entries
BART (Bay Area Rapid Transit), 3, 25
   Air-BART Shuttle, 5
Baseball
   San Francisco Giants, 410
Basic Brown Bear Factory, 230, 292
Basketball
   Golden State Warriors, 410–11
Basque Boulangerie Cafe, 373
Bass Ticket Service, 410
Bathhouse Lake, 374
Bathhouses
   Kabuki Springs and Spa, 33, 220
   See also Sutro Baths
Bauerware Cabinet Hardware, 276
Bay Area Discovery Museum, 234, 238, 375

private gatherings, 415
Bay Area Playwrights' Festival, 299
Bay Area Rapid Transit (BART), 3, 25
  Air-BART Shuttle, 5
Bay Area Reporter, 34
Bay Area Sea Kayakers, 402
Bay Area Theatresports, 299
Bay Model, 376
Bay Trail, 400
Bayporter Express, 4
Beach Blanket Babylon, 322
  private gatherings, 415
Beaches, 238–39
  Baker Beach, 184, 238
  China Beach, 184
  Lighthouse Field State Beach,
    383
  Maverick Beach, 381
  Natural Bridges State Beach,
    383
  Ocean Beach, 184, 238, 401
  Red Rock Beach, 389
  Waddell Creek Beach, 385
Bear Valley Visitors Center, 390
Be-At Line, 321
Beauty Bar, 333
Beauty salons. See Salons
Bebe, 215, 253
Bed-and-Breakfast California, 141
Bed and Breakfast Inn, The, 160
Beer, 294–95
  See also Ale houses; Micro-
    breweries/ brewpubs;
    Pubs; Taverns
Bell'occhio, 274
Belvedere, 377
Bepples Pie Shop, 344
Berkeley, 356–62
  lodgings, 362
Berkeley Marina, 362
Berkeley Repertory Theatre, 299,
  361
Berkeley Symphony, 361
Bernal Heights
  restaurants, 41
Bernal Heights Park, 400
"Best Views of San Francisco and
  the Bay, The," 401
Betelnut, 55, 218
Bette's Oceanview Diner, 359–60
Bette's-to-Go, 359
Beverages, average costs, 11
Bicycle rentals, 380, 384, 396,
  397–98
Bicycling, 27
  Angel Island State Park, 392
  Marin County, 396
  Santa Cruz, 384
  San Francisco, 397–98
  See also Mountain biking
Bicycle Rental & Tour Center, 384
Bicyclery, 380
Big Basin Redwoods State Park, 385
Bill Graham Civic Auditorium, 209
  private gatherings, 415

Billiards, 318–19
Bimbo's 365 Club, 322
  private gatherings, 415
Birkenstock San Francisco, 289
Biscuits & Blues, 322
Bistro Aix, 55
Bistro Chapeau, 232
Bistro Don Giovanni, 366
Bistro Elan, 379
Bix, 56, 333
Bizou, 56, 199
Black Cat Cafe, 56
Blake's, 361
Blondie's Bar & No Grill, 333
Bloom's Saloon, 230
Blowfish Sushi To Die For, 57, 229
Blue & Gold Fleet, 29, 392
Blue Angels, 17
Blue Bar, 322–23
Blue Lamp, 323
Blues, 318
  See also Jazz; Music
Boats
  chartering, 407
  See also Sailing
Body care, 260–61
  See also Salons; Spas
Body Shop, The, 260
Body Time, 260
Bolinas, 389–90
Bombay Bazar, 228, 269
Books, 261–64
  about or set in San
    Francisco, 6–7
  literary events, 315–16
  literary legends, 6–7
  San Francisco Bay Area Book
    Festival, 18
  See also Bookstores
Books by the Bay, 315
Books Inc., 261–62, 378
Bookshop Santa Cruz, 384
Booksmith, 315
Bookstores, 315
  downtown, 35
  Palo Alto, 378
  Santa Cruz, 384
  Sonoma, 371
  See also Books; individual
    entries
Borders Books & Music, 35, 262,
  378
Boretti Amber, 281
Bothe–Napa Valley State Park, 367
Bottom of the Hill, 230, 323, 351
Boudin Sourdough Bakery & Café,
  256–57
Boulevard, 57
Boyes Hot Springs, 373–74
Brain Wash, 31
Brandy Ho's Hunan Food, 58–59
Brasserie Savoy, 59
Brava Theater Center, 299–300
Brennan's, 360

Brewpubs. *See*
  Microbreweries/brewpubs
Brisas de Acapulco, 59
Britex, 274
Brooks Brothers, 253
Brother's Korean Restaurant, 59
Brown Dirt Cowboy, 278
Bryan's, 269–70
Bubba Gump Shrimp Co., 173
Bubble Lounge, 333
Buckhorn, 192
Buena Vista Cafe, 172, 333–34, 222
Bulgari, 282–83
Bullock & Jones, 174, 253
Bulo Men, 289
Burberrys, 253
Bus Stop, 219, 334
Bus tours
  El Volado, 240
  Gray Line, 239
Buses
  Airporter, 3
  Gray Line, 239
  Greyhound/Trailways, 3, 7
  Municipal Railway System
    (Muni), 24–25
  Samtrans, 3
  to and from San Francisco, 7
Business services, 31–32
Butcher shops, 269–71
Butler & The Chef, The, 248–49
Butterfield & Butterfield, 249

C
Cabaret, 318
Cable cars, 169–70
  San Francisco Cable Car
    Museum, 237, 418
  See also Streetcars
Cafe, The, 323
Cafe Barrone, 379
Cafe Bastille, 60
Cafe Claude, 60
Cafe de la Presse, 262
Cafe du Nord, 225, 323–24
Cafe Fanny, 360
Cafe Flore, 225, 344
Cafe Intermezzo, 357
Cafe Jacqueline, 60
Cafe Kati, 61, 215–16
Cafe Majestic, 62
Cafe Marimba, 62
Cafe Mars, 334
Cafe Niebaum-Coppola, 64
Cafe Pescatore, 64
Cafe Rouge, 360
Caffe Freddy's, 64
Caffe Greco, 344
Caffe Macaroni, 65
Caffe Mediterranean, 357
Caffe Puccini, 344
Caffe Sport, 65
Caffe Strada, 357
Caffe Trieste, 344–45, 351
Caffe Verona, 378

California Academy of Sciences, 234, 308
  private gatherings, 415–16
California Canoe & Kayak, 381
California Culinary Academy, 209
California Historical Society, 262
  private gatherings, 416
California Palace of the Legion of Honor, 187–88, 234, 308
California Wine Merchant, 294
Calistoga, 368–69
  lodgings, 369–70
Calistoga Inn Restaurant and Brewery, 369
Calistoga Roastery, 369
Calistoga Spa Hot Springs, 368
Caltrain, 4, 5
Cambodiana's, 359
Camera shops, 32
Camping
  Angel Island State Park, 392
Campton Place Hotel, 66, 140
Candelier, 274
Candy, 264–65
  See also Dessert; individual entries
Cannery, The, 170, 180–81
  private gatherings, 416
  shopping, 242–43
Cannery Wine Cellars, 295
Canoe rentals, 381
  See also Kayak rentals
Canoeing, 402–3
  See also Kayaking
Cantinetta Tra Vigne, 367
Canton Bazaar, 281
Carnelian Room, 66, 196
Carol Doda's Champagne & Lace Lingerie Boutique, 253
Carousels
  Golden Gate Park, 177
  Santa Cruz, 382–83
  Yerba Buena Gardens, 183
Cars
  Auto Impound, 26–27
  rental, 26
  See also Driving; Parking; Scenic drives
Carta, 67
Cartier, 283
Cartoon Art Museum, 308
Casa Aguila, 67, 232
Casa Collection, 218
Casa Lucas, 227
Castro, 23, 223–25
  lodgings, 164–65
  map, 224
  nightlife, 225, 319, 341
  restaurants, 41, 225
  shopping, 224–25, 246
  tours, 240
Castro Street Fair, 245
Castro Theatre, 223, 313
Cat Club, The, 200, 324

Catahoula Restaurant and Saloon, 369
Catalyst, 384
Caviar, 271
CDs, 286–87
Celine Paris Boutique, 253
Cha Am, 359
Cha Cha Cha, 68, 222
"Chain Gang, The," 147
Chanel, 254
Chanticleer Books, 371
Charanga, 68
Charles Nob Hill, 69, 205–6
Charters
  boats, 407
Chateau Tivoli, 186
Checkers, 369
Cheese
  Say Cheese, 271
  Sonoma Cheese Factory, 373
  24th Street Cheese Co., 271
  See also Delicatessens; Food, ethnic and specialty
Chester's Cafe, 359
Chestnut Street, 23, 217, 243
Chevy's, 185
Chez Panisse, 358–59
Children
  clothing for, 265–66
  emergency services for, 11
  family restaurants, 44
Children's museums
  Bay Area Discovery Museum, 234
  Exploratorium, 234, 416–17
  Randall Museum, 216
China Beach, 184
Chinatown, 22, 200–4
  map, 201
  nightlife, 319, 341
  parking, 21
  restaurants, 41
  shopping, 246
  walking tours, 239
Chinese Folk Dance Association, 309
Chinese New Year, 14, 204
Chocolate Covered, 264
Chocolate Heaven, 264
Chocolates, 264–65
  See also Candy; Dessert
Chow, 69
Churches
  Chinatown, 202
  Glide Memorial Church, 351
  Grace Cathedral, 205
  Noe Valley Ministry, 226
  Saints Peter and Paul Roman Catholic Church, 210–11
  St. Mary the Virgin in Exile, 232
  Swedenborgian Church, 215
  See also Synagogues
Church's English Shoes, 289
Cielo, 254

Cigars
  Alfred Dunhill, 282
Cine Acción Festival, 313
Cinema 21, 312
Citizen Cake, 70, 257
City Arts & Lectures, 315–16
City Club, The
  private gatherings, 416
City College of San Francisco, 37
City Discount, 278
City Guides, 239, 308
City Hall, 193, 208
City Lights Bookstore, 35, 211–12, 262, 316
City Tavern, 219
Civic Auditorium (Bill Graham), 209
Civic Center, 208–9
  lodgings, 157–59
  parking, 21
  restaurants, 41, 209
Claremont Resort and Spa, 362
Classical music, 304–9
Clay Theatre, 215, 313
Clean Well-Lighted Place for Books, A, 262, 316
Clement Street, 246
Cliff House, 188–89, 231
Cliff's Hardware, 276
Clift Hotel, 140
Clothing
  appropriate for San Francisco, 9–10
  children's, 265–66
  consignment and discount, 268–69
  maternity and special sizes, 285–86
  stores, 252–56
  vintage, 293–94
  See also Apparel; Outdoor gear; Shoes
Club Deluxe, 324
Club Fugazi, 212
Club Line, 321
Clubs
  information, 321
  nightlife, 321–32
Coach Store, 283
Coast tour, north, 353–54
Coastal Trail, 400
Cobb's Comedy Club, 324
Cocktail lounges, 318
Coffee
  coffeehouses, 301, 343–46, 361, 366, 373
  retail, 173, 266–68, 366
  See also individual entries, neighborhoods, and towns
Coffee Garden, 373
Coffee Roastery, 266
"Coffeehouse Culture," 301
Coit Tower, 177–78, 212
  frescoes, 234
  private gatherings, 416
Cole Valley, restaurants, 41

Collective Antiques, 249
Comedy clubs, 318
Comet Club, 334
Comfort Suites, 165
Commodore International Hotel, 141
Common Scents Soaps and Lotions, 226
Company Store, The, 285
Computer repairs and rentals, 32–33
Concourse Exhibition Center at Showplace Square, private gatherings, 416
Conferences, 413–19
     Napa Valley Conference and Visitors Bureau, 363
Confetti le Chocolatier, 264
Connecticut Yankee, 230
Conservatory of Flowers, 177
Consignment and discount apparel, 268–69
Consulates, 14
Contemporary Music Players, 306
Cookin', 278
Copeland's Sports, 290
Copy services, 31–32
Cost Plus World Market, 281
Costs, general, 10–11
Cottage Industry, 281
Cow Hollow, 22, 218–19
     nightlife, 218–19, 319
     restaurants, 42, 218
     shopping, 218, 243
Cow Palace, private gatherings, 416
Cowell Theater, 190, 300
Craft and Folk Art Museum, 190
Crate & Barrel, 278
Crescent City Cafe, 70
Crissy Army Airfield, 178, 184
Critical Mass, 398
Crocker Galleria, 242
Crow Bar, 334
Cruisin' the Castro, 240
Crunch, 394–95
Curran Theatre, 300
Currency exchange, 13
Cypress Club, 70

D
Daniel Stein Antiques, 249
Dalva, 334–35
Dance, 309–12
     Ethnic Dance Festival, 310
     See also Ballet
Dancing/dance floors, 318
Dandelion, 274
David Stephen Men's, 254
Davies (Louise M.) Symphony Hall, 208
Day trips, 355–92
     Angel Island State Park, 391–92
     Berkeley, 356–62
     Half Moon Bay, 380–82

Marin Coast, 385–90
Marin County, 375–78
     Palo Alto, 378–79
     Point Reyes National Seashore, 390–91
     Santa Cruz, 382–85
     Wine Country, 362–75
     See also Itineraries
de Vera, 274
de Young (M. H.) Memorial Museum, 235–36, 308
Delfina, 71
Delicatessens, 30, 210, 269–71
Dental services, 29–30
Department stores, 247–48
Departures from the Past, 293
Dessert, 343–46
     See also Bakeries; Candy
Detour, 225
Diamond Corner Cafe, 226
Diesel, 254
Different Light Bookstore, A, 224–25, 316
Dillingham & Company, 249
Diner, The, 366
Dining Room at the Ritz-Carlton, The, 71, 206
     Sunday brunch, 351
Disabled people, services for, 11–12
Discount apparel, 268–69
Disney Store, 292
Districts, 194–233
     See also individual entries
Dr. Wilkinson's Hot Springs, 368
Doctors, 29–30
     emergency rooms, 11
Does Your Father Know, 224
Dogs
     off-leash areas for, 12
     services, 33
Doidge's, 72
Dol Ho, 72
Dollhouse, The, 200
Dolores Park, 401
     tennis, 409
Dolores Park Inn, 164
Dolphin Club, 402, 404–5
     swimming, 408–9
Domaine Chandon, 366
Don Sherwood Golf and Tennis World, 290
Dottie Dolittle, 265
Dottie's True Blue Café, 73
Downtown Joe's Restaurant and Brewery, 365–66
Drakes Estero, 391
Driving
     49-Mile Scenic Drive, 349
     See also Cars; Highways; Parking
Drugstores, 30–31
Dry cleaners, 31
Durm & Company, 249–50

E
Eagle Tavern, The, 335
Eastside West Restaurant & Raw Bar, 218
Ebisu, 73, 233
Ed Hardy Antiques, 250
Eddie Bauer, 254
Edward II Inn & Pub, 160
El Dorado Hotel, 374–75
El Drisco, 161
El Volado, 240
Elbo Room, 229, 324
Elite Cafe, The, 74
Eliza's, 74, 230
Elizabeth Arden Red Door Salon & Spa, 260
Ella's, 74
Embarcadero
     running, 405
     skating, 403
Embarcadero Center, 185, 196, 242
Embarcadero Center Cinema, 185
Embassy Suites, 166
Emergency rooms, 11
Emergency services, for children, 11
Emporio Armani, 254
End Up, The, 200, 325–26
Enrico's, 75, 335
Eos Restaurant & Wine Bar, 75, 222
Eppler's, 257
Equinox, 337
Eric's, 76
Espresso Roma, 358
Esprit Outlet Store, 268
Este Noche, 229
Ethnic Dance Festival, 310
Ethnic festivals and events, 14–18, 204, 244–45
     See also individual entries
Ethnic foods, 227–28, 269–71
Ethnic goods, 281–82
Ethnic restaurants, 43–47
Eureka Theatre, 300
Evelyn's Antique Chinese Furniture, 250
Events. See Festivals and events
Evvia, 379
Excelsior District, restaurants, 41
Exploratorium, 181–82, 203, 234, 308
     private gatherings, 416–17

F
Fairmont Hotel & Tower, 152
"Family Attractions," 203
FAO Schwarz, 292
Farallon, 76
Farallon Islands, 388
Farmers markets
     Ferry Plaza Farmers Market, 51, 197, 351
     Santa Cruz, 384–85
Farms, Andreotti Family Farm, 381–82
Fatapples, 359

Ferries, 28, 29, 392
itinerary, 352–53
Ferry Building, 196
Ferry Plaza Farmers Market, 51,
197, 351
Festivals and events,
calendar, 14–18
ethnic, 14–18, 204, 244–45
film, 313–15
food, 17
literary, 315–16
music, 16, 17, 18, 304, 308
street fairs, 244–45
theater, 17, 299, 302, 361
weekly events, 351
See also individual festivals
and events
Fiddler's Green, 326
15 Romolo, 335
Fifth Floor, 77
Fillamento, 278
Fillmore, The, 326
Fillmore District
restaurants, 42
Fillmore Street, 243
Film, 312–15
festivals, 15, 313–15
See also Movie theaters;
Movies
Film Arts Foundation Festival of
Independent Cinema, 313
Film developing, 32
Financial District, 20–22, 194–97
lodgings, 149–51
nightlife, 319, 341
restaurant, 41s, 197
Finocchio's, 326
Fior d'Italia, 210
Fiordella, 271
Fiori, 271
Fire Department Museum, 309
Fire Engine Tours & Adventures,
239
Firefly, 77, 226
Firewood Cafe, 78, 192
Fireworks
Fourth of July Celebration
and Fireworks, 16
First Squeeze Deli & Juice Bar &
Cafe, 366
Fish markets, 288. See also
Seafood
Fisherman's Wharf, 22, 170–72
lodgings, 156–57
map, 171
nightlife, 319, 341
restaurants, 41
shopping, 242–43
Fishing
Half Moon Bay, 381
Flax Art & Design, 275
Flea markets
Treasure Island Flea Market,
239
Fleet Feet, 406

Fleur de Lys, 78
Florio's, 79, 216
Flowers, 271–72
Flying Saucer, 79, 228
Fog City Diner, 80
Folk Art International, 281
Food
average costs, 11
ethnic and specialty, 269–71
fairs, 17
health food stores, 277
See also Bakeries; Candy;
Delicatessens; Desserts;
Restaurants; individual
entries
Football
San Francisco 49ers, 410
Footnotes Literary Walk Highlights,
239
Foreign Cinema, 80
Foreign visitors, services for, 13–14
Fort Mason, 189–90, 217
private gatherings, 417
Fort Point, 179, 184, 308, 400
42 Degrees, 81
42nd Street Moon, 300–1
"49-Mile Scenic Drive, The," 349
49ers, 410
Foster-Gwin, Inc., 250
Fourth of July Celebration and
Fireworks, 16
Franciscan, 81
Fred's Place, 376
Fredericksen Hardware, 276
Freight & Salvage Coffeehouse, 361
French Hotel, 362
French Laundry, 366
French Tulip, 271–72
Fringale, 82, 199–200
Fringe Festival, 302
Fumiki, 218
"Fun for Free," 308–9
Furniture, 272–73. See also
Antiques

G

G&M Sales, The Great Outdoors
Store, 291
Gap, 185, 255
Garages, 26
city-owned, 21
See also Parking
Garden Court Hotel, 82, 379
Gardens
Berkeley, 361
Japanese Tea Garden, 177
Strybing Arboretum and
Botanical Gardens, 177
Yerba Buena Gardens,
183–84
See also Parks
Garibaldi's, 83
Gary Danko, 83
Gaylord India Restaurant, 181
Gays/Lesbians

Different Light Bookstore, A,
316
gay/lesbian bars, 200, 318
International Gay & Lesbian
Film Festival, 314
Lesbian, Gay, Bisexual,
Transgender Pride Parade
and Celebration, 16
Lesbian/Gay Chorus of San
Francisco, 304
San Francisco Bay Blades, 405
San Francisco Gay Men's
Chorus, 304
services and resources for, 13
Theater Rhinoceros, 303
See also Castro
General's Daughter, The, 373
Genova Delicatessen, 366
Ghirardelli Chocolate Shop, 265
Ghirardelli Square, 170, 180–81
private gatherings, 417
shopping, 243
Ghurka, 283
Giants, 410
Gift shops, 273–76
Gimme Shoes, 215, 289
Girlfriends, 218
Glen Canyon Park, 238
Glen Ellen, 374–75
Glide Memorial Church, 351
Globe, 84
Goat Hill Pizza, 230
Godiva, 265
Going in Style, 283
Gold Dust, 335–36
Golden Gate Bridge, 3, 174–75
running, 405
statistics, 259
"Golden Gate Bridge, The," 3
"Golden Gate Bridge by the
Numbers," 259
Golden Gate Fields, 411
Golden Gate Golf Course, 399
Golden Gate Hotel, 142
Golden Gate National Recreation
Area (GGNRA), 179, 184, 386
running, 405
See also Presidio, The
Golden Gate Park, 23, 175–77,
203, 222, 308
horseback riding, 402
itinerary, 350–52
map, 176
roller skating, 351
running, 405
skating, 403
Tennis Complex, 409–10
Golden Gate Park Skate and Bike,
397, 403
Golden Gate Park Stables, 402
Golden Gate Promenade, 179, 400
Golden Gate Theatre, 301
Golden Gate University, 37
Golden State Warriors, 410–11
Gold's Gym, 394

Golf, 398–400
    Half Moon Bay Golf Links, 382
    information line, 399
    Lincoln Park Golf Course, 231
Goodbyes, 268
Gordon Bennett, 180, 278
Gordon Biersch Brewery
    Restaurant, 84
Gordon's House of Fine Eats, 84,
    229
Grace Cathedral, 186–87, 205
Graffeo Coffee Roasting Co., 267
Graham (Bill) Civic Auditorium, 209
Gramercy Grill, 206
Grand Café, 85
Grand Hyatt San Francisco on
    Union Square, 142
Grant & Green Blue Club, 212, 327
Gray Line, 239
Great American Music Hall, 327
Great Eastern, 86
Green Apple Books and Music,
    232, 262–63, 286–87
Greenbelt Alliance, 401
Greenhaven, 228
Greens, 86, 217
Greens Sports Bar, 336
Greyhound/Trailways, 3, 7
Grocery stores, 30
    ethnic and specialty, 269–71
    health food, 277
Guaymas, 377
Gucci, 283.
Gump's, 275
Guys and Dolls, 293
Gyms, 394–95

H

Haas-Lilienthal House, 213, 235
    private gatherings, 417
Haight-Ashbury, 23, 220–22
    itinerary, 350–52
    lodgings, 163–64, 221–22
    map, 221
    nightlife, 319, 341
    restaurants, 41, 222
    walking tours, 239
Haight Street, 246
Haight Street Fair, 244
Half Moon Bay, 380–82
Half Moon Bay Golf Links, 382
Hamburger Mary's, 87
Harbor Court Hotel, 151
Harbor Village Restaurant, 87, 185
Hard Rock Cafe, 87
Harding Park Golf Course and Jack
    Fleming Golf Course, 399
Hardware stores, 276–77
Hardware Unlimited, 276
Harold's Newsstand, 263
Harper Greer, 285
Harrington Bros. Antiques, 228
Harrington's Bar and Grill, 336
Harris's, 88
Harry Denton's Starlight Room, 337

Harry's on Fillmore, 327
Harvest Interiors, 272
Hats, 180, 215, 284
Hawthorne Lane, 88
Hayes and Vine Wine Bar, 336
Hayes Street, 246
Hayes Street Grill, 89
Hayes Valley
    nightlife, 319, 341
    parking, 21
    restaurants, 41
Hear Music, 287
Hearst (Phoebe) Museum of
    Anthropology, 361
Heaven Day-Spa & Center for
    Wellness, 217
Helmand, 89
Herb 'n Inn, The, 163
Hi-Ball Lounge, 212, 327
Highways, 7–8
Hiking, 400–1
    Angel Island State Park, 392
    Palomarin Trailhead, 390
Historic homes, 204, 206, 207,
    213–15, 218, 235, 236, 417
    See also individual entries
Holiday Inn (San Francisco Airport
    North), 166
Home accessories, 278–80
    See also Imported goods
Homechef, 278
Hong Kong Flower Lounge, 90
Hoogasian Florist, 272
Horse racing, 411
Horseback riding, 401–2
Hospitals, 29–30
    emergency rooms, 11
Hotel Bohème, 155
Hotel Diva, 143
Hotel Griffon, 151
Hotel Majestic, 158
Hotel Monaco, 143
Hotel Rex, 144
Hotel Triton, 144
Hotels
    chain, 147
    See also Lodgings; individual
        entries
House, The, 90
House of Nanking, 91
Housewares, 321
Huntington Hotel, 153
Hyatt, 150
Hyde Street Bistro, 91
Hyde Street Pier, 193–94

I

I Love Chocolate, 258
Ice cream
    Joe's Ice Cream, 345
    Lappert's Ice Cream, 376
    Zero Degrees, 346
    See also Dessert
Ice rinks
    Yerba Buena Gardens, 184

Il Fornaio, 92, 257–58
Imaginarium, 292
Imported goods, 281–82
    See also Home accessories
Indian Oven, 92
Indian Springs Resort and Spa, 368
Indigo, 93
Information, 24
    golf, 399
    music and clubs, 321
    running, 406
Infusion Bar & Restaurant, 93, 336
In-line skating, 403
Inn at Southbridge, 370
Inn on Castro, 165
Interieur Perdu, 250
Interior Perspectives Antiques,
    250–51
International Film Festival, 15, 314
International Gay & Lesbian Film
    Festival, 314
Internet access, 34
Irish Bank Bar and Grill, 338
Itineraries, 347–54
    bus itinerary, 349–50
    coast tour, north, 353–54
    eating and shopping itinerary,
        350
    ferry itinerary, 352–53
    Golden Gate Park and
        Haight-Ashbury, 350–52
    San Francisco
        neighborhoods, 352
    San Francisco walking tour,
        348–49
    Wine Country, 353
    See also Day trips

J

Jack London State Historic Park, 374
Jack's, 94, 197
Jack's Cannery Bar, 181
Jackson Court, 161
Jackson Fillmore, 94, 215
Jackson Square, 196–97
    shopping, 246
Jacqueline Perfumery, 260
Jammin' Java Coffee House, 345
Japanese Tea Garden, 177
Japanese Weekend, 285
Japantown, 219–20, 246
    lodgings, 157–59
    restaurants, 42
Japonesque, 275
Jardinière, 95
Jazz, 318
    Kuumbwa Jazz Center, 384
    radio stations, 36
Jazz at Pearl's Restaurant & Bar, 327
Jessica McClintock, 255
Jewelry and accessories, 180,
    282–85
Jewish Film Festival, 314–15
Jewish Museum San Francisco,
    The, 235, 308

Joan & David, 289
Joanie Char, 268
Joe Goode Performance Group, 310
Joe's Ice Cream, 345
John Barleycorn, 206
John Doughty Antiques, Inc., 251
John Lee Hooker's Boom Boom Room, 328
Johnson's Oyster Farm, 390–91
Jonathan Kaye, 292–93
Joseph M. Long Marine Laboratory, 385
Joseph Schmidt Confections, 225, 265
Judah L. Magnes Museum, 360–61
Julie's Supper Club, 338
Just Desserts, 258

K
Kabuki Springs and Spa, 33, 220
Kabuto Sushi, 95
Kan Zaman, 96
Kate's Kitchen, 96
Kayak rentals, 381, 383–84, 388, 391, 402–3
Kayaking, 388, 402–3
    Point Reyes, 391
    Santa Cruz, 383–84
    tours, 392
Kenneth Cole, 290
Kenwood Inn and Spa, 375
Kepler's Books and Magazines, 378
Khan Toke Thai House, 96, 232
Kinder Sport, 266
Kitchen shops, 278–80
Kokkari Estiatorio, 97
Kronos Quartet, 304
Kuleto's, 98
Kuumbwa Jazz Center, 384
Kyo-ya, 98

L
L'Amie Donia, 379
L'Osteria del Forno, 102
L'Uomo, 255
La Folie, 98, 207
La Nouvelle Patisserie, 258
La Palma Mexicatessen, 270
La Residence, 370
La Rondalla, 228
La Rosa, 293–94
La Salle Gallery, 251
La Taqueria, 99
La Vie, 232
La Villa Poppi, 100
Lachryma Montis, 371
Laghi, 100
Lake Merced, 232, 238
Lakeside Hardware & Lumber Co., 276–77
Land's End, 184
Lang Antiques and Estate Jewelry, 283
Lappert's Ice Cream, 376

Laserium, 234
Laundromats, 31
Lavendar Hill Spa, 368–69
Lawrence Pech Dance Company, 310
Le Charm, 100
Le Colonial, 100
Leather goods, 283–84
Legal services, 31
Lesbian, Gay, Bisexual, Transgender Pride Parade and Celebration, 16
Lesbian/Gay Chorus of San Francisco, 304
Lesbians
    bars, 200, 318
    services and resources for, 13
    See also Castro; Gays/Lesbians
Levi Strauss, 255
Lexington Club, 229, 338
Lhasa Moon, 101
Li Po, 338
Liberty Cafe, 101
Libraries
    Noe Valley Library, 226
    public, 34–35
    San Francisco Performing Arts Library and Museum, 208–9
    San Francisco Public Library, 209
Lighthouse Field State Beach, 383
Lighthouses
    Point Bonita Lighthouse, 386
    Point Reyes Lighthouse, 390
Liguria Bakery, 259
Li-Lo Lounge, 231
Limn, 272–73
Lincoln Park Golf Course, 231, 399
Linen shops, 278–80
Lines Contemporary Ballet, 310–11
Liquor, 294–95
Literary events, 315–16
Literary legends, 6–7
Little City Meats, 270
Little Thai, 208
Lively Arts, 379
Living Green, 272
Lodgings, 139–66
    Alamo Square, 186
    average costs, 10–11
    Berkeley, 362
    Calistoga, 369–70
    Castro, 164–65
    chain hotels, 147
    Civic Center, 157–59
    Financial District, 149–51
    Fisherman's Wharf, 156–57
    Haight-Ashbury, 163–64, 221–22
    Japantown, 157–59
    near San Francisco International Airport, 165–66
    Nob Hill, 152–54

    North Beach, 155–56
    Pacific Heights, 160–63
    Palo Alto, 379
    Sonoma Valley, 374–75
    South of Market (SoMa), 151–52
    Union Square, 140–49
Loehmann's, 268
Lombard Street, 175
Lombardi Sports, 291
London Wine Bar, 338
Lone Palm, 229, 339
Long Life Noodle Co. & Jook Joint, 192
Lorries Airport Service, 4
Louis Vuitton, 284
Louise M. Davies Symphony Hall, 208
Lou's Pier 47 Club, 172
Lucca Delicatessen, 270
Lucca Ravioli Company, 228
Luggage and travel accessories, 283–84
LuLu, 102
Luna Loca, 192

M
M. H. de Young Memorial Museum, 235–36, 308
Ma Maison Home Accents, 278
MacArthur Park, 379
Macy's Union Square, 247
Mad Magda's Russian Tea Room and Mystic Cafe, 345
Magazine, The, 273
Magazines, 261–64
Magic Theatre, 190, 301
Maiden Lane, 242
Maiden Lane Salon & Spa, 33
Maison d'Etre, 279
Make-Out Room, 328
Malls, 247
Malm Luggage, 284
Mandarin Oriental, 149
Mandarin Restaurant, The, 181
Manora's Thai Cuisine, 103
Maps
    Castro, 224
    Chinatown, 201
    Financial District, 195
    Fisherman's Wharf, 171
    Golden Gate Park, 176
    Haight-Ashbury, 221
    Mission District, 227
    Nob Hill, 205
    Noe Valley, 224
    North Beach, 211
    Pacific Heights, 214
    Potrero Hill, 198
    Russian Hill, 205
    South of Market (SoMa), 198
Marcello's Pizza, 103
Margaret Jenkins Dance Company, 309
Marin Coast, 385–90

Bolinas, 389–90
Marin Headlands, 386–87
Muir Woods/Muir Beach, 387
Stinson Beach, 387–89
See also Marin County;
    Marin Headlands
Marin County, 375–78
Belvedere, 377
bicycle rentals, 396
biking and mountain biking,
    396
Mill Valley, 378
Sausalito, 375–76
Tiburon, 376–77
See also Marin Coast; Marin
    Headlands
Marin Headlands, 184, 386–87
See also Marin Coast; Marin
    County
Marina Cyclery, 397
Marina District, 23, 217
nightlife, 319
restaurants, 42, 217
Marina Green, 217, 400
skating, 403
Marina Inn, 161
Marina Lounge, 339
Marine Mammal Center, 386
Mario's Bohemian Cigar Store,
    103, 210
Maritime Museum, 235, 309
Mark Reuben Gallery, 180
Market Street, 20
Marsh, The, 229, 302
Marriott, San Francisco, 151
Martini Mercantile (Haight), 294
Martini Mercantile (North Beach),
    294
Martuni's, 339
Masa's, 104
Ma-Shi'-Ko Folk Craft, 281
Massawa, 222
Maternity clothing, 285–86
Maverick Beach, 381
Max's Opera Cafe, 345–46
Maya San Francisco, 104
MC², 105
McCormick & Kuleto's, 181
McPherson Center for Art and
    History, 384
Meadowood Resort, 370
Mecca, 105, 225
Medical services, 29–30
emergency, 11
Medium Rare Records, 287
Meetings, 413–19
Meetinghouse, The, 106
Mel's Diner, 106
Mercury, 328
Merry-go-rounds
    Golden Gate Park, 177
    Santa Cruz, 382–83
    Yerba Buena Gardens, 183
Messenger services, 32
Metier, 255

Metreon, 191–92
restaurants, 192
Metro, 225
Metronome Ballroom, 230–31
Mexican Museum, 190, 235, 308
Michelangelo, 210
Microbreweries/brewpubs, 84,
    117, 129
Anchor Brewing Co., 230
Calistoga Inn Restaurant and
    Brewery, 369
Downtown Joe's Restaurant
    and Brewery, 365–66
San Francisco Brewing
    Company, 325, 340
Thirsty Bear Brewing
    Company, 342
Triple Rock Brewery, 359
Twenty Tank Brewery, 200,
    343
See also Ale houses; Beer;
    Pubs; Taverns
Midsummer Mozart, 304
Mifune, 107
Mike Furniture, 215, 273
Mill Valley, 378
Millennium, 107
Mio, 255
Miss Millie's, 108
Mission Bay Golf Center, 399–400
Mission Cliffs Rock-Climbing
    Center, 397
Mission District, 226–29
map, 227
nightlife, 229, 319, 341
restaurants, 42, 228–29
shopping, 228
Mission Dolores, 190–91, 236
Mister Lee, 261
Modern Times Bookstore, 315, 263
Moe's Alley, 384
Moki Sushi and Pacific Grill, 108
Molinari Delicatessen, 210, 270
Mollie Stone's Market and Deli, 30
Mom Is Cooking, 108
Momo's, 109
Montage, 109, 192
Moose's, 110
Morrison Planetarium, 234
Moscone Convention Center, 199
private gatherings, 417–18
Mount Livermore, 392
Mount St. Helena, 369
Mountain biking, 27
    Marin County, 396
    Point Reyes, 392
    San Francisco, 397–98
    See also Bicycle rentals;
        Bicycling
Movie theaters, 312–13
    Berkeley, 361
    Castro Theatre, 223
    Clay Theatre, 215
    Embarcadero Center
        Cinema, 185

IMAX Theatre, 192
Palo Alto, 379
Roxie Cinema, 229
See also Film; Movies
Movies, 312–15
made in San Francisco, 63
San Francisco International
    Film Festival, 15
See also Film; Movie theaters
Mrs. Dewson's Hats, 215, 284
Mud, Wind, and Fire, 180–81
Muddy Waters Coffee House, 346
Mudpie, 266
Muir Beach, 387
Muir Woods, 387
Municipal Railway System (Muni),
    24–25
Murals
    El Volado, 240
    Precita Eyes Mural Arts
        Center, 236, 240
Mureta's Antiques, 251
Musée Méchanique, 189, 236
Museum of the City of San
    Francisco, 181, 236
Museum of the Money of the
    American West, 196
Museum Store at San Francisco
    Museum of Modern Art, 275
Museums, 233–37
    Bay Area Discovery
        Museum, 234, 375, 415
    California Academy of
        Sciences, 234, 415–16
    California Historical Society,
        416
    Chinese Historical Society
        Museum, 203
    Exploratorium, 181–82,
        203, 234, 308, 416–17
    free admission times, 308–9
    Jewish Museum San
        Francisco, 235
    Judah L. Magnes Museum,
        360–61
    Lawrence Hall of Science, 361
    Maritime Museum, 235
    McPherson Center for Art
        and History, 384
    Mexican Museum, 190, 235
    Mission Dolores, 236
    Musée Méchanique, 189, 236
    Museum of the City of San
        Francisco, 181, 236
    Museum of the Money of
        the American West, 196
    Phoebe Hearst Museum of
        Anthropology, 361
    Presidio Army Museum,
        179, 236–37
    Randall Museum, 216
    Ripley's Believe It or Not!
        Museum, 172, 237
    San Francisco Craft and Folk
        Art Museum, 190

San Francisco Performing
Arts Library and Museum,
208–9
Santa Cruz Surfing Museum,
383
Sharpsteen Museum and
Brannan Cottage, 369
Wax Museum, 172, 237
Wells Fargo History Room,
196
See also Art museums;
Children's museums;
Historic homes
Music
Berkeley, 361
blues, 318
Celtic, 318
classical, 304–9
folk/acoustic, 318
information, 321
jazz, 318, 384
nightlife, 321–32
radio stations, 35–36
reggae/ska/world beat, 319
rock, 319
San Francisco Museum of
Modern Art, 351
Santa Cruz, 384
shopping, 286–87
swing, 319
Mustards Grill, 366

N

Nabolom Bakery, 358
Napa, 363–66
Napa County Landmarks, 365
Napa Valley, 362–70
wineries, 364–65
Napa Valley Coffee Roasting
Company, 366
Napa Valley Conference and
Visitors Bureau, 363
Napa Valley Olive Oil
Manufacturing Company, 367
Napa Valley Wine Train, 363
"Napa Valley Wineries," 364–65
Natural Bridges State Beach, 383
Natural History Museum, 234
Neighborhood districts, 194–233
See also individual entries
Neiman Marcus, 247
Epicure Department, 270
Neptune's Palace, 173
Nest, 279
New Conservatory Theatre
Center, 302
Newspapers, 33–34
Nickie's BBQ, 328
Nightlife, 317–46
alcohol-free/all ages, 319
alternative, 318
bars, pubs, and taverns,
332–43
Castro, 225

coffee, tea, and dessert,
343–46
Cow Hollow, 218–19
dancing, 318
features, 318–19
gay/lesbian bars, 200, 318
Mission District, 229
music and clubs, 321–32
neighborhoods, 319–20
Nob Hill, 206
North Beach, 212
outdoor seating, 318
Potrero Hill, 230
romantic, 319
Santa Cruz, 384
South of Market (SoMa), 200
Niketown, 291
Nikko Fish Co., 230, 288
No Name Bar, 375–76
Nob Hill, 22, 204–6
lodgings, 152–54
map, 205
nightlife, 206, 341
parking, 21
restaurants, 42, 205–6
running, 405
Nob Hill Inn, 154
Noe Valley, 225–26
map, 224
restaurants, 42, 226
shopping, 226, 243, 246
Nordstrom, 248
North Beach, 22, 210–12
festival/street fair, 16, 244
lodgings, 155–56
map, 211
nightlife, 212, 319–20, 341
restaurants, 42, 210
shopping, 246
walking tours, 239
North Beach Restaurant, 110
North End, The, 346
North Face, The, 291
Outlet, 268
North Star, 111
Nuts About You, 265

O

Oakland International Airport
(OAK), 4–5
transportation to and from,
4–5
Oakville, 367
Oakville Grocery Co., 367
Obester Winery, 382
Ocean Beach, 184, 238, 401
Octagon House, 218, 236
ODC–San Francisco, 311
Off the Beach Boats, 388
Old Faithful Geyser, 369
Old Federal Reserve Building,
private gatherings, 418
Old Firehouse, The
private gatherings, 418
Old First Church Concerts, 304

One Market, 111
Opera, 304–9
Caffe Trieste weekly arias, 351
San Francisco Opera, 306
Pocket Opera, 305
Opera House (War Memorial), 208
O'Reilly's Irish Bar, 339
Oritalia, 112
Orpheum Theatre, 302
Outdoor activities, 397–410
bicycling and mountain
biking, 397–98
golf, 398–400
hiking, 400–1
horseback riding, 401–2
kayaking and canoeing,
402–3
roller skating, 403
rowing, 403–5
running, 405–6
sailing, 406–7
swimming, 407–9
tennis, 409–10
Outdoor gear, 290–92, 395–96
Outdoors Unlimited, 395–96,
398, 402–3
Outlet stores, 268–69
Oyster Point Marina Park, 407

P

Pacific, 112
Pacific Film Archive, 361
Pacific Heights, 22, 213–16
lodgings, 160–63
map, 214
nightlife, 320, 341
restaurants, 42, 215–16
shopping, 215
walking tours, 240
Pacific Rowing Club, 405
Palace of Fine Arts, The, 181–82
private gatherings, 418
Palace Hotel, 149
Palace of the Legion of Honor,
187–88
Palo Alto, 378–79
lodgings, 379
Palomarin Trailhead, 390
Palookaville, 384
Pan Pacific, 145
Pane e Vino, 112
Paradise Lounge, 200, 328–29
Park Chow, 113
Park Cyclery, 397
Park Hyatt San Francisco, 150
Parking, 26
Oakland International
Airport, 5
San Francisco International
Airport, 2
San Francisco, 8, 21
Parks, 238–39
Angel Island State Park,
391–92
Aquatic Park, 407–8

Bale Grist Mill State Historic Park, 367
Berkeley, 362
Bernal Heights Park, 400
Big Basin Redwoods State Park, 385
Bothe–Napa Valley State Park, 367
Buena Vista Park, 222
Dolores Park, 401, 409
Glen Canyon Park, 238
Golden Gate Park, 175–77, 222, 409–10
Jack London State Historic Park, 374
Lake Merced, 238
off-leash areas in, 12
private gatherings, 418
San Francisco Maritime National Historic Park, 184, 419
Stern Grove, 238
Washington Square Park, 210
See also Arboretums; Gardens
Parnassus Bike Club, 398
Pastis, 113
Pat O'Shea's Mad Hatter, 232
Patagonia, 291–92
Pauline's Pizza, 114
Paxton Gate, 275
Pea in the Pod, A, 286
Pearl Empire, 284
Pearl's Restaurant & Bar, jazz, 327
Peet's Coffee & Tea, 267
People's Park, 357–58
People's Store, 389
Performing arts, 297–316
    Berkeley, 361
    classical music, 304–9
    dance, 309–12
    film, 312–15
    literary events, 315–16
    opera, 304–9
    theater, 297–303
Performing Arts Library and Museum, 208–9
Perfume, 260
Persian Aub Zam Zam, 339–40
Pet service, 12s, 33
Petite Auberge, 145
Petrified Forest, 369
Pharmacies, 30–31
Philharmonia Baroque Orchestra, 304–5
Phoebe Hearst Museum of Anthropology, 361
Phoenix Hotel, 159
Phone numbers, useful, 37–38
Photography
    Ansel Adams Center for Photography, 233
    equipment and services, 32
Piano bars, 318
Pied Piper Bar, The, 337
Pier 23 Cafe, 329

Pier 39, 172–73
    shopping, 243
Pier 39 Marina, 407
Pillar Point Harbor, 381
Pintxos, 114
Pizzerio Uno, 185
PJ's Oysterbed, 115, 233
Planetariums
    Morrison Planetarium, 234
Plants, 271–72
Playgrounds
    Golden Gate Park, 177
Plouf, 115
Plough & Stars, 232, 340
PlumpJack Cafe, 116, 218
PlumpJack Wines, 295
Pocket Opera, 305
Podesta Baldocchi, 272
Point Bonita Lighthouse, 386
Point Reyes Bird Observatory, 389–90
Point Reyes Lighthouse, 390
Point Reyes National Seashore, 390–91
Polanco, 282
Police, 29
Polk Gulch, restaurants, 42
Polly Esther's, 329
Pool tables/billiards, 318–19
Portsmouth Square, 203
Post offices, 30
Postrio, 116
Potrero Brewing Co., 117
Potrero Hill, 229–31
    map, 198
    nightlife, 230, 320
    restaurants, 230
    shopping, 230
Precipitation, 9
Precita Eyes Mural Arts Center, 236, 240
Prescott Hotel, The, 146
Presidio, The, 23, 184, 178–79, 308
Presidio Army Museum, 179, 236–37, 309
Presidio Golf Course, 399
Presidio Heights, restaurants, 42
Presidio Theater, 313
Printer's Inc., 378
Public art
    Coit Tower frescoes, 234
    El Volado, 240
    Precita Eyes Mural Arts Center, 236, 240
Pubs, 232, 319, 332–43
Punchline Comedy Club, 329
Purisima Creek Redwoods, 380–81

Q
Q San Francisco, 34
Quake City Shuttle, 4
Queen Anne Hotel, 159

R
R&G Lounge, 117
Races
    running, 405–6
Racetracks, 411
Radio stations, 35–36
Rainbow Grocery, 277
Rand McNally Map & Travel Store, 263
Rasselas Jazz Club and Ethiopian Cuisine, 329–30
Rayon Vert, 228
Readers' Books, 371
Real Food Company, The, 226, 277
Receptions, 413–19
Records, 286–87
Recreation, 393–411
    adventure outfitters, 395–96
    bicycling and mountain biking, 397–98
    golf, 398–400
    gyms, 394–95
    hiking, 400–1
    horseback riding, 401–2
    kayaking and canoeing, 402–3
    rock climbing (indoors), 397
    roller skating, 403
    rowing, 403–5
    running, 405–6
    sailing, 406–7
    swimming, 407–9
    tennis, 409–10
    See also Outdoor gear; Rentals; Sports; individual activities
Recreation and Park Department, City and County of San Francisco, private gatherings, 418
Red & White Fleet, 29
Red Herring, 118
Red Room, The, 337
Red Victorian Bed, Breakfast & Art, 164, 222
Redwood Park, 196
Redwood Room, The, 337
REI, 396
Rendezvous Charters, 407
Rentals
    bicycles, 27, 380, 384, 396, 397–98
    canoes, 381
    cars, 26
    computers, 32–33
    facilities for conferences, meetings, and receptions, 413–19
    kayaks and canoes, 381, 383–84, 388, 391, 402–3
    mountain bikes, 391
    sailboats, 406–7

skates, 403
See also Charters
Reservation services, 141
Rest rooms, public, 28
Restaurants, 39–138
  Civic Center, 209
  features and food types, 43–47
  Financial District, 197
  Ghirardelli Square, 181
  Metreon, 192
  neighborhood listings, 41–42
  Nob Hill, 205–6
  Palo Alto, 379
  Russian Hill, 207–8
  South of Market (SoMa), 199–200
  star ratings, 40–41
  See also individual entries
Richard Hilkert Bookseller, 263
Richmond District, 23, 231–33
  nightlife, 320
  restaurants, 42, 231–32
  shopping, 232
Rick & Ann's, 358
Ripley's Believe It or Not!
  Museum, 172, 237
Ristorante Ecco, 118
Ristorante Tra Vigne, 367
Ritz-Carlton, 154
  Dining Room, 71, 206
  Sunday brunch, 351
Rizzoli, 263
Roaring Camp Train, 385
Robert Domergue & Co., 251
Robert Moses' Kin, 311
Robin's Nest, 371
Rochester Big and Tall, 286
Rock climbing (indoors), 397
Roller skating, 403
  Golden Gate Park, 351
Rosa Montoya's Argentinian Bailes
  Flamencos, 309
Rose Garden Inn, The, 362
Rose Paoli's City Discount, 207
Rose Pistola, 118, 210
Rose's Cafe, 218
Rotunda, 119
Rowing, 403–5
Roxie Cinema, 229, 313
Royal Oak, 208, 340
Rubicon, 119
Rumpus, 120
Runner's Schedule, 406
Running, 405–6
Russian Hill, 206–8
  map, 205
  nightlife, 320, 341
  restaurants, 42, 207–8
  shopping, 207

S

Sacramento Street, 243
Safety, 29
Safeway, 30

Sailing, 406–7
St. Helena, 367
Saints and Sinners, 240
Sak, The, 284
Saks Fifth Avenue, 248
  Men's Store, 248
Salons, 33
  Elizabeth Arden Red Door
    Salon & Spa, 260
  Heaven Day-Spa & Center
    for Wellness, 217
  Mister Lee, 261
  77 Maiden Lane Salon &
    Spa, 261
  See also Body care; Spas
Saloon, the, 325
Sam's Anchor Cafe, 377
Sam's Grill & Seafood Restaurant,
  120, 197
Samtrans, 3
San Francisco
  clothing appropriate for, 9–10
  essential services, 28–33
  exploring, 167–240
  general costs, 10–11
  landmarks and orientation,
    20–23
  local resources, 33–38
  neighborhood districts,
    194–233
  parking in, 8, 21, 26
  performing arts, 297–316
  public rest rooms, 28
  shopping, 241–95
  time zone, 9
  Top 25 attractions, 168–94
  transportation in and
    around, 24–28
  transportation to and from,
    2–8
  visitor information, 24
  weather, 8–9
  weekly events, 351
  See also individual activities,
    attractions,
    neighborhoods, and
    businesses
San Francisco Airport North
  Travelodge, 166
San Francisco Asian American Film
  Festival, 314
San Francisco Bach Choir, 305
San Francisco Ballet, 311–12
San Francisco Bay Area Book
  Festival, 18, 316
San Francisco Bay Blades, 405
San Francisco Bay Guardian, 34
San Francisco Bay Swimming
  Association, 409
San Francisco Brewing Company,
  325, 340
San Francisco Business Times, 34
San Francisco Cable Car Museum,
  237, 309
  private gatherings, 418

San Francisco Chronicle, 33–34
San Francisco City Hall, 193, 208
San Francisco Conservatory of
  Music, 305–6
San Francisco Contemporary
  Music Players, 306
San Francisco Convention and
  Visitors Bureau, 24
San Francisco Craft and Folk Art
  Museum, 190
"San Francisco Day by Day," 351
San Francisco Examiner, 33–34
San Francisco Fire Department
  Museum, 309
San Francisco Fire Engine Tours &
  Adventures, 239
San Francisco 49ers, 410
San Francisco Fringe Festival, 302
San Francisco Gay Men's Chorus,
  304
San Francisco Giants, 410
San Francisco International Airport, 2
  construction hotline, 2
  lodgings near, 165–66
  parking, 2
  transportation to, 2–4
San Francisco International Film
  Festival, 15, 314
San Francisco International Gay &
  Lesbian Film Festival, 314
San Francisco Jewish Film Festival,
  314–15
San Francisco Lesbian, Gay,
  Bisexual, Transgender Pride
  Parade and Celebration, 16
San Francisco Marina, 407
San Francisco Maritime National
  Historic Park, 184, 193–94
  private gatherings, 419
San Francisco Marriott, 151
San Francisco Mime Troupe, 303
San Francisco Museum of Modern
  Art, 183, 199, 237, 309, 351
  Museum Store, 275
"San Francisco on Celluloid," 63
San Francisco Opera, 306
San Francisco Performances,
  306–7
San Francisco Performing Arts
  Library and Museum, 208–9
San Francisco Public Library,
  34–35, 209
San Francisco Recreation and Park
  Department
  private gatherings, 418
"San Francisco Reservation
  Services," 141
San Francisco Reservations, 141
San Francisco Shakespeare
  Festival, 17, 303
San Francisco Shopping Centre,
  242
San Francisco State University
  (SFSU), 37, 232
San Francisco Symphony, 307

San Francisco Visitor Information Center, 24
San Francisco Zoo, 203, 232, 238, 308
"San Francisco's Ferry Fleet," 29
"San Francisco's Literary Legends," 6–7
San Remo Hotel, 155
Sanraku, 192
Santa Cruz, 382–85
    Beach Boardwalk, 382–83
    Visitor's Information Center, 384
Santa Cruz Surfing Museum, 383
Sapporo-ya, 121
Sarah Shaw, 256
Saul's, 359
Sausalito, 353, 375–76
Savor, 226
Savoy Hotel, 146
Say Cheese, 271
Scala's Bistro, 121
Scenic drives
    49-Mile Scenic Drive, 349
Scheuer Linens, 279–80
Scott's Seafood, 185
Sea Trek, 392
Seafood, 288
    Johnson's Oyster Farm, 390–91
    Nikko Fish Co., 230, 288
Seafood & Beverage Company, 189
Sears Fine Food, 122
"See Life at the Farallon Islands," 388
Seniors, services for, 11
Sephora, 261
77 Maiden Lane Salon & Spa, 261
SF Weekly, 34
Shalimar, 122
Shanghai Kelly's, 208
Shanghai 1930, 122
Sharp Park Golf Range, 399
Sharpsteen Museum and Brannan Cottage, 369
Sheehan Hotel, swimming, 408
Sheraton Fisherman's Wharf, 156
Sherman House, The, 162
Shoes, 288–90
Shopping, 241–95
    antiques, 248–52
    apparel, 252–56
    bakeries, 256–59
    body care, 260–61
    books and magazines, 261–64
    candy and chocolates, 264–65
    Cannery, The, 242–43
    Castro, 224–25, 246
    children's clothing, 265–66
    Chinatown, 246
    coffee and tea, 266–68
    consignment and discount, 268–69
    Cow Hollow, 218, 243
    department stores, 247–48
    Embarcadero Center, 185

ethnic and specialty foods, 269–71
Fisherman's Wharf, 242–43
flowers and plants, 271–72
furniture, 272–73
Ghirardelli Square, 180, 243
gift and specialty shops, 273–76
hardware stores, 276–77
health food stores, 277
home accessories, 278–80
imported goods, 281–82
Jackson Square, 246
jewelry and accessories, 282–85
malls, 247
maternity and special sizes, 285–86
Metreon, 192
Mission District, 228
music (CDs, records, and tapes), 286–87
Noe Valley, 226, 246
North Beach, 246
Pacific Heights, 215
Palo Alto, 378–79
Pier 39, 243
Potrero Hill, 230
Richmond District, 232
Russian Hill, 207
Santa Cruz, 384
Sausalito, 376
seafood, 288
shoes, 288–90
Sonoma, 371
South of Market (SoMa), 246–47
sports and outdoor gear, 290–92, 395–96
toys, 292–93
Union Square, 242
vintage clothing, 293–94
wine, beer, and spirits, 294–95
See also individual entries
Shoreline Amphitheater, 379
Short Shop, The, 286
Shreve & Company, 174, 284
Shuttles
    to Oakland International Airport (OAK), 5
    to San Francisco International Airport, 4
Sigmund Stern Grove, 16, 232, 238, 308
Silkroute, 282
Silks, 197
Sir Francis Drake Hotel, 147
Six, 330
Skates on Haight, 403
Skating, 402–3
    Golden Gate Park, 351
    rentals, 403
Skylark, 340
Slanted Door, The, 123, 228

Slim's, 200, 330
Slow Club, 123, 229
Small Frys, 226, 266
Smedley Herrera, 272
Smuin Ballets–SF, 312
Soko Hardware, 220, 277
SoMa. See South of Market
Sonoma, 370–74
Sonoma Barracks, 371
Sonoma Cheese Factory, 373
Sonoma City Hall, 371
Sonoma Mission, 371
Sonoma Mission Inn & Spa, 374, 375
Sonoma Mountain, 374
Sonoma Plaza, 371
Sonoma Valley, 370–75
    Visitors Bureau, 370
    wineries, 372–73
"Sonoma Valley Wineries," 372–73
Sound Factory, 330
South End Rowing Club, 404
swimming, 408
South of Market (SoMa), 20, 197–200
    lodgings, 151–52
    map, 198
    nightlife, 200, 320, 341
    parking, 21
    restaurants, 42, 199–200
    shopping, 246–47
South Park Cafe, 124
South San Francisco, lodgings, 165–66
Spa Nordstrom, 33, 261
Spas, 33
    Calistoga, 368–69
    Calistoga Spa Hot Springs, 368
    Claremont Resort and Spa, 362
    Dr. Wilkinson's Hot Springs, 368
    Elizabeth Arden Red Door Salon & Spa, 260
    Heaven Day-Spa & Center for Wellness, 217
    Indian Springs Resort and Spa, 368
    Kabuki Springs and Spa, 33, 220
    Kenwood Inn and Spa, 375
    Lavendar Hill Spa, 368–69
    77 Maiden Lane Salon & Spa, 261
    Sonoma Mission Inn & Spa, 374, 375
    Spa Nordstrom, 33, 261
    See also Body care; Salons
Specialty foods, 269–71
Specialty shops, 273–76
Specs' Twelve Adler Museum Cafe, 325, 342
Spectator sports, 410–11
Spectrum Gallery, private gatherings, 419

Spinnaker Sailing School, 406–7
Splendido, 185
Sports
    bars, 319
    gear, 290–92, 395–96
    spectator, 410–11
    See also Recreation
Sproul Plaza, 356
Stacey's, 263, 315, 378
Stanford Park Hotel, 379
Stanford Shopping Center, 379
Stanford Theater, 379
Stanford University, 378
Stanyan Park Hotel, 164, 221
Star Classics, 287
Starbucks, 267
Stars, 124
Steinhart Aquarium, 234, 415–16
Stella Pastry & Caffe, 259
Stephen Pelton Dance Theater, 309
Steps of Rome, 346
Stern Grove, 232, 238
    Midsummer Music Festival,
        16, 308
Stinking Rose, 125
Stinson Beach, 387–89
Stonestown Galleria, 247
Storyville, 330
Stow Lake, 177
Straits Cafe, 125, 231–32
Stray animals, 33
Street fairs, 244–45
    See also Festivals and events;
        individual entries
Streetcars, 223–24
    Municipal Railway System
        (Muni), 24–25
Strybing Arboretum and Botanical
    Gardens, 177
Stud, The, 200, 330–31
Sue Fisher King, 280
Sunset District, 23, 231–33
    restaurants, 42, 232
Sunset views, 401
Supershuttle, 4
Suppenkuche, 125
Sur la Table, 280
Surfing
    Half Moon Bay, 381
    Santa Cruz, 383
Susan, 256
Sushi Groove, 126
Sushi Ran, 376
Sutro Baths, 189, 231
Swan Oyster Depot, 126, 288
"Swanky Hotel Bars," 337
Swatch, 285
Sweat Shop, 229
Sweet Dreams, 358
Swensen's, 207
Swimming, 407–9
Symphony Hall (Louise M.
    Davies), 208
Synagogues
    Temple Emanu-el, 215

T
Tadich Grill, 127, 197
Tail of the Yak, 358
Tapes, 286–87
Taqueria Cancun, 127
Taverns, 332–43
Tavolino, 127
Taxis, 4, 25–26
    average cost per mile, 11
Tea
    retail, 173, 266–68
    tea rooms, 343–46
Tea and Company, 267
Telegraph Hill, 212–13
    restaurants, 213
Telephone numbers, useful, 37–38
Television stations, 35–36
Temperatures, 8–9
Temples
    Chinatown, 202–3
    1015 Folsom, 331
Ten Ren Tea Co., 267
Tenderloin
    nightlife, 320
    restaurants, 42
Tennis, 409–10
Terra Brazilis, 128
Thai House, 128
Thai House Bar and Cafe, 128
Theater, 298–303
    Berkeley, 361
    See also Theater festivals;
        Theaters
Theater festivals
    Bay Area Playwrights'
        Festival, 299
    San Francisco Fringe Festival,
        302
    San Francisco Shakespeare
        Festival, 17, 303
    See also Theater
Theater Rhinoceros, 303
Theaters
    Cowell Theater, 190
    Fort Mason, 190
    Magic Theatre, 190
    Palace of Fine Arts Theatre,
        182
    Palo Alto, 379
    See also Theater; Theater
        festivals
Theatre on the Square (TOTS), 303
Theatreworks, 379
Thep Phanom, 129
Therapy, 228
Third Hand Rose, 294
Thirsty Bear Brewing Company,
    129, 342
Thomas Bros. Maps & Books, 264
Thomas Livingston, 251
Thos. Moser Cabinetmakers, 273
330 Ritch Street, 331
Ti Couz, 129, 228
Tiburon, 376–77

Tiburon Deli, 377
Tickets
    Bass Ticket Service, 410
Tiffany & Co., 285
Tilden Regional Park, 362
Time zone, 9
Timo's, 130
Tokyo Go Go, 131
Tommaso Ristorante Italiano, 130
Tommy Toy's, 131
Ton Kiang, 132, 232
Tonga Room, 206, 337
Top, The, 331
Top Dog, 359
Top of the Mark, 206, 337
Top 25 attractions, 168–94
Toronado, 342
Torrefazione Italia, 267–68
Tosca Cafe, 212, 342
TOTS (Theatre on the Square), 303
Touch of Asia, 282
Toujours, 256
Tours, 239–40
    Angel Island State Park, 392
    Farallon Islands, 388
    Ghirardelli Square, 180
    Golden Gate Park, 177
    Presidio, 179
    sea kayaking, 392
    See also Bus tours; Walking
        tours
Tower Records, 287
Toy Boat Dessert Cafe, 346
Toys, 292–93
Trad'r Sam, 342–43
Trains
    Amtrak, 5
    Caltrain, 4, 5
    Napa Valley Wine Train, 363
    Roaring Camp Train, 385
    to and from San Francisco,
        5–7
Transamerica Pyramid, 196
Translation services, 13
Transportation
    Bay Area Rapid Transit
        (BART), 3, 25
    bicycles, 27
    buses, 7, 25–25
    cable cars, 169–70
    cars, 7–8, 26–27
    for disabled people, 11–12
    ferries, 28, 29
    to and from Oakland
        International Airport
        (OAK), 4–5
    in and around San Francisco,
        24–28
    to and from San Francisco,
        2–8
    to and from San Francisco
        International Airport, 2–4
    taxis, 25–26
    trains, 5–7
Traveling Jewish Theatre, A, 303

Travelodge, San Francisco Airport North, 166
Treasure Island Flea Market, 239
Triple Rock Brewery, 359
Tsar Nicoulai Caviar, 271
Tu Lan, 132
Tuffy's Hopscotch, 290
Tully's, 268
Tunnel of Elms, 367
Tuscan Inn, 157
Twenty Tank Brewery, 200, 343
2223 Restaurant and Bar, 132, 225
24 Hour Fitness Training, 394
24th Street Cheese Co., 271
Twin Peaks, 216, 401
Twin Peaks Tavern, 343
"Two-Wheel Route: Bicycling in Marin," 396

U

U.C. Theatre, 361
Union Ale House, 219
Union Square, 22, 173–74
 lodgings, 140–49
 nightlife, 320, 341
 parking, 21
 restaurants, 42
 shopping, 242
Union Street, 22, 218, 243
Union Street Goldsmith, 285
Union Street Inn, 162
United Artists Coronet, 312
United Artists Vogue, 312
United Nations Plaza, 209
Universal Cafe, 133, 229
Universities, 36–37
 See also individual entries
University of California at Berkeley, 356
 Art Museum, 360
University of California Botanical Garden, 361–62
University of California at San Francisco (UCSF), 36–37
University of California Medical Center, 232
University of San Francisco (USF), 36
Up & Down Club, 331–32
Upstairs at the Cliff House, 189

V

Valencia Street
 nightlife, 341
Valencia Street Muscle and Fitness, 395
Venticello, 206
Vesuvio Cafe, 212, 343
Veterinarians, 33
Victoria Pastry Co., 259
Victoria Theatre, 313
Victorian and Edwardian Pacific Heights Walk, 240
Victorian Interiors, 280
View Lounge, 337
Views, 401

Vineria, 228
Vintage clothing, 293–94
Vintage 1870, 366
Virgin Megastore, 287
Vision Quest Kayaking, 383–84
Visitor information
 Bear Valley Visitors Center, 390
 Napa Valley Conference and Visitors Bureau, 363
 Santa Cruz Visitor's Information Center, 384
 San Francisco Convention and Visitors Bureau, 24
 San Francisco Visitor Information Center, 24
 Sonoma Valley Visitors Bureau, 370
Vivande Porta Via, 271
Vorpal Gallery, private gatherings, 419

W

W. Graham Arader III, 251–52
W Hotel, 152
Waddell Creek Beach, 385
Walgreens, 30
Walking tours
 Angel Island, 238–39
 Chinatown, 239
 City Guides, 239, 308
 free, 239
 Ghirardelli Square, 180
 Golden Gate Park, 177
 literary, 239
 Precita Eyes Mural Arts Center, 236, 240
 Saints and Sinners, 240
 Upper Haight, 239
 Victorian and Edwardian Pacific Heights Walk, 240
Wappo Bar & Bistro, 369
War Memorial Opera House, 208
Warfield Theatre, 332
Warriors, Golden State, 410–11
Washington Square Inn, The, 156
Washington Square Park, 210
Wasteland, 294
Waterfront Restaurant & Café, The, 133
Wax Museum, 172, 237
Weather, 8–9
Web information, 14
Wells Fargo, 28–29
 History Museum, 309
 History Room, 196
Westin St. Francis, 148
Whale watching, 388
Wheelchair accessible attractions, information on, 12
"Where Do You Want to Go Tonight?" 341
White Buffalo Gallery, 181
White Swan Inn, 148
Whole Foods Market, 30, 277

Wildlife viewing
 Farallon Islands, 388
 whale watching, 388
Wilkes Bashford, 256
William K. Stout Architectural Books, 264
Williams-Sonoma
 Grande Cuisine, 280
Wine bars
 Hayes and Vine Wine Bar, 336
 L'Amie Donia, 379
 London Wine Bar, 338
Wine Club, 295
Wine Country, 353, 362–75
 Napa Valley, 362–70
 Sonoma Valley, 370–75
Wine Impressions, 295
Wine shops, 294–95
Wineries
 Half Moon Bay, 382
 Napa Valley, 364–65
 Sonoma Valley, 372–73
 See also entries for individual wineries
Women, services for, 12
Women's Philharmonic, The, 307–9
Woodward's Garden, 134

X

Xanadu Tribal Arts, 281
Xela Imports, 282
XYZ, 134, 337

Y

Yank Sing, 135
Yerba Buena
 nightlife, 341
Yerba Buena Center for the Arts, 191–92, 199, 237, 309, 313
 private gatherings, 419
Yerba Buena Gardens, 183–84, 199, 203
Yountville, 266, 366
Your Basic Bird, 358
Yum Yum, 288

Z

Zachary's Chicago Pizza, 360
Zao Noodle Club, 217
Zarzuela, 135, 207–8
Zax, 136
Zazie, 136
Zendo Urban Retreat, 33
Zero Degrees, 346
Zinc Details, 275–76
Zinzino, 137, 217
Zodiac Club, 137
Zoe Limited, 215
Zonal, 273
Zuni Cafe, 137

We Stand By Our Reviews

Sasquatch Books is proud of *San Francisco Best Places*. Our editors and contributors go to great lengths and expense to see that all of the restaurant and lodging reviews are as accurate, up-to-date, and honest as possible. If we have disappointed you, please accept our apologies; however, if a recommendation in this 1st edition of *San Francisco Best Places* has seriously misled you, Sasquatch Books would like to refund your purchase price. To receive your refund:

1. Tell us where and when you purchased your book and return the book and the book-purchase receipt to the address below.
2. Enclose the original restaurant or lodging receipt from the establishment in question, including date of visit.
3. Write a full explanation of your stay or meal and how *San Francisco Best Places* misled you.
4. Include your name, address, and phone number.

Refund is valid only while this 1st edition of *San Francisco Best Places* is in print. If the ownership, management, or chef has changed since publication, Sasquatch Books cannot be held responsible. Tax and postage on the returned book is your responsibility. Please allow six to eight weeks for processing.

Please address to Satisfaction Guaranteed, *San Francisco Best Places*, and send to:
Sasquatch Books
615 Second Avenue, Suite 260
Seattle, WA 98104

San Francisco Best Places Report Form

Based on my personal experience, I wish to nominate the following restaurant, place of lodging, shop, nightclub, sight, or other as a "Best Place"; or confirm/correct/disagree with the current review.

_____

_____

_____

(Please include address and telephone number of establishment, if convenient.)

REPORT

Please describe food, service, style, comfort, value, date of visit, and other aspects of your experience; continue on another piece of paper if necessary.

_____

_____

_____

_____

_____

_____

_____

I am not concerned, directly or indirectly, with the management or ownership of this establishment.

SIGNED
_____

ADDRESS
_____

_____

PHONE   **DATE**

Please address to San Francisco Best Places and send to:
SASQUATCH BOOKS
615 SECOND AVENUE, SUITE 260
SEATTLE, WA 98104
Feel free to email feedback as well: **BOOKS@SASQUATCHBOOKS.COM**